D0215155

Supply Chain Focused Manufacturing Planning and Control

W. C. Benton, Jr.
Department of Management Sciences
Fisher College of Business
The Ohio State University

Australia • Brazil • Mexico • Singapore • United Kingdom • United States

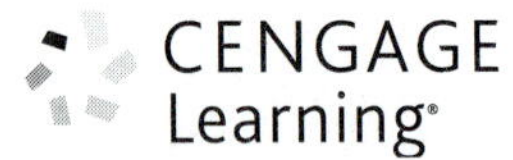

Supply Chain Focused Manufacturing Planning and Control
W. C. Benton, Jr.

Senior Vice President, LRS/Acquisitions & Solutions Planning: Jack W. Calhoun

Editorial Director, Business & Economics: Erin Joyner

Publisher: Joe Sabatino

Senior Acquisition Editor: Charles McCormick

Developmental Editor: Conor Allen

Editorial Assistant: Anne Merrill

Brand Management Director: Jason Sakos

Senior Brand Manager: Robin LeFevre

Market Development Director: Lisa Lysne

Art and Cover Direction, Production Management, and Composition: PreMediaGlobal

Media Editor: Chris Valentine

Rights Acquisition Director: Audrey Pettengill

Rights Acquisition Specialist, Text and Image: John Hill

Manufacturing Planner: Ron Montgomery

Cover Image: © Rosemary Calvert/Getty Images

Library of Congress Control Number: 2013932184

ISBN 13: 978-1-133-58671-5

ISBN 10: 1-133-58671-6

Cengage Learning
200 First Stamford Place, 4th Floor
Stamford, CT 06902
USA

Cengage Learning is a leading provider of customized learning solutions with office locations around the globe, including Singapore, the United Kingdom, Australia, Mexico, Brazil, and Japan. Locate your local office at **www.cengage.com/global**.

Cengage Learning products are represented in Canada by Nelson Education, Ltd.

To learn more about Cengage Learning Solutions, visit **www.cengage.com**.

Purchase any of our products at your local college store or at our preferred online store **www.cengagebrain.com**.

Printed in the United States of America
1 2 3 4 5 6 7 17 16 15 14 13

In memory of my brother Rod Benton

Brief Contents

Contents

Preface

The purpose of this textbook is to provide an understanding of the supply chain focused manufacturing planning and control function. The primary objective of a supply chain focused manufacturing planning and control system (MPCS) in any organization is to ensure that the desired products are manufactured at the right time, in the right quantities, and meeting quality specifications in the most cost-efficient manner. The manufacturing planning and control system (MPCS) in a competitive organization is achieved by integrating the activities such as (1) determining product demand, (2) translating product demand into feasible manufacturing plans, (3) establishing detailed planning of material flows for producing the product, (4) capacity to support the overall manufacturing plans, and (5) executing scheduling and purchasing plans. There have been two recent trends in manufacturing planning and control.

The first is the significant growth in the theory and practice of the concept of supply chain management. Supply chain management is becoming the key driver of competitive advantage for manufacturing organizations. Manufacturing planning and control must now be integrated into the supply chain revolution. In many organizations, manufacturing has been integrated with the supply chain management function. The purpose of this textbook is to provide an understanding of the supply chain focused manufacturing planning and control function.

The second trend is the increasing interest in sustainability. Remanufacturing is the process by which products are recovered, processed, and sold as like-new products in the same or separate markets. Due to increasing legislation and the realization that being "green" can be profitable, an increasing number of companies have been implementing comprehensive programs in order to reap the potential benefits of remanufacturing. In the United States, laws that mandate companies be responsible for take-back of electronic wastes are becoming prevalent at the state level. The Remanufacturing Institute (www.reman.org) reports that as of May 2010, 21 states in the United States had passed laws requiring OEMs to be responsible for taking back and reusing and/or disposing of products at end of life. However, few guidelines are available to the practicing manager to aid in planning, controlling, and managing remanufacturing operations. Production planning and control activities become more complex and difficult for the manufacturer engaging in remanufacturing operations mainly due to the uncertainty in sourcing the cores required for remanufacturing. The remanufacturing planning and control concept is presented for the first time in this textbook. The motivation for covering remanufacturing is to update the manufacturing and control paradigm to include the challenges and opportunities posed by supply chain management and sustainability trends.

The material in this textbook explains how to achieve maximum integration with upstream and downstream supply chain members using the latest methodologies and manufacturing technologies. This textbook can be used to teach the fundamentals of supply chain focused manufacturing planning and control in a logical, simple, and concise format. The textbook is excellent for upper-level supply chain and operations management courses, MBAs, and industrial engineering students (graduate and undergraduate). The textbook serves as an excellent resource for executive education and training seminars. The textbook is also an excellent resource for the certification program sponsored by the American Production and Inventory Control Society (APICS).

Key Emphasis and Features

As supply chain management has become more relational in nature, there has been a paradigm shift from a transactional to a strategic exchange in the manufacturing planning and control environment. Some of the more significant changes are:

1. Faster product life cycles
2. The advent of lean manufacturing
3. A trend toward integrated manufacturing
4. Remanufacturing planning and control (sustainability)
5. Highly variable demand patterns
6. More product variety demanded from the ultimate customer
7. Shorter cumulative lead times from manufacture to customer
8. A reduction in fabrication value added
9. More emphasis on purchasing value-added assembles and outsource providers

Companies throughout the world are using these factors as means of gaining competitive advantages. Given the fluid and diverse nature of domestic and global markets, companies must constantly adapt their manufacturing planning and control systems in order to remain competitive. Faster product life cycles, highly variable demand patterns, and increased product variety can lead to major disruptions in the manufacturing planning and control process. The manufacturing organizations that learn how to adapt and manage in this changing environment can gain a competitive advantage in the marketplace. Many manufacturing organizations are also are embracing lean strategies and integrative manufacturing flows.

The Evolution of Manufacturing Planning and Control

This textbook will contribute to both students' and practitioners' knowledge of the new approaches to the manufacturing supply chain interface. Compared to the manufacturing planning and control approach of the early 1990s, today's supply chain focused manufacturing approach is relatively innovative and has seen several phases of transition. The evolution of the various manufacturing stages, starting from the push (MRP) manufacturing of the early 1970s to the ERP manufacturing that is fast becoming a standard practice for some of the more sophisticated companies (Walmart, Toyota, Lockheed, and others) has been impressive. It is important to understand that the newer manufacturing practices do not replace the older ones but instead continue to blend the best of the current and past manufacturing practices to meet current business needs. Thus, although various manufacturing philosophies currently exist—push, lean, flexible—none are applied in a pure, holistic fashion. Most companies operate hybrid manufacturing systems.

Supply Chain Manufacturing Integration

As supply chains continue to become leaner and the level of waste (inventory, capacity, labor) continues to decrease, companies whose manufacturing capabilities cannot respond quickly to variable demands become increasingly vulnerable. These manufacturing organizations are now searching for ways to integrate all their manufacturing activities and connect them with the supply chain. But the majority of MPC solutions available to help them address this problem is still relatively localized to specific environments and fails to have wide industry application. This is mostly true because manufacturing organizations are diverse and at various stages of evolution.

1. Focus on Lean Manufacturing This textbook integrates lean concepts into the manufacturing planning and control process. The lean approach is about doing more with less: less time, inventory, space, labor, and money. Lean manufacturing is a commitment to eliminating waste, simplifying procedures, and speeding up production. Lean manufacturing, in its most basic form, is the systematic elimination of waste—overproduction, waiting, transportation, inventory, motion, overprocessing, defective units—and the implementation of the concepts of continuous flow and customer pull. This supply chain focused manufacturing planning and control textbook explicitly considers the five drivers of lean manufacturing/production:

1. Cost
2. Quality
3. Delivery
4. Safety
5. Morale

Just as mass production is recognized as the production system of the 20th century, lean production is viewed as the production system of the 21st century. It has been shown that the establishment and mastering of a lean production system allows manufacturing organizations to achieve the following benefits:

- Waste reduction by 80 percent
- Production cost reduction by 50 percent
- Manufacturing cycle times decreased by 50 percent
- Labor reduction by 50 percent while maintaining or increasing throughput
- Inventory reduction by 80 percent while increasing customer-service levels
- Capacity in current facilities increased by 50 percent
- Higher quality
- Higher profits
- Higher system flexibility in reacting to changes in requirements
- More strategic focus

This textbook also focuses on manufacturing excellence in the following areas:

1. Workforce attitude toward efficiency
2. Continuous improvement
3. Elimination of waste
4. Embracing technology
5. Supply chain integration

2. Focus on Information Technology This textbook also focuses on information technology as the driver for the supply chain manufacturing integration mechanism. Integration is sometimes described as the linking of product design, the manufacturing process, and manufacturing planning and control using information technology. At the same time, many organizations are now searching for ways to integrate all their manufacturing activities and connect them with the entire supply chain by using fully integrated enterprise resource planning (ERP) systems. The main objective of an integrative MPC system is to document and understand the information and physical flows of the MPC function. However, the majority of manufacturing companies throughout the world are still in the early stages of ERP driven integration. The initial phase in the MPC integration evolution is to develop a comprehensive understanding of the localized MPC system. A fully integrated MPC system is simply an integration of all departments, functions, and supply chain participants onto a single computer system that can serve all those entities' needs.

3. Focus on Remanufacturing Remanufacturing is the process by which products are recovered, processed, and sold as like-new products in the same or separate markets. In a survey reported in Clottey, Benton, and Srivastava (2012)[1] remanufacturing operations accounted for total sales in excess of $69 billion per year. The EPA cites remanufacturing as an integral foundation of reuse activities and reports that less energy is used and fewer wastes are produced with these types of activities (U.S. EPA, 1998). Production plans and control activities become more complex and difficult for the manufacturer engaging in remanufacturing operations mainly due to the uncertainty in sourcing the cores required for remanufacturing. In this textbook, the acquisition and sourcing of reusable cores will be addressed.

4. Fully Integrated (Adaptive) Manufacturing Systems Thanks to the Internet and information ubiquity, the customer has finally been crowned king, and companies that adapt quickly and efficiently to the king's variable demands are destined for success. Adaptive (integrated) manufacturing is the key characteristic driving this success. Adaptability has two primary characteristics, flexibility and velocity. Flexibility enables a manufacturing unit to scale efficiently, while velocity determines its ability to switch operational modes rapidly and to transition between modes such as high-volume/low-mix to high-volume/high-mix product loadings. Adaptive manufacturing enterprises are expected to achieve required flexibility and velocity by linking technology to manufacturing planning and control processes, production equipment, and manufacturing systems. This adaptive (integrated) technology allows for the profitable manufacture of products for increasingly time-sensitive and competitive markets.

Book Structure

In this book, the integrated MPC concepts are introduced in the logical order of analysis based on how the function is executed in practice. The strategic long-term integrated MPC activities are discussed in **Chapter 1**. The more detailed short-term activities are then covered. Next, in **Chapter 2**, the approaches to independent demand forecasting are discussed. Forecasting drives all of the key business functions. Forecasts are the inputs for sales, budgeting, capacity planning, purchasing, inventory management, and staffing decisions. In **Chapter 3**, sales and operations planning is discussed. Sales and operations planning (S&OP) provides a means to show how manufacturing firms can meet sales and marketing's objectives. The S&OP plan must also provide a precise forecast of financial output for the next 6 to 18 months. Effective sales and operations planning is needed in order to improve future performance for the manufacturing firm. **Chapter 4** discusses the various approaches to supply chain focused master production scheduling, which represents the anticipated build schedule for specific customer orders. The most important element of customer service is product availability. The main tool to control product availability is the master production schedule (MPS). The inventory control function is introduced in **Chapter 5**. The objective of this chapter is to provide a framework for inventory management in a supply chain focused manufacturing

[1]Clottey, T., Benton, W.C., and Srivastava, R.S. 2012. "Forecasting Product Returns for Remanufacturing Operations." *Decision Sciences* 43 (4):589–614.

environment. Chapter 5 also includes a comprehensive appendix that focuses on quantity discounts and supply chain integration. The intent of **Appendix A** is to categorize the major variations on the problem and to develop a consistent procedure for finding the supplier's optimal discount schedule.

In Chapters 6 through 8, the various forms of manufacturing approaches are introduced. **Chapter 6** discusses MRP concepts. Materials requirements planning (MRP) was developed specifically to assist companies in managing dependent demand inventory and scheduling replenishment orders. Specifically, MRP is a computerized information system that creates planned orders for both manufactured and purchased materials. **Chapter 7** discusses just-in-time (JIT) and lean manufacturing. Just-in-time is a manufacturing system in which materials are pulled through the system and delivered at the precise time to each step in the process just as they are needed. JIT manufacturing is designed to manage the flow of materials, components, tools, and information. JIT production is based on planned elimination of all waste and on continuous improvement. **Chapter 8** discusses the differences between the push and pull manufacturing approaches. The terms *push* and *pull* are used to describe alternative systems for executing the production process in manufacturing organizations. A push system is based on forecasted demand that is completed and pushed to the next workstation or, in the case of the final workstation, to finished goods inventory. On the other hand, in a pull system, the movement of work is based on the succeeding work station. Material plans are very important, but there are several systems and managerial issues that must be addressed in order to execute the various production approaches. Specifically, the proper amount of capacity is essential. In **Chapter 9**, the capacity planning process is discussed. The manufacturing capacity planning is a process for determining the required manufacturing resources to meet manufacturing objectives. The objectives of capacity planning are to solve capacity problems in a timely manner in order to meet booked order requirements and to reconcile the difference between required capacity and effective available capacity.

In **Chapter 10**, planning and control for remanufacturing approaches is discussed. Remanufacturing is the process by which products are recovered, processed, and sold as like-new products in the same or separate markets. Due to increasing legislation and the realization that being "green" can be profitable, an increasing number of companies have been implementing comprehensive programs in order to reap the potential benefits of remanufacturing. Managing the outsourcing supply chain is discussed in **Chapter 11**. Outsourcing is defined as the complete transfer of a business process that has been traditionally operated and managed internally to an independently owned external service provider. The outsourcing point of departure from these concepts is the complete transfer of all associated internal business process activities. When considering outsourcing, firms are evaluating whether to reverse a prior decision to "make." In other words, outsourcing reshapes a firm's boundaries. The critical manufacturing issues related to outsourcing are addressed in this textbook.

Finally, **Chapter 12** provides a discussion of manufacturing focused supply chain integration. The concept of manufacturing excellence cannot be achieved without an integrated manufacturing planning and control system. Information sharing, supply chain practice and technology must be integrated across the supply chain. Supply chain integration involves sharing information across the supply chain to monitor, control, and enhance overall manufacturing and supply chain performance. Manufacturing planning and control across the supply chain involves the coordination of purchasing, manufacturing and resource planning information.

Appendix B is a glossary of terms and definitions. The comprehensive glossary of terms is another unique feature of this textbook compared to other manufacturing planning and control textbooks. This glossary also synchronizes the textbook with the APICS educational mission.

Acknowledgments

The following reviewers provided valuable feedback on the manuscript. The reviewers contributed significantly to the final version. They include:

Thomas Brady	*Purdue University North Central*
Cem Canel	*University of North Carolina Wilmington*
Yong Hoon Choun	*The Ohio State University*
Jurriaan L. de Jong	*Suny Buffalo*
Yasser Dessouky	*San Jose State University*
Patrick Penfield	*Syracuse University*
Michael Stodnick	*University of Dallas*
Srinivas Talluri	*Michigan State University*
Robert Vokurka	*Texas A&M University*
Theresa Wells	*University of Wisconsin Eau Claire*

I particularly wish to express my gratitude to Lindu F. McHenry, Esq. of Benton and Associates for her critical review of certain parts of this textbook.

Charles McCormick, the executive editor, provided unwavering enthusiasm and support for this project. Charles is also a valued friend and colleague from the great state of Texas. I want to thank Conor Allen and the entire team at Cengage for producing the final product. Their passion for excellence helped us attain the highest level of quality and excellence. My greatest appreciation goes to my colleagues and the hundreds of students who have shared classrooms with me, from whom I have learned more than I have ever taught. If you have any comments or suggestions you would like to share with me, I welcome them.

Email: benton.1@osu.edu
www.supplychain-mgt.com

W. C. Benton, Jr.
Semper Fidelis

About the Author

W. C. Benton, Jr. is the Edwin D. Dodd Professor of Management and Distinguished Research Professor of Operations and Supply Chain Management in the Max M. Fisher College of Business at The Ohio State University. Professor Benton teaches courses in operations management to undergraduates, MBAs, and doctoral candidates. Dr. Benton received his doctorate in both operations and systems management and quantitative business analysis from Indiana University, Bloomington, Indiana.

Ranked number one out of 753 operations management researchers in terms of quality and quantity, Dr. Benton's vast research and writing accomplishments include more than 150 articles in the areas of healthcare performance issues, economics of cardiovascular surgery, purchasing management, inventory control, supply chain management, quality assurance, and materials management. They have appeared in *The New England Journal of Medicine, Annals of Thoracic Surgery, American College of Physician Executives, Decision Sciences, Journal of Operations Management, Naval Research Logistics, IEE Transactions, European Journal of Operational Research, Quality Progress, Naval Research Logistics, The Journal of Business Logistics, The Journal of Purchasing and Supply Chain Management, Production and Operations Management, Interfaces, Journal of Supply Chain Management,* and *Production and Operations Management.* Dr. Benton has published four textbooks and he has also authored "Bargaining, Negotiations, and Personal Selling" for the *Handbook of Economic Psychology.* He currently serves on the editorial boards for the *Journal of Operations Management, Decision Sciences, Journal of Supply Chain Management, Journal of Business Logistics, Business of Service Industries Journal,* and *International Journal of Productivity and Quality Management* and as a special issue editor for the *European Journal of Operational Research.* For the Engineer and Manufacturing and Service Enterprise Systems Divisions at the National Science Foundation, he is a research panel member.

Professor Benton's expert contributions to the business and governmental arena include consultancy for Grant Hospital, Ashland, IBM, RCA, Frigidaire, the Ohio Department of Transportation, the Florida Department of Transportation, the Indiana Department of Transportation, the South Carolina Department of Transportation, the Alabama Department of Transportation, the Kentucky Department of Transportation, the Federal Highway Administration, Battelle Institute, the United States Air Force, Gelzer Automated Assembly Systems, Bitronics, Inc., the Ohio Bureau of Disability Determination, Bio-Ohio, the Carter Group Canada, and others.

He serves on the board of directors for the Healthcare Accreditation Colloquium, Inc., the Sleep Medicine Foundation, the Academic Council for Healthcare Research, the House of Hope, and the Supply Chain Research Group and is a member of the Decision Sciences Institute, the Institute of Management Sciences, the Institute of Supply Management, the Production and Inventory Control Society, the Operations Management Association, American Society for Quality Control, Society of Logistics Engineers, the Mathematical Association of America, and others.

About the Authors

Note to Students

The material contained in this textbook is practical, relevant, and useful. The lessons you learn from this textbook are based on proven conceptual and analytical principles. The concepts covered in each chapter are relatively simple and highly intuitive.

The primary objective of a supply chain focused manufacturing planning and control system (MPCS) in any organization is to ensure that the desired products are manufactured at the right time and in the right quantities and are meeting quality specifications in the most cost-efficient manner. The ultimate goal for any ongoing concern is to quickly transform all manufactured products into profitable sales. The textbook is also an excellent resource for the many certification programs sponsored by the American Production and Inventory Control Society (APICS).

"The ability to achieve any goal is absolutely contingent on the quality of your mind"

Chapter 1

SUPPLY CHAIN FOCUSED MANUFACTURING PLANNING AND CONTROL

Learning Objectives

- Understand the trends in manufacturing planning and control
- Identify the relationship between the manufacturing planning and control system and the supply chain
- Explore the historical evolution of the current manufacturing philosophies
- Identify the primary performance criteria for each manufacturing philosophy
- Understand the manufacturing planning and control implications of different manufacturing environments
- Discuss the marketing positioning implications of the different manufacturing environments
- Explain the overall financial implications of supply chain focused manufacturing planning and control
- Learn about the Association for Operations Management (APICS) and related careers in operations planning and control

Introduction

The primary objective of a supply chain focused *manufacturing planning and control system* (MP&CS) in any organization is to ensure that the desired products are manufactured at the right time in the right quantities and are meeting quality specifications in the most cost-efficient manner. The MP&CS in a competitive organization is achieved by integrating the activities, such as (1) determining product demand, (2) translating product demand into feasible manufacturing plans, (3) developing detailed material flows plans for producing the product, (4) establishing capacity to support the overall manufacturing plans, and (5) executing scheduling and purchasing plans. In the past 20 years, there have been two significant trends in manufacturing planning and control.

The first is the significant growth in the theory and practice of the supply chain management concept. Supply chain management has become the key driver of competitive advantage for manufacturing organizations. Manufacturing planning and control must now be integrated into the supply chain revolution. In many organizations, manufacturing has been integrated with the supply chain management function.

The second trend is the increasing interest in sustainability. Remanufacturing is the process by which products are recovered, processed, and sold as like-new products in the same or separate markets. Because of increasing legislation and the realization that being "green" can be profitable, an increasing number of companies are implementing comprehensive programs in order to reap the potential benefits of remanufacturing. In the United States, laws mandating companies to be responsible for the take back of electronic wastes are becoming prevalent at the state level. The Remanufacturing Institute (www.reman.org) reports that as of May 2010, 21 states in the United States had passed laws requiring Original Equipment Manufacturers (OEMs) to be responsible for taking back and reusing and/or disposing of end of life products. However, few guidelines are available to the practicing manager to aid in planning, controlling, and managing remanufacturing operations. Production planning and control activities have become more complex and difficult for the manufacturer engaging in remanufacturing operations mainly due to the uncertainty in sourcing returned items required for remanufacturing. The remanufacturing planning and control concept will be presented in chapter 10 in this textbook.

It is easy to see that sustainability and supply chain focused manufacturing planning and control have a significant impact on current approaches to manufacturing planning and control philosophies. This text book will not address the architecture for an exhaustive enterprise resource planning (ERP) approach to manufacturing planning and control, but instead, it is an attempt to present a comprehensive foundation and a series of proven concepts that can be applied to the many innovations and attributes observed in today's fluid and diverse supply chain focused manufacturing environment. The topic of manufacturing planning and control (MP&C) and related functions to the planning activities of supply chain focused organizations will be examined. Specifically, the focus will be on the strategic, tactical, and operational planning control activities of the manufacturing organization and not on the automation or design of the manufacturing environment. The relevant information flows will also be described in the MP&C framework. The hierarchal manufacturing planning and control framework is given in Figure 1.

Successful manufacturing organizations are increasingly adapting customer-driven manufacturing philosophies. The current MP&C framework has evolved into a highly integrated value chain of customers and suppliers. In today's manufacturing environment, the customer has become the most important driver of the manufacturing

Figure 1 Manufacturing Planning and Control Framework

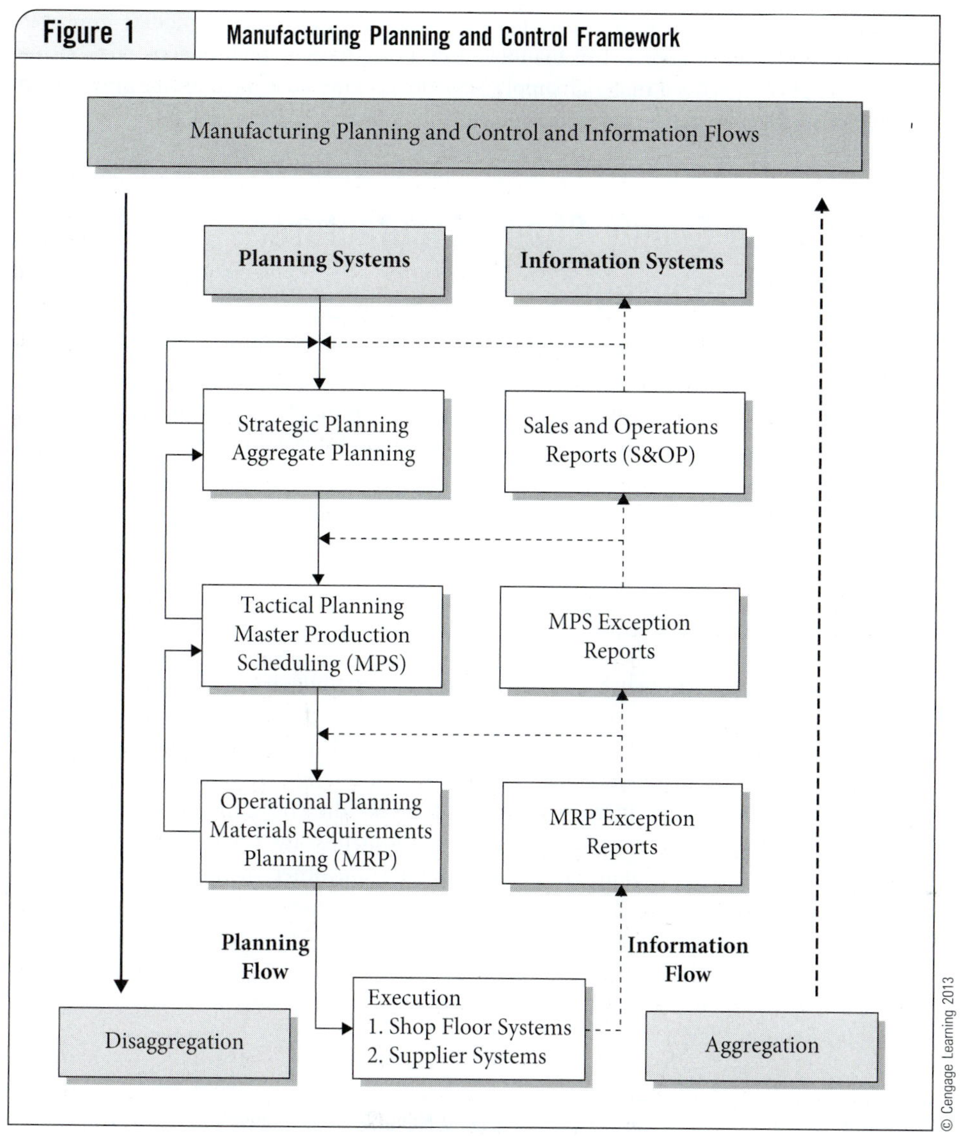

organizations. Customers are increasingly more demanding and no longer willing to accept standard products. In addition, the Internet has led to customers interacting and directly with the manufacturing organizations. As an example, in the case of Dell Computer, customers access the Internet to directly express their preferences on computer specifications and functionality. In effect, the customer places an order for a customized computer. At the same time, the standard Dell computers continue to be sold through alternative distribution channels (e.g., retail outlets).

The greater interaction between the customer and the manufacturer means that in order to quickly respond to customer specifications, the manufacturer must have a close relationship with both suppliers and customers. Customer–supplier relationship management has become one of the most important supply chain functions. The master production scheduling (MPS) function facilitates the supplier- and customer-relationship management process. If a customer requests a specific delivery time, the manufacturing organization must respond to the customer's request. In order to accommodate improved delivery performance requests, the manufacturer must have a high-quality relationship with the supplier to reduce material supply lead times. This is, in fact, an example of the importance of supply chain focused manufacturing planning and control.

The Focused Supply Chain Manufacturer–Supplier Relationship

As supply chain management becomes more relational in nature, there has been a paradigm shift from a transactional to a strategic relationship in the supply chain management environment (see Benton and Maloni, 2005; Trent, 2005). Traditional manufacturer–supplier relationships are based on arms-length transactions between supplying firms and the manufacturer, which does not provide adequate motivation for long-term relationship building. If there is mutual commitment, the manufacturer and supplying firms will work harder to satisfy the ultimate customer, thereby increasing the profitability of the entire supply chain. Manufacturing firms that are committed to the supplying firms will gain a competitive advantage based on information sharing. Both the manufacturing and supplying firms will be better off.

The state of the relationship quality between the manufacturer and supplying firm influences the overall effectiveness (of the competitive performance) of the supply chain. Healthy manufacturer–supplier relationships will secure a competitive supply chain network and allow for the possibility of lower costs, higher quality, and better service, as well as a promise of increased market share for the entire manufacturing supply chain. On the other hand, counterproductive relationships are when both firms are so focused on getting what is best for them that puts the other members of the supply chain are at a disadvantage. This type of relationship is undesirable, because it does not foster a positive relationship between firms involved in the supply chain networks. This dysfunctional relationship will discourage any future dealings between manufacturing firms and supplying firms, creating more instability in each firm's effectiveness (Prahinski and Benton, 2004).

Figure 2 Typical Supply Chain Focused Manufacturing Network

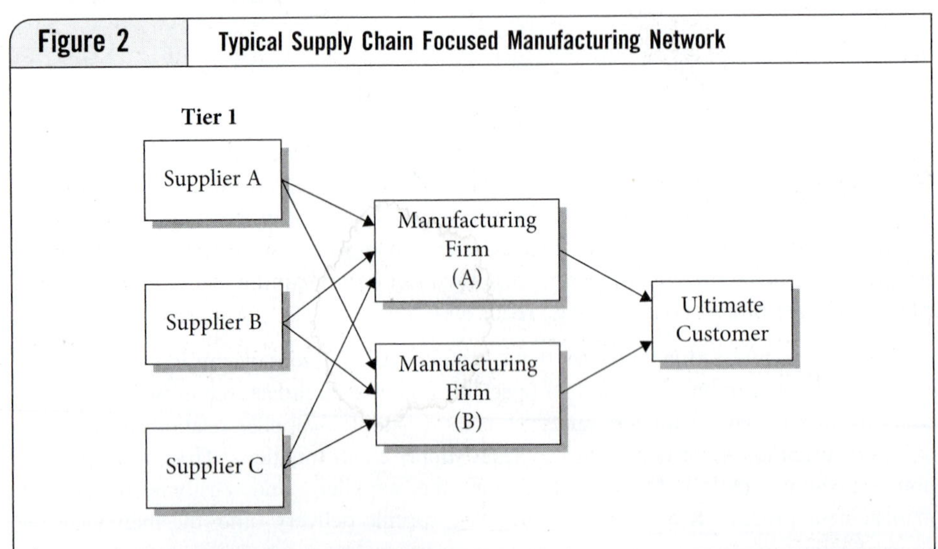

Each member of the supply chain (i.e., supplying firm, manufacturing firm, and customer) is a stakeholder. The objective is to provide a valued product or service to the ultimate stakeholder, the customer, as shown in Figure 2.

As can be seen in Figure 2, the ultimate customer is the end point in the supply chain. The individual members of the supply chain cannot function effectively without the relationship quality and service performance of the other supply chain members. The quality of the relationships between members will determine which supply chains (or firms) survive in a hypercompetitive *market share*–driven business environment. Many manufacturing organizations consider the relationship between themselves and their ultimate customers more important than the business-to-business relationship with their suppliers. The challenge facing manufacturing firms is deciding how to increase the value of the supply chain without sacrificing the interests of the ultimate customer and supplying organization.

Some of the more significant supply chain focused manufacturing changes are:

1. Shorter product life cycles
2. Adoption of lean manufacturing concepts
3. A trend toward integrated manufacturing
4. Highly variable demand patterns
5. More product variety demanded by the ultimate customer
6. Shorter cumulative lead times from manufacturer to customer
7. A reduction in fabrication value added
8. More emphasis on purchasing value-added components and assemblies

Companies throughout the world are using the factors listed here as a means of competitive advantage. Given the fluid and diverse nature of domestic and global markets companies must constantly adapt their manufacturing planning and control systems in order to remain competitive. Shorter product life cycles, highly variable demand patterns, and increased product variety can lead to major disruptions in the manufacturing planning and control process. The manufacturing organization that learns how to adapt, innovate, and manage in this changing environment can gain a competitive advantage in the market place. Many manufacturing organizations are also embracing lean strategies and integrative manufacturing flows. The objective of integrated manufacturing is to focus on the flows of materials, purchase orders, booked orders, and final product flows. The lean manufacturing philosophy is given in the next section.

The Lean Philosophy

Lean is about doing more with less: less time, inventory, space, labor, and money. Lean manufacturing is a commitment to eliminating waste, simplifying procedures, and speeding up production. Lean manufacturing, in its most basic form, is the systematic elimination of waste—overproduction, waiting, transportation, inventory, motion, overprocessing, defective units—and the implementation of the concepts of continuous flow and customer pull.

Five areas drive lean manufacturing/production:

1. Cost
2. Quality

3. Delivery
4. Safety, and
5. Morale

Just as mass production is recognized as the production system of the 20th century, lean production is viewed as the production system of the 21st century. It has been shown from testimonials that the establishment and mastering of a lean production system allows manufacturing organizations to achieve the following benefits:

- Waste reduction of 80 percent
- Production cost reduction of 50 percent
- Manufacturing cycle times decreased of 50 percent
- Labor reduction of 50 percent while maintaining or increasing throughput
- Inventory reduction of 80 percent while increasing customer service levels
- Capacity in current facilities increased by 50 percent
- Higher quality
- Higher profits
- Higher system flexibility in reacting to changes in requirements improved
- More strategic focus
- Improved cash flow through increasing shipping and billing frequencies

However, by continually focusing on waste reduction, there is truly no end to the benefits that can be achieved. The five elements of enabling a lean approach are:

1. Specify value
2. Identify and map the value stream
3. Efficient flows
4. Pull philosophy
5. Quality perfection

Many practitioners and academicians believe that the future of global manufacturing planning and control must be lean, adaptable, and integrated. However, there is no consensus on how integration is defined. Integration is sometimes described as linking the product design, the manufacturing process and manufacturing planning and control using information technology as shown in Figure 1. At the same time, many organizations are now searching for ways to integrate all their manufacturing activities and connect them with the entire supply chain by using fully integrated enterprise resource planning (ERP) systems.

Historical Perspective

Twenty years ago, manufacturing planning and control systems were highly decentralized. Production managers were responsible for the scheduling of production, ordering of materials, and shipment of products within their assigned departments. The manufacturing revolution is now relatively mature and has seen several phases of transition. As these early industrial-era firms evolved from highly specialized fixed-quantity reorder-point systems of production and inventory, control systems gradually replaced these decentralized "seat-of-the-pants" manufacturing planning systems. Reorder-point

Table 1 Historical Perspective

PERIOD	1970s	1980s	1990s	2000 & BEYOND
Manufacturing philosophy	Push manufacturing	Lean manufacturing	Flexible manufacturing	Adaptive manufacturing
Key market differentiator	Cost	Quality	Availability	Lead time
Performance criteria	Production throughput	Return on assets (ROA)	Segment market share	Customer satisfaction

inventory systems are independent and disconnected when used as the primary planning and control mechanism. Table 1 shows the various manufacturing stages starting from the push (MRP) manufacturing of the early days to the hybrid or adaptable ERP-based manufacturing. Adaptable manufacturing is fast becoming a standard practice for some of the more sophisticated companies (Wal-Mart, Toyota, Lockheed Martin, and others). It is important to understand that the *newer* manufacturing practices do not replace the *older* ones but instead continue to *blend* the best of the current and past manufacturing practices to meet current business needs. Thus, although various manufacturing philosophies currently exist—push, lean, flexible—none are applied in a pure, holistic fashion. Today, most companies run hybrid planning and control systems.

Push Manufacturing

Demand push is usually defined as a business response in anticipation of customer demand and demand pull as a response resulting from customer demand. However, from a supply chain viewpoint, deciding whether a particular supply chain is push or pull is often difficult and generally depends on the perspective of what constitutes the supply chain and where particular participants are placed in the supply chain. For example, the manufacture of Toyota automobiles is heralded as a leading example of a customer demand–driven (pull) supply chain. In the 1970s, the simplicity of product designs and operations resulted in relatively simplistic but functional push manufacturing systems. At that time, it was still a sellers' market for the most part, and companies were focused primarily on building capacity and maximizing production throughput. Product variety was limited, and almost all that was produced was built to forecast. This was the era that also saw the real emergence and popularity of material requirements planning (MRP), which became recognized as a key tool for enhancing productivity. Not only did MRP enable companies to do a better job managing inventory, it also enabled companies to do systematic capacity requirements planning (CRP). For the first time, a feedback loop was established from the CRP module to alert when there was not enough capacity available to produce to plan.

Lean (Pull) Manufacturing

The push manufacturing decade was followed by the lean manufacturing era. Popularized by the Japanese as just-in-time (JIT) or pull manufacturing, the principal focus of the lean manufacturing philosophy was to minimize all forms of waste and produce quality products. Rework was considered the worst waste of all, and one of the primary metrics of lean manufacturing was "first-pass" quality. Not surprisingly, the greatest impact of lean manufacturing was in the reduction of waste. The philosophy worked well in an environment of low product variability and relatively stable customer demand.

Table 2 **Differentiators of Push and Pull Manufacturing Models**

DIFFERENTIATOR	PUSH MANUFACTURING	LEAN MANUFACTURING
Prime business driver	Maximize utilization of resources, raw materials, and throughput cost.	High levels of customer service through responsiveness and flexibility in order to meet customer demand.
Supply chain strategy	Operate strict processes in anticipation of demand. Emphasize demand forecasting and sales and operations planning (S&OP). Explore postponement.	Operate in response to customer demand. Emphasize the five lean principles.
Lead times	Relatively long	Short
Pricing strategy	Pricing is subject to market forces based on supply and demand.	Pricing does not normally impact short-term demand. Based on product quality and branding.
Manufacturing strategy	Long production runs	Short and flexible production runs
Inventory	Typically high. Emphasize inventory planning, safety stock policies, and ABC classification. Push as close to customer as possible.	Typically low. Pull as remotely from the customer as possible.

By focusing on narrow product mixes with relatively predictable demand, many of the lean manufacturing facilities of the 1980s outperformed conventional plants that were still following a purely push production philosophy that focused primarily on building capacity. The automotive industry profited most from lean manufacturing, and the best practices from the automotive industry have since penetrated several other industry sectors.

The five-step thought process for guiding the implementation of lean techniques is easy to remember but not always easy to achieve:

1. Specify value from the standpoint of the end customer by product family.
2. Identify all the steps in the value stream for each product family, and eliminating whenever possible those steps that do not create value.
3. Make the value-creating steps occur in tight sequence so the product will flow smoothly toward the customer.
4. As flow is introduced, let customers pull value from the next upstream activity.
5. As value is specified, value streams are identified and wasted steps are removed. Next flow and pull are introduced. The process continues it until a state of perfection is reached in which perfect value is created with no waste.

A comparison of the push and lean approaches are summarized in Table 2.

Flexible Manufacturing

Flexible manufacturing is a method for producing goods that is readily adaptable to changes in the product being manufactured. Machines have the ability to handle varying levels of production. A flexible manufacturing system (FMS) gives manufacturing firms an advantage in a quickly changing manufacturing environment. This postindustrial phenomenon was a response to more volatile markets, higher product proliferation,

Table 3 Different Flexible Manufacturing Approaches

APPROACH	FLEXIBILITY MEANING
Manufacturing	• The capability of producing different parts without major retooling • A measure of how fast the company converts its process(es) from making an old line of products to producing a new product • The ability to change a production schedule, modify a part, or handle multiple parts
Operational	• The ability to efficiently produce highly customized and unique products
Customer	• The ability to exploit various dimensions of speed of delivery
Strategic	• The ability of a company to offer a wide variety of products to its customers
Capacity	• The ability to rapidly increase or decrease production levels or to shift capacity quickly from one product or service to another

shorter life cycles, quicker response capabilities, and more sophisticated buyers. All of these factors increased business complexity significantly and led to the breakdown of the lean principles that focused on stable demand and relatively low product variation.

In a changing manufacturing environment, responsiveness and product availability are important to maintaining sales and market share. Flexibility became the new strategic imperative. Flexible manufacturing exploited the gain from product proliferation and mass customization to reach economies of scope. Flexible manufacturing practices also popularized the concepts of general-purpose machines and equipment, cross-trained workers, information technology, well-developed suppliers, and a highly trained workforce. But flexible manufacturing was not without its drawbacks, chief among them being the cost of flexibility. Companies came to realize that although some excess flexible capacity allowed better management of variability, outsourced manufacturing was often a more financially viable means to the same end. Thus began the era of outsourcing.

Outsourcing had a dramatic impact on a company's cost structure. Large chunks of fixed costs simply disappeared. On the downside, with outsourcing came loss of control. As manufacturing moved outside the four walls of the company, visibility became a major concern. The focus shifted to collaborative capabilities, and technology began having a major impact on visibility and collaboration.

The late 1990s and the early part of this century have seen the dramatic impact of technology on productivity. The efficiency benefits of push manufacturing, the quality benefits of lean manufacturing, and the responsiveness benefits of flexible manufacturing have all become market qualifiers.

The different aspects of the flexible manufacturing approach are shown in Table 3.

Adaptive Manufacturing

The customer is now in charge, and companies that adapt quickly and efficiently to the customer's various demands are destined for success. Adaptive (integrated) manufacturing is the key characteristic driving this success. Adaptability has two primary characteristics: flexibility and velocity. Flexibility enables a manufacturing unit to scale efficiently, while velocity determines its ability to switch operational modes rapidly and to transition between modes, such as high-volume/low-mix to high-volume/high-mix product loadings. Adaptive manufacturing enterprises are expected to achieve required flexibility and velocity by linking technology to manufacturing planning and control processes, production equipment, and manufacturing systems. This adaptive (integrated) technology will allow for the profitable manufacture of products for increasingly time-sensitive and competitive markets.

Adaptive manufacturing is the ability to profitably replenish the supply chain while dynamically responding to supply and demand uncertainties. With global supply chains, the more fragmented the supply chain, the more adaptive it needs to be. Even a small disruption can cause expensive problems, so it is crucial (even for a lean six-sigma enterprise) to detect these exceptions proactively and dampen them at the source.

Different Manufacturing Environments

In order to understand the significance of manufacturing planning and control, it is necessary to have an understanding of the different types of manufacturing environments. The different manufacturing environments are (1) make to stock (MTS), (2) make to order (MTO), (3) assemble to order (ATO), and (4) engineering to order (ETO).

Make-to-Stock

A product market strategy for pursuing a given level of customization is closely linked to the manufacturing approach. A make-to-stock (MTS) manufacturing approach is usually undertaken for fairly standard products whose demand can be forecast with reasonable accuracy. Finished goods inventory is used to fill orders, as customers expect fairly immediate availability. Forecasts are usually developed by product family. MTS manufacturing environments are characterized by sales volume and minimum customer interaction. The customer delivery time is usually determined by availability and forecasts quality. However, the manufacturing firm must respond to customer demand instantaneously in order to be competitive in an MTS marketing environment. Finished goods inventory is used to buffer against uncertain demand.

Make-to-Order

A make-to-order (MTO) approach is undertaken in situations in which a high degree of customization is involved and it is extremely difficult to forecast demand for a specific product or features associated with a product. Items in the bill of materials are procured after the receipt of the customer order. The products are usually customized based on the customer's specifications and unique bill of materials. Manufacturing of MTO products begins with receipt of an order, and configuration of the product is likely to change from the initial specification during the production process. Interaction with the customer is high. There is very little demand uncertainty associated with the MTO manufacturing environment. However, the sales volume and lead times are difficult to forecast.

Assemble-to-Order

An assemble-to-order (ATO) approach is used when the product market strategy pursues customization (offering a large number of potential end-item configurations) by allowing customers to select a combination of features associated with several key product modules. Modular product architecture is emphasized during product development to enable manufacturing to custom-configure these features during final assembly. A forecast of the demand for features is used to drive the master production schedule. Actual orders for a given end item configuration are used to drive the final assembly schedule. ATO organizations manufacture a variety of semifinished modules that can be quickly assembled together to produce a finished product with customer options. Products are designed in such a way that a large number of finished products can be assembled from a small number of core assemblies. Core module demands can be easily forecast similar to the MTS environment. Final assembly is driven by actual customer orders. ATO organizations' competitive priorities are both lead time and customization.

Product strategy in an ATO environment is concerned with both fundamental product variety (platform and model mix) and peripheral product variety (option mix). The peripheral product variety decisions involve determining the combinatorial (geometric) variety level and the manner in which features are offered through development of option alternatives for product modules.

Engineer-to-Order

The engineer-to-order (ETO) approach is similar to a make-to-order scenario, except that the customers also expect a significant level of engineering design from the manufacturer. ETO organizations manufacture unique products designed to customer specifications. Each product requires a unique set of component part numbers, bills of material, and routing file. Each engineered product is tailored to the requirements of specific customer. Products are complex with long lead times, typically months or even years. Unlike the alternative manufacturing approaches, the customer is heavily involved throughout the entire design and manufacturing process. Engineering changes are a way of life. Material is purchased not for inventory but for a specific final product. The actual costs are allocated to the specific product and tracked against the original estimate. Once completed, the product is typically installed at the customer's site. In most cases, aftermarket services continue throughout the product life cycle. The competitive estimating and bidding pricing approach is usually used by customer. The ETO approach is similar to building a commercial construction project.

Implications for Alternative Manufacturing Environments

The implications for master planning are given in Table 4, and a product-related comparison of the various manufacturing environments is given in Figure 3.

In typical manufacturing companies, 40 to 70 percent of the total assets in the supply chain are fixed (plant and machinery). Organizations that leverage these fixed assets productively are capable of generating higher-than-normal returns. Some of the world's

Table 4 **Implications for Master Planning in Different Manufacturing Environments**

ASPECT	MTS	ATO	MTO	ETO
MPS unit	Sales unit	Major components	End products	End products
Final assembly scheduling	Close correspondence to the master schedule	Determined by customer orders received by order entry	Covers most of the assembly operations	Covers all of the assembly operations
Bill of material (BOM) structuring	Standard BOMs (one BOM for each sales item)	Planning BOMs are used	BOMs are unique and created for each customer order	BOMs are unique and created for each customer order

Figure 3 **Positioning Strategy and Manufacturing Technology**

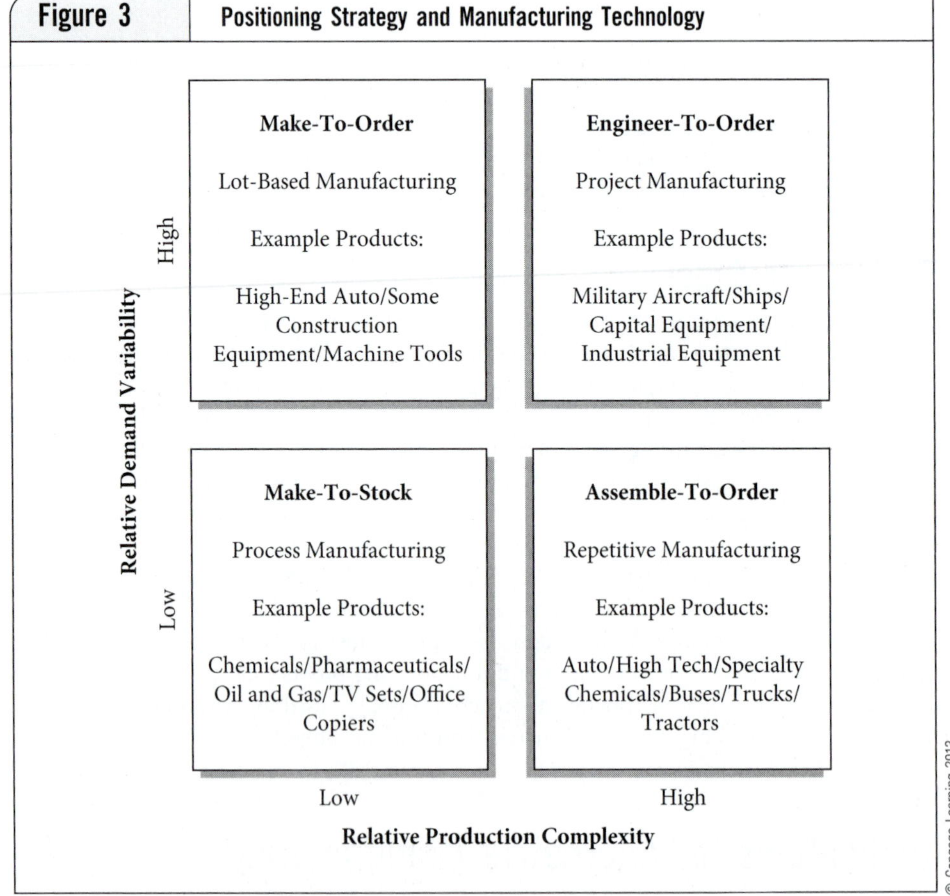

foremost automobile companies (known for their lean production philosophy) and some of the world's most efficient computer manufacturers (known for their mass customization and flexible manufacturing capabilities) have been leveraging their manufacturing competence to generate financial benefits that far outstrip those generated by their peers.

Manufacturing Return on Investment Drivers

Successful manufacturing organizations will always create value through obtaining a higher return on assets (ROA). ROA is an important measure of manufacturing effectiveness. ROA is a function of profit margin and asset turnover. Specifically, profit margin measures operating efficiency and asset turnover measures how well the manufacturing organization is utilizing its capital assets. There are two types of asset turns: fixed and variable. Fixed asset turns commonly refer to the machinery and equipment on the shop floor; variable asset turns refer to the inventory impacted by manufacturing. This inventory can be raw material (RM), finished goods (FG), or work in process (WIP). Figure 4 shows the drivers that constitute the ROA equation and the key operational metrics directly affected by manufacturing operations.

A simple ROA example is given in Example 1.1.

Figure 4 Manufacturing ROA Drivers

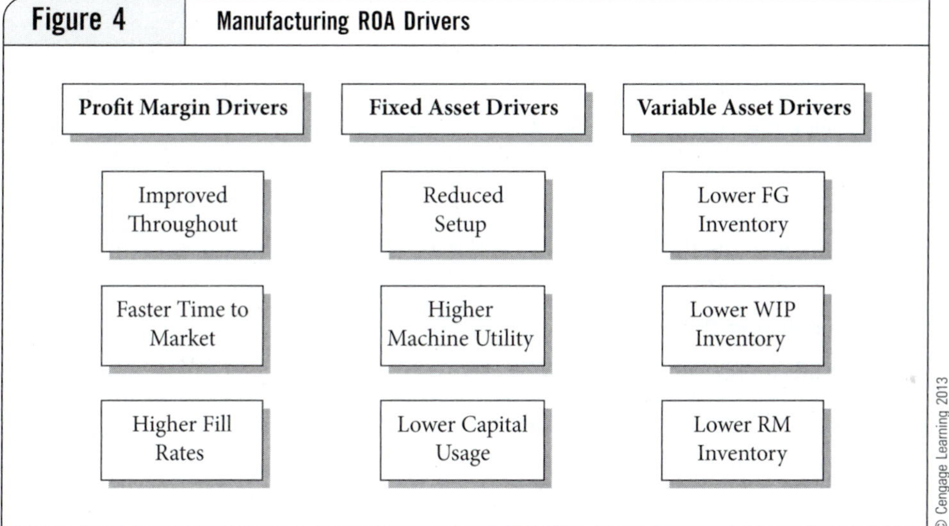

Example 1.1

Return on assets measures the amount of profit the company generates as a percentage of the value of its total assets.

How It Works:

A company's *return on assets (ROA)* is calculated as the ratio of its net income in a given period to the total value of its assets. For instance, if a company has $10,000 in total assets and generates $2,000 in net income, its ROA would be $2,000 / $10,000 = 0.2 or 20%.

Why It Matters:

The profit percentage of assets varies by industry. For this reason it is often more effective to compare a company's ROA to that of other companies in the same industry or against its own ROA figures from previous periods. Investors and analysts should bear in mind that the ROA does not account for outstanding liabilities and may indicate a higher profit level than actually derived.

The Association for Operations Management (APICS)

The Association for Operations Management (APICS) (www.apics.org) is the global leader and premier source of the body of knowledge in supply chain and operations management, including production, inventory, materials management, purchasing, and logistics. For many years, companies have relied on APICS for its superior training, internationally recognized certifications, comprehensive resources, and worldwide network of accomplished industry professionals.

The APICS CPIM certification program prepares the professional with the dynamic ability to understand and evaluate production and inventory activities within a company's global operations. The APICS CPIM prepares the professional with essential terminology, concepts, and strategies related to the following topics:

- demand management
- procurement management
- supplier planning
- material requirements planning
- capacity planning
- sales and operations planning
- master scheduling
- performance measurements
- supplier relationships
- quality control
- continuous improvement

The certification examination modules are:

1. Basics of Supply Chain Management
2. Master Planning of Resources
3. Detailed Scheduling and Planning
4. Execution and Control of Operations
5. Strategic Management of Resources

The information in this textbook provides excellent preparation for the APICS certification examination. A comprehensive glossary of the supply chain focused manufacturing planning and control definitions is also included in Appendix B.

The various CPIM Program Exam Modules are given below:

Basics of Supply Chain Management

Explore the basic concepts in managing the complete flow of materials in a supply chain.

Master Planning of Resources

Explore the processes used to develop sales and operations plans, and learn to identify and assess internal and external demand and forecasting requirements.

Detailed Scheduling and Planning

Focus on the various techniques for material and capacity scheduling.

Execution and Control of Operations

Focus on the areas of prioritizing and sequencing work, executing work plans and implementing controls, reporting activity results, and providing feedback on performance.

Strategic Management of Resources

Explore the relationship of existing and emerging processes and technologies to manufacturing strategy and supply chain-related functions.

The CPIM certification exam is useful as a resume builder for undergraduate and graduate students in manufacturing, as it demonstrates to potential employers that the individual has an in-depth knowledge of how to manage the manufacturing process and the distribution of various products and services. Some operations management programs require students to pass the CPIM exam as a prerequisite for graduation.

SUMMARY

This chapter documents and motivates the evolution of the manufacturing and control paradigm to include the challenges and opportunities posed by supply chain management. Supply chain management is becoming the key driver of competitive advantage for manufacturing organizations. Manufacturing planning and control must now be integrated into the supply chain revolution. Chapter 1 focuses on the strategic, tactical, operational planning, and control activities of the manufacturing organization. The relevant information flows are also described in the MP&C framework. The hierarchal manufacturing planning and control framework is also discussed. Healthy manufacturer–supplier relationships will secure a competitive supply chain network and allow for the possibility of lower costs, higher quality, and better service, as well as offering a promise of increased market share for the entire manufacturing supply chain. The challenge facing the manufacturer (manufacturing firms) is deciding how to increase the value of the supply chain without sacrificing the interests of the ultimate customer and supplying organization.

It is important to understand that the *newer* manufacturing practices do not replace the *older* ones but instead continue to *blend* the best of the current and past manufacturing practices to meet current business needs. Thus, although various manufacturing philosophies currently exist—push, lean, flexible—none are applied in a pure, holistic fashion. Most companies run a hybrid system. Next an indepth discussion of the different manufacturing and marketing environment is presented. The chapter concludes with an indepth discussion of manufacturing return on investment drivers.

DISCUSSION QUESTIONS AND EXERCISES

1. Write a brief memo to your immediate manager discussing why the study of supply chain focused manufacturing planning and control is important in today's competitive manufacturing environment.
2. Discuss the relationship between the manufacturing planning and control system and the supply chain.
3. Discuss in detail the manufacturing planning and control process given in Figure 1.
4. Consider a durable product that you have recently purchased. Classify the product in terms of the positioning strategy and manufacturing technology.

5. Define lean manufacturing. Give as much detail as possible.
6. Discuss the difference between push and pull manufacturing systems. Which manufacturing system requires a higher level of management expertise? Give specific examples in your response.
7. What is the impact of return on asset (ROA) on manufacturing operational excellence?
8. Josh, Inc. is faced with the choice of either producing a newly designed product, XX-30, to stock in anticipation of demand or to customer order. The demand for the product is expected to be 5,000 units per week. Josh decided to produce XX-30 in lots of 500 units. The cost of holding the average unit in inventory per year is $50 times the average inventory level. If Josh, Inc. produces to order, it must discount its unit price on all sales $5 for each week that the first customer to order has to wait before the product is delivered. Should Josh, Inc. produce to stock or to order?
9. Consider a firm that produces a product that costs $300 each at the rate of 10,000 units per week. From the time that production begins, it takes four weeks to complete. The raw material cost is $180. All of the raw materials are added to the product at the time each product is started. Assuming that labor and overhead costs are added in equal parts over the four-week processing period for each unit, determine the average value of work-in-process inventory for the firm.

REFERENCES

Benton, W. C., and M. Maloni. "The Influence of Power Driven Buyer/Seller Relationships on Supply Chain Satisfaction." *Journal of Operations Management* (2005) Vol. 23, No. 1, pp. 1–22.

Prahinski C., and W. C. Benton. "Supply Chain Communication Strategies." *Journal of Operations Management* (2003) Vol. 22, No. 1, pp. 39–62.

Trent, R. J. "Why Relationships Matter," *Supply Chain Management Review*, November, 2005.

Chapter 2

FORECASTING DEMAND

Learning Objectives

- Learn about the uses of forecasts in a supply chain focused manufacturing environment
- Define the manufacturing planning and control forecasting problem
- Understand the difference between forecasts and predictions
- Understand the systematic forecasting process
- Evaluate the differences between qualitative and quantitative forecasting models
- Evaluate short term forecasting models
- Learn how to generate and evaluate exponential smoothing models
- Learn how to measure forecast quality
- Learn how to monitor forecasts using the tracking signal concept

Introduction

Supply Chain Management

In dynamic business-to-business environments, maintaining a competitive advantage is a major survival factor. The advent of supply chain management has led to a more complicated operating environment. The supply chain includes purchasing, inventory coordination, manufacturing, scheduling, facility location, transportation, and distribution. Each of these functions is influenced by product demand. Without accurate forecasting, the entire supply chain would be inefficient and costly. As manufacturing information technology evolves, firms have become more integrated. Therefore, integrating effective supply chain practice with effective demand information sharing becomes critical for improving supply chain performance.

Forecasting drives all of the key business functions. Forecasts are the inputs for budgeting, capacity planning, purchasing, inventory management, and staffing decisions. Some examples of how forecasts are used in the operations management function are given below:

- Demand forecasts are inputs to both business strategy and production resource planning.
- New facility planning—It can take at least five years to design and build a new factory or design and implement a new production process.
- Production planning—Demand for products varies from month to month, and it can take several months to change the capacities of production processes.
- Workforce scheduling—Demand for services (and the necessary staffing) can vary from hour to hour, and the employees' weekly work schedules must be developed in advance. (Also see Chapter 9).

In most organizations, the marketing department is responsible for preparing demand forecasts while operations management is responsible for forecasting inventory requirements and resource requirements based on the demand forecasts. The elements of a good forecast are:

- The forecast interval must be consistent with the demand patterns. Before one can start to forecast, it is necessary to determine what the forecasting or data-collection interval should be. The pattern of demand estimates will determine whether a daily, weekly, monthly, quarterly, or yearly forecast is required.
- While all forecasts inevitably will have errors, the number and influence of these errors must be kept to a minimum.
- The forecast must be reliable. There should be a high degree of measurable consistency over time.
- The forecast must be valid. There must be a high level of face and convergent validity.
- The forecast must be cost effective.

The Forecasting Criteria

Forecasting can be categorized by the following criteria:

a. Accuracy
b. Simplicity of computation
c. Flexibility to adjust the response rate

Accuracy is a measure of how well a forecasted condition mirrors the actual condition when it occurs forecast are rarely perfect. Highly *precise* forecasts will not allow for simplicity of computation. Thus there must be a trade-off between accuracy and precision. As an example, fast-moving seasonal market forces associated with snow tires in Michigan require forecast calculations to be accurate. On the other hand, if a space shuttle launch is scheduled, a *precise* weather forecast is necessary. The flexibility to adjust the rate of response is how adaptable the forecast is to changing conditions. In the snow tire example, if the winter weather was significantly below the norm, it would be relatively easy to adjust the forecast model. The forecasting model has to be able to adapt the model parameters, such as a change in the linear slope of a regression model. On the other hand, if the shuttle launch is delayed or aborted because of the weather condition, there are no simple operational adjustments available. Operational *precision* is necessary for a successful shuttle launch.

The Conceptual Forecasting Framework

The forecasting experiential input is the first step in the forecasting process. Managerial judgment is perhaps the most important component of the forecasting process. Next, the forecast must be validated by comparing the forecasted demand with actual demand for a specific period. This calculation represents a measure of forecast error. The forecast

Figure 1 Conceptual Forecast Framework

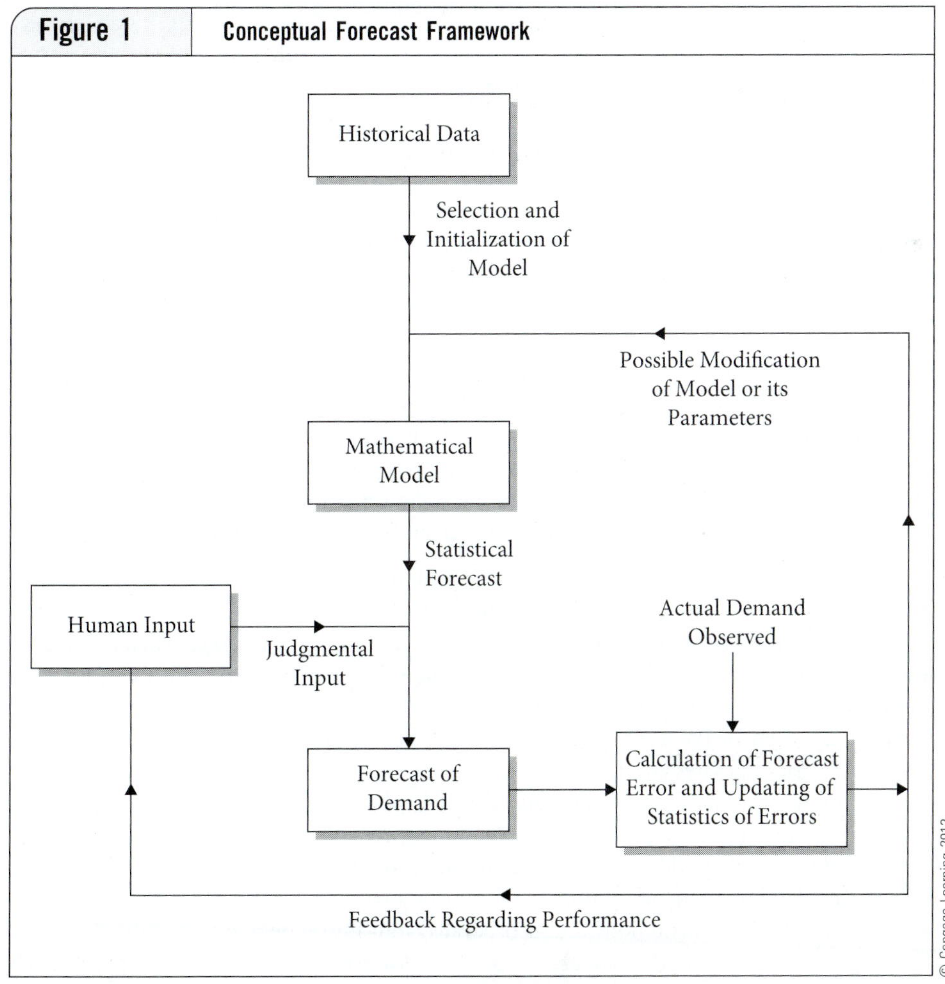

error can then be used to determine the appropriate level of safety stock required for a predetermined level of customer service. Safety stock calculations will be addressed in the supply chain inventory chapter (Chapter 5). The forecast errors are also used to monitor and track the quality of the forecast parameters and other managerial inputs. The conceptual forecasting framework is given in Figure 1.

As can been seen in Figure 1 the forecasting framework requires input from two sources-historical data and human judgment. The initialization phase is first step in developing a forecast. Historical data should be plotted to see if there is a pattern in the past data. These detected patterns should be used to set the initial values related to historical data. It is advisable to use historical data to set the initial values for the base, trend and seasonality indexes. After setting the initial values it is important to build a mathematical model. Next, the forecasting model is tested using another segment of historical data. Finally the forecasting model is modified using relevant parameters.

The Forecasting Problem

The forecasting problem is to achieve a "good" estimate of future conditions. For expository purposes, we will consider here sales or demand forecasting. Although we will follow a common practice of loosely equating sales and demand, it is worth noting that sales is only *one* observed indication of underlying desire or demand.

Forecasts versus Prediction

Forecasting estimates can be segregated into (1) the causal factors that generated past demand and (2) the new causal factors that are expected to come into play in determining future demand. The actual demand for a product or service is generated by a complex interaction of many factors. It is an overwhelming task to understand and model all of these factors, such as the effects of competition, strength of the economy, and advertising expenditures. As a result, there is a considerable appeal in attempting to reduce the complexity associated with estimating future demands. An approach to this problem would be to, in an aggregative fashion, identify some past basic demand level generated by a complex set of known and unknown factors. Consequentially, we can separate our future demand estimating efforts into two categories of models. The first category of *qualitative* forecasting is concerned with estimating the future aggregative basic demand level, while the second category of *quantitative* forecasting is concerned with better assessing the influence of additional or new causal factors on a given or basic demand level.

Forecasts can be largely associated with statistical measurements based upon sound statistical theory. However, intuitive *predictions* or judgments must be made on many occasions, such as when substitutes for an existing product are coming on the market, when a change in economic conditions would indicate that a sizable change in demand will occur, or when demand estimates are required for new products that have no past demand performance data. Thus, when BMW adds a new 5-series sports car, predictions are required both for the new 5-series car sales and for their influence on existing 5-series automobile sales. *Forecasting*, on the other hand, may be usefully defined as being based upon the projection of the past into the future, where the past is assumed to represent a series of unknown or random interactive factors that will be maintained in the future. It is necessary to carefully select or screen past data to obtain an appropriate forecasting base. Just as the probability and influence of "nonrandom" conditions are incorporated into future demand estimates as predictions, past actual demands that are to be used for forecasting are often appropriately screened to eliminate the effect of "nonrandom" conditions. Thus, if the local chamber of commerce were interested in obtaining an estimate of weekly demand for a restaurant in Columbus, Ohio, the market researcher would be well advised to eliminate university football home game weekends, graduations, and the like from the base for forecasting. Similarly, the influence of a major promotion must be isolated to ascertain base-level sales at BMW dealerships. The major emphasis hereafter will be on forecasting rather than on prediction, since prediction is primarily a judgmental matter that is highly situation oriented, and few explicit models are available. We will, however, see that our forecasting methodology will attempt to identify instances in which predictive or judgmental inputs are required.

The remainder of the chapter will focus on the systematic forecasting process using alternative forecasting techniques. Using statistical methods, alternative forecasting techniques will be used to evaluate forecast quality. The systematic seven step process below is recommended.

A Systematic Forecasting Process

1. Determine the forecast purpose. How will the forecast be used?
2. Establish the forecast interval (daily, weekly, monthly)
3. Select a forecasting technique
4. Collect and analyze data. Collecting the appropriate historical data is significant step in the process.
5. Initialize the forecast
6. Generate the forecast
7. Monitor the forecast quality. The forecast must be continuously validated and revised.

Measures of Forecast Accuracy

There is need to develop a general-purpose forecast measurement criterion. An unbiased measurement approach is to evaluate the differences between the observed values and the forecast and calculate their average differences as a reasonable performance measure. The forecast should not be consistently high or consistently low. The forecast must be an accurate representation of past demand. The forecast must be valid and lack bias. The two forecasting measurement criteria are mean error (BIAS) and mean absolute deviation (MAD).

(1) Mean Error (bias)

$$\text{Mean error (bias)} = \frac{1}{n} \times \sum_{i=t}^{(n+t)-1} (D_i - F_i)$$

Where:

n = number of periods with actual date included in the model
i = period number
D_i = actual demand for period i
F_i = forecasted demand for period i (for most models, this forecast will have been made at the end of period $i - 1$)
t = the period number of the first period included in the analysis

For the example, when a two-period simple moving average model is used for forecasting, the bias calculation starts with the third period ($t = 3$) because of the model's characteristics.

Time Period	1	2	3	4	5	6	7	8	9	10	11	12	Count
Demand	10	15	13	15	10	20	17	27	27	22	34	44	12
Forecast			12.5	14.0	14.0	12.5	15.0	18.5	22.0	27.0	24.5	28.0	10

$$\text{Mean error (bias)} = \frac{1}{10} \times \sum_{i=3}^{(10+3)-1} (D_i - F_i) = \frac{1}{10} \times \sum_{i=3}^{12} (e_i) = 4.1 \text{ units}$$

The bias is also an indicator of the forecast model's tendency regarding the direction of its forecast errors. The ideal forecast bias is 0. See Figure 2 below:

It is not sufficient to only consider the forecast bias. Forecast bias is a measure of the quality of the forecast model parameters. Positive errors and negative errors should cancel out overly pessimistic or overly optimistic model performance. Ideally, the average error should approach zero. When the model is consistently high or consistently low, model parameters must be corrected. Secondly, there must be a concern about the magnitude of the errors. As can be seen in Figure 2, the forecast is high for eight periods and low for two periods. If the individual errors are much larger and customer service must remain at a specific level, safety stock is required (see Chapter 5). The mean absolute deviation is used to assess the magnitude of the individual forecast errors.

(2) Mean Absolute Deviation (MAD)

$$\text{Mean absolute deviation (MAD)} = \frac{1}{n} \times \sum_{i=t}^{(n+t)-1} (|D_i - F_i|)$$

Where:

n = number of periods with actual date included in the model
i = period number
D_i = actual demand for period i
F_i = forecasted demand for period i (for most models, this forecast will have been made at the end of period $i - 1$)
t = the period number of the first period included in the analysis
e_i = forecast error

Figure 2 **Error Distribution**

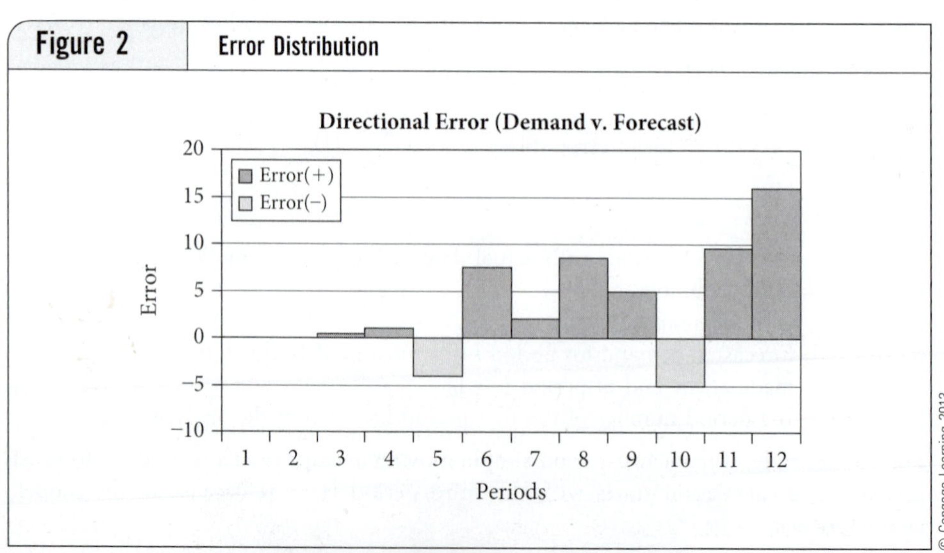

Figure 3 Mean Absolute Deviation

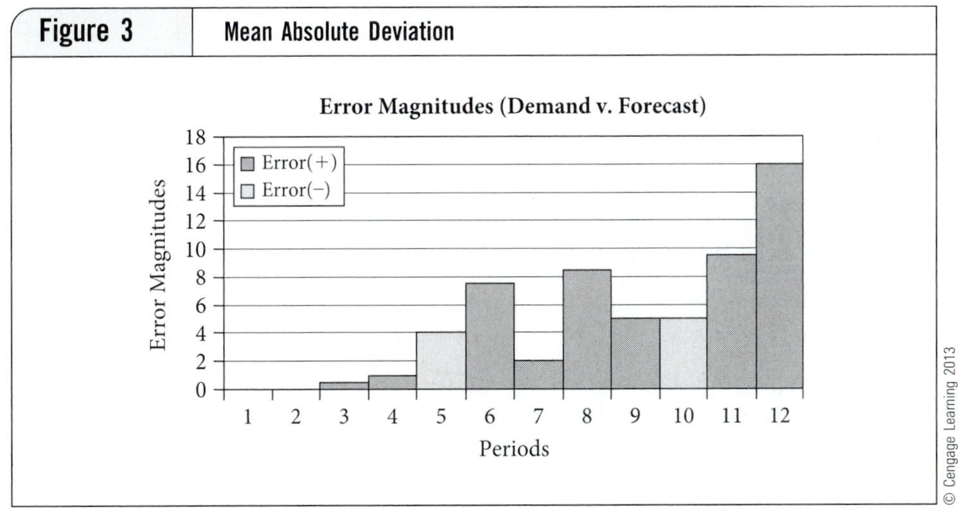

The mean absolute deviation (MAD) can also be used to approximate the standard deviation of forecast errors (σ). The standard deviation of forecast errors (σ) is approximately 1.25 times the value of MAD.

Standard deviation of forecast errors (σ) $\cong 1.25 \times MAD$ or $\text{MAD} \cong 0.8 \times \sigma$

For the example, when a two-period simple moving average model is used for forecasting, the MAD calculation starts with the third period ($t = 3$) because of the model's characteristics.

Time Period	1	2	3	4	5	6	7	8	9	10	11	12	Count
Demand	10	15	13	15	10	20	17	27	27	22	34	44	12
Forecast			12.5	14.0	14.0	12.5	15.0	18.5	22.0	27.0	24.5	28.0	10

$$\text{MAD} = \frac{1}{10} \times \sum_{i=3}^{(10+3)-1} \left(|D_i - F_i| \right) = \frac{1}{10} \times \sum_{i=3}^{12} |e_i| = 5.9 \text{ units}$$

Standard deviation of forecast errors (σ) $\cong 1.25 \times MAD = 1.25 \times 5.9 = 7.375$ units

The mean absolute deviation (MAD) is an indicator of the forecast model's tendency regarding the magnitude of its forecast errors. See Figure 3 above.

An additional technique used to monitor forecast accuracy is the tracking signal. An example of the tracking signal will be presented at the end of the chapter.

Qualitative Forecast Models

Qualitative forecasts are based on human factors and opinions. Qualitative forecasts are referred to as "judgment" or "opinion" forecasts. Qualitative forecasts are based on executive opinions, consumer surveys, and expert opinions. The approach/method that is appropriate depends on the product's life cycle stage and other relevant environmental factors. In addition, these forecasting approaches vary in sophistication from scientifically conducted surveys to intuitive hunches about future events. Some of the qualitative approaches are listed below:

- Educated guesses
- Executive committee consensus
- The Delphi method
- Survey of sales force
- Survey of customers
- Historical analogy
- Market research

The most popular qualitative forecast approach is the Delphi method. The **Delphi method** utilizes a panel of experts who anonymously answer a set of questions in a series of questionnaires; responses are fed back to panel members, who then may adjust their original responses. Each new questionnaire is developed using the information extracted from the previous survey. The ultimate objective is to achieve a consensus forecast.

Quantitative Forecasting Models

Time series forecasts are the most popular quantitative forecast models. A time series is a set of numbers in which the order or sequence of the numbers is important, such as historical demand. The analysis of time series data requires the use of statistical theory to uncover the underlying patterns of the time series data. Once the patterns are identified, they can be used to develop a forecast. The components of time series forecast data are: trend, seasonality, cyclical, irregular variations and random fluctuation. Examples of the time series components are given below:

- Trends are noted by an upward or downward sloping line. An example of the trend-enhanced pattern component is given in Figure 4.
- Seasonality is a data pattern that repeats itself over the period of one year or less. An example of the seasonality data pattern is given in Figure 5.

Figure 4 Trend-Enhanced Demand Pattern

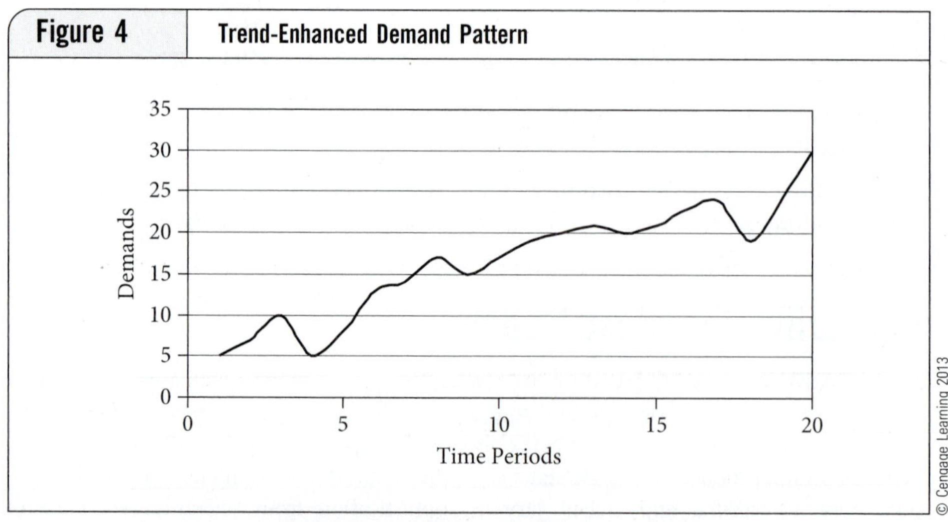

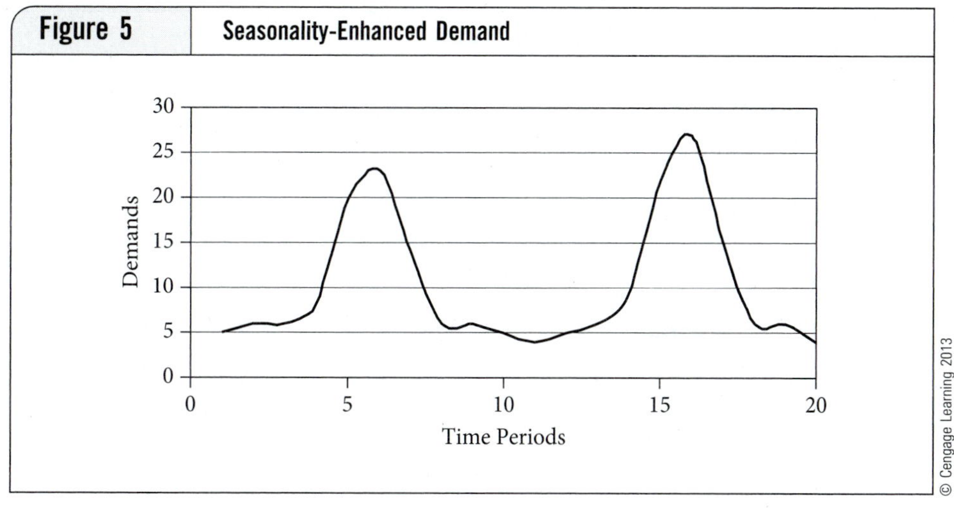

Figure 5 Seasonality-Enhanced Demand

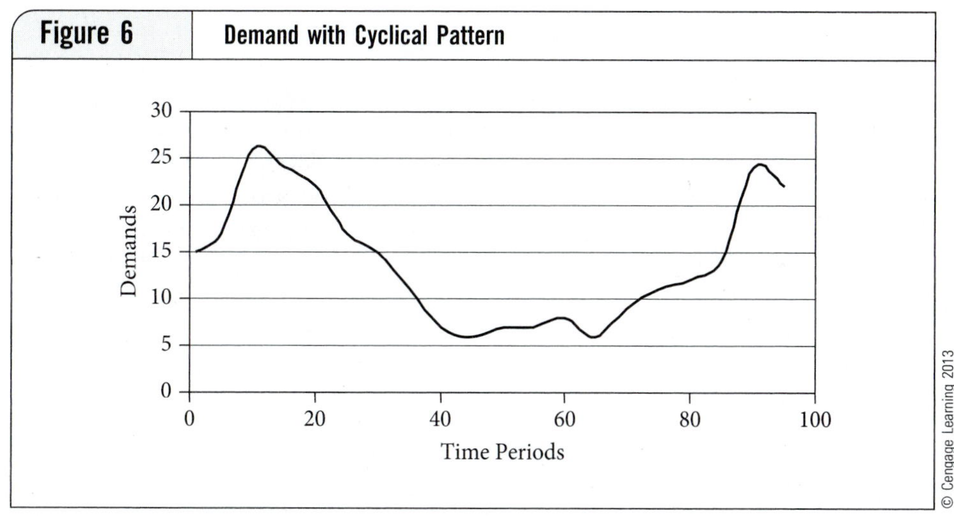

Figure 6 Demand with Cyclical Pattern

- Cyclical is a data pattern that repeats itself. Unlike seasonality, it may take years for a cycle to take its course and start over. An example of the cyclical data pattern is given in Figure 6.
- Irregular variations jump in the level of the series due to extraordinary events. An example of irregular variation patterns is given in Figure 7.
- Random fluctuation from random variation are based on unexplained causes. An example of random fluctuation patterns is given in Figure 8.

Quantitative Forecasting Approaches

Examples of quantitative forecasting approaches are given below:

A. Linear regression
B. Simple moving average

Figure 7 Demand with Irregular Pattern

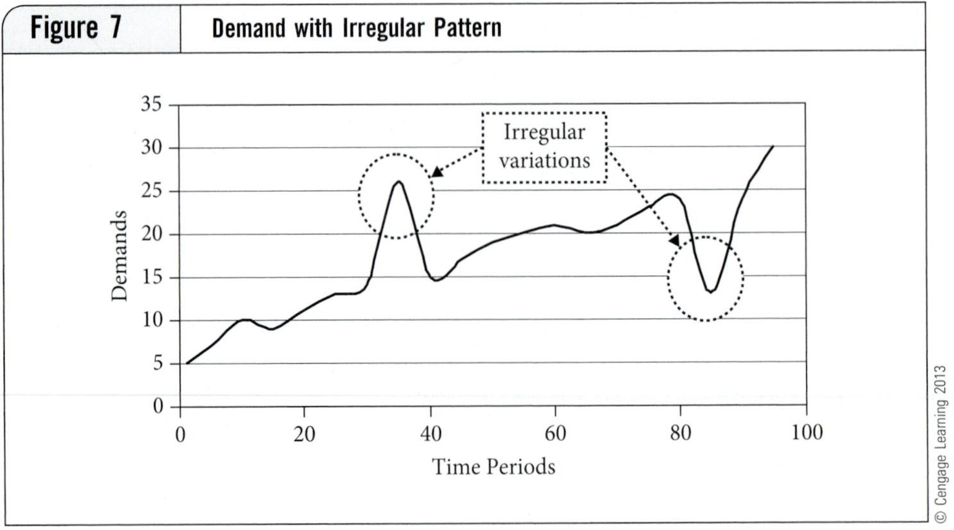

Figure 8 Demand with Random Fluctuations

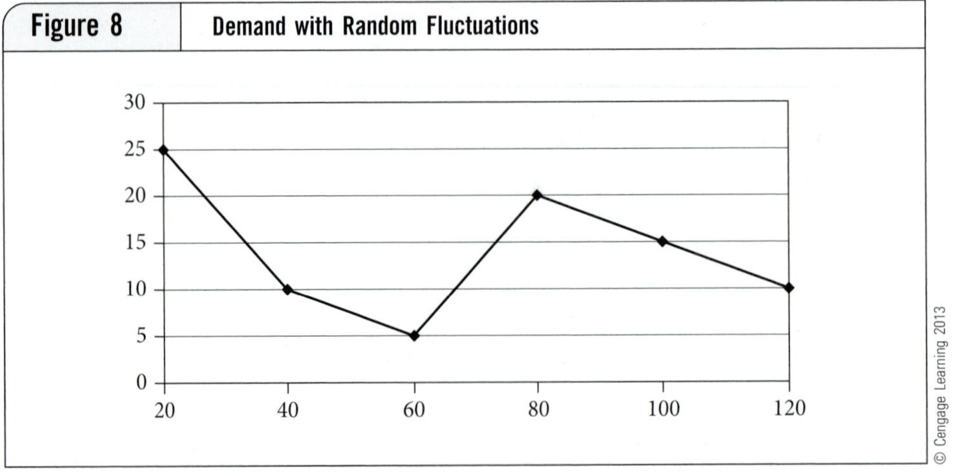

C. Weighted moving average
D. Exponential smoothing
   a. Simple exponential smoothing
   b. Trend-enhanced exponential smoothing
   c. Seasonality-enhanced exponential smoothing
   d. Trend and seasonality exponential smoothing

Linear Regression

Linear regression is a method of fitting the available data to form a linear line. In regard to forecasting, the resulting line is an approximated representation of the demand according to the flow of time, as the *x*-axis displays the time factor (explanatory variables) while the y-axis displays the corresponding demands (endogenous variables).[1] This line would indicate the trend in the actual data that could be expected to continue into the future. Therefore, the future demands would be located around the "trend line."

The most common method for generating the trend line would be the ordinary least squares (OLS) method, which focuses on reducing the sum of the squared differences between the actual data and modeled values (residuals).

The following is the equation for the trend line.

$$y = bx + a$$

n = the number of available data used in the generation of the line

$$b = \frac{\left[n \times \sum xy - \left(\sum x\right) \times \left(\sum y\right)\right]}{n \times \sum x^2 - \left(\sum x\right)^2} \qquad a = \frac{\left[\sum y - b \times \sum x\right]}{n}$$

For the purpose of forecasting demands, the endogenous variable (y) could be interchanged with the value of demand (D_t) and explanatory variables (x) with time period (t).

$$D_t = bt + a \qquad b = \frac{\left[n \times \sum D_t t - \left(\sum t\right) \times \left(\sum D_t\right)\right]}{n \times \sum t^2 - \left(\sum t\right)^2} \qquad a = \frac{\left[\sum D_t - b \times \sum t\right]}{n}$$

Whether the resulting linear regression line or trend line is a good representation (good fit) of the current data can be interpreted from the *coefficient of determination* (R^2).

$$0 \le R^2 \le 1$$

The closer the *coefficient of determination* (R^2) is to the value of 1, the better line fit to the data. For example, if R^2 is 0.8, this can be interpreted as meaning that 80 percent of the variation in the actual demand data (endogenous variable) is explained by the model with the trend line. However, this correlation does not equate to causation between the variables.

The following are the equations for calculating the *coefficient of determination* (R^2).

$$R^2 = 1 - \frac{SS_{err}}{SS_{tot}} \qquad SS_{tot} = \sum_i \left(y_i - \bar{y}\right)^2 \qquad SS_{err} = \sum_i \left(y_i - \hat{y}_i\right)^2$$

Where:

$\bar{y}$ is average demand
$\hat{y}_i$ is forecasted demand in period i
y_i is actual demand in period i

Example

Time Period	1	2	3	4	5	6	7	8	9	10	11	12	Count
Demand	10	15	13	15	10	20	17	27	27	22	34	44	12

$$b = \frac{\left[n \times \sum D_t t - \left(\sum t\right) \times \left(\sum D_t\right)\right]}{n \times \sum t^2 - \left(\sum t\right)^2} = \frac{[12 \times 2009 - 78 \times 254]}{12 \times 650 - 6084} = 2.503496503$$

$$a = \frac{\left[\sum D_t - b \times \sum t\right]}{n} = \frac{[254 - 2.503496503 \times 78]}{12} = 4.893939394$$

[1] An endogenous variable is determined by the state of the other exogenous, or explanatory variables within the model.

Figure 9 Fitted Linear Regression Model for the Sample Problem

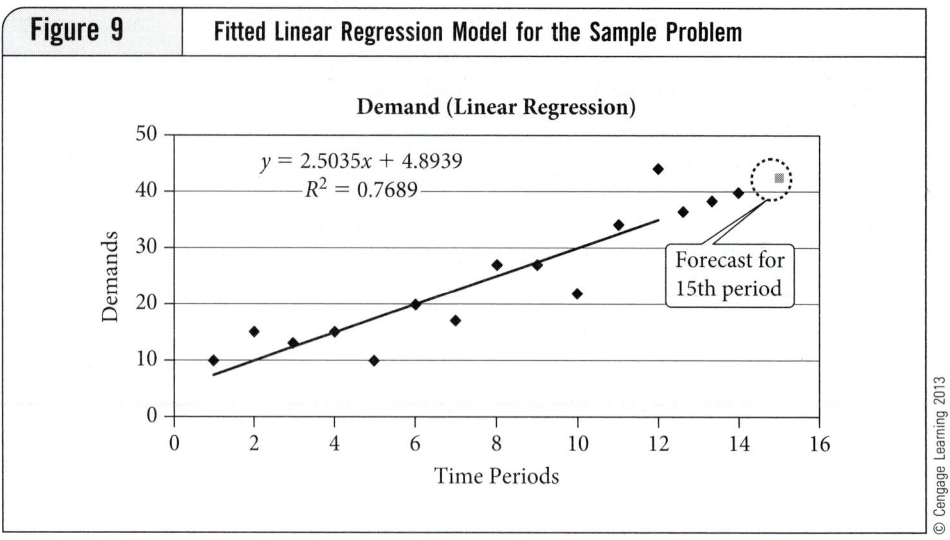

The resulting trend line: $y = 2.5035x + 4.8939$ or $D_t = 2.5035t + 4.8939$

$$SS_{tot} = \sum_i (y_i - \bar{y})^2 = 1165.667 \quad SS_{err} = \sum_i (y_i - \hat{y}_i)^2 = 269.415$$

$$R^2 = 1 - \frac{SS_{err}}{SS_{tot}} = 1 - \frac{269.415}{1165.667} = 0.7689$$

The fitted linear regression model for the sample problem is given in Figure 9 above:

Forecast for 15th period made at the end of 12th period:

$$D_t = D_{15} = 2.5035t + 4.8939 = 2.5035 \times 15 + 4.8939 = 42.45 \text{ units}$$

Off-the-shelf software packages are typically used to implement linear regression and other curve-fitting techniques. The implementation process involves collecting many periods of data for the indicator and forecast variables. The older data are used to initialize the model. Subsequent data are then used to observe the errors that would have resulted had the parameterized model been used in the past. After the most accurate model has been selected, implementation can be recommended. Because of the subtle changes in the environment and the ease of calculation, the parameters should be updated every few periods. Thus, the most recent N periods of historical data are used to update (recalculate) the parameters. Each period, a forecast for future periods is then calculated.

Simple Moving Averages

A naïve forecast uses the current period to calculate the succeeding period. As an example, if demand is 350 units in May, the forecast for June is also forecasted to be 350 using a naïve forecast. If actual demand turns out to be 385 units in June, the forecast for July is 385 units. The naïve forecast ignores historical demand and focuses only on current demand.

The simple moving average uses historical demand values during the recent past in order to generate the forecast. The effect of the moving-average approach is the smoothing of the random increases and decreases in demand. The simple moving-average approach is an adequate method if the demand is relatively stable. There should be no evidence of trend or seasonality.

Moving averages are calculated for a predetermined number of periods (i.e., 3 months, 5 months.)

The longer the forecast interval, the more stable the forecast will be. The simple moving average is calculated as below:

Notation

$MAF(n)_t$ is an n-period moving-average forecast made at the end of period t. Considering the limited forecast range of one period ahead, $MAF(n)_t$ is the same as the forecast of the demand for period $t + 1(F_{t+1})$,

$$MAF(n)_t = \sum_{i=t-n+1}^{t} \frac{D_i}{n}$$

Where:

D_i = actual demand for period i
n = the number of data periods included in generating the forecast

Example

Time Period	1	2	3	4	5	6	7	8	9	10	11	12	Count
Demand	10	15	13	15	10	20	17	27	27	22	34	44	12

$$MAF(2)_{12} = \sum_{i=11}^{12} \frac{D_i}{2} = \frac{(34 + 44)}{2} = 39 \text{ units}$$

$$MAF(3)_{12} = \sum_{i=10}^{12} \frac{D_i}{3} = \frac{(22 + 34 + 44)}{3} = 33.33 \text{ units}$$

$$MAF(6)_{12} = \sum_{i=7}^{12} \frac{D_i}{6} = \frac{(17 + 27 + 27 + 22 + 34 + 44)}{6} = 28.5 \text{ units}$$

The graphical comparison of the three models is given in Figure 10 below:

Figure 10 **Graphical Results Comparing Three Moving-Average Models**

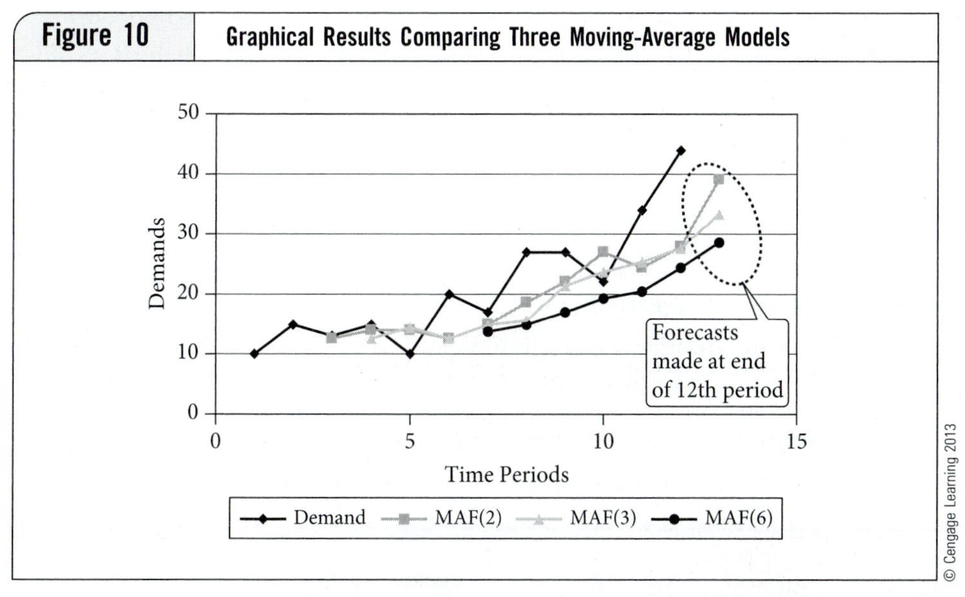

Weighted Moving Averages

This forecasting method is similar to the simple moving-average forecasting method with the addition of weights applied to the demands of previously utilized periods. As with the simple-moving average forecasting method, it can only generate a forecast for the period right after the latest data utilized in generating it. The relative importance of a period's demand is correspondent to its assigned weight.

Notations

$WMAF(n)_t$ or $WMA(n)_t$ is an n-period weighted moving-average forecast made at the end of period t. Considering the limited forecast range of one period ahead, $WMAF(n)_t$ is the same as the forecast of the demand for period $t+1(F_{t+1})$

$$WMAF(n)_t = \sum_{i=t-n+1}^{t} (w_i \times D_i) \quad \sum_{i=t-n+1}^{t} w_i = 1$$

Where:

D_i = actual demand for period i
w_i = weight assigned to the demand for period i $0 \le w_i \le 1$
n = the number of data periods included in generating the forecast.

Example

Time Period	1	2	3	4	5	6	7	8	9	10	11	12	Count
Demand	10	15	13	15	10	20	17	27	27	22	34	44	12

Case 1 when more importance is assigned to more **recent** data:

	Weights	w1	w2	w3	w4	w5	Total
n	3	0.1	0.3	0.6			1
	5	0.05	0.1	0.2	0.3	0.35	1

$$WMAF(3)_{12} = \sum_{i=10}^{12} (w_i \times D_i) = [(0.1 \times 22) + (0.3 \times 34) + (0.6 \times 44)] = 38.8 \text{ units}$$

$$WMAF(5)_{12} = \sum_{i=10}^{12} (w_i \times D_i) = [(0.05 \times 27) + (0.1 \times 27) + (0.2 \times 22) + (0.3 \times 34) + (0.35 \times 44)] = 34.05 \text{ units}$$

The graphical results are given in Figure 11.

Case 2 when more importance is assigned to **past** data:

	Weights	w1	w2	w3	w4	w5	Total
n	3	0.6	0.3	0.1			1
	5	0.35	0.3	0.2	0.1	0.05	1

Figure 11 Graphical Results Comparing Two Weighted Moving-Average Models Using Recent Data

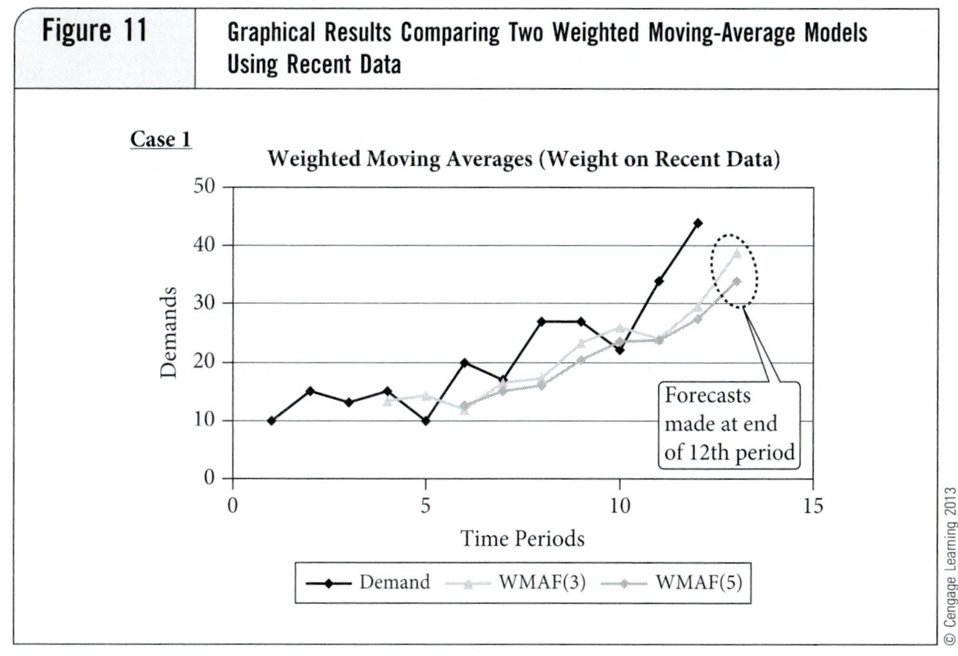

$$WMAF(3)_{12} = \sum_{i=10}^{12}(w_i \times D_i) = [(0.6 \times 22) + (0.3 \times 34) + (0.1 \times 44)] = 27.8 \text{ units}$$

$$WMAF(5)_{12} = \sum_{i=10}^{12}(w_i \times D_i) = [(0.35 \times 27) + (0.3 \times 27) + (0.2 \times 22) + (0.1 \times 34) + (0.05 \times 44)] = 27.6 \text{ units}$$

The graphical results are given in Figure 12 below:

Figure 12 Graphical Results Comparing Two Weighted Moving-Average Models Using Past Data

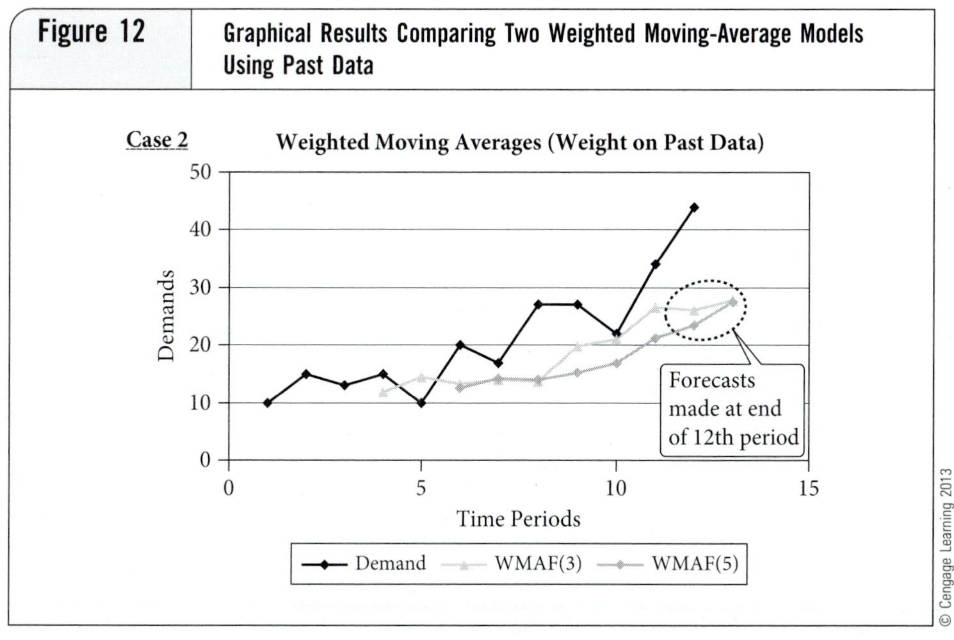

Case 3 Comparison between the methods of assigning weights to the periods utilized in weighted moving average forecasting when n is set at three periods.

	Weights	w1	w2	w3	Total
	3	0.1	0.3	0.6	1
n	3	0.333	0.333	0.333	1
	3	0.6	0.3	0.1	1

If the weights assigned to the periods are all equal to each other, the weighted moving average becomes a simple moving-average forecast (e.g., $w_1 = w_2 = w_3 = w = \frac{1}{3}$).

$$WMAF(n)_t = \sum_{i=t-n+1}^{t} (w_i \times D_i) = w \times \sum_{i=t-n+1}^{t} (D_i) = \sum_{i=t-n+1}^{t} \left(\frac{D_i}{n}\right) = MAF(n)_t$$

The graphical results are given in Figure 13.

The Exponential Smoothing Model

The moving-average model and the weighted moving-average models attempt to remain responsive by deleting information after n periods. As can be seen in Figure 13, stable demand tends to minimize forecast error as the number of periods included in

Figure 13 **Graphical Results Comparing (Recent and Past) Weighted Moving-Average Models Data**

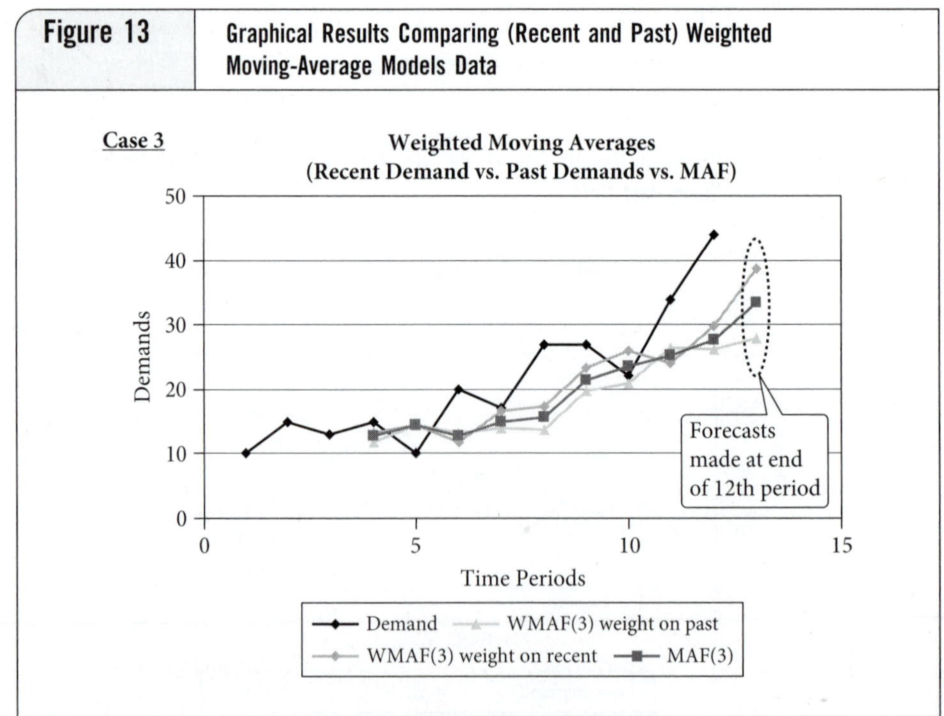

the moving average approaches the long-run overall average. In other words, with stable demand patterns, old demand is viewed as having the equivalent value to new demand observations. This is clearly not the case when there is a trend or seasonality demand pattern. The moving-average model and weighted-average model both assume that actual demand data have no value after n periods. It can be assumed that the value of old demand observations may decrease at a decreasing rate, but not abruptly. Another problem with the moving-average and the weighted moving-average models is the excessive data requirement. Even with fast computers, calculations and storage requirements are unattractive given the resulting quality of the forecast. The exponential smoothing model offers a more elegant and parsimonious treatment of the smoothing forecasting process.

Simple exponential smoothing uses past values of demand to forecast future values as a weighted decreasing average of all available past actual demand data. The moving-average model gives equal weights to all of the past demand data. On the other hand, exponential smoothing gives more weight to the most recent data and less weight to older demand data. The weights assigned to the older demand data decrease (exponentially) at a decreasing rate. The weight of the most recent demand data is assigned by multiplying the value of α between 1 and 0. As an example, α is assigned to the most current observed demand, the next most recent demand observation is assigned $(1-\alpha)$, the next $(1-\alpha)^2$, the next $(1-\alpha)^3$, and so on.

Simple Exponential Smoothing Model

Notation

An exponential smoothing forecast (ESF_t) can be described as a forecast of the expected demand for period $(t+1)$ made at the end of period t. It is also generally denoted as $\overline{F}_t$.

As an example, ESF_{20} or $\overline{F}_{20}$ is the forecast for the 21st period made at the end of the 20th period. $\overline{F}_{20}$ is also referred to as the base for period 20. The notation can sometimes be confusing because it uses the number of the period when the forecast is made rather than the targeted period. F_{21} also represents the forecast of the demand for the 21st period, which indicates the same period's demand as $\overline{F}_{20}$ or ESF_{20}. Thus, the operational relationship is given as:

$$F_{t+1} = \overline{F}_t = ESF_t$$

The calculating method for computing the simple exponential smoothing model is:

$$ESF_t = ESF_{t-1} + \alpha \times (D_t - ESF_{t-1}) = \alpha \times D_t + (1-\alpha) \times ESF_{t-1}$$

Or

$$\overline{F}_t = \alpha \times D_t + (1-\alpha) \times \overline{F}_{t-1} \quad \text{or} \quad F_{t+1} = \alpha \times D_t + (1-\alpha) \times F_t$$

Where:

D_t = actual demand for period t
α = the exponential smoothing constant $(0 \le \alpha \le 1)$
ESF_t & $\overline{F}_t$ & F_{t+1} = the forecasted demand for period $(t+1)$ made at the end of period t

The smoothing constant, α, is set between 0.0 and 1.0. The smoothing constant is a measure of the weight given to the most recent actual demand. As an example, if $\alpha = .20$, the next period's forecast is based on 20 percent of the most recent demand (D_t) and on 80 percent of past demand in the form of ($\overline{F}_t$ = base). If the smoothing constant α is set at 1, the exponential smoothing technique is the equivalent to the naïve forecast technique. Therefore, the tradeoff is between responsiveness and stability. As α approaches zero, the forecast will adjust more slowly to the differences between the actual demand and the forecast for a specific period. Setting the smoothing constant requires experimentation and judgment.

An illustrative example is given below in Example 2-1.

Example 2-1

Lee's sells and repairs refurbished servers. The service manager needs weekly forecasts of service calls so that she can schedule service personnel. The manager uses exponential smoothing with $\alpha = 0.20$.

a. Forecast the number of calls for week 6 made using a two-month moving average.
b. Forecast the number of calls at the end of week 5 using exponential smoothing.

WEEK	ACTUAL SERVICE CALLS
1	35
2	43
3	47
4	54
5	36

Solution

a. Forecast the number of calls for week 6 made using two-week moving average.

MAF (2)

	D	*MAF*(2)
1	35	
2	43	
3	47	39, $MAF_2 = (35 + 43)/2 = 39$
4	54	45, $MAF_2 = (43 + 47)/2 = 45$
5	36	50.5, $MAF_2 = (47 + 54)/2 = 50.5$
6		45, $MAF_2 = (54 + 36)/2 = 45$

b. Forecast the number of calls at the end of week 5 using exponential smoothing.
Initialize at week 1: assumption $= \overline{F_0} = F_1 = D_1 = 35$.

BUILD WEEK 2~5:

	D	*F*
1	35	35
2	43	35, $F_2 = .2(35) + (1 - .2)35$
3	47	36.6, $F_3 = .2(43) + (1 - .2)35$
4	54	38.68, $F_4 = .2(47) + (1 - .2)36.6$
5	36	41.744, $F_5 = .2(54) + (1 - .2)38.68$

Forecast: week 6 $F_6 = 0.2 * 36 + (1 - 0.2) * 41.744 = 40.5952$.

Trend Enhancement

The simple exponential smoothing model assumes that demand is constant, with random variation around the mean. See Figure 4. However, if the observed demand data reveal that there is systematic variation around the trend or seasonally, the simple exponential smoothing model is inappropriate. One way to estimate the trend component would be with a regression model. Another, more efficient way to estimate the trend component is to determine the first-order differences between the actual demand and the forecasted demand for a series of past observations. The differences are then divided by the number of observations minus 1. The trend-adjusted exponential smoothing forecast consists of the exponential smoothing model with a trend-adjusted factor added. The calculating method for computing the trend-enhanced forecast is

$$\overline{F} = \alpha(Actual\ demand_t) + (1 - \alpha)(Base\ value_{t-1} + Trend_{t-1}) \qquad \text{(Equation 1)}$$

Where:

α = base value smoothing constant $(0 \leq \alpha \leq 1)$
t = current period (the most recent period in which actual demand is known)
$Base\ value_{t-1}$ = base value computed for most recent period in the past (at the end of period $t - 1$)
$Trend_{t-1}$ = trend value computed for the most recent period in the past (at the end of period $t - 1$)

We will now focus on updating the trend estimate. The calculating method for updating the trend estimate is:

$$Trend_t = \beta(Base\ value_t - Base\ value_{t-1}) + (1 - \beta)(Trend_{t-1}) \qquad \text{(Equation 2)}$$

Where:

β = trend-smoothing constant $(0 \leq \beta \leq 1)$)
$Base\ value_{t-1}$ = base value computed for the most recent period in the past (at the end of period $t - 1$)
$Trend_{t-1}$ = trend value computed for the most recent period in the past (at the end of period $t - 1$)

The final step in calculating the trend-enhanced forecast is given in Equation 3.

$$Forecast_{t+n} = Base\ value_t + n(Trend_t) \qquad \text{(Equation 3)}$$

An example is shown in Figure 14a:

Figure 14a | **Example Problem: Trend Enhanced Forecast Calculation**

A toy manufacturer recently introduced a new computer game. Management is interested in estimating future sales volume to determine whether it should continue to carry the new game or replace it with another game. At the end of April, the average monthly sales volume of the new game was 500 games and the trend was +50 games per month. The actual sales volume figures for May, June, and July are 560, 600, and 620, respectively. Use trend-adjusted exponential smoothing with $\alpha = 0.2$ and $\beta = 0.1$ to forecast usage for June, July, and August.

Solution

Data: $\alpha = 0.2,\ \beta = 0.1,\ \overline{F}_{April} = 500$, Forecast for May $= 500 + (1)(50)$

Forecast for June

$$\overline{F}_{May} = .2(560) + (1 - 0.2)(500 + 50) = 552$$
$$Trend_{May} = .1(552 - 500) + .9(50) = 50.2$$
$$Forecast\ for\ June = 552 + (1)50.2 = 602.2$$

Forecast for July

$$\overline{F}_{June} = .2(600) + (1 - 0.2)(552 + 50.2) = 601.76$$
$$Trend_{June} = .1(601.76 - 552) + .9(50.2) = 50.16$$
$$Forecast\ for\ July = 601.76 + (1)(50.16) = 651.92$$

Forecast for August

$$\overline{F}_{July} = .2(620) + (1 - 0.2)(601.76 + 50.16) = 645.53$$
$$Trend_{July} = .1(645.53 - 601.76) + .9(50.16) = 49.52$$
$$Forecast\ for\ August = 645.53 + (1)49.52 = 695.05$$

Where:

t = current period (the most recent period in actual demand is known)
n = number of periods beyond period t for which the forecast is determined
$Base\ value_t$ = exponential smoothed-base value computed at the end of period t
$Trend_t$ = exponentially smoothed estimate of trend computed at the end of period t

Seasonality

The term *seasonality* is rooted in a monthly or quarterly cycle, but in forecasting, seasonal patterns can be detected in alternative cycles. See Figure 5. The operations manager must determine the appropriate periods in the cycle as related to the manufacturing planning and control process. As an example, if the planning process is monthly, daily or weekly patterns are meaningless if the forecasts are used as input to the monthly planning process. The following steps should be followed when investigating seasonal demand patterns.

1. Plot the data and visually determine any obvious time-series characteristics.
2. Determine if a significant seasonal trend exists.
3. Deseasonalize the data arithmetically.

Figure 14b Example of Seasonal Enhanced Forecast Calculations

Data: $\alpha = .2$, $\gamma = .3$, $Old\ Index_{quarter1} = 1.5$, $Old\ Index_{quarter2} = .80$,

$\overline{F}_1 = 100\ (quarter2),\quad D_2 = 90$

$\overline{F}_2 = .2(90/1.5) + (1 - .2)\ (100) = 92$

$S_1 = .3(90/92) + (1 - .3)\ (1.5) = 1.34$

$F_{2,2} = 92 * (.80) = 73.6$

4. Develop a seasonality-enhanced forecast model.
5. Continuously update the model as new data are added.

If both trend and seasonality exist, the model should be enhanced to include both seasonality and trend enhancements. A useful measure of the degree of seasonal variation is the seasonal index. The seasonal index estimates how much demand during a season will be above or below the item's average demand. Consider a specific motorcycle manufacturer that sells 1,000 units per month on the average, 2,000 units in peak season (summer quarter), and 500 in off season (winter quarter). The seasonal index for peak sales is 2.0 and .50 for off-season. Thus, the seasonal index is used to adjust the forecast for seasonal patterns. The calculating method for computing the seasonality-enhanced forecast is given in Equations 4 and 5 below:

$$\overline{F}_t = (Base\ value_t) = \alpha\,(Actual\ demand)(D_t)/Old\ Index_t) + (1-\alpha)(Base\ value_{t-1}) \qquad \text{(Equation 4)}$$

$$(New\ Index_s) = \gamma\ (Actual\ demand\ (D_t)/Base\ value_t) + (1-\gamma)\ (Old\ Index_{s-1}) \qquad \text{(Equation 5)}$$

Where:

$\alpha =$ base value-smoothing constant $(0 \le \alpha \le 1)$
$\gamma =$ smoothing constant for seasonal indexes $(0 \le \gamma \le 1)$
$\overline{F}_{t-1} = Base\ value_{t-1} =$ base value computed for one period in the past (at the end of period $t - 1$)
$Old\ Index_s =$ seasonal index value computed for season s, calculated one full cycle ago

The resulting seasonality enhanced forecast for season s in the future at the end of period t is:

$\overline{F}_{t,s} = (Base\ value_t) * (New\ Index_s)$. An example is shown in Figure 14:

Trend and Seasonal Enhancements

When seasonality and trend random variations are detected in the data, a more complex model that involves three components of variation is needed. Conceptually, the same process discussed in the trend and seasonality models is used as input to the trend and seasonality-enhanced model. The expanded trend- and seasonality-enhanced model is given below:

Step 1

$$\overline{F}_t = \alpha \times \left(\frac{D_t}{S_{t-L}}\right) + (1-\alpha) \times (\overline{F}_{t-1} + T_{t-1})$$

Step 2

$$S_t = \gamma \times \left(\frac{D_t}{\overline{F}_t}\right) + (1-\gamma) \times S_{t-1}$$

Step 3

$$T_t = \beta \times (\overline{F}_t - \overline{F}_{t-1}) + (1-\beta) \times T_{t-1}$$

Step 4

The trend-enhanced forecast for n periods in the future at the end of period t is

$$F_t, n = \left[\overline{F}_t + n \times T_t\right] \times S_{(t+n)-L}$$

Where:

$\overline{F}_t$ = most recent deseasonalized base value at the end of period t
D_t = actual demand for period t
S_t = seasonal index for the season s
T_t = trend estimate per period calculated at the end of period t
n = number of periods beyond period t for which the forecast is desired
L = the number of periods that compose a seasonal cycle
α = the exponential smoothing constant for the base value $(0 \leq \alpha \leq 1)$
γ = the exponential smoothing constant for the seasonal factor $(0 \leq \gamma \leq 1)$
β = the exponential smoothing constant for the trend factor $(0 \leq \beta \leq 1)$

The trend- and seasonality-enhanced model incorporates both components of variation in the same model. The subscript in the equation in Step 4 deserves an additional note. The forecast is made at the end of period t, for n periods into the future $(t + n)$. By subtracting L, the index subscript is moved back to the season value computed at the end of quarter 2. We desire to forecast for quarter $4 + 2 - 4$, or the seasonal index computed two months previously at the end of quarter 4.

The limit to the forecast range is L number of periods after the last available demand data period. $S_{(t+n)-L}$ represents the seasonal factor in the previous cycle that is in the same location within a cycle as the targeted period $t + n$.

Operationalizing the Trend and Seasonality Forecasting

A systematic model forecasting approach is recommended. The suggested steps involved in the model-building approach are:

1. Plot and evaluate the observed patterns in the historical demand data.
2. Initialize and build the model using holdout data.
3. Develop an unbiased experimental design to test the model. The bias and MAD are used to test the quality of the alternative models.
4. Forecast future demand using the best model developed in Step 3.

Example Problem Using the Systematic Forecasting Approach is given in the example below.

The MP&L utility company in Miami, Florida, wants to develop quarterly forecasts of power loads for next year. The power loads are seasonal, and the data on the quarterly loads in megawatts (MW) for the last four years are as follows:

QUARTER	2009	2010	2011	2012
1	100	105	128	119
2	75	105	151	151
3	112	127	169	176
4	101	142	188	192

The manager estimates the total demand for the next year at 845 MW. Use the seasonally adjusted exponential smoothing model to develop the forecast for each quarter. Initialize the model using year 2009 and $\alpha = .2, \beta = .15$ and $\gamma = .3$. Calculate the bias and MAD for the test data (year 2010–2012). Choose the best model using the Bias and MAD criteria. Show the calculations for the initialization and first forecast iteration. The remaining calculations can be accomplished using the Excel spreadsheet on the next page.

1. Plot and evaluate the historical data given in Figure 15 below.
2. Initialize the model using the first year's data.
   a. Calculate the initial base using data from the holdout year, 2009.
      The hold out data selection is a tradeoff between the model building and the testing steps. If 2009 and 2010 are both used to build the model, the model testing would cover two years, 2011 and 2012.

$$\overline{F}_i = \frac{\sum_1^i D_t}{i}$$

$$\overline{F}_4 = \frac{\sum_1^4 D_4}{4} = \frac{D_1 + D_2 + D_3 + D_4}{4} = \frac{100 + 75 + 112 + 101}{4} = 97$$

   b. Calculate the initial trend using data from the holdout year, 2009.

$$T_i = \frac{\sum_1^{i-1}(D_{t+1} - D_t)}{i - 1} = \frac{(75 - 100) + (112 - 75) + (101 - 112)}{3} = 0.33$$

Figure 15 **Plot All Available Data**

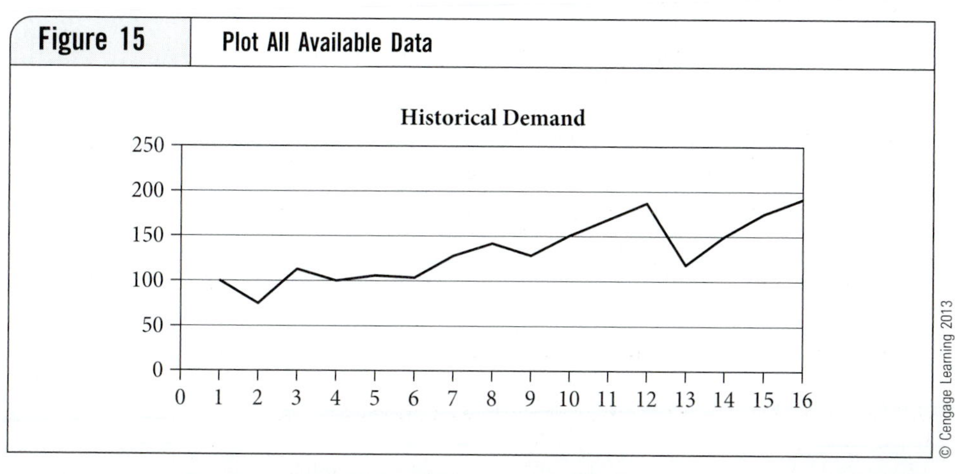

Figure 16 Excel Results for Example Problem

Alpha = 0.2 Beta = 0.15 Gamma = 0.3
$(1-\alpha) = 0.8$ $(1-\beta) = 0.85$ $(1-\gamma) = 0.7$

Year	Qtr	D_t	$F_{t,n}$	$\overline{F}_t$	$\overline{F}_{t-1}$	S_t	S_{t-1}	T_t	T_{t-1}	Dev.	Abs. Dev.
2009	1					1.030					
	2					0.770					
	3					1.150					
	4			97.0		1.040		0.3			
2010	1	105	101.2	98.3	97.0	1.042	1.030	0.5	0.3	3.8	3.8
	2	105	76.0	106.2	98.3	0.835	0.770	1.6	0.5	29.0	29.0
	3	127	124.0	108.4	106.2	1.157	1.150	1.7	1.6	3.0	3.0
	4	142	114.4	115.3	108.4	1.097	1.040	2.5	1.7	27.6	27.6
2011	1	128	122.7	118.8	115.3	1.052	1.042	2.6	2.5	5.3	5.3
	2	151	101.5	133.3	118.8	0.925	0.835	4.4	2.6	49.5	49.5
	3	169	159.3	139.4	133.3	1.173	1.157	4.7	4.4	9.7	9.7
	4	188	158.1	149.5	139.4	1.145	1.097	5.5	4.7	29.9	29.9
2012	1	119	163.1	146.6	149.5	0.980	1.052	4.2	5.5	(44.1)	44.1
	2	151	139.4	153.3	146.6	0.943	0.925	4.6	4.2	11.6	11.6
	3	176	185.3	156.3	153.3	1.159	1.173	4.4	4.6	(9.3)	9.3
	4	192	184.0	162.1	156.3	1.157	1.145	4.6	4.4	8.0	8.0
2013	1		163.3								
Forecast	2		157.1								
	3		193.1								
	4		192.8								
										bias = 10.3	MAD = 19.2
			Index								
Season Avg.	1		1.03								
	2		0.77								
	3		1.15								
	4		1.04								

Figure 17 Graphical Results for Example Problem

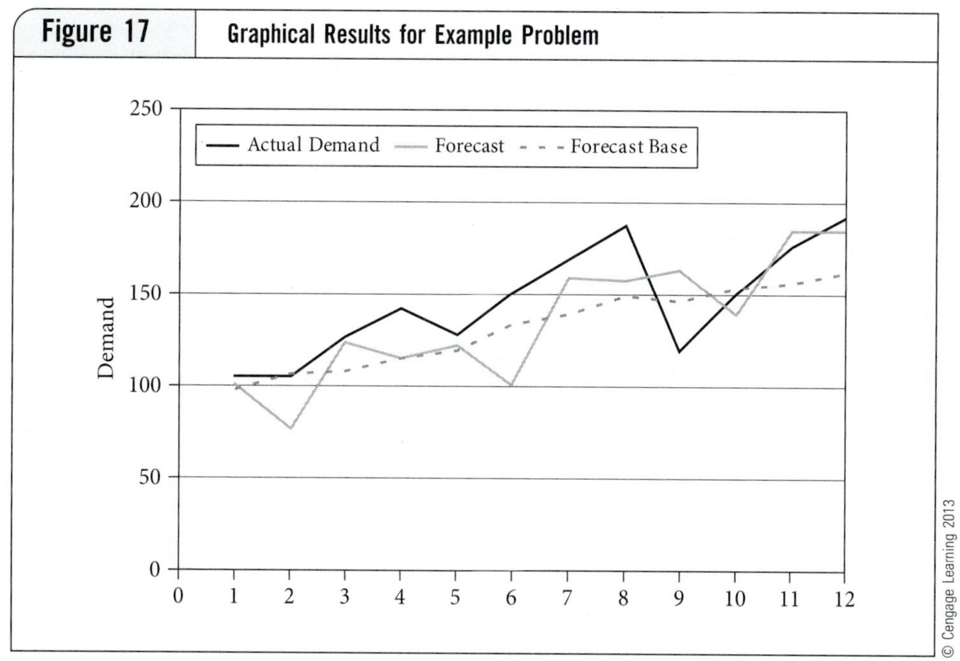

c. Calculate the initial seasonal indexes using data from the holdout year, 2009.

$$S_t = \frac{D_t}{\overline{F}_i}$$

$$S_1 = \frac{100}{\overline{F}_4} = 1.0309, S_2 = \frac{75}{\overline{F}_4} = 0.773, S_3 = \frac{112}{\overline{F}_4} = 1.1546, S_4 = \frac{101}{\overline{F}_4} = 1.04$$

3. Develop an unbiased experimental design to test the model. See Figures 16 and 17.
   a. $\overline{F}_4 = 97$, $\overline{T}_4 = .33$, $S_{1,2009} = 1.03$, $S_{2,2009} = 0.77$, $S_{3,2009} = 1.15$, $S_{4,2009} = 1.04$
   b. Initial smoothing constants: $\alpha = .20$, $\beta = .15$ and $\gamma = .30$
   c. Test the model using the systematic steps in the trend- and seasonality-enhanced model.

The model ($\alpha = 0.2$, $\beta = 0.3$, $\gamma = 0.3$) shown in Figure 16 should be compared to alternative models using Bias and MAD as the performance criteria C.

The MAD and the Bias calculation are used to compare the accuracy of alternative forecasting models. As an example a manager could compare the results of the exponential smoothing with alternative parameter values. Another managerial focus of forecasting is to track error performance over time. The tracking error monitoring approach is addressed in the next section.

Tracking Signal Monitoring

The tracking signal is the ratio of cumulative error to average deviation, which is used to determine whether the forecasting method is under control. Additionally, the unit of a tracking signal is MAD, or mean absolute deviation. The tracking signal is used to monitor forecast quality. The exponential smoothing parameters are used to weight the demand observations. The calculation for the tracking signal is given below.

Figure 18 Tracking Signal Example

TIME PERIOD	1	2	3	4	5	6	7	8	9	10	11	12	COUNT
Demand	10	15	13	15	10	20	17	27	27	22	34	44	12
Forecast			12.5	14.0	1 4.0	12.5	15.0	18.5	22.0	27.0	24.5	28.0	10
Error			0.5	1.0	-4.0	7.5	2.0	8.5	5.0	-5.0	9.5	16.0	
Running Error sum			0.5	1.5	-2.5	5.0	7.0	15.5	20.5	15.5	25.0	41.0	
Absolute Error			0.5	1	4	7.5	2	8.5	5	5	9.5	16	
Running Absolute Error sum			0.5	1.5	5.5	13.0	15.0	23.5	28.5	33.5	43.0	59.0	
MAD			0.50	0.75	1.83	3.25	3.00	3.92	4.07	4.19	4.78	5.9	
Tracking Signal			1.00	2.00	-1.36	1.54	2.33	3.96	5.04	3.70	5.23	6.95	

$$\text{Tracking signal} = \frac{n \times Bias}{MAD} = \frac{\sum_{i=t}^{(n+t)-1} e_i}{MAD} = \frac{\sum_{i=t}^{(n+t)-1} (D_i - F_i)}{MAD} = \frac{\sum_{i=t}^{(n+t)-1} (D_i - F_i)}{\frac{1}{n} \times \sum_{i=t}^{(n+t)-1} (|D_i - F_i|)}$$

Where:

D_i = actual demand for period i
i = period number
F_i = forecast demand for period i (for most models, this forecast will have been made at the end of period $i - l$)
t = the period number of the first period included in the analysis

For example, when a two-period simple moving-average model is used for forecasting, the bias calculation starts with the third period ($t = 3$) because of the model's characteristics. See Figures 18 and 19.

$$\text{Running error sum: } \sum_i e_i \text{ Running absolute error sum: } \sum_i |e_i|$$

$$\text{Tracking signal} = \frac{\sum_{i=t}^{(n+t)-1} (D_i - F_i)}{\frac{1}{n} \times \sum_{i=t}^{(n+t)-1} (|D_i - F_i|)} = \frac{\sum_i e_i}{\frac{1}{n} \times \sum_i |e_i|} = \frac{\text{Running Error sum}}{\frac{1}{n} \times \text{Running Absolute Error sum}}$$

When $\pm 3 \times \sigma$ are used as control limits, these control limits convert to $\pm 3.75 \times MAD$

$$\pm 3 \times \sigma = \pm 3 \times (1.25 \times MAD).$$

Initializing a Forecasting Model

The initialization phase is the first step in developing a forecast. Historical data should be plotted to see if there is a pattern in the past data. These detected patterns should be used to set the initial values related to historical data. A subset of the historical

Figure 19 Graphical Results for Tracking Signal

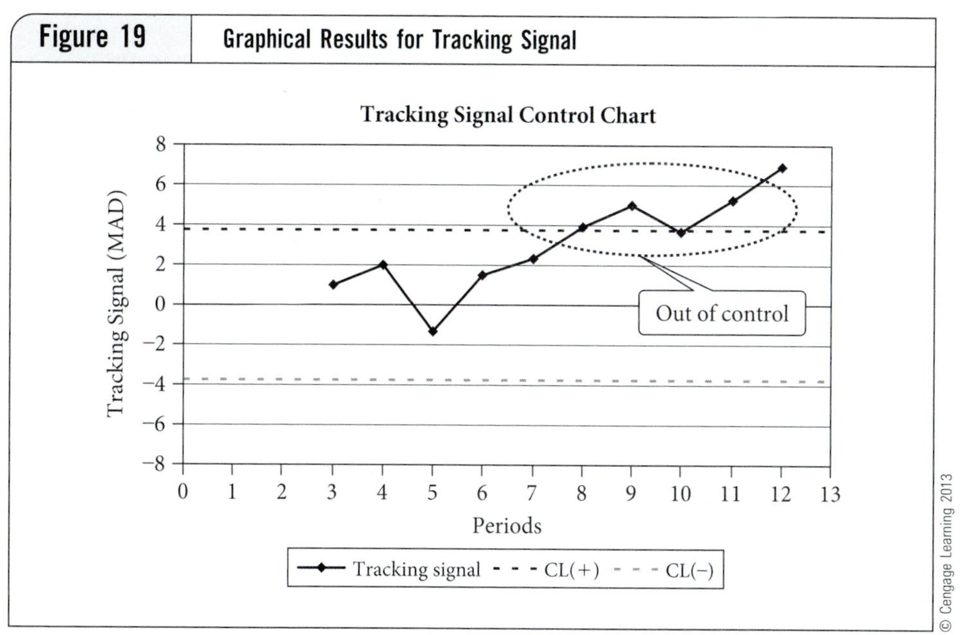

cycle can be used to estimate the initial base for the forecast components. As an example, a plot of the trend enables us to draw a trend line in order to estimate the average trend values between the points on the line. Initial seasonality indexes can be estimated by averaging the indexes calculated for each period in the cycle. The initial base value should also be derived from the historical data plot. By definition, it is always advisable to use historical data to set the initial values for the base, trend, and seasonality indexes. After setting the initial values, it is important to test the model with another segment of historical data. As an example, if there are 20 quarters of historical data available, then the first two years of the data can be used to build the model (set base, trend, and seasonality) and the next three years of data can be used to test the model based on the bias and MAD performance measures.

The smoothing constants should be based on trading off responsiveness and stability. The accepted guidelines for selecting the appropriate smoothing constants are based on practice and experimentation. The alpha for the base value should be between .1 and .2. Beta for the trend component should always be less than alpha, about .05 to .15. The seasonality constant, gamma, should be set based on the frequency of updating the seasonality indexes. If updated monthly, a low gamma of .1 is reasonable. If updated less frequently (quarterly), a gamma between .3 and .4 should be considered. In general, the choice of smoothing constants should be based on the manager's assessment of the responsiveness–stability tradeoff, given the environmental conditions.

SUMMARY

This chapter focuses on the forecasting problem in the manufacturing planning and control environment. Forecasting drives all of the key business functions. The forecasting problem is to achieve a "good" estimate of future conditions. For expository purposes, we consider here sales or demand forecasting. Forecasting estimates are segregated into (1) the causal factors that generated past demand and (2) the new causal factors that are expected to come into play in determining future demand.

Forecasts are usually associated with statistical measurements based upon sound statistical theory. However, intuitive predictions or judgments must be made on many occasions, such as when substitutes for an existing product are coming on the market, when a change in economic conditions would indicate that a sizable change in demand will occur, or when demand estimates are required for new products that have no past demand performance data. Qualitative forecasts are based on human factors and opinions. Qualitative forecasts are referred to as "judgment" or "opinion" forecasts. Quantitative forecasts are based on time-series numerical data, such as historical demand. The measurement of forecast errors can be tested statistically with the data generated during the model-building period when both actual demands and forecasts exist for the same period.

EXERCISES

1. Grey's Audiovisual rents audio and visual equipment to musicians for local concerts. The company is interested in forecasting the rentals for the d2-console so that it can make sure the d2-console is on hand when needed. The d2-console data for the last 10 months are shown here.

MONTH	DEMAND	MONTH	DEMAND
Jan.	23	June	28
Feb.	24	July	32
March	32	Aug.	35
April	26	Sept.	26
May	31	Oct.	24

   a. Prepare a forecast for months 6 through 10 by using three- and five-month moving averages. What is the forecast for month 11?
   b. Calculate the mean absolute deviation (for periods 6–10) for each forecasting method.
   c. What are your recommendations for Gray's?

2. Sales for the past 12 months at Bell, Inc. are given below.

MONTH	SALES ($ MILLIONS)	MONTH	SALES ($ MILLIONS)
January	10	July	26
February	12	August	31
March	14	September	27
April	16	October	18
May	18	November	16
June	23	December	14

a. Use a three-month moving average to forecast the sales for the months May through December.
b. Use a four-month moving average to forecast the sales for the months May through December.
c. Compare the performance of the two methods by using the bias and MAD as the performance criterion. Which method do you recommend?

3. Nelson Fabricators sells a portable EKG machine. The sales manager requires a weekly forecast of the portable EKG machine so that he can schedule production. The manager uses exponential smoothing with $\alpha = 0.30$.

WEEK	ACTUAL PRODUCTION
1	535
2	689
3	601
4	768
5	433

a. Forecast the number of machines for week 6 made at the end of week 4.
b. Forecast the number of machines at the end of week 5.
c. Calculate the bias and MAD for parts a and b. Why is one of the forecasts more accurate than the other?

4. Consider the sales data for Bell, Inc. given in Problem 2.

a. Use a three-month weighted moving average to forecast the sales for the months April through December. Use weights of (3/6), (2/6), and (1/6), giving more weight to more recent data.
b. Use exponential smoothing with $\alpha = 0.30$ to forecast the sales for the months April through December. The forecast for January was $12 million.
c. Compare the performance of the two methods by using the bias and MAD as the performance criteria. Which performance method is the most reasonable? Why?

5. A toy manufacturer recently introduced a new computer game. Management is interested in estimating future sales volume to determine whether it should continue to carry the new game or replace it with another game. At the end of April, the average monthly sales volume of the new game was 500 games and the trend was +50 games per month. The actual sales volume figures for May, June, and July are 560, 600, and 620, respectively. Use trend-adjusted exponential smoothing with $\alpha = 0.2$ and $\beta = 0.1$ to forecast usage for June, July, and August.

6. At the end of April, the average monthly use of an ATM was 320 customers and the trend was +100 customers per month. The actual use rates for May, June, and July are 880, 910, and 990, respectively. Use trend-adjusted exponential smoothing with $\alpha = 0.3$ and $\beta = 0.2$ to forecast the ATM usage for June, July, and August.

7. The number of knee surgeries performed at New Albany Surgical Hospitals (NASH) has increased steadily over the past five years. The hospital's administration is seeking the best method to forecast the demand for such surgeries in years 6 through 9. The data for the past five years are shown below.

YEAR	DEMAND
1	350
2	429
3	642
4	765
5	899

NASH's administration is considering alternative exponential forecasting methods. Use the first three years to initialize your methods. All methods must be tested and compared using the same years. Use the bias and MAD as the performance criteria to determine the best knee surgery forecasting method for periods 6 through 9.

8. The following data are for computer sales in units at an electronics store over the past five weeks:

YEAR	DEMAND
1	56
2	59
3	53
4	60
5	63

Use trend-adjusted exponential smoothing with $\alpha = 0.2$ and $\beta = 0.2$ to forecast sales for weeks 3 through 6. Assume that the smoothed average is 55 units and that the average trend was +6 units per week just before week 1.

9. The demand for refurbished cell phones is experiencing a decline. The company wants to monitor cell phone demand closely. The trend-adjusted exponential smoothing method is used with $\alpha = 0.1$ and $\beta = 0.2$. At the end of December, the updated estimate for the average number of cell phones sold in January was 340 and the updated trend for January was 52 per month. The following table shows the actual sales history for January, February, and March. Generate forecasts for February, March, and April.

MONTH	UNITS SOLD
January	168
February	198
March	230

10. Consider the quarterly data below:

QUARTER	YEAR 1	YEAR 2	YEAR 3
1	3,000	3,300	3,502
2	1,700	2,100	2,448
3	900	1,500	1,768
4	4,400	5,100	5,882
Total	10,000	12,000	13,600

a. Use intuition and judgment to estimate quarterly demand for the fourth year.
b. Now use a three-period moving average to forecast year 4. Are any of the quarterly forecasts different from what you thought you would get in part (a)?

11. The manager of Pat's Organic Farm must make the annual purchasing plans for rakes, gloves, and other gardening items. One of the items the company stocks is Lean-feed for chickens. The sales of this item are seasonal, with peaks in the spring, summer, and fall months. Quarterly demand (in cases) for the past two years is as follows:

QUARTER	YEAR 1	YEAR 2
1	40	60
2	350	440
3	290	320
4	210	280
Total	890	1,100

If the expected sales for Lean-feed are 1,150 cases for year 3, use the adjusted exponential smoothing model to prepare a forecast for each quarter of the year. Make the appropriate initialization assumptions.

12. The Textron company in Mt. Vernon, Texas, asked you to develop quarterly forecasts of combine sales for next year. Combine sales are seasonal, and the data on the quarterly sales for the last four years are as follows:

QUARTER	YEAR 1	YEAR 2	YEAR 3	YEAR 4
1	55	85	178	256
2	37	23	101	193
3	89	130	145	209
4	110	156	167	167

Lisa Williams estimates the total demand for the next year at Textron. Use the seasonally adjusted exponential smoothing model to develop the forecast for each quarter. Use the appropriate assumptions to initialize the model.

13. Demand for car washes at Jenny's Car Wash has been as follows:

MONTH	NUMBER OF WASHES
January	410
February	460
March	570
April	520
May	590
June	510
July	600
August	620

Compare the performance of at least three exponential smoothing models using the bias and MAD as the performance criteria. Make the appropriate initiating assumptions. Which method do you recommend?

14. Mrs. Cole's Bakery bakes and distributes bread throughout central Indiana. The company wants to expand operations by locating another plant in Ohio. The size of the new plant will be a function of the expected demand for baked goods within the area served by the plant. The company wants to estimate the relationship between the manufacturing cost per loaf and the number of loaves sold in a year to determine the demand for bread and, thus, the size of the new plant. The following data have been collected:

PLANT	COST PER THOUSAND LOAVES (*Y*)	THOUSANDS OF LOAVES SOLD (*X*)
1	$515	208.9
2	457	232
3	567	125
4	500	182
5	543	115.8
6	631	126.5
7	432	294
8	450	207.0
9	502	132.2
10	503	183.0
Total		

a. Develop a regression equation to forecast the cost per loaf as a function of the number of loaves produced.
b. What are the correlation coefficient and the coefficient of determination? Comment on your regression equation in light of these measures.
c. Estimate the manufacturing cost per loaf for a plant producing 160,000 loaves per year.

Chapter 3

SALES AND OPERATIONS PLANNING/ AGGREGATE PRODUCTION PLANNING

Learning Objectives

- Understand the evolutionary dimensions of the sales and operations planning process
- Explore the benefits of sales and operations planning
- Learn about the key processes of sales and operations planning
- Understand the aggregate planning process
- Explore the relationship between S&OP and aggregate production planning
- Learn about the relationship between aggregate production plans and capacity planning
- Identify the aggregate planning cost and capacity tradeoffs
- Understand the managerial importance of various aggregate planning strategies
- Learn about alternative aggregate planning solution approaches

Introduction[1]

Sales and operations planning (S&OP) provides a means to show how manufacturing firms can meet sales and marketing objectives. A significant number of successful U.S. manufacturing firms are implementing or operating integrated manufacturing planning and control systems. By formalizing the level-by-level planning process the benefits can become a competitive weapon. The S&OP process is a typically monthly review of all functional areas of the company process by top management. Its ultimate goal is to always keep the detailed sales, manufacturing, purchasing, and capacity planning systems in synchronization with the latest high-level plans of management. The S&OP plan must also provide a precise forecast of financial output for the next 6 to 18 months. Effective sales and operations planning are needed in order to improve the future performance for the manufacturing firm. Sales and operations planning are currently used by a growing number of successful manufacturing firms throughout the world. An effective S&OP allows decision makers to visualize and adapt to changes in the manufacturing environment.

In the past, most manufacturers owned their entire supply chain and production output. Manufacturing organizations had complete, specific knowledge of the capacity, schedules, and costs of manufacturing. With direct control over all operations, manufacturing organizations could adapt quickly to changes in the marketplace and restore the supply sources if needed. During the past 30 years, a fundamental shift has taken place. Specifically, today's manufacturing environment is a result of three primary evolutionary trends that have fundamentally changed how manufacturing organizations operate. The evolutionary trends are:

- Outsourcing of supply and globalization of demand
- The complexity and speed of product innovation
- Demand volatility and uncertainty

In addition, complex supply chains have also evolved into diverse and globally distributed relationships that exist across different time zones, cultures, and technologies. With minimum managerial control of the constraints of the supply chain partners, strategic decision making has become difficult, yet the speed with which decisions must be made has increased significantly.

Impressive supply chain complexities along with unprecedented demand volatility are constantly challenging the manufacturing organization's performance and sustainability. Manufacturing planning and execution coordination has become a competitive advantage. The planning function must be agile enough to quickly take action at any stage in the production cycle. It is not enough to base S&OP decision making on static monthly plans. Using static plans, demand and supply uncertainty will quickly lead to inaccurate data and significant risks. While companies continue to focus on improving the planning process, many manufacturing organizations are putting equal emphasis on how to deal with the fact that established plans can be costly and infeasible. The unforgiving cyclical business environment requires more frequent S&OP cycles, continuous plan performance monitoring, collaborative analysis, and effective decision making at all levels.

[1]Refer to glossary in Appendix B for a more comprehensive definition and terms used in this chapter.

Figure 1 Sourcing Classification

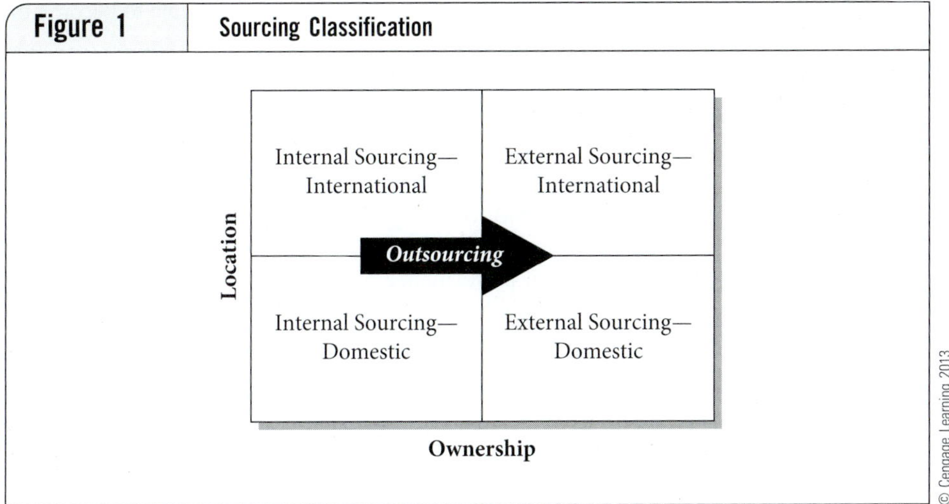

The Evolutionary Trends

The evolutionary trends mentioned above (outsourcing, product innovation, demand volatility and uncertainty) have exposed serious limitations in the manufacturing organization's ability to keep pace with the activities of the complex market forces.

Outsourcing of Supply and Globalization of Demand

Outsourcing and globalization place key operational data that influence S&OP decisions outside of the direct control of the manufacturer and make the data more difficult to access, integrate, and analyze. With falling trade barriers and advances in information technologies, traditional barriers to external sourcing have collapsed over the past few decades. While this environment has provided firms with a wide range of opportunities to improve the effectiveness of their value chain, it has also made sourcing decisions extremely complex. One can broadly consider four sourcing strategy alternatives: (1) internal sourcing—domestic, (2) internal sourcing—international, (3) external sourcing—domestic, and (4) external sourcing—international. See Figure 1 above.

In practice, various combinations or hybrids of these sourcing strategies may be employed for a product or business process. However, for parsimony, only these four alternatives are depicted. Further, there exist several secondary sourcing questions beyond simply ownership and location. These include how many sources should be used, how evolving competitive and market conditions are impacting our existing sourcing policies, and what capabilities will be required of our sources in the future in order for us to improve our competitiveness.

The Complexity and Speed of Product Innovation

The speed of product innovation requires greater operational visibility and precision in the timing of new product releases to gain market share while avoiding excess and obsolete inventory for older products. Apple has always been seen as a highly innovative company compared to its competitors. The decision makers at Apple are masters at sales and operations planning. The company has a rare ability to reinvent its products long before demand for the current version of the product reaches maturity. It is difficult for Apple's competitors to lead the innovation cycle. Their development process is vertically integrated and well branded. This approach to innovation has paved the way for Apple to become the most successful technology company in the world.

Demand Volatility and Uncertainty

Demand uncertainty driven by the evolving preferences of demanding consumers requires flexibility in demand management. The production and sales plans must contribute to achieving general business objectives of profitability, productivity, and competitive customer service as outlined in the company's strategic business plan. Customer demand is usually driven by historical performance metrics. Businesses today operate in a hypercompetitive environment with decreasing customer loyalty. The customer is now in charge! Customers have endless options in price, choice, and availability. The customer expects the highest-quality products for the lowest cost.

The manufacturing implications of this new reality are significant. Power has shifted from the manufacturing organization to the customer, and demand responsiveness is the new basis of competition. Manufacturing organizations must be able to quickly respond to volatile demands. If companies do not respond to volatile demands, they will become irrelevant.

Consider Apple, the ability to meet consumer demand with the right product at the right time and in the right place is paramount to maintaining its leadership in its acutely competitive consumer technology market. With consumers expecting the latest and greatest innovations, manufacturing organizations are continually faced with new product introductions, challenging them to effectively manage inventory levels at the retail level. At the same time, stockouts are unforgiving.

The entire supply chain must be competitive. If there is fragmented functional coordination and inconsistencies across the supply chain, operational excellence cannot be achieved. In many manufacturing organizations, sales and operations planning lacks the communication and the insight into market demands required to effectively execute business plans and achieve strategic goals. The sales and operations planning process can be designed to bring a company's marketing, finance, sales, and operations departments together to continuously monitor and meet customer demand. As the separate departments collaborate, they create business plans with the latest and most accurate data and begin to develop and measure a common set of metrics. With integrated S&OP processes, companies are able to coordinate supply and demand, improve revenue, decrease costs, and increase customer service.

The Benefits of S&OP

While many world-class manufacturing organizations are reaping the benefits of effective S&OP, many others fail to create value. Manufacturing organizations must be able to review and evaluate new products in development and future plans in the context of demand, supply, financial reconciliation, and management analysis. Manufacturing organizations must adapt, innovate, and implement integrated S&OP processes. With integrated S&OP processes, successful manufacturing organizations are able to coordinate supply and demand, improve revenue, decrease costs, and increase customer satisfaction.

The Framework for an Effective S&OP

An effective S&OP framework will lead to a consensus among stakeholders, allow management to understand the tactical plans necessary to satisfy demand, and make it possible to adjust to responsive supply chains. World-class S&OP driven manufacturing entities must perform specific activities within the manufacturing organization. The key S&OP processes are given below:

1. **New product analysis.** Performs a thorough market analysis. The manufacturing organization must determine the market opportunities and threats of launching new products. Specifically, how will the proposed new product affect current products in terms of market share, pricing, and revenue generation?
2. **Demand analysis.** Demand management is the manufacturing organization's critical link with customers, supply chain partners, and suppliers. Production and capacity planning are directly driven by forecasting future demand. Dell is a good example of using information sharing to improve its supply chain practices. Effective information sharing between supply chain partners enhances most supply chain initiatives, including supplier-managed inventory, continuous replenishment programs, collaborative forecasting and replenishment, and efficient customer response. Dell receives customer order information directly from its website. At the same time, component availability information is shared with its customers.
3. **Supply analysis.** The supply manager must analyze the supply chain's capacity, including inventory requirements, procurement policy, and outsourcing capabilities. Strategic sourcing decisions for specific segments of the supply chain must be considered in the supply analysis phase. Outsourcing is the act of reversing a previous decision to "make" or perform a particular function internally.
4. **Financial analysis.** Translates the supply-and-demand plan into financial targets of revenue, margin, and working-capital requirements. Financial targets are usually stated in terms of dollars and grouped by product family.
5. **Management analysis.** Top management usually plans with a focus on sales and profitability. However, an accurate production plan stated in units must be integrated with the overall business plan. The S&OP process adds the most value when integrated with other core business processes. A full-fledged S&OP program in place will result in a more competitive supply chain.

Businesses must collect aggregated data according to different dimensions that are meaningful to them (e.g. time, organization, product, geography, unit of measure, etc.). Thus, the company's S&OP process must link decisions at the strategic level, align tactics with strategy and goals, and allow decision makers to adapt to changing circumstances. Monthly S&OP meetings are designed to allocate and align company resources with a single set of sales and supply plans. The goal of S&OP is to optimize resources to support the company's business objectives. This includes assessing the financial implications of the plan as well as its impact on the supply and demand activities of the organization. As shown in Figure 2, S&OP provides the primary communication links between the manufacturing operation and the planning activities throughout the organization.

The supply chain operations reference (SCOR) model framework is one suggested method for integrating the business planning function with the production function (S&OP). The SCOR model focuses on the supply chain management function from an operational process perspective and includes customer interactions, physical transactions, and market interactions. The SCOR model has been used by companies of various sizes and of various continents. Intel is one of the first major U.S. corporations to adopt the SCOR model (Supply Chain Council, 2006). In the past decade, the SCOR

Figure 2 S&OP Integrated Framework for Production Management

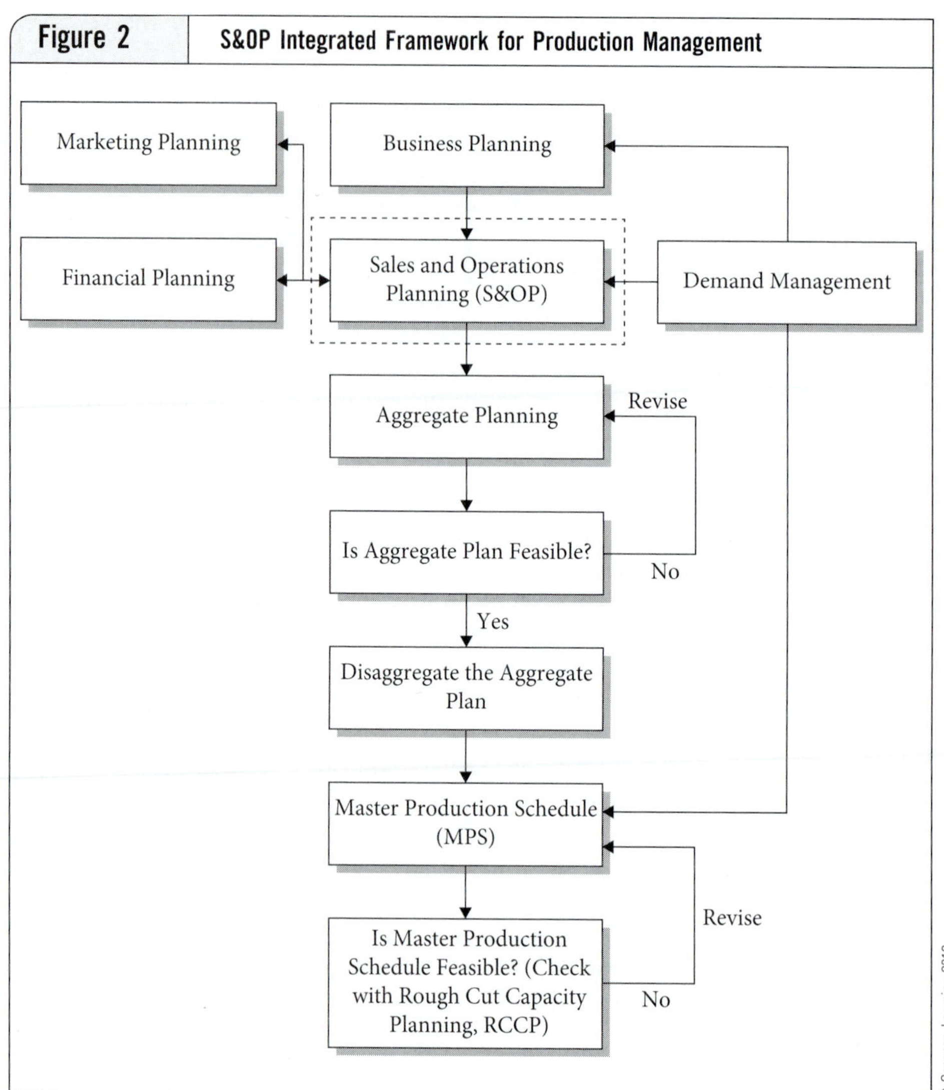

model has been widely adopted by many companies including Intel, General Electric, Airbus, DuPont, and IBM.

The benefits of implementing the SCOR model include faster cycle times, less inventory, improved visibility of the supply chain, and access to important customer information in a timely fashion. According to the definition in the SCOR model, *Plan* includes the processes that balance aggregate demand and supply to develop a course of action that best meets sourcing, production, and delivery requirements. *Source* includes the processes that procure goods and services to meet planned or actual demand. *Make* is composed of the processes that transform products to a finished state to meet planned or actual demand. *Delivery* includes all processes that provide for finished goods and services to meet planned or actual demand (Supply Chain Council, 2006). The SCOR-driven sales and operations planning framework is given in Figure 3. A brief discussion follows. A more comprehensive discussion of the SCOR model is given in chapter 12.

Figure 3 The SCOR S&OP Framework

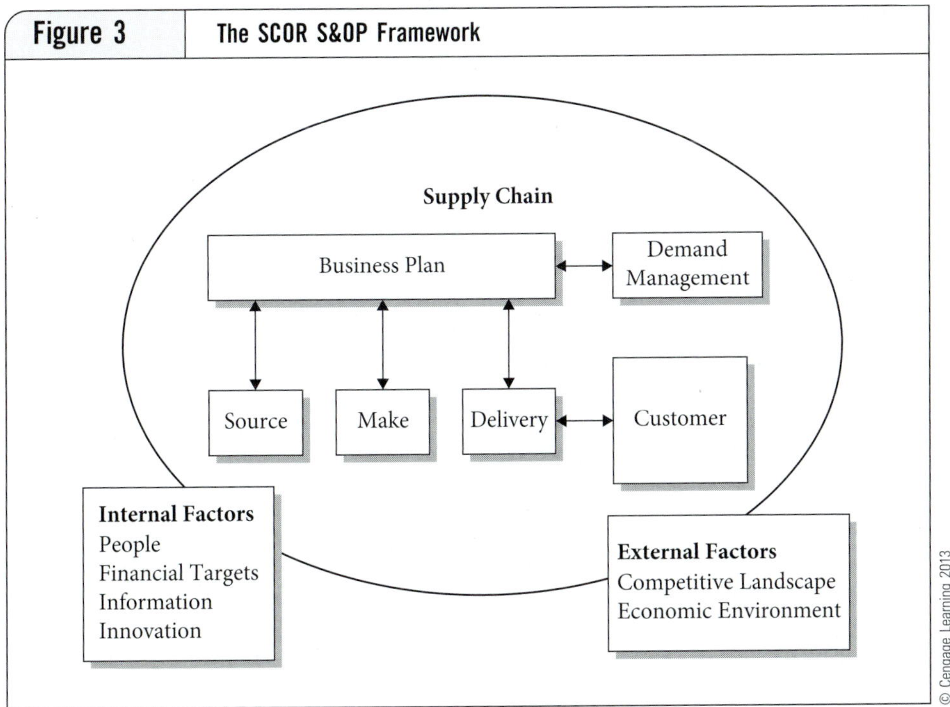

Plan (Planning)

The supply chain planning process uses information from external and internal operations to balance aggregate demand and supply. The ability to use historical data for demand forecast development is a critical component of the planning process. The SCOR model also suggests that the capability to run "simulated" full-stream supply/demand balancing for what-if scenarios is important for supply chain planning. Another important ability is to get real-time information and rebalance supply chains in real time. From the process perspective, it is important to have a designated supply chain planning team. Furthermore, the inter-functional coordination within a firm is critical for supply chain planning because the alignment between the functions is necessary to achieve a firm's strategic goals. For example, marketing and manufacturing must be aligned in order to improve performance.

Source (Buyer–Supplier Relationship)

Sourcing practice connects manufacturers with suppliers and is critical for manufacturing firms, because manufacturing firms often spend a significant portion of their revenue on purchasing materials and services. The criteria for best sourcing practice are (1) it is important to have a designated procurement team; such teams can span several functions to facilitate the timely completion of purchasing related activities; and (2) establishing long-term supplier–buyer relationships and reducing the supplier base. Having a good supplier relationship is important for securing strategic materials.

Make (Transformation Process)

The *Make* process includes the practices that efficiently transform raw materials into finished goods to meet supply chain demand in a timely manner. The SCOR model includes four groups of practices for the *Make* process: just-in-time (JIT) production, total preventive maintenance (TPM), total quality management (TQM), and human resource management (HRM).

JIT production includes several practices: pull system, cellular manufacturing, cycle-time reduction, agile manufacturing strategy, and bottleneck removal. (In a pull system, the production is driven by customer demand.) The objective is to meet customers' demands in a precise and timely manner. The TPM, TQM and HRM processes will be discussed in chapter 12.

Deliver (Outbound Logistics)

Delivery has become a critical link in a successful supply chain management–driven organization. An important capability is sharing real-time information with supply chain partners, which increases the real-time visibility of order tracking. Agility is also an important competence of world-class logistics. JIT delivery is used to measure the agility of a supply chain. Gurin (2000) described how Ford partnered with UPS to develop and implement an Internet-based delivery process, significantly improving Ford's delivery performance. An Internet-based delivery system can significantly enhance real-time order-tracking capability and is an important component to enhance JIT delivery. Dell Computer uses JIT delivery. UPS serves as Dell's logistics department, arranging deliveries around the world. This has resulted in improved responsiveness in Dell's product delivery and higher customer satisfaction.

Implementation Process for the Sales and Operations Plan

The sales and operations plan combines all business plans into one integrated plan. The plan must then be reviewed by the management team. The process begins with a summary of the change in demand. A revised demand plan is then created. Once the demand plan is approved, a supply proposal is developed. The next step is for the management team to approve the supply proposal. After both plans are approved, the supply chain partners review and modify both plans based on resources, budgets, and constraints. The entire implementation process is shown in Figures 4.

The output of the S&OP processes is coordination with the development of more specific aggregate production plans.

Aggregate Production Planning

The aggregate plan specifies the production rates, inventory, employment levels, and other resources needed to meet the expected customer demands.

Aggregate production planning (APP) is an approach to operations management focused on satisfying demand as it relates to production, workforce, inventory, and

Figure 4 A Typical S&OP Cycle

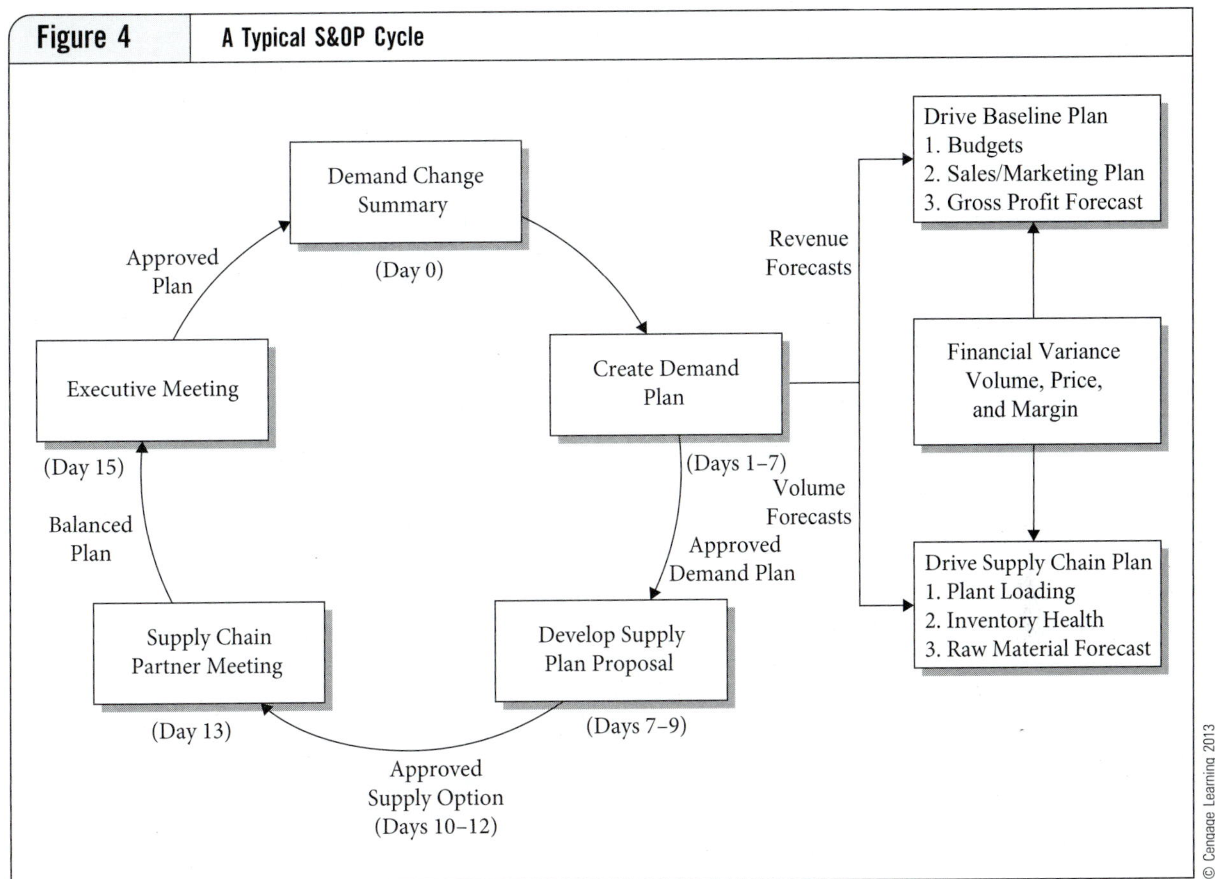

other resources. Aggregate production plans are necessary to maximize workforce opportunity, and they constitute a crucial part of the S&OP process. Aggregate production plans focus on matching supply with demand while minimizing total production costs. The S&OP–level decisions provides input to the aggregrate planning process. See the flow diagram given in Figure 5.

Aggregate resources are defined as the total number of workers, hours of machine time, or tons of raw materials. Aggregate units of output could include gallons, feet, pounds of output, as well as aggregate units appearing in service industries such as hours of service delivered, number of patients seen, and so forth.

In the automobile industry, aggregate planning does not distinguish among make, model, or color. Specifically, aggregate planning for General Motors, for example, considers the total number of cars planned but not the individual models, colors, or options. When units of aggregation are difficult to determine (for example, when the variation in output is extreme), equivalent units are usually determined. These equivalent units could be based on value, cost, worker hours, or some similar measure.

Aggregate planning is considered to be intermediate term (as opposed to long or short term) in nature. In general, most aggregate plans cover a period of 6 to 18 months. Aggregate plans serve as a foundation for future short-range-type planning, such as production scheduling, sequencing, and loading. The master production schedule (MPS)

Figure 5 The Aggregate Production Planning Process

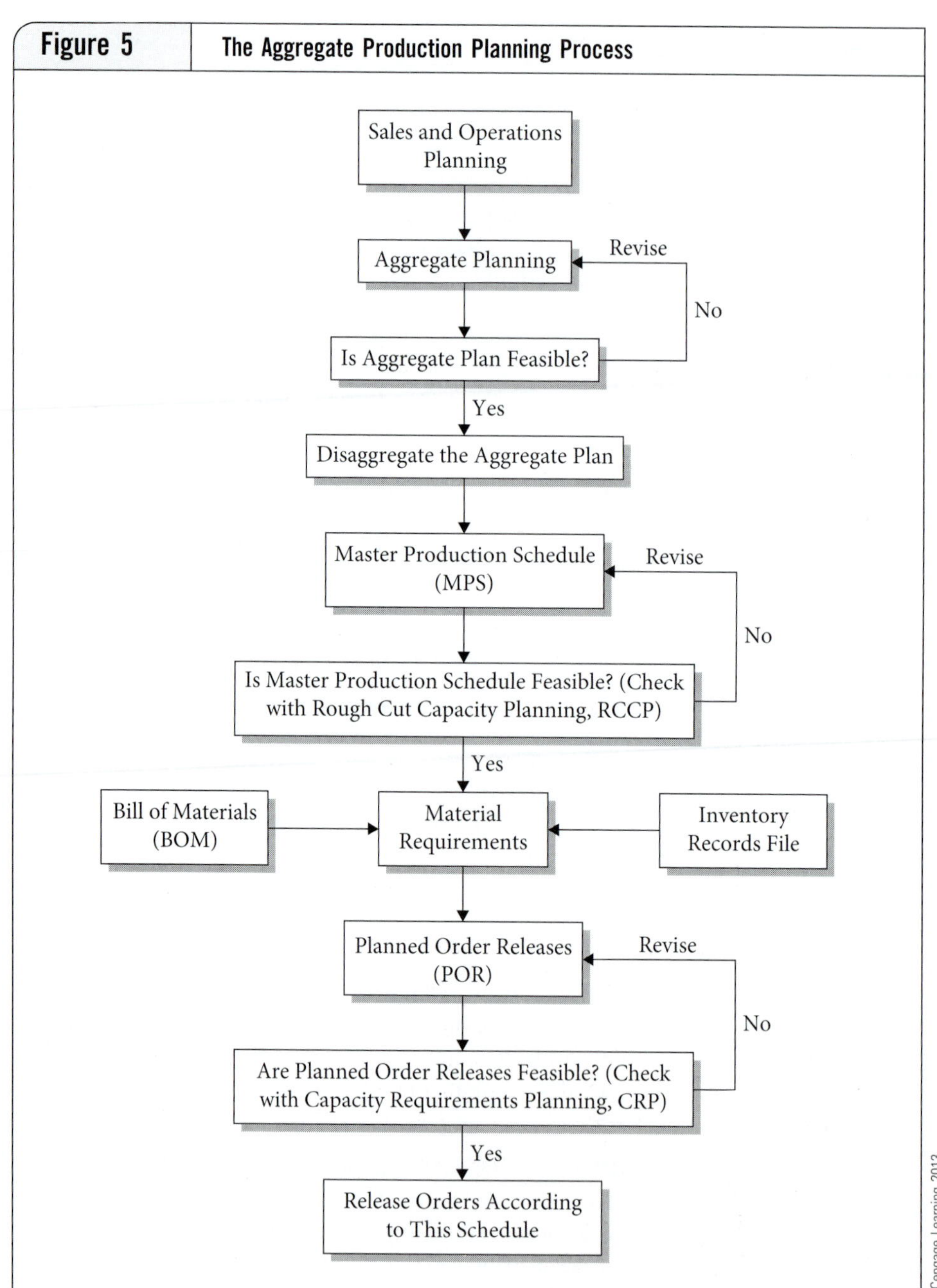

used in material requirements planning (MRP) will be described as the aggregate plan "disaggregated." Also see chapters 4 & 6.

The aggregate planning process begins with an assessment of anticipated demand and the determination of current capacity. Capacity is expressed as total number of units per time period that can be produced. Demand is expressed as total number of units needed per period of time. If capacity and demand are not equal, the firm must decide whether to increase or decrease capacity to meet demand or increase or decrease demand to meet capacity. In order to accomplish this, a number of options are available.

Options for situations in which demand needs to be increased in order to match capacity include:

1. **Pricing.** Varying pricing to increase demand in periods when demand is less than peak. For example, matinee prices for movie theaters, off-season rates for hotels, weekend rates for telephone service, and pricing for items that experience seasonal demand.
2. **Promotion.** Advertising, direct marketing, and other forms of promotion are used to increase demand.
3. **Back ordering.** By postponing delivery on current orders, demand is shifted to a period when capacity is not fully utilized. This is really just a form of smoothing demand. Service industries are able to smooth demand by taking reservations or by making appointments in an attempt to avoid walk-in customers. Some refer to this as "partitioning" demand.
4. **New demand creation.** New but complementary demand is created for a product or service. When restaurant customers have to wait, they are frequently diverted into a complementary (but not complimentary) service, the bar. Other examples include the addition of video arcades within movie theaters and the expansion of services at convenience stores.

Options that can be used to increase or decrease capacity to match current demand include:

1. **Hire/lay off.** By hiring additional workers as needed or by laying off workers not currently required to meet demand, firms can maintain a balance between capacity and demand.
2. **Overtime.** By asking or requiring workers to work extra hours a day or an extra day per week, firms can create a temporary increase in capacity without the added expense of hiring additional workers.
3. **Part-time or casual labor.** By utilizing temporary workers or casual labor (workers who are considered permanent but only work when needed, on an on-call basis, and typically without the benefits given to full-time workers).
4. **Inventory.** Finished-goods inventory can be built up in periods of slack demand and then used to fill demand during periods of high demand. In this way, no new workers have to be hired, no temporary or casual labor is needed, and no overtime is incurred.
5. **Subcontracting.** Frequently, firms choose to allow another manufacturer or service providers to provide the product or service to the subcontracting firm's customers. By subcontracting work to an alternative source, additional capacity is temporarily obtained.
6. **Cross-training.** Cross-trained employees may be able to perform tasks in several operations, creating some flexibility when scheduling capacity.
7. **Other methods.** While varying workforce size and utilization, inventory buildup/backlogging, and subcontracting are well-known alternatives, there are other, more novel ways that find use in industry. Among these options are sharing employees with counter-cyclical companies and attempting to find interesting and meaningful projects for employees to do during slack times.

Aggregate Planning Strategies

APP helps to minimize production costs, the effect of variant demand, and cost of inventory and labor costs. By doing so, aggregate production planning also maximizes plant and equipment utilization and profits. Aggregate production planning is also a useful tool in the creation and evaluation of alternatives such as the adjustment of the labor force through hire/fire/layoff/overtime, the use of subcontractors, anticipatory inventory, and even the development of complementary products, services, and pricing strategies.

There are two pure planning strategies available to the aggregate planner: a pure level strategy and a pure chase strategy. Firms may choose to utilize one of the pure strategies in isolation, or they may implement a hybrid strategy that combines the pure strategies.

Pure Level Strategy

A *pure* level strategy seeks to produce an aggregate plan that maintains a steady production rate and/or a steady employment level. In order to satisfy changes in customer demand, the firm must raise or lower inventory levels in anticipation of increased or decreased levels of forecasted demand. The firm maintains a level workforce and a steady rate of output when demand is somewhat low. This allows the firm to establish higher inventory levels than are currently needed. Higher inventory level is considered as the first alternative. As demand increases, the firm is able to continue a steady production rate/steady employment level while allowing the inventory surplus to absorb the increased demand.

A second alternative would be to use a backlog or backorder. A backorder is simply a promise to deliver the product at a later date when it is more readily available, usually when capacity begins to catch up with diminishing demand. In essence, the backorder is a device for moving demand from one period to another, preferably one in which demand is lower, thereby smoothing demand requirements over time.

In general, a pure level strategy allows a firm to maintain a constant level of output and still meet demand. This is desirable from an employee-relations standpoint. Negative results of the level strategy would include the cost of excess inventory, subcontracting or overtime costs, and backorder costs, which typically are the cost of expediting orders and reduced customer service. The pure level strategy plan supports regular scheduling and no backorders or overtime. The pure level strategy approach generally leads to higher holding cost than the hybrid or customized aggregate strategy, but does not require the use of overtime.

Pure Chase Strategy

The pure chase strategy implies matching demand and capacity period by period. This could result in a considerable amount of hiring, firing, or laying off of employees; insecure and unhappy employees; increased inventory-carrying costs; problems with labor unions; and erratic utilization of plant and equipment. It also implies a great deal of flexibility on the firm's part. The major advantage of a chase strategy is that it allows inventory to be held to the lowest level possible, and for some firms, this means considerable savings. Most firms embracing the just-in-time production concept utilize a chase strategy approach to aggregate planning. The pure chase strategy can also be referred to as just-in-time management; the chase strategy maintains minimal levels of inventory, if any. While this feature is positive for many industries, such as a bakery, employing this strategy decreases the ability of the company to meet unexpected demand due to increases the risk of back orders. Utilization levels are also generally higher.

Most firms find it advantageous to utilize a combination of the level and chase strategies. A combination strategy (sometimes called a hybrid or mixed strategy) can be found to better meet organizational goals and policies and achieve lower costs than either of the pure strategies used independently.

Hybrid Aggregate Planning Strategy

A hybrid aggregate plan will take advantage of a both chasing and leveling. Basically, the current workforce will be used without drastic changes. Demand fluctuations is usually handled by overtime. Should the levels of demand overreach the maximum labor output, back orders will be used. In this system, there will be large amounts of overtime. Hybrid aggregate planning is the most popular form of aggregate production planning.

Solution Methods

Solution methods for aggregate production range from trial and error to the use of quadratic calculus methods. Some of the better-known solution methods that can be used in aggregate planning applications are linear programming, pure level, pure chase and hybrid.

In the next section a comparison between the LP (optimal), pure level, chase, and hybrid (trial and error) methods will be illustrated.

The comparison will be made using the data given below using the demand data in Table 1.

Cost and Productivity Data

Hiring cost: $250 per worker hired
Firing cost: $150 per worker fired
Regular pay: $5,500 per worker per month
Overtime pay: 1.5 times regular pay
Inventory carrying cost: $25 per unit (based on end-of-month balances)
Backorder cost: $40 per unit (based on end-of-month shortage)
Productivity: 1,000 units per worker per month
Beginning workforce size: 200 workers (available at the beginning of January)
Beginning inventory: 0 units (no inventory available at the beginning of January)

Table 1 Illustrative Example Data Set

MONTH	JAN	FEB	MAR	APR	MAY	JUN	JUL	AUG	SEP	OCT	NOV	DEC
Demand Forecast (000s)	200	250	350	500	350	150	190	260	360	490	340	160

The total annual demand from the above set of forecasts is 3,600,000 units.

Linear Programming (LP) Solution

Linear programming is an optimization technique that allows the user to find a solution to obtain the maximum profit or revenue or a minimum cost based on the availability of limited resources and limitations known as constraints. A special type of linear programming problem known as the transportation model can be used to obtain aggregate plans that would allow balanced capacity and demand and the minimization of costs. Few real-world aggregate planning decisions are not compatible with the linear assumptions of linear programming. However, Excel Solver will be used to provide a base case solution to the problem given in the next section.

The LP method will be used to determine the optimal solution.

Variables and Formulation

MONTH	JAN	FEB	MAR	APR	MAY	JUN	JUL	AUG	SEP	OCT	NOV	DEC
Production amount	X1	X2	X3	X4	X5	X6	X7	X8	X9	X10	X11	X12
Workforce size	W1	W2	W3	W4	W5	W6	W7	W8	W9	W10	W11	W12
Hire	H1	...										H12
Fire	F1	...										F12
Ending inventory size	I1	I2	I3	I4	I5	I6	I7	I8	I9	I10	I11	I12
Backorder	B1	...										B12
Carry	C1	...										C12

$$X_i: integer > 0 \quad \forall i$$

$$W_i: integer > 0 \quad \forall i$$

$$C_i = 1 \quad \forall i \quad \text{if} \quad I_{i-1} > 0, \qquad C_i \in \{0, 1\} \ \forall i$$

$$B_i = 1 \quad \forall i \quad \text{if} \quad I_{i-1} < 0, \qquad B_i \in \{0, 1\} \ \forall i$$

$$H_i = 1 \quad \forall i \quad \text{if} \quad W_i - W_{i-1} > 0, \quad H_i \in \{0, 1\} \ \forall i$$

$$F_i = 1 \quad \forall i \quad \text{if} \quad W_i - W_{i-1} < 0, \quad F_i \in \{0, 1\} \ \forall i$$

$$I_i: integer \quad \forall i$$

$$I_0 = 0$$

$$W_0 = 0$$

Minimize Total Cost:

$$Z = 5500\left(\sum_{i=1}^{12} W_i\right) + 25\left(\sum_{i=1}^{12} I_{i-1}C_{i-1}\right) - 40\left(\sum_{i=1}^{12} I_{i-1}B_{i-1}\right) + 250\left(\sum_{i=1}^{12} (W_i - W_{i-1})H_i\right)$$

$$-150\left(\sum_{i=1}^{12} (W_i - W_{i-1})F_i\right)$$

Workforce: $1000 \times X_i = W_i \quad \forall i$
Ending Inventory: $I_i = I_{i-1} + X_i - D_i \quad \forall i$
Backorder cost: $B_i = -40 * I_{i-1} * B_{i-1} \quad \text{if } I_{i-1} < 0 \quad \forall i$
Inventory carrying cost: $B_i = 25 * I_{i-1} * C_{i-1} \quad \text{if } I_{i-1} < 0 \quad \forall i$

$$\text{Hiring/firing cost: } \begin{Bmatrix} 250 \times (W_i - W_{i-1})H_i & \text{if } W_i - W_{i-1} > 0 \\ -150 \times (W_i - W_{i-1})F_i & \text{else} \end{Bmatrix}$$

Solution

Optimal Planning Strategy Constraints

- Demand:

$$\sum_{i-1}^{12} X_i \geq \sum_{i-1}^{12} D_i$$

- X_i: $integer > 0 \quad \forall i$

Results: Total Cost = ($2,006,200)

DEMAND FORECAST

JAN	FEB	MAR	APR	MAY	JUN	JUL	AUG	SEP	OCT	NOV	DEC
200000	250000	350000	500000	350000	150000	190000	260000	360000	490000	340000	160000
X1	X2	X3	X4	X5	X6	X7	X8	X9	X10	X11	X12
200000	250000	350000	500000	350000	150000	190000	260000	360000	490000	340000	160000

MONTHLY VALUES FOR THE VARIABLES

	JAN	FEB	MAR	APR	MAY	JUN	JUL	AUG	SEP	OCT	NOV	DEC
Ending inventory	I1	I2	I3	I4	I5	I6	I7	I8	I9	I10	I11	I12
	0	0	0	0	0	0	0	0	0	0	0	0
Workforce	W1	W2	W3	W4	W5	W6	W7	W8	W9	W10	W11	W12
	200	250	350	500	350	150	190	260	360	490	340	160
Hire?	H1	H2	H3	H4	H5	H6	H7	H8	H9	H10	H11	H12
	0	1	1	1	0	0	1	1	1	1	0	0
Fire?	F1	F2	F3	F4	F5	F6	F7	F8	F9	F10	F11	F12
	0	0	0	0	1	1	0	0	0	0	1	1
Back order	B1	B2	B3	B4	B5	B6	B7	B8	B9	B10	B11	B12
	0	0	0	0	0	0	0	0	0	0	0	0
Holding	C1	C2	C3	C4	C5	C6	C7	C8	C9	C10	C11	C12
	0	0	0	0	0	0	0	0	0	0	0	0

The L.P. results are shown in Table 2.

Table 2 Linear Programming Results

	JAN	FEB	MAR	APR	MAY	JUN	JUL	AUG	SEP	OCT	NOV	DEC	TOTAL COST
Carrying cost	$ -	$ -	$ -	$ -	$ -	$ -	$ -	$ -	$ -	$ -	$ -	$ -	
Backorder cost	$ -	$ -	$ -	$ -	$ -	$ -	$ -	$ -	$ -	$ -	$ -	$ -	
Hiring cost	$ -	$ 12,500	$ 25,000	$ 37,500	$ -	$ -	$ 10,000	$ 17,500	$ 25,000	$ 32,500	$ -	$ -	$ 160,000
Firing cost	$ -	$ -	$ -	$ -	$ 22,500	$ 30,000	$ -	$ -	$ -	$ -	$ 22,500	$ 27,000	$ 102,000
Labor cost	$ 1,100,000	$ 1,375,000	$ 1,925,000	$ 2,750,000	$ 1,925,000	$ 825,000	$ 1,045,000	$ 1,430,000	$ 1,980,000	$ 2,695,000	$ 1,870,000	$ 880,000	$ 19,800,000
Total cost	$ 1,100,000	$ 1,387,500	$ 1,950,000	$ 2,787,500	$ 1,947,500	$ 855,000	$ 1,055,000	$ 1,447,500	$ 2,005,000	$ 2,727,500	$ 1,892,500	$ 907,000	$ 20,062,000

Table 3 Pure Level Strategy (in1000s)

MONTH (N)	(A) DEMAND	(B) = (A) + (A + 1) CUMULATIVE DEMAND	(C) = (B)/N PEAK DEMAND	(D) = (C)/1000 WORKERS REQUIRED
Jan (1)	200	200	200	200
Feb (2)	250	450	225	230
March (3)	350	800	266.6666667	270
April (4)	500	1300	325	325
May (5)	350	1650	330	330
June (6)	150	1800	300	300
July (7)	190	1990	284.2857143	290
August (8)	260	2250	281.25	290
September (9)	360	2610	290	290
October (10)	490	3100	310	310
November (11)	340	3440	312.7272727	320
December (12)	160	3600	300	300
Total demand	3,600,000			

Pure Level Strategy Solution

This strategy will produce at a constant rate, and simply accumulate and deplete inventory throughout the year. A first step is to determine what the monthly production needs to be (in order to produce enough to satisfy the demand for the peak month), and determine whether our initial work force size is sufficient to produce at this rate. The peak cumulative demand of 330,000 occurs in May. See Table 3.

Total annual demand = 3,600,000 units. Peak monthly production needed = 330,000/1000 = 330 workers per month or 330,000 units per month. A graphical representation is given in Figure 6. The current work force size is 200 workers. The results are shown in Table 4.

Pure Chase Strategy Solution

The chase strategy will produce exactly what is demanded each month. It will adjust capacity by hiring and firing workers at the beginning of each month so that the work force is the proper size to produce just what is demanded each month. The results for the pure chase strategy are shown in Table 5.

Chase Strategy with Overtime and Idle Time (Hybrid)Solution

Chase aggregate strategy requires continuous monitoring of demand and adjustment to meet that demand (i.e., overtime, temporary labor, subcontracting). Level aggregate strategy involves taking the cumulative monthly demand and dividing it by the hours required to meet the peak cumulative demand. Hybrid planning uses a

Figure 6 Cumulative Graph of Peak Demand and Peak Production

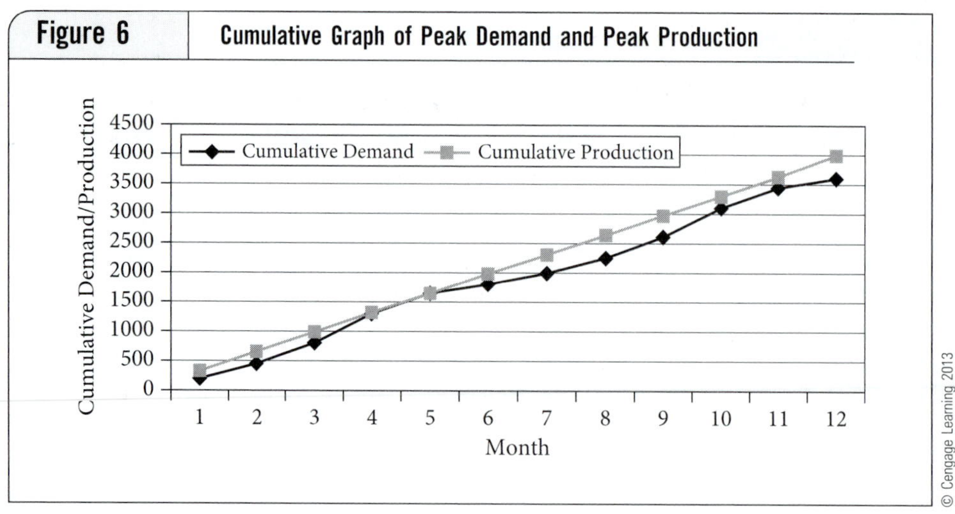

combination of the chase strategy and the level planning techniques. Hybrid planning looks at the cost of back orders compared to the cost of holding inventory and develops the optimal levels of each. While this can be accomplished through trial and error, it is also possible to use the "solver" feature in spreadsheet software to arrive at a good solution.

This strategy will produce exactly what is demanded each month by maintaining its current workforce size of 200 workers at a constant value. It will adjust capacity by using overtime when demand exceeds the regular time capacity and allow workers to sit idle when demand is less than the regular time capacity. The results are shown in Table 6.

Comparing the Results of the Alternative Aggregate Production Planning Strategies

The least costly of the three strategies presented above is the chase strategy and the most costly is the hybrid strategy using overtime; of course, these results are not generalizable. The costs generated are purely a function of the relative costs of hiring, firing, overtime, and inventory carrying; if these costs were to have had different values, the results could have been quite different.

Also, no claims are being made about the practicality of these pure strategies. There are many reasons why one or more of the strategies would be impractical. For example, if skilled workers are in great demand and hard to find, one would probably think twice about firing them whenever they were not immediately needed. It might be quite difficult to replace them when there is a need. Also, close examination of the overtime strategy would reveal that in April and October, the costs are significant. In April, we need the equivalent of 500 worker months of output. Since we have a workforce size of 200, that is equivalent to needing 300 worker months of overtime. To put this in perspective, if our workers normally work 40 hours per week, then each will have to work 70 hours per week in the month of April!

Table 4 Pure Level Strategy Results

MONTH	JAN	FEB	MAR	APR	MAY	JUN	JUL	AUG	SEP	OCT	NOV	DEC
Demand Forecast (in 1000's)	200	250	350	500	350	150	190	260	360	490	340	160
Production	330	330	330	330	330	330	330	330	330	330	330	330
Beginning Inv.	0	130	210	190	20	0	180	320	390	360	200	190
Ending Inv.	130	210	190	20	0	180	320	390	360	200	190	360
Carrying Cost	3250	5250	4750	500		4500	8000	9750	9000	5000	4750	9000
Backorder Cost												
Regular Labor Cost	1,815,000	1,815,000	1,815,000	1,815,000	1,815,000	1,815,000	1,815,000	1,815,000	1,815,000	1,815,000	1,815,000	1,815,000
Overtime Cost												

Total inventory carrying cost	(2550 x 25) = 63,750
Total backorder cost	0
Total hiring cost	(130 × 250) = 32,500
Total firing cost	0
Total regular payroll cost	(330 × 5,500 × 12 months) = 21,780,000
Total overtime payroll cost	0
Total annual cost	$21,876,250

Table 5 **Pure Chase Strategy Results**

MONTH	JAN	FEB	MAR	APR	MAY	JUN	JUL	AUG	SEP	OCT	NOV	DEC
Demand Forecast	200	250	350	500	350	150	190	260	360	490	340	160
Workers Needed	200	250	350	500	350	150	190	260	360	490	340	160
Number Hired		5	10	15			4	7	10	13		
Number Fired					150	200					150	180
Hiring Cost		12,500	25,000	37,500			10,000	17,500	25,000	32,500		
Firing Cost					2,2500	30,000					22,500	27,000
Labor Cost	1,100,000	1,375,000	1,925,000	2,750,000	1,925,000	825,000	1,045,000	1,430,000	1,980,000	2,695,000	1870,000	880,000
Overtime Cost												

Total inventory carrying cost	0
Total backorder cost	0
Total hiring cost	(640 × 250) = 160,000
Total firing cost	(680 × 150) = 102,000
Total regular payroll cost	$19,800,000
Total overtime payroll cost	0
Total annual cost	$20,062,000*

*The pure chase strategy is also the optimal strategy. Please refer to the L.P. strategy on page 64.

Table 6 Hybrid Strategy Results

	JAN	FEB	MAR	APR	MAY	JUN	JUL	AUG	SEP	OCT	NOV	DEC
Demand Forecast (in 1000's)	200	250	350	500	350	150	190	260	360	490	340	160
Capacity*	200	200	200	200	200	200	200	200	200	200	200	200
Capacity Needed	200	250	350	500	350	150	190	260	360	490	340	160
Overtime		50	150	300	150			60	160	190	140	
Idle Time						50	10					4
Regular Labor Cost	1,100,000	1,100,000	1,100,000	1,100,000	1,100,000	1,100,000	1,100,000	1,100,000	1,100,000	1,100,000	1,100,000	1,100,000
Overtime Cost		412,500	1,237,500	2,475,000	1,237,500				1,320,000	1,567,500	1,155,000	

Total inventory carrying cost	0
Total backorder cost	0
Total hiring cost	0
Total firing cost	0
Total regular payroll cost	$13,200,000
Total overtime payroll cost	$9,404,500
Total annual cost	$22,604,000

*In February, we have our first overtime, which is the equivalent of five worker months of overtime. One worker month of labor on a regular time basis costs $5,500. Since the overtime rate is given as time and a half, a worker month of overtime would cost $8,250.

In reality, a company's aggregate plan will probably be a hybrid plan that may have used a combination of the pure strategies mentioned. For example, to ease the burden on the work-force during April, we probably would not have allowed our workers to sit idle during January and February, but instead had them use their full-time capacity to produce in excess of January and February demand. Those excess units would have been held in inventory to lessen the need for overtime in the later months. Even with that, overtime needs might have still been excessive, so it may have been necessary to hire some temporary workers during those peak months to help get by. (Or we might have subcontracted out some of the work, or we might have accepted some backorders, with the unsatisfied demand being satisfied in some of the later months when demand tails off.) In summary, the pure strategies might provide a starting point in the development of an aggregate plan, but those will almost certainly have to be tweaked to get a plan that is practical.

Resource Requirements Planning

Once an aggregate plan has been developed, it is necessary to perform a feasibility check to make sure the plan will not overburden critical or limited resources. A process called **resource requirements planning** is used to see if sufficient resources are available to carry out the proposed aggregate plan. These resources can be many and varied. There may be limitations on storage space (which impacts inventory), limitations on personnel department capabilities (which impacts hiring and firing), limitations on machine capacity (which impacts production scheduled), and/or limitations on energy availability (which impacts production scheduled). An additional case study is given in Appendix 3A at the end of this chapter to illustrate the aggregate planning process.

SUMMARY

This chapter focuses on the **sales and operations planning process for manufacturing firms.**

The S&OP plan is an intermediate planning approach that provides a precise forecast of financial output for the next 6 to 18 months. Effective sales and operations planning is needed in order to improve the future performance for the manufacturing firm. Supply chain complexities along with demand volatility challenge the manufacturing firm's performance and sustainability. Planning and execution coordination is becoming a competitive advantage. The planning function must be flexible enough to quickly take action at any time in the production cycle. Using static plans, demand and supply uncertainty will quickly lead to significant risks to the firm. The fast-moving business environment demands more frequent-continuous planning and performance monitoring.

Aggregate production plans are necessary to maximize workforce opportunity, and they constitute a crucial part of S&OP process. Aggregate planning is an attempt to balance capacity and demand in such a way that production costs are minimized. Aggregate resources are defined as the total number of workers, hours of machine time, or tons of raw materials. Aggregate units of output could include gallons, feet, or pounds of output, as well as aggregate units appearing in service industries such as hours of service delivered or the number of patients seen.

APPENDIX 3A

Free Range, Inc.[2]

On December 28, 2013, Joan Davenport was reviewing the forecast for the GD49-GD175 supplement compound. The forecasts for the GD supplements were to be used as the basis for developing aggregate monthly production plans for the Free Range, Inc.

The demand for the GD supplement showed an exaggerated seasonal pattern. Joan felt that it was particularly important to have well-developed plans for the product line because competition was heating up. Customer service and goodwill were being threatened by the policy of hiring and firing. She was confident that the historical sales data were accurate enough for production planning for the GD product line.

The GD division of the company produced a number of products that were sold to various poultry farms throughout the world. The GD supplements were added to prepared dietary compounds given to organic poultry during the winter months when there was insufficient feed from grazing. The sales of the GD products increased sharply during the winter months, when most of the customers purchased the GD products on an as-needed basis. Although the company had tried a number of incentives to get its customers to stockpile the supplement during the slack season, it had no success. In addition, its customers demanded immediate service and would rarely accept a back order when a particular supplement was out of stock.

The GD supplement division employed manual labor, and the jobs generally required very little training. Although labor was readily available, there were some difficulties in hiring the people when needed. In addition, the company had developed a policy of hiring on a monthly basis. Employment varied considerably during the year, and in 2013, it had been as low as 50 and as high as 250 employees. This great variability led to increased union activity, and the company expected the union to demand increased compensation for layoffs. A recently passed labor law already provided for a large increase in the severance payment to employees laid off. This severance was now mandatory for all employees, even those who had been employed less than a month. The monthly employment and production for the year 2013 are shown in Table A.1.

The wages for manual labor at the plant were approximately the equivalent of $10 per hour for regular time. The employees were paid time and one-half for overtime, and overtime was restricted to no more than 10 hours a week over the normal 40-hour week. The new labor law virtually guaranteed a full month's regular pay for all employees whether or not they were utilized for the entire month. This was in addition to any severance pay. For planning purposes, the company used $1,800 per month as the base wage for each employee. On the average, each employee produced 1,000 pounds of GD supplement in a month. If he or she worked the maximum overtime, the expected production would be 1,200 pounds during the month.

In considering some of the other factors relevant to the production planning problem, Joan estimated that, under the new labor law, the costs of laying off a worker could be as much as $900. This estimate included the direct severance pay benefits under the new law, the paperwork and filing that needed to be done with the union. Although labor was generally available, there was always cost associated with hiring. Joan estimated the screening, paperwork, company introduction, and preliminary training costs to average approximately $175 per person hired.

Any smoothing of employment levels would result in an accumulation of inventories; therefore, some provision would have to be made to carry these inventories. Only limited

Table A.1 2013 Production and Employment

MONTH	2013—PRODUCTION 1,000s	NUMBER OF EMPLOYEES
January	55	50
February	57	50
March	63	50
April	75	90
May	121	120
June	187	150
July	234	200
August	263	250
September	222	250
October	148	130
November	120	130
December	107	100

space was available at the plant; therefore, additional space would have to be rented. In addition, the cost of capital is high because of the company's low credit rating. Taking all of these factors into account, Joan estimated the cost of storing 1,000 pounds of product for one month to be nearly $120. The company had a policy of trying to maintain a buffer inventory to improve customer service. The management team recently decided that, for planning purposes, the minimum inventory level should be 10,000 pounds to provide sufficient buffer inventory.

Simulating the Aggregate Planning Process

Joan felt that a useful approach for determining the cost of alternative production plans was to develop a simulation based on the 2013 sales forecast. The forecast of the monthly sales for 2014 is presented in Table A.2. For simplicity in the simulation, she decided to use 12 average months to represent the year rather than actual months of varying length. This enabled her to use 1,000 pounds per month as the production rate for a worker on regular time for a month. Each employee on the payroll in any month would be paid the $1,800 base wage. Overtime would be limited to 25 percent of regular time and would be compensated for at a premium rate of 50 percent.

The two variables in the production plan are the number of workers and the monthly production rate. Idle time could be specified as a part of the production plan. As an example, if 100 workers are specified to produce 90,000 pounds in a month with all workers receiving their full base wage equivalent. On the other hand, overtime could be scheduled, up to 25 percent over regular time, by specifying production in excess of the production capability on regular time. Joan also knew that she must meet the demand requirements and maintain the minimum inventory for each month in the plan.

There were 100 production employees on the payroll in December 2013, and Joan wondered whether any of those should be laid off for January. With the current production schedule, the company would end up at the end of December with very close to the 10,000-pound minimum inventory requirement. Joan was most interested in comparing

Table A.2 2014 Production and Employment

MONTH	2014—PRODUCTION 1,000s
January	60
February	60
March	60
April	80
May	130
June	200
July	250
August	280
September	240
October	170
November	150
December	120

a pure level production plan, or one with a minimum number of hirings and firings, with the current policy of changing the workforce each month to meet the estimated production requirements. She also wanted to evaluate a hybrid with fewer hirings and firings than what would be required under the current policy.

Exercises

1. Consider the following:

   a. Given the following costs and quarterly sales forecasts, use a pure level strategy to design a production plan that will meet demand. What is the cost of the plan?

QUARTER	SALES FORECAST
1	50,000
2	150,000
3	200,000
4	52,000

Inventory carrying cost	$3.00 per/unit per quarter
Production per employee	1,000 units per quarter
Regular workforce	50 workers
Overtime capacity	50,000 units
Subcontracting capacity	40,000 units
Cost of regular production	$50 units
Cost of overtime production	$75 units
Cost of subcontracting	$85 units
Hiring costs	$200

   b. The company owner has decided to implement a chase production strategy. Assume the costs of hiring and firing are $200 and $500, respectively. Compare the pure chase strategy with the pure level strategy given in part a. Which production plan more economically meets demand?

2. Daniels Inc., a skate board manufacturer, needs help planning production for next year. Demand for skateboards follows a seasonal pattern, as shown here. Given the following costs and demand forecasts, use a pure level, a pure chase, and a hybrid strategy. Which strategy would you recommend?

MONTH	DEMAND FORECAST
January	1,000
February	500
March	500
April	2,000
May	3,000
June	4,000
July	5,000
August	3,000
September	1,000
October	500
November	500
December	3,000

Beginning workforce	8 workers
Subcontracting capacity	unlimited
Overtime capacity	2,000 units/month
Production rate per worker	250 units/month
Regular wage rate	$15 per unit
Overtime wage rate	$25 per unit
Subcontracting cost	$30 per unit
Hiring cost	$100 per worker
Firing cost	$200 per worker
Holding cost	$0.50 per unit/month
Backordering cost	$10 per unit/month
No beginning inventory	

3. King Edward, Inc., publishes textbooks for the college market. The demand for college textbooks is high during the beginning of each semester and then tapers off during the semester. The unavailability of books can cause a professor to switch adoptions, but the cost of storing books and their rapid obsolescence must also be considered. Given the demand and cost factors shown here, use the linear programming and an additional method of choice to design an aggregate production plan for King Edward that will economically meet demand. What is the cost of the production plan?

MONTHS	DEMAND FORECAST
February–April	5,000
May–July	10,000
August–October	30,000
November–January	25,000

Regular capacity per quarter	10,000 books
Overtime capacity per quarter	5,000 books
Hiring cost	$200 per worker
Firing cost	$300 per worker
Subcontracting capacity per quarter	10,000 books
Regular production rate	$20 per book
Overtime wage rate	$30 per book
Subcontracting cost	$35 per book
Holding cost	$2.00 per book
No beginning inventory	

4. New Generation Mountain Bikes, Inc. manufacturer of the Road Warrior bike line, needs help planning production for next year. Demand for the Road Warrior follows a seasonal pattern, as shown in Table on next page. Given the data, evaluate these four strategies for meeting demand: (a) level production with overtime and subcontracting, (b) pure level production strategy, (c) pure chase strategy, and (d) 2,500 units of regular production

Table A.3 Company Data

MONTH	DEMAND FORECAST
January	1,000
February	500
March	500
April	2,000
May	3,000
June	4,000
July	5,000
August	3,000
September	1,000
October	500
November	500
December	3,000

from March through September and as much regular, overtime, and subcontracting production in the other months as needed to meet annual demand. Determine the cost of each strategy. Which strategy would you recommend? (Use a spread sheet to solve.)

Beginning workforce	6 workers
Subcontracting capacity	unlimited
Overtime capacity	2,000 units/month
Production rate per worker	260 units/month
Regular wage rate	$25 per unit
Overtime wage rate	$35 per unit
Subcontracting cost	$40 per unit
Hiring cost	$300 per worker
Firing cost	$400 per worker
Holding cost	$1.50 per unit/month
Backordering cost	$16 per unit/month
No beginning inventory	

5. In Problem 4, assume that the workforce cost increases by $2,000 per worker and backordering is increased to $25 per unit per period. Which strategy is the best now?
6. In Problem 4, suppose the market for the Road Warrior has increased by 2,000 units per month. Consider these three strategies: (a) level production at 3,000 units with overtime and subcontracting, (b) level production at 4,000 units with backorders, and (c) pure chase demand. Which strategy would you recommend?
7. Suppose you were asked to develop an aggregate planning system and you wanted to choose among the approaches suggested in this text. Discuss the analysis you would conduct to select an approach.

Chapter 4

MASTER PRODUCTION SCHEDULING

Learning Objectives

- Understand the concept of master production scheduling (MPS)
- Learn about the interface between the forecast, sales, and operations plan and the MPS
- Learn about alternative MPS strategies
- Understand how the bill of material and planning horizon are related to the MPS
- Understand the order promising process
- Learn how to calculate the available-to-promise process
- Compare two alternative MPS procedures

Introduction[1]

Customer service plays a central role in achieving marketing objectives for all competitive firms. The most important element of customer service is product availability. The main tool used to control product availability is the master production schedule (MPS). By using the beginning inventory and the sales forecast for a particular end item, a planner can calculate the amount of production needed per period to meet anticipated customer demand. This calculation becomes more complex in a multi product environment in which forecast errors and capacity constraints can add a great deal of uncertainty to the planning process. As firms continue to integrate the MPS into supply chain planning, it is becoming increasingly clear that MPS stability plays a major role in managing the trade-off between costs and product availability.

The MPS is an anticipated schedule of demand. The MPS represents the disaggregation of the aggregate plan (see chapter 3). The MPS includes forecasted demand as well as backlogged customer orders. Specifically, the master production schedule is composed of the supply plan, the projected on-hand inventory, and the available-to-promise (ATP) quantity. The MPS is the primary output of the master scheduling process. The MPS specifies the end items the organization anticipates manufacturing each period. End items are either final products or the items from which final assemblies (products) are made, as will be described later in this chapter. Finally, the MPS is the plan for providing the supply to meet the demand.

The MPS Interfaces

The MPS is a key link in the manufacturing supply chain planning and control process. As will be seen later, the MPS is driven by the aggregate plan and interfaces with supply chain planning, production planning, and capacity planning. The MPS also is the primary input to the material requirements planning (MRP) system. In addition to the planning linkages in Figure 1, the key operational inputs to the MPS are given in Table 1.

The MPS enables marketing and sales to make confirmed delivery commitments to field warehouses and final customers. It enables production to evaluate capacity requirements in a more detailed manner. The MPS also provides the necessary information for production and marketing to agree on a course of action when customer requests cannot be met by normal capacity. Finally, the MPS provides to management the opportunity to ascertain whether the business plan and its strategic objectives will be achieved. The master scheduling process is perpetually managed in order to ensure a balance of stability and responsiveness. The master schedule is reconciled periodically with the production plan resulting from the sales and operations planning process (see chapter 3). The MPS management primary criteria are given in Table 2.

Disaggregating the Aggregate Plan

The master production schedule is a disaggregation (break down) of the aggregate plan. It contains more product detail than the aggregate plan (distinct end items rather than composite or average units of product), and it uses finer time intervals (weeks rather than months). In the example below, two different models (Model A and Model B)

[1]Refer to glossary in Appendix B for a more comprehensive definition of terms used in this.

Figure 1 MPS Linkages

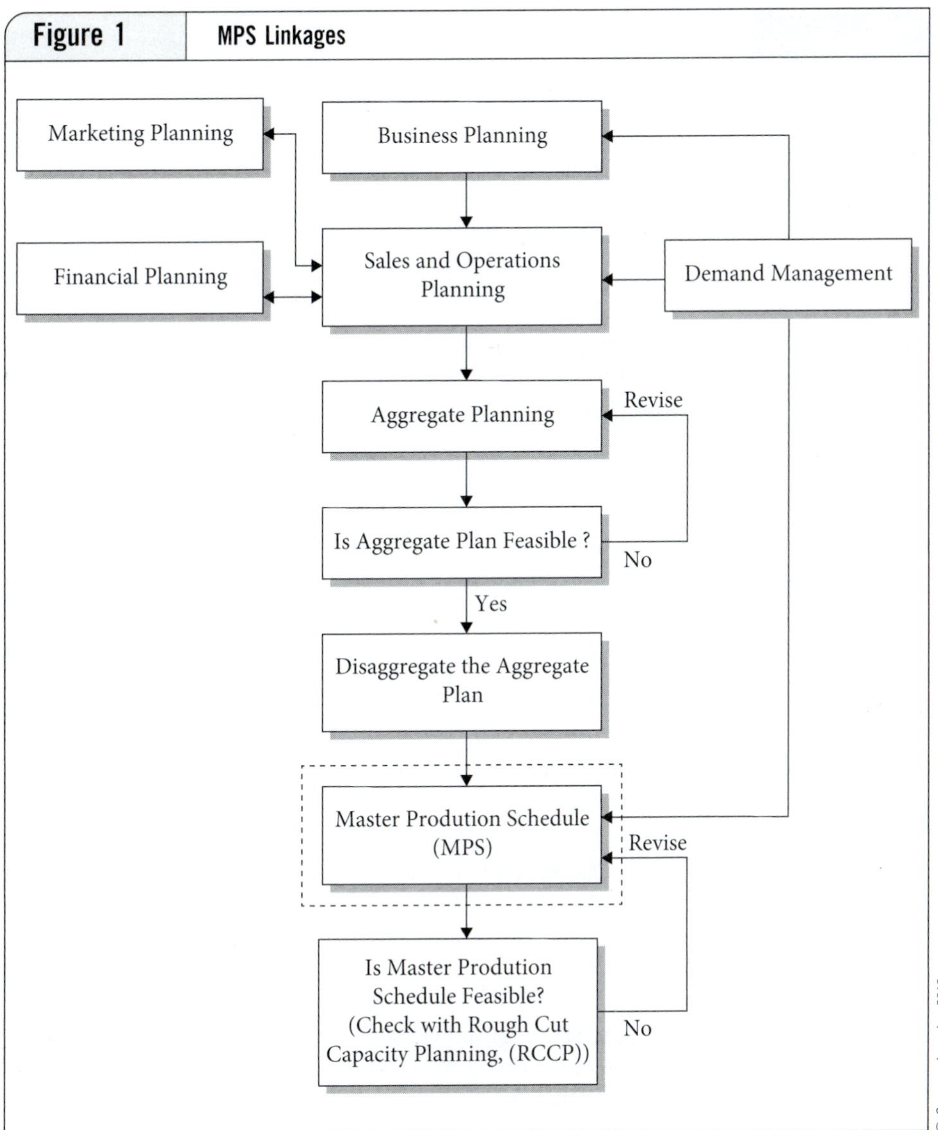

Table 1 MPS Inputs

MPS Inputs
Customer orders
Finished goods warehouse requirements
Service part requirements
Forecasts
Safety stock
Orders for safety stock (stabilization inventory in anticipation of future needs)
Inter-plant orders (component parts rather than products)

Table 2 MPS Management Criteria

- Does the master scheduler participate in and provide important detailed information to the aggregate planning process?
- Does the master schedule take into account all demands, including forecasts, contracts, customer orders, specials, prototypes spares?
- Does the master schedule also take the suppliers', capacity, and material limitations into account?
- Is a written master schedule policy followed to monitor stability and responsiveness; are goals established and is performance measured?
- Is master production software utilized and does it include exception reporting that directs the master scheduler to items requiring attention?
- Are master schedule changes made within the planning time horizons managed; are changes authorized by the appropriate people, measured and reviewed for cause?
- Are changes made only when it has been demonstrated that production capacity and materials are or can be made available?
- Are items on the master schedule past due?
- Do the master scheduler, and other affected company personnel recognize that an item cannot be manufactured, purchased, or shipped within the negotiated time period.
- Is there a defined process to determine what levels in the product structure are to be master scheduled?

of a tractor are manufactured. The aggregate plan generated the following schedule of planned production for the tractors:

AGGREGATE PLAN (000s)

MONTH	JAN	FEB	MAR	APR
Planned Production	100	400	600	800

For the purpose of projecting the needs for individual models, the historical records show that Model A accounted for 40% of the past demand for tractors, while Model B accounted for 60% of the past demand. Using these percentages and past knowledge that demand typically occurs uniformly throughout a month is used to project the week-by-week production needs for our two models.

AGGREGATE PLAN

MONTH	JAN	FEB	MAR	APR
Planned Production	100	400	600	800

	JANUARY				FEBRUARY			
Week	1	2	3	4	5	6	7	8
Model A	10	10	10	10	40	40	40	40
Model B	15	15	15	15	60	60	60	60

These numbers can be viewed as a projection of our MPS needs (we can refer to them as a "forecast" of MPS needs). Of course, this process would continue for 6 to 18 months. In actual practice, the process of developing the MPS is quite a bit more complex than what is pictured in the example. The example only shows the first pass. Additional factors (such as available inventories of finished products, lot sizing issues with production batches, etc.) result in further tweaking of the numbers to get to the final monthly MPS requirements for models A & B.

The Master Scheduling Environment

Before describing the specific activities involved in creating and managing the MPS, we must first examine the different organizational environments in which MPS takes place. These environments are determined in large measure by an organization's strategic response to the interests of customers and to the actions of competitors. An understanding of these environments, of the product bill of material, and of the planning horizon is essential to the first stage of master planning activities: designing the master schedule.

The competitive nature of the market and the strategy of the organization determine which of the MPS alternatives should be used. It is not unusual for an organization to have different strategies for different product lines and, thus, use different MPS approaches. The three most popular strategies are discussed below.

(A) Make to Stock

The competitive strategy of make to stock emphasizes immediate delivery of reasonably priced off-the-shelf standard items. In this environment, the MPS is the anticipated build schedule of the items required to maintain the finished goods inventory at the desired service level. Quantities on the schedule are based on manufacturing economics and the forecasted demand as well as desired safety stock levels. An end-item bill of material (BOM, described later in this section) is used in this environment. Items may be produced either on a mass-production (continuous, repetitive, or intermittently) line or in batch production.

(B) Make to Order

In many situations, the initial design of an item is part of what is purchased. The final product is usually a combination of standard items and custom-designed items made to meet the special needs of the customer; combined material handling and manufacturing processing systems are an example, and special trucks for off-the-road work on utility lines and facilities are another. Thus, there is one MPS for the raw material and the standard items that are purchased, fabricated, or built to stock and another MPS for items that are custom engineered, fabricated, and assembled.

(C) Assemble to Order

In this environment, options, subassemblies, and components are either produced or purchased to stock. The competitive strategy is to be able to supply a large variety of final product configurations from standard components and subassemblies within a relatively short lead time. For example, an automobile may be ordered with or without an option such as seat warmers, and a fast-food restaurant will make your hamburger with or without lettuce. This environment requires a forecast of options as well as of total demand.

The Bill of Material

An inclusive definition of a final product includes a list of the items, ingredients, or materials needed to assemble, mix, or produce the end product. This list is called a bill of material (BOM). The BOM can take several forms and be used in a number of ways. It is created as part of the design process and is used by manufacturing engineers to determine which items should be purchased and which items should be manufactured. Production planning use the BOM in conjunction with the MPS to determine the items for which purchasing requisitions and production orders must be released. The BOM is also used by accounting for product costing.

The BOM is thus a basic required input for many production planning and control activities, and its accuracy is crucial. In computerized systems, the BOM data are contained in BOM files, a database organized by the BOM processor that also produces the BOM in the various formats required by the organization. The way in which the BOM files are organized and presented is called the structure of the bill of material. The simplest format is a two-level BOM, as depicted in Figure 2. It consists of a list of all components needed to make the end item, including for each component (1) a unique part number, (2) a short verbal description, (3) the quantity needed for each single end item, and (4) the part's unit of measure. As can be seen in figure 2, an auxiliary power unit and a turbine housing is needed to make a J750 engine assembly.

The manufacturing and purchasing lead times required to produce the turbine housing and the turbine assembly components are indicated in Figure 2. Note that two weeks are required to fabricate the turbine housings and that all of the turbine housings must be delivered to the engine-assembly plant before the week in which

Figure 2 **J750 Engine Product Structure**

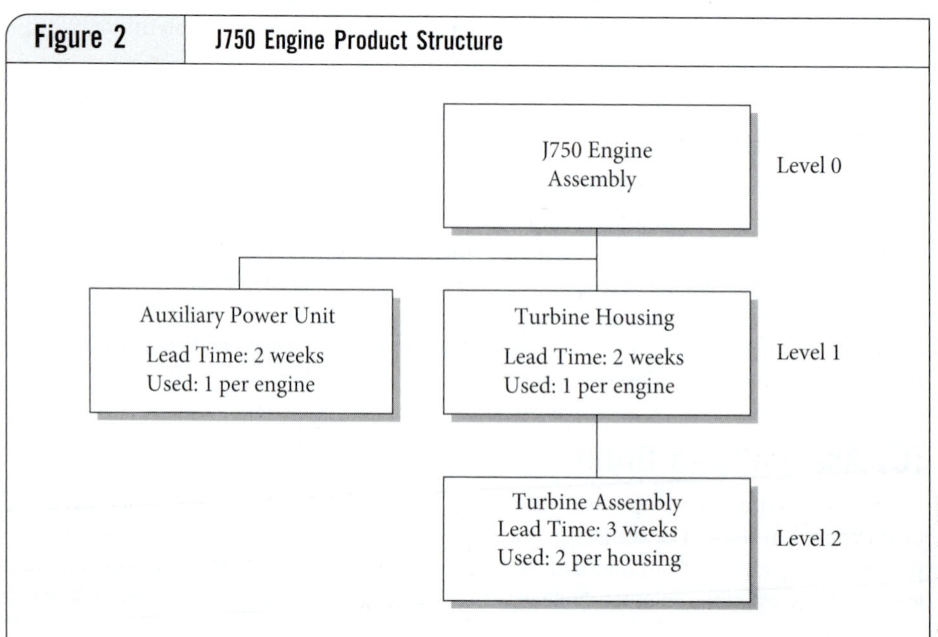

they are to be used. It takes three weeks to produce one lot of turbine assemblies, and all of the assemblies that are needed for the production of turbine housings for a specific week must be delivered to the subassembly department stockroom for the turbine housing before the usage week.

The Planning Horizon

A principle of planning is that a plan must cover a period at least equal to the time required to accomplish a specific objective. This means that the MPS planning horizon must be at least as long as the lead time required to fabricate the MPS items. This includes production and procurement time as well as engineering time in a custom design environment. Delivery-to-customer response times (lead times) in the different production environments will be discussed in the next section. A simple planning horizon MPS example is shown in Example 4-1.

Example 4.1

GFR, Inc. schedules production of its best selling dog food, Rex-2, in batches of 130 units whenever the projected ending inventory balance in a quarter falls below 20 units. It takes one quarter to make a batch of 130 units. GFR currently has 80 units on hand. The sales forecast for the next four quarters is:

	QUARTER			
	1	**2**	**3**	**4**
Forecast	70	120	120	230

a. Prepare a time-phased MPS record showing the sales forecast and MPS for Rex-2.
b. What is the inventory balances at the end of each quarter?
c. During the first quarter, no units were sold. The revised forecast for the rest of the year is:

	QUARTER		
	2	**3**	**4**
Forecast	50	80	100

How does the MPS change?

Solution to Example 4.1

GFR, Inc. schedules production of its best selling dog food, Rex-2, in batches of 130 units whenever the projected ending inventory balance in a quarter falls below 20 units. It takes one quarter to make a batch of 130 units. GFR currently has 80 units on hand. The sales forecast for the next four quarters is:

	QUARTER			
	1	**2**	**3**	**4**
Forecast	70	120	120	230

a. Prepare a time-phased MPS record showing the sales forecast and MPS for Rex-2.

QUARTER	**1**	**2**	**3**	**4**
Forecast	70	120	120	230
***Available**	10	→ 20	→ 30	→ 60
****MPS**	130	130	*260	
On hand	80		*2 batches	
MPS Quantity	130			
Safety Stock (SS)	20			

*Available = (MPS + On hand-forecast)
**There is a one quarter lead time for each MPS quantity

b. What is the inventory balances at the end of each quarter?
*Available = (MPS + On hand-forecast)
$\text{Available}_1 = (0 + 80 - 70) = 10$
$\text{Available}_2 = (130 + 10 - 120) = 20$
$\text{Available}_3 = (130 + 20 - 120) = 30$
$\text{Available}_4 = (260 + 30 - 230) = 60$

	QUARTER			
	1	**2**	**3**	**4**
Inventory Balance	10	20	30	60

c. During the first quarter, no units were sold. The revised forecast for the rest of the year is:

	QUARTER		
	2	**3**	**4**
Forecast	50	80	100

How does the MPS change?

	2	**3**	**4**
Forecast	50	80	100
Available	160	80	→ 110
MPS		130	
***On hand 210**			

*(80 + 130) = 210

The MPS Process and Forecasting

Manufacturing firms face the challenge of providing what the customer wants when the customer wants it. This problem derives from the inability to exactly forecast the desires of prospective customers and to introduce the demand requirements into the manufacturing system. The responsibility for forecasting may be borne by the marketing department, but the problems associated with forecast errors often are the responsibilities of the operations manager.

The forecasting of end item demand is much more complicated for some firms than in others. Many firms, such as automobile companies, have an almost endless number of end item possibilities, but each can be assembled from standard components and options. We call such firms "assemble-to-order" companies.

Production Lead Time and the Final Assembly Schedule

Manufacturing firms have usually been attributed with one of three major characteristics, **make-to-stock** or **make-to-order** or **assemble-to-order**. In the strictest sense, make-to-stock firms accept no orders for work-in-process goods but simply fill orders with goods already in stock. On a time line, the acceptance of orders occurs after goods are placed in stock.

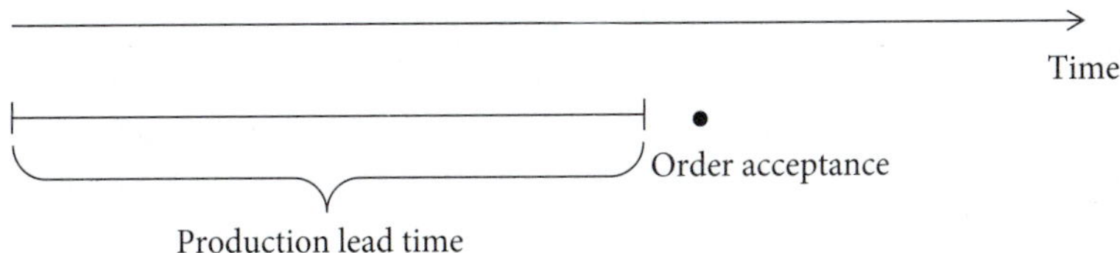

Conversely, make-to-order firms accept orders before any production activity takes place. On a time line, the acceptance of orders occurs before production begins.

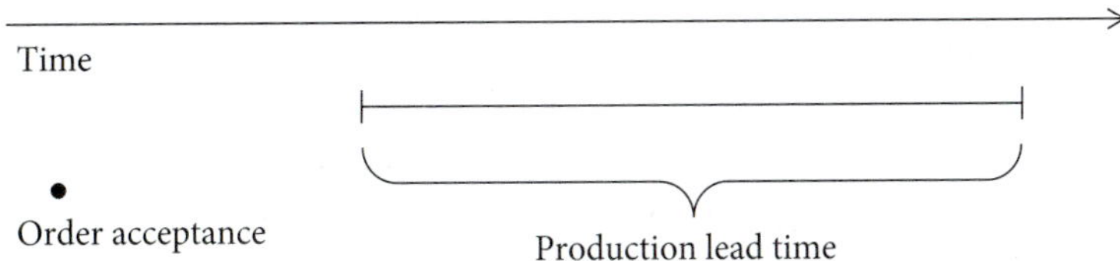

In practice, however, the distinction is not quite so clear. For example, when production lead time is greater than the order acceptance-to-delivery time needed to match competition, then order acceptance occurs somewhere during the production lead time segment.

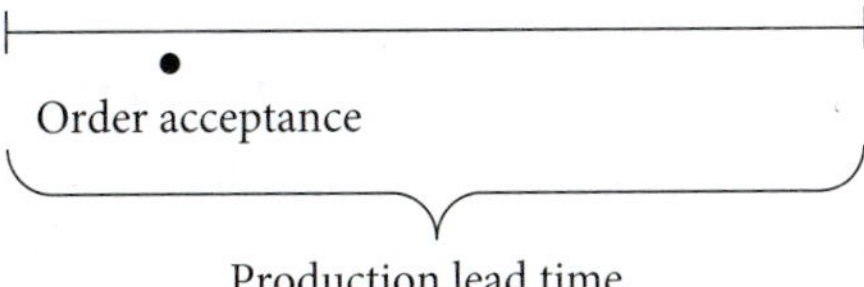

At the beginning (left) of the production lead time segment, only raw materials are purchased, components are fabricated, and minor subassemblies are constructed; thus, major subassemblies have not yet been committed to a specific end item configuration.

If the order acceptance occurs close to the end of the production lead time, major subassemblies are being assembled into a specific configuration.

The point at which the final assemblies are committed to a specific configuration marks the beginning of the final assembly schedule (FAS).

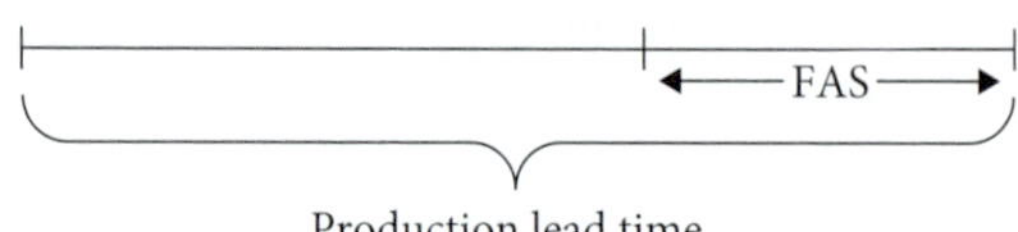

The length of time associated with the FAS varies by firm. The beginning of the FAS may be thought of as a time fence. To the left of (before) the time fence, it is possible to accept orders specifying the configurations that can be assembled during the FAS horizon. Since components and major subassemblies have not yet been committed to individual end item configurations, components and major subassemblies have the potential of being assembled into any configuration allowed by their physical characteristics. After the FAS begins, this flexibility is lost.

When production progresses into the FAS, the components and major subassemblies are committed to being assembled. The potential to be assembled into any end item is now spent on being assembled into a specific end item. The beginning of the FAS marks a point of *no free return*. Once the FAS has begun, any work done on the work-in-process inventory must be undone if the parts are to be assembled into a different end item than what was specified at the beginning of commitment. The commitment is *frozen* during the FAS.

The length of time associated with the FAS is firm specific primarily due to technological considerations. The amount of time needed to assemble components and major subassemblies into end items is a function of how well the engineering department can design the parts and of the technology available to the final assembly operations.

Since orders received during the FAS cannot be filled except when the order directly matches the configuration of a unit not presently assigned to a customer, generally orders can be accepted between the beginning of the production lead time and the beginning of the FAS—but only if all of the component parts and options are available.

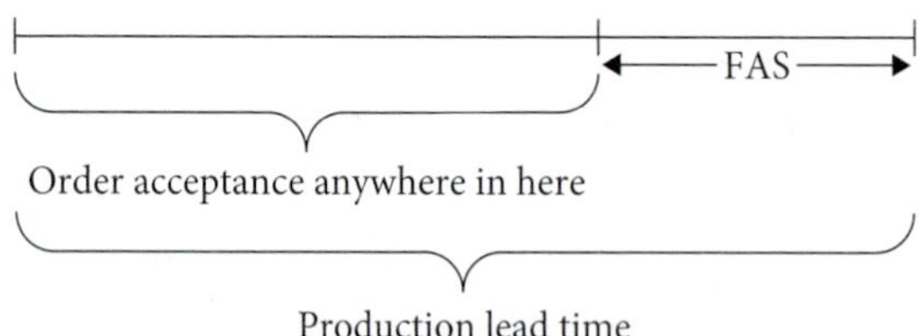

Firms that accept orders after production has begun are anticipating actual demand. They are committing at least raw materials to unplaced orders and will, when actual orders arrive, be able to assign the partially completed product to specific orders, allowing those end item configurations to become part of the FAS. Those firms may accept orders against current production until the work in process becomes totally committed to specific end item configurations. These firms may be said to be operating in an *assemble-to-order* environment. As illustrated above, *assemble-to-order* firms accept orders after production has begun but before exact end items are committed to the final assembly schedule. As a corollary, the time for order acceptance occurs prior to the FAS.

This constraint can only be relaxed by building specific end items "on the come"—that is, by either guessing correctly or by building some "prototype" end items that will be retrofitted later to specific configurations. Since retrofitting generates costs that would not have been incurred if the item was correctly built in the first place, the retrofitting approach corresponds to the concept that the FAS marks the point of no *free* return. However, in some cases, the trade-off may be worth the added costs.

In contrast, *make-to-stock* firms have periods in which commitments to specific configurations are made. The decision as to which configuration to assemble is sometimes made well before the time fence, because there are few, if any, options. Sometimes, when there are several options, the FAS concept is used to provide the latest information as to the product mix for inventory.

Environments in which orders are accepted during the FAS may be thought of as *make-to-stock* environments in a back-order position. The order is accepted but cannot be immediately filled from stock. It is back ordered against the final assembly's work-in-process inventory. The customer cannot specify the final assembly configuration and must accept the stock configuration currently in final assembly.

Master Production Scheduling in Alternative Manufacturing Environments

In a *make to order* manufacturing environment the final product is usually a combination of standard items and items custom-designed to meet the special needs of the customer.

A firm that produces only one standard model with no options or alternatives may be considered to have no special FAS or, equivalently, to have an FAS that is identical to the master production schedule (MPS), which has to be planned for at least the total production lead time. Since no alternatives exist, there is no special final assembly activity that needs to be distinguished from the general production schedule. Even if a firm with the above characteristics were to accept orders during the production lead time, the firm would not be a make-to-order firm. As described in the previous section, a firm that accepts orders during the FAS may also be thought of as a *make-to-stock* firm in a back-order position.

This concept may be extended to the firm with indistinguishable FAS or no FAS at all. Since only one standard model exists, accepting orders anywhere during production lead time is simply back ordering in a *make-to-stock* environment. Or, if orders are accepted early in the production cycle, the firm may be thought to be of the make-to-order variety but with a slight "jump" on the orders.

Regardless of how one classifies such firms, the point to be made is that firms that do not have optional configurations beyond a standard model cannot be classified as *assemble-to-order* firms. Put another way, even though a firm accepts orders during production lead time, it is not an *assemble-to-order* firm unless it has an FAS, and a firm will not have an FAS unless it offers optional configurations beyond a single standard model.

The previous section mentioned that forecasting became more complex as orders were accepted closer to the FAS. Compounding the forecasting problem is the necessity to account for the options in constructing the forecasts. Besides forecasting to account for the options, *assemble-to-order* firms must also provide for the production scheduling of these options. In order to understand the forecasting and scheduling problems faced by an *assemble-to-order* firm, it is first necessary to understand the situation faced by *non–assemble-to-order* firms.

Consider a *make-to-stock* firm that offers only one standard product. The forecasting problem is to forecast demand for the fully assembled end item. If this end item is the only item subject to independent demand, as opposed to additional external demand for service parts, then the forecast of end item demand becomes the master schedule in the absence of lot sizing and capacity considerations. That is, under ideal conditions, the forecast and MPS for a *make-to-stock* firm are identical. Even when capacity and lot sizing constraints enter the argument, *make-to-stock* firms need only to forecast independent demand items in order to construct the MPS.

Under material requirements planning (MRP) control, only the gross requirements for the end item must be scheduled, since lot sizing, on-hand inventories, bill-of-material explosion, and time phasing will control the scheduling for dependent demand items. Once the schedule for production of end items is set, the schedule of production for component parts and assemblies may be derived from the end item bills of materials, routing files, and other lead time measurements. A more detailed discussion of MRP control is covered in Chapter 6.

If, for example, a tractor company forecasted sales of 100 standard models two months from now, then this forecast of independent demand would become the master schedule. MRP lot-for-lot logic would dictate that 100 medium engine blanks, transmission blanks, and frames enter production in time to be assembled into complete tractors two months from now.

But in order to support a MPS of standard tractors, 24 = (3 Medium engine blanks) × (4 Transmission blanks) × (2 Frames) separate forecasts would need to be made. Of the 100 tractors, some configurations will be more popular than others—for example, some of the forecasts will have a history of only one or two units each period, which makes it inappropriate for accurate forecasting thus leads to the observation that accurate forecasting at the end item level for *assemble-to-order* firms is complicated by two problems of size. First, there may be far too many end item possibilities to realistically consider forecasting. Second, even if the number of forecasts is considered to be manageable, the size of individual histories may be too small to allow the forecasts to be accurate. From the discussion on the various alternative manufacturing environments, it is easy to see that assemble-to-order manufacturing is more complex in terms of the competitive landscape and customer service. Thus, the following sections will focus exclusively on the assemble-to-order manufacturing environment.

The Order Acceptance Ratio for Assemble-to-Order Environment

Assemble-to-order environments may be further classified by the ratio of the time between order acceptance and the beginning of the FAS to the production lead time less FAS time (order acceptance ratio).

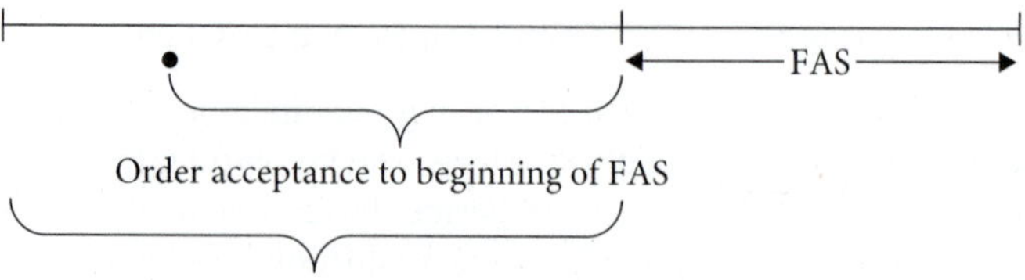

If this ratio is near unity, meaning orders are accepted just as production is commencing, then the environment is nearly make to order. The firm only needs to forecast raw material requirements or a few components with long lead times in anticipation of future orders. Orders are received before any significant subassembly schedules are

Figure 3 Bulldozer Tractor Bill of Material

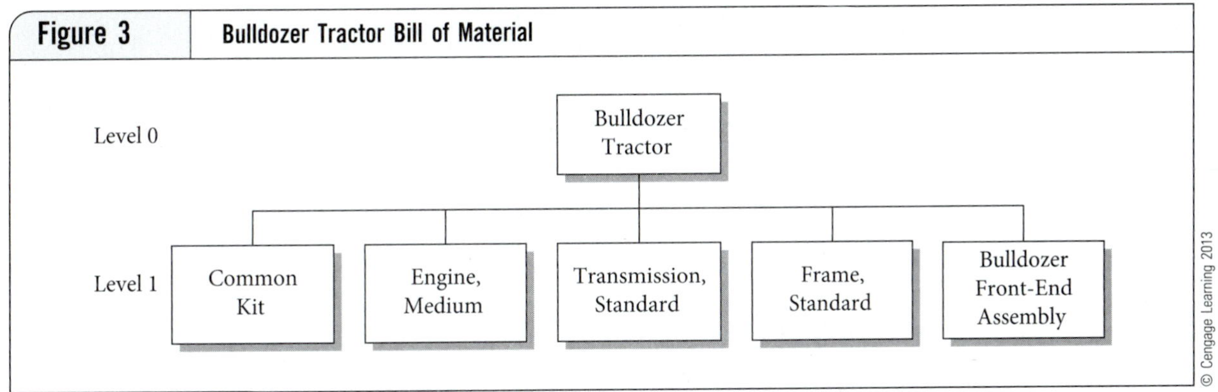

committed. A firm in this position must forecast raw materials usage but does not require accurate forecasting of subassembly demand.

For example, consider a tractor manufacturer with an eight-week production lead time in which the final week constitutes the FAS. During the final week, specific tractor configurations are assembled from numerous options. One such tractor may have a medium-size engine with standard transmission, standard frame, and a bulldozer blade (Figure 3). Once the tractor enters the eighth week of production, the engine, transmission, frame, and blade are committed to the configuration mentioned.

If the example firm operates in the near-unity position of the assemble-to-order environment, then orders are accepted during the first week of production. During this week, only engine, transmission, frame, and blade blanks are being manufactured from raw materials. Since orders for specific engines, transmissions, frames, and front-end assemblies will be known by the time the blanks are produced, the firm does not need to forecast demands for individual options. However, the firm does have to forecast the demand for aggregate engines, transmissions, frames, and front-end assemblies in order that it produce enough blanks to satisfy demand without over producing unneeded blanks. Thus, an assemble-to-order firm in this position faces only an aggregate forecasting problem.

At the other extreme, when the order acceptance ratio approaches zero, a firm must forecast the demand of all assemblies up to the final assembly schedule. This is a more formidable problem. The only reasonable response is to carry extra inventories of the various major components in order to respond to actual customer orders. If the example tractor manufacturer operates in an environment in which the ratio is near zero, orders will be accepted in the seventh week of production, just before the FAS begins. The firm may find itself in this less enviable position due to short delivery schedules of the competition or to the demands of key customers.

The firm must now have every item and the proper number of that component available for assembly into a specific tractor configuration by the end of the seventh week. Since the firm will not have orders promised against the work in process until the seventh week, it must conquer the problems of forecasting the demand for individual options and implementing production schedules to meet this demand.

If, say, an order for 12 tractors with medium-sized engines, standard transmissions, and standard frames is placed in week seven, then the firm must somehow have provided for the manufacture of the component parts six and a half weeks before the order is accepted. The firm will either have to forecast options sold currently or any extra options (safety stock inventories) in order to be able to accept actual customer orders.

The Assemble-to-Order Managerial Problem

We have shown that forecasting the demand for every possible end item configuration is not a feasible approach to constructing an MPS for assemble-to-order firms having a combinatorically large set of possible end items. Since the complexity of assemble-to-order environments often leads to an unmanageable number of end item configurations, it is similarly infeasible to believe that an MPS system can be based upon individual indented bills of material for every end item, since the number of such end item bills grows geometrically.

How then should the manager approach master production scheduling for the assemble-to-order environment?

In the assemble-to-order environment, one critical managerial issue is the length of delivery lead time that must be quoted to a prospective customer. It is realistic to assume that most assemble-to-order firms compete with firms producing similar products. In order to effectively compete with other firms, a firm must be able to at least match delivery lead times quoted by the competition. Since competing firms may manufacture nearly identical products, prospective customers may then choose the firm that can more quickly supply the product. Delivery lead time performance is the competitive edge of the winning firm.

As the order acceptance ratio approaches zero, the only way the firm can offer competitive delivery lead time quotations is to carry safety stocks in the various optional features from which customers may choose to order. For a given investment in safety stocks (over planned or overstated option alternatives), one way to view the managerial problem is how to construct the master production schedule in order to maximize the firm's ability to respond to delivery lead time pressures. The operations manager is interested in the delivery lead time performances that result from alternative techniques for constructing the MPS and in the comparative costs of designing and maintaining these MPS systems.

Available to Promise (ATP) Logic

The MPS serves as a control mechanism in three distinct ways: (1) Actual production is compared to the MPS to determine if the plan is being met; (2) the available-to-promise (ATP) is calculated to determine if an incoming order can be promised for delivery in a specific period; and (3) the projected on-hand inventory is calculated to determine if the supply is sufficient to fill expected future orders.

The ATP value for an item in the most immediate time period is the amount of on-hand inventory plus scheduled production that is not yet promised to actual customer orders. In subsequent time periods, the ATP is the scheduled production less any quantities allocated to specific customer orders. The ATP value measures the uncommitted portion of a scheduled production receipt. By calculating the ATP associated with every scheduled receipt of production, it is possible to determine if a new order can be accepted in the time frame requested by the customer. Moreover, the product-by-product ATP indicates the pattern of how actual orders are consuming the forecast. An illustrative example of ATP is given in Example 4-2.

If a customer wishes to place an order, the order-promising logic examines the "availability" of each option during or before the desired period. If any one of the options is unavailable, the logic examines the availability of each option for one more period in the future. This process continues until a future period is found with available-to-promise units for every option.

For example, if a customer wishes to order five bulldozers with medium-size engines and standard transmissions and frames (Figure 3) in period eight, then the order may be accepted if the ATP for every level-one assembly or option has a cumulative ATP value through period 8 at least as great as 5. See chapter 6 for a discussion on low-level coding. If, say, the bulldozer blade assembly has an ATP value of 0 for periods 1 through 7, three in period 8 and five in period 10, then the order may not be accepted until period 10. The order acceptance date would be even further out if another level-one ATP record so dictates. Figure 4 illustrates the order-promising logic. An illustrative example of ATP is given in Example 4.2.

Example 4.2

Calculating ATP:

1. For the first period, the available-to-promise is the sum of the beginning inventory plus the MPS for the first period (in this case zero) minus customer commitments for the first period and all periods following the first period up to but not including the next period for which an MPS quantity has been planned. See formulation below.
2. For all periods after the first, there are two possibilities: Schedule or do not schedule a MPS quantity.
3. If a master production quantity has been scheduled for the period, the available-to-promise is the quantity scheduled minus all customer commitments for the period and for all following periods up to but not including the next period for which a master production quantity has been scheduled.
4. If no master production quantity has been scheduled for the period, the available-to-promise is zero, even if deliveries in the period have been promised. The promised shipments often are shown as backlog (customer commitments) in the period with the most recent production (MPS).
5. Calculating the (available inventory) projected on-hand inventory

$$I_t = I_{t-1} + MPS_t - \max(F_t \text{ or } CO_t)$$

Where:

I_t = projected-on-hand at end of week t
MPS_t = MPS quantity due in week t
F_t = forecast of orders in week t
CO_t = customer orders already booked for shipment in week t

6. Calculating available-to-promise (ATP) quantities
   - **Conceptual framework**
     The MPS quantity that can still be used to meet new booking requests, considering **current** on-hand, MPS_t, and CO_t must be considered.
   - **First Week**
     ATP = Current on-hand + MPS in first week − cumulative CO_t up to next MPS receipt
     $ATP = I_{t-1} + MPS_t - \Sigma(CO_t)$
   - **Subsequent weeks**
     Only for weeks when an MPS quantity arrives
     ATP = MPS of the next week − cumulative CO_t up to next MPS receipt
7. MPS Order Promising Illustrative Example

Order-Promising Example—Week 1

For week 1, verify the available and available-to-promise.

	Week number											
	1	2	3	4	5	6	7	8	9	10	11	12
Forecast	5	5	5	5	5	5	15	15	15	15	15	15
Customer Orders	5	3	2									
Available*	15	10	5	30	25	20	5	20	5	20	5	20
ATP**	10			30				30		30		30
MPS				30				30		30		30
On hand =	20											

*Available = $I_{t-1} + MPS_t - \max(F_t \text{ or } CO_t) = (20 + 0) - \max(5, 5) = 15$
**Available-to-Promise (ATP) = $I_{t-1} + MPS_t - \Sigma(CO_t) = (20 + 0) - (5 + 3 + 2) = 10$

For week 1, sales were 10 units instead of 5 and ending inventory was 10 units. Sales forecasts were revised accordingly as shown below.

Order-Promising Example—Week 2

	Week number											
	2	3	4	5	6	7	8	9	10	11	12	13
Forecast	10	10	10	10	10	15	15	15	15	15	15	15
Customer Orders	5	5	2									
Available*	30	20	10	30	20	5	20	5	20	5	20	5
ATP**	28			30			30		30		30	
MPS	30			30			30		30		30	
On hand =	10											

*Available = $I_{t-1} + MPS_t - \max(F_t \text{ or } CO_t) = (10 + 30) - \max(5, 10) = 30$
**Available-to-Promise (ATP)= $I_{t-1} + MPS_t - \Sigma(CO_t) = (10 + 30) - (5 + 5 + 2) = 28$

Order-Promising Example—Week 3

	Week number											
	3	4	5	6	7	8	9	10	11	12	13	14
Forecast	10	10	10	10	15	15	15	15	15	15	15	15
Customer Orders	20	2		35		10						
Available*	10	0	20	30	20	5	20	5	20	5	20	5
ATP**	3		0			20		30		30		
MPS			30			30		30		30		
On hand =	30											

*Available = $I_{t-1} + MPS_t - \max(F_t \text{ or } CO_t) = (30 + 0) - \max(20, 10) = 10$
**Available-to-Promise (ATP) = $I_{t-1} + MPS_t - \Sigma(CO_t) = (30 + 0) - (20 + 2) = 8^{\dagger}$
†The ATP of seven units must be adjusted for the expected stockout of five units in period 6. All expected stockouts must be satisfied before additional orders can be promised. In the case of period 3, three units (8–5) are available to promise.

Figure 4 Available to Promise ATP Process

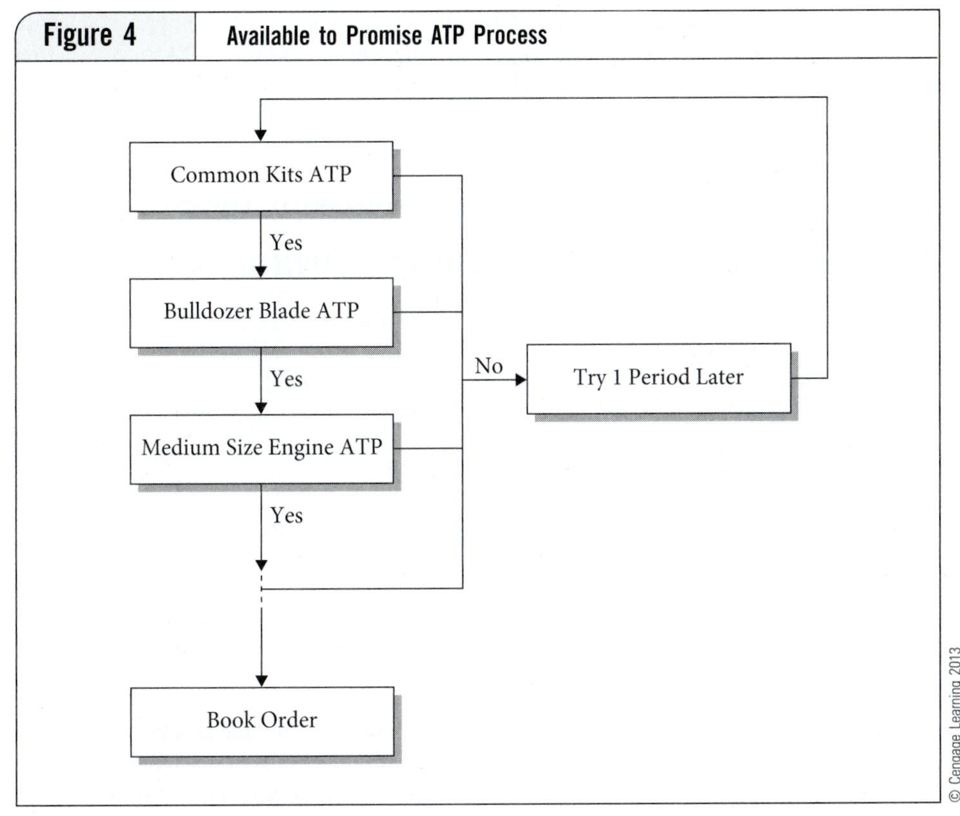

Figure 5 For the Most Part, a Firm's FAS Time Is Unalterable

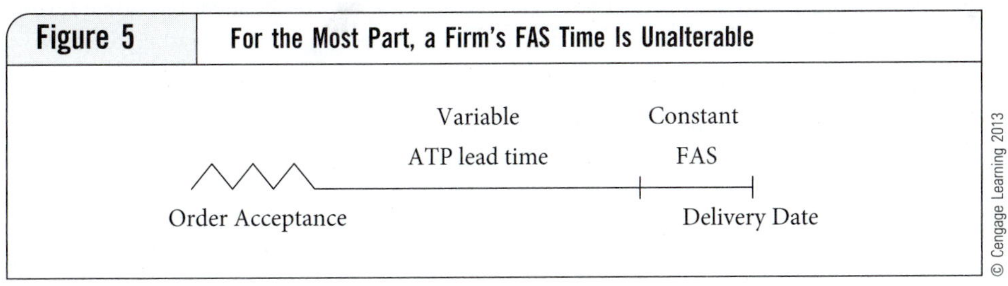

It can be seen that the ATP order-entry logic determines how long a customer must wait until the order is received. The timing between order acceptance and the delivery date in the assemble-to-order environment is composed of two segments. First, the FAS takes a constant amount of time. This time segment is dependent on the technology, manufacturing approach, and efficiency of the firm. For the most part, a firm's FAS time is unalterable. See Figure 5.

Second, the FAS for a specific end item may not begin until all necessary options and components are physically available. The time waiting for the arrival of all necessary items is variable and controllable through the MPS. A well-developed MPS will result in the proper quantities of assemblies being available to enter the FAS. The ATP order-entry logic provides the means to measure the performance of this variable portion of the order-acceptance-to-delivery-date lead time.

In the next section, the performance of two MPS techniques will be compared. Since the managerial problem discussed above is concerned with delivery lead times, the primary performance criterion will be how well each technique keeps the order-acceptance-to-delivery-date lead time short.

Alternative MPS Technique Comparison for an Assembly-to-Order Manufacturing Environment

The FAS for a specific end item may not begin until all necessary options and components are physically available. The time waiting for the arrival of all necessary items is called ATP lead time and is controllable through the master schedule. A well-developed master schedule will result in the proper quantities of assemblies available to enter the FAS and thus reduce the time. For a thorough development of the alternative ATO MPS technique comparison see King and Benton (1987).[2]

In this section, we introduce two MPS techniques for the assemble-to-order environment. The alternative MPS procedures are the superbill and the covering-set approaches. The specific purpose of this section is to relate and examine both the superbill approach and the covering-set approach in terms of the MPS problem in the assemble-to-order environment.

(A) Superbills

The superbill approach is in direct response to the large combinatorial number of end items that need to be handled if the MPS is to be based upon the standard end item indented bill structure. The superbill allows the MPS for the assemble-to-order environment to be stated in terms of a much smaller number of MPS units. The special product structure of the superbill approach requires the development of special planning bills of material or super bill to be used for constructing the MPS. This is a key characteristic of this approach. Super bill structures, different from indented bill structures, are designed, maintained, and used for setting the MPS.

When setting the MPS, the executive team must commit to how many tractors in the super bill, or overall units are to be produced in each time bucket of the planning horizon. See chapter 3. This aggregate total may be the production plan, company game plan, or contract between various functional areas of the firm. Marketing agrees to sell that many overall units, production commits to make them preserving as much flexibility in the end item configuration as possible, and finance agrees to provide adequate resources. The criteria for setting the production plan or lot sizes at the end item level are beyond the scope of this discussion. See chapters 3, 6 and 9. What is important to superbill development is that the overall or total MPS contains no safety stock.

For the tractor firm example, numerous indented bills of material may exist in the form shown in Figure 6a. Rather than forecasting and constructing an MPS for arctic bulldozers (Figure 6a), standard bulldozers (Figure 6b), and the other numerous end-item configurations, the superbill approach constructs special planning bills in the form shown in Figure 7. The superbill shown as a super tractor is not a tractor at all; it is simply a method of identifying an artificial end item created for planning and for accounting for all options that make up all of the tractors produced by the firm.

[2]King, B.E, and W.C. Benton. "Alternative Master Production Scheduling Techniques in an Assembly-to-Order Environment, Journal of Operations Management" 7.2 (1987) 179-201.

Figure 6a Indented Bill of Material for Arctic Bulldozer

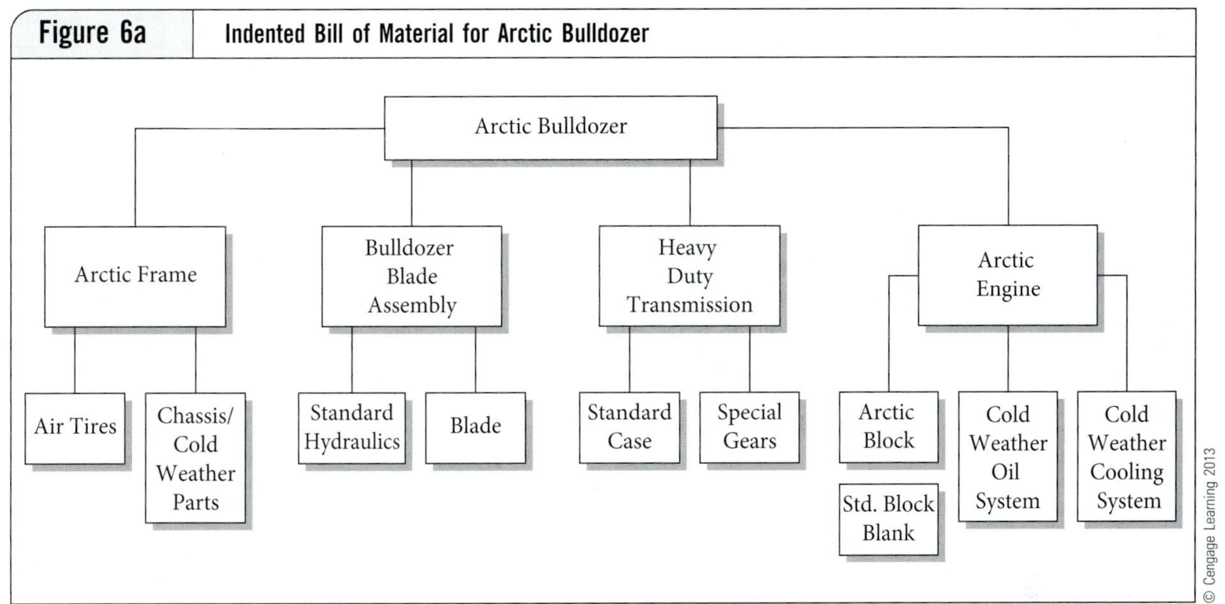

Figure 6b Indented Bill of Material for Standard Bulldozer

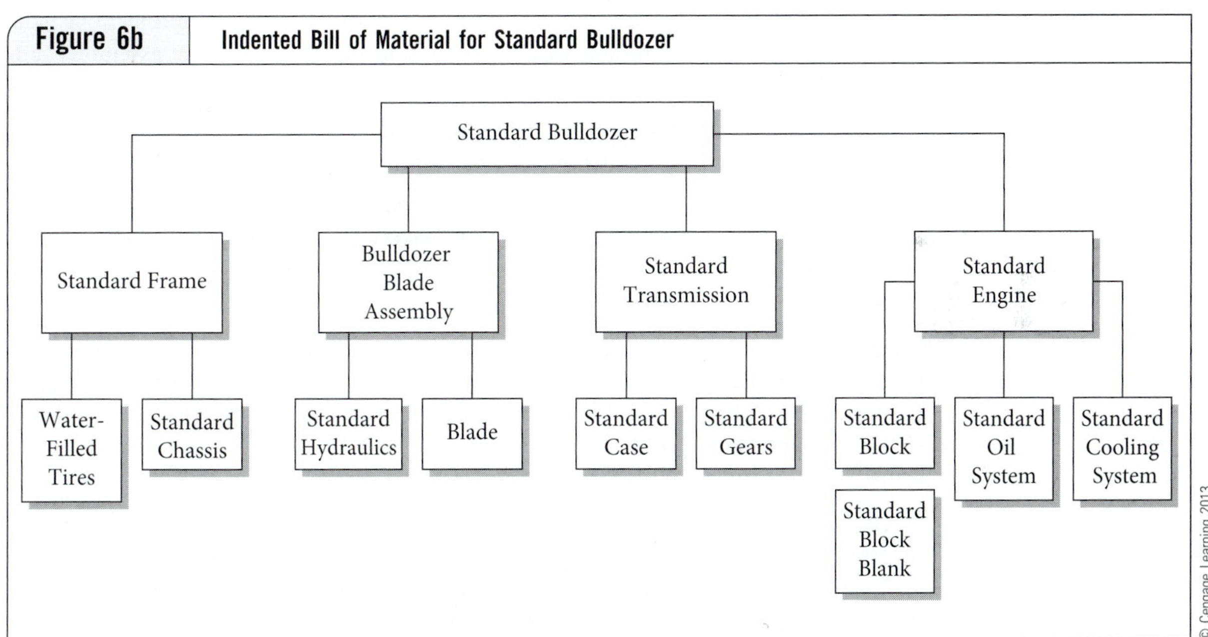

Notice that the options shown on the superbill are not necessarily buildable or stockable. For example, since the engine block blank is the same for all tractors, it is placed in the common module. All tractors have the same standard block blank. The block is drilled to accept both standard and arctic oil and cooling systems. The cooling and oil systems are add-on systems, but the drilling of the block is an integral part of the fabrication process.

The other components of an engine, the oil systems and the cooling system, are planned and accounted for under the appropriate engine kit. Since it is impossible

Figure 7 Superbill Supertractor Illustration

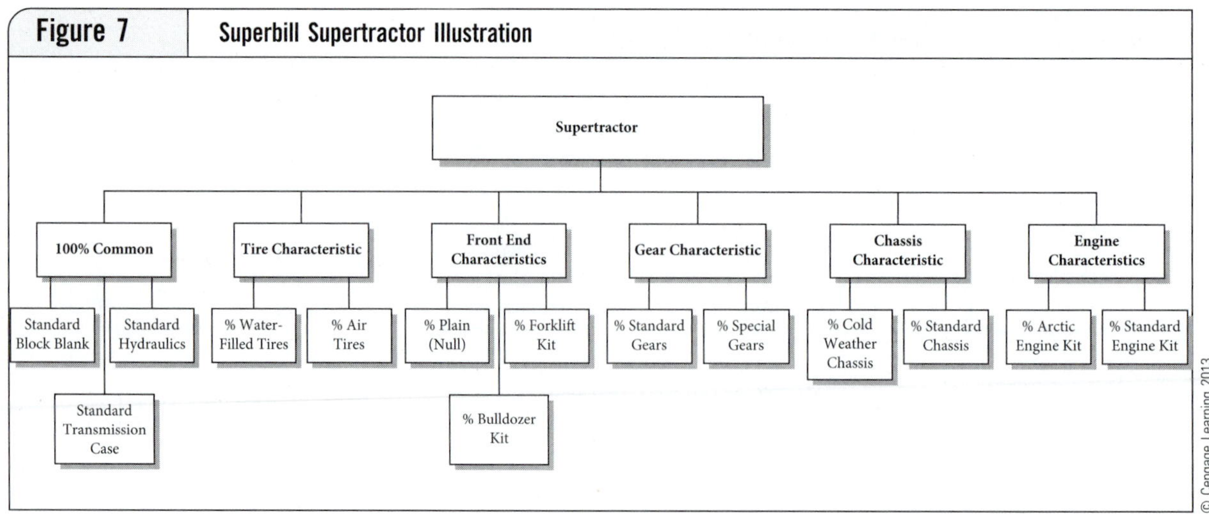

to build an engine without these two systems, fully assembled engines will never be built or stocked except briefly during final assembly. The engine kits consist of the oil systems and cooling systems. Independently, nothing useful can be constructed, but all in combination with a properly drilled block may be assembled into a functioning engine.

Under a standard MPS approach based upon indented bill structures, indented bills drive the planning and construction activities during the entire cascaded lead time.

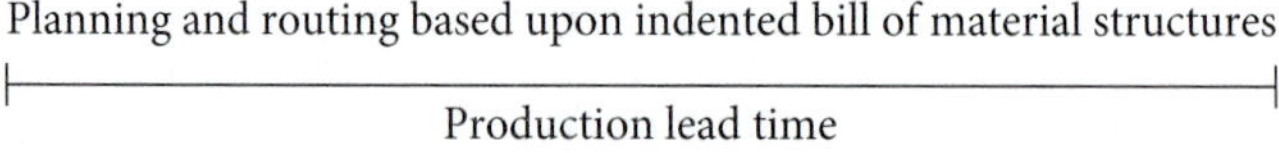

When using superbills, the indented bill of material is inappropriate for planning purposes. The superbill is a substitute for planning activity in the range between the start of component part fabrication and the FAS. During the final assembly process, either indented bill structure or some special routing information is used to assemble definable actual end items.

The use of superbills in MPS development affects not only the planned orders for the superbill options but also the resultant entire time phasing of component production lead times. As an example, consider the indented bill time chart shown in Figure 8 for the arctic bulldozer manufacturing process, when it is based upon indented (goes into) bill structures.

Other component fabricating and procurement processes can occur before the processes illustrated in the indented bill time chart. The cold-weather chassis requires many component items that are not accounted for on the chart; the transmission case is cast from raw materials, which are further planned and controlled through standard MRP systems and procedures. It is necessary to point this out, since lower-level components not on the indented bill time chart are identical to those not on the superbill time chart of Figure 9. That is, the required components of the indented-bill and superbill time charts are equivalent after some level in the product structure.

Figure 8 **Indented Bill Time Chart the Artic Bulldozer**

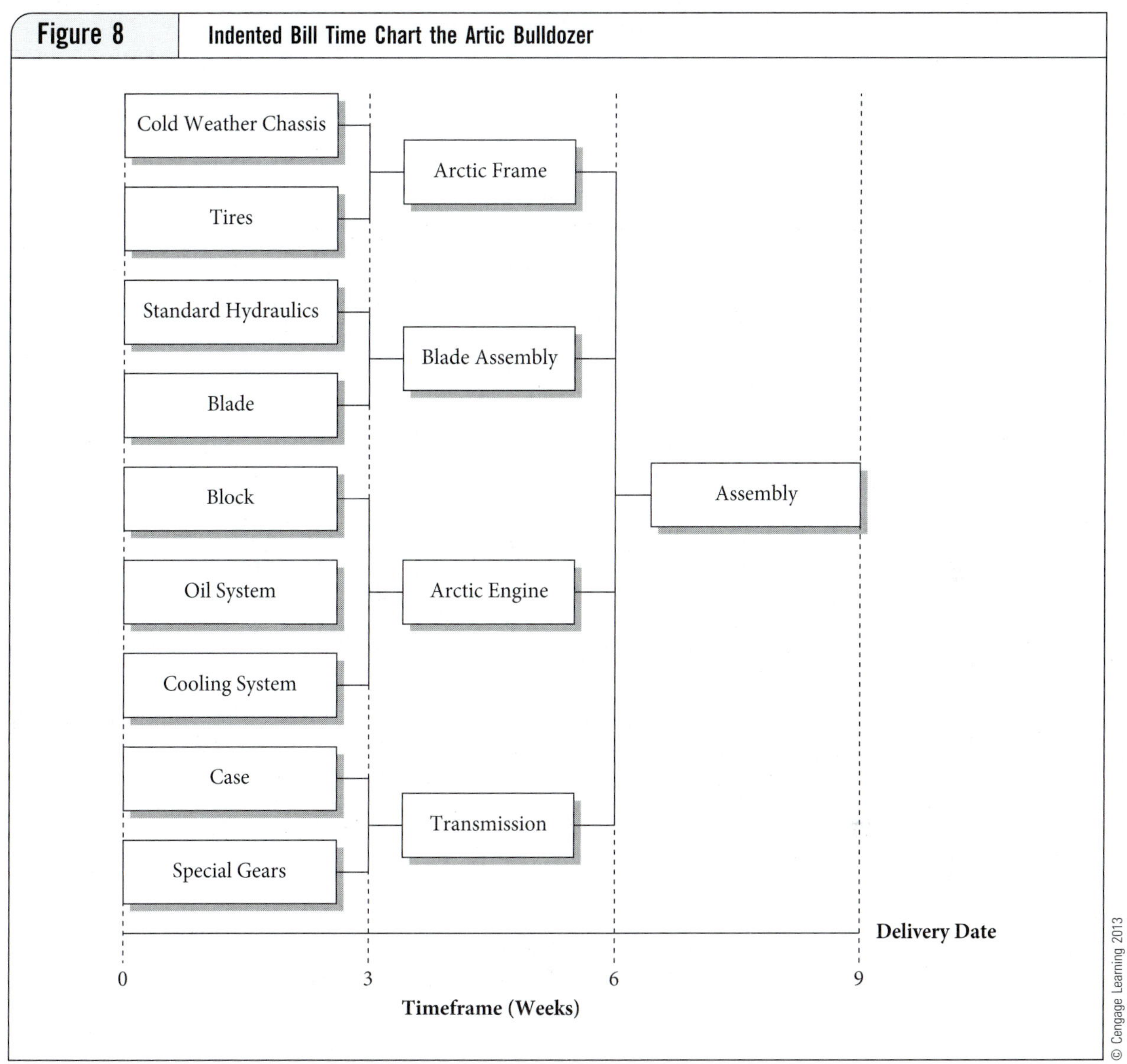

Setting up the corresponding superbill for the intended bill time chart produces the superbill time chart in Figure 9. Notice in the indented bill time chart that the engine block finishes production at the same time that the bulldozer blade enters production. But in the superbill time chart, the "goes into" relations are partially lost, and the bulldozer kit, including the blade, completes production at about the same time as the engine block.

In the superbill approach, the company truly begins to consider itself as being in the business of producing options rather than the end items. The end items are explicitly considered only during the FAS, which is based on actual customer orders. The managerial consideration is how to maximize the response flexibility in options for a given level of investment in safety stocks.

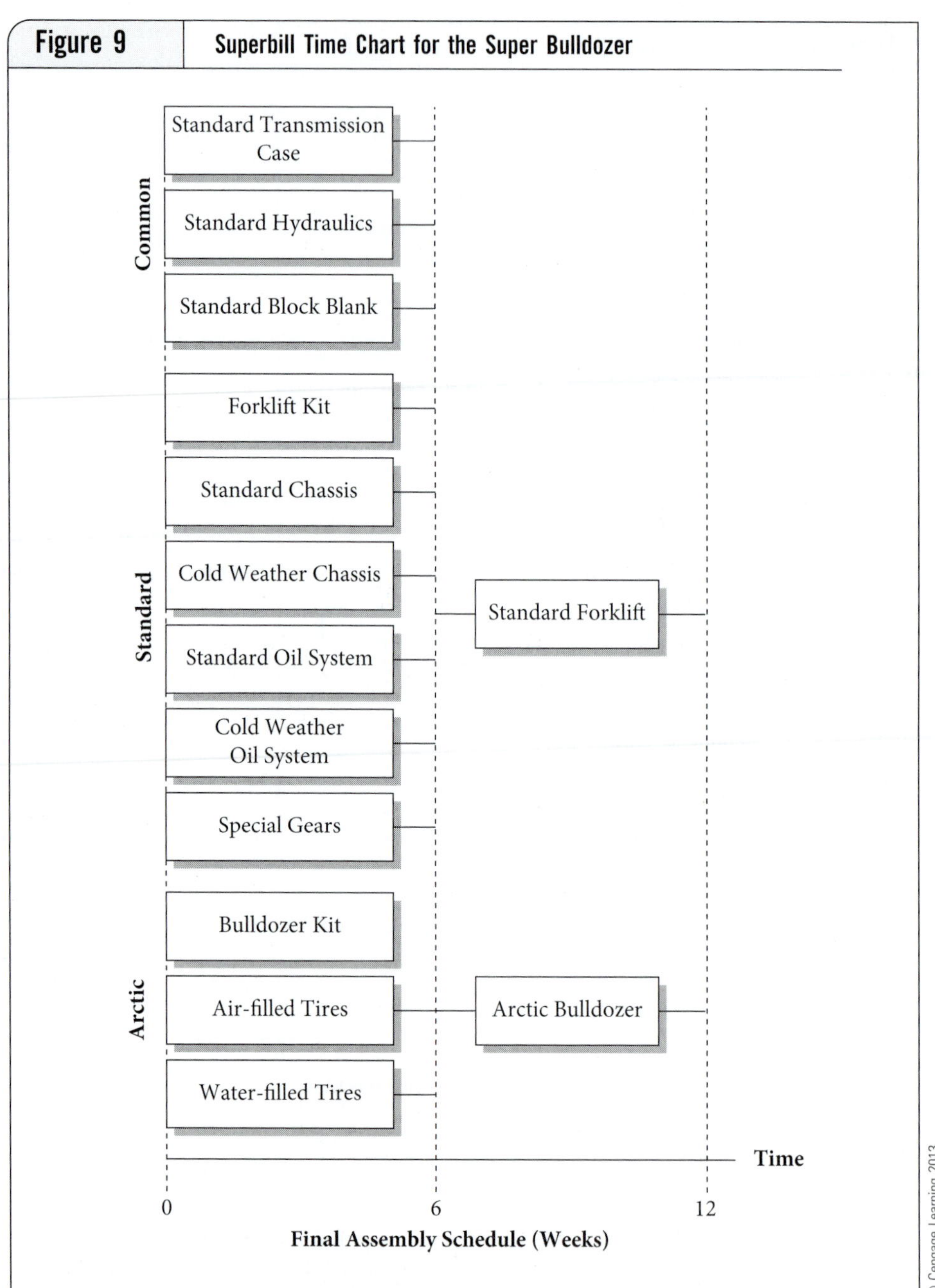

The distinction between the MPS and the FAS in the superbill approach leads to the observation that the MPS development may disrupt the time phasing of component production. This disruption is more than superficial. It is not simply a matter of losing indented product structures for momentary planning and thereafter regaining them. If a component part is truly to be considered a common part—that is, part of the common parts kit that is not over-planned—it must be committed to a final end item only as a part of the FAS. If that part is consumed earlier in the production phase, say in some subassembly that is being over planned, then the component part cannot be part of the common kit.

A firm's decision to incorporate superbills as a planning technique may force changes to the standard production process, to construction routing, and to the industrial engineering approaches for product assembly.

(B) Covering Sets

The main feature of the covering-set technique is that it enters actual end items (with resultant typical indented bill structures), as opposed to special planning items, into the MPS. These end items can be exploded with standard MRP logic to create component part requirements. The actual end items that are in fact assembled are determined with an FAS that differs from the original MPS. The scheme avoids the need to maintain non-indented or superbills while still supplying the arithmetic consistency and percentage of products mix forecasting as in the case of superbills.

As an example, consider the arctic and standard bulldozers' indented bills of material as illustrated in the superbill discussion (Figure 6a & b). Notice that each of these two tractors has four product characteristics: frame, front-end assembly (here, a bulldozer blade), transmission, and engine. Further assume that these characteristics have more than one standard configuration or option. For our example, consider the options below:

Frame (F)
- F1 standard frame
- F2 arctic frame

Front-end assembly (E)
- E1 bulldozer blade
- E2 forklift
- E3 plain (null)

Transmission (T)
- T1 standard transmission
- T2 heavy duty transmission

Engine (M)
- M1 standard engine
- M2 arctic engine

Given the options of two frames, three front-end assemblies, two transmissions, and two engines, the tractor firm can assemble $2 \times 3 \times 2 \times 2 = 24$ different end items. Rather than enter all 24 combinations into the MPS, the covering-set technique chooses a subset of these 24 and enters appropriate quantities into the MPS for the sole purpose of introducing the expected quantities of subassemblies and components into the MRP.

Let us consider, for example, that the 10 tractor configurations along with their associated option mix, shown in Table 3 have been chosen as the covering subset. Notice that each option of every one of the four product characteristics appears at least once in the option mix table. The 10 tractors represented in the table may be

Table 3 Option Mix Table for 10 Tractor Configurations

TRACTOR	F1	F2	E1	E2	E3	T1	T2	M1	M2
1	X		X			X		X	
2		X			X		X		X
3	X			X		X		X	
4	X				X	X			X
5	X		X			X			X
6	X		X				X		X
7		X		X			X	X	
8		X			X		X	X	
9	X				X		X	X	
10	X			X		X			X

said to cover all the options. See King and Benton for a more comprehensive discussion related to Table 3.

Because standard indented bills are used both for planning and for production purposes, there may not be a distinction between the time chart for production under traditional MRP and under covering sets (See Figure 8). Unlike superbills, use of the covering set technique does not disrupt, or require changes to, the standard routing files and bill structures. However, the use of covering sets makes it a requirement to stock fully built subassemblies has disadvantages. Since common parts, such as the engine block for M1 and M2, are not placed in the common kit, and since overbuilding M1 and M2 engines are necessary to offset forecast variability, then as a consequence, engine blocks will be overbuilt. That is, since the common parts are not segregated out, overplanning the options will result in overplanning of the common parts.

Because the engines are actually built, if orders for M1's exceed the forecast plus safety stock and orders for M2's fall below the forecast, then it is no easy task to convert M2's to M1's. The M2's must be disassembled, with associated costs, before blocks can be retrofitted as M1's.

Critical Comparison of the Two Approaches

The two MPS techniques superbill and covering sets, are not necessarily interchangeable. Each MPS technique affects more of the firm's operation than just aiding in the development of the MPS. The two techniques affect buffering inventories, systems development, final assembly schedules, routing files, and delivery quote times in respective unique ways. An operations manager in an assemble-to-order firm, before deciding whether to adopt one of the two MPS techniques, would be interested in the performance characteristics of each technique under different environmental conditions such as the level of safety stock investment and the degree of commonality in

Table 4 Performance characteristics of the Superbill MPS Technique

SUPERBILL MPS TECHNIQUE	
ADVANTAGES	***DISADVANTAGES***
• Facilitate savings in common parts manufacturing and inventory building	• Requires the construction of special bill structure for planning purposes
• Avoid making forecast of an unmanageable number of specific items	• The scheduling of subassembly and component parts will be different than when performed with standard indented bill structures . Additional data files are require to aid actual assembly.
• Allows for overplanning or building safety stocks of modules with high demand variance.	• The routing of modules through final assemebly can be different than when performed with standard indented bill structures
• Avoid incorporating parts into subassemblies before actual demand for the subassembly is known. Reduces retrofitting.	• FAS and, consequently, order acceptance to delivery time may be longer than that for covering sets.
	• Requires sophistication and experience to develop the support systems.

Table 5 Performance characteristics of the Covering Set MPS Technique

COVERING SET MPS TECHNIQUE	
ADVANTAGES	***DISADVANTAGES***
• Avoids the need to construct special planning bills	• Overplans common parts resulting in increased inventory holding costs.
• Is capable of being quickly implemented through already existing indented bill-of-material structures.	• Major subassemblies are fully constructed, leading to retrofitting costs if changes are needed.
	• For some firms it is mathematically possible but improbable, that the covering set will be no smaller than the full set of end items.

the product bill structures (see Tables 4 & 5). Furthermore, the manager would be interested in the costs to design, adopt, and maintain a specific master scheduling technique.

Many environmental factors potentially affect the lead time performance of the scheduling techniques. The investment in buffering inventories will affect the quoted lead time when demand varies above the forecasted demand (percentage mix). Analogously, the demand pattern experienced by assembly–to-order firms will consume the cycle and buffering inventories. In this respect the demand pattern can affect the available-to-promise lead time. Moreover the degree of product commonality that exists within the bill-of-material structure, the relative cost of common parts (ABC analysis), the total number of end items in the environment, and the managerial decision in support systems all are environmental factors that might affect the quality of the (available–to-promise measure) customer service performance.

Product Commonality

Part commonality is an important factor in MPS design because high degrees of commonality (associated with a product) in an assemble-to-order manufacturing environment lead to fewer options with less market flexibility. To investigate the performance of superbills and covering sets under product structures of low and high degrees of commonality, it is necessary to generate product structures exhibiting low and high degrees of commonality. Consider the tractor product structure given in Table 6.

There are nine possible engine configurations, since each of the three fuel systems can be matched with each of the three carburetors. Similarly, there are 6 possible transmissions, 20 front-end assemblies, and 6 chassis. This leads to a possibility of assembling $9 \times 6 \times 20 \times 6 = 6{,}480$ distinct end-item configurations.

To establish the degree of commonality for the example above, it is necessary to count the parent/component linkages and establish the number of distinct components in the product structure.

Demand Variability

The MPS procedures use a forecast of aggregate demand and forecasts of individual option mixes. It is assumed that the actual aggregate demand and the forecasted aggregate demand are the same. However, the actual option mixes may vary from the forecast mix of option demand.

For example, consider that the forecasted aggregate demand for the next period is 300 end items and that the product may be assembled in three optional configurations.

Table 6 Tractor Product Structure

Engine
- Common kit
- Fuel system, 3 alternatives
- Carburetor, 3 alternatives

Transmission
- Common kit
- Gears, 3 alternatives
- Shifting mechanism, 2 alternatives

Front-end assembly
- Common kit
- Hydraulic system, 2 alternatives
- Controls, 2 alternatives
- Front end, 5 alternatives

Chassis
- Common kit
- Frame, 3 alternatives
- Wheels and tires, 2 alternatives

The forecast of option mixes is 50 percent, 30 percent, and 20 percent, implying that $.5 \times 300 = 150$ orders are expected to specify option configuration 1, that $.3 \times 300 = 90$ orders are expected to specify configuration 2, and that $.2 \times 300 = 60$ orders are expected to specify configuration 3. The actual option mixes vary from the forecasted mix based on a uniform distribution in which the distribution ranges over ±P percent of the forecasted demand. P is the parameter of the distribution and corresponds to aggregate demand. As an example, consider $P = .20$. This implies that the expected demand for configuration 1 (forecast = 150) corresponds to some point in the range $150 \pm .2 \times 150 = (120, \min[180,300])$ (since the maximum demand cannot exceed the aggregate of 300), say 135. Now that 135 of the 300 end items are committed to configuration 1, $300 - 135 = 165$ end items must be parceled out to options 2 and 3. The mean aggregate demand for the three options is 300 $(135 + 105 + 60)$. The master schedule is the disaggregation of the aggregate. It is possible, and occurs in practice, that the sum of the individual option schedules does not correspond to the mean aggregate demand. For the purpose of the covering-set approach, we assume that the aggregated demands equal the sum of disaggregated demands to avoid confounding the primary issue of this approach, the mean available-to-promise time.

MPS Design

Designing the MPS includes the following steps:

- Select the items, that is, select the levels in the BOM structure to be represented by the items scheduled (both components and final assemblies may be included).
- Organize the MPS by product groups.
- Determine the planning horizon, the time fences, and the related operational guides.
- Select the method for calculating and presenting the available-to-promise (ATP) information.

Creating the MPS includes the following steps:

- Obtain the necessary informational inputs, including the forecast, the backlog (customer commitments), and the inventory on hand.
- Prepare the initial draft of the (MPS).
- Develop the rough-cut capacity requirements plan.
- If required, increase capacity or revise the initial draft of the MPS to obtain a feasible schedule.

Controlling the MPS includes the following activities:

- Track actual production and compare it to planned production to determine if the planned MPS quantities and delivery promises are being met.
- Calculate the ATP to determine if an incoming order can be promised in a specific period.
- Calculate the projected on-hand to determine if planned production is sufficient to fill expected future orders.
- Use the results of the preceding activities.

The Master Scheduler

Most manufacturing organizations should have a master scheduler; this individual is the link among marketing, distribution, engineering, manufacturing, and planning. The tasks of the master scheduler include the following:

- Provide delivery promise dates for incoming orders; match actual requirements with the master schedule as they materialize.
- Evaluate the impact of top-down inputs, such as a request for the introduction of a new product in much less than the normal delivery time.
- Evaluate the impact of bottoms-up inputs, such as anticipated delay reports from the shop or purchasing, indicating that particular components will not be available as scheduled or that planned production rates are not being attained.
- Revise the master schedule when necessary because of the lack of material or lack of capacity.
- Call basic conflicts of demand and capacity to the attention of other members of management, especially marketing and manufacturing, who need to participate in resolving the problems.

Managing the MPS

- Reschedule past-due orders. Do not schedule additional units without planning for additional capacity.
- Make changes as soon as possible as the need is recognized.
- Maintain the integrity of the MPS.
- An overstated MPS without additional capacity will cause many past-due orders. When someone wants to add something, the question is, "Of what do you want less?"
- An understated MPS will result in a reduction of efficiency of the system.
- MPS performance measurement has to be established in concrete terms that reflect the fundamental goals of the firm. An important measure is customer service. Some firms evaluate production against the production plan, which is to deliver a specific number of products to marketing in the agreed-upon time frame.

Whether or not a firm has someone formally designated as the master scheduler, the tasks are essential. Combining them under the jurisdiction of one individual improves the likelihood that they will be coordinated and managed properly. Most importantly, it provides a focal point for the required coordination of marketing, manufacturing, distribution, and planning as well as a place to look for answers when things are not going as planned.

SUMMARY

Although the preparation and maintenance of all the elements of the MPS may be complex in some situations, the principles and concepts are not. All have been developed in practice and well documented in the literature and have been discussed in this section.

The MPS is a vital link in the operations planning and control systems in connecting manufacturing, production, marketing, and engineering (product and process design). The items on the MPS, in particular their level in the BOM, should be consistent with the organization's competitive strategy. The efficacy of the master scheduling process and the MPS requires an accurate and reliable capacity planning system. (See chapter 9).

Available-to-promise information is very useful for responding to customer requests for delivery. Projected on-hand data are very helpful in indicating when the MPS is inadequate or will result in excessive inventory.

The master scheduler plays a key role in the marketing and manufacturing tactical planning process. Two MPS scheduling approaches for an assembly to order manufacturing environment were compared.

If actual production is consistently below the planned MPS, it suggests that actual capacity is less than the "capacity available" used in creating the MPS. And if actual orders completed in each period consistently differ substantially from those in the MPS, it suggests that the priority plan established by the MPS is not being followed throughout the system or that the MPS is not being controlled (revised) as unplanned changes in material, equipment, or personnel occur.

DISCUSSION QUESTIONS AND EXERCISES

1. The Remington Manufacturing Company has a plant in Fort Worth, Texas. Product A is shipped from the firm's plant warehouse in Fort Worth to satisfy demand in California. Currently, the sales forecast for product A at the Fort Worth plant is 80 units per week.

   The master production scheduler at Fort Worth considers product A to be a make-to-stock item for master scheduling purposes. Currently, 120 units of product A are on hand in the Fort Worth plant warehouse. Desired safety stock level is 40 units for this product. Product A is produced on a lot-for-lot basis. Currently, an order for 80 units is being produced and is due for delivery to the plant warehouse on Monday, one week from today.

   An MRP record that uses the forecast for gross requirements and has a lead time of zero can be used for master production scheduling. Complete the following MRP record. How can this be used for master production scheduling? (Refer to Chapter 6 if MRP knowledge is limited).

	WEEK					
PRODUCT A	**1**	**2**	**3**	**4**	**5**	**6**
Gross requirements						
Scheduled receipts						
Projected available balance						
Planned order release						

Q = lot for lot; LT = 0; SS = 40

2. The scheduler at Haley's Airframes uses MPS time-phased records for planning end-item production. The planner is currently working on a schedule for a strut assembly,

one of Haley's top-selling spare parts. The planner uses a production lot size of 170 and a safety stock of 15 for the strut assembly.

ITEM: P24	WEEK 1	2	3	4	5	6	7	8
Forecast	130	130	130	140	140	140	145	145
Orders	45	38	18					
Available								
Available to promise								
MPS								

a. Complete the MPS time-phased record for product P24.
b. Can the planner accept the following orders? Update the MPS time-phased record for accepted orders.

ORDER	AMOUNT	DESIRED WEEK
1	120	4
2	144	6
3	100	2
4	75	3

3. The American Manufacturing Company (AMC) produces laser computers. The manufacturing process consists of assembling the computer base (produced by the firm's plastic molding department) into a finished frame (purchased from an outside supplier). The company is interested in using material requirements planning to schedule its operations and has asked you to prepare an example to illustrate the technique.

The firm's sales manager has prepared a 10-week sales forecast for one of the 200 orders per week. AMC has customer orders of 165 units, 120 units, 80 units, and 40 units in weeks 1, 2, 3, and 4, respectively. The computers are assembled in batches of 600. Presently, three such batches are scheduled: one in week 2, one in week 5, and one in week 8.

a. Complete the following time-phased record:

CLASSIC MODEL MPS RECORD	WEEK 1	2	3	4	5	6	7	8	9	10
Forecast										
Orders										
Available										
Available to promise										
MPS										

On hand = 150

b. Prepare the MRP record for the assembly of the computer using the following record. The final assembly quantity is 600, lead time is 2 weeks, and there is a scheduled receipt in week 2. Note that no inventory is shown for the assembled sunglasses in this record, since it's accounted for in the MPS record. (Refer to Chapter 6 if MRP knowledge is limited).

		WEEK									
		1	2	3	4	5	6	7	8	9	10
Gross requirements											
Scheduled receipts			600								
Projected available balance	0										
Planned order release											

Q = 600; LT = 2; SS = 0

4. Consider the following (partial) time-phased MPS record:

	WEEK					
	1	2	3	4	5	6
Forecast	10	15	10	15	10	15
Orders	7	4	3			
Available						
Available to promise						
MPS	25		25		25	25

On hand = 5

a. Complete the record.
b. Are there any problems?
c. What's the earliest week that 44 units can be promised?
d. Assume that an order for 12 is booked for week 4. Assume the order for 22 units in part c is not booked; recompute the record.

5. Consider the greeting card company described below.

a. Complete the following MPS time phased record.

	WEEK							
ITEM: MUSICAL BIRTHDAY CARD	1	2	3	4	5	6	7	8
Forecast	40	40	40	60	60	60	60	60
Orders	10	6	4					
Available								
Available to promise								
MPS	50			50	50		50	

On hand = 40; MPS lot size = 50

The following events occurred during week 1:
Actual demand during week 1 was 35 units.
Marketing forecasted that 80 units would be needed for week 9.
An order for 40 in week 4 was accepted.
An order for 12 in week 3 was accepted.
The MPS in week 1 was produced as planned.

b. Update the record below after rolling through time.
Please calculate the beginning on-hand inventory for week 2.

	WEEK							
ITEM: MUSICAL BIRTHDAY CARD	**2**	**3**	**4**	**5**	**6**	**7**	**8**	**9**
Forecast								
Orders								
Available								
Available to promise								
MPS								

On hand = , MPS lot Size = 50

6. The following data have been prepared for master production scheduling purposes at the Shaster Golf Club Company. Assume 40 hours per week for the assembly-line capacity.

END PRODUCT	BEGINNING INVENTORY	WEEKLY FORECAST	LOT SIZE	HOURS PER LOT SIZE
A	60	10	30	30
B	20	5	20	20
C	30	15	50	50

Current capacity = 40 hours per week

a. Prepare the master production schedule for these items during the next four weeks using a scheduling method of your choice.
b. Should Shaster Company increase or decrease the capacity of the final assembly line? Justify your answer.
c. Suppose that the Shaster master production schedule is frozen for the next three weeks. What specific impact would the policy have on the firm's performance?

Chapter 5

SUPPLY CHAIN FOCUSED INVENTORY MANAGEMENT

Learning Objectives

- Learn about the function of inventory management in supply chain focused manufacturing
- Learn about the relevant inventory cost components
- Understand the differences between independent and dependent demand
- Learn about the necessary requirements for effective inventory management
- Identify the cost components of the classical fixed-order inventory model
- Learn about the basic assumptions of the classical fixed-order quantity inventory model
- Investigate the effect of relaxing many of the assumptions of the classical fixed-order quantity model
- Learn about safety stock and service levels
- Identify the differences between the classical fixed order quantity and fixed-interval periodic inventory systems

Introduction

The inventory management function is taking on increasing importance in today's industrial economy. Since materials constitute the largest single percentage of their purchasing dollars, profit-oriented firms have turned to professionally operated inventory management in order to make sure they are getting full value for their investment in materials.

Inventory is the life blood of any manufacturing business. Most firms store thousands of different items. There are many inexpensive supply-or operating-type items. The type of industry a firm is in will usually determine how much of the firm's assets are invested in inventories. As an example, hospitals carry beds, surgical instruments, food, pharmaceuticals, and other miscellaneous items. On the other hand, manufacturing firms carry office supplies, raw materials, component parts, finished products, and many other industry-related items. As shown in Figure 1, in many industries, firms spend between 40 and 80 percent of their sales dollars on purchased materials. These data only include raw materials and component parts. The data in Figure 1 shows that the inventory-management activity is an important factor affecting the prosperity and survival of an industry or firm. The data also suggests that sound management of the inventory control function will give a firm a significant competitive advantage in any industry.

Dependent versus Independent Demand

In order to manage inventory, attributes of the items must first be analyzed in terms of cost, lead time, past usage, and the nature of demand. The nature of demand is perhaps the most important attribute. The nature of demand can be either independent or dependent. *Independent* demand is unrelated to the demand for other items (finished items). In other words, demand for an independent item must be forecasted independently. *Dependent* demand is directly derived from demand for another inventoried item. In manufacturing firms, raw materials, components parts, and subassemblies are dependent on the final item's demand. Thus, demand for dependent item should not be forecasted independently. As an example, a completed automobile is an independent demand item that should be forecasted. However, we know that each automobile requires chassis assembly. It would make no sense to forecast the chassis assembly independently, simply because the chassis assembly is dependent and is derived from demand for the automobile. In distribution firms, demand is usually *independent*. The order quantities for each inventory item should be forecasted separately. Stock replenishment in independent-demand systems is usually determined by statistical inventory control.

Inventory Management Overview

Management of inventories is of major interest to operations managers. In many industries, the investment in inventories comprises a substantial share of the firm's assets. If the productivity of the inventory asset can be enhanced, the improvement will go directly to the bottom line. How does the operations manager know how much inventory to carry? How does the decision maker know when to place a replenishment order? Specifically, what guidelines should be used for making inventory management decisions? The supply chain focused manufacturing planning and control function is directly influenced by inventory management decisions. Before inventory productivity can be improved, one must take a careful and critical look at the specific

Figure 1 Purchases as a Percent of Total Sales Dollars

SELECTED INDUSTRIES EACH WITH SALES EXCEEDING $1 BILLION	
Pharmaceutical	22.0
Photographic equipment and supplies	26.4
Book publishing	33.6
Aircraft equipment	35.0
Cement, hydraulic	36.5
Oil field machinery	38.1
Value and pipe fittings	42.1
Motors and generators	42.1
Shipbuilding and repairs	42.6
Furniture and fixtures	43.0
Miscellaneous plastics products	44.7
Fabricated rubber products	44.9
Organic chemicals	45.8
Electronic computing equipment	46.6
Electronic components	46.7
Inorganic chemicals	47.0
Tires and inner tubes	47.7
Weaving and finishing mills, wool	48.1
Automotive stampings	49.6
Construction machinery	50.1
Paper board mills	51.8
Sheet metal work	52.2
Weaving mills, cotton	52.2
Refrigeration and heating equipment	52.4
Farm machinery	52.9
Primary aluminum	55.1
Synthetic rubber	56.0
Fabricated sheet metal	56.1
Paper bags	56.2
Sanitary paper products	58.1
Blast furnace steel mills	58.5
Metal cans	60.1
Radio and TV sets	61.1
Tufted carpets and rugs	68.0
Copper rolling and drawings	74.6
Petroleum refining	81.6
Primary cooper	82.9

Source: U.S. Bureau of the Census, Census of Manufacturers, 2000.

business entity. In the area of inventory management, the operations manager should make explicit decisions regarding the following:

1. *What to stock.* At the very minimum, the decision maker must meet the requirements and needs of the manufacturer in the supply chain–management environment.

2. *How much to invest.* The operations manager must first review the level of capital support for inventory. This decision is usually made at the vice president level.
3. *How much service to offer.* What level of protection against stockouts is acceptable for the competitive environment? It is practically impossible to achieve a service level of 100 percent.

As can be seen, none of these decisions is independent of the others. Moreover, combining these decisions is complex and may be closely correlated with the industry and the type of firm within the industry. In the case of a manufacturing firm, it must be determined whether the production process is make-to-order, make-to-stock, assembly-to-order, or some hybrid of the three (see Chapters 1, 3 and 4). For instance, if the process strategy in a specific industry follows a make-to-stock strategy, customer service becomes a key management concern. The choice of inventory management system should be dependent on the firm's production process. The production-inventory system taxonomy is shown in Figure 2.

The production-processing technology is divided into two categories: continuous systems and intermittent systems. Continuous systems produce standardized products through an assembly line, while intermittent systems are used to produce non-standardized products through a job shop. Another inventory system category (not shown in the taxonomy) associated with continuous systems is pure inventory systems. Pure inventory systems are distribution stocking points, such as warehouses or distributors.

Batch operations or job shops are associated more with nonstandard products produced in discrete batches. The second-level classification of the taxonomy is the way in which goods and materials flow through production systems, and the function of inventories in facilitating this flow. There has been an extensive body of literature dedicated to inventory over the past 40 years.

Currently, inventories account for between 60 and 80 percent of a typical industrial firm's assets. Inventory serves as the life blood that allows business to operate competitively. Its existence either in the form of finished products, work in process or raw materials is the lubricant of any production system. Inventories affect costs, profits, customer service, and investments in facilities. The inventory control manager must have a clear understanding of the role of inventory in the competitive supply chain network.

ABC Classification of Inventory Items

The inventory items that are the most important for a specific industry or firm should be items that account for the greatest dollar value. In order to determine which items these are, two variables must be considered: unit cost of each item and item demand. Inventory items can be classified into this category. "A" items have a high dollar usage, B items have an intermediate dollar usage, and "C" items have a low dollar usage. In other words, those items that are the most demanded and most costly are the most important inventory items, and the items that are the slowest moving and least expensive are least important. To determine the usage value of an item, multiply the unit cost by annual sales volume. If a particular item costs \$100 and 150 are sold in one year, then its usage value is \$100 × 150, or \$15,000. With only these two data points (sales and costs), you can rank all of your inventory items by importance but also take the first step towards controlling independent demand inventories.

It has been observed that a small percentage of the total number of items usually accounts for a large proportion of total usage value. Typically, 80 percent of the total inventory cost is vested in approximately 20 percent of the items. Thus, operations managers should allocate a larger percent of their managerial resources to the A items. It may make economic

Figure 2 Production-Inventory System Taxonomy

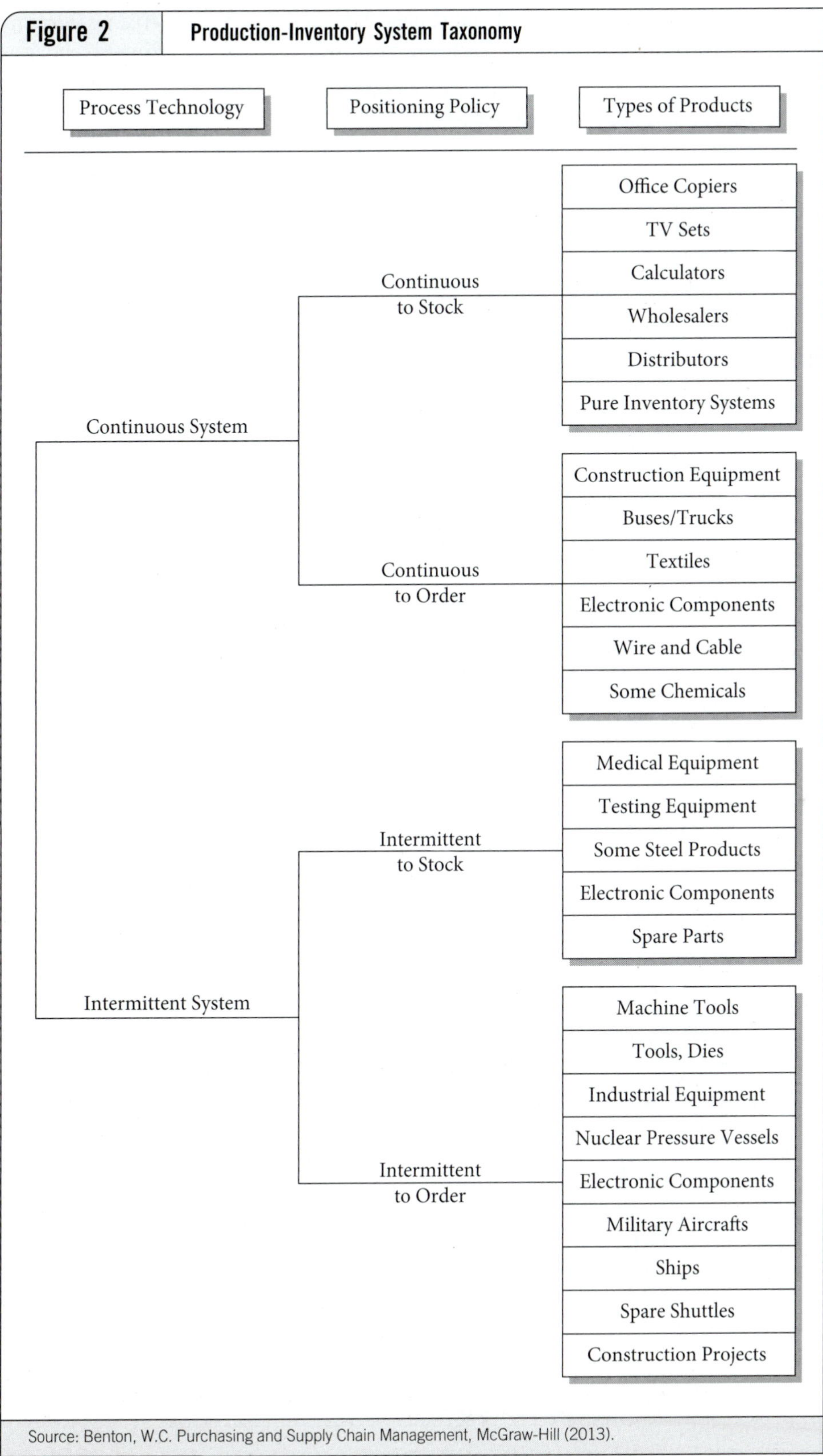

Source: Benton, W.C. Purchasing and Supply Chain Management, McGraw-Hill (2013).

sense to carry larger quantities of B and C items but apply fewer managerial resources for less important B and C inventories. The following procedure is one way of implementing an ABC analysis.

1. Calculation of the annual usage value.
2. Sorting of the items based on their annual usage value in decreasing order.
3. Calculation of the ratios of the annual usage per item and accumulated percentages.
4. Calculation of the ratios of the annual usage value per item and accumulated percentages.
5. Classify items into A, B and C item groups.

The actual percentage of the total items included in any class is quite arbitrary, but the typical breakdown is:

Class A items (15–20 percent of the items) account for the highest dollar (70–80%) of the investment in inventory.

Class B items (10–20 percent of the items) account for approximately (10–15%) of the investment in inventory.

Class C items (50–60 percent of the items) account for roughly (3–5%) of the investment in inventory.

A similar to the curve shown in Figure 3 would be the result of the ABC analysis.

Figure 3 **Typical ABC Analysis Curve**

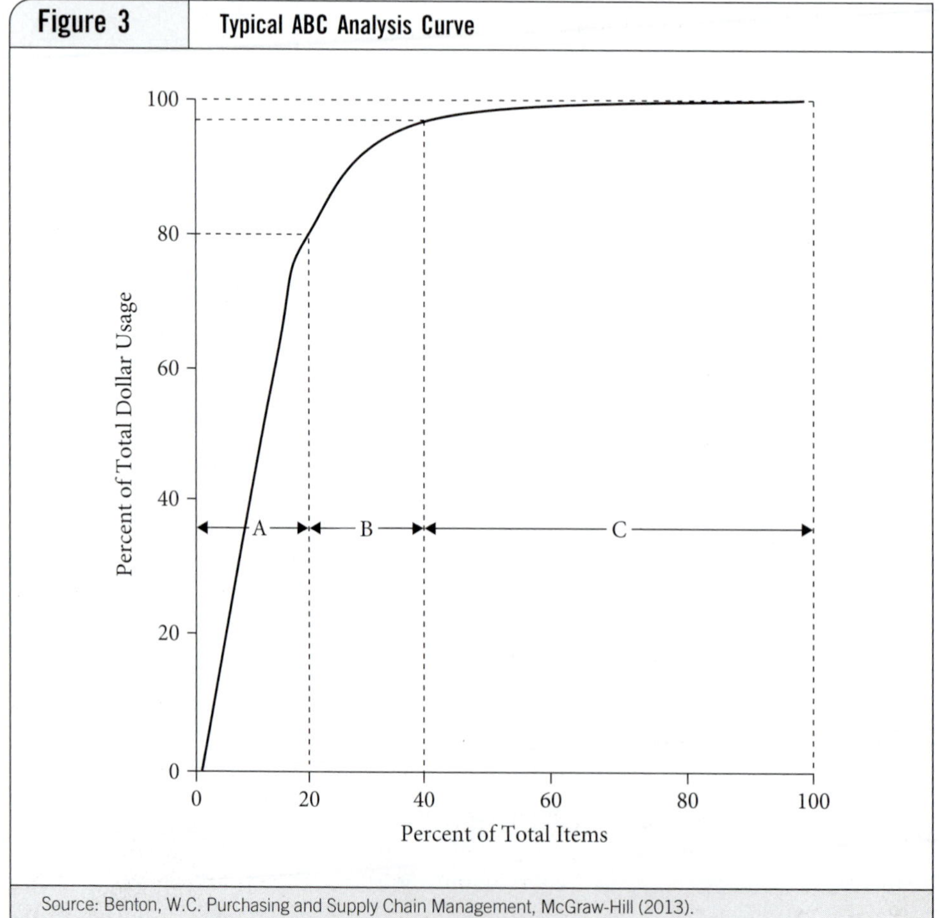

Source: Benton, W.C. Purchasing and Supply Chain Management, McGraw-Hill (2013).

Figure 4a An illustrative example of ABC Analysis

ITEM	ANNUAL USAGE (UNITS)	COST PER UNIT ($)	ANNUAL USAGE VALUES ($)
1	10,120	$0.20	$2,024.00
2	3,520	0.40	1,408.00
3	3,830	9.50	36,385.00
4	4,368	0.25	1,092.00
5	3,590	0.90	3,231.00
6	4,820	0.70	3,374.00
7	1,050	0.30	315.00
8	1,100	0.44	484.00
9	710	31.60	22,436.00
10	4,700	0.38	1,786.00

Figure 4b

ITEM	ANNUAL USAGE (UNITS)	COST PER UNIT ($)	ANNUAL USAGE VALUES ($)	CUMULATIVE RATIO OF ANNUAL USAGE (%)	CUMULATIVE RATIO OF USAGE VALUE (%)	CLASSIFICATION
3	3,830	$9.50	$36,385.00	50.16%	50.16%	A
9	710	31.60	22,436.00	30.93%	81.09%	
6	4,820	0.70	3,374.00	4.65%	85.65%	B
5	3,590	0.90	3,231.00	4.45%	90.01%	
1	10,120	0.20	2,024.00	2.79%	92.89%	
10	4,700	0.38	1,786.00	2.46%	95.35%	
2	3,520	0.40	1,408.00	1.94%	97.29%	C
4	4,368	0.25	1,092.00	1.50%	98.79%	
8	1,100	0.44	484.00	0.6%	99.39%	

Source: Purchasing and Supply Chain Management. McGraw-Hill (2013).

An illustrative example of ABC Analysis is shown in Figure 4a & b.

The objective of the remainder of this chapter is to provide a framework for inventory management in a supply chain focused manufacturing environment. First, a discussion of the classical *fixed-order quantity* order point system will be presented. Next, a number of the assumptions used in the classical fixed-order quantity system will be relaxed. The classical fixed-order quantity model will be relaxed to include back ordering, quantity discounts, demand uncertainty, and lead time uncertainty. The *fixed-interval periodic review* inventory control system will be presented in the Third section.

Inventory Management Models

In this section, we are concerned with the control of independent demand. While based on a manufacturing entity the inventory management concepts covered in this section are also applicable to retailing and distribution entities.

There are five primary functions of inventories:

1. *Pipeline inventory.* The supply pipelines of the entire supply chain system require a considerable investment in inventory. If the system's volume is 1,000 units per week and it takes one day to transport from the supplier to the plant, there are $1/7 \times 1{,}000$, or about 143, units in transit on the average.
2. *Cycle stocks.* Assume that the average unit sales volume is five units per week or 15 units in the three-week order period. Thus, the firm must have no fewer than 15 units of cycle stock on hand when an order is placed for an average on hand cycle stock level of $15/2 = 7.5$ units. The concept of average inventory will be addressed in the next section. During the 3-week replenishment cycle stock is required.
3. *Seasonal inventories.* If the demand follows a seasonal pattern, inventories can be accumulated during low sales periods and depleted during high usage periods to avoid problems associated with adjusting capacity.
4. *Safety stocks.* Safety stocks are designed to absorb random demand uncertainties.
5. *Decoupling stocks.* Stocks of inventories at major stocking points throughout the system make it possible to carry on each activity independently. That is, the presence of inventories allows for each work center to begin at the same starting time.

Costs in an Inventory System

The objective of an inventory system is the minimization of total operating costs. The avoidable costs of operating pure inventory systems are ordering costs, and holding costs. To illustrate the cost behavior of a fixed-order-size system, let's look at the simple classical economic order size (EOQ) model. The EOQ derives the optimal lot size for purchasing by minimizing the sum of the cost components involved (ordering costs and holding costs).

The classical inventory model assumes the idealized situation shown in Figure 5a and b, where Q is the order size.

Assume an annual requirement of $A = 52{,}000$ units, or an average of 1,000 units per week. If we ordered supplies on products in quantities of $Q = 1{,}000$ units, the cycle inventory, on the average, is $Q/2 = 500$ units. On the other hand, if the purchasing manager chooses to order in quantities of 500 units, the associated average cycle inventory level falls to $500/2 = 250$ (see Figure 5). The inventory holding cost (C_H) will be proportional to the lot size as shown in Figure 6a. The relationship between the holding cost and ordering cost is shown in Figure 6a–c. Figure 6c shows the total cost curve.

Inventory holding cost C_H is defined as the cost of carrying one unit of inventory for one year. The costs include insurance, taxes, interest, and obsolescence. As Q increases, the annual holding cost increases. The ordering cost C_P is defined as the cost of preparing and following up on an order. Thus, as Q increases, the annual incremental ordering cost decreases because fewer orders need to be placed.

Figure 6c shows the resulting total cost by adding the annual holding and ordering costs.

Figure 5 Simple Classical Inventory Model

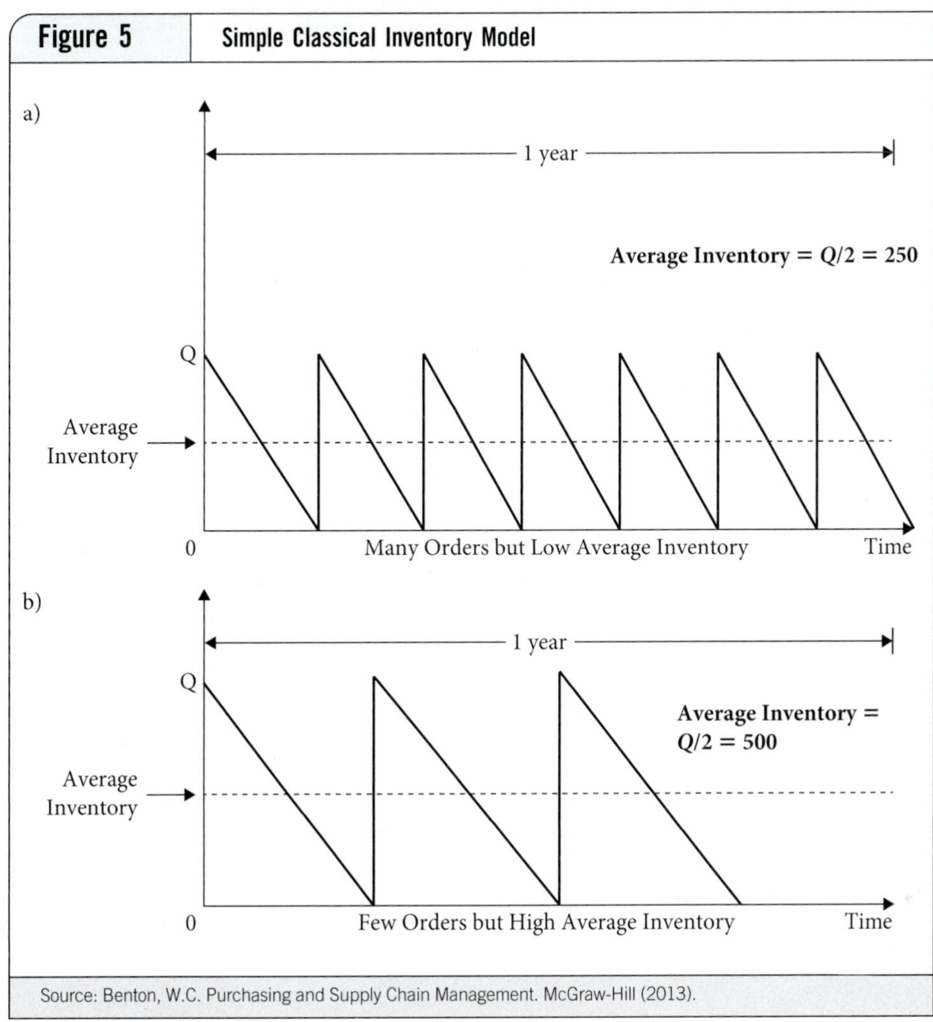

Source: Benton, W.C. Purchasing and Supply Chain Management. McGraw-Hill (2013).

$$TC = [(A/Q \times C_P) + (Q/2 \times C_H)] \qquad (1)$$

Where:

A/Q = Number of orders per year
C_P = Cost of placing an order
$Q/2$ = Average inventory
r = The annual inventory carrying cost rate (%)
C_H = per unit inventory cost per year, or item cost (P) times the annual inventory carrying cost rate (r).

Upon receipt of an order, units are assumed to be withdrawn at a constant rate from the beginning level of Q units; this is illustrated in Figure 5a and b. When inventory reaches the reorder point, a new order is placed for Q units. After a fixed lead-time period, the units are replenished with the entire order quantity Q. The vertical line represents the instantaneous replenishment of Q. The new quantity Q is received as the inventory reaches zero, so the average inventory is $Q/2$. Figure 7 shows a flow diagram for the basic EOQ model.

Figure 6 Total Cost Curve

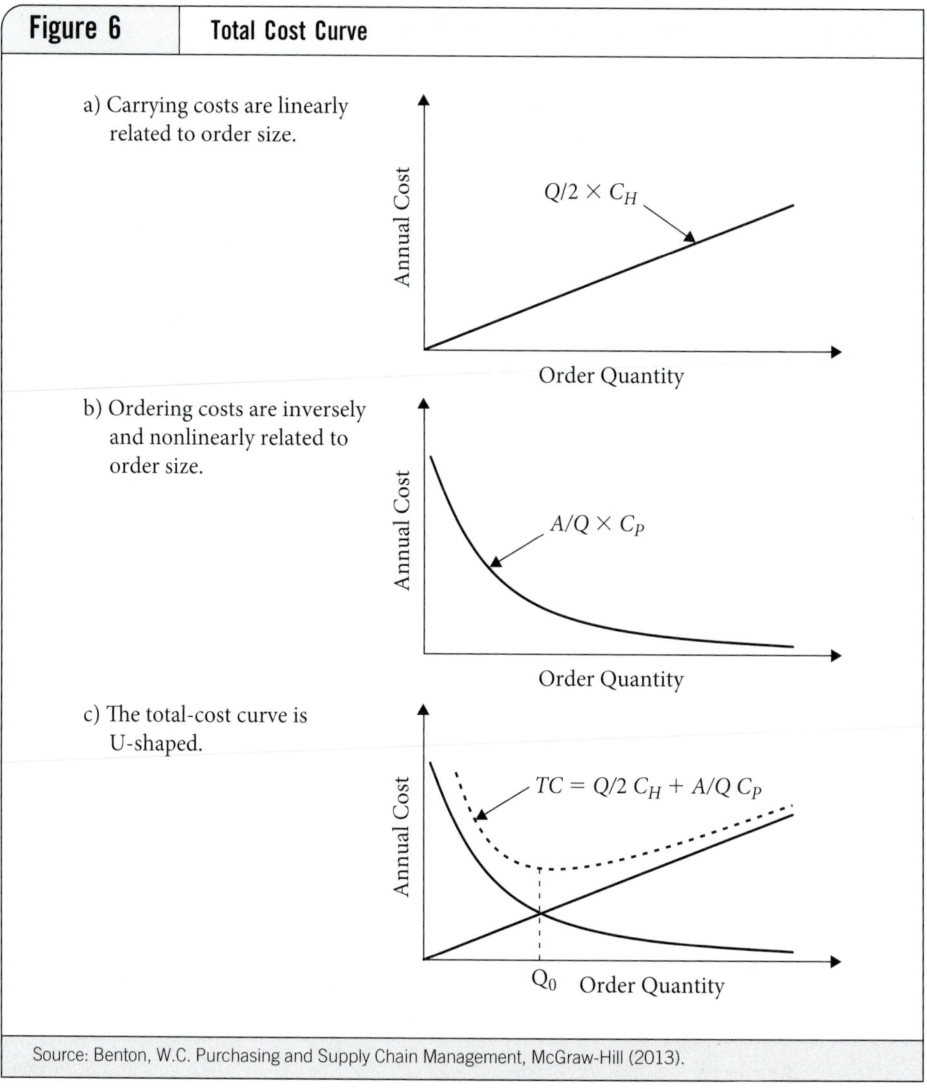

Source: Benton, W.C. Purchasing and Supply Chain Management, McGraw-Hill (2013).

The sum of the two costs (ordering and holding) will be the total inventory cost per year for any purchased item. To derive the minimum-cost lot size (EOQ), take the first derivative with respect to Q and set it equal to zero. This calculation to determines the point of inflection on the total cost curve where it is no longer decreasing and beginning to increase.

$$\frac{\delta(TC)}{\delta Q} = -\left(\frac{A}{Q^2}\right)C_P + \frac{C_H}{2} = 0 \qquad (2)$$

$$C_P \frac{A}{Q^2} = \frac{C_H}{2} \qquad (3)$$

$$Q^2 = 2C_P \frac{A}{C_H} \qquad (4)$$

Figure 7 Flow Diagram for Classical EOQ Inventory Systems

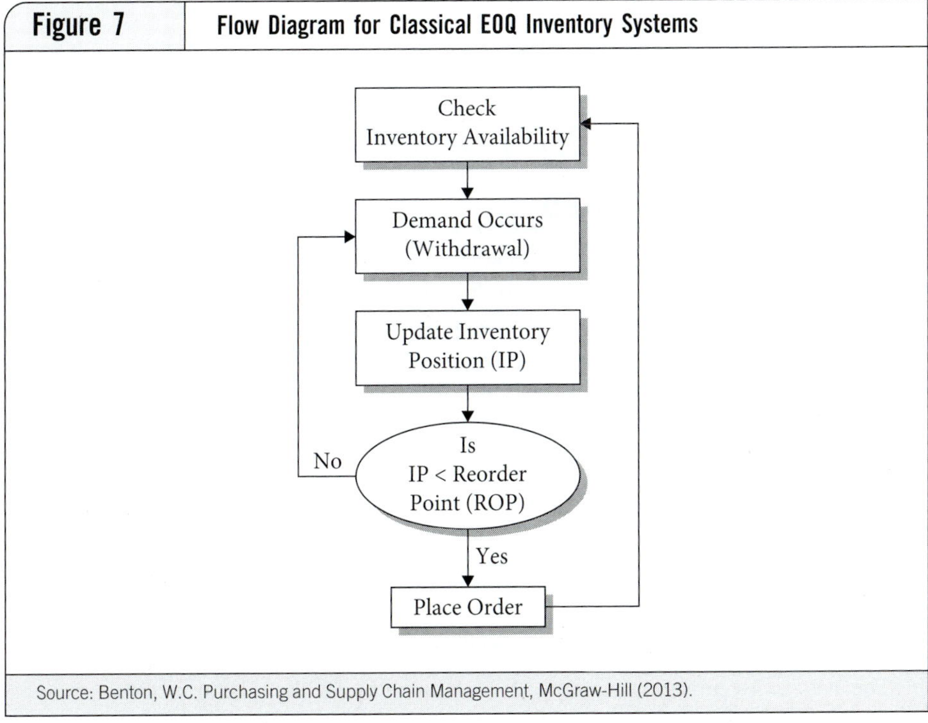

Source: Benton, W.C. Purchasing and Supply Chain Management, McGraw-Hill (2013).

The solution to Equation (2) is

$$EOQ = \sqrt{\frac{2AC_P}{C_H}} \tag{5}$$

As can be seen by Equation (5), expensive items will be ordered frequently and in small quantities, and inexpensive items will be ordered less frequently and in larger quantities, since holding cost C_H depends on the value of the item.

Once the economic order quantity is known, several other measures can be determined:

1. The expected number of orders during the year, $N_O = A/Q$
2. The expected time between orders, $(TBO) = 1/N_O = Q/A \times 365$ days
3. The reorder point, $ROP = (A/12) \times L$, where L (lead time) is expressed in months. If L is expressed in weeks, $ROP = (A/52) \times L$.

The minimum total cost per year is obtained by substituting Q^* for Q in equation (1).

The classical EOQ model assumes the following:

1. Demand is continuous at a constant rate
2. Constant lead time
3. Constant unit price
4. Fixed-order cost per order
5. Fixed holding cost per unit
6. Instantaneous replenishment
7. No shortages allowed

8. No demand uncertainty
9. No quantity discounts available

The Classical Fixed-Order Quantity (EOQ) Model with Stockouts Allowed

For this case, we relax the "no stockouts allowed" assumption and keep the other assumptions unchanged. Figure 8 shows how the inventory levels vary over time. The stock positions range from a low of $-B$ (amount of demand deliberately unsatisfied and put on the backorder list) to a high of $Q - B$, which represents the amount on hand immediately after a lot of size Q is delivered. Notice that B units out of Q are never carried in stock; as soon as delivery takes place, the backlog of orders is filled. A low stockout cost is an incentive for backordering demand, since this saves on the inventory holding cost.

In this model, it is assumed that the backordering cost incurred by the inventory system is proportional both to the number B of units short and the duration t_b of the shortage.

Let bc = the cost to have one unit backordered for one year, dollars per unit year.

The average inventory on hand can be computed by dividing the area of the inventory triangle (mnp) by the duration T of the cycle. Time t_i of inventory availability is given by $(Q - B)/A$ and the cycle time $T = Q/A$.

Figure 8 The Backordering Case

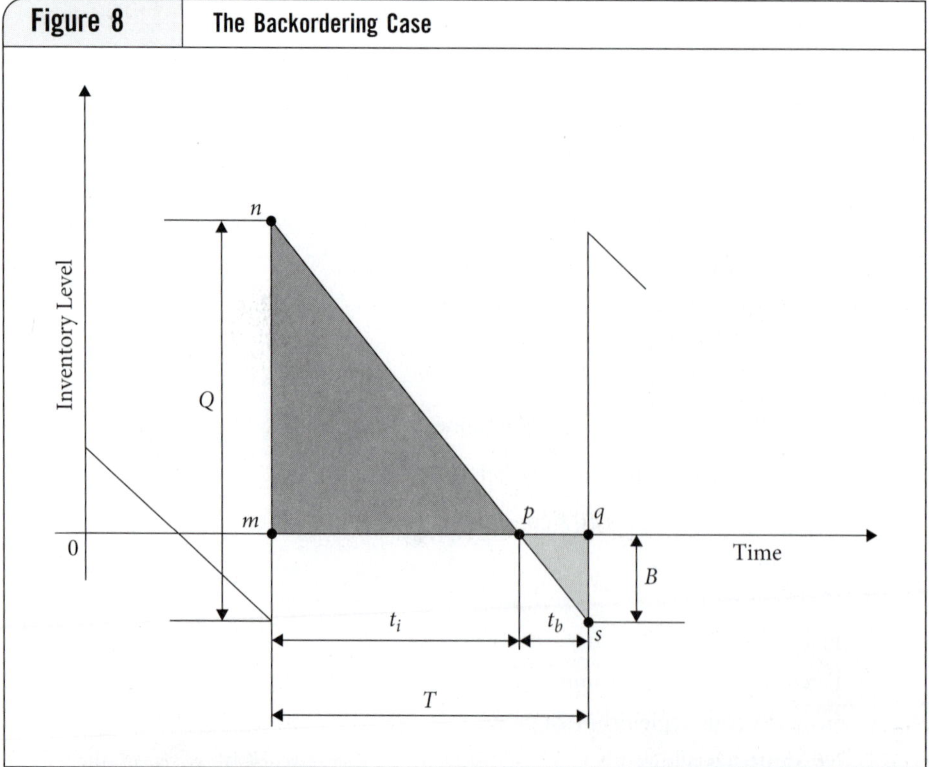

Therefore:

$$\text{Average inventory } = \frac{1}{T} \cdot \frac{(Q-B)t_i}{2} = \frac{(Q-B)^2}{2Q} \quad (6)$$

The average backorder level is obtained similarly by dividing the area of the backorder triangle pqs into T; note that $t_b = B/A$:

$$\text{Average backorder level } = \frac{1}{T} \cdot \frac{Bt_{bc}}{2} = \frac{B^2}{2Q}$$

The total annual cost is

$$TC = C_P \frac{A}{Q} + C_H \frac{(Q-B)}{2Q} + bc \frac{B}{2Q}$$

There are two policy parameters: Q and B. The first order (necessary) conditions for the optimality of Q^*, T^* are given below.

$$\frac{\partial(TC)}{\partial Q} = 0$$

$$\frac{\partial(TC)}{\partial B} = 0$$

The optimum solution is:

$$Q^* = \sqrt{\frac{2C_P A}{C_H}} \sqrt{\frac{C_H + bc}{bc}} \quad (7)$$

$$B^* = \frac{C_H Q^*}{C_H + bc} = \sqrt{\frac{2C_P A}{C_H}} \sqrt{\frac{C_H}{C_H + bc}} \quad (8)$$

As an example, if we consider a setting in which, $A = 50$, $C_P = 100$, $r = .30$, and $bc = \$75$, $P = \$411$, determine Q^* and B^*.

$$Q^* = \sqrt{\frac{2 \times 50 \times 100}{411 \times .30}} * \sqrt{\frac{(411 \times 0.3) + 75}{75}} = 14.63 \approx 15$$

$$B = \frac{(411 \times 0.30) \times 14.63}{(411 \times 0.3) + 75} = 9.097 \approx 10$$

Expressions (7) and (8) are defined only for $bc > 0$. Of course, $bc = 0$ does not make sense if stockouts are permitted. Indeed, in such a case, $B^* = Q^* \rightarrow \infty$ no backorders. This means that, with no charge for backorders, one would keep piling up unfilled demand until the backlog gets infinitely large. Then one single order would be released to satisfy all accumulated demand, thus driving the per unit share of the ordering cost to zero. Notice that if $bc \rightarrow \infty$, no backorders may be carried in the optimum solution and (7) becomes the classic lot size formula.

The Classical Fixed-Order Quantity (EOQ) Model with Quantity Discounts

The classical EOQ model assumes that the per-unit material price is fixed. However, from time to time, buying firms receive discounted price schedules from their suppliers. This usually means that the price per unit is lower if larger orders are purchased. It may or may not be to the buyer's advantage to accept the quantity discount. The buyer must be careful not to compromise the economies of his or her firm's

Figure 9 Total Cost Curve for All Units with Quantity Discounts

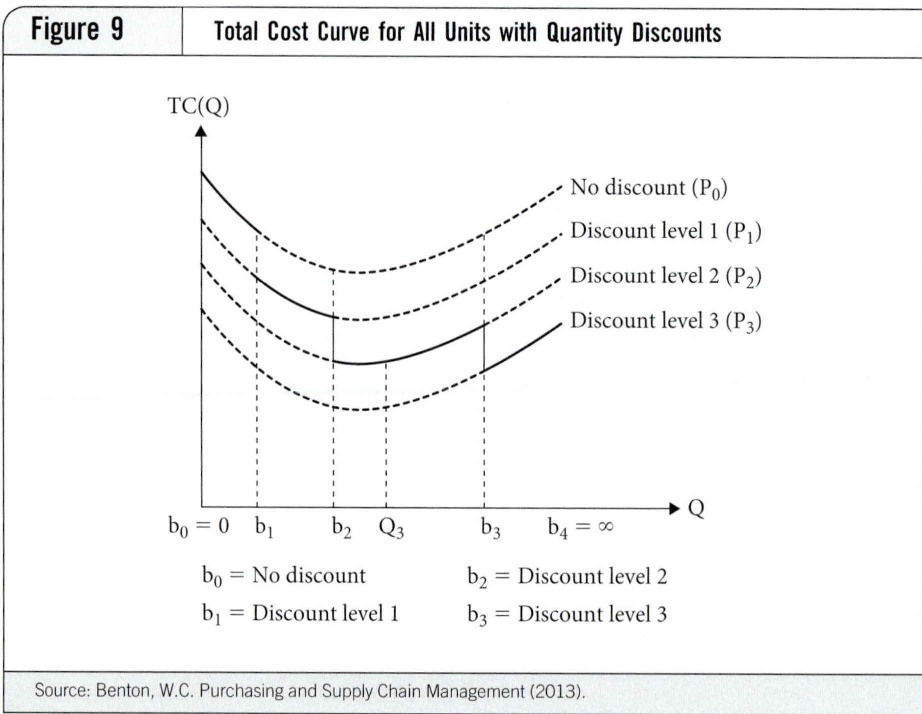

Source: Benton, W.C. Purchasing and Supply Chain Management (2013).

cost structure. Although the discount schedule may appear attractive in terms of material cost savings, higher holding costs may reduce overall profitability. On the other hand, a specific discount schedule could produce economic advantages for both the buyer and seller. See Appendix A for a comprehensive quantity discount discussion.

The quantity discount condition invalidates the total cost curve in Figure 6a and c. Quantity discounts induce a discontinuous total cost curve. Assuming the discount applies to *all units* (and not just *incremental* units beyond the discount point), the minimum total cost point will be either at the point of discontinuity or at the nondiscount EOQ point.

Figure 9 shows the new total cost curve. As can be seen, the behavior of the EOQ does not change. The effect is a constant increase in the total cost curve. Specifically, there are separate total cost curves for each price break. No one curve applies to the entire range of quantities; each curve applies to a portion of the curve (the solid portion).

A five-step method can easily be used for determining the minimum cost order quantity for *all units* discount schedule:

1. Calculate the economic order quantity (EOQ) using the minimum unit prices. If this quantity falls within the range for which the vendor offers that specific discount price, it is a valid economic order quantity and will result in the minimum cost for the particular item.
2. If the EOQ calculated in Step 1 is not valid (i.e., is less than the break quantity), find the total annual cost for each price break quantity.
3. Calculate an EOQ for each unit price other than the minimum price.
4. Calculate the total annual cost for each valid EOQ determined in Step 3.
5. Find the minimum-cost order quantity which is valid is that associated with the lowest cost in either Step 2 or Step 4.

An example of quantity discounts is given in example 5-1 on next page.

Example 5-1

All Units Quantity Discount Example

The Value City Hardware Company purchases 10,000 units of product #605 each year. The supplier offers the units for sale at $10.00 per unit for up to 799 units and $8.75 per unit for orders of 800 units or more. What is the economic order quantity if the order cost is $50.00 per order and holding cost is 40 percent per unit per year? The Total cost for the single price break quantity of 800 units is as follows:

1. Calculate the economic order quantity using the minimum unit prices. If this quantity falls within the range for which the vendor offers the discount price, it is a valid economic order quantity and will result in the minimum cost for the particular item.

$$Q_{\$8.75} = \sqrt{2C_p\ A/C_H} = \sqrt{\frac{2 \times (50)(10{,}000)}{\$8.75(.40)}} = 535 \text{ units, not valid}$$

   The EOQ with the price of $8.75 is invalid since the $8.75 price is not available for quantities less than 800 units. (i.e., $535 < 800$)
2. If the EOQ calculated in Step 1 is not valid (i.e., is less than the break quantity), find the total annual cost for each price break quantity.

$TC_{DQ=800}$

$$TC_{DQ} = AP + C_P \times (A/Q) + C_H \times Q/2$$
$$TC_{800} = 10{,}000(8.75) + 50(10{,}000/800) + (800/2)(0.40)(\$8.75)$$
$$TC_{800} = 87{,}500 + 625 + \$1{,}400 = \$89,525$$

3. Calculate the EOQ for each unit price other than minimum price.

$$Q_{\$10} = \sqrt{2C_p\ A/C_H} = \sqrt{\frac{2 \times (50)(10{,}000)}{\$10(.40)}} = 500 \text{ units}$$

   The EOQ for the $10 unit price is valid. (i.e., $500 < *799$)
4. Calculate the total annual cost for each valid EOQ determined in Step 3.

$$TC_{10} = 10{,}000(\$10) + \$50(10{,}000/800) + (800/2)\ (0.40)\ (\$10) = \$102{,}000$$

5. The minimum cost order quantity is that associated with the lowest cost in either Step 2 or Step 4.

   Comparing the total costs of the single price break quantity and the valid EOQ, the minimum cost order of 89,525 occurs at 800 units. The discount is attractive and a lot size of 800 should be ordered.

See Appendix A for a more comprehensive discussion of all-units and incremental solution policies.

Determining the Level of Safety Stock

The assumption of constant lead time and constant demand is usually not realistic in an actual operating environment. Replenishment lead-time variations are a result of supply and operating challenges. Volatile demand for individual products occurs because of changing consumer preferences. In order to protect against these uncertainties, we must first establish a metric for determining how much protection against uncertainty is economically prudent. The most widely used protection criteria are the probability of stocking out during the given order cycles and the desired level of customer service that management would like to achieve directly from the current inventory.

Demand Uncertainty and Safety Stock

Realistically, demand and lead time will tend to be uncertain. In any case inventories will deplete a faster or slower rate than expected.

When there is uncertainty in demand, safety stock must be considered. For this case, we relax assumptions (1 & 8), suggesting that demand is not constant, and keep the other assumptions unchanged (see pages 119–120).

There are several ways to determine the level of safety stock to carry. Perhaps the most popular approach is the **probability of stocking out during any lead time cycle**. As an example a service level of 80 percent means that there is a 0.80 probability that demand will be met during the lead time, and a 0.20 probability that a stockout will occur. Another approach is for the operations manager to determine the **desired level of customer service** in regard to satisfying demand directly from the current inventory levels. Both of the safety stock setting criteria will be considered in the next two sections.

1. **Probability of Stocking Out Approach**
   Safety stock is extra inventory held to protect against randomness in demand or lead time. Safety stock is needed to cover the demand during the replenishment lead time in case actual demand is greater than expected demand. Figure 10 illustrates the impact of safety stock. In the case below, safety stock covers demand during the replenishment cycle. If a variation in demand occurs, safety stock can be used to protect against stockouts.

Figure 10 The Impact of Safety Stock

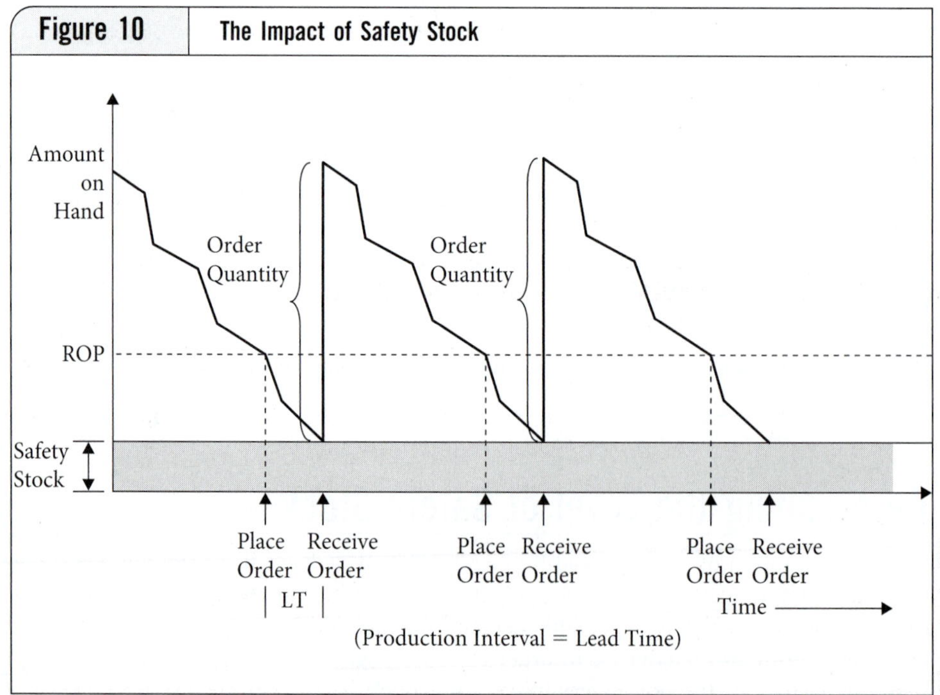

As an example, consider an inventory system with an average daily demand of five units; if lead time is six days, then the expected demand during the lead time will be five units times six days, or 30 units. The distribution of demand during the lead time is assumed to follow a normal distribution, as shown in Figures 11 & 12.

Figure 11 illustrates the concept of safety stock. As can be seen the reorder point is the sum of the demand during lead time and the safety stock. In Figure 11 the lead time is constant while the demand during lead is uncertain. Now turning our attention to the normal distribution shown in Figure 12 and supper imposed in Figure 11, it can be seen that the probability of stocking out is directly related to the level of safety available between the order replenishment cycle. Stated differently, if the maximum level of demand occurs during the replenishment cycle a stock out will occur unless the appropriate level of safety stock is available.

Figure 11 The Impact of Safety Stock

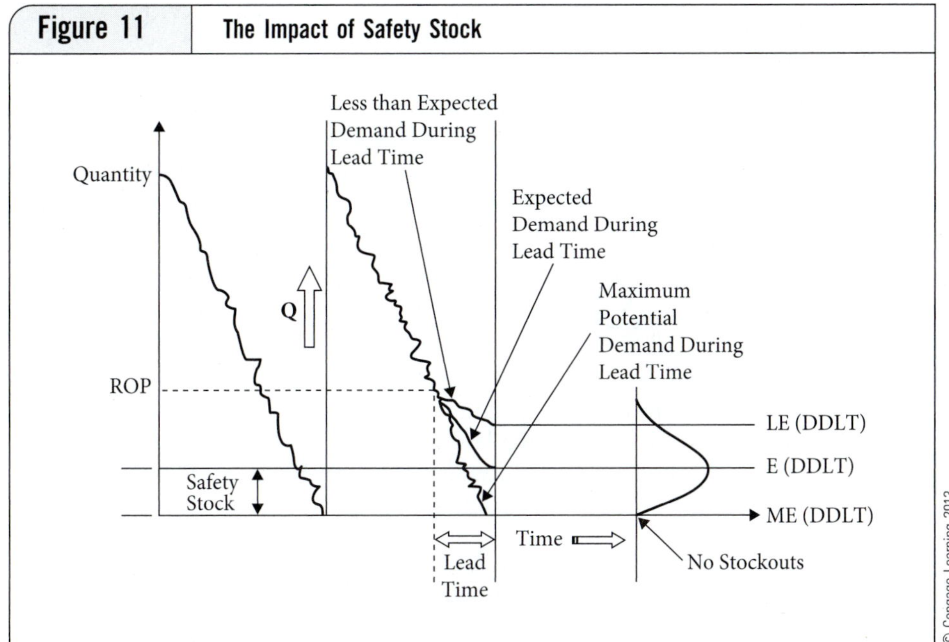

Figure 12 Normal Distribution of Demand During Lead Time (DDLT)

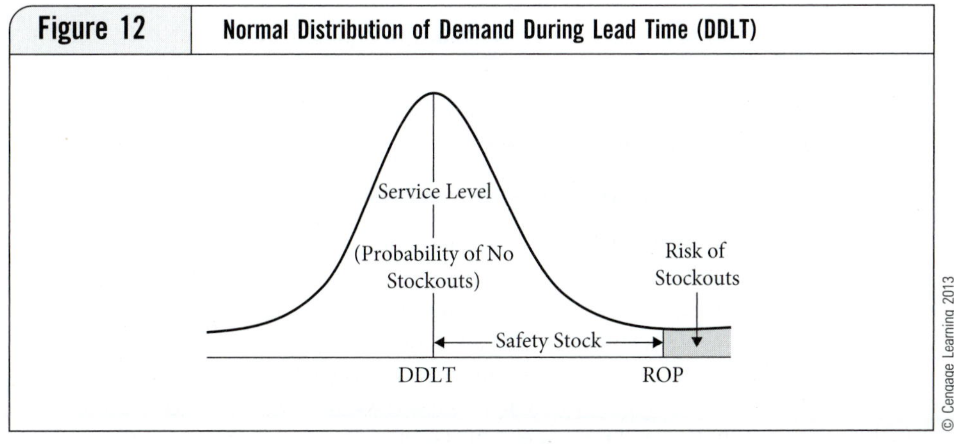

The safety stock adjusted reorder point is

$$ROP = (\text{Expected demand during lead time}) + (\text{Safety stock})$$

$$\text{Safety stock } = Z\sqrt{L} \times \sigma_d$$

$$ROP = DDLT + Z\sqrt{(\text{Lead time expressed as some multiple of forecast interval})} \times (\text{Standard deviation of demand})$$

$$= DDLT + Z\sqrt{L} \times \sigma_d$$

Where:

$DDLT$ = expected mean demand during lead time
L = Lead time expressed as some multiple of forecast interval (e.g., days, weeks)
Z = Number of standard deviations from the mean demand. The appropriate value from a table of standard normal distribution probabilities. See Appendix 5A.
σ_d = Standard deviation of demand

An example of the fixed-order-quantity model with demand uncertainty is given in Example 5-2 on next page.

2. **Customer Service Level (CSL) Approach**
The probability of stocking out in any given order cycle was shown in the previous section. However, the customer service level can also be determined by calculating the expected number of units short per reorder cycle [E{s}]. The expression for the [E{s}] is given in (9) below:

$$\text{E}\{\text{s}\} = \sum_{D=ROP+1}^{D_{MAX}} P(D)(D - ROP) \tag{9}$$

Where:

Q = Fixed-order quantity
D = demand during lead time
$P(D)$ = Probability of demand during lead time equaling D.
D_{MAX} = Maximum demand during replenishment lead time

$$\text{CSL } (\%) = 100 \times \left[1 - \frac{1}{Q}\sum_{D=R+1}^{D_{MAX}} P(D)(D - ROP)\right]$$

$$= 100 \times \left[1 - \frac{1}{Q} \times \text{E}\{\text{s}\}\right] \tag{10}$$

There are two approaches to calculating the expected number of units short per reorder cycle [E{s}]:

(a) Utilizing continuous distributions (normal distribution)
(b) Utilizing discrete distributions

(a) Utilizing Continuous Distributions (Normal Distribution)

If the distribution of the demand is approximated as a normal distribution, a partial expectation of the normal distribution called the service function [$E(Z)$] can be utilized. $E(Z)$ is the expected number of units short per reorder cycle, when $\sigma_d = 1$ and $Z \times \sigma_d$ units of safety stocks (S) are held in the standard normal curve. Z is the number of standard deviations. Therefore, the expected number of units short per reorder cycle [E{s}] associated with customer service level is "The Service Function" [$E(Z)$] multiplied by the actual standard deviation.

Example 5-2

Consider a small retail outlet that has normally distributed demand during lead time, a mean of 1,000 units, and standard deviation of 20 units per week. Lead-time interval is two weeks. What reorder point should be used in order to average no more than one stockout every 20 reorder cycles? Also, determine the service level if we choose to carry 30 units of safety stock.

Solution

$$\text{Stockout Probability} = 1/20 = .05$$
$$\text{Service Level} = 1 = \text{stock level} = 1 - .05 = 95\%$$
$$Z = 1.645 \quad \text{(see } Z \text{ table)}$$

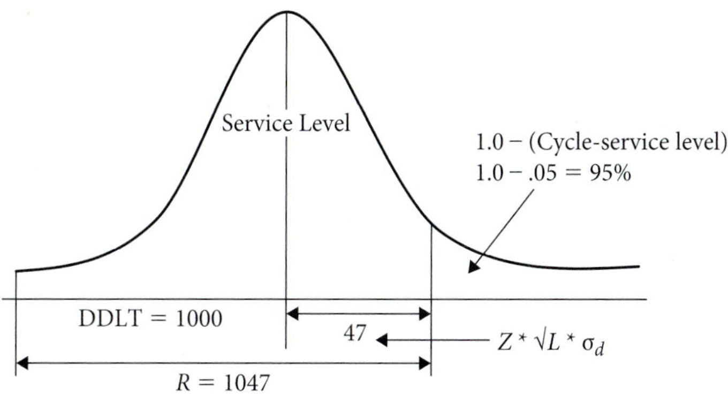

$$\text{Reorder point} = DDLT + Z\sqrt{L}\times\sigma_d \quad (1)$$
$$= 1{,}000 + 1.645\sqrt{2}\times 20 = 1{,}047$$
$$\text{Safety stock} = Z\sqrt{L}\times\sigma_d = 1.645\times\sqrt{2}\times 20 = 47$$

The Z-score associated with SS = 30 units is calculated below using equation 1:

$$Z = (ROP - DDLT)/[\sqrt{(L)}\times\sigma_d] = (1{,}030 - 1{,}000)/(\sqrt{2}\times 20) = 1.06$$

This equates to a service level of 85.54 (see Z table).

Where:

$DDLT$ = Average demand during lead time
LT = Lead time expressed as some multiple of forecast interval (e.g., days, weeks)
Z = Number of standard deviations from the mean demand
σ_d = Standard deviation of demand rate

$$E\{s\} = \sum_{D=ROP+1}^{D_{MAX}} P(D)(D - ROP) = \sigma_d \times E(Z)$$

In order to calculate the safety stocks (S) and the reorder point (R), the service function $[E(Z)]$ can be determined and converted to a Z value using the table and graph in Table 1.

Table 1 The Service Function $E(Z)$

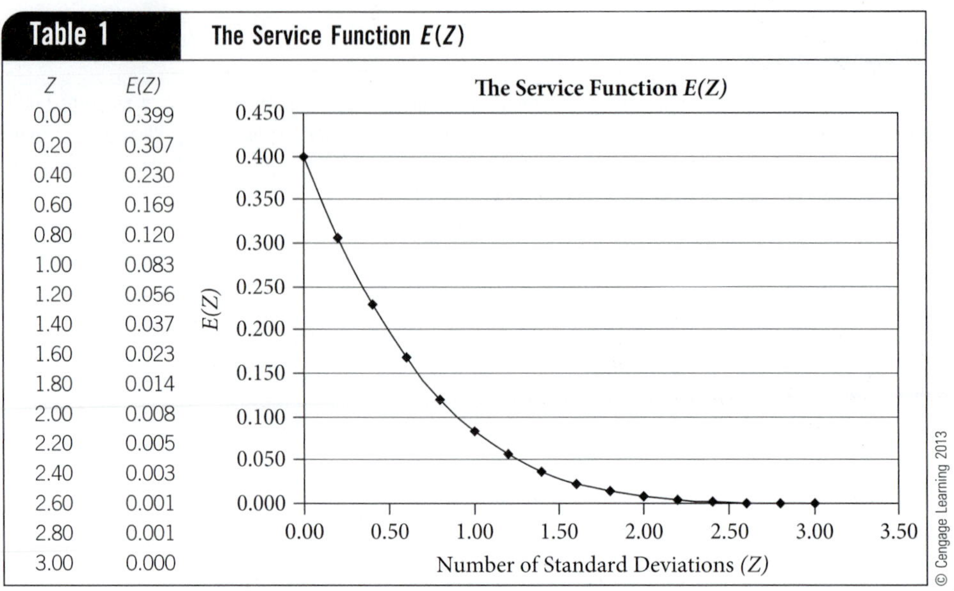

Z	E(Z)
0.00	0.399
0.20	0.307
0.40	0.230
0.60	0.169
0.80	0.120
1.00	0.083
1.20	0.056
1.40	0.037
1.60	0.023
1.80	0.014
2.00	0.008
2.20	0.005
2.40	0.003
2.60	0.001
2.80	0.001
3.00	0.000

$$\text{CSL }(\%) = 100 \times \left[1 - \frac{1}{Q} \times \text{E}\{\text{s}\}\right] = 100 \times \left[1 - \frac{1}{Q} \times \sigma_d \times E(Z)\right]$$

$$E(Z) = \frac{(100 - CSL(\%)) \times Q}{100 \times \sigma_d}$$

The safety stocks (S) will be $Z \times \sigma_d$ units.

So if Q is set at 20 units and the required customer service level (CSL) is 97 percent and σ_d is 5 units, then the service function [$E(Z)$] is 0.12 and the correlating Z value is 0.8. In this case, the Z value can be approximated to set to 0.8 standard deviations. As a result, in order to achieve a service level of 97 percent, the reorder point (ROP) should be set at 8 given a 4 unit demand during lead time.

$$E(Z) = \frac{(100 - 97) \times 20}{100 \times 5} = 0.12 \quad Z = 0.8$$

(see Table 1)

$$\text{E}\{\text{s}\} = \sum_{D=R+1}^{D_{MAX}} P(D)(D - ROP) = \sigma_d \times E(Z) = 0.6$$

$$S = \sigma_d \times Z = 5 \times 0.8 = 4 \text{ units} \quad ROP = DDLT + S = 4 + 4 = 8 \text{ units}$$

(B) Utilizing Discrete Distributions

Unlike fitting the data into a normal distribution, the discrete approach requires the calculation of the expected number of units short per reorder cycle [E{s}]. The [E{s}] is calculated for each possible reorder point (ROP).

$$\text{E}\{\text{s}\} = \sum_{D=R+1}^{D_{MAX}} P(D)(D - ROP)$$

Table 2 Discrete Distribution

(1) SELECTED REORDER POINT (*R*)	(2) SAFETY STOCK (*S*)	(3) DEMAND PROBABILITY *P*(*D* = *ROP*)	(4) EXPECTED NUMBER OF UNITS SHORT PER RECORDER CYCLE E{S}	(5) CUSTOMER SERVICE LEVEL (*CSL*)
5	0	0.30	0.56	88.8%
6	1	0.20	0.21	95.8%
7	2	0.10	0.06	98.8%
8	3	0.04	0.01	99.8%
9	4	0.01	0.00	100.0%

As an example, if Q is 5 units and ROP is set at 7 units, the expected number of units short per recorder cycle is 0.06 units and customer service level (CSL) is 98.8 percent. The demand probability time is shown in Table 2:

$$\mathrm{E}\{s\} = \sum_{D=8}^{9} P(D)(D-7) = P(8)(8-7) + P(9)(9-7)$$

$$= (0.04 \times 1) + (0.01 \times 2) = 0.06 \text{ units}$$

$$CSL\,(\%) = 100 \times \left[1 - \frac{1}{Q}\sum_{d=R+1}^{d_{MAX}} P(D)(D-R)\right] = 100 \times \left[1 - \frac{1}{Q} \times \mathrm{E}\{s\}\right]$$

$$= 100 \times \left[1 - \frac{1}{5} \times 0.06\right] = 98.8\%$$

The table above lists the customer service level (CSL) for the reorder points (ROP) set between 5 and 9 units. So if Q is set at 5 units and the required customer service level (CSL) is 95 percent, the reorder point (ROP) will be approximately 6 units, which includes 1 unit of safety stock (S).

Demand and Lead Time Uncertainty

In the case that the assumption regarding order lead time is also relaxed in addition to relaxing the demand assumption, the previously explained methods remain valid. However, the probability for each possible demand during lead time ($DDLT$) needs to be calculated before proceeding. For example, if the lead time (LT) was one or two days rather than one day as previously stated and the previous daily demand distribution was used, the possible demand during lead time ($DDLT$) would be between 5 and 9 units for the example in Table 2. The lead time and demand variation require that all possible lead time demand combinations be calculated. A decision tree as shown in the following section can be used for the convolution. Once all of the probabilities for the possible demand during lead time ($DDLT$) are determined, the determination of safety stock, the ROP, E({s}), and the customer service level can be determined as before.

The process of determining the convoluted demand during lead-time distribution is determined by preparing a schedule of daily demands for the item from actual inventory

Table 3 Demand Distribution (%)

DEMAND PER DAY (UNITS)	FREQUENCY	PROBABILITY, *P*
0	40	.4
1	30	.3
2	30	.3
	100	1.0

Table 4 Lead Time Distribution

LEAD TIME (DAYS)		FREQUENCY	PROBABILITY, *P*
1		12	.6
2		8	.4
	Total	20	1.0

records by counting the number of days that a certain demand occurs. For example, the demand for some product A for an observed 100 day period was 0 units 40 percent of the time, 1 unit 30 percent of the time, and 2 units 30 percent of the time. The demand distribution is given in Table 3.

Next, a distribution of lead times from actual data is prepared. As an example, if the lead time for 20 orders was 1 day for 60 percent of the time and 2 days for 40 percent of the time. The lead times distribution is given in Table 4 above.

From the distribution of demands, the expected demand per day, $E(D)$, is calculated as follows:

$$E(D) = (0 \times .4 + 1 \times .3 + 2 \times .3) = .9 \text{ units}$$

The expected lead time per order, $E(LT)$, is then calculated as shown below:

$$E(LT) = (1 \times .6 + 2 \times .4) = 1.4 \text{ days}$$

Next, the expected demand during lead time, $E(DDLT)$, the product of $E(D)$ and $E(LT)$, is calculated:

$$E(DDLT) = .9 \times 1.4 = 1.26 \text{ units}$$

Given the actual demand and lead time distributions given above, we form the decision tree shown in Figure 13 to depict all possible demands during lead time:

Combining the outcomes by *DDLT*, we obtain the following probabilities, $P(DDLT)$, associated with each demand during lead time.

DDLT (UNITS)	*P* (*DDLT*)
0	.304
1	.276
2	.312
3	.072
4	.036
	$\Sigma = 1.00$

Figure 13 Decision Tree for All Possible Demands During Lead Time

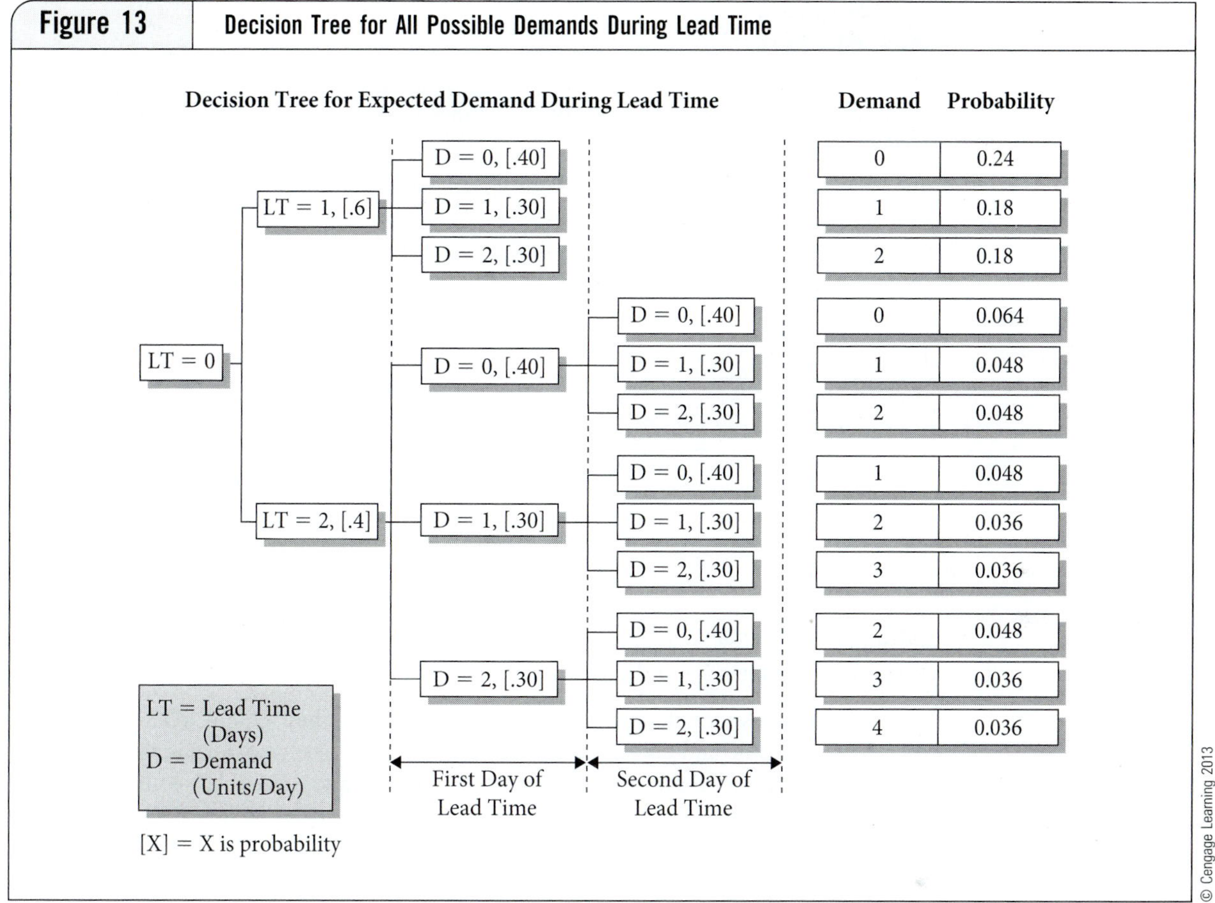

The expected stockout during lead time, E({s}), for each reorder point can now be determined. The maximum protection level is 4 units of safety stock. To calculate the expected stockouts per lead time for a particular reorder point *ROP*, we use the probabilities *P*(*D*), calculated above, to determine the expected value of demand greater than the reorder point. That is, for each possible value of demand *D*, there is an associated probability *P*(*D*), and reorder point *ROP*. Since the probability of this occurring is *P*(*D*), the expected number of units stockout is (*D* − *ROP*) × *P*(*D*). For each possible *ROP*, we must investigate each possible demand using the following equation.

$$E\{s\} = \sum_{D=ROP+1}^{D_{MAX}} P(D)(D - ROP)$$

Thus, for example, using *ROP* = 0, we get the following:

(4 − 0) × .036 = .144

(3 − 0) × .072 = .216

(2 − 0) × .312 = .624

(1 − 0) × .276 = .276

1.260 units stockout = *E*(*S*)

Table 5	Safety Stock Determination		
REORDER POINT (ROP)	DEMAND PROBABILITY $P(D = ROP)$	PROBABILITY OF STOCKING OUT $P(D > ROP)$	AVERAGE NUMBER OF SHORTAGES PER REPLENISHMENT CYCLE $E(\{S\})$
0	.304	.696	1.26
1	.276	.42	0.564
2	.312	.108	0.144
3	.072	.036	0.036
4	.036	.00	.000

and for $ROP = 1$ the following:

$$(4 - 1) \times .036 = .108$$
$$(3 - 1) \times .072 = .144$$
$$(2 - 1) \times .312 = \underline{.312}$$
$$.564 \text{ units stockout} = E(S)$$

and similarly for $ROP = 2$, 3, and 4. The average number of shortages per replenishment cycle for all reasonable reorder P points (ROP) is shown in Table 5.

We can now use the iterative method to determine the best Q and ROP combination when both lead time and demand are uncertain. On the other hand, testing different combinations of Q and ROP that yield minimum total cost is also a possible solution approach.

The Iterative *Q*, *R* Procedure

Figure 14 summarizes the iterative procedure. It starts with the EOQ. The value of $P(D > ROP)$ at Step 2 is found by equating the extra annual inventory carrying cost C_H incurred by increasing the reorder point by 1 unit to savings in shortage costs that can be attributed to the additional unit of inventory; that is,

$$C_H = (A/Q)C_S(E\{s\}R - E\{s\}_{R+1})$$

Since $(E\{s\}_{ROP} - E\{s\}_{ROP-1}) = P(D > ROP)$,

$$C_H = C_S * (A/Q)P(D > ROP)$$

Figure 14 The Iterative Procedure for Finding *Q* and *R*

1. Compute $Q = \sqrt{\dfrac{2AC_p}{C_H}}$.
2. Compute $P(D > ROP) = QC_H/AC_S$ and determine the value of ROP by comparing the value of $P(D > ROP)$ with the cumulative demand during lead-time distribution values.
3. Determine $E\{s\}$, the expected inventory shortage, using the value of ROP from Step 2.
4. Compute $Q = \sqrt{\dfrac{2A[C_p + C_S E\{s\}_{ROP}]}{C_H}}$
5. Repeat Steps 2 through 4 until convergence occurs, that is, until sequential values for Q at Step 4 and ROP at Step 2 are equal. (Also see Kim and Benton, 1995.)

The calculation of Q at Step 4 is obtained by differentiating the following total cost equation with respect to Q, setting the resulting expression equal to 0, and solving for Q:

$$TC = (A/Q)\left[Cp + Cs\left(\sum_{d \approx R+1}^{D_{MAX}} (D - ROP)P(D)\right)\right] + C_H\left[\frac{Q}{2} + (ROP - \overline{D})\right]$$

$$Q = \sqrt{\frac{2A[C_p + C_S E\{s\}_{ROP}]}{C_H}}$$

Where:

A = Annual demand
Q = Order quantity
C_H = inventory carrying cost per unit per period
C_p = Fixed ordering cost
D = Demand during lead time
$\overline{D}$ = Average demand during lead time
$P(D)$ = Probability of demand during lead time equaling D.
ROP = Reorder point
$ROP - \overline{D}$ = Safety Stock
C_S = Shortage cost per unit

To illustrate the procedure, we'll use the example problem in 5-3 below. Since the procedure iterates from calculating Q to calculating ROP, it's sometimes called the Q, R (ROP) procedure.

The five-step procedure converges quickly on the solution values for Q and ROP. Using the five-step iterative procedure we have demonstrated how the traditional sequential lot size and safety stock decisions can be modified when the replenishment lead time is not fixed but a function of the lot size. In supply chain focused manufacturing environments, the assumption of fixed lead time is inappropriate. Consequently, the savings in safety stock investment and total cost can be significant if the order quantity and lead time decisions are made simultaneously.

Example 5–3

For our example, we will assume the following additional values:

A = annual demand = 50 units

Q = order quantity

$\overline{D}$ = Average demand during replenishment lead time

C_p = fixed-ordering cost = \$100

C_H = annual inventory carrying cost per unit = \$.30

C_i = item cost = \$411

C_S = Shortage cost = \$75

Step 1. $Q = \sqrt{2AC_P/C_H} = (2 \times 50 \times \$100/(\$411 \times .30)) = 9$

Step 2. $P(D > ROP) = (9)(.30)(\$411)/(50)(\$75) = .295$. The closest value in Table 5 is .42 at $ROP = 1$.

Step 3. $E\{s\} = 0.564$ (from Table 5 when $ROP = 1$).

Step 4. $Q = \sqrt{(2 \times 50 \times (\$100 + (0.564 \times \$75)/(.30 \times \$411)))} = 10.74$

Step 5. $P(D > ROP) = (10.74)(.30)(\$411)/(50)(\$75) = 0.353.\quad ROP = 1.$

$$\text{The customer service level } (CSL) = 100 \times \left[1 - \frac{1}{Q}\sum_{d=R+1}^{d_{MAX}} P(D)(D-R)\right]$$

$$= 100 \times \left[1 - \frac{1}{10.74} \times .564\right] = 9$$

Periodic Review Inventory System

The contrast to the fixed-order quantity system is the *fixed-interval reorder system* or *periodic-reorder system.* The periodic-review system examines the inventory position only at periodic or random intervals. At the fixed review time, the decision maker must decide how much to order to replenish inventory. Of course, the replenishment decision depends on the inventory on hand at the review period, the nature of the replenishment leadtime, and the interval between reviews. An example of a periodic-review system is that of a vending machine supplier making weekly rounds of machine locations. Each week, the supplier reviews the machine's inventory of products and restocks the machine with enough items to meet demand and safety stock requirements until the next week.

Three of the original EOQ assumptions are maintained: (1) the holding and ordering costs are fixed, (2) decisions for one item are independent of decision for other items, and (3) constant lead time. However, demand is again uncertain. In the periodic-review system, there are holding costs for both active and reserve inventories, as well as costs associated with stockouts. Periodic-review systems are required in situations in which continuous monitoring is impossible or not preferred. Continuous monitoring is usually difficult for B and C items (see Figure 4b on page 115). If we will assume that the time interval between reviews has been fixed and the problem will be to determine the best ordering policy when the review takes place.

The primary guidelines for the periodic-review system are:

1. The demand forecast is made for a specific period equal to the lead time plus one reorder cycle.
2. The order is then placed equal to the demand forecast during the reorder cycle plus lead time less the inventory on hand.

Thus the three components of inventory are safety stock, cycle stock, and scheduled orders. The three components are defined below:

1. The *safety stock* is designed to protect against demand uncertainty over the protection interval. In the fixed-period system, the amount of stock on hand at the minimum points will fluctuate by the same amount as the differences between actual and expected demand during the period. Thus, the required safety stock can be determined from an analysis of these fluctuations, together with a specified risk of running out.
2. The *cycle stock* is equal to half the average quantity ordered.
3. The *scheduled orders* is equal to the average consumption during the lead time.

In the periodic-review system, orders will arrive periodically if the lead time is constant, and the time between orders will equal the review cycle time. However, there will be a lead time lag between the order arrival and the time the review is made.

A discussion and illustration example of the Fixed-Time Period Model with a service level is given below:

Fixed-Time Period Model with Service Level

In a fixed-time period system, inventory is reviewed at specific times, such as every week or every month. Counting inventory and placing orders on a periodic basis is desirable in situations such as when suppliers make routine visits to customers and take orders for their complete line of C items, or when buyers want to consolidate orders to save transportation costs. The order quantities, in a fixed time period inventory system vary from period to period, depending on the usage rates. Fixed time period inventory systems generally require a significantly higher level of safety stock than a fixed-order quantity system. The fixed-order quantity system assumes continual counting of inventory on hand, with an order *immediately* placed when the reorder point is reached. In contrast, the standard fixed-time period models initiate order quantities only at the time specified for review. It is possible that demand can sometimes draw the stock down to zero right after an order is placed. This condition could easily go unnoticed until the next review period. In addition the new order, when placed, still takes time to arrive. Thus, it is possible to be out of stock throughout the entire review period, Time Between Review (TBR), and the order lead time. Safety stock, therefore, must provide protection against stockouts during the review period itself, as well as during the lead time from order placement to order receipt.

In a fixed-time period system, orders are placed at the time between review (*TBR*), and the safety stock that must be reordered is

$$\text{Safety stock} = Z\sigma_{DR}(TBR + L)$$

A fixed time period system with a constant lead time, L is shown in Figure 15.

Order quantity (Q) = Average demand over the review period + safety stock − Inventory currently on hand (+ on order, if any)

$$Q = \overline{D}(TBR + L) + Z\sigma_{DR}(TBR + L) - OH$$

Figure 15 Fixed-Time Period Inventory Model

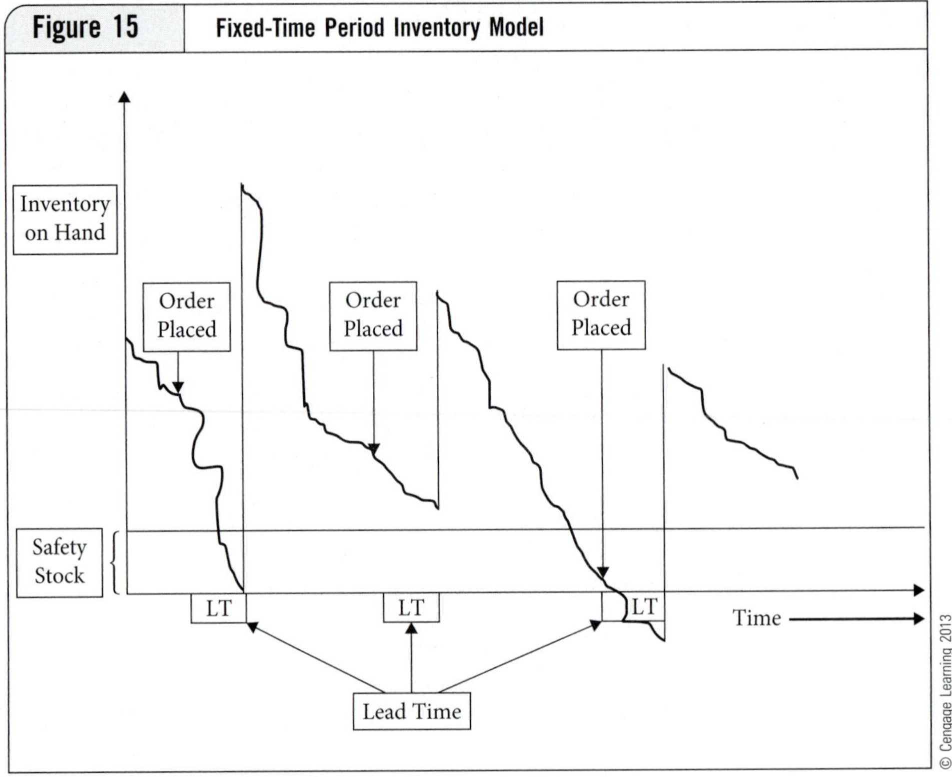

Where:

Q = Quantity to be ordered
TBR = The number of weeks between reviews
L = Lead time in days (time between placing an order and receiving it)
$\overline{D}$ = Forecasted average weekly demand
z = Number of standard deviations for a specified service level
$\sigma_{DR}(TBR + L)$ = Standard deviation of demand over the review and lead time
OH = Current Inventory level (includes items on order)

In this model, demand ($\overline{D}$) can be forecast and revised each review period, if desired, or the yearly average may be used if appropriate.[1]

The value of Z can be obtained by solving the following equation for E(z) and reading the corresponding Z value.

$$E(Z) = \overline{D}_{TBR}(1 - SL)/[Z\sigma_{DR}(T + L)]$$

Where:

$E(z)$ = Expected number of units short table where the mean = 0 and σ = 1
SL = Service level desired
$\overline{D}_{TBR}$ = Demand during the review period where $\overline{D}$ is Weekly demand and TBR is the number of Weeks
$\sigma_{DR}(TBR + L)$ = Standard Deviation of demand over the review period and lead time

An example problem is given in Example 5-4 on next page.

[1]The demand, lead time, review period, and so forth can be any time units such as days, weeks, or years, so long as it is consistent throughout the equation.

Example 5-4

Weekly demand for a specific C item is 100 units with a standard deviation of 35 units. The review period is 4 weeks, and lead time is 2 weeks. The policy is to satisfy 99% of demand from items in stock. At the beginning of this review period, there are 600 units in inventory. How many units should be ordered?

Solution:

The quantity to order is

$$Q = \overline{D}(TBR + L) + Z\sigma_{DR}(TBR + L) - OH$$
$$= 100(4 + 2) + Z\sigma_{DR}(TBR + L) - 600$$

Before we can complete the solution, we need to find $Z\sigma_{DR}(TBR + L)$ *and z. To find* $Z\sigma_{DR}(TBR + L)$, we use the notation, that the standard of sequence of independent random variables is equal to the square root of the sum of the variances. Therefore, the standard deviation during the period *TBR* + *L* is the square root of the sum of variances for each week, or

$$\sigma_{TBR+L} = \sqrt{\sum_{i=1}^{TBR+L} \sigma^2_{DRi}}$$

Since each week is independent and σ_{DR} is constant,

$$\sigma_{TBR+L} = \sqrt{(TBR + L)\sigma^2_{DR}} = \sqrt{(4 + 2)(35)^2} = 85.73$$

Now in order to find *z*, we first need to find *E*(*z*) and look this value up in Table 1 on Page 128. In this case, demand during the review period is $\overline{D}_{TBR}$. Therefore,

$$E(z) = \overline{D}_{TBR}(1 - SL)/\sigma_{DR} + L = (100(4)(1 - .99))/85.73 = .046658$$

From Table 11 at *E*(*z*) = .046658, by interpolation $z = 1.30$.

The quantity to order, then, is

$$Q = \overline{D}(TBR + L) + Z\sigma_{DR}(TBR + L) - OH$$
$$= 100(4 + 2) + 1.30(85.73) + L - 600$$
$$= 111.44 \text{ or } 112 \text{ Units}$$

To satisfy a 99 percent service level from inventory an order quantity of 112 units is needed to be placed.

The fixed-time period model is recommended when it is convenient to place orders at fixed time intervals (weekly, twice a month, etc.) Fixed-time period ordering is widely used in retail businesses. There are many reasons for using the fixed-time period model. A key supplier's policy might encourage placing orders at fixed intervals in order to minimize shipping costs for groups of inexpensive items.

SUMMARY

Supply chain focused manufacturing planning and control has among its objectives the determination of the appropriate inventory levels. In this chapter we focus on inventories that are involved with manufacturing, namely raw materials, purchased component parts, manufactured parts, subassemblies, assemblies and finished products for the supply chain. However, most of the concepts presented in this chapter are also adaptable to retailing, distribution and services systems. The five functions of manufacturing inventories are: 1) pipeline stock, 2) cycle stock, 3) seasonal stocks, 4) safety stock, and 5) decoupling stocks.

Inventory management is a key element of a well-run manufacturing organization. An increasingly large number of firms are spending between 60 and 80 percent of their sales dollars on materials purchased outside of the firm. This significant change has increased the importance and profile of supply chain relationships. This also means that the need for tight control over inventories is extremely important to profitability. In many industries, the investment in inventories comprises a substantial share of the firm's assets.

Many of the assumptions of the classical fixed order quantity point inventory system were relaxed. The fixed order interval system was also addressed. In the fixed-quantity models, orders are triggered by a quantity (ROP), while in the fixed-interval models orders are triggered by *time*. Therefore, the fixed-interval system must have stockout protection for lead time plus the next order cycle, but the fixed-quantity system needs protection only during lead time.

The operations manager must first ascertain the item characteristics and the operating environment before determining the appropriate supply chain focused inventory management system.

DISCUSSION QUESTIONS AND EXERCISES

1. SRC Inc. buys shrink wrap in 1,000-pound rolls. Annual demand is 3,500 rolls. The cost per roll is $1,000, and the annual holding cost is 25 percent of the cost. Each order costs $50.
   a. How many rolls should SRC order at a time?
   b. What is the economic time between orders?
2. Big City Productions, Inc. buys 4,000 blank CDs per month for use in producing rap music. The ordering cost is $12.50. Holding cost is $0.12 per CDs per year.
   a. How many CDs should Big City order at a time?
   b. What is the expected time between orders?
3. At DallasBooks.com, a large retailer of popular model airplane books, demand is constant at 48,000 books per year. The cost of placing an order to replenish stock is $15.50, and the annual cost of holding is $6 per book. Stock is received five working days after an order has been placed. No backordering is allowed. Assume 300 working days a year.
   a. What is DallasBooks.Com's optimal order quantity?
   b. What is the optimal number of orders per year?
   c. What is the optimal interval (in working days) between orders?
   d. What is demand during the lead time?
   e. What is the reorder point?
   f. What is the inventory position immediately after an order has been placed?
4. Welding Plus, a local retailer of welding supplies, faces demand for its 820 High-Intensity Welding Rod at a constant rate of 53,500 units per year. It costs Welding Plus $22.50 to process an order to replenish stock and $1.75 per unit per year to

carry the item in stock. Stock is received four working days after an order is placed. No backordering is allowed. Assume 300 working days a year.

a. What is Welding Plus's optimal order quantity for the 820 rod?

5. No Tell Motel operates 52 weeks per year, 6 days per week, and uses a continuous-review inventory system. It purchases bath soap for $5.65 per box. The following information is available about these boxes of soap.

Demand = 132 boxes/week
Order cost = $74/order
Annual holding cost = 24 percent of cost
Desired cycle-service level = 95 percent
Lead time = 3 weeks
Standard deviation of weekly demand = 25 boxes
Current on-hand inventory is 159 boxes, with no open orders or backorders.

a. What is the EOQ? What would be the average time between orders (in weeks)?
b. What should R be?
c. An inventory withdrawal of 18 boxes was just made. Is it time to reorder?
d. The motel currently uses a lot size of 600 boxes (i.e., $Q = 600$). What is the annual holding cost of this policy? Annual ordering cost? Without calculating the EOQ, how can you conclude from these two calculations that the current lot size is too large?
e. What would be the annual cost saved by shifting from the 600-box lot size to the EOQ?

6. Consider again the soap ordering policy for No Tell Motel in Problem 5.

a. Suppose that the weekly demand forecast of 132 boxes is incorrect and actual demand averages only 83 boxes per week. How much higher will total costs be, owing to the distorted EOQ caused by this forecast error?
b. Suppose that actual demand is 83 boxes but that ordering costs are cut to only $25 by using the Internet to automate order placing. However, the purchasing agent does not tell anyone, and the EOQ is not adjusted to reflect this reduction in *Cp*. How much higher will total costs be compared to what they could be if the EOQ were adjusted?

7. At Pam's Organic Cookie Shop, the demand rate for a box of triple chocolate cookies is normally distributed, with an average of 4,250 boxes per week. The lead time is five weeks. The standard deviation of *weekly* demand is 25 boxes.

a. What is the standard deviation of demand during the five-week lead time?
b. What is the average demand during the five-week lead time?
c. What reorder point results in a cycle-service level of 99 percent?

8. Allen Enterprises uses a continuous-review inventory control system for one of its most popular computer games. The following information is available on the item. The firm operates 50 weeks in a year.

Demand = 12,000 games/year
Ordering cost = $30/order
Holding cost = $38/game/year
Average lead time = 9 weeks
Standard deviation of weekly demand = 245 games

a. What is the economic order quantity for this item?
b. If Allen wants to provide a 95-percent cycle-service level, what should be the safety stock and the reorder point?

9. In a continuous-review inventory system, the lead time for custom six-panel doors is five weeks. The standard deviation of demand during the lead time is 50 doors. The desired cycle-service level is 99 percent. The supplier of the custom doors decided for competitive reasons to now quote a one-week lead time. How much can safety stock be reduced without reducing the 99-percent cycle-service level?

10. AutoZone Auto Parts uses a periodic-review inventory-control system for one of its stock items. The review interval is set at four weeks, and the lead time for receiving the materials ordered from its wholesaler is two weeks. Weekly demand is normally distributed, with a mean of 250 units and a standard deviation of 50 units.
    a. What is the standard deviation of demand during the protection interval?
    b. What should be the target inventory level if the firm desires 98.2 percent stockout protection?
    c. If 150 units were in stock at the time of a periodic review, how many units should be ordered?

11. The lead time for a case of antifreeze is two weeks and the review period is one week. Demand during the protection interval averages 123 cases, with a standard deviation of 25 cases. What is the service level when the target inventory level is set at 250 cases?

12. Echo Electronics is a retailer of hand held texting devices. You are in charge of inventory control for one of Echo's most profitable multitasking devices (MT-46). Weekly demand for the MT-46 varies, with an average of 34,500 units and a standard deviation of 75 units. The MT-46 is purchased from a wholesaler at a cost of \$99.50 per unit. The supply lead time is six weeks. Placing an order costs \$620, and the inventory carrying rate per unit per year is 45 percent of the item's cost. Echo operates five days per week, 50 weeks per year.
    a. What is the optimal ordering quantity for the MT-46?
    b. How many units of the MT-46 should be maintained as safety stock for 97.5 percent protection against stockouts during an order cycle?
    c. If supply lead time can be reduced to three weeks, what is the percentage reduction in the number of units maintained as safety stock for the same 97.5 percent stockout protection?
    d. If, through appropriate sales promotions, the demand variability is reduced so that the standard deviation of weekly demand is 25 units instead of 75, what is the percentage reduction (compared to that in part b) in the number of units maintained as safety stock for the same 97.5 percent stockout protection?

13. Suppose that No Tell Motel in Problem 5 uses a fixed order interval system instead of a fixed order quantity system. The average daily demand is 15 boxes, and the standard deviation of *daily* demand is 6.124 boxes $\sqrt{6}$.
    a. What *TBR* (in working days) and *L* should be used to approximate the cost trade-offs of the EOQ?
    b. How much more safety stock is needed than with a fixed order quantity system?
    c. It is time for the periodic review. How many boxes should be ordered?

14. Buckeye Novelty Shop uses a continuous-review system and operates 52 weeks per year. One of the best-selling items has the following characteristics:

    Demand (D) = 14,000 units/year
    Ordering cost (S) = \$320/order

Holding cost (H) = \$4/unit/year
Lead time (L) = 3 weeks
Cycle-service level = 95%

Demand is normally distributed, with a standard deviation of *weekly* demand of 120 units. Current on-hand inventory is 1,308 units, with no scheduled receipts and no backorders.

a. Calculate the item's EOQ. What is the average time, in weeks, between orders?
b. Find the safety stock and reorder point that provides a 95-percent cycle-service level.
c. For these policies, what are the annual costs of (i) holding the cycle inventory and (ii) placing orders?
d. A withdrawal of 95 units just occurred. Is it time to reorder? If so, how many should be ordered?

15. Suppose that your firm uses a periodic-review system, but otherwise the data are the same as in Problem 14.

a. Calculate the *TBR* that gives approximately the same number of orders per year as the EOQ. Round your answer to the nearest week.
b. Find the safety stock and the target inventory level that provides a 95 percent cycle-service level.
c. How much larger is the safety stock than with a Q system?

16. Jake, Inc. begins a review of ordering policies for its continuous review system by checking the current policies for a sample of its A items. Following are the characteristics of one item:

Demand (D) = 94 units/week (assume 52 weeks per year)
Ordering and setup cost (S) = \$720/order
Holding cost (H) = \$23/unit/year
Lead time (L) = 3 weeks
Standard deviation of *weekly* demand = 30 units
Cycle-service level = 82 percent

a. What is the EOQ for this item?
b. What is the desired safety stock?
c. What is the reorder point?
d. What are the cost implications if the current policy for this item is $Q = 300$ and $R = 120$?

17. Using the same information as in Problem 16, develop the best policies for a periodic-review system.

a. What value of P gives the same approximate number of orders per year as the EOQ? Round to the nearest week.
b. What safety stock and target inventory levels provide a 90-percent cycle-service level?

18. Grant County Hospital consumes 2,000 boxes of 45 clamps per week. The price of clamps is \$76 per box, and the hospital operates 52 weeks per year. The cost of processing an order is \$62, and the cost of holding one box of clamps for a year is 28 percent of the value of the clamp.

a. The hospital orders the 45 clamps in lot sizes of 1,000 boxes. What *extra* cost does the hospital incur that it could save by using the EOQ method?
b. Demand is normally distributed, with a standard deviation of weekly demand of 100 boxes. The lead time is two weeks. What safety stock is necessary if the

hospital uses a continuous-review system and a 99-percent cycle-service level is desired? What should be the reorder point?

c. If the hospital uses a periodic-review system, with P = two weeks, what should be the target inventory level, T?

19. Tinsel Town is a tennis racket wholesaler that operates 50 weeks per year. Management is trying to determine an inventory policy for its ACE-2 rackets, which have the following characteristics:

Demand (D) = 2,000 units/year
Demand is normally distributed
Standard deviation of *weekly* demand = 19 units
Ordering cost = $50/order
Annual holding cost (H) = $35/unit
Desired cycle-service level = 90%
Lead time (L) = 6 weeks

a. If the company uses a periodic-review system, what should P and T be? Round P to the nearest week.
b. If the company uses a continuous-review system, what should R be?

20. Clark Lawnmower Supply, Inc. stocks everything retail garden stores require for lawnmower repairs. A particular mower blade has been very popular with local garden stores as well as those who buy on the Internet from hardware stores. The cost to place orders with the supplier is $30/order; the demand averages 12 blades per day, with a standard deviation of 6 blades; and the inventory holding cost is $8.00/blade/year. The lead time from the supplier is five days, with a standard deviation of two days. It is important to maintain a 98-percent cycle-service level to properly balance service with inventory holding costs. Use a continuous-review inventory system for this item.

a. What order quantity should be used?
b. What reorder point should be used?
c. What is the total annual cost for this inventory system?

21. Using the data below, develop a spreadsheet for finding the least-cost order quantities when there are quantity discounts (order cost = $60, inventory holding cost = 30 percent of item value, and annual demand = 800):

QUANTITY ORDERED	PRICE
Fewer than 50 units	$53.00
50–99 units	51.50
100–199 units	49.50
200–499 units	48.00
More than 499 units	47.00

22. Demand during lead time for Apex Enterprises is distributed as follows:

Probability	.05	.10	.2	.3	.15	.15	.05
Demand	40	41	42	43	44	45	46

a. Use a spreadsheet program to evaluate the expected number of units short per reorder cycle for reorder points of 40 to 46. What is the expected shortage cost per reorder cycle when the reorder point is 40 and cost per unit short is $36?

b. What happens to the expected shortage cost (when $R = 40$ and $C = \$36$) if the demand distribution shifts as follows?

Probability	.2	.4	.2	.1	.1	0	0
Demand	40	41	42	43	44	45	46

23. RGK, Inc. manufactures smart cell phones. RGK has recently introduced a new line of smart phones that is popular for college students. RGK purchases batteries from an outside supplier. RGK has noted the following demand distribution for its new phones.

DEMAND/MONTH	PROBABILITY
1,200	.10
1,300	.15
1,400	.15
1,500	.20
1,600	.20
1,700	.10
1,800	.05
1,900	.05

The purchase price to RGK is $90 per battery. The clinic has an ordering cost of $35. Cost of carrying inventory is 35 percent of the item value per unit per year. Order lead time is constant at one month. The work year consists of 12 months.

a. Compute the economic order quantity for the RGK purchases.

b. Compute the reorder point and buffer stock level for a 99-percent customer service level. Assume order quantity and reorder point can be computed independently.

c. What is the total annual cost of carrying the buffer stock computed in part b?

24. Shark, Inc., a custom paint distributor, orders a 15-day supply of custom paints whenever on-hand inventory falls below the reorder point. Lead time for paint is one day. On Monday, September 30, 23 gallons of paint are in stock. The sales are normally distributed with a mean of 25 gallons per day and a standard deviation of 12 gallons per day. Desired customer service level is 99 percent.

a. What reorder point for paint provides a 99-percent customer service level?

b. How many gallons of paint should be ordered on September 30 if the store is open five days per week?

25. The Sonic Video Game Company is in the process of developing an inventory-control system for purchasing integrated circuits (IC) that will cope with uncertainty. There are 24 ICs in each box. The following information represents the IC use:

Average demand during lead time = 500 IC boxes
Lead time = 1 month
Economic order quantity = 1,500 IC boxes
Forecast interval = 1 month
Mean absolute deviation of forecast error = 60 IC boxes
Desired probability of stocking out = 0.05.

a. How much safety stock will be required?
b. What is the reorder point?
c. What is the customer service level for this policy?
d. What decision rule should Sonic use in ordering ICs, assuming constant IC usage throughout the year?

26. Consider the following demand and lead time data for Carnival Campers, Inc.

a. Calculate average demand during lead time and determine the distribution for demand during lead time.
b. For each reorder point from two to six units (assume the item is ordered 12 times per year and stock-out cost is $33 per unit), what are the expected stockouts and shortage costs per year?

DEMAND PER DAY	PROBABILITY	MANUFACTURING LEAD TIME (IN DAYS)	PROBABILITY
1	.4	2	.3
2	.6	3	.7

27. Consider the data given below and determine the best ordering policy for Camps Antique Clocks (CAC). CAC has an annual inventory carrying cost of $55 per unit per year, stock-out cost is $33 per unit, ordering cost is $15 per order, and the annual requirement is 290 units. Demand during replenishment lead time has the following probability distribution:

DEMAND DURING LEAD TIME (IN UNITS)	PROBABILITY
0	.07
2	.25
4	.27
6	.24
8	.09
10	.05
12	.03

Determine the minimum-cost lot size and reorder point for the antique clocks.

28. The demand during lead time for Vibe Pottery has the following probability distribution:

DEMAND DURING LEAD TIME (IN UNITS)	PROBABILITY
0	.01
1	.03
2	.06
3	.13
4	.15
5	.20
6	.15
7	.12
8	.08
9	.04
10	.03

Vibe stocks a product having ordering cost of $309, inventory carrying cost of $25/unit/year, stockout cost of $200 per unit short, an annual requirement of 90 units, and one-month production lead time.

What is the minimum-cost lot size and reorder point for this item?

29. Bell Helicopter produces a spare part with ordering cost of $2,000, inventory carrying cost of $400/unit/year, stockout cost of $1,850 per unit short, an annual requirement of 494 units, and one-week replenishment lead time. Demand during replenishment lead time has the following probability distribution:

DEMAND DURING LEAD TIME (IN UNITS)	PROBABILITY
10	.01
11	.05
12	.09
13	.15
14	.32
15	.16
16	.12
17	.06
18	.04

Find the minimum-cost lot size and reorder point for this item.

30. Stevens manufactures component parts for the Department of Defense (DOD). There are a number of "C" items that are used for the product. The Skid Brace Tube (SBT) is one such component part. Daily demand for the SBT is 75 units with a standard deviation of 15 units. The review period is 30 days, and the lead time is 5 days. At the time of the review there are 96 units in stock. If 98 percent of all SBT demand is to be satisfied from items in stock, how many units should be stocked?

APPENDIX 5A

Areas Under the Normal Curve

Area under the standard normal curve from 0 to z, shown shaded, is $A(z)$. *Examples.* If Z is the standard normal random variable and $z = 1.54$, then

$$A(z) = P(0 < Z < z) = .4382,$$
$$P(Z > z) = .618,$$
$$P(Z < z) = .9382$$
$$P(|Z| < z) = .8764.$$

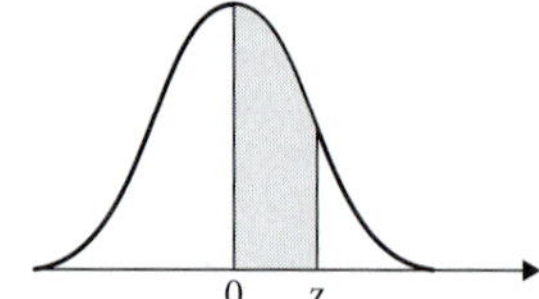

z	.00	.01	.02	.03	.04	.05	.06	.07	.08	.09
0.0	.0000	.0040	.0080	.0120	.0160	.0199	.0239	.0279	.0319	.0359
0.1	.0398	.0438	.0478	.0517	.0557	.0596	.0636	.0675	.0714	.0753
0.2	.0793	.0832	.0871	.0910	.0948	.0987	.1026	.1064	.1103	.1141
0.3	.1179	.1217	.1255	.1293	.1331	.1368	.1406	.1443	.1480	.1517
0.4	.1554	.1591	.1628	.1664	.1700	.1736	.1772	.1808	.1844	.1879
0.5	.1915	.1950	.1985	.2019	.2054	.2088	.2123	.2157	.2190	.2224
0.6	.2257	.2291	.2324	.2357	.2389	.2422	.2454	.2486	.2517	.2549
0.7	.2580	.2611	.2642	.2673	.2704	.2734	.2764	.2794	.2823	.2852
0.8	.2881	.2910	.2939	.2967	.2995	.3023	.3051	.3078	.3106	.3133
0.9	.3159	.3186	.3212	.3238	.3264	.3289	.3315	.3340	.3365	.3389
1.0	.3413	.3438	.3461	.3485	.3508	.3531	.3554	.3577	.3599	.3621
1.1	.3643	.3665	.3686	.3708	.3729	.3749	.3770	.3790	.3810	.3830
1.2	.3849	.3869	.3888	.3907	.3925	.3944	.3962	.3980	.3997	.4015
1.3	.4032	.4049	.4066	.4082	.4099	.4115	.4131	.4147	.4162	.4177
1.4	.4192	.4207	.4222	.4236	.4251	.4265	.4279	.4292	.4306	.4319
1.5	.4332	.4345	.4357	.4370	.4382	.4394	.4406	.4418	.4429	.4441
1.6	.4452	.4463	.4474	.4484	.4495	.4505	.4515	.4525	.4535	.4545
1.7	.4554	.4564	.4573	.4582	.4591	.4599	.4608	.4616	.4625	.4633
1.8	.4641	.4649	.4656	.4664	.4671	.4678	.4686	.4693	.4699	.4706
1.9	.4713	.4719	.4726	.4732	.4738	.4744	.4750	.4756	.4761	.4767
2.0	.4772	.4778	.4783	.4788	.4793	.4798	.4803	.4808	.4812	.4817
2.1	.4821	.4826	.4830	.4834	.4838	.4842	.4846	.4850	.4854	.4857
2.2	.4861	.4864	.4868	.4871	.4875	.4878	.4881	.4884	.4887	.4890
2.3	.4893	.4896	.4898	.4901	.4904	.4906	.4909	.4911	.4913	.4916
2.4	.4918	.4920	.4922	.4925	.4927	.4929	.4931	.4932	.4934	.4936
2.5	.4938	.4940	.4941	.4943	.4945	.4946	.4948	.4949	.4951	.4952
2.6	.4953	.4955	.4956	.4957	.4959	.4960	.4961	.4962	.4963	.4964
2.7	.4965	.4966	.4967	.4968	.4969	.4970	.4971	.4972	.4973	.4974
2.8	.4974	.4975	.4976	.4977	.4977	.4978	.4979	.4979	.4980	.4981
2.9	.4981	.4982	.4982	.4983	.4984	.4984	.4985	.4985	.4986	.4986
3.0	.4987	.4987	.4987	.4988	.4988	.4989	.4989	.4989	.4990	.4990

Chapter 6

MATERIAL REQUIREMENTS PLANNING PRODUCTION SYSTEMS

Learning Objectives

- Explore the historical development of material requirements planning (MRP)
- Understand the difference between independent and dependent demand
- Learn about the different types of manufacturing and control systems
- Learn the basic mechanics of how MRP is executed
- Learn how to execute alternative lot sizing methods
- Learn how MRP evolved into MRP II
- Learn the relationship between MRP, MRP II, and enterprise resource planning (ERP)

Introduction

In order to manage the various types of inventory for a manufacturing operation, attributes of the items first must be analyzed in terms of cost, lead time, past usage, and the nature of demand. The nature of demand is perhaps the most important attribute. The nature of demand can be either independent or dependent. *Independent* demand is unrelated to the demand for other items. In other words, an independent item must be forecasted independently. *Dependent* demand is directly derived from demand for another inventoried item demand. In manufacturing firms, raw materials, components parts, and subassemblies are dependent on the final item's demand. Thus, dependent demand should not be forecasted independently. As an example, a completed automobile is an independent-demand item that is forecasted. However, we know that each automobile requires a product structure for which it would make no sense to forecast the wheel assemblies independently, simply because the wheel assemblies are dependent on and are derived from demand for the automobile. Inventory management for dependent items is usually managed by MRP. In distribution firms, demand is usually *independent*. The order quantities for each inventory item should be forecasted separately. Stock replenishment in independent-demand systems is usually managed by statistical inventory control or order point systems. The characteristics and examples of the types of demand and types of inventory control systems are given below.

Types of Demand

1. Independent-demand characteristics:
   - Automobiles, televisions, computers
   - Demand often occurs at constant rate
   - Affects inventories that are managed separately from other items (e.g. finished goods made to stock)
   - Inventory is managed based on demand forecasts
2. Dependent-demand characteristics:
   - Affects inventories that are managed to support production of other items (e.g., component parts)
   - Inventory is managed based on plans (e.g., master production schedule, or MPS)
   - Most raw materials, components, and subassemblies
   - Demand often occurs in lumps

Materials requirements planning (MRP) was developed to assist companies in managing dependent-demand inventory and scheduling replenishment orders. Specifically, MRP is a computerized *information system* that creates planned orders for both manufactured and purchased materials. The logic of the MRP approach is significantly different from the reorder-point approach (see Chapter 5). MRP has been shown to be beneficial to a variety of manufacturing companies.

Types of Inventory Control Systems

Reorder-Point Inventory Control System

The reorder-point system is based on the independent-demand concept. Independent-demand inventory is not directly related to the internal manufacturing operation. A flow diagram of an independent-demand system is given in Figure 7 in Chapter 5.

Reorder-point systems are driven by using historical data to forecast future inventory demand. The forecast assumes that past data are representative of future demand. As shown in Figure 10, Chapter 5, if, at any time, an item's inventory level falls below some predetermined level, either additional inventory is ordered or new production orders are released in fixed order quantities (FOQ). Although most early ROP systems were manual, automated ROP systems soon followed when commercial computer use increased in the 1960s.

Evolution from ROP Inventory Control to MRP Systems

During the early 1970s, computerized materials requirement planning systems (MRP) began to replace ROP systems as the preferred manufacturing control system. MRP systems presented a clear advantage in that they offered a forward-looking, demand-based approach for planning the manufacturing of products and the ordering of inventory. This approach allowed lumpy inventory levels experienced under ROP's FOQ capabilities to be smoothed and managed more effectively under MRP's more precise time-phased order-generation capabilities. In addition, MRP systems introduced basic computerized production-reporting tools that could be used to evaluate the viability of the master schedule against projected materials demand.

MRP is a computer-driven information system that translates end-item demand from the MPS into time-phased requirements for raw materials, component parts, and subassemblies, working backward from the due date using lead times, lot sizes, bills of materials, and other relevant production information. The MRP system is different from the reorder-point manufacturing planning and control approach. Prior to the introduction of MRP in the early 1970s, variations of the reorder-point system were used to plan and control production inventories. The MRP system makes it possible to construct a time-phased requirement record for any part number. The MRP logic also allows for detailed capacity-planning models (see chapter 9). Developing the requirements plan (materials and capacity) is basically an iterative process in which the planning is executed level by level in the product structure. For example, planning for a backhoe tractor would determine requirements for tires, transmission, bucket size, and so forth. However, planning for tires has to be done after the planning for wheel assemblies. Suppose the company planned to build 40 backhoe tractors and each backhoe tractor required four wheel assemblies. Thus 160 wheel assemblies will be required. If 100 wheel assemblies are currently on hand and 20 wheel assemblies have already been ordered, only 40 more wheel assemblies must be ordered to complete the 40 backhoe tractors.

MRP Lot Sizing

The general lot-sizing problem for time-phased requirements for a component part involves converting the requirements over the planning horizon (the number of periods into the future for which there are requirements) into planned orders by batching the

Figure 1 **Net Requirements for 12 Periods**

Order cost = $92
Inventory carrying cost = $.5/period/unit

Period	1	2	3	4	5	6	7	8	9	10	11	12
Net requirements	80	100	124	50	50	100	125	125	100	100	50	100

Source: Benton, W.C. Purchasing and Supply Chain Management, McGraw-Hill, (2013).

requirements into lots. The specific method for determining the order quantities for a component part is given by a lot-sizing procedure. In many cases, the lot-sizing procedure performance is based on the minimization of the sum of ordering and inventory-carrying costs subject to meeting all requirements for each period (see Chapter 5). An ordering cost is incurred for each order placed. A carrying cost is charged against the ending inventory balance in each period. The sum of these two cost components is the total inventory cost.

Lot-sizing procedures evaluate orders that cover the requirements for one or more periods. For example, in Figure 1, a minimum of 80 units must be ordered for period 1 (to meet that period's requirement), but other alternatives would include an order of 180 (for the first two periods' requirements), 304 (first three periods' requirements), and so on.

In order to avoid being out of stock, there must be an order received in the first period in which there is a requirement not covered by inventory (net requirement). In order to fill the first net requirement, the firm will incur the cost of ordering (all costs associated with placing and receiving an order). It may be less expensive to combine the first net requirement with another requirement and hold the additional units in inventory until they are needed rather than pay for another order. Additional net requirements for periods beyond the first should be included as long as the cumulative units times the number of periods to be held times the cost to hold a unit for one period are less than or equal to the order cost. When this is no longer true, placing another order is less costly. In general, this is the criterion used to establish the purchase order quantity for the lot-sizing procedures. The MRP concept is illustrated in the example given in Figure 2 below. *A more comprehensive discussion of the various lot-sizing models is given in Appendix 6A.*

Figure 2 **Lumpy Requirements Example**

On hand = 50 units
Safety stock = 5 units
Lead time = 1 period

Periods	1	2	3	4	5	6	7	8
Projected customer demand*	15	15	15	10	15	10	10	10
Build schedule				50				50
Component requirements			50				50	

*Periods 1, 2 and 3 customer demand is supplied directly from the 50 units on hand.
Source: Benton, W.C. Purchasing and Supply Chain Management, McGraw-Hill (2013).

For components of assembled products, the demands are not usually constant per unit time, and depletion is anything but gradual. Inventory depletion for component parts tends to occur in discrete "lumps" because of lot sizing of the final product. Requirements dependent on the final product are usually discontinuous and lumpy since requirements for these components depend on when the product is built. In some periods, there may be a few or no component requirements, and in the next, a requirement for many will occur. As an example, Figure 2 shows a case in which customer demand is fairly uniform but, because of the economics of the build schedules, the requirements for the components are "lumpy." Lumpy demand is caused by the way the manufacturing process is operated. There are a variety of end items competing for manufacturing, timing, scheduling and capacity. The build schedule shows three periods of zero requirements before a requirement of 50 component parts is encountered. This requirement sequence, very common to component parts, is not handled well with the non–time-phased reorder-point techniques.

With the reorder-point system, the production control manager does not plan for future requirements but reacts to the current situation, which may require expediting to prevent a materials shortage. In these situations, expediting is used as a substitute for planning future requirements. An improved basis for planning to meet future needs would be to extend the requirement information throughout enough time periods to cover the entire manufacturing lead time. This provides the time-phased requirement information that is the basis for MRP systems.

MRP systems utilize substantially better information on future requirements than is possible by the non–time-phased reorder-point system. MRP systems are helpful for companies with assembled products that have component requirements dependent on the final product. The system provides information to better determine the quantity and timing of component parts and purchase orders than is possible with the non–time-phased reorder-point system.

Material Requirements Planning Basics

The MRP concept provides the basis for projecting future inventories in a manufacturing operation. MRP can help improve the traditional non-time-phased order-point system because it allows the operations manager to plan requirements (raw materials, component parts) to meet the final assembly schedule. That is, MRP provides a plan for component and subassembly availability that allows certain end products to be scheduled for final assembly in the future. Once a firm's final assembly schedule has been determined and the product bills of materials have been finalized, it is possible to precisely calculate the future materials needs for the final assembly schedule. The product bill of materials for a given finished product can be broken down, or "exploded," and extended for all component parts to obtain that product's exact requirements for each component part. The MPS is generated from the aggregate production. MRP translates that MPS plan into a detailed production plan. An overview of the MRP system is illustrated in Figure 3. Also see Figure 1 in Chapter 1 and Figure 7 in Chapter 3.

Figure 3 MRP Overview

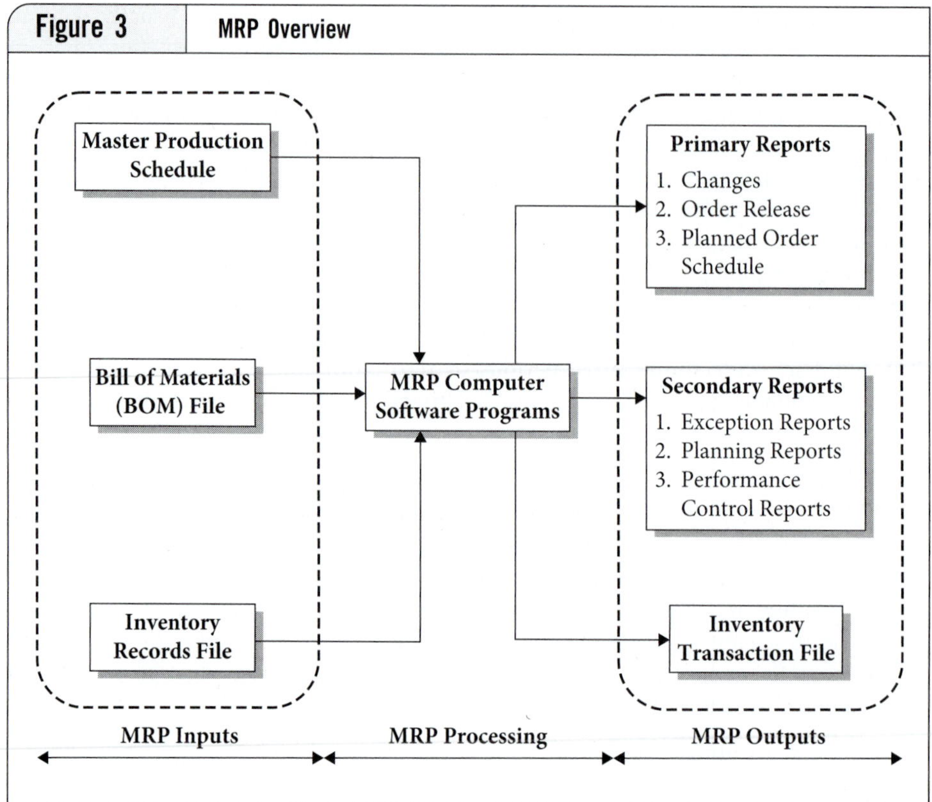

MRP Inputs

The MRP inputs are the master production schedule (MPS), the bill of materials (BOM) file, and the inventory records file as shown in Figure 3.

1. Master production schedule (MPS)—The MPS is the anticipated build schedule that is derived from forecasted demand and actual customer-booked orders. The MPS is the exact time-phased build schedule needed to satisfy booked orders and forecasted demand. Also see chapter 4 for a comprehensive discussion of MPS.
2. Bill of materials (BOM)—A listing of all the raw materials, parts, subassemblies, and assemblies needed to produce one unit of a product. The computerized MRP system processes the BOM file from left to right starting with the highest or zero level. Subassemblies and parts that go directly into the assembly of the finished product are called level 1 components. The parts and components that go into the assembly items are level 2, and so on. The MRP explosion involves determining the quantity and lead time for each item required to satisfy the item at that level. The BOM explosion process generates time-phased requirements of specific quantities of each item necessary to assemble the finished product. A BOM is illustrated in Figure 4.

Figure 4 Bill of Materials

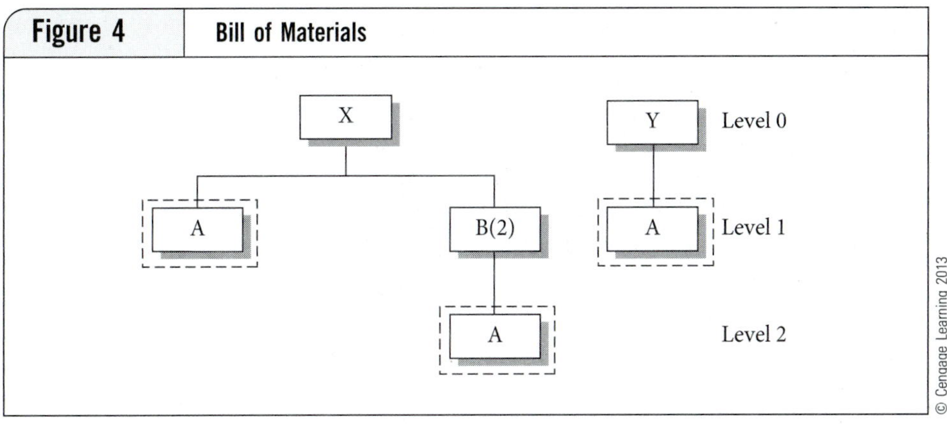

As can be seen from Figure 4, a component part may be used in more than one level in a bill of material. The planned order level of end items X and Y will be passed down as gross requirements to component part A. But there are additional requirements for component part A from component part B. If we process the time-phased record for component part A before all of its gross requirements have been accumulated, the production quantities for component part A would be insufficient. By convention, the top final assembly level is denoted as level 0. As can be seen in Figure 4, final assemblies X and Y have low level codes as 0. All immediate component parts A and B are assigned a low level code of 1. The next level down is coded Level 2. Note that component part A has been coded at both Levels 1 and 2, indicating that it is also used at a lower level in the product structure. The higher the assigned code, the lower the level in the product structure the part is used. Thus, the last level code assigned to a component part reveals the lowest level of usage and is the actual level of usage retained for the component part. There could be an endless number of level 0 end items in a manufacturing organization. The level code assigned to any component part is based on the usage of the component part in all Level 0 end items (products). MRP record processing must always begin at Level 0.

As can be seen from Figure 4, a component part may be used in more than one level in a bill of material.

3. Inventory Records File—The inventory records file contains specific information on the quantity of each item on hand, on order, and committed to use in future time periods. The MRP gross-to-net processing logic determines the quantity available for use in a given period, and if enough items are available to meet the order requirements, it commits these for use during the time period by updating the inventory record file. If there is not enough of the item available, the system includes the item order information (e.g., lot size, lead time, scheduled receipts). A planned order release is then initiated.

The MRP system is the key driver in the manufacturing planning and control process. MRP transforms the overall plan for production into executable activities.

MRP Outputs

MRP systems have capabilities of generating a wide range of outputs. These typically include primary reports and secondary reports. Some of the managerial reports are summarized below.

Primary Reports

The primary reports include the following specific reports:

1. Order release notice- requesting planned orders
2. Rescheduling notice- changes in open order due dates
3. Planned order released reports- a documentation of future planned order releases
4. Cancellation notices cancellation of open orders or changes to the MPS
5. Inventory reports- inventory status documentation

Secondary reports

The secondary output reports are performance-control reports, planning reports, and exception reports.

1. Performance reports of various types reflecting cost, item usage, actual vs. planned leadtime, and other relevant performance measures.
2. Exception reports reflecting MPS deviations, supplier performance and overdue orders.

The Basic MRP Record

The basic MRP record is given in Figure 5.

Figure 5 Time-Phased MRP Record

J750 ENGINE ASSEMBLY MASTER SCHEDULE

Week	1	2	3	4	5	6	7	8	9	10	11	12
Quantity												

MRP RECORD **TURBINE HOUSING REQUIREMENTS**

Week	1	2	3	4	5	6	7	8	9	10	11	12
Gross Requirements												
Projected Available (on hand)*												
Scheduled Receipts**												
Net Requirements												
Planned Order Release												

*Measured at the end of each week.
**Received at the beginning of each week.

The explanation of each row follows:

- Gross requirements (GR)—The gross requirement is the total quantity needed for an item on a weekly basis. It is assumed that the quantity will be available on Monday morning for the week in question.
- Projected available on hand (PA)—The projected available is the inventory of the component at the end of the week.
- Scheduled receipts (SR)—The scheduled receipts are orders that have already been launched, either as a shop order or purchased item. Scheduled receipts are important because they represent a commitment of resources. It should be assumed that the exact quantity and timing of these orders are certain and will be delivered in the expected period.
- Net requirements (NR)—The net requirements are the amount of the inventory item needed for the week after the gross requirements have been netted against available inventory and scheduled receipts.
- Planned order releases (POR)—The planned order releases are the quantity of net requirements that are planned to be ordered in the beginning of the period, taking into account lot sizes and time phasing. Unlike scheduled receipts, planned order releases are not firm orders. The planned order releases are the primary output of the MRP system, as they represent the expected timing and quantities of future purchases and production plans.

As can be seen in Figure 5, the MRP record is driven by the MPS (J750 Engine assemble). Each period is referred to as a **time bucket**. The typical time bucket is usually a week. The number of periods in a MRP record represents the decision-making planning horizon. The GRs are time phased based on the specific period in which the requirements are needed for the MPS. In other words, all materials must be ordered, received and assembled in order to meet demand for the period MPS requirement. The PA row is an indication of the number of required units that can be supplied directly from the current stock. The projected available balance is accounted for at the end of each period. The planned order release row is determined directly from the net requirement row (NR=GR−(PA+SR)). The scheduled receipt row describes the open orders or work in progress for each future period at a specific time. The scheduled receipt (SR) is a committed shop order or an open purchase order. Scheduled receipts are added to the projected available stock.

The MRP system generates the planned order releases based on the gross requirement, projected available, scheduled receipts, and net requirements. The resulting positive POR quantity is then executed in terms of a shop or purchase order. An illustrative MRP example is given in the next section.

The MRP decision-making criteria are focused on *when to order* and *how much to order*. With respect to the timing decision, orders should always be made as late as possible without stocking out. Stockouts should be avoided. With respect to the quantity decision, the order quantity should be as little as possible, that is, just enough to avoid a stockout. This is known as the lot-for-lot (LFL) rule.

MRP Illustrative Example

Jan Smith, the operations manager for Karo, Inc., recently attended a seminar on MRP systems. Karo manufactures chairs. Jan decided to implement the MRP concept at Karo. Jan estimates that the lead time between releasing an order to the shop floor and producing a finished chair is two weeks. The company currently has 475 chairs in stock and no safety stock. The forecast customer demand is for 400 chairs in week 1, 270 in week 3, 375 in week 5, 135 in week 7, and 150 in week 8. The data are translated into the time-phased record below.

WEEK	1	2	3	4	5	6	7	8
Gross Requirements	400		270		375		135	150
Scheduled Receipts								
On Hand (475)	75							
Planned Order Release								

Safety stock = 0
Lead time = 2 weeks
Order quantity = lot for lot

There are 475 chairs available, so if these are used to meet the demand of 400 in week 1, we have 475 – 400 = 75 chairs left on hand (i.e., in stock) at the end of week 1. The demand for week 3 is 270. In order to avoid a stockout in week 3, Jan must place an order for 195 (270 – 75) in week 1. Since the lead time is two weeks, conceptually Jan must determine when to order and how much to order. Continuing in the same way, weeks 5, 7, and 8 were calculated.

WEEK	1	2	3	4	5	6	7	8
Gross Requirements	400		270		375		135	150
Scheduled Receipts								
On Hand (475)	75		0					
Planned Order * Release	195		375		135	150		

Safety stock = 0
Lead time = 2 weeks
Order quantity = lot for lot

*Since net requirements = POR, the net requirement row is omitted from the example.

Extending the Chair Example

For the chair production problem considered before, suppose now that Jan must also plan the production of the components that make up the chair. The components include a seat, a back, and four legs. The lead time for seats and backs is two weeks and the lead time for legs is one week. The company currently has an inventory of 225 seats, 200 backs, and 800 legs. Scheduled receipts are 100 seats in week 1 and 30 backs in week 1. Jan decided to adopt an Lot-For-Lot (LFL) lot-sizing method for all items. The specific bill of materials for the chair is given below:

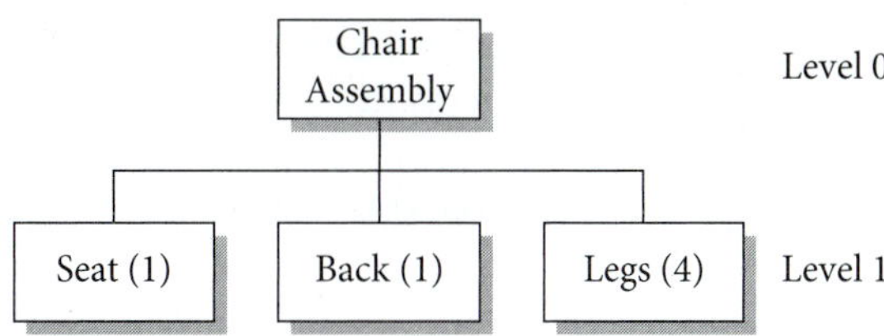

Legs

Since there are 195 chairs planned for production, 780 (195*4) legs were supplied directly from the available inventory and 20 legs remain on hand in week 1. The time-phased record for the leg component is given below:

CHAIR ASSEMBLY

WEEK	**1**	**2**	**3**	**4**	**5**	**6**	**7**	**8**
Planned order Release	195		375		135	150		
Chair Legs (4)	↓ (4*195)[1]		↓ (4*375)		↓ (4*135)	↓ (4*150)		
Week	1	2	3	4	5	6	7	8
Gross Requirements	780		1500		540	600		
Scheduled Receipts								
On Hand (PA) (800)	20		0					
Planned Order Release		*1480		540	600			

*POR = (GR−OH) = 1480; (1500–20)
Safety stock = 0
Lead time = 1 week

The lead time is the time between placing an order and receiving that order note that this lead time assumes that all the items needed for production are available at the time at which we place an order. For example, the chair in our example requires one seat, one back, and four legs to make it the lead time of 2 weeks for a chair assumes that all of the parts are available when we place an order for a chair the 2 weeks covers the time required to assemble them into a chair.

[1]Pegging reflects the relationship of the chair legs to all the planned order releases for the Chair Assembly. The pegging records contain the specific part number or part numbers of the sources of all gross requirements. Pegging is the process of identifying the parent item that has generated a given set of materials requirements for an item.

Backs

Since there are 195 chairs planned for production, 195 backs were supplied directly from inventory and 35(5 + 30) backs remained on hand at the end of week 1.

BACKS (1 BACK FOR EACH CHAIR)

WEEK	1	2	3	4	5	6	7	8
Gross Requirements	195		375		540	600		
Scheduled Receipts	30							
PA (On Hand) (200)	35		0					
Planned Order Release	340		540	600				

Safety stock = 0
Lead time = 2 weeks
Quantity = lot for lot

Seats

Since there are 195 chairs planned for production, 195 seats were supplied directly from inventory in week 1.

SEAT (1 SEAT FOR EACH CHAIR)

WEEK	1	2	3	4	5	6	7	8
Gross Requirements	195		375		540	600		
Scheduled Receipts								
PA (On Hand) (225)	30		0					
Planned Order Release	345		540	600				

Safety stock = 0
Lead time = 2 week
Quantity = lot for lot

MRP Design Decisions

Additional MRP adoption decisions include the following:

1. How big should the time buckets be?
2. How often should the materials plan be regenerated?
3. Where should safety stocks be located, if at all? How big should they be?
4. Should the fabrication department be buffered from assembly by inserting buffer inventory?
5. What (if any) lot-sizing methods should be used?

Since master scheduling is usually accomplished in monthly time periods, the *MRP time buckets* should be less than a month. Thus, MRP time buckets should be weekly.

Weekly MRP buckets will provide greater accuracy for timing the delivery of materials and will result in lower inventory levels throughout the system. Daily time buckets would result in a level of planning precision that is not recommended given the level of inherent forecast error. Given the trend toward volatile demand and increased customer demands, forecasts are becoming difficult to predict with a high degree of accuracy (see Chapter 2). Daily time buckets may also create nervousness throughout the system. *Nervousness* is when the requirements change by small amounts, causing the materials requirements plan to change back and forth. In today's consumer-driven environment, backlogging must be avoided, if at all possible. This is especially true for seasonal products. Thus, most consumer-oriented companies must regenerate weekly during peak demand periods. *Regeneration* involves re-exploding the MPS down through all bills of material to maintain valid priorities. New requirements and planned orders are completely recalculated or "regenerated" at that time. There is no need to establish buffers between departments, since the primary objective is to integrate production flows based on a common MPS. However, *safety stocks* in each department during the peak selling cycle can be recommended.

The appropriate *lot-sizing method* is usually determined by the different levels in the product structure. At the end-item level at which products are master scheduled, the best lot size is one that minimizes the number of set-ups in the plan subject to the constraint that total production not exceed the planned capacity level. See the Appendix 6A for a more detailed discussion of the economics of alternative lot-sizing methods.

MRP Implementation Case Study

The production control manager at Point Clear, Inc.,[2] decided to implement a time-phased requirements planning (MRP) system. In May, he had attended a short course on world-class manufacturing. He now needed to convince the plant manager that materials requirements planning could work for Point Clear's jet engine assembly operation. The production control manager decided that a simple example was needed to illustrate his ideas.

He first prepared a master schedule for one of the engine types produced by Point Clear—the J750 turbo engine. The resulting master schedule is shown in Figure 6. This 12-week schedule shows the number of units of the J750 engines to be assembled. He also decided to consider two "A" category items to represent the projected requirements for the J750. The two A items were representative of the many other components. These two components, the *turbine housing* and the *562 turbine assemblies*, are shown in the product structure diagram in Figure 7. The production control manager noted that

Figure 6 **J750 Engine Master Schedule**

Weeks	1	2	3	4	5	6	7	8	9	10	11	12
Quantity	75	25	35	50	0	45	100	50	0	40	10	80

[2]Copyright © 2006 W.C. Benton Jr. All rights reserved.

Figure 7 J750 Engine Product Structure

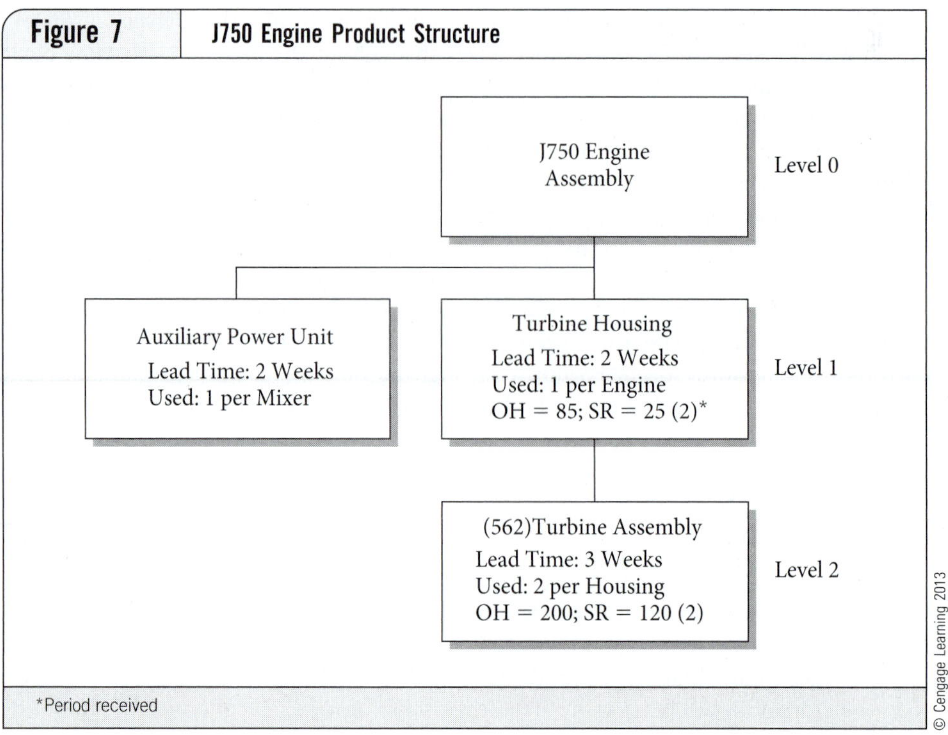

*Period received

the turbine auxiliary power unit is purchased from a tier-one supplier and is shipped to the main engine assembly plant. The manufacturing stages that are involved in producing a J750 involve the engine assembly department and the auxiliary power unit.

The manufacturing and purchase lead times required to produce the turbine housing and the turbine assembly components also are indicated in Figure 7. Note that two weeks are required to fabricate the turbine housings and that all of the turbine housings must be delivered to the engine assembly plant before Monday morning of the week in which they are to be used. It takes three weeks to produce one lot of turbine assemblies, and all of the assemblies that are needed for the production of turbine housings for a specific week must be delivered to the sub assembly department stockroom before Monday morning of that week. The BOM and economic data for the Point Clear case example is shown in Figure 8.

In preparing the MRP example, the following assumptions are made:

1. Eighty-five turbine housings are on hand at the beginning of week 1 and 25 turbine housings are currently on order to be delivered at the start of week 2.
2. Two hundred turbine assemblies are on hand at the start of week 1 and 120 are scheduled for completion at the beginning of week 2.
3. Point Clear is currently ordering using the lot-for-lot (LFL) method. The period order quantity (POQ) method will be compared with the LFL ordering method.

Solution to the Point Clear Engine Company MRP Example

Point Clear Data

1. There are no capacity issues
2. 85 turbine housings are on hand at the beginning of week 1

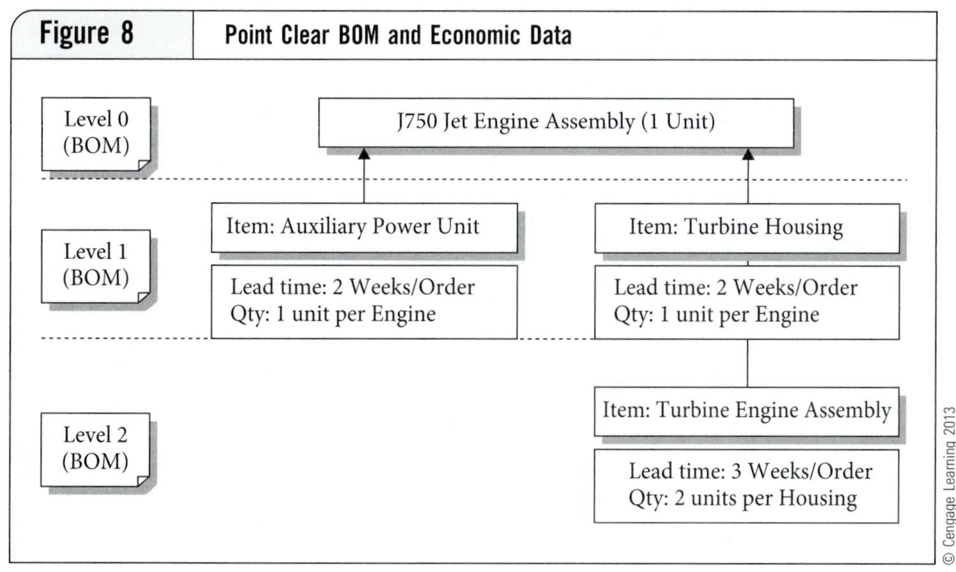

3. 25 turbine housings are scheduled to be received in week 2
4. 200 turbine assemblies are on hand at the beginning of week 1
5. 120 turbine assemblies are scheduled to be received in week 2
6. The bill of materials is given in Figure 8.
7. Costs for each assembly are as follows:

TURBINE HOUSING	DATA
Ordering costs	$650.00
Carrying costs	$7.00
Average demand	50
On hand	85

TURBINE ASSEMBLY	DATA
Ordering costs	$700.00
Carrying costs	$2.00
Average demand	100
On hand	200

Alternatives

- Order using LFL (See Figure 9)
- Order using the POQ method (See Figure 10)

Figure 9 Lot-For-Lot

TURBINE HOUSING RECORD

Week	1	2	3	4	5	6	7	8	9	10	11	12
Gross Requirements	75	25	35	50	0	45	100	50	0	40	10	80
Projected Available (85)*	10#	10	10									
Scheduled Receipts**		25										
Net Requirements				50		45	100	50		40	10	80
Planned Order Release	25	50		45	100	50		40	10	80		

*Measured at the end of each week
**Received at the beginning of the week
#$PA_1 = 85 - 75 = 10$

Ordering Costs	$ 5,200.00 (8 x $650)
Holding Costs	$ 210.00 (30 x $7)
Total Costs	$ 5,410.00

TURBINE ASSEMBLY RECORD (2 x 40) (2 x 80)

Week	1	2	3	4	5	6	7	8	9	10	11	12
Gross Requirements	50	100		90	200	100		80	20	160		
Projected Available (200)*	150#	170	170	80								
Scheduled Receipts**		120										
Net Requirements					120	100		80	20	100		
Planned Order Release		120	100		80	20	100					

*Measured at the end of each week
**Received at the beginning of the week
#$PA_1 = 200 - 50 = 150$

Ordering Costs	$ 3,500.00 (5 x $700)
Holding Costs	$ 1,140.00 (570 x $2.00)
Total Costs	$ 4,640.00

Total Cost for Lot-For-Lot = (Turbine Housing + Housing Assembly) = $10,050

Figure 10 **Period Order Quantity Solution**

EOQ = 96.36 POQ = EOQ/Average Demand = 1.92 ≈ 2.00[1]

TURBINE HOUSING RECORD

Week	1	2	3	4	5	6	7	8	9	10	11	12
Gross Requirements	75	25	35	50	0	45	100	50	0	40	10	80
Projected Available (85)*	10	10	50				50			10		
Scheduled Receipts**		25										
Net Requirements			25	50		45	100	50		40	10	80
Planned Order Release	75			45	150			50		80		

*Measured at the end of each week
**Received at the beginning of the week

Ordering Costs	$ 3,250.00 (5 x $650)
Holding Costs	$ 910.00 (130 x $7)
Total Costs	$ 4,160.00

EOQ = 264.67 POQ = EOQ/Average Demand = 2.64 ≈ 3.0

TURBINE ASSEMBLY RECORD (2 x 80)

Week	1	2	3	4	5	6	7	8	9	10	11	12
Gross Requirements	150			90	300			100		160		
Projected Available (200)*	50	50	50	300								
Scheduled Receipts**		120										
Net Requirements				40								
Planned Order Release	340				100		160					

*Measured at the end of each week
**Received at the beginning of the week

Ordering Costs	$ 2,100.00 (3 x $700)
Holding Costs	$ 1,200.00 (2 x $1400)
Total Costs	$ 3,000.00

Total Cost for POQ = (Turbine Housing + Housing Assembly) = $ 7160.00

[1]Round POQ to nearest integer

The point clear case study clearly illustrates the economic impact between alternative lot sizing models. The POQ lot sizing model is 28.75% $[(\frac{\$7160-10050}{\$10050}) \times 100]$ less costly than the Lot-For-Lot model.

Limitations of MRP

At first glance, MRP appears to be technically robust. However, the implementation of MRP is fraught with many problems. The sources of the failures of MRP can be traced to both organizational and behavioral factors. The primary MRP failure factors are (1) the lack of top management commitment; (2) the failure to realize that MRP is merely a computer program that requires accurate input data; and (3) that there is a need to integrate MRP with a detailed shop floor control system, such as JIT. See Chapters 7 and 8.

Some of the specific limitations of MRP are given below:

1. MRP software assumes that lead times are certain or fixed. It is well known that for most manufacturing environments, lead times are uncertain for internal and external reasons. There are also many sources of manufacturing leadtime. Some of the more common sources of manufacturing lead time are queue time, setup time, run time, wait time, and move time.
2. MRP software assumes that all products are produced on a predetermined bill of material structure. In some manufacturing, the most efficient production sequence may not be consistent with the bill of materials structure.
3. In many cases, it is difficult to make engineering and part changes within the software.
4. MRP software schedules the shop floor based on the bill of materials, ignoring efficient shop floor control issues.
5. MRP software assumes infinite shop floor capacity.
6. If the MRP software does not consider capacity constraints, the master scheduler must balance capacity by hand each time a change is made to the master schedule. In addition, the complexities of resolving capacity constraints become more complex as the number of master schedulers increases.
7. MRP software does not consider "floating bottlenecks." Depending on changes to the master production schedule, bottlenecks are intractable.

As can be seen from this discussion, MRP is not a stand-alone system. MRP must be integrated with top management and shop floor control if it is to be an effective manufacturing tool.

Manufacturing Resource Planning II (MRPII)

Manufacturing resource planning II (MRP II) evolved from MRP through the addition of several new management modules. See Figure 11. The evolution of the new management modules was a natural extension. As an example, MRP was extended to support master planning, rough-cut capacity planning (RCCP), capacity requirements planning (CRP), and production activity control (PAC) modules. As recommended by the American Production and Inventory Control Society, the term *production activity control* replaces the term *shop floor control*. Production activity control is the function of routing and dispatching the work to be accomplished through the production facility and of performing supplier control. PAC encompasses the principles, approaches, and techniques needed to schedule, control, measure, and evaluate the effectiveness of production operations. See Figure 12.

Figure 11 MRP II Overview

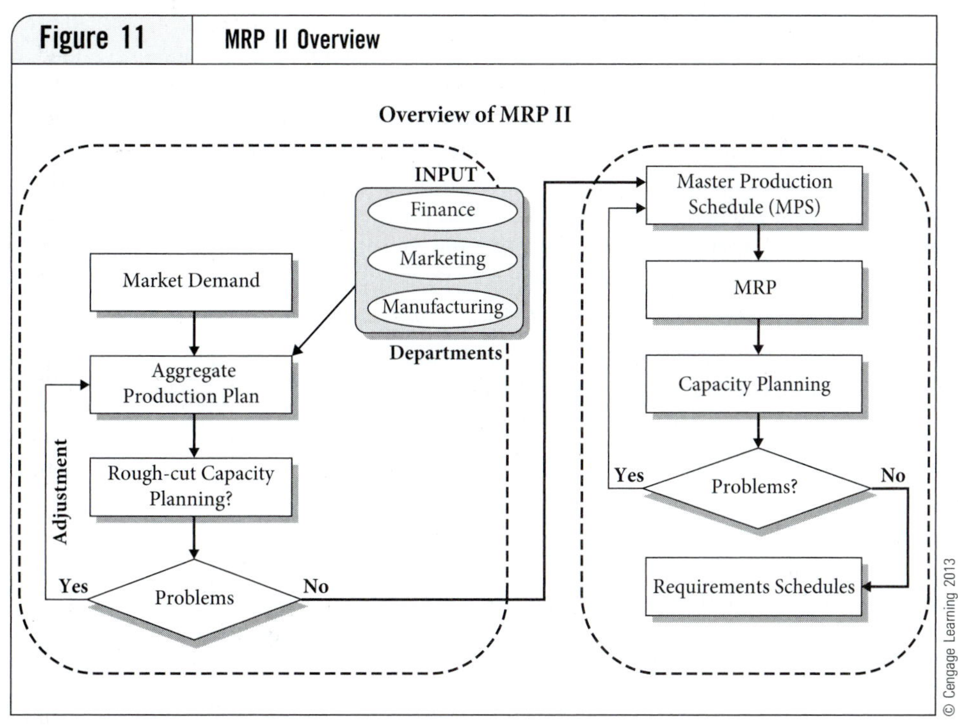

Figure 12 Production Activity Control

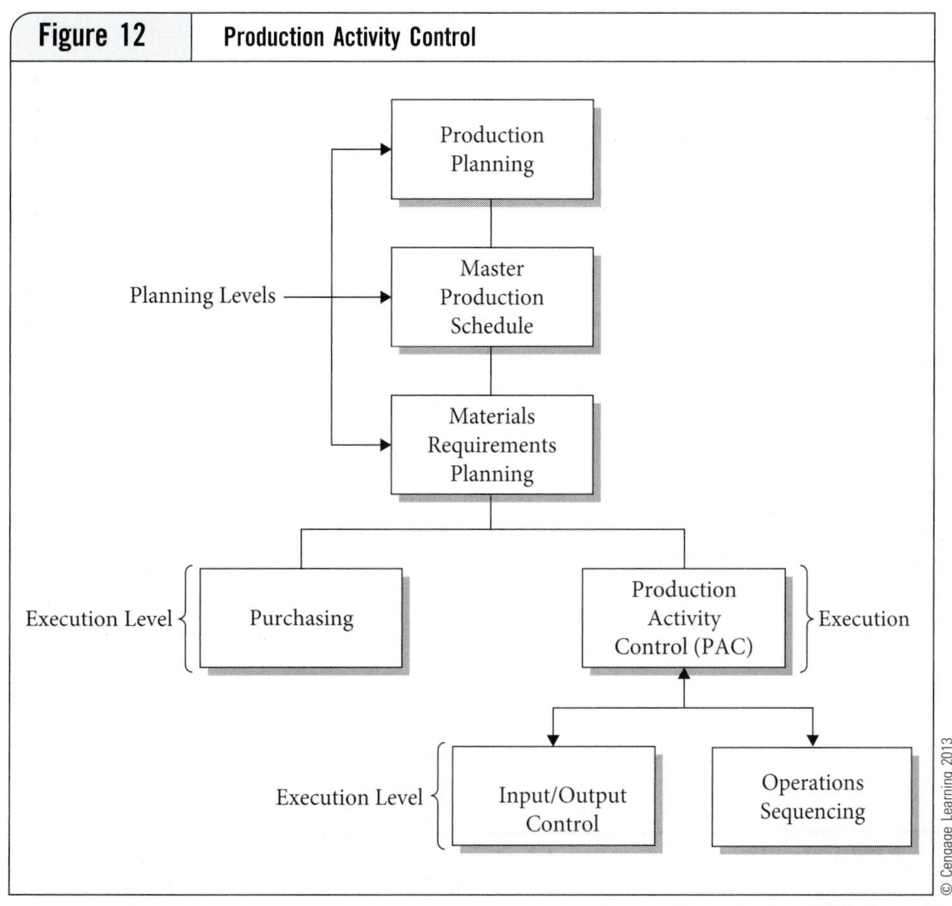

MRP II also facilitates a stage of MRP system development in which the planning functions of master scheduling, MRP, and capacity requirements planning are linked with the execution functions of production activity control (shop floor control) and purchasing. This is also referred to as a closed-loop MRP system. The new MRP execution modules include features for input-output measurement, detailed scheduling and dispatching on the shop floor, and planned delay reports from both the shop floor and the supply chain members (suppliers), as well as purchasing follow-up and control functionality. MRP II ensures that not only are the execution modules part of the overall planning and control system, but there is also feedback from the execution functions so that plans can be kept valid at all times.

With these extensions, MRP II includes all master planning, business planning, and financial control functions. The financial module generates outputs such as the purchase commitment reports and inventory projection reports. MRP II offers an integrated approach to the management of all manufacturing resources.

The MPS drives MRP and is thus the key input into the MRP process. Any errors within the MPS, such as poor forecasts, cannot be compensated for by sophisticated MRP analysis as in lot sizing, calculation of safety stock, or rescheduling. The MPS must be realistic in terms of the goals it sets for the manufacturing facility. It must not be merely a wish list of desirable production levels set by top management. With MRP II, the MPS must now be accurate and realistic.

Of course, the MPS is less accurate beyond the frozen planning horizon. The actual booked orders within the frozen planning horizon are difficult to revise. At some point, the ship has to sail! Forecasts may be based on analysis of historical trends, consideration of the state of the economy and market, and the actions of competitors. The master planning manager must become an expert on each product category and where it is segmented in terms of market share. This approach is especially true for electronics and telecommunications industries, in which product life cycles tend to be relatively short. See chapter 4.

Many MPS systems allow for a system-generated forecast, a manually entered forecast, a schedule of actual customer orders received, and a very simple procedure to combine the above into a reasonable available-to-promise system. There is a netting process very similar to MRP, as the forecast demand is netted with the MPS and current inventory to generate a projection of inventory on hand and available to promise. Projected on-hand inventory is based on initial inventory plus the firm-planned orders less total demand. Available to promise is based on initial inventory plus firm-planned orders less actual orders.

The final step is to check the feasibility of the proposed MPS before it is frozen and released to the manufacturing system for implementation. This feasibility check may be carried out through rough-cut capacity planning. Master planning and rough-cut capacity planning are thus two techniques that are employed in parallel. Actual MRP II systems vary somewhat in the support they give to these functions. Master planning systems often allow for planning at multiple levels and similar techniques to MPS, and RCCP can be applied at the sales and operations planning and production planning levels. See Chapters 4 and 9 for a more detailed MPS discussion.

The Transformation to Enterprise Resource Planning (ERP)

Material requirements planning is a manufacturing planning tool. The basic MRP concept has evolved over the past 40 years into manufacturing resource planning (MRP II).

Enterprise resource planning (ERP) software systems were developed in the 1990s to run MRP II business-management processes in a more integrated manner across all units and sites of a manufacturing enterprise.

ERP is an information-management system used to integrate an organization's different processes into a centralized pool that facilitates management effectiveness. The processes include manufacturing, finance, accounting, human resources, sales, supply chain management, customer information, and other organizational functions.

ERP, properly integrated, can easily become a competitive weapon for manufacturing organizations. The successful implementation of ERP results in an enterprise that has streamlined the data flow between the various business functions. ERP is an enterprise-wide solution. Thus, ERP systems provide the right information at the right time to the right people. The main reason for the popularity of ERP is that it forces an organization to approach operational excellence.

There are a number of ERP vendors (SAP, Oracle, etc.). Each ERP vendor provides a range of ERP modules that are functional software packages for each individual business unit. ERP systems start with a set of core applications, and offer additional applications from which an organization can choose. ERP vendors also offer specialized modules to account for unique processes specific to a particular industry. The three main types of ERP applications are finance, human resource, and manufacturing and logistics. The advantages and disadvantages of ERP are given below.

Advantages of ERP

- Elimination of redundant data operations
- Easily customized
- Efficient access to company-wide information
- Reliable file structure
- Increased efficiency and reduced costs
- Adaptable in a changing business environment
- Reduced cycle times
- Promotes module functionality interaction

Disadvantages of ERP

- Expensive
- Implementation difficulty
- Maintenance is costly and time consuming
- Commitment to a single vendor
- Employees need extensive implementation training

SUMMARY

Materials requirement planning is concerned with the overall logistics of the flow of materials in order to satisfy demand schedules for finished products. The MRP system coordinates all of the information on the state and activities of the purchasing, production control, and inventory control areas in order to determine what, how much, and when all materials flow in each of these areas.

MRP is a manufacturing tool designed to help production managers operate efficiently in a manufacturing environment. Some of the potential benefits involve the minimization of inventory levels, tracking of material requirements, determining the most economical lot sizes for orders, computing quantities needed as safety stock, and planning for future capacity needs. There are numerous useful output reports generated by the MRP system. Production managers, customer service representatives, purchasing managers, and inventory managers rely heavily on MRP output.

MRP relies upon accurate input information. At a minimum, an MRP system must have an accurate MPS, reasonable lead time estimates, and accurate inventory records in order to function effectively and produce useful information. The key to making MRP implementation work is to provide training and education for all affected employees.

In the 1980s, MRP technology was expanded to MRP II, to include several new management modules MRP II supports master planning, RCCP, CRP, and PAC modules. ERP software systems were developed in the 1990s to run MRP II business management processes in a more integrated manner across all units and sites of a manufacturing enterprise.

REFERENCES

Benton, W. C., Purchasing and Supply Chain Management, New York: McGraw Hill-Irwin, 2013.

Benton, W. C., H. Shin, "Manufacturing Planning and Control: The Evolution of MRP and JIT Integration," *European Journal of Operational Research.* 110(1998) 411–440.

Goddard, Walter E. "Focus on the Fundamentals of MRP II." *Modern Materials Handling.* December 1993.

Hasin, M. Ahsan A., and P.C. Pandey. "MRP II: Should Its Simplicity Remain Unchanged?" *Industrial Management.* May–June 1996.

"Manufacturing Execution Systems: Managing the Product through the Plant." *Industry Week.* September 18, 1995.

Orlicky, Joseph. *Material Requirements Planning.* McGraw-Hill, 1975.

Stevenson, William J. *Production/Operations Management.* 9th ed. McGraw-Hill, 2012.

EXERCISES

1. Complete the following MRP Record for item A:

ITEM: A LT: 2 Lot Size: 250					PERIOD				
		1	2	3	4	5	6	7	8
Gross requirements		100	150	500	750	600	850	450	600
Scheduled receipts			150						
Projected on hand 120									
Net requirements									
Planned order releases									

2. Mega Games, Inc., produces two games, *Extreme Combat* and *Judgment Weekend*, with product structures as shown. An order for 100 units of *Extreme Combat* and 175 units of *Judgment Weekend* has been received for period 8. An inventory of available stock reveals 15 units of *Extreme Combat* on hand, 20 of *Judgment Weekend*, 15 of R, 50 of S, 45 of T, 60 of U, 75 of V, and 80 W. Of the Ts on order, 125 are due in by period 2; 40 Ss should arrive in period 1. Determine when orders should be released for items V and W, and the size of those orders.

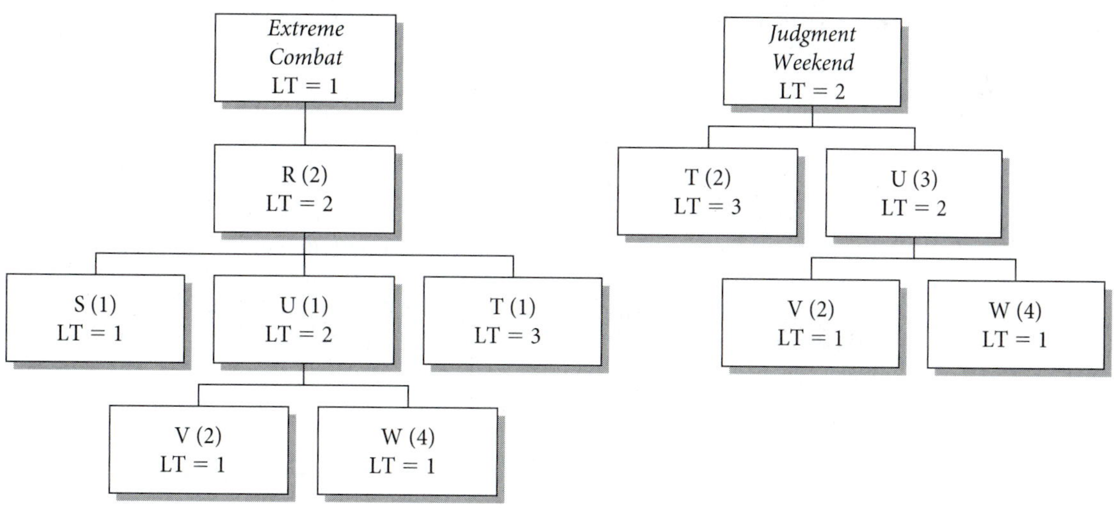

3. PIMS, Inc., has been manufacturing plumbing equipment since 1999. Because of the depressed economic conditions, component parts are assembled in batch runs. At any given time, each level of production has several partially assembled components. Given the following assembly and inventory information, construct a product structure diagram for the oil leak valve, and plan the order releases necessary to assemble 400 oil leak valves for period 10.

Description of the Production Process

Production of the valve begins with the base. The base is placed and secured in a housing. Ball bearings are then installed on opposing sides of the base housing. The rear base cover is fitted on and held while the front cover is secured with U-bolts. Next, the anchor assembly is connected. Finally, two sets of brackets are screwed on and the oil leak valve is checked before shipping.

MASTER FILE

ITEM DESCRIPTION	LEAD TIME	ON ORDER	SCHEDULED RECEIPT DATE	ON HAND	LOT SIZE (MULTIPLES)
Oil Leak Valve	1	-	-	0	1
Brackets	2	-	-	30	25
Shield Valve	1	-	-	40	1
Anchor assembly	3	50	Period 2	90	25
Sealing Valve	1	-	-	10	1
U-bolts	3	-	-	105	50
Front cover	2	-	-	40	50
Rear cover	2	50	Period 1	0	50
Capping Valve	1	-	-	0	1
Ball bearing	3	50	Period 1	90	50
Back flush Valve	1	-	-	50	1
Base	3	25	Period 2	40	25
Base housing	4	25	Period 2	35	25

4. Sandy's Cabinet Company uses MRP to schedule its production. Due to the current recession and the need to cut costs, Sandy has targeted the inventory investment area for cost reduction. However, the company does not want to reduce its customer service level in the process. Demand and inventory data for a standard two-drawer file cabinet are given in the following table. Complete an MRP matrix for the cabinet using (a) no lot sizing, (b) minimum of 200, and (c) multiples of 175 lot sizing. Which lot-sizing rule do you recommend?

Ordering cost = $100 per order
Holding cost = $1 per cabinet per week
Lead time = 1 period
Beginning inventory = 150

PERIOD	1	2	3	4	5
Demand	145	165	155	135	170

5. Sam's Bicycle Company produces bicycles in different styles for boys and girls, in heights of 26 inches or 20 inches, and with 10 speeds, 3 speeds, or 1 speed.

a. How many different kinds of bicycles does Sam's make?

b. Construct a modular bill of material for Best Wheels (one level).

c. If bicycle sales are expected to reach 10,000 over the holiday shopping season, how many 26-inch bikes should Sam's plan to produce? How many 10-speed bikes? Make reasonable assumptions if needed.

6. Consider the following information about an end product item:

Ordering cost = $90/order

Annual demand = 936

Inventory carrying cost = $2/unit/week.

a. How many orders should we place per year (52 weeks) to replenish inventory of the item based on average weekly demand?

b. Given the following time-phased net requirements from an MRP record for this item, determine the sequence of planned orders using economic order quantity and periodic order quantity procedures. Assume lead time equals zero and current on-hand inventory equals zero. Calculate the inventory carrying cost on the basis of weekly ending inventory values. Which procedure produces the lowest total cost for the eight-week period?

	WEEK							
	1	2	3	4	5	6	7	8
Requirements	18	5	13	115	9	0	18	9

7. Final assembly (X) requires one week to assemble and has a component part (A) requiring two weeks to be fabricated. Three units of final assembly A and four units of part B are currently on hand. The gross requirements for assembly A for the 10 weeks are as follows (two of part A are used on each X):

	WEEK									
	1	2	3	4	5	6	7	8	9	10
Assembly (A)	1	4	2	8	1	0	6	2	1	3

a. What are the planned order releases for part A using lot-for-lot sizing for both parts X and B?

b. What are the planned order releases for part A using POQ = 2 for both parts X and A? (See Appendix 6A for POQ example)

8. A company has estimated net requirements for a particular part as follows:

	MONTH											
	1	2	3	4	5	6	7	8	9	10	11	12
Requirements	50	5	8	10	35	125	125	125	125	20	0	50

Ordering cost associated with this part is $200. Estimated inventory carrying cost is $2.50 per unit per month calculated on average inventory. Currently, no parts are available in inventory. The company wishes to know when and how much to order over the next 12 months.

a. Apply the economic order quantity and the part period balancing procedures to solve this problem. (See Appendix 6A for example of the EOQ and PPB procedures).
b. What important assumptions are involved in each of the approaches used in part a?

9. The Big Country Manufacturing Company is trying to decide which of several lot-sizing procedures to use for its MRP system. The following information pertains to one of its fast-moving component parts:

Setup cost = $75/order.
Inventory cost = $1.25/unit/week
Current inventory balance = 0 units.

	WEEK							
	1	2	3	4	5	6	7	8
Demand forecast	160	138	126	45	200	122	195	100

a. Apply the EOQ (only integer multiples of the EOQ can be ordered), POQ, and PPB lot-sizing procedures and show the total cost resulting from each procedure. Calculate inventory carrying costs on the basis of average inventory values. Assume orders are received into the beginning inventory. (See Appendix 6A for example of the EOQ, POQ and PPB procedures).
b. Indicate advantages and disadvantages of using each procedure suggested in part a.

10. Apply the McLaren's order moment (MOM) lot-sizing procedure to the following 12 periods of requirements data, indicating order receipts' size and period. Assume order costs are $100/order placed and inventory carrying cost is $2.00/unit/period. Calculate the inventory carrying costs on the basis of *ending* inventory values. (See Appendix 6A for an example of the MOM procedure).

	PERIOD											
	1	2	3	4	5	6	7	8	9	10	11	12
Requirements	60	20	25	50	50	15	25	60	35	60	70	45

11. Use the requirements data from Problem 11 and order costs of $75/order, inventory carrying cost of $1.25/unit/period, and a unit cost of $100 in lots of less than 100 and $95 for lots of 100 or more, and inventory carrying costs calculated on the basis of *ending* inventory values to:

a. Apply McLaren's order moment (MOM) lot-sizing procedure (with look-ahead).
b. Apply the least unit cost (LUC) procedure without look-ahead.
(See Appendix 6A for an example of the MOM and LUC procedures).

12. Consider the information below:

Order cost = $50
Inventory carrying cost = $5/unit/week
Item price = $100/unit ($95/unit if orders are issued for 80 units or more).

	WEEK								
	1	2	3	4	5	6	7	8	9
Forecast	82	9	18	90	88	6	50	17	2

Calculate the most economical order quantities using the least unit cost, the least period cost, and the MOM procedures. Find total cost of each solution procedure, assuming inventory carrying cost is based on the average inventory.
(See Appendix 6A for an example of the MOM procedures).

APPENDIX 6A

Illustration of Various MRP Lot-Sizing Models[1]

There has been a significant amount of attention given to the variable-demand order size lot-sizing problem.

Among the better-known lot-sizing methods for the single-item, non discount, time-phased, certain-demand models are (1) lot-for-lot, (2) economic order quantity, (3) periodic order quantity, (4) least unit cost, (5) McLaren's order moment, (6) Silver-Meal, and (7) the Wagner-Whitin dynamic programming algorithm. The procedures of these lot-sizing methods all determine how the period net requirements should be combined into production lots or purchase orders. A description will be given for each lot-sizing method, along with an example problem using the data shown in Figure A.1 below:

1. Lot-for-Lot

The lot-for-lot (LFL) method places an order for each period in which there is a net requirement. Thus, no inventory is carried from period to period. This method is usually used when setup costs are low or inventory carrying costs are high. Figure A.2 shows the lot sizes of the LFL lot-sizing method for the example problem. The resulting lot sizes of the LFL method produce an order in each period in which there is a positive net requirement.

2. EOQ Lot-Sizing Model

The economic order quantity (EOQ) method for determining the quantity to order was first worked out by F. W. Harris. With this method, the quantity ordered will always be greater than or equal to the economic order quantity. The objective of the method is to balance opposing costs (inventory carrying versus ordering). Figure A.3 shows the lot sizes and costs for the example problem.

3. Periodic Order Quantity

The periodic order quantity (POQ) lot-sizing method is based on the economic order quantity (EOQ). As shown in Figure A.4, the EOQ method is insensitive to time-phased demand for the 12 periods of demand. The POQ method is an adjustment to the EOQ method for time-phased demand. The EOQ is converted to the equivalent number of

Figure A.1

Net Requirements for 12 Periods
Order cost = $92
Inventory carrying cost = $0.5/period/unit

Period	1	2	3	4	5	6	7	8	9	10	11	12
Net requirements	80	100	124	50	50	100	125	125	100	100	50	100

[1] Benton, W.C. Purchasing and Supply Chain Management, McGraw-Hill (2013).

Figure A.2 Example of Lot-for-Lot Lot-Sizing Procedure

Required Receipts Schedule

PERIOD	NET REQUIREMENTS	REQUIRED RECEIPTS
1	80	80
2	100	100
3	124	124
4	50	50
5	50	50
6	100	100
7	125	125
8	125	125
9	100	100
10	100	100
11	50	50
12	100	100

Total ordering cost = 12 × 92 (avg. dem) = $1,104
Total inventory carrying cost = 0 ↓ = 0
Total ordering plus inventory cost = $1,104

periods of demand to be included in a lot. The EOQ is calculated and then divided by the average demand. This result is then rounded to the nearest integer value. Figure A.4 shows the lot sizes and costs for the example problem. In the example problem, the POQ method performs better than the EOQ method.

4. Least Unit Cost

The objective of the least unit cost (LUC) lot-sizing method is to determine the economic lot size on the basis of the least unit cost per item. For the LUC procedure, net requirements are accumulated and unit costs are calculated for each period. The calculations are continued until the unit cost increases. The quantity purchased is that quantity that provides the lowest unit cost. Figure A.5 shows the lot sizes and costs for the example problem. In the example problem, an order was coincidently scheduled every two periods.

5. McLaren's Order Moment (MOM)

The McLaren order moment (MOM), in its simplest version, accumulates requirements for consecutive periods into a tentative order until the accumulated part-periods (one unit carried in inventory for one period) reach or exceed a specified part-period target. The MOM method compares the carrying cost incurred by including the requirements above the target with the cost of placing a new order. Either the requirements are

Figure A.3 **Example of the EOQ Lot-Sizing Procedure**

Ordering cost (Cp) = \$92
Inventory carrying cost (CH) = \$5/unit/period
Average demand ($\bar{A}$ = 92/period) EOQ = $\sqrt{2 * \bar{A} * C_p / C_H} = \sqrt{2 * 92 * \$92/.5} = 184$
Required Receipts Schedule

PERIOD	NET REQUIREMENTS	REQUIRED RECEIPTS
1	80	184
2	100	
3	124	184
4	50	
5	50	184
6	100	
7	125	184
8	125	184
9	100	
10	100	184
11	50	
12	100	

Total ordering cost = 6 × \$92 = \$552.00
Total carrying cost = 971 units × 0.5 period = 484.00
Total ordering plus inventory carrying costs = \$1,036.00

included in the current lot or a new lot is started, depending on which cost is less. Figure A.6 shows the lot sizes and costs for this example.

6. Silver-Meal

The Silver-Meal (SM) lot-sizing method is based on minimum cost per period. As shown earlier, the fixed-EOQ approach does not perform well when the demands vary from one period to the next. The SM method selects the order quantity so as to minimize the total relevant costs per unit of time. The basic objective of SM is to evaluate the total cost per period for successive periods until the first time the new period's total cost exceeds the current period's total cost. Figure A.7 shows the lot sizes for the example problem.

7. Wagner-Whitin

Wagner and Whitin (W-W) developed a dynamic programming–based lot-sizing method that explores various alternatives in setting order quantities to minimize total cost over a planning horizon. The WW method guarantees optimal solutions for lot-sizing problems when requirements are known with certainty over a fixed number of

Figure A.4 **Example of Periodic Order Quantity Lot-Sizing Procedure**

EOQ = 184 units
R bar = 92 units/period
Periodic order quantity = EOQ/$\bar{A}$ = 184/92 = 2 periods
Required Receipts Schedule

PERIOD	NET REQUIREMENTS	REQUIRED RECEIPTS
1	80	184
2	100	
3	124	174
4	50	
5	50	150
6	100	
7	125	250
8	125	
9	100	200
10	100	
11	50	150
12	100	

Total ordering cost = 6 × \$92 = \$552.00
Total carrying cost = 575 units × 0.5 period = 287.50
Total ordering plus inventory carrying costs = \$839.50

periods and the carrying cost is non-decreasing over time. The technical description of the procedure is beyond the scope of this chapter, but Figure A.8 shows the resulting lot sizes for the example problem for comparison purposes.

There have been numerous articles and papers written on the comparison of various time-phased lot-sizing methods. Under certain experimental conditions, even the EOQ procedure performed just as well as the optimizing method (the Wagner-Whitin algorithm). The lot-sizing methods in this section have been used extensively in material requirements planning systems. The principles of the EOQ, the least unit cost, and MOM lot-sizing methods have emerged as the most effective managerial approaches to the variable-demand lot-sizing problem.

Figure A.5 Example of Least Unit Cost Lot-Sizing Procedure

PERIOD	NET REQUIREMENT	CUMULATIVE REQUIREMENT	EXCESS INVENTORY	PERIODS CARRIED	CARRYING COST UNIT CUM.	SETUP COST	TOTAL COST	UNIT COST
1	80	80	0	0	0	$92	$ 40,092	$501.15
2	100	180	100	1	50	92	90,142	500.79
3	124	304	124	2	174	92	152,266	500.88
3	124	124	0	0	0	92	62,092	500.74
4	50	174	50	1	25	92	87,117	500.67
5	50	224	50	2	75	92	112,167	500.75
5	50	50	0	0	0	92	25,092	501.84
6	100	150	100	1	50	92	75,142	500.95
7	125	275	125	2	175	92	137,767	500.97
7	125	125	0	0	0	92	63,592	500.74
8	125	250	125	1	67.50	92	125,159	500.64
9	100	350	100	2	167.50	92	175,259	500.74
9	100	100	0	0	0	92	50,092	500.92
10	100	200	100	1	50	92	100,142	500.71
11	50	250	50	2	100	92	125,192	500.77
11	50	50	0	0	0	92	25,092	501.84
12	100	150	100	1	50	92	75,142	500.95

Figure A.5 Example of Least Unit Cost Lot-Sizing Procedure (Continued)

Required Receipts Schedule

PERIOD	NET REQUIREMENTS	REQUIRED RECEIPTS
1	80	180
2	100	
3	124	174
4	50	
5	50	150
6	100	
7	125	250
8	125	
9	100	200
10	100	
11	50	150
12	100	

Total ordering cost = 6 × $92 = $552.00
Total carrying cost = 575 units × 0.5 period = 287.50
Total ordering plus inventory carrying costs = $839.50

Figure A.6 Example of McLaren's Order Moment Lot-Sizing Procedure

Target = Order moment target
EOQ = 184
$\bar{A}$ = Average demand/period = 92/period
TBO = Expected time between orders = EOQ/$\bar{A}$ = 184/92 = 2 periods

$$\text{Target} = \bar{A}\left[\sum_{t=1}^{T^*-1} t + (TBO - T^*)T^*\right]$$

Where T^* is defined as the largest integer less than TBO.
Thus, the target for the example problem is

$$\text{Target} = 92\left[\sum_{t=1}^{T^*-1} 1 + (2 - 1^*)1^*\right] = 184$$

PERIOD	REQUIREMENT	CUMULATIVE REQUIREMENT	PART-PERIODS	CUMULATIVE PART-PERIOD
1	80	80	80 × 0 = 0	0
2	100	→180	100 × 1 = 100	100
3	124	304	124 × 2 = 248+	348
3	124	124	124 × 0 = 0	0
4	50	174	50 × 1 = 50	50
5	50	→224	50 × 2 = 100	150
6	100	324	100 × 3 = 300	450
6	100	100	100 × 0 = 0	0
8	125	→225	125 × 1 = 125	1250
8	125	350	125 × 2 = 250	375
8	125	125	125 × 0 = 0	0
9	100	→225	100 × 1 = 100	100
10	100	325	100 × 2 = 200	300
10	100	100	100 × 0 = 0	0
11	50	→150	50 × 1 = 50	50
12	100	250	100 × 2 = 200	250
12	100	→100	100 × 0 = 0	0

→ indicates the lot size
\+ The 124 units required in period three must be carried for two periods.

Figure A.6 Example of McLaren's Order Moment Lot-Sizing Procedure (Continued)

Required Receipts Schedule

PERIOD	NET REQUIREMENTS	REQUIRED RECEIPTS
1	80	180
2	100	0
3	124	224
4	50	0
5	50	0
6	100	225
7	125	0
8	125	225
9	100	0
10	100	150
11	50	0
12	100	100

Total ordering cost = 6 × $92 = $552.00
Total inventory cost = 525 × 0.5/period = 262.50
Total ordering plus carrying costs = $814.50

Figure A.7 Example of the Silver-Meal Lot-Sizing Procedure

PERIOD	NET REQUIREMENT	CUMULATIVE REQUIREMENT	EXCESS INVENTORY	ORDERING COST	TOTAL COST	COST PER PERIOD
1	80	80	0	$92	$ 40,092	$ 40,092
2	100	180	100	92	90,142	45,071
2	100	100	0	92	90,902	90,092
3	124	224	124	92	112,159	56,079
4	50	274	174	92	137,204	45,736
5	50	324	224	92	162,284	40,571
6	100	424	324	92	212,392	42,478
6	100	100	0	92	50,092	50,092
7	125	225	125	92	112,659	56,329
7	125	125	0	92	62,592	62,592
8	125	250	125	92	125,159	62,579
9	100	350	225	92	175,192	58,397
10	100	450	325	92	225,409	75,136
10	100	100	0	92	50,092	50,092
11	50	150	50	92	75,117	37,558
12	100	250	150	92	125,167	41,722
12	100	100	0	92	50,092	50,092

Figure A.7 **Example of the Silver-Meal Lot-Sizing Procedure (Continued)**

Required Receipts Schedule

PERIOD	NET REQUIREMENTS	REQUIRED RECEIPTS
1	80	80
2	100	0
3	124	324
4	50	0
5	50	0
6	100	0
7	125	100
8	125	350
9	100	0
10	100	0
11	50	150
12	100	100

Total ordering cost = 6 × \$92 = \$552.00
Total inventory cost 749 × 0.5/period = 374.50
Total ordering plus carrying costs = \$926.50

Figure A.8 **Example for the Wagner-Whitin Lot-Sizing Procedure**

Required Receipts Schedule

PERIOD	NET REQUIREMENTS	REQUIRED RECEIPTS
1	80	180
2	100	0
3	124	224
4	50	0
5	50	0
6	100	225
7	125	0
8	125	225
9	100	0
10	100	150
11	50	0
12	100	100

Total ordering cost = 6 × \$92 = \$552.00
Total inventory cost = 525 × 0.5/period = 262.50
Total ordering plus carrying costs = \$814.50

Chapter 7

JUST-IN-TIME/LEAN PRODUCTION

Learning Objectives

- Explore the historical evolution of the just-in-time (JIT) philosophy
- Understand the just-in-time production framework
- Identify the relationship between purchasing and supplier relationship management
- Understand the role of culture in the implementation process
- Learn how to implement a successful production system
- Evaluate the results from an actual JIT implementation
- Understand overall financial implications of an actual JIT implementation

Introduction

In its simplest form, the manufacturing process is a collection of the material flows. Just-in-time (JIT) manufacturing is designed to manage the flow of materials, components, tools, and associated information. JIT production is based on planned elimination of all waste and on continuous improvement. JIT is also referred to as *lean production.* An organization driven by a JIT philosophy can improve profitability by reducing inventory levels, reducing variability, improving product quality, reducing production and delivery lead times, and reducing setup costs. With JIT, the entire manufacturing system from purchasing to shop floor management can be measured and controlled. Therefore, the JIT system is a powerful management tool that could easily determine the success or failure of the manufacturing system.

JIT applies primarily to repetitive manufacturing processes in which the same products and components are produced over and over again. The general idea is to establish flow processes (even when the facility uses a job-shop or batch-process layout) by linking work centers so that there is an even, balanced flow of materials throughout the entire production process, similar to that found in an assembly line. To accomplish this, an attempt is made to drive all inventory buffers toward zero and achieving the ideal lot size of one unit.

For more than three decades, JIT and MRP production systems have followed two independent research streams. As the popularity of JIT, motivated by the success of Japanese manufacturing firms has grown, numerous global practitioners have initiated complete changeovers from the traditional MRP based methods to JIT methods. For instance, Harley-Davidson and Hewlett-Packard are two of the most popular American examples of JIT success testimonials.

There rarely exists a pure JIT production system in practice. Even at Toyota, the inventor of the JIT system, production smoothing is planned by the master production schedule (MPS), and the material requirement plan is executed based on the MPS using bill of materials (BOM). This type of manufacturing planning has been adopted by most automobile manufacturers. The integration between MRP and JIT in literature reflects the trend toward a more realistic hybrid manufacturing environment.

The current shift toward the so-called "lean thinking" manufacturing environment is one of the major motivations for future JIT research. There is also a strong need to organize the previous JIT studies and provide directions for innovative JIT implementations and research focus. The conceptual framework for JIT is shown in Figure 1.

Conceptual Framework for JIT Production

The following practices are considered essential for a comprehensive JIT implementation.

1. *Uniform production* (also known as ***heijunka***) Create a uniform load on each workstation through constant daily production and producing the same mix of products each day, using a repeating sequence. Meet demand fluctuations through end-item inventory rather than through fluctuations in production level. The use of a stable production schedule also permits the use of ***backflushing*** to manage inventory: an end item's bill of materials is periodically exploded to calculate the usage quantities of the various

Figure 1 Conceptual Framework for JIT

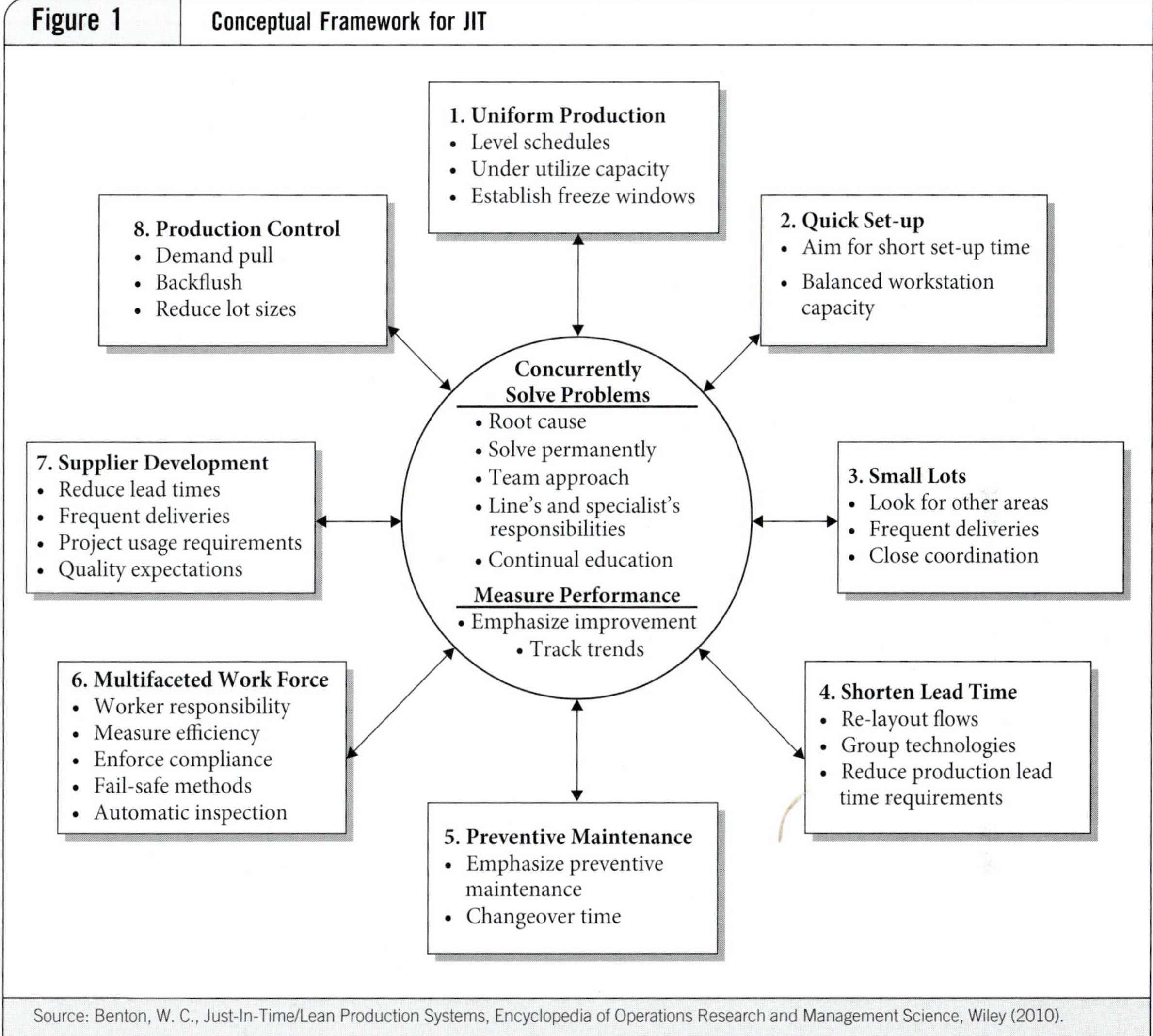

Source: Benton, W. C., Just-In-Time/Lean Production Systems, Encyclopedia of Operations Research and Management Science, Wiley (2010).

components that were used to make the item, eliminating the need to collect detailed usage information on the shop floor.

2. *Quick setup times* This can be done through better planning, process redesign, and product redesign. A good example of the potential for improved setup times can be found in the airline industry, where Southwest Airlines can turn around 30 full-capacity flights per day between Dallas and Houston whereas American Airlines can turn around only 4 half full flights per day between Dallas and San Franscisco. Southwest's efficiency is the result of a team effort using the correct aircraft (container) size and a coordinated, well-rehearsed process.

3. *Small lot sizes* Reducing setup times allows economical production of smaller lots; close cooperation with suppliers is necessary to achieve reductions in order lot sizes for purchased raw materials and component parts, since this will require more frequent deliveries.

4. *Short lead times* Production lead times can be reduced by moving workstations closer together, applying group technology and cellular manufacturing concepts,

reducing queue length, and improving the coordination and cooperation between downstream processes. Delivery lead times can be reduced through close cooperation with supplying organizations, possibly by inducing suppliers to locate closer to the factory.

5. *Preventive maintenance* Use machine and worker idle time to maintain equipment and prevent breakdowns.

6. *Multifaceted work force* Workers should be trained to operate several machines, to perform maintenance tasks, and to perform quality inspections. In general, JIT requires teams of competent, empowered employees who take responsibility for their own work.

7. *Supplier development* All defective items must be eliminated, since there are no buffers of excess parts. A *quality-at-the-source* (***judoka***) program must be implemented to give workers the personal responsibility for the quality of the work they do and the authority to stop production when something goes wrong. Techniques such as JIT lights (to indicate line slowdowns or stoppages) and tally boards (to record and analyze causes of production stoppages and slowdowns to facilitate correcting them later) may be used.

8. *Kanban production control* Use a control system such as a ***kanban*** (card) pull system (or other signaling system) to convey parts between workstations in small quantities (ideally, one unit at a time). In a larger sense, JIT is *not* the same as a kanban system, and a kanban system is not required to implement JIT (some companies have instituted a JIT program along with an MRP system), although JIT is required to implement a kanban system, and the two concepts are frequently equated with one another.

Finally, the ultimate goals of JIT are to solve problems concurrently and measure performance in a continuous way. See the inner circle in Figure 1.

This chapter proceeds in the following order: First, the JIT production system is discussed. Then, the kanban production control system will be presented. Third, the JIT purchasing framework will be evaluated. Next, the role of culture will be discussed. Finally, a critical implementation analysis of the JIT philosophy will be conducted.

Lean Production System

The eight types of waste are shown in Figure 2. The primary objective of lean manufacturing systems is to eliminate these eight types of waste. The elimination of waste is referred to as *muda*. The second objective of a lean manufacturing system is to continuously improve the value of the products and services.

Focusing on specific areas that need improvement, continuous improvement in quality and productivity can be expected. This is referred to as *kaizen*. A work element can be defined as the smallest increment of work that could be moved to another person. Work should always be broken down into work elements. This helps us to identify and eliminate waste that is otherwise hidden within the total operator cycle. When determining the work elements, obvious wastes should never be included as a work elements. This is called paper kaizen because waste is eliminated, by design, from the process before the process is implemented. There is usually a significant amount of

Figure 2 Eight Types of Manufacturing Waste

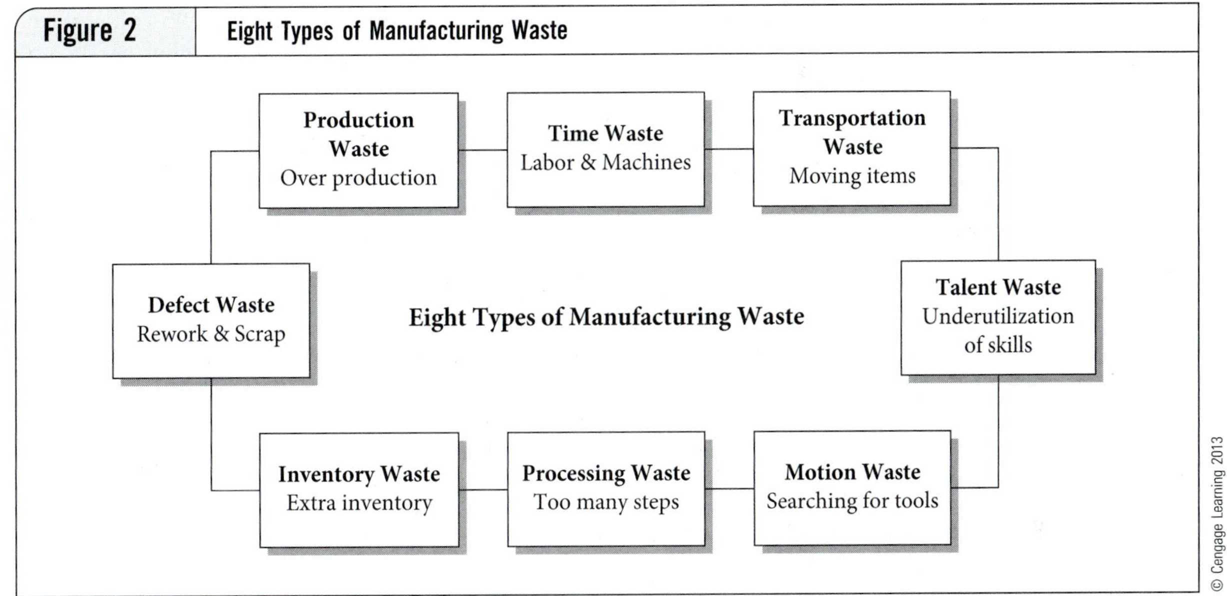

waste that can be eliminated at the paper kaizen stage. The paper kaizen guidelines are given below:

1. *Do not include any walking as a work element.* The actual amount of walking is unknown at this stage in the process.
2. *Do not include any out-of-cycle work for operators as work elements.* Out-of-cycle work destroys continuous flow. Out-of-cycle work should be accomplished by material handlers, support staff, and others outside of the continuous flow process. However, during the refinement stage, some out-of-cycle work could become in-cycle work within the continuous process.
3. *Do not include operators waiting for machines to cycle as a work element.* Waiting for a machine represents operator waste. On the other hand, a machine is sitting idle after a cycle. In most cases, machine idle time does not affect continuous flow.
4. Do not include time for removing finished parts from machines wherever you believe automation could be used to remove the finished parts. Stopping to remove finished parts from a machine is a source of wasted time.

Value-stream mapping (VSM) is a lean tool used to eliminate waste. VSM creates a visual map of every work element involved in the flows throughout the supply chain. The value stream map consists of the current state, the future state, and an implementation plan. The value stream map is usually the first step in the kaizen process.

JIT is Toyota's manufacturing philosophy to minimizing waste, and the JIT production system is a subsystem controlled by kanban. The kanban-controlled JIT production system is based on the premise of minimizing work-in-process inventories (waste) by reducing or eliminating discrete batches. The reduced lot sizes not only contribute to production efficiency and product quality but also reduce the overall costs associated with production in the JIT manufacturing environment. This proposition holds true only when certain conditions are sustained. According to Monden (1983), the success of Toyota's kanban-controlled production system is supported by smoothing of production, standardization of jobs, reduction of setup times, improvement of activities, design of machine layout, and automation of processes (automation with human touch). In fact, the JIT production system appears most suitable for repetitive manufacturing environments.

Improvements in the kanban-controlled production systems have followed a pragmatic approach—"continuous improvement." Therefore, success of the JIT production system must be explained in conjunction with continuous improvement. Experience and commitment of the workers on the shop floor to continue to improve performance and methods are the major drivers of the JIT production system. A host of cases and evidence from the literature indicate that JIT success has been achieved not by the predetermined scheduling technique but also by the aggressive continuous improvement effort.

The JIT production system is not a panacea. As with the MRP system, there are also operational problems with the JIT system. In fact, there is a list of reasons why the Toyota manufacturing system may not work for all firms. The reasons include cultural differences, geographical dispersion of suppliers, supplier power, different management styles, and so on.

The Toyota manufacturing system has been viewed in different ways by a variety of researchers. The JIT production system is often called the lean production system because it uses less of every resource compared with the conventional mass production system (Womack et al., 1990). On the other hand, the JIT system is viewed as a conventional reorder-point system with extremely small lot sizes (Zipkin, 1991). The most common standpoint in understanding the JIT production system is that JIT production is a pull system as opposed to the conventional push system (see Chapters 6 & 8). In the MRP/JIT comparison or integration literature, the pull nature of JIT production systems has been discussed extensively. Thus, it is only natural to portray the push/pull debates in conjunction with the MRP/JIT studies. JIT production requires significant involvement between Tier 1 suppliers and the buying organization. JIT purchasing is discussed in the following section.

JIT Purchasing

The function of purchasing is to provide a firm with component parts and raw materials. Purchasing also must ensure that high-quality products are provided on time at a reasonable price. A comparison of critical elements associated with JIT purchasing and traditional purchasing approaches follows.

1. *Reduced order quantities.* One of the most crucial elements of the just-in-time system is small lot sizes. Traditionally, long and infrequent production runs were considered beneficial for the overall productivity of a manufacturing organization. However, long production runs sometimes lead to high levels of raw-material and finished-goods inventories. Large setup times have been the primary motivating factor for longer production runs. The just-in-time concept reduces setup times and the associated costs by introducing clever changeover techniques and simpler product designs. This permits more frequent production runs and smaller lot sizes. In turn, the JIT purchasing function becomes responsible for

Figure 3 Reduction in Order Costs Using the JIT Approach

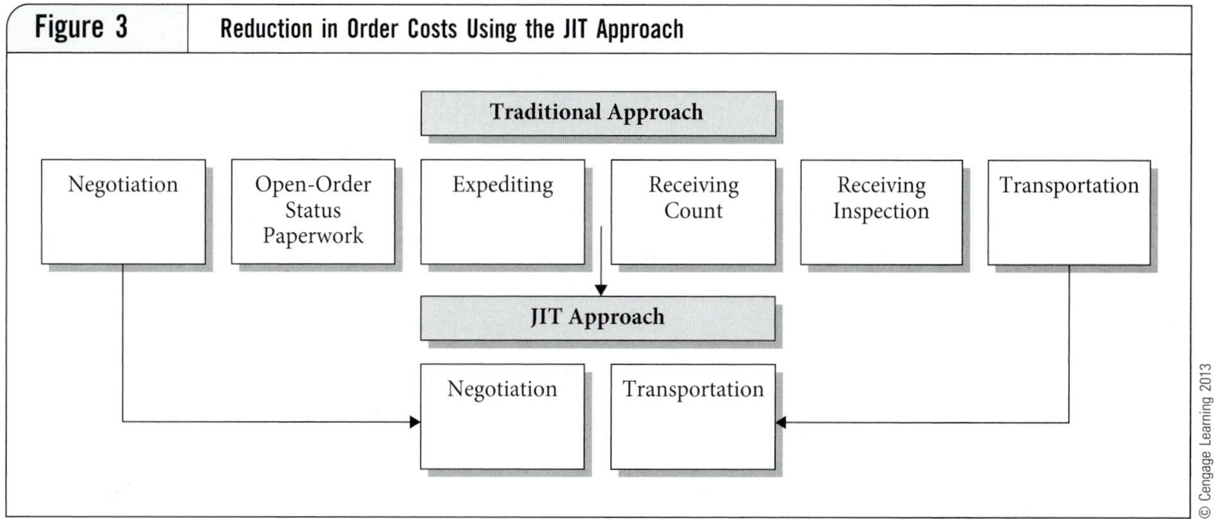

more frequent but smaller orders compared to the traditional case. Under the traditional manufacturing system, suppliers, on average, ship enough materials to cover two months of production. Since adopting JIT, the lot size has been trimmed to less than three weeks. If frequent purchase orders are to be a viable option, traditional inventory theory suggests that order costs be minimal for JIT purchasing to be cost effective. Indeed, the JIT philosophy strives to drive the ordering costs down to a bare minimum. A breakdown of the ordering costs associated with conventional purchasing practices is shown in Figure 3. Under the JIT purchasing approach, the relationship between the supplier and buyer allows the ordering costs to be reduced to simplify the negotiation and transportation costs.

All the intermediate costs are expected to be eliminated once the supplier meets the requirements of a Class A supplier (strategic supplier). A substantial decrease in the ordering costs permits a greater number of orders to be placed over shorter intervals.

2. *Frequent and "on-time" delivery schedules.* Supplier performance can be measured more accurately under the JIT purchasing approach compared to the traditional one. In order to obtain small lot sizes for production, the order quantity size needs to be reduced and corresponding delivery schedules need to be made more frequently. The on-time windows have been decreasing systematically over the years. In the pre-JIT days, "on time" meant anything arriving up to 12 days ahead of the nominal schedule, and as late as 6 days. On average, today's JIT buyers set the window at five days early and two days late. Yet the surprising fact is that on-time deliveries increased from 62 percent to 79 percent in spite of the 11-day reduction in delivery window time.
3. *Reduced lead times.* To be able to maintain low inventory levels, it is critical that replenishment lead times be as short as possible. The JIT philosophy inherently attempts to reduce lead times for order completions. Under traditional purchasing practices, the lead time is made up of the following components: paperwork lead time, manufacturing time for supplier, transportation lead time, and time

Figure 4 Reduction in Lead Time Using the JIT Approach

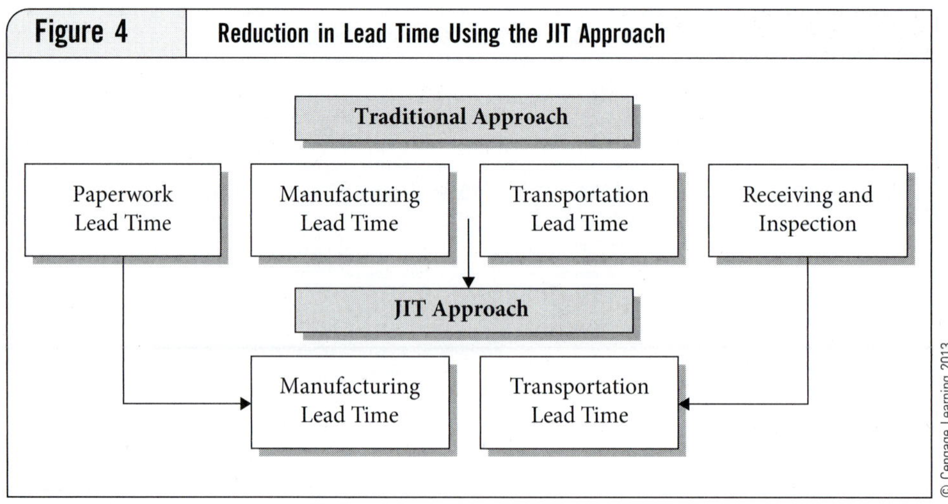

spent on receiving and inspection. A comparison between the JIT approach to lead time and the traditional approach is shown in Figure 4.

Under the JIT system, suppliers are usually associated with the company on a long-term basis. Consequently, it is possible for them to reduce paperwork significantly. Also, the supplier may be able to reduce the manufacturing time because of the guaranteed volumes. As a result of building quality into the products, the receiving and inspection time spent by the buyer usually decreases. Replenishment lead times also may be reduced by locating a supplier close to the buying firm's plant.

4. *High quality of incoming materials.* Japanese manufacturers attempt to reduce incoming material inspection as much as possible. In order to eliminate the associated receiving-inspection costs, a very high emphasis is placed on the quality of incoming materials under the JIT system.

   Xerox provides a good example of the unnecessary resources spent on the incoming inspection of goods in its pre-JIT days. All deliveries from suppliers had to pass through Xerox's Webster plant in upstate New York before they could be redirected to the appropriate plants around the United States.

   In some instances, component parts from West Coast suppliers were first shipped to the East Coast for inspection and shipped back to the West Coast manufacturing plants. The JIT approach favors material inspection at the suppliers' plant. Motivation for the suppliers to furnish high-quality materials is cultivated by long-term agreements and strategic relationships between buyers and suppliers. JIT purchasing, therefore, plays a very critical role in improving product quality at the manufacturing source.

5. *Reliable suppliers.* Since the JIT system does not provide for buffer stocks, unreliable supply, in terms of delivery time and quality of incoming material, may lead to frequent problems in production. Consequently, reliability of supply is a critical consideration in the selection of JIT suppliers. Since JIT purchasing has gained popularity within the United States, the purchasing function has been preoccupied with reducing the overall supplier base in quest of so-called superior suppliers. Xerox, for example, reduced its supplier base by nearly 4,700 over a

Table 1 **Comparison between Traditional and Just-in-Time (Lean) Purchasing Approaches**

	TRADITIONAL PURCHASING	JIT PURCHASING
Order quantities	Based on trade-offs between ordering and carrying costs	Based on small lot sizes for production
Delivery schedules	Infrequent, primarily because of high ordering costs involved	Frequent because of small lot sizes and low ordering costs
Delivery windows	Relatively wide	Very narrow
Delivery lead times	Relatively long and relaxed	Stringent and reduced significantly
Parts quality	Responsibility of the quality function in the buying organization	Responsibility of supplier
Supplier base	Fairly broad	Considerably smaller

period of one year.[1] Ford has reduced its supplier base by nearly 40 percent since 1980. The number of superior suppliers is on the rise as JIT promotes the concept of fewer but better suppliers.

A brief summary of the comparison between the traditional and just-in-time purchasing approaches is shown in Table 1. JIT purchasing systems are much more difficult to manage. In a typical JIT manufacturing environment, excess inventory and other waste have been eliminated. Thus, managerial competency is a requirement for success. If JIT purchasing systems are not properly implemented and managed, the synergies will be lost and the system will collapse. However, significant advantages are realized if these elements are implemented successfully.

JIT Supply Management Benefits

Implementation of just-in-time purchasing assists the purchasing function in its major objectives of improving quality of incoming materials and supplier delivery performance, along with reducing lead times and cost of materials. Some of the critical JIT purchasing advantages for the manufacturer are discussed below.

1. *Reduced inventory levels.* JIT purchasing facilitates the reduction in inventory levels and the associated inventory holding costs. Asian firms like Toyota have been able to reduce inventory levels to such an extent that their inventory turnover ratios have gone up to more than 60 times per year, compared to corresponding ratios of 5 to 8 times per year reported by most American manufacturers. U.S. manufacturers have been trying to reduce inventory levels by using JIT purchasing techniques. NCR's Ithaca, New York, plant, for instance, has been successful in reducing its number of days of inventory from 110 to 21 within three years of implementing JIT. However, a strong debate exists as to whether manufacturers shift the burden of inventories to suppliers using the guise of just-in-time. This issue will be addressed later. Reduced inventory levels is indeed one of the benefits of the JIT system, which basically stresses continuous improvement and elimination of waste.

[1]Anthony R. Inman, "Time-Based Competition: Challenges for Industrial Purchasing," *Industrial Management* 34, no. 2 (March–April 1992): 31–32.

2. *Improved lead-time reliability.* Compared to traditional manufacturing approaches, delivery lead times under the JIT system are considerably shorter. Lead-time reliability is usually much better for just-in-time systems. This implies higher levels of customer service and lower safety stock requirements for the company. Lower levels of safety stock contribute significantly to reduced working capital requirements for the firm.
3. *Scheduling flexibility.* JIT emphasizes scheduling flexibility by reducing purchasing lead times and setup times. Such flexibility prevents confusion in the manufacturing plant and offers unique competitive advantages to manufacturing firms, since they are capable of adapting to changes in the environment more quickly.
4. *Improved quality and customer satisfaction.* JIT manufacturing results in improved quality and corresponding levels of higher customer satisfaction. Since high-quality products are critical in achieving a competitive advantage in today's global business world, manufacturers gain immensely by implementing the JIT production control system. High-quality incoming materials result in savings associated with reduced rework and scrap.
5. *Reduced costs of parts.* As cooperation and relationships between suppliers and manufacturers build up in a JIT system, so do the opportunities to conduct an extensive value analysis and to focus on reducing the cost of parts purchased. A comprehensive JIT progress report indicates that supplier costs were reduced by 11 percent when they adopted the JIT system in cooperation with their customers. Long-term commitments on the part of the manufacturer allow volume purchases, development of supplier learning curves, and overall productivity increases.[2]
6. *Constructive synergies with suppliers.* A just-in-time purchasing program involves close technical cooperation with suppliers. This particularly means cooperation between manufacturing and design engineers. Because of smaller lot sizes and frequent delivery schedules, suppliers are in a position to receive quick feedback regarding any potential manufacturing or design problems. Also, manufacturing is in a position to implement engineering changes more quickly because of the reduced inventory levels. The JIT progress report mentioned above indicates that supplier quality improved by 26 percent since the JIT system was adopted.

It is well documented that JIT reduces the physical inventory level. Reductions in physical inventory will also have a favorable impact on:

- Reduced insurance premiums associated with storage of inventory
- Reduced inventory holding costs
- Reduced labor cost in stock rooms and material handling costs
- Reduced clerical and administrative costs
- Reduced waste from the manufacturing process
- Reduced obsolescence costs
- Reduced depreciation of handling and storage equipment

Each of the cost savings will result in a leaner, more profitable operation.

[2] Ibid.

The Role of Culture

A crucial issue to be considered is the relevance of culture in the successful implementation of the just-in-time system in a country. Honda's culture and its focus on group-oriented activities are particularly suitable to the implementation of the just-in-time production control system. The need to have harmony in organizations provides for better manufacturer–supplier relationships at Toyota and Honda. Moreover, long-term relationships between a supplier and a manufacturer are the norm of doing business in Japan. Severance of a business relationship between manufacturer and supplier has a strong stigma associated with it, which both manufacturers and suppliers try to avoid as much as possible.

Within the United States, however, such relationships between manufacturers and suppliers are a little more difficult to cultivate. Traditionally, the business firms in the United States are so short-term that they primarily have their immediate interests in mind. Moreover, the level of employee and supplier commitment to the JIT concept is not as uniform and high as it is in Japan. This does not mean that JIT is not a viable concept in the United States. It is not advisable, however, for U.S. firms to blindly emulate the Japanese JIT approach. In fact, U.S. firms should try and tailor JIT to their needs and circumstances. Some firms in the United States have developed and implemented their own version of JIT under different names, such as Lean, ZIPS (zero inventory production systems), MAN (material-as-needed), and nick of time. A case study on JIT indicates how Hutchinson Technology (a publicly held company that manufactures a variety of products for computer peripheral and military markets) organized and implemented JIT manufacturing.[3] The major difficulties encountered in the process included the inability of purchasing personnel to make the immense cultural transformation and the lack of resources to effect the change properly. Despite these difficulties, their JIT purchasing program has been successful. Greater geographic separation between supplier and manufacturer in the United States is also a major impediment to the implementation process, according to one survey.[4] The survey also indicates that JIT does not imply single sourcing in the United States as it does in Japan. This reflects the reality of the marketplace in the United States and efforts of manufacturers to adjust to JIT it as best they can.

Critical Analysis of the JIT Concept

Most of the testimonials published on JIT systems exalt the simplicity inherent in the system processes and procedures. However, the key issue for a firm in the United States is whether it is simple to implement JIT in an existing manufacturing environment. Does JIT really provide the solution to most manufacturing problems in the United States? It is also worth investigating whether traditional purchasing approaches have been outdated in light of just-in-time production.

JIT came under intense scrutiny when Japanese manufacturers stormed into the U.S. markets and took away a substantial share from the U.S. automobile industry. Subsequent investigations revealed, much to the relief of U.S. manufacturers, that it was not only the work culture in Japan that provided the Japanese an edge, but also the JIT

[3]Steven Ray, "Just-in-Time Purchasing—A Case Study," *Hospital Management Quarterly* 12, no. 1(August 1990): 7–12.

[4]James R. Freeland, "A Survey of Just-in-Time Purchasing Practices in the United States," *Production and Inventory Management* 32, no. 2(1991): 43–50.

approach to manufacturing management. Many U.S. manufacturers have been in strong pursuit of this manufacturing revolution and manufacturing excellence that JIT was portrayed to bring. Several manufacturing firms that adopted the JIT approach early include General Motors, Hewlett Packard, Ford, and Xerox. Unfortunately, the excitement about the radically new manufacturing approach, coupled with the romantic version of JIT put forward by many, lulled quite a few manufacturers into believing that JIT would bring instantaneous results for their companies. Too many companies turned to JIT looking for a relatively painless financial surgery that would yield substantial short-term benefits. Over the years, these companies have come to realize the tremendous effort and commitment required to make a JIT system run smoothly.

The radical proponents of JIT manufacturing in the United States during the past three decades, the so-called JIT revolutionaries, are to some extent responsible for this initial misunderstanding. The practitioners painted an extremely romantic picture of JIT emphasizing simplicity and efficiency, along with a state of affairs in which employee morale would be high and relations between buyers and suppliers would be completely harmonious. They also called for immediate action and changeover to JIT without really considering the possible ramifications of implementation in the United States. Nor did they convey the message that driving obstacles and impediments out of the system would take serious and substantial effort, commitment, and time.

The pragmatic version of JIT put forth by Japanese authors focuses on the details of the production process. Here, the emphasis is on identifying impediments to the smooth flow of materials and innovative techniques to overcome those problems. The Japanese perspective clearly stresses the need for careful and slow implementation following thorough preparation. It takes time to change attitudes of the workforce and nurture long-term relationships with suppliers.

The transition to JIT has not necessarily been a smooth one for many companies in the United States. But this does not imply that switching from a pure MRP system to a JIT or hybrid system was a mistake for most companies. There are two serious drawbacks with the MRP production control system. First, the master production schedule that drives MRP is based on *estimated* customer requirements; and second, MRP's production control system utilizes a push system for manufacturing goods. That is, the purchasing function places orders for materials in large lot sizes even though the material may not actually be required, and one workstation pushes materials to the next regardless of actual production requirements. Changes in demand estimates or forecasts may allow inventory to pile up in the plant. Very frequent adjustments to the master production schedule make the production system extremely nervous and place enormous pressures on purchasing. However, it must be admitted that MRP is an elegant technique for exploding materials requirements for production. This system has increasingly become easier to implement with the advent of sophisticated computing technology. It is not surprising to find some Western manufacturers who still utilize MRP for ordering purchased materials but require that delivery schedules be based on the kanban system and lean concepts. See chapters 4, 6 and 8 for a comprehensive discussion.

Another critical issue for JIT manufacturers is the variability in product demand. The JIT system seems to work best when its smooth production and low inventory requirements are aimed at meeting a relatively stable product demand. However, demand patterns are not stable for all products. In order to induce a relatively stable demand, companies using JIT manufacturing often consolidate their product lines. They emphasize high quality and low cost of the product, but not variety and availability. This suggests that not all marketing strategies are compatible with the JIT system. Also see chapter 5.

Does this mean that JIT, as a concept, is not particularly suited to manufacturers in the United States? No, the basic concept is as applicable in the United States as it is in Japan. The JIT system does yield substantial benefits where it has been implemented properly. Undoubtedly, proper implementation of JIT is the key to its success. We have seen the advantages JIT offers to a firm from a purchasing point of view. There are significant benefits to other functional areas as well. However, it should be realized that JIT is not a panacea for all manufacturing problems and scenarios. A comprehensive study by Krajewski and colleagues (1987) revealed that selection of a production or inventory system can be of less importance than the improvement in the manufacturing environment itself.[5] Keeping this in mind, manufacturers in the United States should evaluate the potential benefits of a JIT system from their own perspective, not from that of the romantic visionaries. A brief comparison of the JIT manufacturing planning and control (MP&C) Philosophy with the traditional MP&C approach is shown in Table 2.

The financial statement implications of successful JIT implementation are significantly more than a reduction in inventory and quality improvement. With regard to expected savings, there will be an initial increase in operating costs. Once the JIT system is embedded in the manufacturing culture, the consequences of improved productivity, cost reduction, and effective production rate will more than likely increase the profit growth margin. With respect to asset balances, there is likely to be a positive impact on cash, accounts receivables, and plant assets. With respect to liability and equity accounts, increases can be predicted in accounts payable, taxes payable, long-term debt, and retained earnings.

Table 2 Brief Comparison of the JIT Manufacturing Planning and Control (MP&C) Philosophy with the Traditional MP&C Approach

CATEGORY	TRADITIONAL MP&C APPROACH	JIT MP&C PHILOSOPHY
Inventory	An asset	A liability
Lot size	Select lot sizes based on economic order quantity or based on the master production schedule	Minimize inventory order quantity
Set-up	Set-up and change over time are important	Classified as waste
Queues	Necessary investment	Eliminate them
Suppliers	Adversaries	Partners
Quality	Tolerate some scrap	Zero defects
Equipment maintenance	As required, but not critical because we have queues available	Must perform scheduled maintenance; eliminate machine breakdowns
Lead times	The longer the better	Keep them short
Worker involvement	Minimum involvement by workers	Top management and worker involvement important for success

[5] L. Krajewski, B. E. King, R. P. Ritzman, and D. S. Wong, "Kanban, MRP, and Shaping the Manufacturing Environment," *Management Science* 33(1987): 39–57.

JIT Implementation

JIT is much more than a set of techniques or procedures. Techniques such as waste reduction, continuous improvement, and set-up reduction are important, but the passion for JIT must be used to drive a successful JIT implementation. JIT implementation requires total commitment to change. The entire culture of the organization must change. Kotter's eight steps of change is an excellent method for facilitating organizational change. The eight steps leading to successful change are[6]:

1. *Create a sense of urgency:* Winners first make sure that a sufficient number of people feel a true sense of urgency to look for an organization's critical opportunities and hazards now.
2. *Put together the guiding team:* With a strong sense of urgency, people quickly identify critical issues and form teams that are strong enough and that have enough commitment to guide an ambitious charge initiative, even though the team members may already be overworked.
3. *Develop the change visions and strategy:* Strong and highly committed teams orchestrate the effort to find smart visions and strategies for dealing with a key issue even when the best strategies are elusive.
4. *Communicate for understanding and buy-in:* High-urgency teams inherently feel a need to relentlessly communicate the visions and strategies to relevant people to obtain buy-in and generate still more urgency in their organizations.
5. *Empower others to act:* Those with a true sense of urgency empower others who are committed to making any vision a reality by removing obstacles in their paths.
6. *Produce short-term wins:* High-urgency teams guide empowered people to achieve visible, unambiguous short-term wins that silence critics and disarm cynics.
7. *Don't let up:* After initial successes, groups with a true sense of urgency refuse to let their organizations slide back into comfortable complacency.
8. *Create a new culture:* High-urgency organizations feel compelled to find ways to make sure any change sticks by institutionalizing it into the structure, systems, and, most of all, culture.

Elements of JIT Manufacturing and Control

1. The passion for operational efficiency
2. Elimination of waste
3. Continuous improvement
4. World-class customer service
5. Set-up time reduction
6. Treating people as valuable assets
7. Designing quality into culture
8. World-class supply chain partnerships
9. A well-conceived plant and equipment strategy
10. A lean manufacturing strategy
11. A level production strategy

[6]Kotter, J. P. "A sense of urgency". Harvard Business Press, August 5, 2008.

12. A well-designed scheduling and sequencing strategy
13. An innovative purchasing strategy

Steps in Implementing JIT Production

1. Complete commitment from top management is needed.
2. Involve the work force.
3. Reduce set-up time.
4. Implement level production.
5. Reduce lot sizes throughout the production process.
6. Make capacity adjustments in each department.
7. Remove WIP inventories from the storage room to the production floor.
8. Extend JIT philosophy to suppliers.
9. Assist suppliers with quality assurance.
10. Negotiate long-term supplier contracts.
11. Remove purchased inventory from store-room and place it on the shop floor.

JIT Implementation Example (The Valencia Facility)

Ford has become a leader in the automobile industry. Ford avoided bankruptcy during the 2008 economic downturn. The Ford case represents a significant JIT implementation testimonial. In 2003, Ford experienced a 50% reduction in production efficiency. Ford found that the initial bottleneck was caused by material handling, assembly time and inbound logistics. The materials were handled too many times which led to significant quality problems. In 2004 Ford implemented JIT at its Valencia Facility.

Ford is currently achieving the highest efficiency in the car manufacturing industry. In 2012, Ford posted its highest level of profitability in its almost 100 year existence. The Valencia plant case has become the standard and is being implemented in Ford plants throughout the world. The tangible benefits from the JIT implementation include a significant reduction in logistics costs savings, significant waste reduction, a lean integrated manufacturing process and improved product quality. JIT has also resulted in improved customer satisfaction.

SUMMARY

The JIT philosophy has changed the way manufacturing is conducted throughout the world. JIT applies primarily to *repetitive manufacturing* processes in which the same products and components are produced over and over again. JIT is driven by a philosophy of eliminating waste and continuous improvement. Waste results from any activity that adds cost without adding value, such as the unnecessary movement of materials, the accumulation of excess inventory, or the use of faulty production methods that create products requiring subsequent rework. JIT improves profits and return on investment by reducing inventory levels, reducing variability, improving product quality, reducing production and delivery lead times, and reducing other costs. In a JIT system, under-utilized (excess) capacity is used instead of buffer inventories to hedge against problems that may arise. Perhaps one of the most important realizations of JIT is the fact that high quality supply chain relationships have become an important consideration for the manufacturing planning and control function, wherein they should be viewed as partners and not adversaries.

DISCUSSION QUESTIONS AND EXERCISES

1. Describe the conceptual framework for JIT implementation.
2. Compare the JIT manufacturing philosophy with traditional manufacturing.
3. Discuss the eight types of waste. Based on your experiences, give a specific example of each type.
4. What is value stream mapping? How is it related to JIT and lean manufacturing?
5. How is muda related to kaizen? How did JIT evolve into continuous improvement?
6. What are the differences between push, pull and hybrid systems?
7. How are the kanban system and the reorder-point system similar? How are they different?
8. What are the advantages of small lots?
9. How are suppliers affected by JIT?
10. How does JIT purchasing differ from traditional purchasing? Be specific.
11. You are currently working for a fishing rod manufacturer that has two departments (fabrication and assembly). There are 50 different end items that have 80 percent commonality. The company uses a reorder-point system. The demand is seasonal. Each year there are many stockouts and high levels of inventories (raw materials, work in process, and finished goods). Your manager has requested an analysis of this dilemma. Based on your knowledge of push and pull production systems, write a two-page memo to your manager.
12. Develop an implementation strategy for the problem given in Problem 11.

REFERENCES

Benton, W. C., Just-In-Time/Lean Production Systems, Encyclopedia of Operations Research and Management Science, Wiley (2010).

Kotter, J. P. "A sense of urgency." *Harvard Business Press*, August, 5, 2008.

Krajewski, L., B. E. King, R. P. Ritzman, and D. S. Wong. "Kanban, MRP, and Shaping the Manufacturing Environment." *Management Science* 33(1987): 39–57.

Monden, Y. Toyota Production System, 2nd ed. Institute of Industrial Engineers, 1993.

Ray, S. "Just-in-Time Purchasing—A Case Study." *Hospital Management Quarterly* 12, no. 1 (August 1990): 7–12.

Womack, J. P., Jones, D. T., Roos, D. *The Machine That Changed the World: The Story of Lean Production.* Harper Perennial, 1990.

Zipkin, P. H. "Does Manufacturing Need a JIT Revolution?" *Harvard Business Review* (January–February 1991): 40–45.

Chapter 8

PUSH AND PULL PRODUCTION SYSTEMS

Learning Objectives

- Explore the relevant manufacturing/customer service questions
- Understand the push and pull production systems
- Understand the relationship between total quality management and the push and pull production systems
- Understand how the kanban system works
- Understand how to determine the number of kanbans (containers) required
- Compare the advantages and disadvantages of the push and pull production control systems

Introduction

In any manufacturing environment, it is important to be proactive instead of reactive. The manufacturing organization must make adjustments to the manufacturing operation in order to provide unmatched world-class customer service. In today's competitive environment, customers may refuse to adjust to the manufacturer's production schedule. At the same time, it is important for the manufacturing operation to have a passion for efficiency. Waste must be eliminated. Waste can be defined as excessive work in process, expediting, firefighting, backlogs behind every work center, past-due manufacturing schedules, backorders, missed and past-due customer orders, and other inefficiencies. The solution to the day-to-day manufacturing planning and control problem consists of the following manufacturing-/customer-focused questions:

- Which unit of production should be made next?
- When should the next unit of production be made?
- How many specific units of production should be made?
- Where should the units of production be made?
- How should the units of production be built?

1. The solution to the first question focuses on scheduling and sequencing. Scheduling issues are complicated, but the solution methodologies are well defined.
2. When should the next unit of production be made? The appropriate response to this question can be determined by one of two dispatching rules:
   a. Push rule—Make the next unit of production immediately after making the last item.
   b. Pull rule—Make the next unit of production only when authorized by the downstream (internal customer) work center.
3. The solution to the third question is determined by the lot size, order quantity, and replenishment quantity that matches the customer needs with the manufacturing capability. The objective should be to make the exact quantity the customer needs, not more or less.
4. The solution to the fourth question is based on the specific line or work center at which the product is to be run productively and cost effectively.
5. The solution to the fifth question is having high-quality and on-time documentation (bills of material, drawings, specifications, procedures, routings/processes/sequence of events, method sheets, etc.).

The focus of this chapter is on Question 2: When should the next unit be processed—push vs. pull? There have been many discussions about the advantages and disadvantages of push and pull production methods. Some companies feel the push rule has the following *advantages*: It leads to high equipment utilization and the absorption of overhead cost. The *disadvantages* are that the downstream work center may not want, have a need for, or have a place to store the items that were pushed to them, which results in increased work-in-process inventory and critical value-added resources being wasted on inventory that is sitting in the queue.

The terms *push* and *pull* are used to describe alternative systems for executing the production process in manufacturing organizations. A push system is based on forecasted demand that is completed and sent to the next workstation or, in the case of the final workstation, is pushed to finished goods inventory. On the other hand, in a pull system, the movement of work is based on the requirements of the downstream workstation. Each succeeding workstation pulls (demands) output from the previous workstation as needed. The next work station determines when and how much output is requested. The output from the final workstation is pulled by customer demand or the master production schedule. Specifically, in a push system, work output moves to the next station when it is completed without knowing whether the next station is ready to receive the additional work output. If the succeeding workstation is not ready to receive the new work, excess inventories can result in cost and quality problems. In a pull system, work moves to the next station only in response to demand from the succeeding station.

A hybrid production system combines both push and pull production systems. Careful analysis and planning are required prior to implementing hybrid production system. In a push production system, the emphasis is on material planning and procurement. In a pull production system, the emphasis is on shop floor scheduling. The hybrid production system thus makes best use of both material planning and shop floor scheduling efficiencies.

On the other hand, some companies feel the pull rule has the following *advantages*:

- The internal customers/suppliers are in sync because the upstream work center or firm produces only what the downstream work center or firm needs when they need it; work-in-process inventory is forced to remain at a given level.
- The inventory levels are determined by a business strategy that matches the external customer's needs and expectations and keeps a balanced and synchronized manufacturing flow.
- Value is added only to items when they are needed.

The *disadvantages of pull production systems* are:

- People are not always busy producing inventory and may be idle at times. They are temporarily not producing; equipment may be temporarily shut down.
- Overhead may not be absorbed, creating an accounting variance.

There is common agreement among operations management researchers that JIT functions as a pull system and MRP as a push system. Developed along with JIT, a kanban system is a production-control approach that uses containers, cards, or visual cues to control the production movement of goods through a manufacturing system (see Chapters 6 and 7). Yet this proposition does not always hold true. For example, Rice and Yoshikawa (1982) suggest that there are many practical similarities between the kanban system and MRP and that both are "pull-through" approaches. Also, Karmarkar (1989) suggests that JIT can be either a pull system or a push system because it is an integral philosophy rather than a timing-based manufacturing technique. Summarizing the existing viewpoints on push/pull principles, Pyke and Cohen (1990) conclude that an entire manufacturing system cannot be labeled as a push or pull system. They also suggest that the push/pull principles are an attribute of all underlying manufacturing and distribution systems.

There are *three* ways to define or distinguish the nature of push and pull systems in general. The most common way is characterizing the differences in terms of the order release (De Toni, et al., 1988; Karmarkar, 1989; Ding and Yuen, 1991, etc.). According to this viewpoint, in a pull system, removing an end item (or a fixed lot of end items) triggers the order release by which the flow of materials or components is initiated. In contrast, push systems allow for the production or material flow in anticipation of future demand.

The second way is to examine the structure of the information flow (Olhager and Ostlund, 1990; Hodgson and Wang 1991a, 1991b, etc.). In a pull system, the physical flow of materials is triggered by the local demand from the next server (individual station). The local demand in this system is signified by the local information (i.e., empty kanbans). In this context, the pure pull system is a decentralized control strategy in which the ultimate goal of meeting demand (orders) is disregarded in the local servers (individual stations). A push system, on the other hand, uses global and centralized information. Global information of customer orders and demand forecasts is released and processed to control all the levels of production in the push system.

Based on this notion, manufacturing planning and control (MPC) systems may consist of both push and pull elements simultaneously. According to Pyke and Cohen (1990), centralized planning systems always have push elements. Therefore, even in the pull-manufacturing environment, outcomes of the central planning decisions may limit certain operating variables of the production control systems. For example, the JIT production system has a push element in setting capacity limit of a batch, the container (bin) sizes.

Finally, the third way to interpret push/pull systems is a practical approach associated with WIP (work-in-process) level on the shop floor. The WIP are orders or materials that have been started in the production process but are not yet complete. WIP includes orders or materials waiting to be started, orders being set up, orders being worked on, and orders or materials waiting to be moved to the next work station. A variant of a pull system is the CONstant Work in Process (CONWIP) system (Spearman et al. 1990), which is known for its ease of implementation. Stockpiling WIP is a major drawback of MRP systems. In a simulation study comparing push, pull, and CONWIP systems, Spearman and Zazanis (1992) found that the merits of the pull system are generated by the bounded WIP, not by the characteristics of pull logic. They show that a hybrid approach, CONWIP, functions in a very similar manner to the pull approach due to its bounded WIP level. Simply put, a push system is considered to have infinite production capacity, and a pull system is considered to have finite production capacity. Therefore, the MRP-controlled shop floor system without a WIP blocking mechanism would create more WIP inventory than a pull system unless the production strictly follows the original schedule. One of the critical implications of this result is that a comparison based on WIP level between an MRP and kanban system at the shop floor level may not be fair, since the WIP level of the kanban system is inhibited by the size and number of containers. See Benton and Shin (1998) for a more detailed analysis.

Based on the three viewpoints suggested above, it can be concluded that if materials flow is initiated by the central planning system without controlling WIP level, the resulting system is close to the pure push system.

At the shop floor level, a kanban system functions as a pull system, and MRP works as a push system. At other levels, the assumptions that MRP means push and JIT means pull are not always true. In practice, for example, JIT production systems also use global information for long-term production planning. The push/pull and MRP/JIT studies are related in a way of deliberating issues associated with material flow. But an MRP or a JIT production system plays a role as a structure of a supply chain focused manufacturing planning control (SFMPC) system, whereas push or pull logic is a principle only for material flow in the SFMPC system. Thus, it is possible for an SFMPC system to operate under both the push and pull principles simultaneously depending on the stage of production. Notice that the combination of push/pull principles has been adopted and tested in the push/ pull integration literature (see Table 1) and Benton and Shin (1998). In this push/pull hybrid-manufacturing environment, the distinction between push and pull is more ambiguous.

Table 1 MRP/JIT Analytical Integration Literature

CATEGORY	REFS.	TITLE	DISCUSSION	METHODOLOGY
MRP-JIT	Chaudhury and Whinston, 1990	Towards an adaptive kanban system	Manufacturing planning and control shop floor control	Mathematical analysis and simulation
	Ding and Yuen, 1991	A modified MRP for a production system with the coexistence of MRP and kanban	Manufacturing planning and control	Simulation
	Betz, 1996	Common sense manufacturing, a method of production control	Manufacturing planning and control	Field study
Push-Pull				
	Hodgson and Wang, 1991a	Optimal hybrid push/pull control strategies for a parallel multistage system: Part 1	Shop floor control	Optimization
	Hodgson and Wang, 1991a	Optimal hybrid push/pull control strategies for a parallel multistage system: Part 2	Shop floor control	Optimization
	Hirakawa et al., 1992	A hybrid push/pull control system for multistage manufacturing processes	Manufacturing planning and control shop floor control	Mathematical analysis
	Deleersnyder et al., 1992	Integrating kanban-type pull systems and MRP type push systems: Insights from a Markovian model	Shop floor control	Mathematical analysis
	Hirakawa, 1996	Performance of a multistage hybrid push/pull production control system	Manufacturing planning and control shop floor control	Mathematical analysis

Source: Benton and Shin, Manufacturing planning and control: The evolution of MRP and JIT integration, European Journal of Operational Research (1998), with permission from Elsevier.

Push Production Planning System

The primary purpose of push systems is to control inventory levels, assign priorities, and execute product flow through a production facility subject to the capacity constraints. The objectives of the push production planning system are to minimize inventory investment and maximize facility and worker utilization. The push manufacturing activities are guided by a master schedule, a bill of material file, inventory records, and output reports. We discuss the elements of the push production system in more detail in Chapter 6 on MRP. In general, in the push production system, a master schedule is created from forecasted demand and booked orders. The MPS is essentially a statement of production of items for a specific future planning horizon. A bill-of-material file identifies the specific materials and quantities of each that are used to produce the items. The inventory records are used to determine the amount of new production required given the current and projected on-hand balances. The push process converts the requirements of a variety of final products into a materials requirements plan that specifies the replenishment schedules of all the subassemblies, components, and raw materials needed for final assembly. See chapters 4 and 6 for a comprehensive discussion of the push production planning system.

Pull Production Control System

The kanban production system was developed by Toyota (Monden, 1993). In the most basic kanban production system, a card is attached to each container of items that has been produced. A kanban is used to communicate (signal) the needed demand at the next workstation. *Kanban* is the Japanese word for *card.* The kanban contains a part number, the part description, type of container, and various workstation information. The container is filled with a percentage of the daily requirements for an item. When the items in the container are used, the card is removed from the container. The card is the indicator or signal that another container of items is needed. The empty containers are then moved to the storage area. When the container is refilled, the card is attached to the container. The container is then returned to the storage area. The cycle is repeated when the user obtains the refilled container.

In a pull system, work output is based on the demand of the next workstation. A kanban production control system uses simple, visual signals to control the movement of materials between work centers as well as the production of new materials to replenish those sent downstream to the next work center. The kanban is attached to a storage and transport container. The kanban is used to provide an easily understood, visual signal that a specific production activity is required. Kanbans are similar to fixed-order inventory systems in which an order for *Q* is placed when the inventory level falls below the reorder point. The reorder point is determined based on the demand during the lead time. The only inventory required is the inventory required during the replenishment lead time.

In a dual-card kanban system, there are two main types of kanban:

1. Production kanban: signals the need to produce more parts. Each kanban is physically attached to a container.
2. Withdrawal kanban: signals the need to withdraw parts from one work center and deliver them to the next work center.

A kanban-controlled manufacturing system functions as a pull system. As discussed above, in a pull system, removing an end item (or a fixed lot of end items) triggers the order release by which the flow of materials or components is initiated. In contrast, push systems allow for the production or material flow in anticipation of future demand.

In some pull systems, other signaling approaches are used in place of kanbans. For example, an empty container alone (with appropriate identification on the container) could serve as a signal for replenishment. Similarly, a labeled, pallet-sized square painted on the shop floor, if uncovered and visible, could indicate the need to go and get another pallet of materials from its point of production and move it on top of the empty square at its point of use.

A kanban system is referred to as a pull system because the kanban is used to pull parts to the next production stage only when they are needed. In contrast, an MRP system (or any schedule-based system) is a push system in which a detailed production schedule for each part is used to push parts to the next production stage when scheduled. Thus, in a pull system, material movement occurs only when the work station needing more material asks for it to be sent, while in a push system, the station producing the material initiates its movement to the receiving station, assuming that it is needed because it was scheduled for production. The weakness of a push system (MRP) is that customer demand must be forecast and production lead times must be estimated. Inaccurate guesses (forecasts or estimates) result in excess inventory, and the longer the lead time, the more room for error. The weakness of a pull system (kanban) is that following the JIT production philosophy is essential, especially concerning the elements of short setup times and small lot sizes, because each station in the process must be able to respond quickly to requests for more materials. The dual-card kanban rules follow:

1. No parts are made unless there is a production kanban to authorize production. If no production kanbans are in the inbox at a work center, the process remains idle, and workers perform other assigned activities. This rule enforces the "pull" nature of the process control.
2. There is exactly one kanban per container.
3. Containers for each specific part are standardized, and they are always filled with the same (ideally, small) quantity. (Think of an egg carton, filled with exactly one dozen eggs.)

Decisions regarding the number of kanbans (and containers) at each stage of the process are carefully considered, because this number sets an upper bound on the work-in-process inventory at that stage. For example, if 10 containers holding 12 units each are used to move materials between two work centers, the maximum inventory possible is 120 units, occurring only when all 10 containers are full. At this point, all kanbans will be attached to full containers, so no additional units will be produced (because there are no unattached production kanbans to authorize production). This feature of a dual-card kanban system enables systematic productivity improvement to take place. By deliberately removing one or more kanbans (and containers) from the system, a manager will also reduce the maximum level of work-in-process (buffer) inventory. This reduction can be done until a shortage of materials occurs. This shortage is an indication of problems (accidents, machine breakdowns, production delays, defective products) that were previously hidden by excessive inventory. Once the problem is observed and a solution is identified, corrective action is taken so that the system can function at the lower level of buffer inventory. This simple, systematic method of inventory reduction is a key benefit of a dual-card kanban system. See the following kanban determination example given in the next section.

Determining the Number of Kanbans (Containers)

The formula for determining the number of kanbans needed to control the production of a particular product/component part is shown below:

$$\text{Number of kanbans} = \frac{\text{average demand during lead time} + \text{safety stock}}{\text{Container size}}$$

$$N = \frac{(dL + S)}{C}$$

where:

N = number of kanbans or containers
d = average demand per unit of time
L = lead time; the time it takes to replenish an order
S = safety stock; usually given as a percentage of demand during lead time or the level of expected variance
C = container size

To achieve continuous improvement; the container size is usually set at a smaller level than the demand during lead time, say, 10 percent of daily demand. This approach will

Example 8-1

Marcus works as an operator at Health First, a supplement manufacturer. He is asked to process an average of 90 bottles an hour through his workstation. If one kanban is attached to each container, a container holds six bottles, and it takes 20 minutes to receive new bottles from the upstream workstation. The safety stock level is set at 10 percent. How many kanbans are required for the bottling process?

Solution

$$N = \frac{(90 \times .33) + (90 \times .33 \times .10)}{6}$$

$$= \frac{29.7 + 2.97}{6} = 5.44$$

We can either round up or round down. If we round down, we would be approaching continuous improvement. If we round up, we will be allowing more inventory (waste) into the process.

result in reducing the number of kanbans. The reduced number of kanbans causes work methods and process problems to become visible. An example calculation is given in Example 8-1 above.

In a pull production system, the focus is on the production process associated with producing a specific number of products. All processes are connected and are programmed to only produce what is needed. To ensure that the pull production system operates accurately, most companies establish specific pull production rules. Some of the rules are outlined below:

1. The downstream process withdraws only the necessary products from the upstream process in specific quantities at a specific point in time. The success of pull production systems is based on the production worker following well-defined processing rules. Before a pull production system is implemented, production sequencing and order quantities are monitored by each manager (department) involved in the process. In a pull system, all product flow is controlled by the pull production system logic. Top management determines the specific logical rules that are implemented.
2. The preceding process is required to produce its products in the quantities withdrawn by the subsequent process. Rules 1 and 2 will ensure that all processes are connected; thus, inventory buildup and waste is eliminated.
3. Defective products should never be dispatched to subsequent processes. The pull production system does not tolerate defective parts or products. If defective parts or products enter the process, the pull production system is ineffective. If the quality of the material is defective, the following could happen:
   - Rejects and scrap
   - Rework
   - Delays
   - Equipment down
   - Longer cycle times

- More cost
- More expediting
- More schedule changes
- Missed customer delivery
- More queue (WIP)

The suggested solution to the above problems is to trigger the kanban (pull) signal earlier.

4. In a pull system, the number of kanbans is minimized. An increased number of kanbans can easily be the primary source of waste.
5. However, kanbans can be used to adapt to small fluctuations in demand. Fine tuning of production by kanbans is an excellent way to buffer against small demand fluctuations. In cases in which demand fluctuates with more than 10 percent, the whole production system has to be rebalanced and revised. Rebalancing is accomplished by increasing or decreasing the number of workers and kanbans in the system.

Comparison of Push and Pull Production Systems

An illustration of the push and pull manufacturing concepts is given in this example. Traditional MRP manufacturing systems use push systems in which the goal is to ensure all workstations and equipment are fully utilized. A result of this is that serial operations (i.e., fabrication, assembly, and finished goods) are independently optimized. Thus, if earlier operations are faster than a later operation, increasing levels of inventory will build up at the succeeding work as in Figure 1a.

Figure 1a Traditional Production Planning System (Push System)

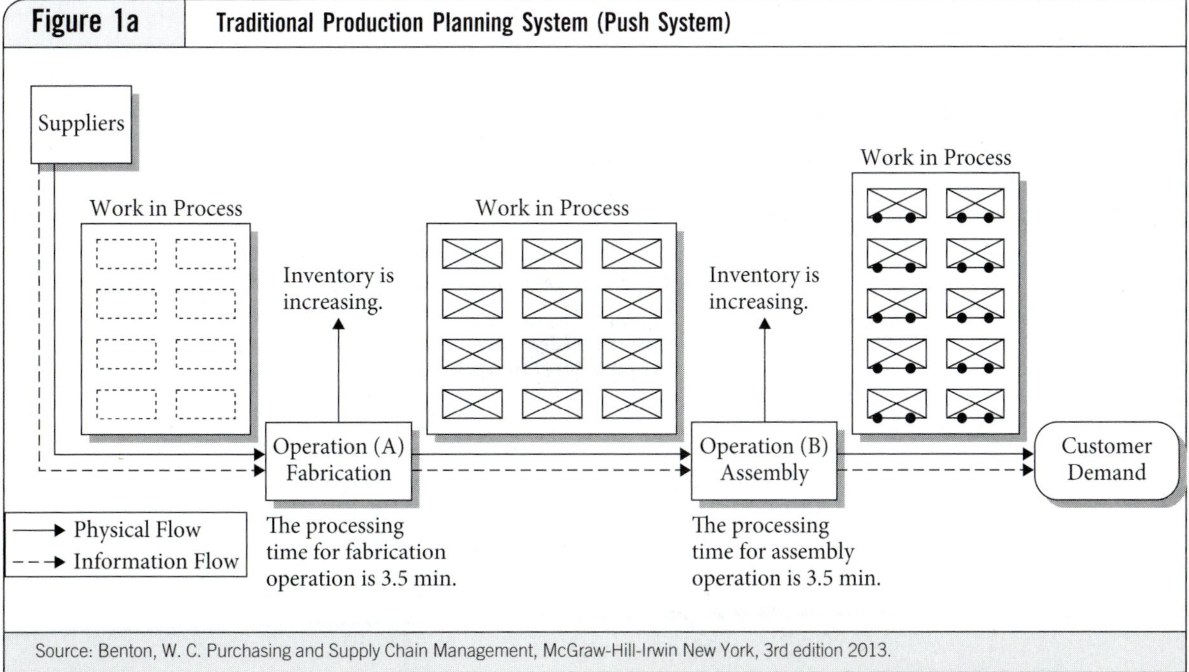

Source: Benton, W. C. Purchasing and Supply Chain Management, McGraw-Hill-Irwin New York, 3rd edition 2013.

Figure 1b **JIT Kanban Production Phasing System (Pull System)**

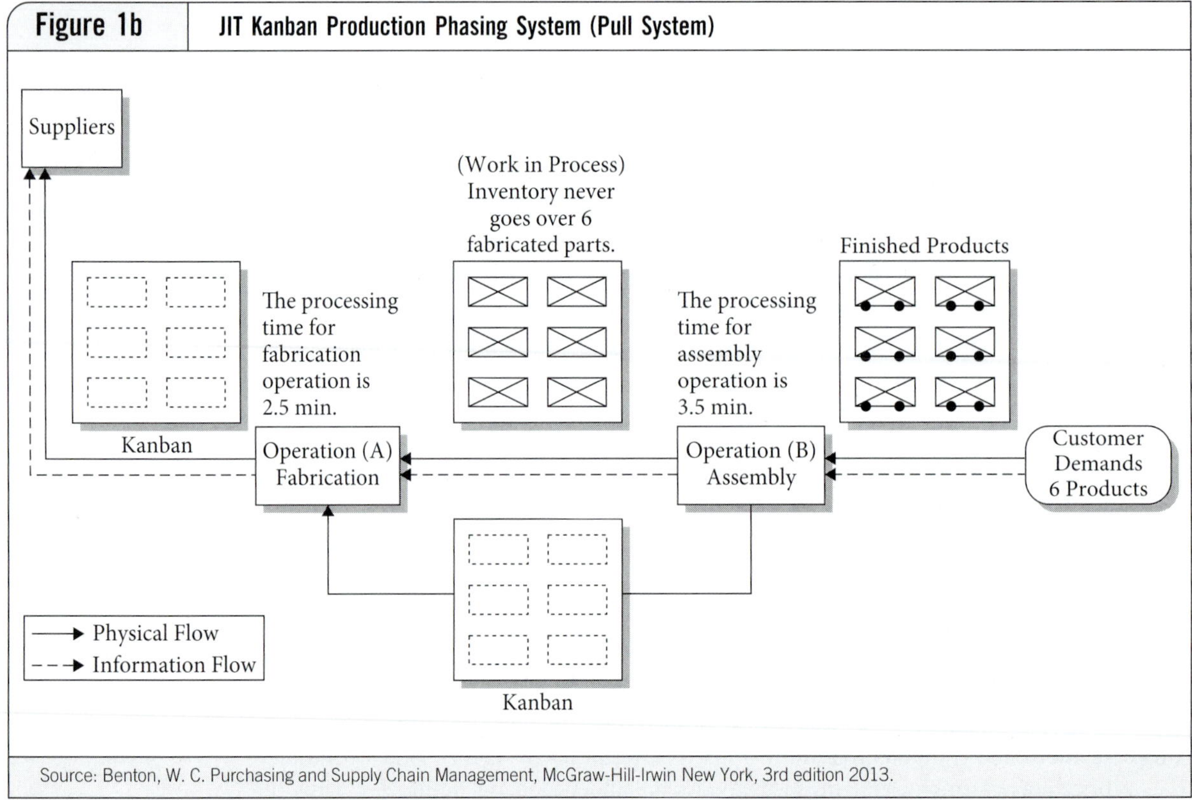

Source: Benton, W. C. Purchasing and Supply Chain Management, McGraw-Hill-Irwin New York, 3rd edition 2013.

As shown in Figure 1a, overproduction is an element of waste. As can be seen in Figure 1a, there are significant levels of excess raw materials, work in process, and finished goods inventories compared to the pull system shown in Figure 1b. The resulting excess inventory uses up working capital and is liable to damage and devaluation. The ultimate inventory pile is at the end of the assembly process, where finished goods are stacked up in warehouses, waiting for customers to buy them.

The principle of 'pull' is that control is transferred from the beginning of the line to the end. Thus, in the example above, Operation B needs to control what Operation A sends them. The secret of this is the kanban. A kanban is a control device that effectively says to the recipient. "Give me *N* items and *N* items only. When you have done that, stop! Wait until you get the next kanban." Figure 1b now shows the changed conversation between the suppliers, Operation A, and Operation B.

Operation A now may stand idle for a while, which may seem like a cost, but it is not as great as the cost of idle inventory.

The objective of the pull system is to see how small a number of items you can pull with a kanban. A certain number are needed to manage natural variation in the process, but no more than the minimum needed for the natural variation. Reducing the number of items pulled, even by one, is an effective way of highlighting problems and bottlenecks in the system. For example, reducing the kanban number in the example to five may lead to Operation B being idle sometimes, but if some process improvement is done on it, it may even be able to handle as few as four kanban items.

SUMMARY

Production control systems are classified as pull and push systems. In a push system, the production order is scheduled and the material is pushed into the production line. In a pull system, the start of each product assembly process is triggered by the completion of another at the end of production line.

There is common agreement among operations management researchers that the kanban-controlled manufacturing system functions as a pull system and MRP as a push system. In this chapter, push and pull production systems are discussed in detail.

MRP or JIT production systems play roles as structures of a supply chain focused manufacturing planning control (SFMPC) system, whereas push or pull logic is a principle only for material flow in the SFMPC system. Thus, it is possible for an SFMPC system to operate under both the push and pull principles simultaneously, depending on the stage of production.

To summarize, many companies get outstanding benefits with pull, push, and hybrid manufacturing planning and control systems. Success with any production planning system is achieved by implementing world-class customer service. Successful companies have a passion for efficiency and focus on reducing waste, which includes minimizing the effect of waste in the following areas:

- Minimizing setups and changeovers
- Minimizing rework and scrap
- Eliminating material shortages
- Reducing excessive paperwork
- Minimizing equipment problems
- Eliminating quality problems
- Eliminating inefficient suppliers

Supply chain focused manufacturing organizations must also focus on developing high-quality schedules, managing inventories, and supplying with demand in order to synchronize and balance the work flow throughout the supply chain system. Successful companies must also change the traditional performance measures from utilization to customer service. The challenge will be to become marketplace-driven and have a strong customer focus while being very flexible and agile in the factory and throughout the supply chain. Flexibility and agility must be achieved without increasing the cost of running the business, having excess inventory, and having long cycle times. The manufacturing organization must learn to adjust to the customer needs. We can no longer afford to adjust the customer to the manufacturing organization and remain competitive. The chapter ends with a push and pull MPC illustrations comparison.

DISCUSSION QUESTIONS

1. Differentiate between a push and pull production system.
2. Describe how the kanban concept works.
3. Why do large lot sizes work well with push production systems?
4. Why do small lot sizes work well with pull production systems?
5. Comment on the relationship between total quality management and pull production systems.

6. Comment on the relationship between total quality management and push production systems.

EXERCISES

1. The *Game Over* computerized football game has far exceeded demand expectations. In order to increase the availability of different models of the game, the manufacturer has decided to begin producing its most popular models as often as possible on its one assembly line. Given the monthly requirements of 10,500, 5,600, and 6,600 units for *Game Over—Big 10, Game Over—PAC 10, and Game Over—SEC,* respectively, determine a model sequence for the final assembly line that will smooth out the production of each model. (Assume 30 working days per month and 8 working hours per day. Also assume that the time required to assemble each model is approximately the same.)
2. Moe Electronics produces APP switches for NASA. The current assembly capacity is 100 switches per hour. It takes 40 minutes to receive the necessary component from the previous workstation. Completed switches are placed in a rack that will hold 25 switches. The rack must be full before it is sent on to the next workstation. If Moe uses a safety factor of 5 percent, how many kanbans are needed for the APP switch assembly process?
3. Referring to Problem 2, how many kanbans would be needed in each case?
   a. Demand is increased to 200 avionic switches per hour.
   b. The lead time for components is increased to 60 minutes.
   c. The rack size is doubled.
   d. The safety factor is increased to 10 percent.
4. It takes Susan 30 minutes to solder 10 circuit boards to fill a container and 2 minutes to transport the container to the next station, where John works. John's process takes about 45 minutes. The facility uses a safety factor of 10 percent. Currently, 5 kanbans rotate between Susan and John's stations. What is the approximate demand for circuit boards?
5. Bill works as a sorter for UPS. He can sort a tub of 50 packages in 20 minutes. He typically sorts 100 packages an hour. A truck arrives with more tubs each hour. UPS uses a safety factor of 5 percent. How many kanbans are needed for the package-sorting operation?
6. The sorting supervisor wishes to decrease the number of kanbans in the package-sorting process described in Problem 5. Which of the following alternatives has the greatest effect on reducing the number of kanbans?
   a. Eliminating the safety factor.
   b. Receiving truck deliveries every 30 minutes.
   c. Increasing the bin capacity to 100 packages.

   What is the effect on inventory levels of decreasing the number of kanbans?
7. Megan is asked to produce 100 iPads an hour. It takes 30 minutes to receive the necessary components from the previous workstation. Each output container holds 20 iPads. The facility currently works with a safety factor of 20 percent. How many kanbans should be circulating between Megan's process and the previous process?
8. Referring to Problem 7, what happens to the number of kanbans and to inventory levels in each case?
   a. The time required to receive material is increased to 40 minutes.
   b. Output expectations decrease to 250 iPads an hour.
   c. The size of the container is increased to 20 iPads.

9. At Apple's assembly plant in China, the assembly line for iPad motherboards has a demand for 500 units an hour. Two feeder lines supply parts A and B to the assembly line (one A and one B for each motherboard). Standard divided container trays are used. A container will hold 40 As or 200 Bs. It takes 20 minutes to fill up a container with As and 30 minutes to fill up a container with Bs. Transit time to the assembly cell is 10 minutes for both A and B. The safety factor is set at 10 percent. Set up a kanban control system for the assembly process.

REFERENCES

Benton, W. C., Purchasing and Supply Chain Management, McGraw-Hill-Irwin, New York, 3rd edition (2013).

Benton, W. C., and H. Shin. "Manufacturing Planning and Control: The Evolution of MRP and JIT Integration." *European Journal of Operational Research* 110 (1998): 411–40.

Betz, Jr., H. J. "Common Sense Manufacturing: A Method of Production Control." *Production and Inventory Management Journal* First Quarter (1996): 77–81.

Chaudhury, A., and A. B. Whinston. "Towards an Adaptive Kanban System." *International Journal of Production Research* 28, no. 3 (1990): 437–58.

Deleersnyder, J. L., T. J. Hodgson, R. E. King, P. J. O'Grady, and A. Savva. "Integrating Kanban Type Pull Systems and MRP Type Push Systems: Insights from a Markovian Model." *IIE Transactions* (1992): 43–56.

De Toni, A., M. Caputo, and A., Vinelli. "Production Management Techniques: Push-Pull Classification and Application Conditions." *International Journal of Operations and Production Management* (1988): 35–51.

Ding, F.-Y., and M. N., Yuen. "A Modified MRP for a Production System with the Coexistence of MRP and Kanbans." *Journal of Operations Management* 10, no. 2 (1991): 267–77.

Hirakawa, Y. "Performance of a Multistage Hybrid Push/Pull Production Control System." *International Journal of Production Economics* 44 (1996): 129–35.

Hirakawa, Y., K. Hoshino, and H. Katayama. "A Hybrid Push/Pull Production Control System for Multistage Manufacturing Processes." *International Journal of Operations and Production Management* 12, no. 4 (1992): 69–81.

Hodgson, T. J., and D. Wang. "Optimal Hybrid Push/Pull Control Strategies for a Parallel Multistage System: Part 1." *Production and Inventory Management Journal*, Second Quarter (1991): 74–83.

Karmarker, U. "Getting Control of Just-in-Time." *Harvard Business Review* (1989): 122–31.

Monden, Y. *Toyota Production System, 2nd ed.* Institute of Industrial Engineers, 1993.

Olhager, L., and B. Ostlund. "An integrated Push-Pull Manufacturing Strategy." *European Journal of Operational Research* 45 (1990): 135–42.

Pyke, D. F., and M. A., Cohen. "Push and Pull in Manufacturing and Distribution Systems." *Journal of Operations Management* 9, no. 1 (1990): 24–43.

Rice, J. W., and T. Yoshikawa. "A Comparison of Kanban and MRP Concepts for the Control of Repetitive Manufacturing Systems." *Production and Inventory Management Journal* First Quarter (1982): 1–13.

Spearman, M. L., and M. A. Zazanis. "Push and Pull Production Systems." *Issues and Comparisons. Operations Research* 40, no. 3 (1992): 521–53.

Chapter 9

CAPACITY MANAGEMENT

Learning Objectives

- Understand the role of capacity planning in the manufacturing planning and control system
- Learn about how managers decide which capacity-management technique(s) to use and how to use them
- Learn about alternative rough-cut capacity techniques
- Learn how to implement the various rough-cut capacity techniques
- Understand how the bill of material and planning horizon are related to capacity planning and control
- Understand the capacity-requirements planning (CRP) process
- Understand the supplier capacity-planning (SCP) process

Introduction

Manufacturing capacity planning and control is the systematic process of matching planned system outputs with the necessary capacity requirements. Capacity planning is an iterative process based on interactive hierarchical planning levels. The capacity-planning process is implicitly based on the concept that in order to generate feasible capacity plans at the work-center level, it is important to make sure that long-range capacity plans are feasible. Thus, capacity planning consists of a series of interrelated hierarchical plans. The general capacity-planning framework is given in Figure 1. Depending on product diversity and product variety, short-term plans may not be feasible even though the long-term and tactical plans are feasible. However, the higher the level of reliability and certainty at the work-center level, the more accurate the planning at all levels in the capacity-planning process. Adjustments are made at various levels to accommodate exceptions to the sales and operations plan. If required, adjustments are made to the planned and required capacity levels in order to achieve feasibility.

Capacity Planning and Supply Chain Management

The capacity-planning process extends throughout the entire supply chain. Manufacturing organizations must also consider the capacity-planning activities of the organization's tier-one suppliers, distributors, and customers. Suppose Hewlett-Packard (HP) decides to

Figure 1 Manufacturing Capacity Planning and Control Framework

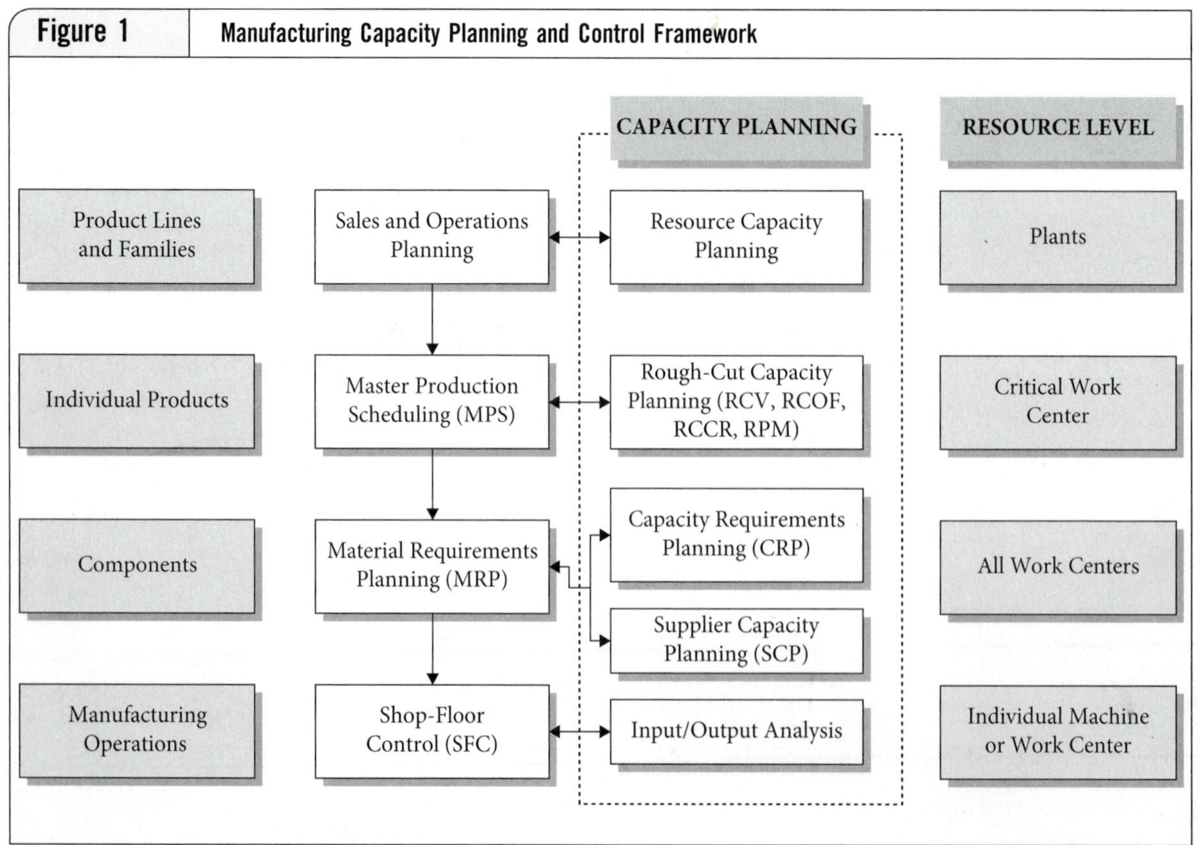

launch a new product line. HP must now fill the downstream supply chain with product. HP must make sure that suppliers have the adequate capacity to provide adequate quantities of raw materials and subassemblies. HP must also make sure that there is adequate trucking, warehousing, and retail capacity to accommodate the new product line. The capacity plans for manufacturing organizations must be carefully integrated up and down the supply chain.

The Elements of Manufacturing Capacity Planning and Control

Capacity planning is a key component of an effective manufacturing capacity planning and control system. In order to fully appreciate the concept of dynamic capacity planning and control, it is important that the basic concepts be thoroughly understood and placed in perspective. Most manufacturing planning and control systems assume that the various input modules are accurate and that the sales and operations plan is valid and executable (see Chapter 3). The sales and operations plan is valid, provided that it is not constrained by resource and MPS capacity availability. The criticality of these constraints is dependent upon the actual manufacturing process and the lead time necessary to obtain materials and/or adjust capacities. These constraints are integral to the capacity planning and control process. Capacity planning and control is the function of establishing, measuring, monitoring, and adjusting limits or levels of capacity in order to execute the manufacturing plans and schedules. Capacity planning and control is an iterative process that considers capacity on three different planning horizons:

- Long-range capacity planning
- Medium-range capacity planning
- Short-range capacity planning

Long-Range Capacity Planning

Long-range capacity planning is concerned with decisions affecting capital expenses that take long periods of time to acquire and that require top management approval. The time period normally associated with this level of planning is one year into the future and beyond. The methods used to change long-range capacities are:

- Change or renovate facilities, including opening and closing existing facilities
- Change capital equipment within the plant facility
- Change work force

Long-range capacity planning is normally associated with the MPS activities at the sales and operations planning and master production scheduling levels. Resource planning and rough-cut capacity planning are the capacity planning techniques used to estimate capacity requirements in this time frame.

Medium-Range Capacity Planning

Medium-range capacity-planning decisions are concerned with increasing or decreasing capacity over a shorter time frame and may not require top management approval.

The time frame normally associated with this level of planning is 1 to 12 months. The methods used to change medium-range capacities are:

- Change make/buy decisions
- Plan alternate product routings
- Contract manufacturing and subcontracting
- Re-allocate work time
- Change work force where feasible
- Add additional tooling and machines

This level of planning most closely relates to MRP where the objective is to achieve detailed individual part number schedules or material plans. The capacity-planning technique used to derive detailed capacity requirements for specific machines or work centers is referred to as capacity requirements planning (CRP).

Short-Range Capacity Planning

In the short range (next four weeks), the planner is more concerned with capacity control than with planning. The activities associated with this time frame are monitoring output, comparing actual output to planned output levels, and executing short-term corrective actions. These corrective actions include:

- Scheduling overtime
- Short-term subcontracting through temporary agencies
- Selecting alternate routings
- Re-allocating the work force

Short-range capacity planning relates to the detailed schedules established by shop floor control (SFC) or production activity control. The techniques used in monitoring work-center performance are input–output analysis. This process assumes that work-center capacity is finite and monitors work-center performance in terms of the amount of work at the work center, the amount of work expected to arrive at the work center, and amount of work completed or expected to be completed at the work center. The supplier capacity planning (SCP) system is also an element of short-range capacity planning. The SCP is concerned with information sharing with key suppliers. SCP is a purchasing planning system built around a planning report obtained from MRP schedules for purchased components.

The long range, medium range, and short range levels in the capacity planning process are interrelated for several reasons. (1) The accuracy of the planning data diminishes with extended capacity projections. Thus, it is especially important to continuously update the planning data. (2) When making capacity planning decisions at the sales and operations planning and MPS levels, it is important to use localized capacity planning techniques that can predict, monitor, and adjust capacity requirements for end items or product families. (3) As the execution date gets closer the number, feasible capacity alternatives rapidly decrease because of the loss of flexibility. At this point, the execution of actual work-center plans becomes more critical. The remainder of the chapter will focus on the relevant managerial factors, capacity measurement, resource capacity planning, rough-cut capacity planning, capacity planning requirements, input & output analysis and the supplier capacity planning process.

Managerial Factors

A variety of managerial factors must be considered in the capacity-planning process. Some of the most common managerial factors are:

- Regular time per employee per period
- Overtime per employee per period
- Number of shifts per day
- Maximum effective facility capacity
- Maximum subcontracting capacity available
- Outsourcing capacity available

Many factors are also beyond the control of management. The uncontrollable factors must be accurately estimated. Some of the more common uncontrollable factors include:

- Absenteeism
- Material shortages
- Scrap and rework
- Additional set-ups
- Labor productivity
- Unplanned equipment breakdowns

Capacity Measurement

Capacity management is an organization's ability to convert its valuable resources into marketable products and/or services. Capacity is the measure of productive capability of a facility for a unit of time. Specifically, capacity is the rate of work projected to be produced by workers, machines, work centers, or entire plants. In the automotive industry, capacity may be defined as the number of cars that can be assembled in an hour, day, week, or month. Capacity is critically important for a manufacturing organization because it directly impacts the cost and efficiency of manufacturing capability of the organization.

Capacity per unit of time is affected by the following:

- Product specifications
- Product mix
- Plant and equipment availability
- Work effort and productivity
- Employee age

1. Design Capacity
   Design capacity is the total effective capacity under perfect conditions. Normally, perfect conditions are not achievable, and few organizations operate at design capacity levels. Operating at design capacity levels can cause morale problems and equipment breakdowns. Operating at design capacity essentially simply means operating at the organization's manufacturing limits. An example is operating an automobile at the highest RPM before the red line.

2. Effective Capacity Utilization
   Effective capacity utilization is the ratio between the effective capacity of a firm and its design capacity. Effective capacity is affected by an organization's product utilization mix, production scheduling, age of equipment, and maintenance standards. The calculation for effective capacity utilization is:

$$\text{Effective capacity utilization} = \text{effective capacity}/\text{design capacity}$$

Example

The Smart Computer manufacturing company has a design capacity of 200 computers per hour. However, because of competitive quality standards, it normally produces only 150 computers per hour. The effective capacity utilization of the computer manufacturing company is calculated in the following manner:

$$\begin{aligned}\text{Effective capacity utilization} &= \text{effective capacity}/\text{design capacity}\\ &= 150/200 = 75\%\end{aligned}$$

3. Capacity efficiency is a ratio of production output to effective capacity. It is a measure of effective management in utilizing effective capacity. It is calculated using the following formula:

$$\text{Capacity efficiency} = \text{actual output}/\text{effective capacity}$$

Example

The effective capacity of the Smart Computer Company is 150 computers per hour; however, it actually produces only 125 computers per hour. The efficiency of the Smart Computer Company can be computed in the following manner:

$$\begin{aligned}\text{Capacity efficiency} &= \text{actual output}/\text{effective capacity}\\ &= 125/150 = 83.33\%\end{aligned}$$

4. Rated capacity is a determination of the maximum usable capacity of manufacturing capability. Rated capacity can never exceed design capacity. It is a product of design capacity times effective utilization capacity times efficiency. The formula used to calculate rated capacity is:

$$\text{Rated capacity} = \text{design capacity} \times \text{effective capacity utilization} \times \text{capacity efficiency}$$

Example

The Smart Computer Company has a manufacturing facility operating at a effective capacity utilization of 75 percent with 83.33 percent efficiency and a design capacity of 200 computers.

$$\begin{aligned}\text{Rated capacity} &= \text{Design capacity} \times \text{effective capacity utilization} \times \text{capacity efficiency}\\ &= 200 \times 0.75 \times 0.833 = 125 \text{ computers per week}\end{aligned}$$

Resource Capacity Planning (RCP)

The RCP level is directly linked to the overall business plans for the manufacturing organization. Top-level operations managers are charged with developing long-range plans that include process innovation, manpower requirement, plant and equipment investments, and many other strategic decisions. The steps involved at this level of planning require extensive data collection, forecasting, and effective communication with marketing and finance.

Resource-planning decisions require careful coordination and integration throughout the organization. Consider an automobile manufacturing facility that produces full-size vehicles, SUVs, and trucks. The company's capacity allocation for 2013 was 50 percent for full-size vehicles, 20 percent for SUVs, and 30 percent for trucks. Currently, there is excess capacity for SUVs and trucks and insufficient capacity for full-size vehicles. How should the company's resources be allocated for 2014? Is this capacity change permanent? What if fuel prices double in 2014? The resource plan for 2013 must be based on whether the product line shift is expected to be permanent or temporary. Managerial decisions at the resource-planning level require input from all functional levels in the organization, including strategic planning and business forecasting. As shown in Figure 1, capacity-planning levels are based on hierarchical planning levels. The rough-cut capacity level will be discussed in the next section.

Rough-Cut Capacity Planning (RCCP)

Rough-cut capacity planning is defined by The Association of Operations Management (APICS) as the process of converting the master production schedule into requirements for key resources, including labor, machinery, warehouse capacity, suppliers' capabilities, and many other transformations. RCCP techniques focus on the impact of high-level plans on detailed work-center plans. The RCCP process attempts to validate the feasibility of the MPS prior to executing work-center plans. There are alternative RCCP techniques. Each alternative RCCP technique has its own strengths and weaknesses. It is important to note that the product mix, work-center reliability, and robustness are all key determinants of the effectiveness of the alternative RCCP approaches. The most widely used RCCP techniques to evaluate available capacity are given in the following sections.

Rough-Cut Capacity and Production Volume (RCV)

The rough-cut capacity validation approach is straight forward and easy to measure. This technique is used in a flow-shop manufacturing environment. Assembly-line cycle times are known and bottle necks can be easily identified. In other words, the total volume of the flow line cannot exceed the bottleneck capacity. Consider the following assembly:

Line: Station 1		Station 2		Station 3		Station 4		
530/units	→	480/units	→	450/units	→	510/units	→	410/Output units

The system's capacity is the bottleneck of 450 units per day. The efficiency of the system is

$$\begin{aligned}\text{Capacity efficiency} &= \text{actual output/effective systems capacity}\\ &= 410/450 = 91.11\%\end{aligned}$$

Rough-Cut Capacity Check Using Overall Factors (RCOF)

The MPS is used for this approach. RCOF uses data from the MPS. The RCOF approach is based on planning factors derived from historical data for the end item. The planning factors are applied to MPS data and are used to estimate overall labor or

Table 1 Capacity Loads for Each Products

PRODUCT (LABOR HOURS)	PERIOD 1	PERIOD 2	PERIOD 3
AA (1)	6	7	6
BB (2)	5	9	4
CC (3)	8	7	7

Table 2 Total Capacity Load for Each Period

	PERIOD 1	PERIOD 2	PERIOD 3
Total Load	$(1 \times 6) + (2 \times 5) + (3 \times 8) = 40h$	$(1 \times 7) + (2 \times 9) + (3 \times 7) = 46h$	$(1 \times 6) + (2 \times 4) + (3 \times 7) = 35h$

Table 3 Work Center Capacity

WORK CENTER	PERIOD 1	PERIOD 2	PERIOD 3
WC1: 50%	$0.5 \times 40h = 20h$	$0.5 \times 46h = 23h$	$0.5 \times 35h = 17.5h$
WC2: 30%	$0.3 \times 40h = 12h$	$0.3 \times 46h = 11.8h$	$0.3 \times 35h = 10.5h$
WC3: 20%	$0.2 \times 40h = 8h$	$0.2 \times 46h = 9.2h$	$0.2 \times 35h = 7h$

machine hour capacity requirements. The MPS in Table 1 is used to calculate the capacity loads for three products.

The total capacity load for each period is given in Table 2.

The capacity requirements for work centers WC1, WC2, and WC3 are 50 percent, 30 percent, and 20 percent, respectively. The work-center requirements are given in Table 3:

The RCOF technique is widely used. It is simple to implement and easily understood. However, if there is wide variation in the product mix at the specific work center, the results will be less reliable. The primary advantages of the RCOF are minimal data requirement and ease of implementation.

Rough-Cut Capacity Using Routings (RCCR)

The RCCR technique is a more detailed approach. This method uses the bill of material (BOM) and routing file as input. Using product AA from the MPS in Table 1 and the BOM in Figure 2, the routings can be determined. Table 4 shows the resulting routings of products AA, C, and D. For this example, the product routings include the set up times and process times for each item as shown in Table 5.

As can be seen, the work load for MPS item AA is aggregated from the production items C and D. Work Center 1 is needed for 0.8 hours to produce item AA, 0.9 hours to produce item C, and 0.2 hours to produce item D. Thus, to produce one unit of AA requires 1.9 hours of workstation 1. The capacity requirements can now be calculated

Figure 2 Bill of Material Diagram

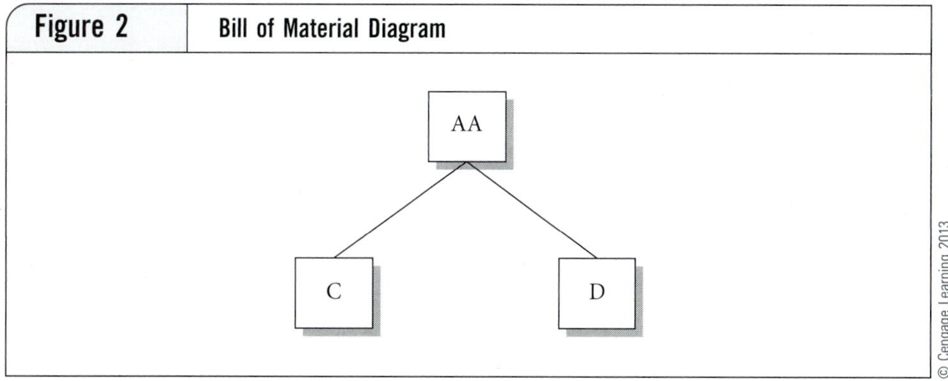

and compared to the workstation availability using the RCCR routings and the item quantities in the MPS. The resulting capacity requirements for AA are shown in Table 6.

As can be seen, the RCCR method is significantly more detailed and therefore more applicable for high levels of product variation and alternative product routings. The effectiveness of the routing-enhanced technique can easily be acknowledged by the work-center calculations when comparing to the ROCF.

The RCCR technique establishes a more direct link between specific end items in the MPS and specific work centers. It also considers the product mix in the capacity-requirements determination. The RCCR technique is simple to implement,

Table 4 Production Routings (hours)

PRODUCT (ITEM)	WC1	WC2	WC3
AA	0.8	0.9	0.5
C	0.9	0.2	0.5
D	0.2	0.3	0.7

Table 5 RCCR Routings

PRODUCT (ITEM)	WC1	WC2	WC3
AA	0.8 + 0.9 + 0.2 = 1.9	0.9 + 0.2 + 0.3 = 1.4	0.5 + 0.5 + 0.7 = 1.7

Table 6 Capacity Requirements for AA

WORK CENTER	PERIOD 1	PERIOD 2	PERIOD 3
WC1	6 × 1.9 = 11.4h	7 × 1.9 = 13.3h	6 × 1.9 = 11.4h
WC2	6 × 1.4 = 8.4h	7 × 1.4 = 9.8h	6 × 1.4 = 8.4h
WC3	6 × 1.7 = 10.2h	7 × 1.7 = 11.9h	6 × 1.4 = 8.4h

but it does require significantly more data than the ROCF. Additional data requirements include the bill of materials, the routing file, direct labor hours, and machine hours for each work center. If there is wide variation in product mix, the RCCR technique is recommended. On the other hand, if the product mix is stable and historical work allocation between work centers remains constant, the ROCF technique is recommended.

Resource Profile Method (RPM)

The RPM adds a timing dimension to the routing method. The resource profile method shows in which period the specific requirements will be needed. The example given in Table 7 shows that the requirements to complete one unit of AA at the end of period *t* are 1.7 hours of WC3, 1.4 hours of WC2 in period $t - 1$, and 1.9 hours of WC1 in period $t - 2$. Period *t*1 is the period in which the quantity of AA is to be delivered. Capacity requirements can now be calculated by multiplying resource profiles by quantities from the MPS using the RPM routing method.

In each of the RCCP techniques, the time buckets can vary (e.g., weekly, monthly, quarterly) based on clockspeed and technology. However, as time periods increase, the timing component becomes less of a decision criterion. Monthly time buckets are basically smoothed weekly (buckets) estimates.

In the examples given above, the calculations for each of the methods have been simplified for the purpose of illustration. In each of the examples, the following assumptions are enforced: (1) The lotsizes are fixed; (2) lower-level assemblies are not considered; (3) the current work-center load has not been considered. The alternative RCC methods are given in Table 8.

Table 7 Resource Profile for Product (Item)—AA

WORK CENTER	PERIOD *t*	PERIOD *t*–1	PERIOD *t*–2
WC1			1.9h
WC2		1.4h	
WC3	1.7h		

Table 8 Alternative RCC Methods

RCC METHOD	WORK-CENTER CAPACITY REQUIREMENTS
Rough-cut capacity and production volume (RCV)	Σ(MPS-item quantities)
Rough-cut capacity check using overall factors (RCOF)	Σ(MPS-item quantity × total capacity req) × WC × share)
Rough-cut capacity using routings (RCCR)	Σ(MPS-item quantity × workstation × requirement)
Resource profiles method (RPM)	Σ(MPS-item quantity × workstation × (*t*) requirement)

Even though rough cut capacity planning indicates that sufficient capacity exists to execute the MPS, CRP may show that capacity could be insufficient during specific time periods. The Capacity requirements planning (CRP) planning horizon extends several weeks in the future. For manufacturing organizations using MRP to execute detailed production and materials planning, the more focused CRP approach should be used. CRP differs from the rough-cut planning approaches by utilizing time-phased capacity plans based on output from the MRP system. CRP is presented in the next section.

Capacity Requirements Planning (CRP)

Capacity requirements planning and rough-cut capacity planning (RCCP) techniques focus on different levels in the capacity planning systems. The rough-cut capacity system focuses on the MPS level in the planning hierarchy. Rough-cut capacity planning techniques can easily overstate required capacity since it includes the stored capacity in inventory. CRP utilizes the time phased requirements planning information generated by the MRP system. Actual input information (lotsizes, scheduled receipts, planned order releases, lead time) from the MRP system is used. CRP inputs also include product routing, job processing and set up times information. As a medium range capacity planning technique, CRP relies heavily on MRP information (See Figure 1). MRP input includes the timing of both open and planned orders, by calculating requirements for actual open work-center orders and requirements stored in the form of work-in-process inventories and finished items. The primary outputs include various load reports for each work center. Improved capacity accuracy is therefore realized.

CRP is also a system that projects the load from a given materials requirements plan onto a production system and evaluates load imbalances (underloads and overloads). The amount of product that the facility can manufacture at any given time is determined by the weekly facility capacity. If the demand increases or decreases significantly, the facility can accommodate this change within limits. In general, CRP is the process of reconciling the difference between the capacity available for the process and the capacity required to properly manage a load to satisfy the timing of the output for the specific customer whose orders represent the load. Once the load and the available capacity are compared, the planning process essentially requires the planner to adjust either the capacity available to meet the load, or, in some cases, adjust the load to the available capacity. In the latter case (adjusting the load) there is typically little flexibility in the capacity available. It may not be possible to change the available capacity, especially in the short run. In those cases the planners instead have to concentrate on managing the load through order promising or some other mechanism. Most manufacturing organizations will attempt to adjust the capacity to meet the load in order to maintain a high level of customer service with respect to customer needs. The major *inputs* and *outputs* to the CRP are shown in Figure 3.

CRP Inputs

As can be seen in Figure 3, the inputs include, planned order releases, routing data, current work center information and open order. These files provide the information needed to produce the work center load file for each machine or work center in the shop. The routing file provides specific information required to produce a component

Figure 3 Inputs and Outputs to CRP

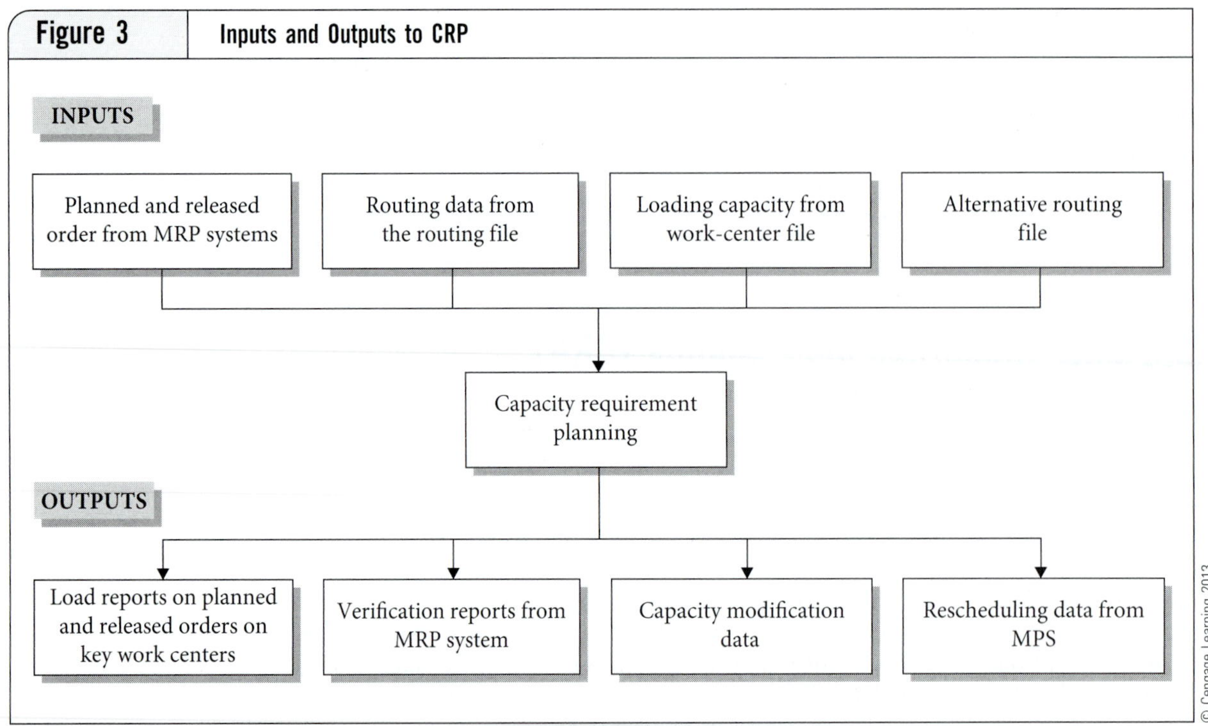

part or item. The routing file includes the operations to be performed, their sequence, the various work centers involved, and the standards for setup and run times. In some companies, the routing file also includes information on tooling, operator skill levels, inspection operations and testing requirements, and so on. Alternative routing is used when the primary work-center is overloaded or unavailable. The work center file is one of the key inputs to CRP. The work center file compiles the relevant work center data. The work center file includes information related to cost, capacity, lead time, work force size and the specific work center function. The work center file also provides work center capacity data that focuses on production scheduling and shop load status.

CRP Outputs

The primary output of the CRP is a comparative analysis of planned versus actual capacity usage in specific work centers. The remaining three outputs (MRP verification reports, capacity modification data and rescheduling data) shown in Figure 3 are directly related to the disposition of the Load report. The load report compares released orders and planned orders with the available capacity in the work center. The work center load report shows detailed future capacity requirements based on the released and planned orders for each time period in the production planning horizon. An example Load report is shown in Table 9. The graphical load profile for the report given in Table 9 is shown in Figure 4.

The CRP technique must first identify under and over loads at the MRP level. Work centers loaded above 100 percent require adjustments in the capacity or load. Graphical load profiles will provide a static visual reflection of work center problems. The normal capacity for work center is shown in Figure 4. The normal capacity for the work center is 40 hours per week. The work center is overloaded in weeks 2, 3 and 4 and under loaded

Figure 4 Work Center Load Profile

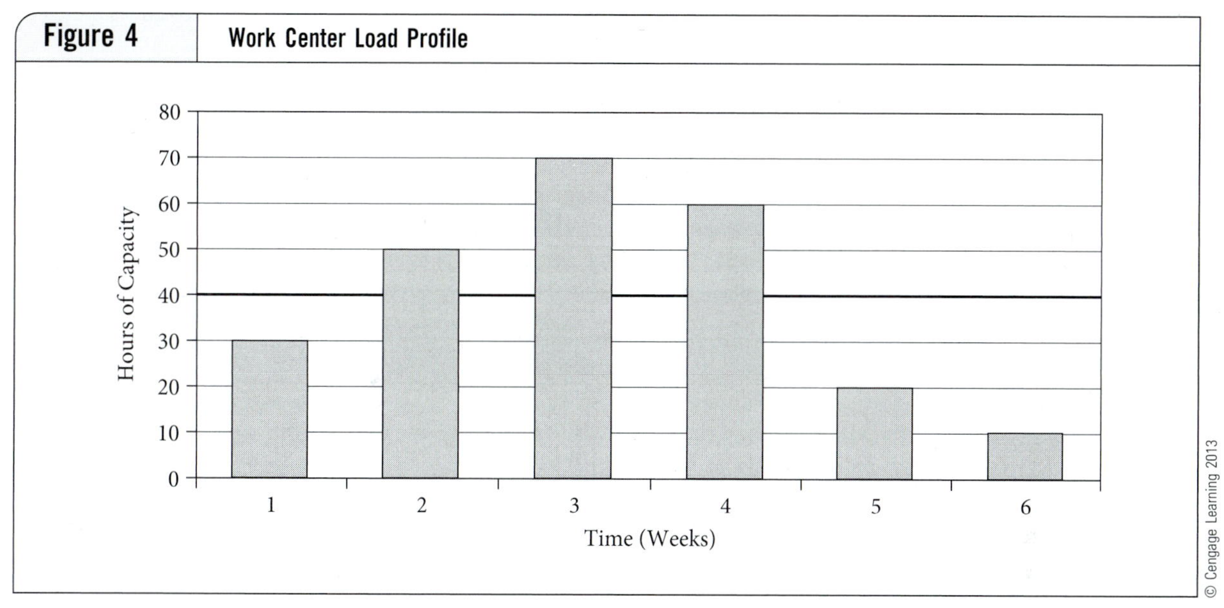

Table 9 Work Center Load Report

PERIOD	1	2	3	4	5	6	TOTAL
Released Load	10	20	30	20	5	10	95
Planned Load	20	30	40	40	15	0	145
Total Load	30	50	70	60	20	10	240
Rated Capacity	40	40	40	40	40	40	240
Overload	−10	10	30	20	−20	−30	0

in weeks 1, 5, and 6. It is easy to see that the most critical capacity problem is period 3. Working overtime is a reasonable option for period 3. Without knowing feasibility with certainty, it may be possible to smooth the load in the work center by pulling work forward from period 2 to period 1. The overload in period 4 could be rescheduled to periods 5 and 6. However this adjustment may create a customer service concern. The results of the adjustments to work center are shown in Figure 5. For most manufacturing organizations overloaded conditions create serious efficiency and customer service problems. Overloaded work centers can be resolved by:

1. Pulling work up or pushing work back (if feasible)
2. Increasing normal capacity
3. Subcontracting
4. Revising the MPS
5. Increasing the efficiency of the operation
6. Rerouting work to another work center
7. Splitting customer orders (if feasible)

Figure 5 Adjustments to the Work Center Profile

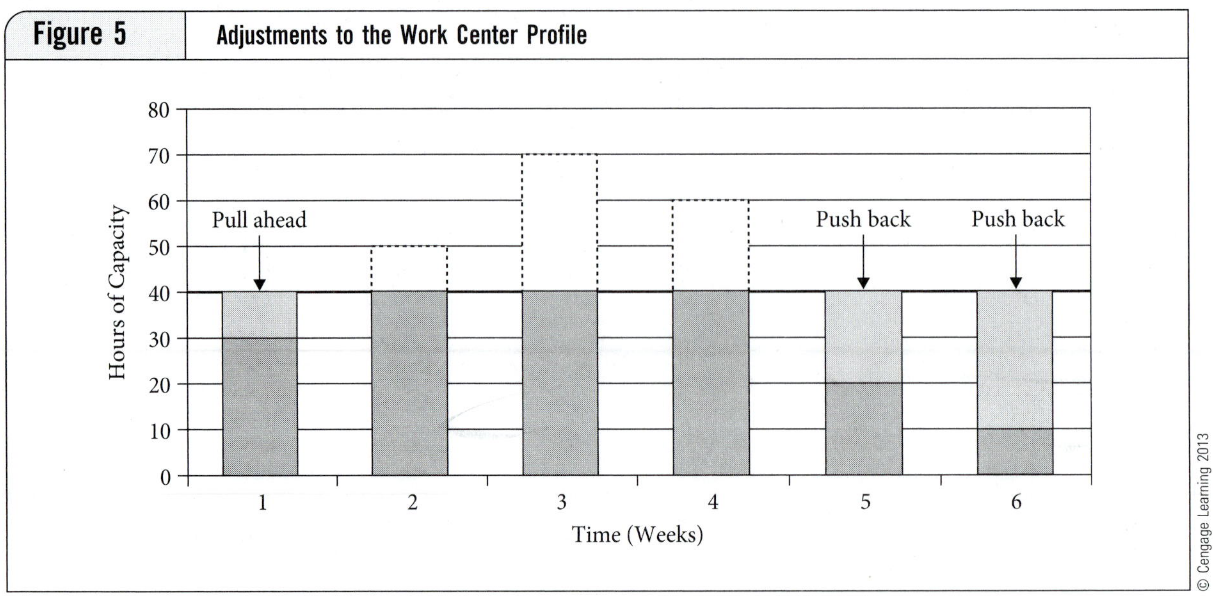

There are drawbacks associated with each of these alternatives. In most cases the planner will attempt to resolve the capacity issue in the most expedient way given the dynamic nature of the work center. The CRP load reporting illustrated in Example 9–1.

Example 9-1

The bill of materials, master schedule and routing file are given for the J750 Engine assembly.

Calculate the capacity requirements per week for the Turbine Housing, Turbine Assembly and auxiliary power unit work centers.

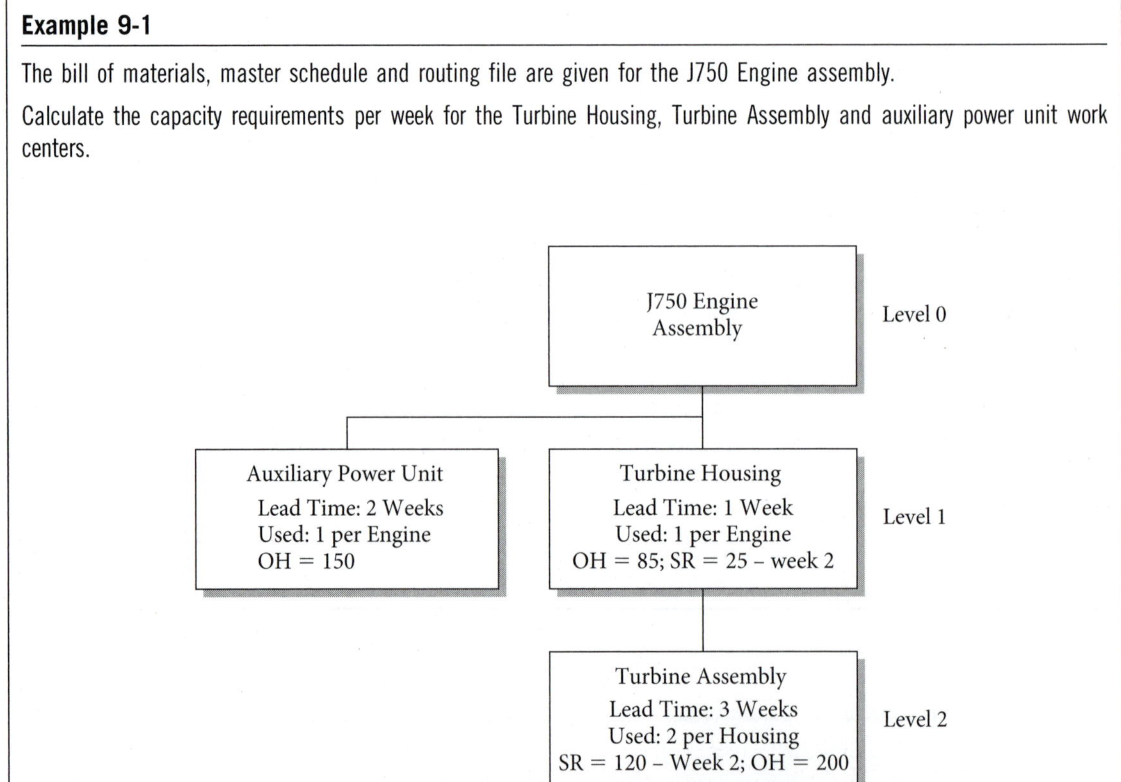

J750 Engine-Routing file

OPERATION	WORK CENTER	LEAD TIME WEEK AFTER PLANNED ORDER RELEASE	OPERATION RUM TIME (HOURS)	SET UP TIME (HOURS)
1	Turbine Assembly	3	0.3	3
2	Turbine Housing	1	0.1	2
3	Auxiliary PowerUnit	2	0.2	1

Component Part MRP Records

J750 Engine Master Schedule

WEEKS	1	2	3	4	5	6	7	8	9	10	11	12
Quantity	75	25	35	50	0	45	100	50	0	40	10	80

Component: Turbine Housing Requirements

WEEK	1	2	3	4	5	6	7	8	9	10	11	12
Gross Requirements	75	25	35	50	0	45	100	50	0	40	10	80
Scheduled Receipts*		25										
Projected Available** On Hand=85	10	10										
Planned Order Release			50		45	100	50		40	10	80	

*Measured at the end of each week.
**Received at the beginning of each week- Order quantity=Lot-for-Lot

Component: Turbine Assembly Requirements

WEEK	1	2	3	4	5	6	7	8	9	10	11	12
Gross Requirements			100		90	200	100		80	20	160	
Scheduled Receipts*		120										
Projected Available** On Hand=100		100	120	120	30	20	0	0				
Planned Order Release			170	100		80	20	160				

*Measured at the end of each week.
**Received at the beginning of each week=Order quantity- Lot-for-Lot

Component: Auxiliary Power Unit

WEEK	1	2	3	4	5	6	7	8	9	10	11	12
Gross Requirements	75	25	35	50	0	45	100	50	0	40	10	80
Scheduled Receipts*												
Projected Available** On Hand=150	75	50	15									
Planned Order Release		35		45	100	50		40	10	80		

*Measured at the end of each week.
**Received at the beginning of each week. . Order quantity=Lot-for-Lot

Turbine Housing

PERIOD	1	2	3	4	5	6	7	8	9	10	11	12
Planned Order Releases			50		45	100	50		40	10	80	
			(50*.1+2) ↓		(45*.1+2) ↓	(100*.1+2) ↓	(50*.1+2) ↓		(40*.1+2) ↓	(10*.1+2) ↓	(45*.1+2) ↓	
PERIOD	**1**	**2**	**3**	**4**	**5**	**6**	**7**	**8**	**9**	**10**	**11**	**12**
Load in Hours			7		6.5	12	7		6	3	10	

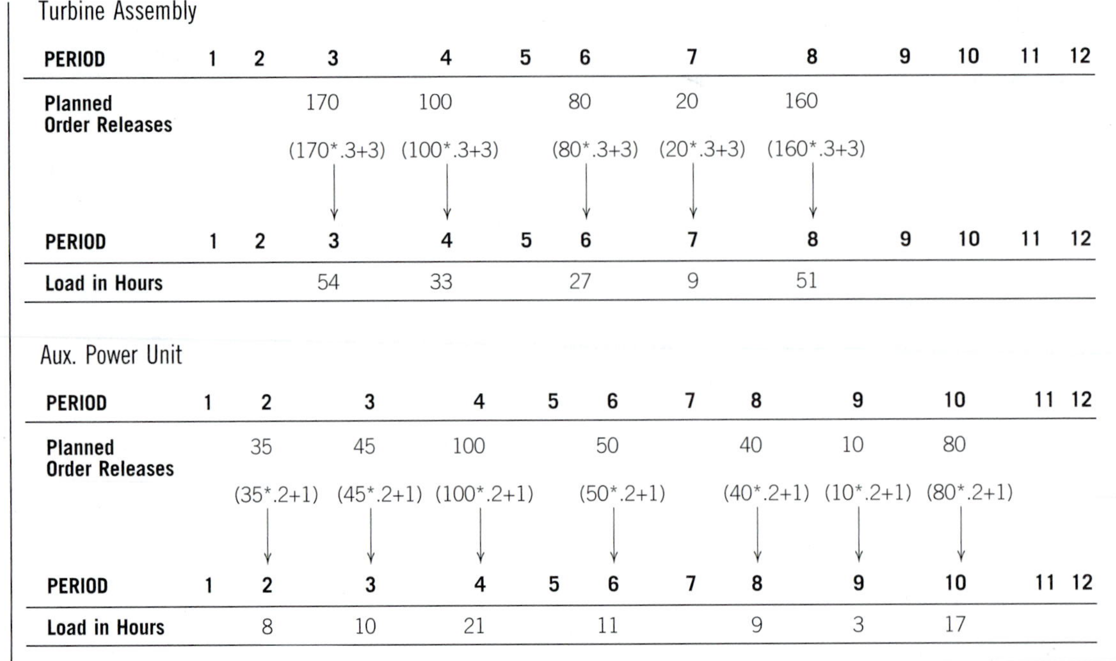

Turbine Assembly

PERIOD	1	2	3	4	5	6	7	8	9	10	11	12
Planned Order Releases			170	100		80	20	160				
			(170*.3+3)	(100*.3+3)		(80*.3+3)	(20*.3+3)	(160*.3+3)				

PERIOD	1	2	3	4	5	6	7	8	9	10	11	12
Load in Hours			54	33		27	9	51				

Aux. Power Unit

PERIOD	1	2	3	4	5	6	7	8	9	10	11	12
Planned Order Releases		35	45	100		50		40	10	80		
		(35*.2+1)	(45*.2+1)	(100*.2+1)		(50*.2+1)		(40*.2+1)	(10*.2+1)	(80*.2+1)		

PERIOD	1	2	3	4	5	6	7	8	9	10	11	12
Load in Hours		8	10	21		11		9	3	17		

Input–Output Analysis

The primary problem in capacity planning is to meet customer order due dates. (see Figure 1). The purpose of CRP is to level more overloaded work centers, work backward or forward. The CRP load-leveling method does not consider queue times for individual orders at the work centers. In capacity-constrained work-centers, planned output is based on the rate of capacity established by the management team. On the other hand, for non-capacitated work centers, planned output is equal to planned input. Thus input–output analysis is an important managerial lever that monitors work-center capacity imbalances. Input–output capacity data are measured in hours. Input hours include set up times, processing times, and time remaining for all scheduled orders. The work center becomes more complex given that each customer order has a unique capacity requirement, arrival, and start and due date. Input–output analysis is used to monitor the detailed work-center plan. Specifically, the planned work input and planned work output are compared to the actual work input and output. Input data is based on the arrival of the expected planned orders and open orders. The actual input is based on the actual arrival of the planned orders and open orders currently in the work center. Output is based on the actual output quantities converted to labor hours. The actual output of a work center usually deviates from the planned work-center output. Work-center output deviations are usually caused by low productivity, poor quality, random variation, and other unexpected circumstances. As an example, if work-in-process inventory is increasing at a work center, it could reflect the need for increased work-center capacity. Insufficient input from preceding work centers can lead to lower-than-expected work-center productivity. The downstream work centers will also be underutilized or starved. Consider the input–output report for the turbine housing work center given in Table 10.

The input–output report shows the capacity status at the end of four weeks for the turbine housing work center (684). Customer orders have been converted from units to labor hours. As can be seen, the planned inputs and outputs were set at the same levels.

Table 10 Input–Output Report for the Turbine Housing Work Center (684)

WORK CENTER 684	JUNE 3, 2013	JUNE 10, 2013	JUNE 17, 2013	JUNE 24, 2013
Planned input labor hours	400	400	400	400
Actual input labor hours	300	250	200	250
Cumulative Input–deviations	–100	–250	–450	–600
Planned output labor hours	400	400	400	400
Actual output labor hours	400	250	300	250
Cumulative–output deviation	0	–150	–250	–400

However, the actual work-center output is much lower. It appears that Work Center 684 is not getting enough work from the upstream work centers. Additionally, there is no WIP at the work center.

It is easy to see that input–output capacity planning is more accurate than the CRP method. The queue length is considered with the input–output method. However, the input–output method does not consider individual work orders in the load-leveling process. The supplier capacity-planning process will be discussed in the next section.

Supplier Capacity Planning

Supplier capacity planning (SCP) is a purchasing-planning system driven by the MRP schedule for purchased components. The SCP system establishes a supply chain relationship with tier-one suppliers. The SCP assists the tier-one suppliers with the development of more stable production schedules. The SCP also allows the manufacturing firm to monitor the quality, quantity, and lead time of deliveries. Figure 6 illustrates the role that the SCP concept plays in the supply chain focused manufacturing capacity planning and control system. The elements of the SCP are the purchase-order schedule, supplier capacity report, and supplier capacity planning.

Purchase-Order Schedule (POS)

The POS represents the planned order releases from the MRP system. The POS also shows the time-phased requirements by supplier. If the quantity required is allocated between the relevant suppliers, as shown in Table 11. The POS for each supplier can be generated by multiplying the predetermined percentage allocation by the MRP output quantities as shown in Figure 6. The MRP system aggregates the part families and distributes the requirements to the appropriate tier 1 supplier. The aggregation of individual component parts and assemblies into part families is also an objective of SCP. However, in practice, many buying organization do not include "C" items in the SCP (See chapter 5). If the part family is used in the SCP, the buying organization must combine the requirements of each individual part in the specified family to obtain the aggregate demand. The schedules shown in Figure 7 labeled Supplier A and C are purchase order schedules used in the development of the SCP for part family A. The aggregate supplier production order schedules are shown in Figure 7, and this serves as input to the SCP. The accumulation of all individual supplier capacity reports by product family or part number is transformed into the SCR summary. See Figure 8.

Figure 6 Purchase Order Schedule

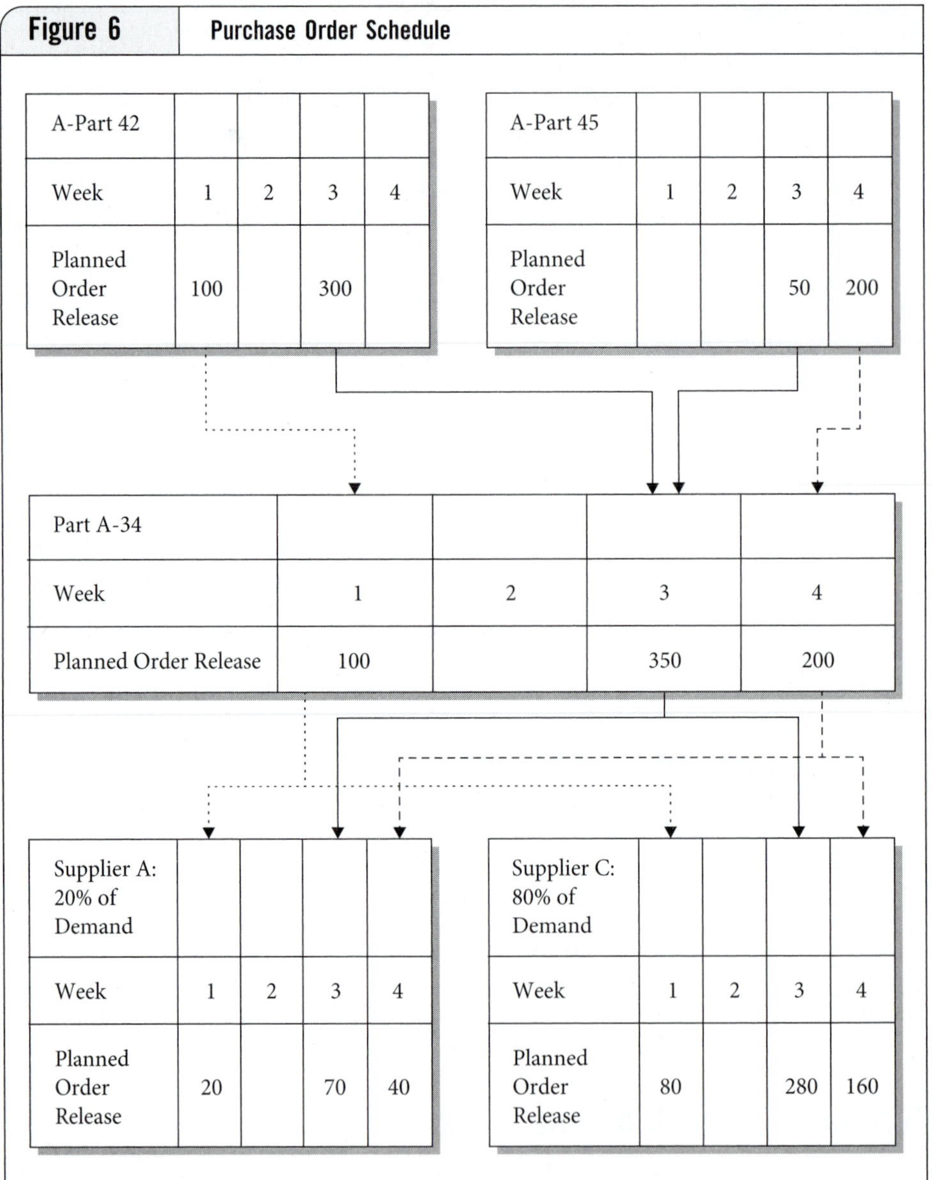

Table 11 Supplier Requirement Allocation

COMPONENT PART FAMILY	SUPPLIER A	SUPPLIER B	SUPPLIER C
A	20%		80%
B	30%	40%	30%
C	30%	70%	
D	100%		
F		100%	

Figure 7 Aggregate Purchase Order schedule

COMPONENT PART	WEEK 1	WEEK 2	WEEK 3	WEEK
A34	100		350	200
B23				
C56				
D90				
E78				

Figure 8 Aggregate Supplier Capacity Report Summary

PART A-34 SUPPLIER	WEEK 1	WEEK 2	WEEK 3	WEEK 4
Supplier A	20		70	40
Supplier C	80		280	160

Supplier Capacity Report (SCR)

The aggregate SCR is used to ensure adequate capacity requirements planning. The purpose of the SCR is to assess the ability of each supplier to produce the needed requirements on time and in the right quantities. If a supplier's capacity is insufficient, the decision maker can take corrective action.

The supplier capacity report is a time-phased statement of available production capacity for each purchased part family or part number over a given planning horizon. The supplier capacity provides valuable information for manufacturer and the suppliers. The supplying organization can easily develop a sustainable supply chain relationship with the manufacturing organization. High-quality SCR performance can help qualified suppliers to become long-term or strategic suppliers with the buying organization. On the other hand, the manufacturing organization can easily monitor the production plan of supplying organizations.

The SCR is the primary information link between the manufacturer and the supplier. When the buying organization selects a supply chain partner, it should assess the supplying firm's ability to execute and provide a supplier capacity report. The supplier should be required to express requirements in terms of units, machine hours, and labor hours during the related planning horizon. The manufacturing firm should share the capacity report for a specific product family with the supplier on a weekly basis. The supplier prepares the SCR by comparing the uncommitted production resources, period by period, with the MPS. The SCR must be submitted to the manufacturer prior to weekly MRP regenerations. On-time return of the SCR from all suppliers enables the manufacturing organization to develop an aggregate SCR summary. The SCR is also an excellent supplier evaluation mechanism.

SUMMARY

Capacity management is the focus of this chapter. We show how the capacity-planning process extends throughout the supply chain. The primary objective is to show how manufacturing planning must integrate capacity planning into the decision-making process. We focus on the elements of capacity planning and control. Capacity planning and control is the function of establishing, measuring, monitoring, and adjusting limits or levels of capacity in order to execute the manufacturing plans and schedules. Rough-cut capacity planning is the process of converting the master production schedule into requirements for key resources, including labor, machinery, warehouse capacity, and supplier's capabilities. Specifically, we focus on a variety of techniques for determining capacity requirements for long-range, medium-range, and short-range capacity decisions. Specific capacity-planning techniques must match the level of detail in the manufacturing planning and control system. Finally, the supplier-capacity planning (SCP) process was discussed. The SCP is concerned with information sharing with key suppliers.

EXERCISES

1. The Best Beer Corporation has a beer-processing facility located in Columbus, Ohio. The beer facility has a system efficiency of 90 percent, and the utilization is 80 percent. Three sub-facilities are used for processing. The facilities operate five days a week and three 8-hour shifts per day. What is the rated weekly capacity for the facility?
2. Best has decided to increase its facilities by adding one sub-facility. Doing this, however, will reduce the overall system efficiency to 78 percent. Compute the new *rated capacity* under this situation.
3. During the last several years, demand for beer has been steady and predictable. Furthermore, there has been a direct relationship between barrels of beer processed and rated capacity expressed in hours per week. This relationship has allowed the executives of Best to forecast rated capacity with a fair degree of accuracy. The production manager provided the following historical data for rated capacity.

MONTH	RATED CAPACITY(HR. /WK.) 2013
Jan.	500
Feb.	510
Mar.	514
Apr.	520
May	524
June	529

With the above data, it is possible to project rated capacity into the future. Use the three period moving-average techniques to forecast for July 2013 (see Chapter 2, if forecasting knowledge is limited).

4. Best is considering using a basic exponential smoothing model with $\alpha = .2$ to forecast capacity (see Chapter 2, if forecasting knowledge is limited).
   a. Use the sales average of 480 through December 2012 as the forecast for January. Prepare capacity forecast for February through April at the end of January.
   b. Calculate the average error and Mean Absolute Deviation (MAD) for the three forecasts using the actual capacity data provided. Estimate the standard deviation of the calculated MAD.
   c. Redo the capacity forecast and MAD calculations, updating the forecast for February through May and June and updating the forecast at the end of March and April.
5. A landing gear manufacturer has the following MPS for one of its items (shaft housing), as well as the accompanying product structure.

	WEEK 1	WEEK 2	WEEK 3	WEEK 4
MPS	200	300	350	200

The resource profile for the frame is as follows:

ITEM	WORK CENTER	SETUP HOURS	RUN HOURS/UNIT	LEAD TIME
Frame	201	4	1.5	0 weeks
Part X	302	3	1.0	1 week
Part Y	302	3	.8	1 week
Part Z	400	2	1.2	2 weeks
Part R	500	2	1.0	1 week

Determine the capacity requirements for all work centers, assuming all usages are one, and that a new setup is required in each week at each work center.

6. Consider the following MRP record for a notebook manufacturer.

COVER	1	2	3	4	5	6
Gross requirements	20	25	25	25	25	0
Scheduled receipts	50					
Projected available balance 10						
Planned order releases		0		0	0	0

Q = 50, LT = 2, SS = 0

The notebooks are fabricated in the following work centers, listed with accompanying time requirements.

OPERATION	WORK CENTER	SETUP TIME	RUN TIME
Notebook assembly	100	2 hours	10 minutes
Pad production	200	3 hours	5 minutes
Cover production	300	2 hours	9 minutes

Determine the weekly capacity requirements in each of the work centers.

7. The following input–output data were gathered at the end of Week 6 for a work center:

	WEEK					
	1	2	3	4	5	6
Planned input	60	60	60	60	60	60
Actual input	68	70	75	70	68	60
Planned output	65	65	65	65	65	65
Actual output	60	62	63	63	64	65

Beginning backlog = 50 hours

a. Complete the input–output report.
b. What was the planned objective? Was it met?
c. What do you recommend?'

8. A company with three product lines has estimated its weekly capacity requirements for three work centers as follows:

	PRODUCT LINE		
WORK CENTER	A	B	C
500	28 hours	35 hours	14 hours
801	37 hours	24 hours	56 hours
636	46 hours	35 hours	35 hours

a. How many workers (and duplicate machines) are needed in each work center if they are to work 40 hours per week?
b. What is the difference if the firm decides to work two shifts (80 hours per week)?

Chapter 10

PRODUCTION PLANNING AND CONTROL FOR REMANUFACTURING

Learning Objectives

- To understand production planning and control for remanufacturing systems
- To identify the relationship between the traditional manufacturing planning and control system and those for remanufacturing
- To explore the development Material Requirements Planning (MRP) in a remanufacturing environment
- To understand the core acquisition process
- To understand the overall financial implications of supply chain focused remanufacturing planning and control

Introduction

What Is Remanufacturing?

Almost everyone who has owned an automobile has purchased remanufactured auto replacement parts. Remanufactured replacement parts are less expensive and, in most cases, just as reliable as new parts. However, if the expertise and remanufacturing process are flawed, the replacement parts will be defective and fail long before the promised warranty date. Examples of remanufactured replacement parts include starters, alternators, brake calipers, drive shafts, and many electrical components. Another example is the US Army. In June 2005, the U.S. Army Tank-automotive and Armaments Command (TACOM) awarded BAE Systems contracts worth $1.127 billion to remanufacture and upgrade more than 500 Bradley Combat System vehicles.

There are many high-quality remanufactures that produce certified products that are just as reliable as many brand-new parts. The cost of remanufactured replacement parts is usually 40 to 50 percent less than comparable new original equipment manufacturer (OEM) replacement parts, and they typically offer warranties ranging from one year up to a lifetime warranty. The warranties on electrical components typically range from 30 to 90 days at most. The issue of quality is an important one for most automobile repair shops because dissatisfied customers will damage the repair shop's reputation.

An additional benefit of using remanufactured parts is that the process recycles metal that would otherwise be thrown away. This may require exchanging the old part (or core) to receive a core credit with your parts supplier. Remanufacturing typically reuses castings and other major components that can be cleaned, remachined, and returned to like-new condition. Most high-quality remanufactures then test the parts to make sure they function correctly before boxing and shipping them for distribution. However, components that are subject to wear and tear, such as seals, bushing, calipers, wheel cylinder pistons, valves, bleeder screws, springs, and the like, are usually replaced with all-new components.

Remanufacturing is the process by which products are recovered, processed, and sold as like-new products in the same or separate markets. Remanufacturing does not involve the process of repairing, reconditioning, or recycling. Remanufactured products have higher quality levels than repaired or reconditioned products. Due to increasing legislation and the realization that being "green" can be profitable, an increasing number of companies have been implementing comprehensive programs in order to reap the potential benefits of remanufacturing. Remanufacturing is an environmentally sound way to achieve many goals of sustainable development. In the United States, laws mandating that companies be responsible for the take back of electronic wastes are becoming prevalent at the state level. Today, there are more than 70,000 remanufacturing companies with revenues exceeding $55 billion in annual sales. The selling price of a remanufactured product is usually 30 to 40 percent lower than the price of a new product. The Remanufacturing Institute (www.reman.org) reports that as of May 2012, 26 states in the United States had passed laws requiring OEMs to be responsible for taking back and reusing and/or disposing of end of life products. Remanufacturing can become a competitive advantage as well as provide for a less polluted environment. However, few guidelines are available to the practicing manager to aid in planning, controlling, and managing remanufacturing operations. A typical remanufacturing process is shown in Figure 1. As can be seen from the process flow diagram, the remanufacturing elements involve core inspection, cleaning disassembly, reassembly, final inspection, and packaging.

Figure 1 Typical Remanufacturing Process

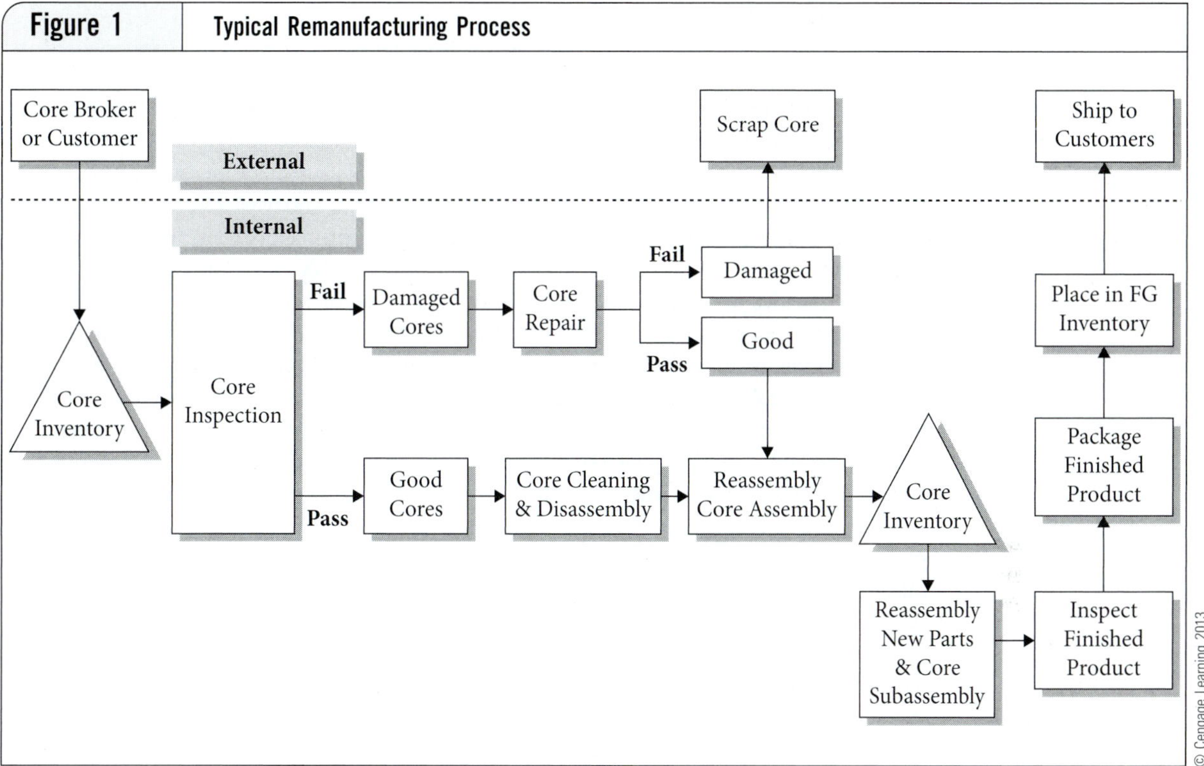

The remanufacturing process is characterized by unexpected uncertainties and alternative throughput choices. The remanufacturing process begins with the acquisition and disassembly of cores. The disassembly process involves cleaning, inspecting, and reassembling component parts. In the final remanufacturing phase, parts are assembled into components, inspected, and packed for shipment or placed into inventory. The damaged cores are scrapped.

Of course, the sequence of steps may change depending on the specific remanufactured product. The following product categories are well suited for remanufacturing considerations.

- Aircraft equipment
- Automotive parts
- Bakery equipment
- Compressors
- Construction equipment
- Data communication equipment
- Gaming machines
- Durable electronics
- Industrial machinery and machine tools
- Musical instruments
- Office furniture
- Photocopiers
- Refrigeration equipment

Disassembly

The used core is the key input into the remanufacturing process. Cores come in at an uncertain rate. In addition, some of the acquired cores are incompatible for the current remanufacturing requirements. There are also uncertainties regarding core quality after disassembly. Some of the damaged cores are repairable while others are too costly to repair. In general the yield rate can be highly uncertain and variable. Core acquisition yield rate is the primary source of remanufacturing complexity. The remanufacturing planning and control process is driven by the disassembly schedule. The disassembly schedule specifies both core type and quantity required for future periods. The disassembly schedule is also influenced by the acquisition forecast and the number of parts currently in inventory. Forecasting of product returns has been studied for disposable cameras, returnable bottles, electronic components, and many other products. In these product environments, typically, only the sales and return volume in each period is known and not the timing of returns and sales. This type of data is usually defined as *period-level* data. One method for forecasting returns with period-level data is to use a time series consisting of past return volumes to forecast future return volumes; however, such a method would ignore past sales data. The key to forecasting returns is the observation that returns in any one period are generated by sales in the preceding periods. However, in practice, the data are not fixed but are, rather, augmented in each period as new sales and return information. For a more comprehensive discussion of core acquisition, see Clottey, Benton, and Srivastava (2012).

Reassembly

The remanufacturing operation has to deal with demand uncertainties as well. It is also important for the production manager to determine the appropriate safety stock quantity of completed assemblies for each core type. There must be an attempt to match supply with demand. The assembly schedule must be developed to ensure that the remanufactured components to meet the required demand and safety stock. After the assembly schedule is formulated, the parts required to support the schedule can be finalized. The remanufacturing assembly schedule is usually divided into weekly time buckets.

Remanufacturing Production Planning and Control

Production planning and control activities are even more complex and difficult for remanufacturing operations compared to traditional manufacturing operations, mainly due to the uncertainty in sourcing the cores required for remanufacturing. Forecasting the proportions of product returns is important for procurement decisions, capacity planning, and disposal management. An accurate forecast of the returned product quantities (in each period) is critical for an effective production-planning and inventory system.

A summary of production planning and control activities is shown in Figure 2. This framework is flexible enough to describe various remanufacturing operations, including furniture, computer, steel, and automotive parts remanufacturing. In order to ensure a sufficient quantity of cores, remanufacturers often use multiple sources for their supply of cores. The primary and usually the least expensive source of cores is product returns from customers due to end life or end use. A secondary source of cores is from third parties (e.g., brokers, salvage operators, and salvage auctioneers).

Table 1 Complications to the Production Planning and Control (PPC) System Due to the Uncertainties in Sourcing Cores for Remanufacturing

ACTIVITY	DESCRIPTION	COMPLICATIONS AS A RESULT OF SOURCING UNCERTAINTIES IN REMANUFACTURING
Demand management	Order entry, forecasting end product demand, order promising, physical distribution activities	i. Difficulties in order promising of remanufactured items can lead to operational inefficiencies and costs ii. Order cancellations and/or back orders of remanufactured items can increase the volatility in forecasting end demand for **both** the remanufactured and new product
Aggregate production planning	Determining the number of units to be produced in each major product line per period (i.e. monthly or quarterly, annually)	i. Difficulty in balancing cores with demand for the remanufactured product can lead to disruptions in the production plan for remanufacturing ii. The production plan for new products can also be affected by disruptions in the plan for remanufactured products
Resource planning	Determining the aggregate capacity to support the production plan (annually)	i. Difficulties in the accurate forecasting of long-term core availability ii. Increased costs due to volatile resource plans
Master production scheduling	Anticipated build schedule for manufacturing end products	Affects MPS stability leading to poor customer service and operational inefficiencies
Detailed capacity planning	Determination of time-phased capacity requirements (weekly or monthly)	i. Planning difficulties due to stochastic routings and processing times ii. Variable material recovery rates lead to volatile capacity plans
Detailed material planning	Determining the parts and component requirements for production (weekly or monthly)	i. Accumulation of both new and used parts/component inventory ii. Increased used parts disposal
Shop-floor systems	Establish priorities for all shop orders and control material flow	Difficulty in scheduling and/or control of material flow due to stochastic routings and processing times
Sourcing systems	Providing detailed planning information for supplier scheduling	i. Risk of shortages from the vendor ii. Need for up-to-date information sharing with the supplier iii. Need for supplier flexibility

Source: Clottey and Benton (2013).

Table 1 provides a summary of these uncertainties in quality and quantity of cores affect the front-end, engine, and back-end components of the production planning and control system shown in Figure 2. The front end and engine level activities focus on planning. The back end focuses on execution.

Demand Management

Demand management encompasses forecasting customer/end-product demand, order entry, and order promising and accommodating inter-company demand and spare parts. When remanufacturing is added to an existing manufacturing operation, the sales

Figure 2 A Production Planning and Control Framework

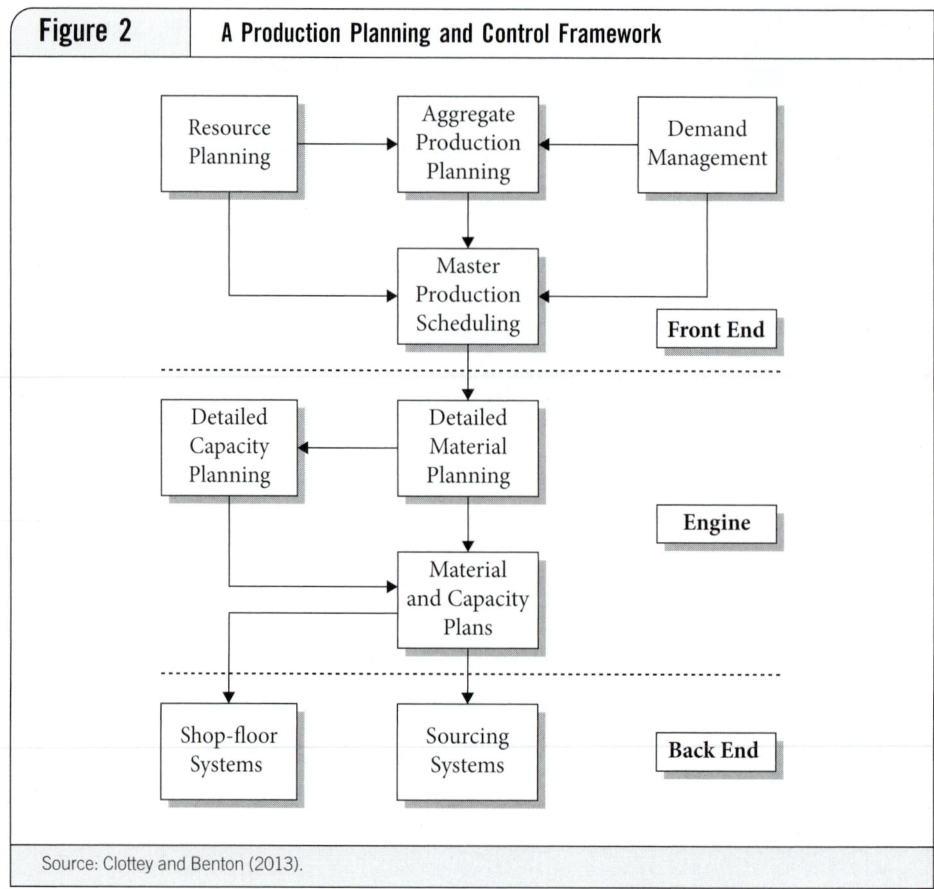

Source: Clottey and Benton (2013).

forecast of new products/components used for demand management needs to be augmented with the sales forecast of remanufactured products/components. Backlogged demand resulting from shortages of cores can complicate the sales forecasting of remanufactured products, since these backlogged items need to be accounted for in the forecast. The uncertainty in the timing, quantity, and quality of cores sourced for remanufacturing also makes order promising for demand management more difficult.

Aggregate Production Planning

Aggregate production planning provides the desired aggregate output from manufacturing in order to support the company's strategic plan. Production plans are often stated in terms of the number of units to be produced in each major product line for the next year. The production plan matches the resources and capacity of the firm to the demand on an aggregate level. Creating an aggregate production plan is more complex for remanufacturing operations due to the uncertainty in the quantity, quality, and timing of cores. The new-parts inventory is often linked to the remanufacturing operation, since manufacturers will use new parts to satisfy demand for remanufactured products if there are insufficient cores available. This further complicates the production-planning process, as resources for new products need to be managed to support both the manufacturing and remanufacturing operations. Also see Chapters 3 & 4 for a detailed discussion of aggregate production and master production schedule.

Resource Planning

Resource planning involves converting monthly, quarterly, or even annual data from the production plan into aggregate long-term resources, such as gross labor-hours, floor space, and machine hours. Uncertainties in the quantity, quality and timing of the sourcing of cores make the determination of the required long-term capacity for remanufacturing a difficult task. The uncertainty in sourcing cores also makes it difficult to create the long-term forecasts of core availability required for resource planning. Also see Chapter 9.

Master Production Scheduling

The master production schedule (MPS) is the disaggregated version of the production plan and must add up to the production plan. Since the outputs from demand management, production planning, and resource planning feed into the MPS, the volatility of these outputs as a result of the uncertainties inherent in sourcing cores for remanufacturing can affect the stability of the MPS, which in turn can lead to poor customer service and operational inefficiencies. Also see Chapter 4.

Detailed Capacity Planning

Detailed capacity planning involves the monthly or weekly determination of time-phased labor or machine-center-capacity requirements for all component parts and raw materials required to produce all the products in the MPS. Varying quality levels of cores lead to varying disassembly and processing times for remanufacturing. This makes it difficult to create accurate time-phased plans for the required labor or machine capacity. Also, varying material-recovery rates from the disassembly of returned products and unanticipated shortages from third-party core suppliers make it difficult to create an accurate material plan, which then makes it difficult to create accurate capacity plans for utilizing the materials. Insufficient or excess capacity results in poor customer service and needless expenses. Also see Chapter 9.

Detailed Material Planning

Detailed material planning involves determining the weekly or monthly raw materials and component parts required for production. Uncertainties in material recovery rates and timing of returned products, along with uncertainties in the quality level and quantities of acquired cores, increase the complexity of creating and implementing a detailed materials plan for remanufacturing. An inaccurate materials plan for remanufacturing leads to the accumulation of core inventory or disposal of otherwise usable returned products if there is insufficient space. If new parts are used for remanufacturing due to insufficient cores, then additional safety stock of new parts is required to cater for the uncertainties in sourcing the cores. Also see Chapter 6.

Shop-Floor Systems

A wide variety of manual and computer-based shop-floor scheduling systems exist. Two basic approaches are MRP and just-in-time (JIT) systems. The MRP-based approach supports the release of shop orders based on a schedule developed by the material and capacity plan. The JIT-based approach supports the release of shop orders based on actual demand for end items and relies on the rate at which capacity and materials are used in order to minimize flow times. Both systems are negatively impacted by supply uncertainties. Stochastic routings and variable material recovery rates due to variable quality and uncertainties in the timing and quantity of cores make it difficult to effectively schedule or control the material flow. (Also see Chapters 6 & 7).

Sourcing Systems

Sourcing systems are used to release orders to suppliers of cores, which are aligned with the correct due dates from the material plan. Contractual agreements with the core suppliers typically define the type and degree of flexibility that can be offered to the manufacturer. Developing appropriate contractual agreements to allow for a flexible remanufacturing operation is also important. Quantity uncertainty from suppliers of cores is a risk that must be managed. An example of the remanufacturing planning and control system will be given in the next section.

Production Planning for Component Remanufacturing

There are two distinct decision processes that must be merged into the remanufacturing system. The demand decision process converts used parts into the *assembly* schedule needed to complete the part. The supply process is the *disassembly* schedule that converts cores into parts. The demand and supply processes are then integrated in order to provide parts for future component demand.

The demand for remanufactured components is met through a finished-goods inventory that is managed with an MPS. A standard MRP approach, time phased in weekly buckets, shown in Table 2 is used to determine the demand for each part in every period. To meet the part requirements, the part inventory is first considered. If additional parts are needed, the parts that are still in core assemblies are considered, and, finally, additional cores (or parts) are purchased if needed. Management of the core inventory requires not only determining what cores should be purchased to meet the need for parts but also what cores should be sold or scrapped to prevent excess inventory from accumulating. When the final core inventory is determined, the disassembly schedule is developed to supply parts to the

Table 2 Time Phased MRP Record for Part-656

PERIOD		1	2	3	4	5	6
Part number	656						
Parent part	A 700						
Expected yield	68%						
Expected disassembly yield	70%						
Core sourcing leadtime	2 weeks						
Gross core assembly requirements		50	100	45	300	170	60
Scheduled core receipts		200					
Assembled cores on hand	20		70	25			
Net core requirements			275*	170	60		

*(Gross Requirements – ON Hand) = 300 – 25 = 275; The 275 + 25 will be used for the 300 unit requirement in Period 4.

part inventory. The information and approach to managing the inventories and creating the production schedules for each of these areas are presented in the following sections.

Part Demand Determination

Each week, the MRP record for each part shows the gross requirement to meet the demand for all products in which it is used. Table 2 shows the MRP record for a specific component part. As can be seen, the part number, parent component, disassembly yield, and core lead time are documented in the time-phased record. Next, the gross requirement is determined by the master schedule. The gross requirements are subtracted from the scheduled receipts plus on-hand inventory. If the difference between them is negative, there is a net requirement that needs to be filled through core disassembly or part purchase.

Part Supply Determination

The primary source for parts to meet the net requirements is the core inventory. If current core inventory plus anticipated trade-ins is not sufficient to meet the needs, either more cores or parts will need to be purchased. Thus, effective core inventory management is important for controlling the costs of remanufacturing. Adapting standard MRP concepts and logic to the remanufacturing environment requires the following design changes:

1. How big should the time buckets be? Weekly or monthly?
2. How often should the remanufacturing assembly plan be regenerated?
3. What (if any) lot sizing methods should be used?
4. Where should safety stock be located? How much safety stock should be held, if any?
5. Should the disassembly department be buffered from the assembly department by inserting a buffer inventory?

If there are no usable cores available, there would be nothing to remanufacture. Core acquisition is the most critical step in the remanufacturing process. A recent core acquisition study is presented in the next section.

Core Acquisition Study[1]

A comprehensive survey of the automobile parts industry was conducted. Effective management of the core-sourcing process can be used to better manage the front-end, engine, and back-end components of the integrated remanufacturing production planning and control system. Planning for the acquisition of cores is critical for reducing the uncertainty associated with core-sourcing. The following study provides insights into the critical issues faced by automotive parts remanufacturers in acquiring cores for production. This is included to provide practical guidance for the effective management of the integrated remanufacturing planning and control system.

The automotive parts industry was chosen for two predominant reasons. First, results from remanufacturing in the automotive parts industry are generalizable due to the

[1]The results in this section are based on a survey conducted by Toyin Clottey, and W. C. Benton.

following: Automotive parts were the first products suited to large-scale remanufacturing in the United States and, therefore, remanufacturing of automotive parts has occurred since the early 1900s (www.reman.rit.edu). The Automotive Parts Remanufacturers Association (APRA) has been in existence since 1941 and is the oldest remanufacturing association in the United States. APRA currently boasts a membership of more than 1000 members worldwide and represents a stable industry in which diverse products are remanufactured (www.apra.com). This stability and diversity makes results, from a sampling frame consisting of APRA members, generalizable to a variety of businesses. Second, the use of the automotive parts industry allows for sufficient insights to be gained concerning the use of third-party brokers for the sourcing of cores. This is because the automotive parts industry is the second-largest user of brokers and salvage operators for the sourcing of cores in the United States.

Remanufacturing Study Results

The profile of respondents is provided in Table 3.

Respondent Demographics

Table 3 demonstrates that the sample represents a variety of remanufacturing operations in the automotive parts industry. Remanufacturing is the primary activity of 69 percent of the respondents. All but two of the respondents indicated having a secondary activity in addition to remanufacturing; those two respondents chose the "other" category for the secondary activity question. The remanufacturing operations of the respondents are mostly small or medium in size in terms of number of employees (fewer than 100), approximate annual unit sales (fewer than 50,000 units), and approximate revenue (less than $3 million). The majority of respondents remanufacture electrical, brake, and transmission systems as their primary product. Most respondents who chose the "other" category for their primary product indicated remanufacturing of clutches, axles, and fuel systems. Only two of the respondents indicated that remanufacturing accounted for 100 percent of sales. This indicates that the remanufacturers in the automobile industry are multifaceted, since they operate other revenue-generating activities in addition to remanufacturing. A similar conclusion was found by Hauser and Lund (2003). The majority of respondents have been engaged in remanufacturing for more than 11 years. The distributions shown in Table 3, when compared to those obtained in Hauser and Lund (2003), for respondents from the automotive industry, were not markedly different. This illustrates that the sample is representative of the automotive parts remanufacturing industry. The next section presents the results for the cores and other materials section of the survey.

Cores and Other Materials

Responses from this section showed that cores mostly represented up to 19 percent of the cost of a remanufactured product. This finding is consistent with a study by Hauser and Lund who found that, on average, cores represented 14 percent of the cost of a remanufactured product in the automotive industry. The fact that the costs of cores constitute a significant portion of the remanufactured product costs provides further motivation for research that investigates the management of the supply of cores.

Table 3 Profile of Respondents

Firm's primary activity		Firm's secondary activity	
Remanufacturing	69%	Service and repair	51%
Service and repair	7%	New product manufacturer (OEM)	34%
New product manufacturer (OEM)	11%	Selling new products made by others	74%
Selling new products made by others	10%	Other (Describe)	12%
Other (describe)	3%	**Total Responses: 91**	
Total Responses: 91			

Principal products remanufactured		Approximate revenue	
Air conditioning systems	5%	0 to 299 thousand	19%
Electrical systems	41%	300 to 999 thousand	16%
Brake systems	19%	1–2.99 million	23%
Clutch systems	15%	3–10 million	16%
Transmission systems	19%	More than 10 million	26%
Electronic control modules	10%	**Total Responses: 88**	
Engines	9%		
Other (Describe)	33%		
Total Responses: 91			

Approximate unit sales	
0 to 9 thousand	42%
10 to 29 thousand	28%
30 to 50 thousand	3%
More than 50 thousand	27%
Total Responses:78	

Number of employees used for remanufacturing		Remanufactured products as a proportion of total sales	
fewer than 100	79%	0–19%	10%
100–249	10%	20–39%	13%
250–499	6%	40–59%	13%
500–999	5%	60–79%	32%
1,000 or more	0%	80–99%	29%
Total Responses: 80		100%	3%
		Total Responses: 78	

Years of operation	
0–3 years	3%
4–10 years	7%
11–30 years	41%
Over 30 years	49%
Total Responses: 91	

The primary source of cores for remanufacturing was trade-in returns from the customer (60%–79% of all cores). The other sources, including core brokers, fell in the 0 to 19 percent category. This differs slightly from the Hauser and Lund (2003) result for the automotive industry, in which trade-ins accounted for an average of 30 percent of cores in the automotive parts industry. In the same report, core brokers

Table 4 Quality of Cores

Portion of cores rejected as unusable	
0–5%	45%
6–10%	28%
11–20%	24%
21–30%	0%
31–40%	1%
41 to 50%	0%
More than 50%	1%
Total Responses: 74	

Salvage value as a percentage of core value	
0–5%	30%
6–10%	27%
11–20%	11%
21–30%	10 %
31–40%	4%
41 to 50%	9%
More than 50%	9%
Total Responses: 70	

Number of groups for sorting cores	
2 groups	65%
3 groups	20%
4 groups	9%
5 groups	2%
More than 5 groups	5%
Total Responses: 74	

accounted for an average of 14.8 percent of cores, which is consistent with the results of this study. The high percentage of cores from trade-ins reported by respondents in this study could mean that the arrangements for cores supplied via trade-ins may have sufficiently increased in the seven years since the survey of Hauser and Lund (2003) was reported, so that trade-ins are now the primary source of returns for remanufacturers of automotive parts.

Quality of Cores

Table 4 shows the results for the questions that address the quality of cores. Ninety-eight percent of respondents indicated that less than 20 percent of cores are immediately rejected as unusable. This high acceptance rate could be due to the low salvage value of the cores. Seventy-eight percent of respondents indicated that the salvage value of a core is at most 30 percent of the value of the core.

With such low rejection rates, the main supply issue faced by remanufacturers in industries such as automotive parts remanufacturing is likely one of *quantity* as opposed to the *quality* of cores. Eighty-five percent of respondents indicated that three or fewer quality groups were used for sorting cores.

Figure 3 shows the responses to questions concerning sourcing relationships.

Figure 3 Sourcing Relationships

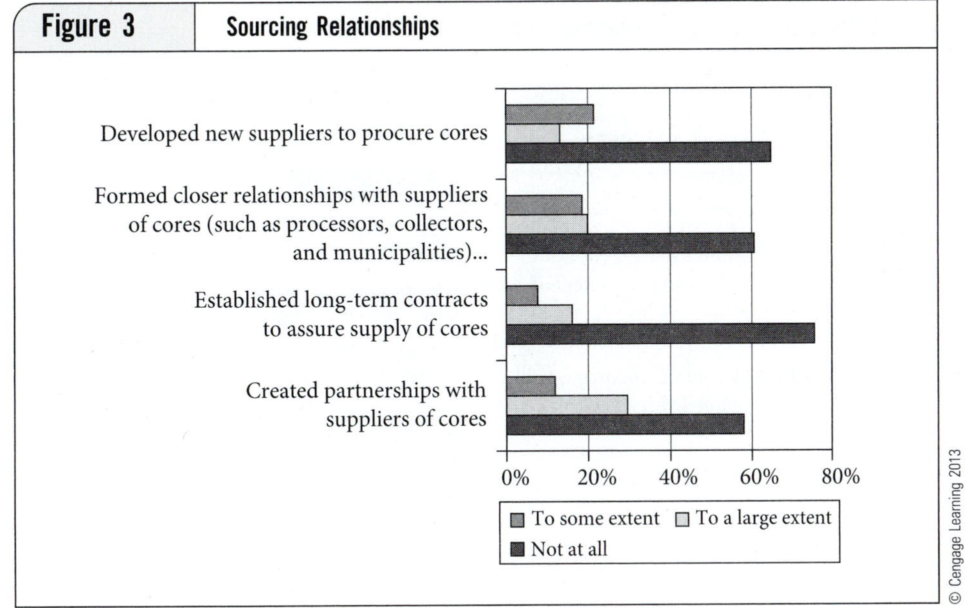

Sourcing Relationships

The majority of the respondents (approximately 60%) indicated not having a close relationship with their suppliers of cores. This has implications for the successful management of the integrated remanufacturing production and control system. Arms-length relationships with suppliers may represent a lost opportunity to better synchronize the sourcing of cores with product returns.

Core Supply Uncertainty

Figure 4 provides the responses to a question concerning the uncertainty in the supply of cores if relations with current suppliers were terminated. The majority of respondents (approximately 51%, averaged over the three categories) indicated that they would find it difficult to source a sufficient quantity of cores if relations with suppliers were terminated. This illustrates that there is some dependence by remanufacturers on suppliers of cores. However, approximately 49 percent indicated the opposite. The managerial implication of this near-equal split will be explained later in this chapter.

Core Forecasting Methods

Figure 5 provides responses to a survey question on the methods used to forecast core quantities. These results indicate that remanufacturers are less likely to use quantitative (e.g., regression) or qualitative models (e.g., market surveys) for making forecasts and more likely to use management opinion. This is conceivable because of the difficulties involved in using quantitative models due to the uncertainties in the timing, quantity, and quality of cores. The availability of quantitative models that are able to provide accurate results by accounting for these uncertainties could encourage remanufacturers to increase their use of quantitative methods for

Figure 4 Supply Uncertainty of Cores from Suppliers

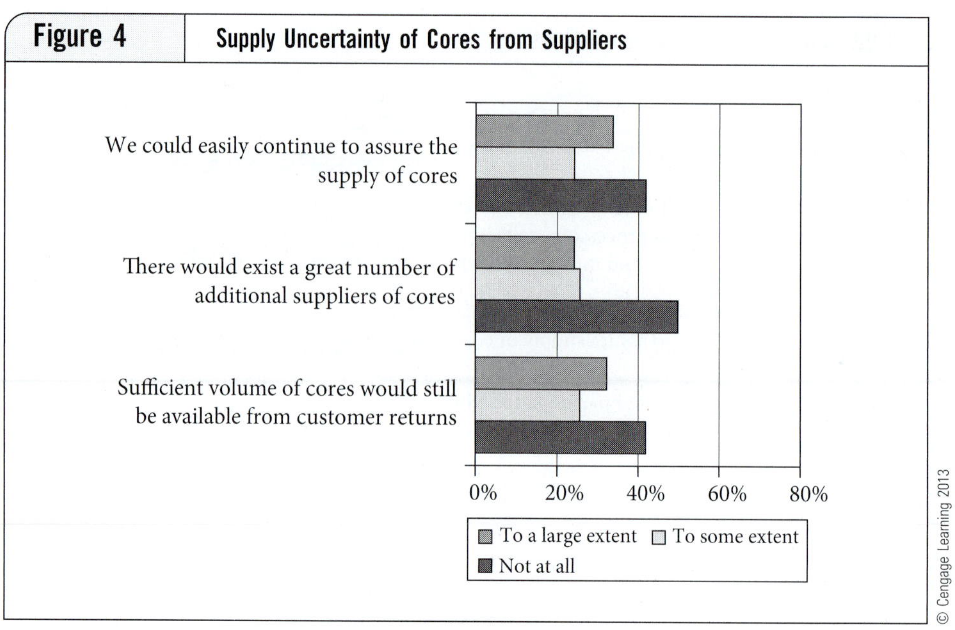

Figure 5 Methods Used for Forecasting Cores

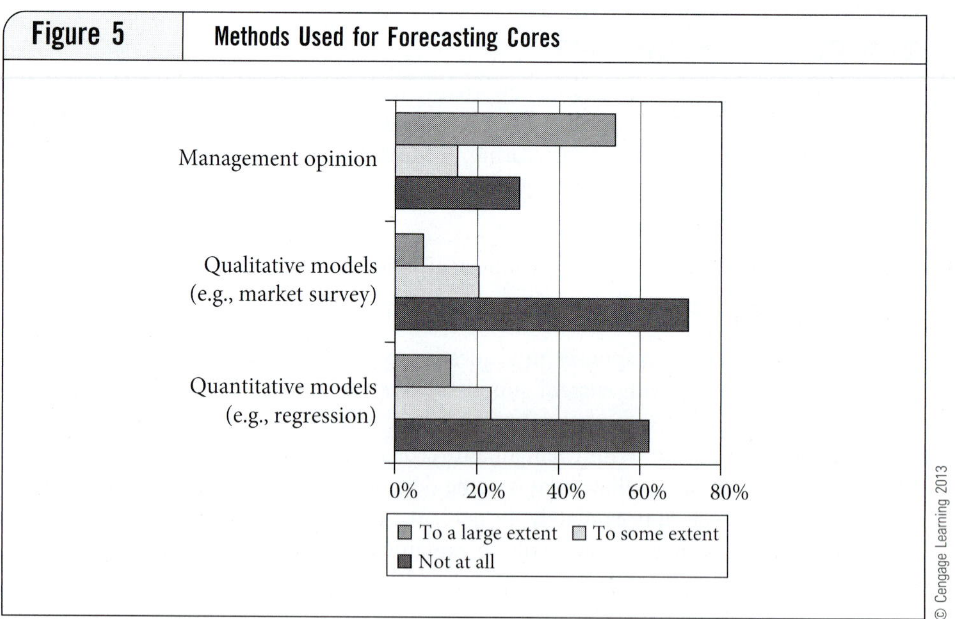

forecasting. Figure 6 provides responses to a survey question concerning the information used to forecast core quantities.

Information Used to Forecast Cores

The results shown in Figure 6 indicate that market research information is least likely to be incorporated into a forecast. This could be because there are only a few market surveys on remanufacturing that have been undertaken and/or that are

Figure 6 Information Used to Forecast Cores

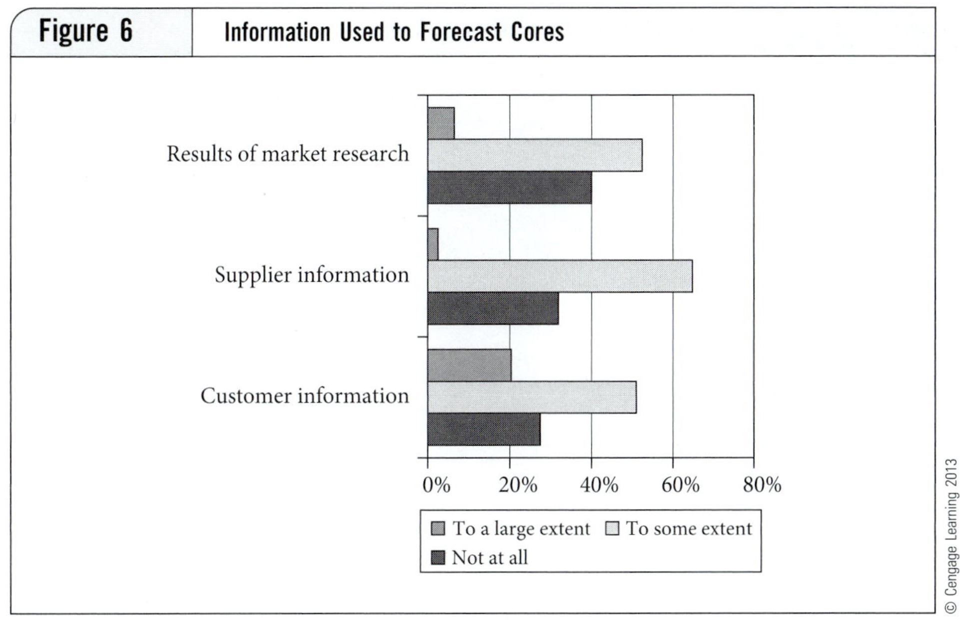

available for the remanufacturer to use. Follow-up phone conversations with select respondents confirmed that this was the reason those respondents did not use market surveys to forecast their cores. This survey provides market information in the form of the management practices used by remanufacturers and is thus a source of this information for remanufacturers.

Core Forecasting Timing

Table 5 shows that 24 percent of respondents do not forecast cores. Of those that do forecast cores (i.e., 55/72 = 76%), the majority (45/55 = 81.8%) make forecasts for six or fewer months. The majority of respondents (35%) make monthly forecasts. Twenty-eight percent of the respondents indicated that they make weekly forecasts, while 11 percent indicated making daily forecasts of cores. Nine percent (= 33%–24% from the not applicable (N/A) categories shown in Table 5) of respondents who make forecasts do not modify the forecast for production. Therefore, the majority of respondents (91%) who make forecasts modify the forecast at least once for production during the year. Of those that do modify their forecast of cores (i.e., 48 = 67% of 72 respondents), the majority (44/48 = 92%) modify, on average, at most 40 percent of the forecasted quantity, each time. The frequency and magnitude of these modifications suggest that there may be an issue with the confidence that the remanufacturers have in their forecasts.

Production Planning

Figure 7 shows the responses to a survey question concerning methods used to determine production data for remanufacturing.

There were a total of 71 respondents for a question concerning production planning and control activities. The majority of respondents indicated that cost planning, shop-floor control, labor planning, and material planning were done manually for their remanufacturing operations. The uncertainty in the timing, quantity, and quality of cores could be the driver of the manual approach. The use of non manual systems for

Table 5 Timing for the Forecasting of Cores

Time horizon for forecasting cores (months)		Frequency of forecast modification (per year)	
1	15%	1 time	6%
3	26%	2–4 times	22%
6	22%	5–12 times	26%
12	7%	More than 12 times	13%
More than 12	6%	N/A	33%
N/A	24%	**Total Responses 72**	
Total Responses 72		**Percentage of forecasts modified**	
Smallest time period dividing time horizon		0–19%	26%
Days	11%	20–39%	28%
Weeks	28%	40–59%	7%
Months	35%	60–80%	3%
Years	3%	More than 80%	1%
N/A	24%	N/A	35%
Total Responses 72		**Total Responses 72**	

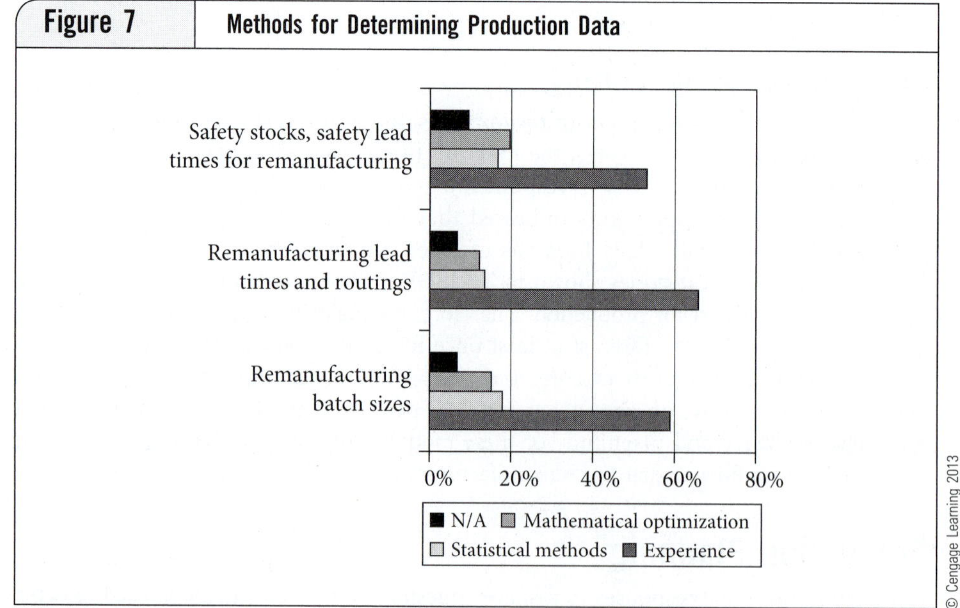

Figure 7 Methods for Determining Production Data

planning and control activities represents an opportunity for the remanufacturers to better manage the supply of cores.

Figure 7 shows that the majority of respondents rely solely on experience for determining the remanufacturing production data shown. On average, 59.52 percent of the respondents indicated using experience to determine the above data; 7.98 percent of respondents chose the N/A category indicating that they did not use such data for their remanufacturing operations. Subsequent follow-up via email revealed that those respondents who selected the N/A category were likely using a "pull" system for remanufacturing production and therefore did not produce in large batches, hold safety stock, or estimate production lead times. In a pull system, material movement occurs only when the workstation requiring more materials asks for it to be sent (Benton, 2013). Therefore, a pull system is characterized by small batch sizes and does not require the forecasting of customer demand or the estimation of production lead times. Since only a small percentage of respondents indicated using a pull system for remanufacturing, this issue was not investigated further in this study. Guide and colleagues (2000) described the difficulty involved in determining shop-floor routings, safety stock, and lead time in remanufacturing due to the uncertainties in the timing, quantity, and quality of cores. This is the likely reason for the heavy reliance on experience by the remanufacturers for the determination of these production-planning elements.

The responses to survey questions concerning the distribution of production types dedicated for remanufacturing show that the majority of respondents indicated that one-of-a-kind and large batches accounted for a smaller percentage of their production (approximately 20%) as compared to small batches. Approximately 10 percent of respondents indicated that one-of-a-kind items accounted for 80 to 100 percent of their production. Assemble-to-order items accounted a smaller percentage of production (i.e., 0%–40%) compared to made-to-stock and made-to-order items. Made-to-stock items mostly accounted for 60 to 79 percent of production. Approximately 10 percent of respondents indicated that made-to-stock items accounted for between 80 to 100 percent of production. Collectively, these results show that respondents use a variety of production strategies to remanufacture their products. Also see Chapter 1.

There were 31 OEMs in the sample that also remanufactured their products. The majority of these OEMs (68%) indicated that remanufacturing occurred on a separate production line than manufacturing. Therefore, remanufacturing models that are developed for traditional and remanufacturing on the same line would not apply to the majority of the remanufacturers surveyed in this study.

A major finding of this study is that there are lost opportunities for supply chain focused remanufacturers to better manage their supply of cores. Based on the results of this study and our review of the literature, several managerial implications and recommendation were created, which are presented in the next section.

Managerial Implications and Recommendations

This survey provides market information in the form of the management practices used by remanufacturers and is thus a source of this information for remanufacturers. This survey therefore addresses a need by practitioners for market information used to source cores. Survey responses concerning the uncertainty in the supply of cores from suppliers were equally split. This split in responses may be explained by the arms-length relationship that the majority of respondents have with their suppliers. Such relationships would suggest that the remanufacturer is not heavily dependent on the supplier. Therefore, the remanufacturer will perceive that sufficient quantity of cores could be obtained elsewhere. This could indicate that the remanufacturers may not be sufficiently aware of their dependence on core suppliers (e.g., brokers and salvage operators) even though they can represent up to 40 percent of their supply of cores. This lack of awareness means that remanufacturers are vulnerable to the risk of core shortages from third-party suppliers of cores.

Close Supplier Relationships

A close relationship with suppliers involves information sharing, long-term contracts, and collaboration for mutual advantage. Such a relationship with suppliers can lead to improved relations, better delivery performance, and lower transaction costs (Benton, 2010).

Better delivery performance from suppliers in terms of delivery speed, reliability, and quality of delivered cores will mean that sufficient core inventory will be available to satisfy customer demand. Therefore, the quantity of cores available will better match the required quantity of cores for the materials plan. Also, better delivery performance by suppliers can lead to lower throughput times, which allow for more flexibility in accommodating customer requirements (Benton, 2013). The flexibility allows for better matching of the materials plan to customer demand. The accuracy of the materials plan can be measured by the percent past due over a planning period.

Information sharing and better delivery performance as a result of a close relationship with suppliers allow for better matching of supply to demand. Improvement in the matching of supply to demand means those actual capacity requirements will better match the planned capacity requirements. The benefits of a more accurate capacity plan include reduced overtime, inventories, and expediting costs. Saved labor hours can be used for training and improvement work, and the effective use of equipment can mean lower total maintenance costs. Material shortages make it difficult to create accurate material and capacity plans. The risk of a supply shortage can be mitigated via activities such as selecting reliable core suppliers, buying from alternative suppliers to guarantee undisrupted supply, and collaborative communication between buyer and suppliers. A close relationship with suppliers fosters increased communication. Also, the process of prequalifying core suppliers for a close relationship is likely to result in the most reliable, preferred suppliers being chosen for such a relationship (Benton, 2013). Therefore, remanufacturers with close relationships with their suppliers of cores are likely to have a lower risk of core shortages.

Forecasting Product Return Rates

Forecasts of product returns by the automotive parts remanufacturers were mostly short term and mainly based on management opinion. Frequent modifications of these forecasts indicated a lack of confidence in the accuracy of the forecasts. The development and application of more accurate forecasting methods could help managers to resolve this lack of confidence.

Forecast Accuracy and Performance

There has been extensive research evaluating the effect of forecast accuracy on MRP systems under various scenarios. The general conclusion from these studies is that accurate forecasts do improve the accuracy of materials planning; however, all of the studies focused on the forecasting of demand. Remanufacturing production planning and control systems require the forecasting of core supply along with demand forecasts for remanufactured products. Long-term forecasts (e.g., annual forecasts) of product returns will need to accommodate factors such as product life-cycle position, rate of technological change, and economic conditions of the product. Short-term forecasts (e.g., monthly or weekly) can be made more effectively by considering previous sales and return rates. Therefore, the process used to make short-term and long-term forecasts of return rates are different, and the accuracy of these forecasts affects different parts of the integrated remanufacturing production control system shown in Figure 2.

Production Planning Activities

Apart from inventory planning, the majority of respondents did their activity planning and control manually. The use of automated systems for planning and control activities represents an opportunity for the remanufacturers to better manage the supply of cores. Also, the majority of remanufacturers relied solely on experience to determine batch sizes, shop-floor routings, safety stocks, and safety lead times. The use of statistical or mathematical optimization techniques represents an opportunity for remanufacturers to better manage their integrated remanufacturing production planning and control systems.

Use of Statistical or Mathematical Techniques

Although statistical techniques (e.g., queuing models) and mathematical techniques (e.g., optimization) have been developed for production planning and control in remanufacturing (Dekker et al., 2004) this study did not look at the effect of these methods on the performance of the integrated remanufacturing production planning and control system. Various studies have compared techniques used for determining safety stock, safety lead times, and batch/lot sizes in manufacturing environments. The general conclusion of previous studies is that statistical and/or mathematical techniques do improve the performance of the production planning and control system. The proposed methods for remanufacturing, however, differ from those used for manufacturing due to the quantity, quality, and timing uncertainties associated with cores. Although the methods proposed in previous studies (e.g., Dekker et al., 2004; Ferrer and Whybark, 2001) for remanufacturing are different from those used for manufacturing, a similar general conclusion might be reached concerning the use of statistical and mathematical techniques and the performance of the integrated remanufacturing production planning and control system.

SUMMARY

In this chapter, we focused on remanufacturing planning and control. Remanufacturing is an environmentally sound way to achieve many goals of sustainable development. In the United States, laws mandating that companies be responsible for the take back of electronic wastes are becoming prevalent at the state level. The remanufacturing process begins with the acquisition and disassembly of cores. The disassembly process involves cleaning, inspecting, and the reassembling of component parts. In the final remanufacturing phase, the parts are assembled into components, inspected, and packed for shipment or placed into inventory. Developing accurate forecasts of the returned product quantities is critical for an effective production-planning and inventory system.

An empirical study provided key insights into the sourcing practices of cores and production-planning practices for remanufacturing. First, the sourcing arrangements are mostly arms-length, which has implications for the successful management of the supply of cores from third-party suppliers.

Second, forecasts are mostly short term and mainly based on management opinion. Frequent modifications of these forecasts indicate a lack of confidence in the accuracy of the forecasts. Third, only a few remanufacturers used optimization or statistical techniques to determine batch sizes, routings, safety stock, and lead times for remanufacturing. The uses of such techniques represent an opportunity for remanufacturers to better manage their supply of cores.

DISCUSSION QUESTIONS

1. In the United States, laws mandating that companies be responsible for take back of electronic wastes are becoming prevalent at the state level. Today, there are more than 70,000 remanufacturing companies with revenues exceeding $55 billion in annual sales. How does remanufacturing relate to this legislation? How is remanufacturing related to green manufacturing initiatives?
2. Describe the typical remanufacturing process for a replacement alternator for an automobile. Use as much detail as possible.
3. Compare the remanufacturing production planning and control framework with the conventional production planning and control framework. What are the major differences between the two systems?
4. Describe the inventory process for the remanufacturing planning and control framework. Consider both independent demand and dependent demand in your response. A comprehensive response is required.
5. How is the remanufacturing MRP system set up and operationalized? How are remanufacturing MRP systems similar to and different from the traditional MRP framework?
6. What are the major findings from the core acquisition study discussed in the chapter? What are the managerial implications of the study?
7. Write a two page memo based on your evaluation of the State of the art of acquiring cores in the automotive industry.

REFERENCES

Benton, W. C. (2008), *Purchasing and Supply Chain Management*, second ed., McGraw-Hill Irwin, 2008.

Clottey, W. C. Benton, and R. S. Srivastava. "Forecasting Product Returns for Remanufacturing Operations" *Decision Sciences* 43 (2012): 32–59.

Clottey, T., and Benton, W. C. *Core Acquisition in the Automotive Parts Remanufacturing Industry*, www.APRA.org.

Dekker, R., K. Fleischmann, K. Inderfurth, and L. N. Van Wassenhove. *Reverse Logistics, Quantitative Models for Closed Loop Supply Chains*. Springer, 2004.

Ferrer, G., and D. C. Whybark. "Material Planning for a Remanufacturing Facility." *Production & Operations Management* 10, no. 2(2001): 112–124.

Guide, V. D., V. Jayaraman, R. Srivastava, and W. C. Benton. "Supply Chain Management for Recoverable Manufacturing Systems." *Interfaces* 30(2000): 18.

Hauser, W. M., and R. T. Lund. *The Remanufacturing Industry: Anatomy of a Giant*. Boston: Department of Manufacturing Engineering, Boston University, 2003.

Chapter 11

SUPPLY CHAIN FOCUSED OUTSOURCING

Learning Objectives

- Learn the precise definition of outsourcing
- Learn why organizations outsource manufacturing and services business processes
- Learn why the outsourcing process is not considered contracting or joint venturing
- Learn about the benefits and pitfalls of outsourcing
- Learn about the hidden cost of outsourcing
- Learn about core and non-core competencies
- Learn about the elements of strategic outsourcing
- Learn about the role of the outsourcing relationship manager

Introduction

Outsourcing can be defined as *the complete transfer of a business process that has been traditionally operated and managed internally to an independently owned external organization*. A complete transfer means that the people, facilities, equipment, technology, and other assets are no longer maintained once the process is outsourced. While some have considered outsourcing decisions synonymously with make-or-buy decisions, it has been recognized that the two are not the same. Outsourcing is also sometimes thought to be similar to subcontracting, joint venturing, and contract manufacturing. Contracting is the purchasing of goods or services to facilitate a business process owned by the buyer. The outsourcing point of departure from these concepts is the complete transfer of all associated internal business process activities. When considering outsourcing, firms are evaluating whether to reverse a prior decision to "make." In other words, outsourcing reshapes a firm's boundaries.

In a recent study, executives categorized their outsourcing activities.[1] Table 1 illustrates the diverse set of outsourced activities that were reported on. Not surprisingly, information technology outsourcing (ITO) represented the largest number of responses at 25.8 percent. Approximately 35 percent of the responses represented the outsourcing of some type of manufacturing activity, with the remainder being business process outsourcing (BPO).

Outsourcing can be conceptualized as a process rather than simply an event. This process begins with the development of a strategic and financial business case for outsourcing. The crafting of the business case is followed by implementing the external sourcing model and, ultimately, managing the relationship with the provider. This view is summarized in Figure 1 and is consistent with the definition of the outsourcing process offered by the International Association of Outsourcing Professionals (IAOP, 2007).

Table 1 **Categories of Outsourced Activity Reported**

CATEGORY OF OUTSOURCED ACTIVITY	FREQUENCY	PERCENTAGE
Business process - information technology or systems	51	25.8%
Other - business process	38	19.2%
Manufacturing of end items	33	16.7%
Manufacturing of component parts	24	12.1%
Other - manufacturing	13	6.6%
Business process - human resources	11	5.6%
Logistics services	11	5.6%
Call center or customer service center	9	4.5%
Business process - accounting or finance	8	4.0%
Total	198	100.0%

Source: Handley, S. M., The Evaluation Analysis and Management of the Business Outsourcing process, Unpublished Dissertation, The Ohio State University, 2008.

[1]Handley, S. M., and W. C. Benton Jr., 2009 "Unlocking the business outsourcing process model." *Journal of Operations Management*, Vol. 27(5), 344 (Forthcoming): 1–18

Figure 1 Outsourcing Process

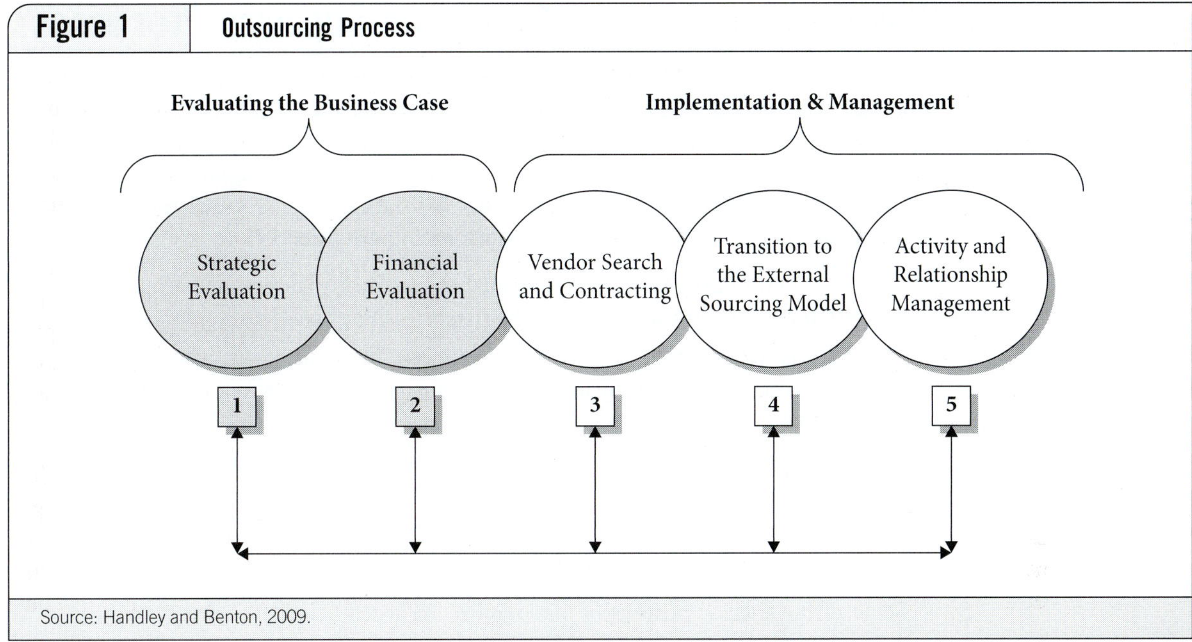

Source: Handley and Benton, 2009.

Global business process outsourcing alone has surpassed the US$6 trillion mark.[2] A recent Booz Allen report posits the expectation that U.S. business-process outsourcing will continue to grow at about 10 percent per year in the near term. A report by the International Association of Outsourcing Professionals (IAOP) suggests that between 25 percent and 34 percent of the "typical executive's budget is outsourced." There is also a significant amount of attention reported by the industry and the popular press. According to a recent Deloitte Consulting study, 64 percent of respondents indicated that they had brought outsourced services back inhouse.[3] Fifty percent of respondents identified hidden costs as the primary problem encountered with outsourcing, while 44 percent did not realize cost savings. Another study reported similar findings from a Bain survey of large and medium-sized firms.[4] They found that only 10 percent of the firms were highly satisfied with the costs they were saving, and nearly 50 percent failed to achieve cost-savings expectations. Moreover, Dunn and Bradstreet found that 20 to 25 percent of all outsourcing relationships *fail* within two years and approximately 50 percent fail within five years. Finally, a 2005 study reported that based on the experience of the global consulting firm Booz Allen Hamilton, they would estimate that approximately one in three outsourcing efforts fail to achieve outsourcing expectations.[5] These anecdotal findings suggest that there is a troubling gap between expectations and reality. However, outsourcing is here to stay. It has become the key driver for globalization. The Internet has made outsourcing an important competitive weapon. This means that outsourcing cannot be dismissed as a passing fad. Outsourcing is one of the most important business concepts in the last 50 years.

[2]Baron, A., 2005. The people impact of outsourcing. *Strategic Communication Management* 9 (1), 13–13.

[3]Landis, K. M., Mishra, S., Porrello, K., 2005. "Calling a change in the outsourcing market: The realities for the world's largest organizations". Deloitte Consulting Report.

[4]Gottfredson, M., Puryear, R., Phillips, S., 2005. Strategic sourcing from periphery to the core. *Harvard Business Review* 83 (2), 132–139.

[5]Disher, C., Prosko, D., Trombetti, E., 2005. "Next generation outsourcing: Ensuring success after signing the deal". Booz Allen Hamilton Report.

Why Do Organizations Outsource Business Processes?

It is virtually impossible to determine why organizations outsource various business processes. The outsourcing decision depends on whether the CEO, CFO, or CIO initiates the outsourcing proposal. However, the majority of outsourcing proposals are driven by a reduction in *direct operating costs*. The cost reduction must be significantly lower than the current *direct operating costs* in order for an outsourcing proposal to be attractive. Some of the generic strategic benefits of outsourcing are listed below:

1. Cost minimization—is accomplished by reducing direct operating costs and eliminating overhead costs and then transforming fixed costs into variable costs.
2. Refocus organization to core competencies—by focusing on what the organization does best and transforming the business to focus on new products and services.
3. Improvement in operating performance—by increasing quality, productivity, and obtaining new capabilities from external sources.
4. Increased market share and revenue—by assessing the providers' network and accelerating expansion into new markets.

Some of the specific benefits of outsourcing are listed below:

1. Reduce and control operating costs
2. Improve quality
3. Change company focus
4. Acquire external capabilities
5. Refocus scarce resources
6. Reduce cycle time
7. Obtain cash infusion
8. Reduce risks
9. Gain flexibility
10. Turn fixed costs into variable costs

While a contract is required to legally protect one's interests, an extensive strategic assessment and true commitment to a cooperative relationship with the service provider are necessary to realize expected outsourcing benefits. These insights offer valuable guidance to outsourcing practitioners in terms of where and how sourcing resources should be applied in order to maximize the value derived from their outsourcing initiatives. These types of management and relationship and capabilities must be developed through training and/or recruitment within outsourcing organizations. The hidden costs of outsourcing are given in the next section.

The Hidden Cost of Outsourcing

Quality Costs

The cost of quality is an essential consideration in sourcing decisions. The costs associated with ensuring quality are often categorized as follows: (1) preventative, (2) appraisal, (3) internal failure, and (4) external failure. If sourcing internally, firms must estimate the costs of defect prevention (i.e., designing quality into products and processes), the costs of quality appraisal (e.g., inspections, audits, monitoring mechanisms), the cost of internal failure (e.g., scrap, rework, internal downtime), and the cost of external failure (i.e., failure perceived by the external customer). All of these costs exist with external sourcing as well. Persistent internal quality issues at the external source will ultimately impact the buying firm. The buying firm will need to ensure that proper mechanisms are in place to make sure that they are capable of detecting quality failures by an external source. This may be more difficult than with internal sourcing, because if sourcing externally, the buying firm may not have maintained sufficient internal capabilities to even appropriately assess the quality of a product or service provided by the external source.

Supplier Vendor Relationship Management

It has long been recognized, in both the strategy and operations literature, that the most effective external sourcing relationships involve considerable management time and coordination.[6] Unfortunately, this comes at an expense. Not all external sourcing relationships are created equal, and those involving commodity products or services may not require extensive relationship building and coordination. The external sourcing of strategic products and services is on the other end of the spectrum. In these situations, relationship building and coordination activities are quite extensive. Thus, it is critical that firms considering outsourcing also evaluate the type and depth of the relationship that will be required to effectively manage the exchange. According to the Deloitte outsourcing study, 62 percent of the respondents cited requiring more management time than expected.[7] It is also suggested that managing the supply relationship costs at least 3 percent and sometimes more than 10 percent of the annual contract value. On average, the IT outsourcing engagements studied resulted in an annual supplier-management expense that equaled 8 percent of the contract value. Many of the costs associated with managing the external sourcing relationship are manifested in the labor expense of purchasing personnel. For instance, Toyota spends more than 7,200 man-days of face-to-face contact with suppliers each year. Other costs associated with managing the relationship include travel, IT infrastructure and management, and supplier-development programs (e.g., training and performance evaluation systems).

Internal Coordination

While internal coordination costs are unique to external sourcing alternatives, they must be contrasted against the internal coordination and overhead costs associated with internally sourcing a product or service. In general, one can think of internal coordination costs as those overhead expenses incurred solely due to the decision to internally source a product or service. Presumably, sourcing internally induces higher cost levels of many overhead administrative functions such as payroll, benefits management, utility IT and so forth. The relationship between higher levels of vertical integration and an increase in bureaucratic costs has been noted in the extant academic literature. Some firms have cast the decision to vertically integrate (i.e., source internally) versus the decision to externally source as a comparison between the costs of bureaucracy and the cost of external coordination. However, according to the Deloitte study, 57 percent

[6]Benton, W. C., Maloni, M., 2005. The influence of power driven buyer/seller relationships on supply chain satisfaction. *Journal of Operations Management* 23 (1), 1–22.

[7]Landis, K. M., Mishra, S., Porrello, K., 2005. "Calling a change in the outsourcing market: The realities for the world's largest organizations". Deloitte Consulting Report

of respondents were unable to free up the anticipated level of internal resources after outsourcing. In comparing traditional internal sourcing with external sourcing options, firms need to have a thorough understanding of these marginal overhead expenses and how they would be incrementally impacted by outsourcing a particular business activity.

Implementation of External Sourcing Model

An often-underestimated expense that is incurred when switching sources (internal or external) is that associated with the transition itself. This cost category could include supplier search, evaluation and contracting, the transfer of physical assets, domestic and international travel during startup, and training of the new source to ensure a smooth transition and seamless integration. A 2001 study of 50 IT outsourcing efforts found that supplier search, evaluation and contracting costs alone represented an average of 3 percent of the annual contract amount. This research also found that typical transitions took more than 10 months to complete. During the transition period, firms incur additional costs related to internal staff providing additional support and duplicate resources. There is usually lower efficiency and effectiveness at the beginning of the contract. Moreover, Dunn and Bradstreet found that 20 to 25 percent of all outsourcing relationships fail within two years and nearly half fail within five years.[8] This implies that the likelihood of incurring these expenses again or experiencing costs associated with re-internalizing an outsourced activity is relatively high. Another critical financial consideration with outsourcing is the impact on the internal workforce. Some of the often hidden costs of outsourcing include training internal employees to become relationship managers rather than technical managers. The hidden costs also include retention bonuses, severance packages, employee turnover, and management time required to thwart labor disputes. Khosrowpour and Subramanian surveyed 146 IT professionals and found that only 19 percent would describe their perceptions toward outsourcing as "positive." Furthermore, the majority believed that their welfare was *not* a major consideration in outsourcing.[9] In a 2004 study, 500 truck drivers were surveyed, 80 percent of whom had been transferred to an external service provider as part of a transportation outsourcing initiative. Their results indicated that employees who were highly satisfied and involved in pre-outsourcing expressed a significantly higher intent to exit the external provider.[10] Another study found that 38 percent of firms who would classify their outsourcing effort as "failed" admitted to over looking personnel issues, as opposed to only 20 percent of firms who classified their efforts as "successful."[11] These observations underscore the importance of considering the impact on internal staff when making outsourcing decisions.

Product Service Design and Development

One of the most influential factors in vertical integration decisions is the coordination requirements. Perhaps nowhere is this more evident than when considering new product or service development. There appears to be a significant interplay

[8]Doig, S. J., Ritter, R. C., Speckhals, K., Woolson, D., 2001. Has outsourcing gone too far? (cover story). McKinsey Quarterly, 24–37.

[9]Khosrowpour, M., Subramanitan, G. H., 1996. Managing information technology with outsourcing: An assessment of employee perceptions. *Journal of Applied Business Research* 12 (3), 85–96.

[10]Logan, M. S., Faught, K., Ganster, D. C., 2004. Outsourcing a satisfied and committed workforce: A trucking industry case study. *International Journal of Human Resource Management* 15 (1), 147–162.

[11]Barthélemy, J., 2003. The seven deadly sins of outsourcing. *Academy of Management Executive* 17 (2), 87–98.

between the architecture of the product or service and the cost of coordination. The cost of coordination has been captured in the extant literature as the number of engineering hours required to bring a new product to market. It has been suggested in the literature that tightly coupled or integrated product designs require higher levels of coordination and therefore may not be appropriate for external sourcing.[12] These findings are consistent with another set of literature, which describes the difficulty and cost with which knowledge is shared between firms, particularly when this knowledge is tacit and less easily codified. Thus, it is imperative that firms develop a deep understanding of the coordination cost implications of various sourcing alternatives. This consideration may not be separable from key product and process architecture decisions.

Government- and Politics-Related Expenses

International sourcing alternatives are significantly complex. It is important that the decision making team develop a complete understanding of the costs involved with ensuring compliance with governmental laws, regulations, and even local business customs. Specifically, these costs could include but are not limited to legal expenses incurred to learn about a foreign location's laws and regulations, lobbying efforts, travel, taxation, tariffs, local content obligations, quota systems, and so on. Tariff rates in developed countries are typically less than 10 percent but can be much higher for less developed nations and for certain products such as agricultural products. These environmental parameters may be highly dynamic requiring analysts "on the ground" and a deep understanding of the evolving environment. Some multinational corporations with large international exposures have large departments dedicated to assessing and managing political risks around the globe.

Supply Chain Risk Management

A report by Cranfield University to the Department for Transport in England recognized outsourcing as one of the key factors driving increased levels of supply chain risk.[13] The idea of risk management should underlie all of the previously discussed cost categories. However, there are some costs that are more directly tied to the management of risk in the supply chain. Broadly, risk can be defined as a measure of the probability and severity of adverse effects. One can divide risk management into four iterative phases: (1) risk assessment, (2) risk mitigation, (3) risk monitoring, and (4) contingency planning. Each of these phases has associated costs that will vary depending on the specific sourcing decision. Risk assessment involves answering three questions: (1) What adverse events could happen? (2) What is the probability of these events happening? (3) What is the financial impact if these events occur? Risk mitigation involves a detailed analysis of what can be done to reduce or eliminate the probability and severity of these adverse events while also considering the trade-offs involved. Managers must learn to tailor appropriate risk-mitigation strategies to a particular situation. It is crucial to fully appreciate these

[12]Anderson, E. G., Parker, G. G., 2002. The effect of learning on the Make/Buy decision. *Production & Operations Management* 11 (3), 313–339.

[13]Christopher, M., 2002. Supply chain vulnerability. *Executive report on behalf of: Department for transport, local government and the regions.* Bedford, UK: School of Management 1–7.

possible financial uncertainties when considering outsourcing opportunities, for they could fundamentally impact the attractiveness of alternatives. Risk monitoring involves continuously evaluating supply chain conditions so that potential issues may be avoided or at least lessened by being more proactive. Best practices for monitoring include regular supplier financial assessments, use of supplier scorecards, use of advanced tracking technology such as RFID, increased supply chain visibility at second- and third-tier sources, and the like.[14] The final phase is contingency planning. More than likely, it will be impossible to eliminate all risks associated with a sourcing alternative and, thus, contingency plans must be put into place that detail early-warning detection systems, internal and external actions upon recognition, and so on. This comprehensive risk-management approach will introduce costs that are different for various sourcing alternatives, because the different options will carry with them different types and sizes of risks. Some specific costs associated with risk management could include insurance, dedicated risk-management personnel, financial hedging, and operations hedging.

Miscellaneous Financial Considerations

A final consideration for evaluating the costs of each sourcing alternative is learning and the appropriation of its benefits. The idea that firms tend to improve their cost position with cumulative volume and engineering time has been well established. A commonly cited source of financial benefit from outsourcing is the vendor's improving economies of scale. External specialists can often enjoy more efficient use of assets from being able to pool the less than perfectly correlated demands of multiple customers. Also, external suppliers can aggregate the demands of their multiple customers, which allows them to offer immediate cost benefits and to travel more quickly down the learning curve than can a firm with its individual demand alone. This is particularly true in industries with relatively standardized processes such as telecommunications equipment and consumer electronics. However, the buying firm also needs to consider what portion of the cost improvement it will be able to appropriate if it decides to outsource. This may be determined by competitive conditions in the supply market, power structures, and the overall threat of opportunistic behavior by the external supplier. These considerations have been found to have the potential to greatly impact the sourcing decision. It is critical that firms also consider their internal ability to improve by means of innovative work practices such as total quality management, lean production, and so forth. If a firm can generate nearly equal financial improvement through internal efforts as would be realized with outsourcing, then the decision to outsource may need to be called into question. According to a Deloitte study, many organizations could realize incremental savings on the order of 20 to 30 percent of direct labor from implementing innovative programs such as lean production.[15]

This section served to develop a comprehensive overview of the multitude of factors that can materially impact the financial viability of outsourcing that are often overlooked in developing the business case for outsourcing.

[14]Elkins, D., Handfield, R. B., Blackhurst, J., Craighead, C. W., 2005. 18 ways to guard against disruption. *Supply Chain Management Review* 9 (1), 46–53.

[15]Doig, S. J., Ritter, R. C., Speckhals, K., Woolson, D., 2001. Has outsourcing gone too far? (Cover story). McKinsey Quarterly, 24–37.

Core Competencies

A concept very similar to the resource-based view of the firm is that of core competencies. Core competencies are the collective learning in an organization. The core competency concept is especially concerned with how to coordinate diverse production skills and integrate multiple streams of technology. Organizations continuously change in order to attract customers, increase revenues, and market share. Core competencies are unique combinations of thought, focus, and implementation methodologies. Most organizations have numerous capabilities. The organization must have a set of *core* capabilities that ensure survival in a competitive market-place. Core competencies are only built and learned over the long term. Alternatively, outsourcing can provide short-term competitive benefits but does not contribute significantly to developing "people-embodied" skills for a sustainable advantage. This implies that upon outsourcing, a firm is accepting a position of competitive parity for the activity in question. Organizations should concentrate on the development of a few core competencies and strategically outsource noncore activities.[16] Outsourcing core activities is the beginning of the end of existence for any organization. Thus, the concept of core competencies along with the resource-based view of the organization provides the basis for the assertion that in considering outsourcing, the decision-making team must have a thorough understanding of *core and noncore capabilities* and how they relate to an organization's competitive advantage.

Outsourcing Trends

Outsourcing is not immune to the effects of economic volatility. However, in an economic downturn, internal and external costs will become the primary bases for considering the outsourcing business case. At the time of this writing, things look gloomy for the global economy, and the outsourcing market represents a dichotomy: on the downside, organizations' cost-cutting outsourcing strategies may negatively impact market growth, but at the same time, the upside is that outsourcing will be adopted by more organizations to help them meet their competitive challenges. In a financially challenged economic environment, the knowledgeable buyer and provider will have a competitive advantage. The potential for outsourcing to address immediate cost pressures as well as long-term recovery goals will be unprecedented. However, only organizations that are diligent about understanding and avoiding the pitfalls of cost-focused outsourcing and that apply total business-outcome-focused outsourcing will be successful. Many outsourcing buyers must continuously re-evaluate their contracts to improve efficiency quality and costs. This will affect provider selection and retention, how services are or will be delivered, delivery location, and contract pricing. Beyond the drivers of efficiency, quality and cost, however, many organizations will also experience core business changes as a result of a worldwide economic crisis.

For organizations that are outsourcing, contract terms may be altered in response to corporate change: Some will downsize, others will expand, acquisition and divestiture will impact others, and still others will cease to exist. Many organizations that are not outsourcing will consider or move aggressively to outsource their IT or business

[16]Quinn, J. B., Hilmer, F. G., 1994. Strategic outsourcing. *Sloan Management Review* 35 (4), 43–55.

processes. Outsourcing buyers and providers must be attentive to contract issues to ensure a certain level of flexibility, since business change is inevitable.

According to Gartner, in 2008, approximately 76 percent of announced outsourcing contracts represented new deals; the remaining percentage was a combination of contract extensions, expansions, or renewals. Almost one-quarter of these contracts were a continuation of outsourcing with an incumbent provider. Key providers are basically betting their future on forming enduring, long-lasting relationships. In uncertain economic times, outsourcing relationships can prove (and test) the durability of relationships and the outsourcing value proposition.[17]

Elements of Strategic Outsourcing

The following steps are suggested for successful outsourcing:

1. Strategic evaluation
2. Financial evaluation
3. Supplier selection and contracting
4. Transition to external sourcing model
5. Managing relationships

These steps are based on the model given in Figure 1. These steps can and should be modified to fit the specific organization and outsourcing objectives. As can be seen from Figure 1, these steps are highly interrelated. The nature of the various steps is important in order to achieve continuous improvement and communication between the required outsourcing activities. Concurrent relationships also reduce the implementation cycle time. It is important to assign different team members to implement each of the steps. It is also important to assign members to more than one step in the process in order to enhance communication and information flows. Figure 2 illustrates the concurrency concept.

Figure 2 **Illustrates the Concurrency Concept**

Outsourcing Steps	Outsourcing Cycle Time Start |---------------------------| Finish
1. Strategic evaluation	|-----------------|
2. Financial evaluation	|----------------|
3. Supplier search and contracting	|----------------|
4. Transition to external sourcing model	|--------------|
5. Managing relationships	|-------------|

Source: Benton, W. C. Purchasing and Supply Chain Management, McGraw-Hill, 2013.

[17] www.gartner.com

Strategic Evaluation

Outsourcing is the act of reversing a previous decision to "make" or to perform a particular function internally. The first step in the make-or-buy decision is to understand the strategic importance (value) of the activity or system.

Initially, outsourcing decisions focused predominantly standardized processes, commoditized products, and activities of extremely low strategic value. However, firms are increasingly considering more strategic capabilities for outsourcing, making the strategic evaluation much more complex. Organization discouraged firms from making outsourcing decisions piecemeal but, rather, encourage organizations to make them as part of a comprehensive sourcing strategy.

Financial Evaluation

Along with performing a complete strategic evaluation of a potential outsourcing effort, it is also critical to ensure that outsourcing makes short- and long-term financial sense as well. In terms of the financial categories discussed above, it should be noted that outsourcing decisions are not necessarily mutually exclusive and independent constructs but, rather, may be significantly interrelated. Furthermore, one may notice that some of the outsourcing considerations are only pertinent in certain circumstances. For instance, many of the costs are only relevant when considering international sourcing alternatives or are only pertinent when considering the outsourcing of a manufacturing activity as opposed to a business process such as accounting, human resources, information technology, and so forth.

Supplier Selection and Contract Development

Supplier Selection

Potential outsourcing suppliers must be identified and investigated. One way to identify and investigate a potential supplier is for the buying firm to compile a supplier profile for each potential supplier. These profiles should include items such as key management contacts, a company overview, SWOT (strengths, weaknesses, opportunities, threats) analysis, Porter's five key financial figures, information on current contracts, "owners" of the relationship within the firm, and an organizational chart. While the process of compiling these profiles should be owned by the outsourcing project team, the content of the profiles should be shared and evaluated by all related business functions within the buying firm. Functional evaluation of the content will ensure that all impacted areas within the buying firm will have input into the outsourcing process. This method also ensures that the outsourcing project team is knowledgeable about all potential suppliers and aware of how they are rated by each function within the buying firm. In addition to the supplier profiles, the buying organization should clearly establish expectations for the potential suppliers and discuss the *scope of work* and the *appropriate pricing* for the outsourcing activity.

Contract Development

The outsourcing alliance must arrive at an enforceable contract. The contract is the key to effective governance of the relationship between the two independent firms. The language of the contract must include *at a minimum* the following components:

- A clearly defined scope of work and elements of the processes to be supplied
- An agreed-upon approximate price for each aspect of what is being supplied
- An understanding of an acceptable level of flexibility as circumstances and requirements change
- Consider a short-term contract with provisions for extensions and renegotiations
- Ground rules that encourage relationship and alliance maintenance
- Determination of a means for measuring performance for each aspect of the agreement

Unfortunately, it is often observed, particularly in unpredictable environments, that it is nearly impossible, or at least impractical, to construct a contract that fully addresses all possible states of nature and contingencies. When a system design is complex (many tightly coupled or technologically novel components), the ability to effectively contract with an independent provider (supplier) becomes untenable.

When a completely precise and legally binding contract is lacking, certain parties to the agreement may be enticed to act in a manner that is potentially counter to the objectives of the other party. One such risk is that of opportunistic renegotiation, especially when one party has made relationship-specific investments. The outsourcing supplier may shirk its responsibilities even if the contract is complete. This is due to incentive misalignment coupled with difficulty in *measuring* or monitoring the supplier's performance or efforts. While contractual incompleteness and misaligned interests can make maintaining a healthy relationship challenging, it has been recognized that spending the extra time to make sure the contract is precisely developed up front can save substantial costs and time down the road. The contract should be treated like a prenuptial agreement by both parties. Outsourcing arrangements form alliances, not partnerships. Thus, while having a perfectly complete contract may not be feasible, making it as inclusive as possible is critical. This often involves using a cross-functional team that includes external experts, experienced employees, and members of senior management.

Perhaps the most widely suggested means of improving goal alignment is to have clear, easy-to-understand roles and responsibilities. A critical part of this is having a contract with precise performance- or service-level agreements along with penalty and reward clauses. This fundamentally must begin with a clear understanding of existing performance and that which is possible, which often requires benchmarking.

It is important to make the contract as complete as possible, yet due to the uncertainty that surrounds most outsourcing efforts as well as the lack of clairvoyance by decision makers, contracts must also be flexible. In order to enhance flexibility, a shorter contract length is suggested. Further, many stipulate that contracts must clearly outline a dispute-resolution process for those situations when actual operating conditions deviate significantly from contract provisions. Reversibility clauses in the contract are sometimes used to spell out the transfer of human and physical resources should the relationship come to an end. These clauses are argued to ease supplier switching or re-internalizing efforts.

A final contractual element that is posited to improve outsourcing efforts is the treatment of transferred employees. In addition to reversibility clauses, it has also been suggested that contracts should include clauses that protect transferred employees or stipulate guidelines as to their treatment. These clauses can include items such as rules for employee retention, benefits, transfer to other accounts, and so on. It is the objective of these employee-related contractual items to minimize the service impact to the organization as well as to enhance the perception of procedural equity in the eyes of the impacted associates.

While hardly any contract can be airtight in its precision, following the prescriptions outlined in this section can ensure that the contract is as effective as possible. Recognizing the reality of contractual incompleteness however, highlights the need for effective relationship management.

Transition to External Sourcing Model

The success of the outsourcing initiative depends heavily on the implementation effort, beginning with the contract execution to the transfer of the agreed-upon activities and resources. The buying and selling organizations must follow the specific roles outlined in the contract. The buying organization must also appoint a relationship manager. The relationship manager and the suppliers must merge their independent plans into one consensus plan. The consensus transition plan must include, at a minimum, the following:

- Communication criteria—How should the external initiatives be communicated to the affected and unaffected employees?
- Personnel criteria—What packages will be offered to affected and unaffected employees?
- Transition criteria—When will the activities and resources be moved to the provider?

Communication Criteria

The goal of effective communication is to avoid misinformation and to control the rumor mill. Prior to developing the outsourcing project team, the CEO should meet with all employees. The initial announcement to the employees should be thorough and convincing. After the contract has been signed, the CEO should meet with the affected employees. The announcement to the affected employees should include the following points:

- The contract has been signed and awarded to the supplying firm.
- Discuss how severance packages will be offered to affected employees.
- Conduct extensive question-and-answer session.

Personnel Criteria

Outsourcing often has a profound effect on employees. A recent study found that 38 percent of firms who would classify their outsourcing effort as "failed" admitted to over looking personnel issues as opposed to only 20 percent of firms who classified their efforts as "successful."[18] This observation underscores the importance of considering the management and impact on internal staff when making outsourcing decisions.

[18]Barthélemy, J., 2001. The hidden costs of IT outsourcing. *MIT Sloan Management Review* 42 (3), 60–69.

Effective management of employee-related concerns is crucial when outsourcing, particularly considering the often negative perceptions that many employees have about outsourcing. Being laid off as a result of outsourcing has clear economic and emotional implications for victims and the organizations that must manage these situations. However, being transferred to the service provider also has apparent consequences that must be addressed. Transferring employees increases the level of uncertainty that surrounds their career prospects with their new employer. Transferring employees to the supplier can have an adverse impact on transferred employee morale, productivity, and turnover. This not only has direct cost implications but also can negatively affect the provider's ability to provide high-quality service. In 2004, 500 truck drivers were surveyed, 80 percent of whom had been transferred to an external service provider as part of a transportation outsourcing initiative.[19] Their results indicated that employees who were highly satisfied and involved (perception that one's job represents a portion of who one is) preoutsourcing expressed a statistically significant decrease in satisfaction after being transferred to the external provider. Additionally, those who were highly involved preoutsourcing expressed a significantly higher intent to exit the external provider. This could manifest itself in higher turnover at the external service provider and perhaps difficulty in providing efficient and effective services.

By observing their peers being transferred or laid off, remaining employees may call into question the organization's commitment to them and their own risk of being impacted in a similar manner in the future. Employees perceive that their existing psychological contract with their employer has been fundamentally altered, which can lead to a drop in their commitment to the organization, reduction in job satisfaction, and lower productivity. While it is clear that there are significant personnel implications of outsourcing given the frequent occurrence of downsizing (i.e., layoffs) and employee transfer, this direct relationship has been relatively neglected in the business literature.

A fundamental element of creating the perception of procedural and interpersonal justice is communication. Specifically, organizations need to communicate early and clearly to employees about why the decision has been made. This aspect of procedural and interpersonal justice has received wide empirical support as it relates to layoffs or downsizing decisions.

A second element that impacts the perceived equity of a decision is the involvement or "voice" of all interested parties. It is important to make sure that all stakeholders feel as though their interests were represented and considered in making the decision.

It is crucial to treat employees (both survivors and those directly impacted) with respect and dignity during the decision-making and implementation process. Some have noted that smooth outsourcing efforts have made explicit attempts to assist impacted employees and to protect those who are transferred to the provider or supplier.

Finally, it has been recognized that providing the retained team with new skills so that they may be effective in their new role is important. Retained employees need to be trained to enhance their lateral skills such as relationship management, negotiation, and consensus building. Failing to appreciate these concerns and proactively manage them will have an adverse impact on the outsourcing engagement.

---

[19]Logan, M. S., Faught, K., Ganster, D. C., 2004. Outsourcing a satisfied and committed workforce: A trucking industry case study. *International Journal of Human Resource Management* 15 (1), 147–162.

Transition Criteria

The relationship managers for both entities revisit the list of activities outlined in the project management schedule. The list of activities is implemented either sequentially or concurrently. Some of the highlights for implementation are as follows:

1. An organization meeting should be conducted for employees moving from the buying firm to the supplier's organization.
2. A meeting with the buying firm's manager whose activities are being outsourced should be conducted on site at the new location.
3. There should be a plan generated to address the issues involved in transferring significant physical assets. There should be a specific third-party agreement in the contract to accomplish the physical movement and acquisition of the equipment.

The transition process will never be flawless. A high level of professionalism is required for a successful relationship between the alliance parties.

Relationship Management

In order to effectively cultivate the relationship, the relationship manager and buying organization should be active in monitoring and evaluating performance and solving problems. The original contract establishes the performance measures, deliverables, due dates, and expected supplier requirements. Performance measurement is the cornerstone of the buyer–supplier relationship. Without measurement, there is no control. Without control, there can be no relationship to manage. The buyer and supplier relationship managers should develop and execute the reporting system established in the contract. The performance report should be designed to compare the actual performance to the contractual standards. An example report is given in Figure 3.

Knight[20] defined the difference between risk and uncertainty: Risk is measurable, but uncertainty cannot be measured. Therefore, buyers' outsourcing risks can be defined as

Figure 3 Sample Performance Report January 25, 2014

SAMPLE PERFORMANCE REPORT, JANUARY 25, 2014								
PERFORMANCE MEASURE	**WEIGHT**	**PERFORMANCE STANDARD**	**2013 ACTUAL**	**2013 VARIANCE**	**2012 ACTUAL**	**2012 VARIANCE**	**2011 ACTUAL**	**2011 VARIANCE**
Output Quantity	0.1	10000	10000	**0.00%**	9910	**–0.09%**	9820	**–0.18%**
Number of errors	0.4	10	45	**–140.00%**	15	**–20.00%**	70	**–240.00%**
Number of on-time deliveries	0.2	50	49	**–0.40%**	43	**–2.80%**	39	**–4.40%**
Number of days-cycle time	0.2	5	4	**4.00%**	6	**–4.00%**	8	**–12.00%**
Number of outputs per employee	0.1	100	105	**0.50%**	93	**–0.70%**	82	**–1.80%**

Source: Benton, W. C. Purchasing and Supply Chain Management, McGraw-Hill, 2013.

[20]Knight, Frank (1965) *Risk, Uncertainty and Profit*, Harper and Row, New York (first published in 1921).

BOR = PA × NC, where BOR = buyers' outsourcing risks, PA = the probability that an adverse event will occur, and NC = negative consequences if the adverse event occurs, assuming that each of the adverse events is independent.

Outsourcing risks include breaches in intellectual property, provider shirking, and opportunistic renegotiation. Shirking is defined as a salient form of opportunism. The combination of contractual incompleteness, asset specificity, and uncertainty gives rise to these risks when firms pursue external sourcing. Outsourcing organizations must have a clear understanding of true supplier intentions.

Traditional thinking about the most appropriate form of governance has cast the decision as somewhat of a dichotomous choice between hierarchy (i.e., internal sourcing) and market (i.e., external sources). Prior works have developed the image of market governance as an arms-length relationship between the customer and supplier organization. However, in the past few decades, due largely to the observation of Japanese-style supply chain relationships, we have come to see that many organizations effectively pursue a governance form that is neither purely hierarchical nor a purely arms-length market mechanism. This hybrid governance form recognizes the inherent limitations as well as the advantages of both of these extreme forms. It seeks to realize the control, goal alignment, and improved coordination associated with retaining an activity internally while also benefiting from the potentially superior skills and cost position of specialized, external organizations. In this environment, the relationship is more of a long-term, collaborative partnership than a short-term, focused, opportunistic arrangement. In an evaluation of the automotive industry, trust and goodwill over a prolonged period and the investment in *co*specialized assets lead to a reduction in transaction costs.[21] Further, the greater social capital leads to improved dissemination of information and reduced motivation for opportunistic behavior. Social capital is "the sum of the actual and potential resources embedded within, available through, and derived from the network of relationships possessed by an individual or social unit. Collaborative relationships can improve learning and control opportunism.

Thus, it appears that through the development of mutually beneficial long-term relationships with service providers, firms can, to a large extent, mitigate many of the traditional concerns with external sourcing while still realizing many of the proclaimed benefits.

For these long-term relationships to work, it initially requires a strong commitment from both parties. Although these longer-term relationships can bear significant benefits for the customer and service provider, the road will not always be a smooth one. Without commitment from both leadership teams, it would be easy to regress into traditional adversarial thinking.

Sharing of timely, rich, and often proprietary information is required for building trust between the organizations. Information sharing also allows for more effective planning and execution. Information exchange in these deep relationships goes beyond simple transactional information exchange to include sharing demand forecasts, detailed cost information, new product plans, strategic changes, and more and be on the "efficacy of information exchange rather than the quantity or amount."

Closely related to rich information exchange is the idea that true buyer–provider partnerships work collaboratively in many areas. While the idea of information sharing may connote one party providing information to the other, collaboration entails joint effort

[21] Prahinski, C., Benton, W. C., 2004. Supplier evaluations: Communication strategies to improve supplier performance. *Journal of Operations Management* 22 (1), 39–62.

by the organizations. Ultimately, people and organizations tend to act in their own best interests. Thus it is imperative for the outsourcing alliances that the parties tie their destinies together. Equitable distribution of pain and gain will ultimately lead to enhanced partnership performance. Along with having a contract that defines performance incentives by means of penalty and reward structures, the relationship must also be able to work through unforeseen conditions in a productive manner. Put differently, it is necessary for the outsourcing alliances to have a constructive and flexible change-management and dispute-resolution process.[22]

A final key element of an effective buyer–supplier relationship is the performance evaluation. There is a strong statistical relationship between a collaborative communication strategy for supplier performance evaluations and the strength of the buyer–supplier relationship, which subsequently influences the supplier's commitment and performance.[23] In their study, Prahinski and Benton found that collaborative communication was characterized as being formal, providing opportunities for feedback, and indirect influence (evaluation, certification, recognition, training, etc.). It appears clear that effective buyer–supplier relationships should include a formalized procedure for communicating the buyer's expectations and evaluating the supplier's performance.

Managing the Outsourcing Provider

Many outsourcing organizations fail to appreciate the magnitude of the costs associated with achieving adequate levels of interorganizational control and coordination, which contributes to disappointing outsourcing outcomes. Higher costs incurred to control and coordinate the outsourcing relationship appear to be significantly associated with less-satisfactory outsourcing performance. These observations that relatively little is known about the sources of these costs underscore the importance of research aimed at the factors that drive control and coordination costs. The next sections discuss how our understanding of task- and location-specific factors of outsourcing complexity influence these elusive management costs. Findings from a recent study show two important decisions firms make when preparing to outsource a business activity: (1) how to define and appropriately scope the manufacturing work to be outsourced and (2) where globally the outsourced work should be performed.

Implications of Task-Specific Complexity on Control and Coordination Costs

The effects of task-specific complexity demonstrate that the scale of the outsourcing service and breadth of tasks involved each uniquely contribute to greater control and coordination costs, with the effect on control costs being more significant. These elements of complexity make it more difficult to develop and maintain a completely specified contract. They also make it more difficult to deploy monitoring mechanisms to reduce information asymmetry. The combined effect translates into a greater concern for provider opportunism and the need for more elaborate (and costly) formal

[22]Benton, W. C., Maloni, M., 2005. The influence of power driven buyer/seller relationships on supply chain satisfaction. *Journal of Operations Management* 23 (1), 1–22.

[23]Prahinski, C., Benton, W. C., 2004. Supplier evaluations: Communication strategies to improve supplier performance. *Journal of Operations Management* 22 (1), 39–62.

controls. The scale of the service, and to a lesser degree the breadth of activities, is also associated with uncertainty. This elevated uncertainty corresponds to greater information-processing and coordination requirements.

These insights have important implications for outsourcing managers. Understanding that larger and more broadly defined outsourcing engagements require more extensive interorganizational management resources allows organizations to scope the outsourcing initiative more appropriately and build in adequate expenses when evaluating outsourcing opportunities from a financial perspective. These additional expenses may include (but are not limited to) a larger retained management team, developing and maintaining a more complex formal contract, establishing a more elaborate performance-monitoring and -evaluation program, and more extensive information systems integration, among others. As Landis and colleagues (2005) found, nearly two-thirds of outsourcers indicated the need for more managerial resources than originally planned. In some cases, it may be that the resources needed to control and coordinate effectively with the provider will largely nullify the benefits of lower labor rates, provider economies of scale, and so forth. Hence, outsourcing organizations must be especially cautious about establishing large, task-diverse arrangements. Outsourcing contracts are trending toward smaller deals. Outsourcing firms should also consider establishing more narrowly scoped relationships (Aron et al., 2005; Kakabadse & Kakabadse, 2005). Should other business requirements drive the need for a larger, more broadly defined arrangement, outsourcing organizations must incorporate the aforementioned expenses into the outsourcing decision. From a managerial perspective, exhaustively evaluating outsourcing opportunities from a strategic perspective allows manufacturing organizations to enter the arrangement with more realistic financial expectations and allows them to focus on critical management factors to mitigate potential strategic risks (Handley and Benton, 2009).

Based on prior theory, it can be argued that customization contributes to complexity, which creates transaction difficulties. Although this may be true, other forces appear to override this effect. In particular, one may posit that it is the providers who makes specialized investments when services are customized. They are tailoring their processes and resources, for example, to align with customer needs. Service customization may be associated with specialized provider investments that in turn increase the "lock-in" for the service provider, not the buyer. This diminishes the provider's proclivity to act opportunistically. This reasoning is consistent with evidence from Handley and Benton (2012) that greater provider relationship-specific investments are associated with a lower risk of opportunism. Moreover, customized services require greater information exchange and open lines of communication early in the outsourcing process. This may enhance the relationship quality from the outset, which mitigates the need for costly formal controls.

Implications of Location-Specific Complexity on Control and Coordination Costs

The impact of location-specific outsourcing characteristics bears out several common concerns anecdotally identified in the literature. First, the level of inter-firm control costs has a positive relationship with the geographic dispersion of the outsourcing service. As the relationship involves more countries, it becomes characterized by greater diversity in the legal and regulatory regimes, as well as more dispersed operational responsibility. These factors serve as obstacles to managing fully specified contracts and monitoring provider behavior and outcomes. Uncertainty also increases with the number of geographic locations. This enhanced uncertainty may contribute to greater information-processing and coordination requirements. The results from a recent study suggest that geographic dispersion has a stronger negative effect on achieving interfirm control than it does on coordination. Greater geographic separation complicates monitoring the service provider's activities and exacerbates information asymmetry. This leads to a more pronounced risk of opportunism and the need for more elaborate and costly formal control mechanisms. Geographic proximity is also noted to facilitate communication and knowledge transfer, which are central to effective coordination. Thus, all else being equal, as the geographic distance between customer and provider locations increases, the costs associated with achieving adequate interfirm coordination also increase.

In some cases, geographic coverage may be a service requirement that the outsourcing firm has stipulated. In such situations, the outsourcing firm needs to be prepared to have the proper resources in place and their cost accounted for. This may include the expenses associated with developing a more complex contract, ensuring that the various legal and regulatory frameworks are being followed, deploying more elaborate monitoring mechanisms, investing in integrated information systems, accounting for the need for more extensive travel to the provider's operations, and retaining a larger management team. Depending on the competitiveness of the supply market, the outsourcing firm may be able to ask the service provider to bear some of these expenses. In other cases, the outsourcing firm may bear the entire cost. Either way, these insights should assist outsourcing organizations in developing realistic business cases. In other cases, these geographic characteristics may simply be a result of the chosen service provider's existing global footprint and not a customer requirement. If this is the case, buying organizations should factor in the impact on control and coordination costs when comparing potential providers.

Cultural Distance Between Customer and Provider

The impact of the cultural distance between the customer and provider organizations is quite interesting. Contrary to intuition, after controlling for the influence of several other factors, cultural distance has a negative effect on control and coordination costs. In other words, outsourcing organizations experience lower control and coordination costs when engaging with more culturally distant providers. These findings are verified by considering alternative measures of cultural differences. In other words cultural differences in and of themselves do not automatically lead to inter-firm management difficulties. Offshore providers frequently locate personnel at the customer's location to overcome these difficulties. It is also important to recognize that individuals are affected by other associations, such as organizational culture, professional culture, and religious affiliation, that are in some cases not tied to nationality. The results show that although all five dimensions of cultural differences had a negative association with both control and coordination costs, only differences along the *individualism–collectivism* dimension had a significant effect. The United States has the highest (i.e., most individualistic) score on this dimension. Thus, outsourcing relationships involving service providers from more collectivist cultures (e.g., Latin American and East Asian countries) would exhibit greater cultural distance on this measure. Hence, it was found that a negative effect of cultural distance on control and coordination costs in the present analysis. One could argue that this result indicates that raw cultural differences do not *create* control and coordination difficulties, but, instead, organizations in more individualistic cultures (e.g., the United States, Australia, Great Britain, and Canada) are more difficult to control and more likely to complicate efforts to coordinate. In sum, the managerial implication is that outsourcing organizations may not need to be as concerned about the effect of raw cultural differences on control and coordination costs as much as they should be when the provider is located in a highly individualistic culture. An outsourcing case study is given in Appendix A.

SUMMARY

Outsourcing is the complete transfer of a business process that has been traditionally operated and managed internally to an independently owned external service provider. A complete transfer means that the people, facilities, equipment, technology, and other assets are no longer maintained once the business process is outsourced. Strategic outsourcing has rapidly become the building block for globalization. Fueled by the Internet, outsourcing has evolved into the most pervasive business paradigm in the past 50 years.

The anticipated economic implications of outsourcing initiatives are complex. There are significant hidden outsourcing costs that are sometimes not accounted for. The motivation for outsourcing is commonly driven by the savings in direct labor and other tangible operating costs. Yet significant hidden costs are often overlooked when preparing a financial business case for outsourcing. Hidden costs include relationship-management costs, quality costs, implementation- or transition-related expenses, and internal coordination costs, among others. If not considered, these financial implications can eat away at the anticipated gains from outsourcing.

DISCUSSION QUESTIONS AND EXERCISES

1. Some people consider outsourcing decisions synonymously with make-or-buy decisions; it has been recognized recently that the two are the same. What is your response to this statement? Be specific in your response.
2. Outsourcing is also sometimes thought to be similar to subcontracting, joint venturing, and contract manufacturing. What is your response to this statement?
3. In a recent study, executives categorized their outsourcing activities. Table 11.1 in the textbook illustrates the diverse set of outsourced activities that were reported on. Not surprisingly, information technology outsourcing (ITO) represented the largest number of responses at 25.8 percent. Approximately 35 percent of the responses represented the outsourcing of some type of manufacturing activity, with the remainder being business-processing outsourcing. Explain these results in significant detail.
4. According to a recent Deloitte Consulting study, 64 percent of respondents indicated that they had brought outsourced services back inhouse. Fifty percent of respondents identified hidden costs as the primary problem encountered with outsourcing, while 44 percent did not realize cost savings. What are some of the more significant hidden cost of outsourcing? Provide a detailed description of at least three hidden costs.
5. It is virtually impossible to generalize why organizations outsource various business processes. Who in the organization makes the final outsourcing decision? Explain the outsourcing decision-making process.

6. The cost reduction must be significantly lower than the current *direct operating costs* in order for an outsourcing proposal to be attractive. What are the generic strategic benefits of outsourcing? What are the specific benefits of outsourcing?
7. According to the Deloitte study, 57 percent of respondents were unable to free up the anticipated level of internal resources after outsourcing. In comparing traditional internal sourcing with external sourcing options, firms need to have a thorough understanding of marginal overhead expenses and how they would be incrementally impacted by outsourcing a particular business activity. Discuss this finding as it relates to the outsourcing business case.
8. Some of the often hidden costs of outsourcing include training internal employees to become relationship managers rather than technical managers. What are some of the other employee-related hidden costs required to thwart labor disputes?
9. A comprehensive risk-management approach will introduce costs that are different for various sourcing alternatives because the different options will carry with them different types and sizes of risks. What are some of the specific costs associated with risk management?
10. This (economies of scale) is particularly true in industries with relatively standardized processes such as telecommunications equipment and consumer electronics. What are some of the other criteria in the outsourcing decision-making process? A comprehensive response is required. What are some of the reasonable outsourcing financial improvement targets in the decision-making process?
11. One way to identify and investigate a potential supplier is for the buying firm to compile a supplier profile for each potential supplier. Provide a comprehensive list of criteria for qualifying a potential supplier.
12. List the components of a typical outsourcing contract.
13. List the components of the outsourcing consensus transition plan.
14. A fundamental element of creating the perception of procedural and interpersonal justice is communication. Discuss the nature of the communication process. Why is communication important?
15. In the past few decades, due largely to the observation of Japanese-style supply chain relationships, we have come to see that many organizations effectively pursue a governance form that is neither purely hierarchical nor a purely arms-length market mechanism. If you agree, give a comprehensive explanation of this statement. If you don't agree justify your position.

MICROFUSE, INC.[24]

Time: 3:42 p.m.
Date: Thursday, April 22, 2009
Place: Office of the VP for Manufacturing

> *Val, Our orientation has always been one in which control is a critical part of maintaining our market leadership position, hence vertical integration. The guiding belief throughout the company is that, by being able to say that we actually make the products, we imply a certain level of proficiency and expert knowledge. In addition to using our vertical structure as a marketing tool, we at Microfuse also regard ourselves as the best providers of quality manufacturing because of our long-standing quality and reliability tradition. Such control translates into greater power, especially in terms of profits, yet it comes at a cost. I understand that our inventory levels are too high. High inventory levels are a price we pay for us to add value to our vertically integrated business model. It should be noted that Microfuse operates a very efficient inventory system, but there is always room for improvement in this area. Although, in general, the company is open to outsourcing, our vertically integrated orientation will remain intact until a supplier comes along that can provide equal or better value to our products and the company. So, you and Bob James are to develop a business case for a limited outsourcing strategy involving some of our non-core products with this guideline in mind. I would like a report on my desk by May 1.*

As stated, Tom Cecil, VP of Microfuse's manufacturing division, asked Valerie (Val) Simmons, purchasing manager, to investigate the implementation of an outsourcing approach to solve a problem that had rapidly become the center of attention of the company's operating executives. Ms. Simmons would be working with Bob James, the plant superintendent.

The problem is as follows. The current industry trend is to have costs cut by outsourcing more than 40 percent of their manufacturing capabilities, which is being done by all of the major competitors. In the past year alone, XFfuse, Micofuse's closest competitor, has reduced their labor force by 50 percent.

The Microfuse Industry

In order to truly understand the operational decisions Microfuse makes, it is necessary to be familiar with the industry. Microfuse's primary industry, which is driven by technology, is the production of circuit-protection products. It is a highly competitive industry in which firms from around the world compete, and survival is a matter of competing not just on quality and value-added functions but also on price. This translates into a need to be innovative and competitive at the same time. There is always a threat of becoming viewed as a commodity product; thus, the goal of many companies is to provide unique and valuable products that attract and retain customers. Obsolescence is the norm for the industry.

Company Background

Microfuse is the industry leader, offering the broadest line of circuit protection in the world. They offer seven major circuit-protection technologies (more than twice

Figure 1 Competitor Comparison

COMPANY	FUSES	POLYMER PTCS	MOVS	GAS TUBES	DIODES	THYRISTORS	POLYMER ESD	TOTAL TECHNOLOGIES
MICROFUSE	X	X	X	X	X	X	X	7
XFFUSE		X		X		X		3
BUSSMAN	X						X	2
RAYCHEM		X				X		2
EPCOS			X	X				2
AVX	X		X					2
ST MICRO					X	X		2
VISHAY					X			1
TECCOR						X		1
WICKMANN	X							1
BEL FUSE	X							1

their nearest competitor) that span three industries: electronics, automotive, and electrical (see Figure 1). Microfuse's technology is a critical component in many of the products we use on a daily basis, from cell phones to digital cameras. Nearly 90 percent of automobiles, industrial machinery, computers, and virtually any other devices using electrical energy include Microfuse's products. The diverse product line is coupled with a worldwide presence. However, because of the characteristics of the industry, Microfuse is facing increased competition and pressures to remain innovative and efficient.

Wednesday, April 29—New Information

During the data-collection phase of Val's research, she discovered that Microfuse currently has one site in China and another facility located in Southern China through a recent acquisition. Initially, the Chinese acquisition was driven by the fact that many more customers are setting up in China. For instance, the automotive sector in China alone is expected to increase in size from selling 4.4 million automobiles this past year to selling 10 million in 2010. Val was wondering how this new information would impact the outsourcing business case. The company was also projecting that almost all European functions may be required to move to lower-cost sites in the near future. More specifically, there appears to be an increased focus on moving the European division to Vietnam. Because of the increase in global business, Microfuse expects that, in the future, 70 percent of production will be done abroad. Domestically, a reduction in operations is forecasted. According to Val's interviews with some of the operating executives, while most of the forecasted shifts in manufacturing are contingent on many factors, there is a strong possibility of realization. However, there is a common belief that the Foundry site in Champaign-Urbana, Illinois, will never be completely relocated due to the fact that it is the base for planning and development and is heavily involved in the manufacturing function. The reasoning behind this belief is that the control-orientated mentality of the company would make moving all manufacturing away from headquarters unlikely. However, at the same time, it is not an impossibility.

As Valerie Simmons:

Drawing from the case facts and the lessons learned from the strategic outsourcing chapter, critically evaluate the business case *for* or *against* an outsourcing strategy at Microfuse. In a two-page memo, addressed to Mr. Cecil, summarize your overall analysis of the case *for* or *against* an outsourcing strategy.

REFERENCES

Benton, W. C., and M. Maloni. The influence of power driven buyer-seller relationship on satisfaction. *Journal of Operations Management* 23, no. 1 (2005): 1–22.

Benton, W. C. (2013). Purchasing and Supply Chain Management, Third edition, McGraw-Hill, Irwin.

Handley, S. M., and W. C., Benton. "The influence of task and location specific complexity and coordination costs in global outsourcing." *Journal of Operations Management*, January 2013.

Handley, S. M., and W. C., Benton Jr. Understanding the Hidden Costs of the Outsourcing Business Model Working Paper, The Ohio State University, January 2009.

Chapter 12

MANUFACTURING FOCUSED SUPPLY CHAIN INTEGRATION

Learning Objectives

- Understand the relationship between manufacturing excellence and supply chain integration
- Learn about how managers decide which capacity-management technique(s) to use and how to use them
- Learn about elements of supply chain practice
- Learn about the impact of information sharing on manufacturing excellence
- Understand the concept of supply chain dynamism
- Learn about the elements of the SCOR model
- Learn about supply integration and the SCOR model
- Use actual data to understand the concept of manufacturing integration

Introduction

Manufacturing excellence cannot be achieved without an integrated manufacturing planning and control system. Information sharing, supply chain practice, and technology must be integrated across the supply chain. Supply chain integration involves sharing information across the supply chain to monitor, control, and enhance overall manufacturing and supply chain performance. Manufacturing planning and control across the supply chain involves the coordination of purchasing, manufacturing, and resource-planning information. In addition to information sharing, systems design and implementation of relevant related processes must be enhanced in order to achieve seamless connectivity and collaboration. One such collaborative tool is the well-known supply chain operations reference (SCOR) model. SCOR was developed to provide a supply chain framework for integrating supply chain processes with related terminology, metrics, and best practices. In this chapter, the focus will be on (1) the integration of effective supply chain practice with effective manufacturing information sharing and (2) the impact of SCOR on manufacturing planning and control.

Supply Chain Practice and Information Sharing

During the past 20 years, supply chain management and manufacturing information technology management have attracted much attention throughout the world. As manufacturing information technology evolves, firms and supply chains are becoming more integrated. Therefore, integrating effective supply chain practice with focused manufacturing information sharing becomes critical for improving manufacturing performance. Supply chain practice focuses on material movement, while manufacturing information sharing focuses on information flow.

In this chapter, three categories of supply chain practice are considered: supply chain planning, just-in-time (JIT) production, and delivery practice. Supply chain practice is regarded as effective if the selected best practices have been implemented. Information sharing is another focus of the chapter. Manufacturing information technology investment in corporate America has increased significantly. It is estimated that U.S. information technology (IT) spending will reach $697 billion by 2013 (http://www.itfacts.biz). Therefore, manufacturing information technology has had an impressive impact on supply chain practice. The business environmental dynamism will also be considered in the supply chain. Dynamism is defined as the unpredictable changes in products, technologies, and demand for products in the market.

Effective supply chain practice and focused manufacturing–supplier information sharing are two sources of supply chain improvement. Some organizations place more emphasis on improving supply chain practice, while others emphasize leveraging the information sharing as it relates to the manufacturing planning and control process. World-class organizations emphasize both supply chain practice and information sharing. Since these two major approaches are not independent, firms must work on both supply chain practice and manufacturing information sharing simultaneously. As an example, Toyota, a world-class supply chain-practice company, began to implement SAP in late 1990s.

Supply Chain Practice

There are three categories of supply chain practice (supply chain planning and JIT production and delivery practice) considered in this chapter, because they have been shown to be closely related to delivery performance.[1]

Supply Chain Planning

Supply chain-planning practices are used to process information from suppliers, customers, and internal operations. Supply chain planning is driven by two objectives: (1) make a good forecast of future demand and (2) coordinate various functions within a firm and its suppliers and customers. The importance of supply chain demand forecast has been well documented.[2,3] The impact of forecast on delivery performance has also been well researched. Inter-functional coordination within a manufacturing firm is important because the alignment among the functions is necessary to achieve a firm's goal. Forecasting drives all of the key business functions. Specifically, forecasts are the inputs for sales, budgeting, capacity planning, purchasing, inventory management, and staffing decisions. See Chapter 2 for a more comprehensive discussion of the forecasting process. As an example, sales forecasts are inputs to both business strategy and production resource forecasts. The value of the inter-firm collaboration and sharing information among supply chain partners is also well documented. Collaborative relationships (win-win) are usually formed with a firm's strategic/tier-one suppliers. This is when the buying and supplying firms truly realize the benefits of working together to optimize outcomes for both firms. The two firms work together to develop a product strategy and frequently share resources and information.

Delivery Practice

The delivery process starts with order inquiry processing and finishes with customer invoicing. It includes processing inquiries, entering orders, consolidating orders, routing shipments, selecting carriers, transporting products, and so on.

The extant literature and anecdotal evidence show that a good delivery system has a significant positive impact on a firm's business performance. According to Johnson and Davis (1998), poor ordering processes cost Hewlett Packard a million dollars a day,[4] whereas the cross-docking technique used by Wal-Mart, using its warehouse as a switching station rather than a stocking place, reduced inventory carrying costs and the number of docking spaces (Stalk et al., 1992).[5] Gurin (2000) described how Ford partnered with UPS to develop and implement an Internet-based delivery process, significantly improving Ford's delivery performance.[6] Both academic and practitioner literature have shown the value of good delivery systems.

---

[1]Supply Chain Council, E-business and supply chain processes, 2006.

[2]H. Lee, V. Padmanabham, and S. Whang, "The Bullwhip Effect in Supply Chains," *Sloan Management Review* 38, no. 3(1997): 93–102.

[3]Y. Aviv, "The Effect of Collaborative Forecasting on Supply Chain Performance," *Management Science* 47, no. 10(2001): 1326–1333.

[4]E. Johnson and T. Davis, "Improving Supply Chain Performance by Using Order Fulfillment Metrics," *National Productivity Review* 17, no. 3(1998): 3–16.

[5]G. Stalk, P. Evans, and L. Shuman, "Competing on Capabilities: The New Rules of Corporate Strategy," *Harvard Business Review* 70, no. 2(1992): 54–65.

[6]R. Gurin, "Online System to Streamline Ford's Delivery Process," *Frontline Solutions* 1, no. 4(2000): 1–3.

JIT Production

JIT production includes five practices: pull system, cycle time reduction, cellular manufacturing, agile manufacturing strategy, and bottleneck removal. In a pull system, production is driven by customer demand. The objective is to meet the customer's demand in a precise and timely manner. Reductions in cycle time allow for running smaller batches, which in turn improves the quality and timeliness of feedback. Cellular manufacturing identifies similar products or similar processes and groups them together. Cellular manufacturing can also reduce throughput time. An agile manufacturing strategy allows production systems to cope with rapid demand changes, which enhances effective supply chain management. Bottleneck removal balances resources and maximizes output of production. Overall, JIT production practices improve the responsiveness and efficiency of supply chains. See Chapter 7, for a more detailed discussion on JIT production.

Information Sharing

This discussion considers three aspects of information sharing: information-sharing support technology, information content, and information quality. Information-sharing support technology includes the hardware and software needed to support information sharing. Information content refers to the information shared between manufacturers and customers. Information quality measures the quality of information shared between manufacturers and customers.

Information-Sharing Support Technology

Since this chapter focuses on manufacturing environments, information-sharing support technology focuses on advanced manufacturing technology and emerging supply chain management IT applications. Information must be adequately deployed in order to contribute to a manufacturing performance improvement. For example, high-performing firms have a higher percentage of information exchanged via Electronic Data Interchange (EDI) with customers and suppliers. Besides advanced manufacturing technology, many supply chain management (SCM) IT applications have emerged and become widely adopted in recent years. The SCM IT applications can be sorted into three categories based on the length of the planning periods (Supply Chain Council, 2006). The first category is supply chain execution, which focuses on short-term daily activities such as efficient warehouse management, transportation management, and collaborative manufacturing. The second category is supply chain planning, which focuses on medium- to long-term activities. The third category is supply chain execution management, which bridges the first two categories as a supporting tool.

Information Content

Many managers mistakenly concentrate their information sharing on only the hardware and software, ignoring the decision making in the information-sharing process. Information technology investment alone is not enough. Only when management teams emphasize both technology investment and choose the appropriate information to share can a firm achieve effective firm performance.

Figure 1 Typical Supply Chain Network

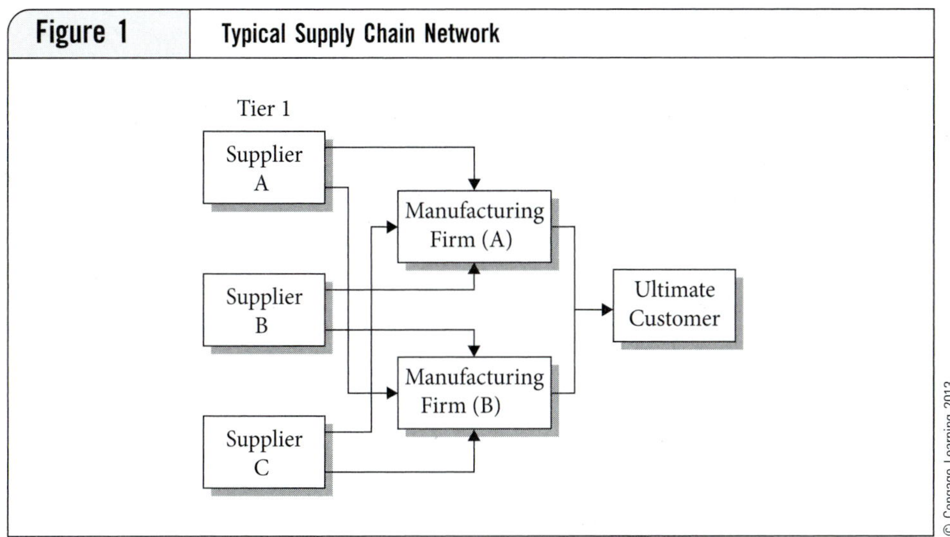

Information content can be classified as supplier information, manufacturer information, customer information, distribution information, and retailer information. The two information-flow measures are the information that manufacturers share with their customers (manufacturer information) and the information that customers share with their manufacturers (customer information). Each member (i.e., supplying firms, buying firms, and customers) of the supply chain is a stakeholder. The objective is to provide a valued product or service to the ultimate stakeholder, the customer, as shown in Figure 1. Also see Chapter 1 for a more comprehensive overview of supply chain focused manufacturing planning & control.

As can be seen in Figure 1, the ultimate customer is the end point in the supply chain. The individual members of the supply chain cannot function effectively without the relationship quality and service performance of the other supply chain members. The quality of the relationships between members will determine which supply chains (or firms) survive in a hypercompetitive market share–driven business environment. Many manufacturing organizations consider the relationship between the ultimate customers more important than the business-to-business relationship with their suppliers. The challenge facing the manufacturer (buying firms) is deciding how to increase the value of the supply chain without sacrificing the interests of the ultimate customer and supplying firms.

Information Quality

Information quality measures the degree to which the information exchanged between organizations meets the needs of the organizations. There are several important information quality characteristics. The most important information quality characteristics are content, accuracy, recency, and frequency. Information quality is an important determinant of the effectiveness of an information system. The information system is perceived useful when the information is high quality, readily accessible, accurate, and relevant. There are nine aspects of information quality: accuracy, availability, timeliness, internal connectivity, external connectivity, completeness, relevance, accessibility, and frequency of updates.

Supply Chain Environmental Dynamism

Supply chain environmental dynamism is defined as the unpredictable changes in products, technologies, and demand for products in the market. Clockspeed is defined as the rates at which companies and supply chain relationships evolve. Fine (1998) measured three environmental clockspeeds: product clockspeed, process clockspeed, and organization clockspeed. All three clock speeds measure the pace of the changes in the business environment and are shown to have a significant impact on operations.[7] Supply chains facing different environmental dynamism (e.g., volatile demand versus stable demand) should use different supply chain practices. Supply chain dynamism measures the pace of changes in both products and processes.

The Impact of Supply Chain Practice, Information Sharing and Supply Chain Dynamism on Integration

Effective information sharing between supply chain partners enhances most supply chain initiatives, including supplier-managed inventory, continuous replenishment programs, collaborative forecasting and replenishment, and efficient customer response. Emerging manufacturing technologies clearly influence supply chain activities and supply chain structures. In addition, Web-based emerging manufacturing technologies make information transmission among the supply chain partners much easier. Spring and Sweeting (2002) synthesized a number of existing and emerging themes in supply chain management, information, and customer relationships.[8] They showed that the use of enterprise resource-planning software profoundly changes the supply chain partner relationships. Two anecdotal examples of information sharing and supply chain practice are shown below.

Dell

Dell is a good example of using information sharing to improve its supply chain practices. Dell receives customer order information directly from its website. At the same time, component availability information is shared with its customers. Specifically, Dell can also update pricing in real time based on demand and available inventory levels. As an example, the component feature price is lower for components with high inventory levels. The Dell website also allows customers to customize their orders. The interaction between Dell and its customers makes the pull production system more effective and enables supply chain planning. Dell also shares information with its suppliers. Once it receives the order information, it transmits the information directly to appropriate suppliers. Suppliers also have backlog and inventory information. Sharing information with suppliers (especially long-lead-times) improves supply chain planning capability. As an example, Sony's logistics information system is linked directly to Dell's information system. In some instances, Sony ships its monitors directly to Dell's customers. Finally, Dell

[7]C. Fine, *Clockspeed: Winning Industry Control in the Age of Temporary Advantage* (Reading, MA: Perseus Books, 1998).

[8]M. Spring, and Sweeting, R., "Empowering Customers: Portals, Supply Networks and Assemblers," *International Journal of Technology Management* 23, no. 1/2/3(2002): 113–128.

outsources its warranty and repair service systems. When Dell receives service requests, it forwards the requests directly to its service and parts providers. This information-sharing feature improves customer service and makes the supply chain more responsive. Overall, Dell's information system interacts with its customers and suppliers to improve its JIT production delivery practices and supply chain planning.

Cisco

Cisco also uses information sharing to enhance supply chain practices. Cisco outsources more than 50 percent of its production capacity. This virtual manufacturing model is driven by information sharing. Cisco's manufacturing model allows it to focus on its core competencies and innovation. Information sharing supports Cisco's supply chain practices in the following ways:

1. A significant number of Cisco's orders originate from online customer interfaces.
2. Cisco shares its order information electronically with its component suppliers. Information sharing allows Cisco to coordinate its supply chain in real time and respond to demand changes.
3. Cisco shares production schedule, inventory, quality, performance, and capacity information with its suppliers.
4. Cisco's logistics system is also driven by information sharing with its suppliers. Many products are shipped from its suppliers directly to its customers.
5. Through the virtual manufacturing model, suppliers are also involved in Cisco's product design process.
6. Cisco's ability to rapidly respond to the demand changes in the supply chain.

Overall, Cisco shares information with its customers to enhance supply chain dynamics. Cisco also has significant two-way information sharing with its suppliers, which enhances supply chain planning, JIT production, and delivery practices.

Based on the operations management literature and anecdotal evidence, information sharing is critical for managing the e-supply chain and effective supply chain practices. E-supply chains are critical for the global economies of the future. An important prerequisite for an e-supply chain implementation is universal integration of the information system with all supply chain partners.[9]

Information-processing theory supports the influence of supply chain dynamism on information sharing and supply chain practice.[10] As supply chain dynamism increases, information-processing capacity must increase in order to achieve superior firm performance. Information systems are suggested as an effective approach to increase information-processing capability. In supply chains, sharing information among supply chain members is one way to increase information-processing capacity. Effective supply chain practices are the "structures" that can increase information-processing capacity. For instance, effective supply chain planning and delivery practices can improve lateral relationships in supply chains.

[9] H. Zhou and W. Benton, Jr., "Supply Chain Practice and Information Sharing," *Journal of Operations Management (2007)* 25, no. 6(2002): 1195–1208.

[10] J. Galbraith, *Designing Complex Organizations* (Addison-Wesley, MA:, 1973).

Managerial Implications of Information Sharing and Supply Chain Practice

There are several managerial insights about the role of information sharing and supply chain practices in supply chain focused manufacturing planning and control. First, effective supply chain practices and information sharing play different roles in managing supply chains. To improve manufacturing and supply chain performance, executives often choose to implement either effective information sharing or effective supply chain practice, because limited resources usually prevent firms from pursuing both simultaneously. However, if the resources are available, world-class manufacturing organizations pursue both strategies simultaneously. Effective supply chain practice standardizes the supply chain processes and exploits the efficiency. The standardization of supply chain processes tends to help companies better leverage the manufacturing information shared among supply chain partners. Manufacturing information sharing is a means to capture the supply chain dynamics and thus reduce uncertainty in external and internal environments. When coupled with the standardization inherent in effective supply chain practice, this uncertainty reduction allows performance improvement. Without standardization, however, uncertainty reduction is less valuable, because the processes themselves are too uncertain to control effectively. Clearly, manufacturing organizations should seek to achieve supply chain performance improvement by implementing both effective supply chain practice and effective information sharing. As discussed earlier in the chapter, Dell computer is a good example of using information technology to get information from its customers and share the information with its suppliers. It uses effective supply chain practices to standardize the supply chain processes and reduce process uncertainties.

Second, the importance of effective supply chain practices increases as the level of manufacturing information sharing increases. Supply chains can be categorized into efficient supply chains and responsive supply chains. In efficient supply chains, products are standardized and firms tend to deploy more effective supply chain practices because effective supply chain practices tend to standardize processes.[11] In responsive supply chains, firms tend to emphasize flexibility and buffering rather than standardization. However, it is suggested that effective supply chain practices that standardize the processes have greater value in responsive supply chains. Looking at the auto industry, Japanese automakers such as Toyota and Honda have more competitive advantage than U.S. automakers such as General Motor and Ford these days when the needs for product variety and information sharing have increased significantly. The effective supply chain practices that Toyota and Honda have are giving them more competitive advantage than their major U.S. competitors in today's more dynamic world where the needs for product variety and information sharing have increased.

Fisher (1997) also found that firms do not have to excel in all dimensions of supply chain processes in order to achieve superior delivery performance. Finally, it was suggested that firms need to be clear about the performance measures they want to excel and invest in the supply chain practices related to those critical performance measures.

[11] M. Fisher, "What Is the Right Supply Chain for Your Product?" *Harvard Business Review* 75, no. 2(1997): 105–116.

Supply Chain Integration and the SCOR Model

The supply chain operations reference (SCOR) model was developed by the Supply Chain Council in 1996. The SCOR model focuses on the supply chain management function from an operational process perspective and includes customer interactions, physical transactions, and market interactions. In the past decade, the SCOR model has been widely adopted by many companies, including Intel, General Electronic, Airbus, DuPont, and IBM. According to the Supply Chain Council's website,

> *"While remarkably simple, it [the SCOR model] has proven to be a powerful and robust tool set for describing, analyzing, and improving the supply chain. The SCOR model has been used by companies of various sizes and of various continents. Intel is one of the first major U.S. corporations to adopt the SCOR model. (Supply Chain Council, 2006)*

In 1999, the Council started its first SCOR project for its Resellers Product Division. Then the second SCOR project was held for the Systems Manufacturing Division. Several other SCOR projects were conducted afterward. The benefits of implementing the SCOR model included faster cycle times, smaller inventories, improved visibility of the supply chain, and access to important customer information in a timely fashion. General Electric (GE) used the SCOR model in its Transportation Systems unit, which had sales of $2.6 billion in 2001. The use of the SCOR model streamlined the purchasing process with its suppliers, which led to shorter purchasing-cycle time and lower cost. It was also reported that since 1999, Philips Lighting has used the SCOR model in its overall business framework, which has helped the company to improve customer service and reduce inventory. In Europe, Degussa (a German chemical company) used the SCOR model to streamline its newly merged businesses. It set up a team of cross-functional employees to implement the SCOR project. After three weeks of a pilot project, the team found opportunities in the existing supply chain processes. It was expected that the project could save the firm millions of euros. Hoovers Financial reported supply chain cost as a percent of total cost. For Four Fortune 10 companies, see Figure 2.

The SCOR model is used not only in manufacturing-related operations but also in service operations. A New York hospital used the SCOR model to define, measure, and improve supply chains. The first phase of the project led to 2 percent reduction in overall drug inventory cost the first year. It anticipated getting about 8 to 10 percent reductions in excess and obsolete inventory in the near future. Meanwhile, the improved visibility and planning generated a 21 percent increase in capacity. It also generated 8 percent increase in demand. The prep times for key procedures were cut by as much as 40 percent, which resulted in reduced labor and reduced costs.

The SCOR model has been widely practiced by many companies in different locations of supply chains, and anecdotal evidence has shown the value of adopting the

Figure 2 **Supply Chain Cost as a Percentage of Total Cost**

COMPANY	GM	FORD	WAL-MART	CHEVRON	IBM
Company Supply Chain Cost as % of Total Cost	94	93	90	88	88

Source: Hoovers 2006 Financial study. www.hoovers.com

SCOR model. The SCOR model has been systematically investigated and rigorously validated.[12]

In the next section, the SCOR model will be briefly discussed.

A Brief Review of the SCOR Model

Since the SCOR model plays a significant role in manufacturing and supply chain integration, a brief introduction of the SCOR framework is necessary. The SCOR generalized model diagram is given in Figure 3. Level 1 consists of five supply chain processes: Plan, Source, Make, Deliver, and Return. Since the Return process was not in the first four versions of the SCOR model and is not as mature as the other four processes, this chapter focuses on the other four processes (Plan, Source, Make, and Deliver), which have been in the SCOR model since its first version and have been widely adopted by practitioners. Both the SCOR model and the literature suggest the relationship among the four supply chain processes as illustrated in Figure 4. The performance attributes and metrics for level 1 are given in Table 1. Level 2 of the SCOR model describes core processes. Level 3 of the SCOR model specifies the best practices of each process.

According to the definition in the SCOR model, *Plan* includes the processes that balance aggregate demand and supply to develop a course of action that best meets sourcing, production, and delivery requirements. *Source* includes the processes that procure goods and services to meet planned or actual demand. *Make* is composed of the processes that transform the product to a finished state to meet planned or actual demand. *Delivery* includes all processes that provide finished goods and services to meet planned or actual demand (Supply Chain Council, 2006).

Plan (Planning)

The supply chain planning process uses information from external and internal operations to balance aggregate demand and supply. The ability to use historical data for demand forecast development is a critical component of the planning process. The SCOR model also suggests that the capability to run "simulated" full-stream supply/demand balancing for what-if scenarios is important for supply chain planning. Another important ability is to get real-time information and re-balance supply chains in real time. It is important to have a designated supply chain planning team. It was found that one primary reason that Japanese automobile firms have an advantage is that they use designated planning teams to coordinate different functions.[13] For example, many studies have shown the importance of aligning marketing and manufacturing operations to improve performance. See chapter 3 for a more comprehensive discussion of the sales and operations planning process.

Source (Buyer–Supplier Relationship)

Sourcing practice connects manufacturers with suppliers and is critical for manufacturing firms, because manufacturing firms often spend a significant portion of their revenue on purchasing materials and services. The academic literature and the

---

[12]H. Zhou, W. C. Benton, D. A. Schilling, and G. Milligan, "An Empirical Test of the Supply Chain Operations Reference Model," 32, no. 4(2011, December): 332–344. (The purpose of the study is to empirically validate the SCOR model (i.e., test the structure of the SCOR model) and explore the relationship between firm strategies and the use of SCOR model. (Data from 125 North American manufacturing firms were collected.)

[13]J. Womack, D. Jones, and D. Roos, *The Machine that Changed the World* (New York: Rawson Associates, 1990).

Figure 3 Supply Chain Operations Reference (SCOR®) Model

	Level #	Level Description	Schematic	Comments
Supply Chain Operations Reference Model	1	Top Level (Process Types)	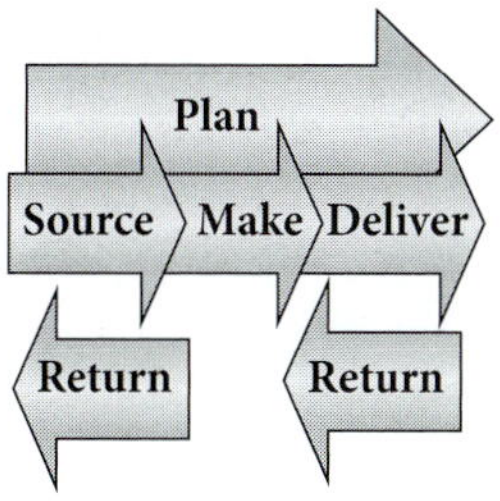 Plan; Source, Make, Deliver; Return, Return	Level 1 defines the scope and content for the supply chain operations reference model. Here, basis of competition performance targets are set.
	2	Configuration Level (Process Categories)	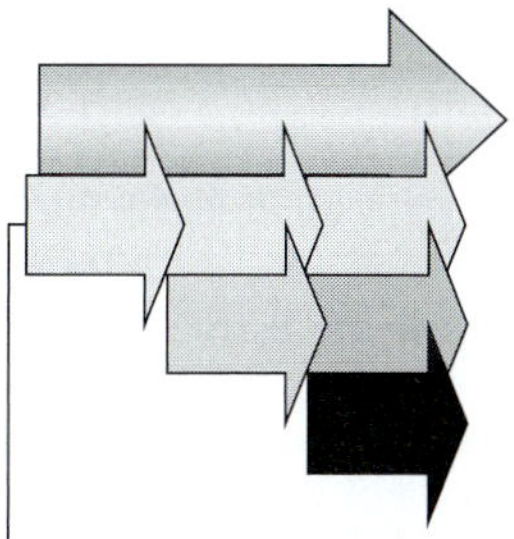	A company's supply chain can be "configured to order" at level 2 from core "process categories." Companies implement their operations strategy through the configuration they choose for their supply chain.
	3	Process Element Level (Decompose Processes)	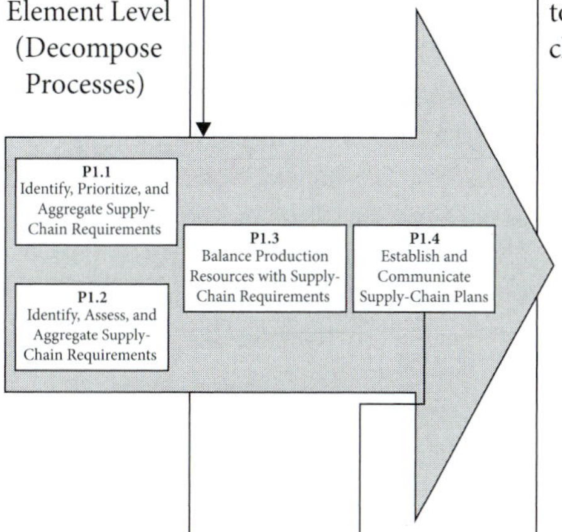 P1.1 Identify, Prioritize, and Aggregate Supply-Chain Requirements; P1.2 Identify, Assess, and Aggregate Supply-Chain Requirements; P1.3 Balance Production Resources with Supply-Chain Requirements; P1.4 Establish and Communicate Supply-Chain Plans	Level 3 defines a company's ability to compete successfully in its chosen markets and consists of: • Process element definitions • Process element information inputs, and outputs • Process performance metrics • Best practices, where applicable
Not in Scope	4	Implementation Level (Decompose Process Elements)	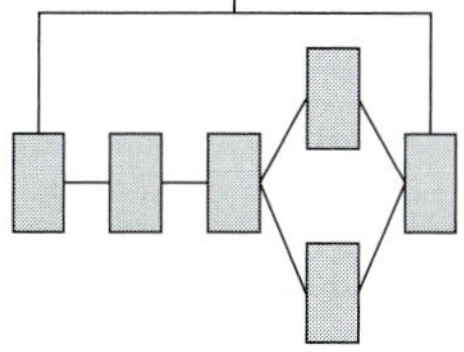	Companies implement specific supply chain-management practices at this level. Level 4 defines practices to achieve competitive advantage and to adapt to changing business conditions.

Source: *Supply Chain Operations Reference Model*, © Supply Chain Council, published with permission.

Figure 4 Supply Chain Operations Reference (SCOR) Model Process Relationships

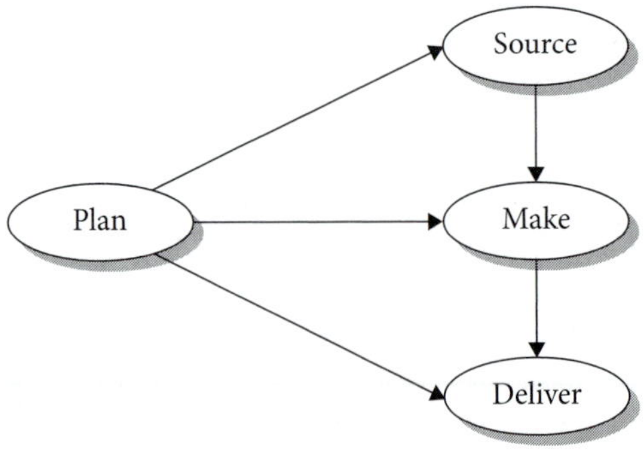

Table 1 Level 1 SCOR Model Attributes and Performance Metric

SCOR ATTRIBUTE	ATTRIBUTE DEFINITION	LEVEL 1 METRIC
Supply Chain Reliability	The performance of the supply chain in delivering: the correct product, to the correct place and customer, at the correct time, in the correct condition and packaging, and with the correct quantity and documentation.	• Delivery Performance • Fill Rates • Perfect Order Fulfillment
Supply Chain Responsiveness	The velocity at which a supply chain provides products to the customer.	• Order Fulfillment Lead Times
Supply Chain Flexibility	The agility of a supply chain in responding to marketplace changes to gain or maintain competitive advantage.	• Supply Chain Response Time • Production Flexibility
Supply Chain Costs	The costs associated with operating the supply chain.	• Cost of Goods Sold • Total Supply Chain Management Costs • Value-Added Productivity • Warranty/Returns Processing Costs
Supply Chain Asset Management Efficiency	The effectiveness of an organization in managing assets to support demand satisfaction. This includes the management of all assets: fixed and working capital.	• Cash-to-Cash Cycle Time • Inventory Days of Supply • Asset Turn

SCOR model have identified several sourcing practices as best.[14] First, similar to the Plan process, it is important to have a designated procurement team. Such teams can span several functions to facilitate the timely completion of purchasing-related activities. Second, establishing long-term supplier–buyer relationships and reducing the supplier

[14]C. Prahinski and W. C. Benton, "Supplier Evaluations: Communication Strategies to Improve Supplier Performance," *Journal of Operations Management* 22(2004): 39–62.

base are good sourcing practices. Having a good supplier relationship is important for securing strategic materials. The role of tier-one suppliers in a supply chain should be assured through long-term relationships. Manufacturing organizations gain added benefits from giving a larger volume of business to fewer suppliers using long-term contracts. By reducing the supplier base, economies of scale based on order quantity can be realized. Moreover, it is less costly to manage a smaller supplier base than a larger supplier base in terms of account management and other management costs. Third, just-in-time (JIT) delivery from suppliers is considered a good sourcing practice. The benefits of JIT delivery have been widely documented in Chapter 7. Last, conducting supplier performance evaluations and providing feedback is a good sourcing practice. Prahinski and Benton (2004) tested the relationship among supplier the evaluation system, supplier–buyer relationship, and financial performance. It was found that executives at buying firms need to incorporate indirect influence strategy, formality, and feedback into supplier-development programs. Based on the evaluation process, the buying firm can determine if the supply base is capable of meeting current and future business needs. Without an effective measurement and communication system, the inter-organizational coordination and improvement initiatives would be ineffective. Thus, supplier development has significant impact on buying firm performance. Also see Chapter 9.

Make (Transformation Process)

The Make process includes the practices that efficiently transform raw materials into finished goods to meet supply chain demand in a timely manner. Both academic literature and the SCOR model include four groups of practices for the Make process: just-in-time (JIT) production, total preventive maintenance (TPM), total quality management (TQM), and human resource management (HRM).

JIT production includes several practices: pull system, cellular manufacturing, cycle time reduction, agile manufacturing strategy, and bottleneck removal.[15] In a pull system, production is driven by customer demand. The objective is to meet customers' demand in a precise and timely manner. Cellular manufacturing is used to identify similar products or similar processes and group them together. Using cellular manufacturing, managers can lessen the setup time because the cell produces similar products in terms of size, shape, and processing requirements. Reductions in cycle time allow for running smaller batches, which in turn may result in reduced inventory levels. Reducing cycle time can also prevent the possibility of producing a large number of undetected quality problems. Agile manufacturing strategy allows production systems to cope with fast demand changes, which is a key for today's supply chain management. Bottleneck removal balances resources and maximizes output of production.

Total preventive maintenance is a manufacturing program that primarily maximizes equipment effectiveness throughout its entire life. Several studies have explored the good practices of TPM and their positive relationship with business performance.[16,17]

---

[15]H. Shin and W. C. Benton, "Manufacturing Planning and Control: The Evolution of MRP and JIT Integration," *European Journal of Operational Research* 110, no. 3(1998): 411–440.

[16]K. Cua, K. McKone, and R. Schroeder, "Relationships between Implementation of TQM, JIT, and TPM and Manufacturing Performance," *Journal of Operations Management* 19, no. 6(2001): 675–694.

[17]K. McKone and R. Schroeder, "The Impact of Total Productive Maintenance Practices on Manufacturing Performance," *Journal of Operations Management* 19, no. 1(2001): 39–57.

Quality has always been an emphasis in production. The quality literature shows a strong relationship between quality-improvement efforts and operating performance. The review of quality-management literature has led to the identification of good quality-management practices: total quality management (TQM), statistical process control (SPC), continuous improvement programs, Six Sigma, and lean techniques. TQM is a manufacturing program used to improve and sustain quality products and processes. SPC is defined as a set of statistical problem-solving techniques whose effective applications to manufacturing or service delivery processes affect improvement in quality. Continuous improvement programs increase the firm's ability to survive in a competitive environment in which success depends on a series of small improvements. Six Sigma is another important quality-management practice. It was initially implemented by Motorola and then widely adopted in many industries. It seeks to improve quality by identifying and removing causes of the defects and variations in manufacturing process. General Electric spent half a billion dollars in 1999 to implement Six Sigma program and received more than $2 billion in benefits.

The human resource–management practices emphasize employee team work and workforce capabilities. Employee team work is important for improving production, because frontline employees working as a team can leverage the experience of all employees and greatly contribute to process and product improvement. Hayes and Wheelwright (1984) recognized the importance of workforce participation for achieving good business performance.[18] Integrating employee teams into planning and working is essential for making improvements. Workforce capability is another important measurement for workforce management. The importance of employee development, such as cross-training and job rotations, has also been emphasized. Employee skills development should progress with technology development. Both team work and workforce capabilities are critical for effective supply chain processes, because firms cannot operate and coordinate with other supply chain members effectively if the firms do not have capable workforces. Also see Chapter 1.

Deliver (Outbound Logistics)

The extant literature and anecdotal evidence show that delivery has become a critical link in supply chain management. One capability is sharing real-time information with supply chain partners, which increases the real-time visibility of order tracking. Agility is also an important competence of world-class logistics. In this chapter, JIT delivery is used to represent the agility of a supply chain. See Chapter 7, for a more detailed discussion of JIT. As an example, Ford partnered with UPS to develop and implement an Internet-based delivery process, significantly improving Ford's delivery performance.[19] An Internet-based delivery system can significantly enhance real-time order-tracking capability and is an important component to enhance JIT delivery. Dell Computer uses JIT delivery. Airborne Express or UPS serves as Dell's logistics department, arranging deliveries around the world. This has resulted in improved responsiveness in Dell's product delivery and higher customer satisfaction. Other best delivery practices identified by the SCOR model include a single contact point for all order inquiries, order consolidation, and the use of automatic identification. Bar code technology significantly improves the relationship between suppliers and buyers and allows for the growth of some emerging inventory-management programs such as supplier-managed inventory programs.

[18]R. Hayes and S. Wheelwright, *Restoring Our Competitive Edge: Competing through Manufacturing* (New York: Wiley, 1984).

[19]R. Gurin, "Online System to Streamline Ford's Delivery Process," *Frontline Solutions* 1, no. 4(2000): 1–3.

Firm Strategy and the SCOR Model (Case Study)[20]

Next, the relationship between firm strategies and the SCOR model will be discussed. In the supply chain–management literature, several studies suggested that the firm strategies should drive supply chain practices. Therefore, in this section, the differences between cost-leadership firms and differentiation-driven firms in the use of the SCOR model will be empirically investigated. The strategy component will provide additional insights on how to use the SCOR model.

In this case study, we consider two types of supply chain practice: supply chain sourcing practice and supply chain delivery practice. As before, a company is considered to have effective supply chain practice if selected best practices are being used. By using sourcing practices and delivery practices, both the incoming and outgoing portions of the supply chain are represented. As for information technology, we use the quality of the information shared among supply chain partners as the surrogate for IT investment.

The question facing companies is how to strategically balance investments in information technology and supply chain practice. To illustrate the question facing manufacturing organizations, we (1) cluster alternative supply chain strategies on the basis of supply chain practice and information technology investment level and (2) identify which alternative supply chain strategies are consistent with good business performance. Sourcing practice, delivery practice, and information quality are used to cluster a sample of 125 North American manufacturing firms into four strategic clusters. Each cluster represents a specific supply chain strategy. The business performance of the four strategic clusters is compared to identify the most desirable supply chain strategy.

Supply Chain Strategy Clusters

In order to perform further analysis, the average score of the survey items in each scale as the score of the scale was calculated. Then, sourcing practice, delivery practice, and information quality as the independent variables were used to cluster the companies into four strategic clusters as shown in Figure 5. The clustering results are shown in Figure 6 and Table 2.

Figure 5 Hypothesized Four Supply Chain Strategy Clusters

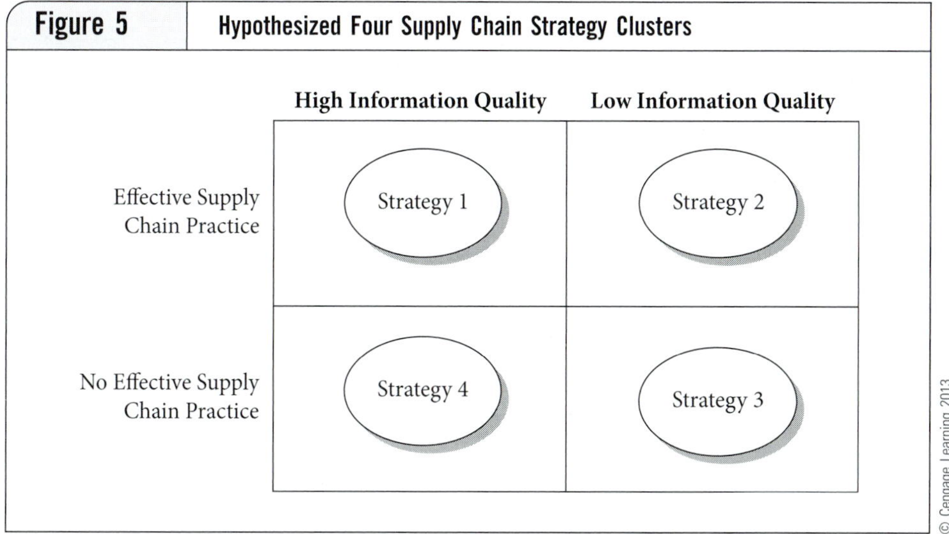

[20]Zhou, H and W. C Benton, (2012) Sourcing Delivering and Information Quality: A Supply Chian Strategy Study Working Paper. The Ohio State University.

Figure 6 Four Company Clusters from Clustering Analysis

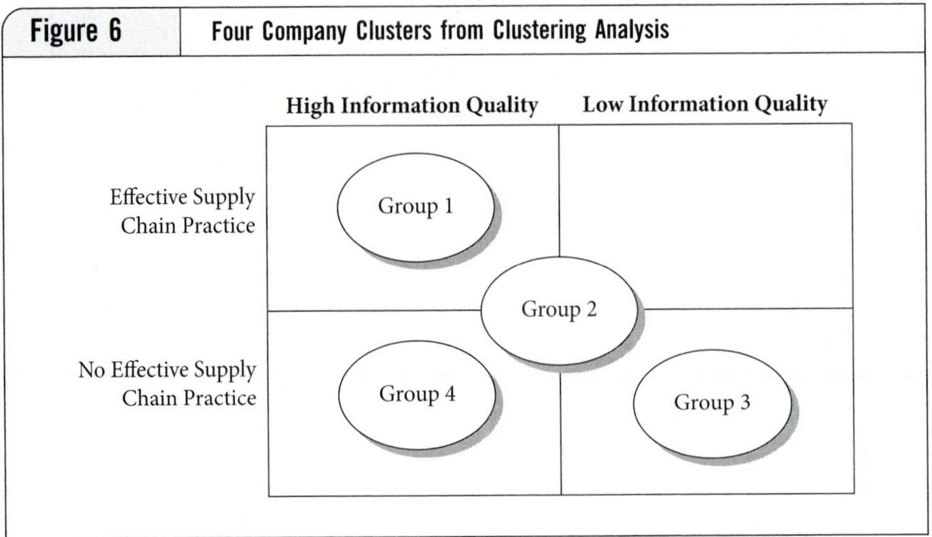

Figure 5 shows one strategic cluster with both high information quality and effective supply chain practice, one strategic cluster with low information quality and no effective supply chain practice, and another strategic cluster with high information quality and no effective supply chain practice. However, Figure 6 does not represent the strategic cluster with low information quality and effective supply chain practice as hypothesized in Figure 5. Instead, Figure 6 shows a strategic cluster (cluster 2) with medium information quality and a medium level of effective supply chain practice. As shown in Figure 6, three supply chain strategies (strategic clusters 1, 2, and 3) align the level of effective supply chain practice with the level of information quality, while one supply chain strategy (strategic cluster 4) has a high level of information quality but a low level of effective supply chain practice.

Table 2 Characteristics of the Four Groups of Companies

GROUP	NUMBER	SOURCE	DELIVER	INFORMATION QUALITY
1. Effective supply chain practice, high information quality	39	5.48 (2, 3, 4)	5.98 (2, 3, 4)	5.91 (2, 3)
2. Medium level of effective supply chain practice, medium information quality	60	4.92 (1, 3, 4)	4.09 (1, 3, 4)	5.03 (1, 3)
3. Non effective supply chain practice, low information quality	8	2.98 (1, 2)	2.50 (1, 2)	2.93 (1, 2, 4)
4. Non effective supply chain practice, high information quality	18	2.77 (1, 2)	3.10 (1, 2)	5.39 (3)
F-statistic (*P* value)		62.065 ($P < 0.001$)	83.909 ($P < 0.001$)	45.859 ($P < 0.001$)

Numbers in the parentheses indicate the group numbers from which this group was significant at the 5 percent level according to Scheffe's pairwise comparison procedure.

Table 3 Classification Results for Discriminant Analysis for Four Groups of Companies

		PREDICTED GROUP MEMBERSHIP*			
GROUP	NO. OF CASES	GROUP 1	GROUP 2	GROUP 3	GROUP 4
1	39	39	0	0	0
2	60	0	59	1	0
3	8	0	0	8	0
4	18	1	0	0	17

* 98.4 percent of cross-validated grouped cases correctly classified.

Table 2 shows the number of companies in each group and the mean score of each independent variable for each group. Thirty-nine companies have high scores on both effective supply chain practice and high information quality. Sixty companies have medium scores on both effective supply chain practice and information quality. Eight companies have low scores on both effective supply chain practice and information quality. Eighteen companies have a high score on information quality but low scores on both sourcing practice and delivery practice.

After clustering the companies into four strategic clusters, a statistical analysis was conducted to assess the differences among the four groups. The results are presented in Table 2. All three independent variables—sourcing practice, delivery practice, and information quality—were found to be statistically important. The numbers in the parentheses indicate the strategic cluster numbers from which the strategic cluster is significantly different. For example (2, 3, 4) at the intersection of group 1 and source means that the sourcing practice of group 1 is significantly different from group 2, 3, and 4.

Except for one strategic cluster, all other strategic clusters align the level of effective supply chain practice with the level of information quality. Information quality, sourcing practice, and delivery practice were entered as independent variables along with the membership from Table 1 (strategic clusters 1, 2, 3, and 4) as the dependent variable. The membership of company was estimated using statistical information drawn from all other 125 companies except company X. In this way, there will be much larger predictive power for the cluster membership. The results in Table 3 show that only two companies among the 125 companies were misclassified, that is, 98.4 percent of the cross-validated grouped cases were correctly classified.

Business Performance

As shown in Figure 5, this study classifies supply chain strategies into four strategic clusters based on the alignment between the level of effective supply chain practice and the level of information quality. If resources are available, firms can choose to invest simultaneously in effective supply chain practices and good information systems. When resources are constrained such that a firm can only improve either supply chain practice or the information system, a firm must choose based on its most pressing needs. If no resources are available, firms cannot invest in either.

Table 4 ANOVA Results for Performance Measures by Four Groups of Companies

PERFORMANCE	GROUP 1	GROUP 2	GROUP 3	GROUP 4	*F*-STATISTIC	*P* VALUE
Market share	5.29	4.50	5.50	4.20	4.254	.007
Sales revenue	5.05	4.23	5.00	4.00	3.428	.020
Return on assets	4.42	4.42	5.13	4.14	0.971	.411
Return on sales	4.47	4.49	4.75	4.14	0.405	.750

Using the four alternative supply chain strategy clusters in Figure 5, business performance associated with each strategy was investigated. Furthermore, this case study shows that effective supply chain practice and high information quality complement each other in supply chain management. For example, high-quality information provides the accurate and timely information that an effective supply chain practice such as JIT delivery requires. On the other hand, an effective supply chain practice can provide high-quality information that supports the supply chain. Automatic identification techniques that track order status are good examples.

After clustering the companies, the business performance of the four strategic cluster groups was compared. The results are shown in Table 4. The profitability measures include both return on assets and return on sales. Performance data can be categorized as perceptual data (e.g., business performance relative to competitors) versus objective data (absolute operating profit margin). Looking further into the mean of the four strategic clusters in market share and sales revenue, it is noted that strategic cluster 2 (medium level of effective supply chain practice and medium information quality) and strategic cluster 4 (no effective supply chain practice and high information quality) have significantly lower market share and sales revenue than strategic cluster 1 (effective supply chain practice and high information quality) and strategic cluster 3 (no effective supply chain practice and low information quality). The descriptive statistics in Table 4 show that strategic cluster 4 did have a lower return on assets and lower return on sales than all other three strategic clusters. While the analysis does not suggest any causal relationship between the business performance and the level of effective supply chain practice and/or information quality, these results do provide more evidence to the growing consensus that aligning the investment in supply chain practice and in information quality is critical in supply chain management.

The results provided several insights about the relationship between supply chain strategy and business performance. First, it is shown that on all business performance dimensions (including market share, sales revenue, and profitability), firms that align the level of effective supply chain practice with the level of information quality (strategic clusters 1, 2, and 3) perform better than the firms with high information quality but no effective supply chain practice (strategic cluster 4). It is interesting to note that firms with a medium level of effective supply chain practice and medium information quality perform worse than the firms with either high level of effective supply chain practice and high information quality or low level of effective supply chain practice and low information quality. This finding suggests that firms in a highly competitive environment need to be good at both information quality and supply chain practice to survive. However, if the environment is not as competitive, firms with low information quality and low supply chain practice may find their investment in supply chain practice and information quality is adequate to retain good performance in market share, sales revenue, and profitability. This would be true in monopoly industries. As can be seen in Table 4, strategic cluster 3 does have a significantly higher market share than strategic cluster 2 while keeping high profitability, which suggests that the companies in cluster 3 might not face a competitive business environment. This might also explain why strategic cluster 3 does not need a high level of information quality and effective supply chain practice. The finding suggests that firms with medium levels of effective supply chain practice and medium information quality should move either towards the supply chain strategy that has a high level of effective supply chain practice and high information quality or toward the supply chain strategy that has a low level of effective supply chain practice and low information quality, depending on how competitive the market environment is.

Second, this empirical study provides evidence that good information quality alone is not enough to improve business performance. Firms need to align the investment in effective supply chain practice with that in information quality. Otherwise, the investment in good information quality is not likely to pay off. While it is relatively easier for companies to buy a suite of IT solutions, it is difficult for companies to change their supply chain processes to leverage the benefits of IT solutions. In a Supply Chain Council study (2006), an Intel manager stated, "The biggest challenge is changing the process, not changing the technology." This study provided a theoretical explanation for the differences in the IT investment returns. As shown in Table 4, if a firm does not have effective supply chain practice in place, it is not likely that a reasonable return on IT investment will occur. Major ERP vendors such as SAP and Oracle ask customers to change their business processes according to the standardized processes used for the ERP systems. If the companies cannot change their business processes, they will not be able to use ERP systems effectively. This finding clearly illustrates the importance of effective processes for utilizing good information quality.

Third, this study showed that firms do not have to trade off different business performance metrics when choosing between implementing effective supply chain practice or information quality, because the supply chain strategy that performs well on one dimension also performs well on other dimensions. In the literature, there are two major opinions about the relationship among different performance dimensions. One research stream argues for the tradeoff model, that is, companies have to sacrifice certain performance dimensions in order to improve other performance dimensions.[21] The other research stream argues for the sand cone model: firms may be able to improve certain performance dimensions without sacrificing other performance dimensions.[22] Although the literature focuses on operational performance such as quality and cost, the same concept applies to business performance. Some manufacturing firms believe that obtaining a higher level of market share and sales revenue might require sacrificing overall profitability. The finding in this study suggests more evidence for the sand cone model in the supply chain environment. Aligning effective supply chain practice and good information quality seems to improve business performance on all dimensions simultaneously.

To summarize, executives in pursuit of improved business performance often choose effective supply chain practice and/or good information systems as a means to the end.

[21]R. Hayes and S. Wheelwright, *Restoring Our Competitive Edge: Competing through Manufacturing* (New York: Wiley, 1984).

[22]D. Miller, "Configuration of Strategy and Structure. Towards a Synthesis," *Strategic Management Journal* 7(1986): 233–249.

This study provides two significant managerial insights about the role of effective supply chain practices and good information systems in improving business performance.

First, the most important message of this study is that firms need to align their investment level on effective supply chain practices with the level on information quality. The study shows that the strategic cluster of firms that does not align the level of effective supply chain practices with the level of information quality performs consistently worse than the other three strategic clusters. A good example illustrating the importance of this alignment is from Toyota and Honda, which have been well known for their effective supply chain practices. However, recognizing the importance of aligning IT investment level with effective supply chain practices, Toyota started to implement SAP in 1996 and Honda started to implement Baan in 1997.

Second, this study shows that it is not necessary for all firms to pursue a high level of investment in both effective supply chain practices and information systems. A group of firms (strategic cluster 3) with low levels of effective supply chain practices and information quality performed well on all business performance dimensions: profitability, market share, and sales revenue. It suggests that what firms really need to pursue is a level of effective supply chain practices and information quality adequate to their environment.

SUMMARY

Supply chain integration involves sharing information across the supply chain to monitor, control, and enhance overall manufacturing and supply chain performance. The widely accepted SCOR model provides firms with a framework for implementing supply chain processes including related terminology, metrics, and best practices. This chapter describes the basic tenet about the role of information sharing and supply chain practice in supply chain management: both effective information sharing and effective supply chain practice are necessary to achieve improvement in supply chain performance. However, the levels of effective information sharing and effective supply chain practice are different under alternative supply chain dynamism.

The lessons learned include: (1) effective information sharing significantly enhances effective supply chain practice; (2) supply chain dynamism has a strong influence on the importance of information sharing; (3) supply chain dynamism has positive influence on the level of investment in supply chain practice but not as much as on information sharing; (4) effective information sharing and effective supply chain practice have significant influence on delivery performance; and (5) the higher the level of information sharing, the more effective supply chain practice is required in order to the achievement of superior performance.

Finally, an empirical study that mapped 125 North American manufacturing companies into four strategic clusters according to their sourcing practice, delivery practice, and information quality was conducted. Four alternative supply chain strategies were identified. The business performances of the four supply chain strategies were compared.

This SCOR strategy study provided the following findings: (1) firms should align the investment in the level of effective supply chain practice with the level of information quality in order to achieve superior business performance; (2) a strategic cluster of firms having low information quality but high levels of effective supply chain practice does not exist; (3) firms can perform well at all business performance dimensions simultaneously; and (4) firms with high information quality but no effective supply chain practice tend to perform the worst among all four supply chain strategic clusters.

DISCUSSION QUESTIONS

1. Supply chain integration involves sharing information across the supply chain to monitor, control and enhance overall manufacturing and supply chain performance. Discuss the relationship between supply chain integration and manufacturing planning and control.
2. What are the major components of supply chain integration? Provide a detailed discussion for each component.
3. What are the categories of supply chain practice? How are the categories related to the other topics in the textbook?
4. How is information sharing used in world class manufacturing organizations? Give specific examples.
5. Why is business dynamism important in a world class manufacturing environment? Give three examples of supply chain dynamism.
6. What is the SCOR model? Discuss each level in detail. Why is the SCOR model important for a world class manufacturing organization? Which SCOR Model level is the most important for manufacturing organizations?
7. What are the Level 1- attributes, definitions and metrics for the SCOR Model?

REFERENCES

Aviv, Y. "The Effect of Collaborative Forecasting on Supply Chain Performance." *Management Science*, no. 10(2001): 1326–1333.

Cua, K., K. McKone, and R. Schroeder. "Relationships between Implementation of TQM, JIT, and TPM and Manufacturing Performance." *Journal of Operations Management* 19, no. 6(2001): 675–694.

Ellram, L. and J. Pearson. "The Role of the Purchasing Function: Toward Team Participation." *International Journal of Purchasing and Materials Management* 29, no. 3 (1993): 3–10.

Fine, C. *Clockspeed: Winning Industry Control in the Age of Temporary Advantage.* Reading, MA: Perseus Books, 1998.

Fisher, M. "What Is the Right Supply Chain for Your Product?" *Harvard Business Review* 75, no. 2(1997): 105–116.

Galbraith, J. *Designing Complex Organizations.* Addison-Wesley, Reading, MA, 1973.

Gurin, R. "Online System to Streamline Ford's Delivery Process." *Frontline Solutions* 1, no. 4(2000): 1–3.

Hayes, R. and S. Wheelwright. *Restoring Our Competitive Edge: Competing through Manufacturing.* New York: Wiley, 1984.

Johnson, E. and T. Davis. "Improving Supply Chain Performance by Using Order Fulfillment Metrics." *National Productivity Review* 17, no. 3(1998): 3–16.

Lee, H., V. Padmanabham, and S. Whang. "The Bullwhip Effect in Supply Chains." *Sloan Management Review* 38, no. 3(1997): 93–102.

McKone, K. and R. Schroeder. "The Impact of Total Productive Maintenance Practices on Manufacturing Performance." *Journal of Operations Management* 19, no. 1(2001): 39–57.

Miller, D. "Configuration of Strategy and Structure. Towards a Synthesis." *Strategic Management Journal* (1986): 233–249.

Prahinski, C. and W. C. Benton. "Supplier Evaluations: Communication Strategies to Improve Supplier Performance." *Journal of Operations Management* 22(2004): 39–62.

Shin, H. and W. C. Benton. "Manufacturing Planning and Control: The Evolution of MRP and JIT Integration." *European Journal of Operational Research* 110, no. 3(1998): 411–440.

Stalk, G., P. Evans, and L. Shuman. "Competing on Capabilities: The New Rules of Corporate Strategy." *Harvard Business Review* 70, no. 2(1992): 54–65.

Supply Chain Council. E-business and supply chain processes 2002.

Womack, J., D. Jones, and D. Roos. *The Machine that Changed the World.* New York: Rawson Associates, 1990.

Zhou H. W. C. Benton, D. A. Schilling and G. W. Milligan, "An Empirical Test of the SCOR Model", 32, no. 4 (December 2011) Journal of Business Logistics.

Appendix A

QUANTITY DISCOUNTS AND SUPPLY CHAIN INTEGRATION[1]

Learning Objectives

- Use price to influence a buyer's purchasing behavior and thus improve supply chain integration
- Show that supply chain members are independent economic entities, maximizing its own profit
- Present a unified quantity discount treatment of the supply chain integration problem

[1]The Appendix is based on the results of a study by Rubin and Benton (2003).

Introduction

The treatment of quantity discounts in the inventory and supply chain literature has tended to be from the buyer's perspective. Most of the work deals with the case of a single supplier selling to a single buyer. The intent of this Appendix is to categorize the major variations on the problem and to develop a consistent procedure for finding the supplier's optimal discount schedule.

Consider the case of a supplier that has negotiated a long-term contract with a customer for regular purchases of a single item, which the supplier either manufactures or resells. The buyer selects its economic order quantity (EOQ) as the standard purchase quantity, but the supplier would like to move the buyer to an order size more efficient from the supplier's perspective. The ideal is for the two parties to negotiate the supplier's profit margin, determine an order quantity that minimizes the sum of the supplier's and buyer's costs (other than the supplier's margin), and then negotiate a method of splitting the overall savings between the parties. In practice, however, cooperation at this level may not be possible due to legal prohibitions, reluctance of either party to disclose cost data, or other managerial concerns. The supplier therefore seeks other means to induce the buyer to shift to a different order size.

Assuming that the supplier prefers larger orders than does the buyer, a reasonable choice for the supplier is to offer a quantity discount. Most authors consider one (but not both) of the two common discount policies: *incremental* discounts, in which a lower unit price is applied to all units in excess of a qualifying amount (the *breakpoint)*, or *all-units* discounts, in which the lower price is applied to the entire order once the order exceeds the breakpoint. Monahan (1984) and Lee and Rosenblatt (1986) take a slightly different approach, offering a discount only for a specific quantity rather than for all quantities above some cutoff. Lal and Staelin (1984) use a continuous decaying function of quantity for the unit price, which can be approximated at implementation by an incremental discount with multiple breakpoints.

When a single buyer is involved, only a single discount range is required, and so the supplier needs to determine just two parameters, the breakpoint and the discount price. How they are determined depends on a number of modeling assumptions. In the following sections, we categorize the different variations on the problem (and note which variants are considered by which authors), examine the problem from first the buyer's and then the supplier's perspective, present a solution procedure, and illustrate the solution procedure through a numerical example.

Problem Framework Assumptions

Certain assumptions are common to the bulk of the work cited above. A single supplier sells a single product to a single buyer. The buyer's demand is deterministic, is constant over the indefinite future, and occurs at a steady rate. A critical assumption is that *discounts do not affect the buyer's annual demand.* Thus, the supplier's sole purpose in offering a discount is to increase the periodic order quantity, not to increase overall sales.

Replenishment lead times are assumed to be deterministic and hence can be neglected. Neither stockouts nor backorders are allowed. The buyer is assumed to use an EOQ as presented in Chapter 5. In addition to the purchase price, the buyer incurs a fixed cost for each order placed, independent of the order size, and incurs material holding costs that increase with order size.

The supplier additionally is assumed to have adequate capacity to meet the buyer's annual demand and to have negotiated a unit price adequate to cover the supplier's variable cost. The supplier incurs a fixed charge for each replenishment order, which may combine acquisition costs (Crowther, 1967), processing costs (Dolan, 1978), and setup costs. The supplier is also assumed to be able to estimate the buyer's cost parameters. This is consistent in today's supply chain focused manufacturing environment. This knowledge is also necessary for the supplier to anticipate the buyer's reaction to any possible discount schedule. Contrary to these assumptions, Corbett and de Groote (2000) assume that the buyer's demand is stochastic and that the supplier has incomplete knowledge of the buyer's cost parameters.

It is assumed (as do the authors cited in Table 1) that the order quantity and discount price are divisible rather than discrete and that the buyer can be induced to switch from one order size to another if the buyer at least breaks even. These assumptions are for mathematical convenience and can be dealt with through minor adjustments to the solution with little impact on total cost.

Finally, we assume that, absent any discounts, the negotiated contract is profitable for the supplier, meaning that the supplier's total annual cost is strictly less than the annual revenue at the contracted price. This allows us to avoid certain pathological situations, such as an optimal discounted price set below the supplier's variable cost to mitigate unavoidable losses on setups and inventory.

Points of Departure

One obvious difference among the cited works is whether they consider all-units or incremental discounts. Another difference is their treatment of holding costs on both sides in the supply chain dyad. On the buyer's side, the issue is whether holding costs per unit per year are fixed or proportional to the average unit price paid; the former is independent of discounts, while the latter is clearly influenced by discounts. On the supplier's side, three distinct possibilities emerge. One version has the supplier incurring no holding costs; only order-setup and direct production costs apply. A second version has the supplier incurring holding costs, proportional to the size of the order, during the portion of each order cycle in which the item is being produced. This version is reasonable if the item is manufactured rather than acquired, if the time to fill an order is nontrivial, and if the supplier incurs work-in-process costs during production. The question of fixed versus proportional holding costs does not arise here, since the supplier's costs are independent of any discounts. A third variant has the supplier receiving a *credit* proportional to the order size, representing either a reduction in capital cost stemming from receipt of payment for each order or, for suppliers who make to stock, a reduction in holding costs by shifting inventory to the buyer.

Finally, most authors assume that the supplier produces or procures the item on a lot-for-lot basis. Some authors (Abad, 1994; Weng, 1995), though, assume instead that the supplier produces or purchases an integer multiple of the buyer's order quantity; the integer multiple to use is part of the supplier's pricing decision.

Table 1 shows the combination of assumptions used in each of several pertinent papers. All those tabulated assume lot-for-lot production. Though all save Monahan (1984) and Lee and Rosenblatt (1986), and Shin and Benton (2004) delve into the problem of setting a single discount schedule for use with multiple buyers, the cited works all cover the case of interest here, that of a single buyer. We will see subsequently that while the type of discount has a significant effect on the solution process, the types of buyer and seller holding costs, while affecting the actual solution, do not materially affect the solution *process*.

Table 1 Assumptions Posed by Various Authors

AUTHOR	DISCOUNT	BUYING HOLDING	SUPPLIER HOLDING
Kim & Hwang	Incremental	Proportional	None
Lal & Staelin	Continuous	Fixed	Credit
Monahan	Single-Quantity	Proportional	None
Lee & Rosenblatt	Single-Quantity	Proportional	Proportional
Shin & Benton	All-Units	Proportional	Proportional

Notation

Buyer's Parameters

A buyer's annual demand (units)

S_b buyer's order setup cost

H_b buyer's holding cost (absolute) per unit per year

H'_b buyer's holding cost (fraction of price) per unit per year

Q_e buyer's economic order quantity without discounts

B buyer's annual cost using the undiscounted EOQ

Supplier's Parameters

P unit price negotiated with buyer (before discounts)

S_s supplier's setup cost per order

H_s supplier's holding cost (absolute) per unit per year

H'_s supplier's rate of return on capital (fraction)

C supplier's direct cost per unit to produce/acquire the item

R supplier's annual production/acquisition rate operating at full capacity

Variables

q buyer's order quantity

p supplier's discounted price

$\overline{q}$ breakpoint above which orders qualify for discount

Functions

$ap(q; p, \overline{q})$ average price per unit for an order of q units given discount policy $(p, \overline{q})$

$ceoq(p, \overline{q})$ buyer's conditional economic order quantity with discount policy $(p, \overline{q})$

$bc(q; p, \overline{q})$ buyer's annual costs at order size q given discount policy $(p, \overline{q})$

$sc(q; p, \overline{q})$ supplier's annual costs at order size q given discount policy $(p, \overline{q})$

Buyer's problem

The buyer seeks to minimize total annual costs, given by

$$bc(q; p, \overline{q}) = \frac{AS_b}{q} + A * ap(q; p, \overline{q}) + \frac{(H_b + H'_b * ap(q; p, \overline{q}))q}{2}, \tag{1}$$

Traditionally, authors have assumed that the buyer's inventory holding costs are either absolute ($H'_b, = 0$) or proportional to the value of the material ($H_b = 0$), but there is no mathematical difficulty in accommodating both types of cost. This allows, for example, the inclusion of capital costs and shelf loss (proportional) as well as warehousing expenses (absolute).

In the absence of discounts, $ap(q;\ p, \overline{q}) = P$ and so the cost formula has the hyperbolic form

$$\frac{\alpha}{q} + \beta + \gamma q \tag{2}$$

with $\alpha = AS_b$, $\beta = A_p$, and $\gamma = (H_b + H'_b\ p)/2$. Throughout the Appendix, we will repeatedly encounter functions of the form (2) with domain $q > 0$. When $\alpha > 0$, as will always be the case here, the function is strictly convex and thus unimodal, with global minimum at

$$\sqrt{\frac{a}{\gamma}} \tag{3}$$

when $\gamma > 0$. (When $\gamma = 0$, the function is asymptotically minimized as $q \to \infty$, and when $\gamma < 0$, the function is unbounded below.) This leads to

$$Q_e = \sqrt{\frac{2AS_b}{H_b + H'_b p'}}$$

which reduces to the well-known Wilson EOQ formula when one of H_b or H'_b is set to zero.

The introduction of discounts changes the average unit price. In the all-units case,

$$ap(q;\ p, \overline{q}) = \begin{cases} P, & 0 < q < \overline{q} \\ P, & q \geq \overline{q}; \end{cases}$$

in the incremental case,

$$ap(q;\ p, \overline{q}) = \begin{cases} p, & 0 < q < \overline{q} \\ p + \dfrac{(P-p)q}{q}, & q \geq \overline{q}. \end{cases} \tag{4}$$

In both cases, $bc(q;\ p, \overline{q})$ retains the form (2) over each quantity range, with coefficients (for the discount range $q \geq \overline{q}$) as indicated in Table 2.

Figures 1(a) and (b) show the buyer's annual total cost as a function of the order size, assuming an all-units discount. Cost functions using both the originally negotiated

Table 2 Buyer Cost Coefficients (When Discounts Apply)

	ALL UNITS	INCREMENTAL
α	AS_b	$A(S_b + (P-p)\overline{q})$
β	A_P	$A_P + \frac{1}{2}H'_b(P-p)\overline{q}$
γ	$\frac{1}{2}(H_b + H'_b p)$	$\frac{1}{2}(H_b + H'_b p)$

Figure 1 Buyer Annual Cost with All-Units Discounts

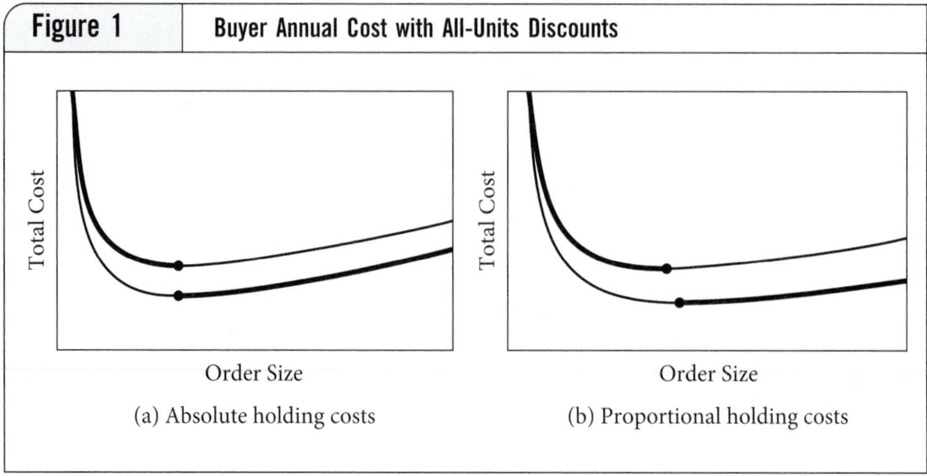

(a) Absolute holding costs (b) Proportional holding costs

price (top curve) and the discounted price (bottom curve) are displayed. The original EOQ and conditional EOQ are indicated. The *conditional EOQ* is the economic order quantity based on the discounted price; it minimizes the actual buyer cost only if it is *feasible* (i.e., large enough to qualify for the discount). The thick curve in the figures is the actual annual cost to the buyer; the jump discontinuity occurs at the breakpoint.

With all-units discounts, the total cost curves are nested. We assume that the supplier wants the buyer to increase its order size and thus will set the breakpoint above the original EOQ. It follows that there are only three order quantities the buyer need consider: the original EOQ (Q_e), the conditional EOQ ($eoq(p, \bar{q})$), and the breakpoint ($\bar{q}$).

Remark 1. If the conditional EOQ is feasible, it is the optimal choice for the buyer. Otherwise, the buyer will choose the less costly of the original EOQ and the breakpoint.

Remark 2. When the buyer's holding cost is absolute, the conditional EOQ is the same as the original EOQ (since neither α nor γ depends on the discount price p when $H_b' = 0$) and thus presumably is infeasible. (This is visible in Figure 1(a).)

Figures 2(a) and (b) show the undiscounted and conditional total costs assuming an incremental discount policy. The conditional cost curve extrapolates (backward) the formula for the average unit price of qualifying orders; that is, the dotted portion uses $P + (P - p)\bar{q}/q$ as the unit price for orders below the qualifying amount. Unlike the all-units case, the cost curves are not nested but rather intersect. As is visible in Figure 2(b), the conditional EOQ, even if feasible, is no longer automatically the buyer's best choice.

Remark 3. Since the composite total cost function (the thick curve in Figure 2) is continuous when discounts are incremental, the breakpoint will never be the buyer's best choice. (This observation is straightforward: The cost at the breakpoint is the same with or without the discount, and this is more than the original EOQ's cost). The buyer will choose the less costly of the original EOQ and, if feasible the conditional EOQ.

Figure 2 Buyer Annual Cost with Incremental Discounts

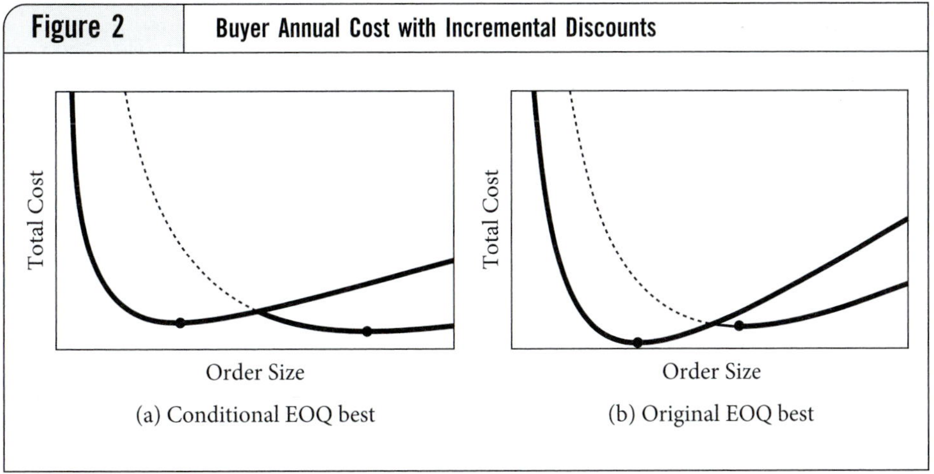

(a) Conditional EOQ best (b) Original EOQ best

Supplier's problem. We begin by assuming that the supplier operates lot-for-lot, and defer the question of lot aggregation to later. The supplier's task is to steer the buyer, through a carefully crafted discount schedule, to an order quantity q that minimizes the supplier's annual cost, given by

$$sc(q;p,\bar{q}) = \frac{AS_s}{q} + A(C + P - ap(q;p,\bar{q})) + \frac{1}{2}H_s + \frac{A}{R}q - \frac{1}{2}H'_s((ap(q;p,\bar{q}) - C)q - Ss) \tag{5}$$

The supplier's setup cost (first term) is straightforward, but the other terms bear explanation. In the second term, we charge the lost revenue on the (captive) demand A as a cost, along with the variable cost of producing or procuring the product. The third term expresses the supplier's holding cost, based on the assumption that the supplier builds the order at a constant rate R over a time period q/R, incurring holding costs until the order is completed and shipped, and does so A/q times per year. The final term expresses the supplier's capital credit. It assumes that the supplier collects a payment of $ap(q;p,\bar{q})q$ each time an order arrives, nets out the order production/acquisition cost Cq and setup cost S_s, and draws down the balance linearly over time to cover other expenses (so that, on average, half the margin is invested). Drezner and Wesolowsky (1989), citing Crowther (1967) and Dolan (1987), omit the setup cost adjustment in the capital credit. Lal and Staelin (1984) write the last term as $-H_sq/2$ and define H_s as the "seller's cost of capital per year" without explaining how it is calculated.

The cost function $sc(q;p,\bar{q})$ again takes the hyperbolic form (2). Table 3 lists the coefficients for both types of discounts. Previous work has assumed that one or both of H_s and H'_s are zero, but we can accommodate in one model both holding costs for work-in-process inventory and a capital credit for accelerated payments.

We noted earlier that in the case of all-units discounts, the buyer will choose the conditional EOQ if it is feasible and will otherwise choose the less expensive of the original EOQ and the breakpoint. It turns out that it is never in the best interest of the supplier to have the conditional EOQ be feasible in the all-units case. (This result is stated, without formal proof, as Property 1 in Drezner & Wesolowsky, 1989.)

Table 3 Supplier Cost Coefficients

	ALL-UNITS	INCREMENTAL
α	AS_S	$A(S_S - \overline{q}(P-p))$
β	$A(C+P-p)+\frac{1}{2}H'_sS_S,$	$A(C+P-p)+\frac{1}{2}H'_s(S_S-(P-p)\overline{q})$
γ	$\frac{1}{2}H_S\frac{A}{R}-\frac{1}{2}H'_s(p-C)$	$\frac{1}{2}H_S\frac{A}{R}-\frac{1}{2}H'_s(p-C)$

Proposition 1 The supplier should never design an all-units discount policy that makes the buyer's conditional EOQ feasible.

Proof In the all-units discount case, the conditional EOQ is given by

$$ceoq(p, \overline{q}) = \sqrt{\frac{2AS_b}{H_b + H'_b\, p'}} \tag{6}$$

where one (but not both) of H_b and H'_b may be zero and is independent of the breakpoint $\overline{q}$. We dispense immediately with the case $H'_b = 0$ (buyer's holding costs are absolute) by noting that the conditional EOQ matches the original EOQ; since the supplier's intent was to stimulate a larger order size, clearly the supplier needs to set the breakpoint $\overline{q}$ above the EOQ. Henceforth we assume that the buyer incurs some proportional holding costs ($H'_b > 0$) and, as a consequence, that the conditional EOQ is a decreasing function of p.

Consider any discount policy $(p, \overline{q})$ and suppose that the conditional EOQ is feasible and that the policy minimizes the supplier's total cost. Because the buyer's total cost functions with and without discount are strictly convex and nested, the buyer's total cost at the conditional EOQ is strictly less than it is at the original EOQ:

$$bc(ceoq(p, \overline{q});\ p, \overline{q}) < B = bc(Qe; p, \overline{q})\cdot$$

Since the buyer's cost function is continuous in both p and $\overline{q}$, the supplier can make small adjustments in either one without raising the buyer's cost enough to shift the buyer back to the original EOQ.

Now suppose that the supplier's total cost is a decreasing function of order size at the conditional EOQ, that is,

$$\frac{d}{dq}sc(q;\ p, \overline{q})|_{q=ceoq(p,\ \overline{q})} < 0. \tag{7}$$

Then if the supplier leaves the discount price at p and sets the breakpoint $\overline{q}$ slightly greater than $ceoq(p, \overline{q})$, the conditional EOQ is infeasible, and the breakpoint remains more attractive to the buyer than is the original EOQ while being less costly to the supplier. Hence for the original policy to be optimal for the supplier, the partial derivative in (7) must be nonnegative. Assuming that to be true, consider the total derivative with respect to p of the supplier's cost function, restricted to the conditional EOQ:

$$\frac{d}{dp}(sc(ceoq(p,\bar{q});\ p,\bar{q})) = \frac{d}{dp}sc(q;\ p,\bar{q})|_{q=ceoq(p,\ \bar{q})}X\frac{d}{dp}ceoq(p,\bar{q})$$
$$+\frac{d}{dp}sc(q;\ p,\bar{q})|_{q=ceoq(p,\ \bar{q})}. \tag{8}$$

The first of the three derivatives we have just assumed to be nonnegative, the second we observed previously to be negative, and the third is strictly negative: from (5), setting $ap(q;p,\bar{q}) = p$, $(d/dp)sc(q;p,\bar{q}) = -A - \frac{1}{2}H'_s < 0$. Thus the total derivative in (8) is negative. This implies that a small increase in the discounted price p will decrease the conditional EOQ slightly, and will reduce the supplier's total cost while keeping the conditional EOQ more attractive to the buyer than was the original EOQ. This contradicts the assumption that the original policy was optimal. It therefore follows that an all-units discount policy that leaves the conditional EOQ feasible can never be optimal for the supplier.

Before proceeding, we note that both $bc(q;p,\bar{q})$ as given in (1) and $sc(q;p\bar{q})$ as given in (5) depend on the discount policy $(p,\bar{q})$ only through the average price $ap(q;p,\bar{q})$. Let $bc(q,\bar{p})$ and $sc(q,\bar{p})$ denote $bc(q;p,\bar{q})$ and $sc(q;p,\bar{q})$, respectively, with $\bar{p}$ substituting for $ap(q;p,\bar{q})$. We will pose the supplier's problem in two phases. The first phase is to determine the supplier's ideal buyer order size q and the ideal discounted average price $\bar{p}$ to charge *at that order size,* without regard to whether the discount is posed as all-units or incremental. The second phase is to determine a discount policy $(p,\bar{q})$ of the appropriate type that will drive the buyer to order quantity q with average price $\bar{p}$.

An important property of this approach is that *the outcome does not depend on the type of discount offered.* More precisely, the breakpoint $\bar{q}$ and discounted unit price p will differ between all-units and incremental discounts, but the effective average price paid by the buyer, the buyer's ultimate order quantity, and the supplier's ultimate annual cost will be the same either way. Weng (1995) reaches a similar conclusion in a somewhat different scenario, although he initially treats the all-units and incremental cases separately.

Supplier's optimal quantity and average price. The supplier's ideal order size and average price form the optimal solution to the following mathematical programming problem:

$$\begin{aligned} \text{Minimize}\quad & sc(q,\bar{p}) \\ \text{s.t.}\quad & bc(q,\bar{p}) < B \\ & \bar{p} \geq C \\ & q \geq Q_e. \end{aligned} \tag{9}$$

The first constraint requires the target order quantity, at the discounted average price, to be attractive to the buyer, to the extent that the buyer must at least break even switching to that quantity. This prevents the supplier from raising the price.

As noted above, the supplier will, in practice, have to "sweeten the pot" a bit to induce the buyer to shift. The second constraint requires that the supplier at least recover variable costs. The final constraint requires an order size no less than the undiscounted EOQ. Problem (9) is well posed in the sense that it has an optimum.

If the optimal solution sets $\overline{p} = P$, then the supplier cannot improve its costs by offering any discount. Recall the earlier assumption that the supplier's initial contract (equivalent to $q = Q_e$, $\overline{p} = P$ here) is profitable. Barring a pathological case in which H'_s is so large that capital credits by themselves are worth more than the contract's profits, $\overline{p} = C$ is unprofitable, since there are no margins to compensate for setups and inventory. Henceforth we will assume that any solution of (9) has $C < \overline{p} < P$. A consequence of this is that $q > Q_e$: If the supplier improves its profits by offering a discount of any size, it must do so by inducing the buyer to increase, not decrease, its order quantity.

Buyer does not gain. Before proceeding to the second phase, we must take note of an obvious but important result. In any optimal solution of (9), the first constraint will be binding. That is, within the limitations of the mathematical program (which ignores the need to provide an incentive to the buyer to switch), the buyer will break even but not gain from an optimal discount policy.

Proposition 2 Any optimal solution $(\overline{p}, q)$ of (9) that improves the supplier's results over the undiscounted case satisfies the first constraint of the respective problem as an equality.

Proof Suppose $(\overline{p}, q)$ is an optimal solution of (9) such that $bc(q, \overline{p}) < B$. For the supplier to see improvement, we must have $C < \overline{p} < P$, and so for sufficiently small $\varepsilon > 0$ we have $C < p + \varepsilon < P$ and, because bc is continuous with respect to $\overline{p}$, $bc(q; \overline{p} + \varepsilon) < B$. From Table 3, clearly $sc(q, \overline{p})$ is a decreasing function of p for qualifying order sizes $q > \overline{q}'_,$ and so $sc(q, \overline{p} + \varepsilon) < sc(q, \overline{p})$, contradicting the assumption of optimality.

Supplier's optimal discount schedule: All-units. Let $(q, \overline{p})$ be an optimal solution to (9), and assume that the supplier's preference is to use an all-units discount. Since the average and marginal prices are the same with an all-units discount, we must choose $p = \overline{p}$. In view of Proposition 1, the supplier's target quantity must be the breakpoint, and so $\overline{q} = q$. In other words, the optimal solution to (9) is the optimal discount policy. What remains is to verify that the buyer will in fact order q under this policy; that is, we must check that $ceoq(p, \overline{q}) = ceoq(\overline{p}, q) \leq \overline{q} = q$. This is a direct consequence of Proposition 2. Since the cost curves are nested in the all-units case, $bc(Q_e, \overline{p}) < bc(Q_e, p) = B$. Because $bc\bullet, \overline{p})$ is strictly convex as a function of the first argument, $bc(q, \overline{p}) = B > bc(Q_e, \overline{p})$ and $q > Q_e$ together imply that $bc(\bullet, \overline{p})$ is rising at q and hence that $q > ceoq(\overline{p}, q)$.

Supplier's optimal discount schedule: Incremental. The supplier's problem with incremental discounts differs from the all-units version in that the supplier steers the buyer not to the breakpoint (which is never attractive to the buyer) but rather to the conditional EOQ. Thus the second phase is to find a breakpoint $\overline{q}$ and unit price p such that $ceoq(p, \overline{q}) = q$ and $ap(q; p, \overline{q}) = \overline{p}$. The second condition allows us to express $\overline{q}$ in terms of $\overline{p}$ and q. From (4),

$$\overline{p} = ap(q; p, \overline{q}) = p + \frac{(P - p)\overline{q}}{q}$$

implies that

$$\bar{q} = \frac{(\bar{p} - p)q}{P - p}. \tag{10}$$

From (3) and Table 2, the conditional EOQ in the incremental case is

$$ceoq(p, \bar{q}) = \sqrt{\frac{2A(S_b + (P - p)\bar{q}}{H_b + H'_b p}}$$

so the first condition (after substituting the right-hand side of (10) for (4) becomes

$$q = \sqrt{\frac{2A(S_b + (P - p)\bar{q}}{H_b + H'_b q}}$$

The solution to that equation is

$$p = \frac{2A(S_b + \bar{p}q) - H_b q^2}{q(2A + H'_b q)} \tag{11}$$

Lot aggregation. To this point, we have assumed that the supplier produces or acquires the item in the same size lots that the buyer orders. We now turn to the case in which the supplier attempts to reduce setup costs by producing or purchasing N lots at a time, for some integer $N > 1$. Two changes need to be made to the supplier's total cost function (5). First, the supplier's setup costs need to be divided into two parts: those, such as paperwork processing, incurred each time a buyer replenishment occurs (which we represent by S'_s), and those, such as production setups, that occur once per N buyer orders (which we represent by S''_s). Second, the supplier's inventory holding costs now must reflect not only work-in-process (WIP) inventory during a production cycle (assuming the item is manufactured) but also the carrying of inventory between buyer replenishments. The WIP inventory term in (5) remains unchanged. We assume that the supplier produces or purchases Nq units just in time to ship q of them, so that the maximum inventory carried is $(N - 1)q$. The on-hand inventory level is then a step function, dropping q units every q/A years, until it reaches zero and remains there for q/A years. The average on-hand inventory is $\frac{N-1}{2}q$, charged at the same holding rate H_s as the WIP inventory is. Note that the capital credit term is unaffected, since payments still arrive with each replenishment order. The supplier's adjusted annual cost function is

$$\begin{aligned} sc(q; p, \bar{q}) = {} & \frac{AS'_s}{q} + \frac{AS''_s}{Nq} + A(C + P - ap(q; p, \bar{q})) + \frac{1}{2}H_s + \frac{A}{R}q \\ & + \frac{1}{2}H_s(N - 1)q - \frac{1}{2}H'_s((ap(q; p, \bar{q}) - C)q - S_s). \end{aligned} \tag{12}$$

For fixed N, (12) has the same basic form as (5). More precisely, if we replace S_s and H_s in (5) with $S'_s + \frac{S''_s}{N}$ and $H_s\left[1 + \frac{(N-1)R}{A}\right]$, respectively, we have (12).

Solution Procedure

Again, we start with a lot-for-lot assumption and subsequently generalize. The second phase of the supplier problem, as described above, is trivial for the all-units case and a simple computation for the incremental case. The work lies in solving (9). Proposition 2 allows us to reduce the problem to one dimension. We use the first constraint of (9) to express q as a function of $\overline{p}$. The resulting quadratic equation has two solutions. When $\overline{p} = P$ (no discount), both solutions equal Q_e. As $\overline{p}$ decreases, the solutions diverge on either side of Q_e. Clearly, we are interested in the larger solution. We substitute that expression for q in $sc(q, \overline{p})$, reducing it to a function of just $\overline{p}$.

From the supplier cost function, expressed in terms of just $\overline{p}$ with numeric values replacing the symbolic parameters, we can either derive and solve the first-order optimality condition using a symbolic algebra program such as Mathematica or Maple, or we can numerically minimize using a variety of software tools, including symbolic algebra packages, programs such as Matlab, or spreadsheet optimizers (such as the Solver in Excel). Since discount schedules would be computed infrequently in practice and would require a degree of human judgment to determine the incentives needed to move the buyer to the supplier's target order size, automated solution of the problem is not necessarily a goal; thus, it would also be reasonable to solve the single-dimension restriction graphically.

Our approach differs from those of other authors cited above, all of whom tie the calculation of the optimal order quantity to the type of discount being offered. Crowther (1967) employs trial and error to find an acceptable, but not necessarily optimal, discount schedule. Dolan (1978) assumes that the breakpoint for an incremental discount will be set equal to the buyer's undiscounted EOQ (which in general will not be optimal), reducing the problem to one dimension (discounted price); if the result is unfavorable to the vendor, Dolan uses ad hoc methods to seek a better schedule. Drezner and Wesolowsky (1989) take a similar approach to ours for the specific scenario covered in their paper, obtaining a quartic equation involving $\overline{q}$, which can be solved in closed form. Unfortunately, when applied to the case of incremental discounts (retaining their other assumptions), the equation for $\overline{q}$ involves a sixth-degree polynomial and so cannot be solved in closed form. The solution procedure specified by Kim and Hwang (1988) for the case of multiple buyers (and a single discount) essentially reduces to that described above when there is only one buyer. As noted above, Lal and Staelin (1984) employ a radically different approach, approximating the discount schedule with a decaying exponential function for price in terms of quantity, while Monahan (1984) and Lee and Rosenblatt (1986) offer a discount only for a particular multiple of the undiscounted EOQ.

Solution of the lot-for-lot case requires relatively little computational effort. This allows us to solve the lot aggregation variant by enumeration. For $N = 2, 3, \ldots$ we adjust the supplier cost coefficients as explained earlier and repeat the solution procedure.

This continues until we reach a lot multiple at which the supplier's production/acquisition quantity becomes unrealistically high. When finished, we simply adopt the lot multiple whose optimal supplier cost is minimal.

Numerical Examples

We illustrate our method by computing all-units and incremental discount schedules for a single scenario. Scenario parameters are given in Table 4. To demonstrate the flexibility of the models, we include both fixed and proportional holding costs for the buyer and both holding costs and capital credits for the supplier. Both combinations are plausible in practice. A buyer's holding cost drivers would reasonably include space and labor, both largely independent of the value of the product, and capital investment and insurance, both tied to the price. A supplier could well incur both holding costs on work-in-process inventory and capital savings from acceleration of payments.

Table 4 Parameters for Examples

BUYER		SUPPLIER	
Annual demand *(A)*	1,540	Base price *(P)*	1
Setup (S_b)	3	Setup (Ss)	48
Holding (H_b)	0.05	Holding (H_s)	0.03
Holding ($\boldsymbol{H_b}$)	0.068	Capital credit (H'_s)	0.04
Undiscounted EOQ ($\boldsymbol{Q_e}$)	280	Unit cost *(C)*	0.54
Undiscounted annual cost (***B***)	1,573	Annual production rate (R)	6,158

We start by assuming that the supplier operates lot-for-lot. In the absence of a discount, the buyer's annual cost is 1,573 and the vendor's annual cost is 1,095.2. Given contractual revenue of 1,540, the supplier's annual profit margin is 444.8.

Phase 1 The Phase 1 problem (9) becomes

$$\begin{aligned}\text{Minimize } & \frac{73{,}920}{q} + (2{,}372.56 - 1{,}540\overline{p}) + (0.0145512 - 0.02\overline{p})q \\ \text{s.t. } & \frac{4{,}620}{q} + 1{,}540\overline{p} + (0.025 + 0.034\overline{p})q \leq 1{,}573 \\ & \overline{p} \leq 1 \\ & \overline{p} \geq 0.54 \\ & q > 0.\end{aligned}$$

Solving the first constraint as an equality yields

$$q = \frac{23{,}132.6 - 22.647.1\overline{p} + 22.647.1\sqrt{1.04315 - 2.04315\overline{p} + \overline{p}2}}{0.735294 + \overline{p}} \tag{13}$$

(There is a second solution, which we rule out because it produces an order quantity smaller than Q_e.) Substitution into the objective function gives the univariate objective function

$$\frac{10^7(5.59674+5.4754871-(6.2608+0.779474\eta)\overline{p}-(0.679744+1.43609n)\overline{p}2+1.43609\overline{p}3)}{(0.735294+\overline{p})(23{,}132.6-22{,}647.1\overline{p}+22{,}647.1\eta)}$$

where

$$\eta = \sqrt{1.04315 - 2.04315\overline{p} + \overline{p}2} \tag{14}$$

Figure 3 depicts the univariate objective function. Both algebraic solution of the first-order conditions and numerical optimization of (14) yield a target average price of $\overline{p} = 0.973$; substitution into (13) gives a target order quantity of $q = 1{,}222$. Those values make the vendor's annual cost 928.8 (a 15% reduction) and the supplier's profit 611.2 (a 37% increase).

Phase 2: All-units discounts. For an optimal all-units schedule, the supplier sets the discounted price at 0.973, a 2.7% discount, and the qualifying quantity (breakpoint) at 1,222. From (6), we can calculate the conditional EOQ to be $ceoq(p;\ \overline{q}) = 282$, which, as expected, is infeasible.

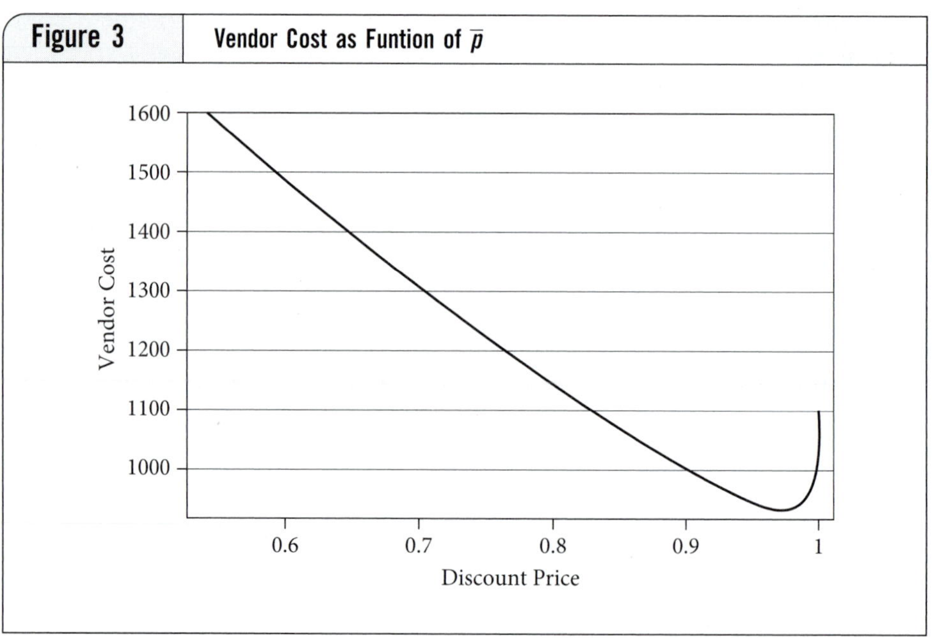

Figure 3 Vendor Cost as Funtion of $\overline{p}$

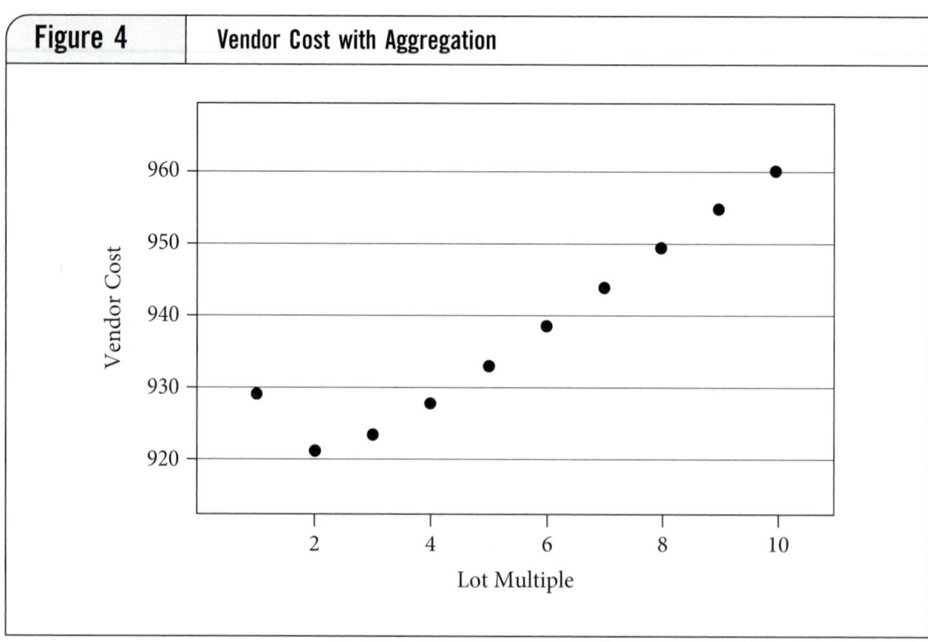

Figure 4 Vendor Cost with Aggregation

Phase 2: Incremental discounts. Given $\overline{p} = 0.973$ and $q = 1,222$, equation (11) sets the discounted unit price at $p = 0.930$, a 7% discount. From that, (10) sets the qualifying quantity (breakpoint) at 746.

Lot Aggregation. Continuing the example, suppose that the supplier's setup cost $S_s = 48$ breaks down into a cost of 12 (S_s') to process a buyer order and 36 (S_s') to set up a production lot. If we repeat the Phase 1 calculations using the aggregation substitutions with N ranging from 2 to 10, we obtain the supplier costs depicted in Figure 4. We see that the supplier can reduce its cost from 928.8 to 920.9 by producing or purchasing two times the buyer's order quantity at a time. The revised Phase 1 solution calls for a buyer order size of 891 (down from 1,222) and average discounted price per unit of 0.984 would set the breakpoint at 891 and the discounted unit price at 0.984. Using an incremental schedule, the supplier would set the breakpoint at 583 and the unit price for units in excess of 583 at 0.954. Note that the Phase 2 calculations are performed identically with or without aggregation.

REFERENCES

Abad, P. L. (1994). Supplier pricing and lot sizing when demand is price sensitive. *European Journal of Operational Research*, 78(3), 334–354.

Corbett, C. J., & de Groote, X. (2000). A supplier's optimal quantity discount policy under asymmetric information. *Management Science*, 46(3), 444–450.

Crowther, J. F. (1967). Rationale for quantity discounts. *Harvard Business Review*, 42 (March/April), 121–127.

Dolan, R. J. (1978). A normative model of industrial buyer response to quantity discounts. In S. C. Jain (Ed.), *Research frontiers in marketing: Dialogues and directions* (pp. 121–125). Chicago: American Marketing Association.

Dolan, R. J. (1987). Quantity discounts: Managerial issues and research opportunities. *Marketing Science*, 6(1), 1–22.

Drezner, Z., & Wesolowsky, G. O. (1989). Multi-buyer discount pricing. *European Journal of Operational Research*, 40(1), 38–42.

Kim, K. H., & Hwang, H. (1988). An incremental discount pricing schedule with multiple customers and single price break. *European Journal of Operational Research*, 35(1), 71–79.

Lal, R., & Staelin, R. (1984). An approach for developing an optimal discount pricing policy. *Management Science*, 30(12), 1524–1539.

Lee, H. L. & Rosenblatt, M. J. (1986). A generalized quantity discount pricing model to increase supplier's profits. *Management Science*, 32(9), 1777–1785.

Monahan, J. P. (1984). A quantity discount pricing model to increase vendor's profits. *Management Science*, 30(6), 720–726.

Rubin, P. A., & Benton, W. C. (2003). A generalized framework for quantity discount pricing schedules. *Decision Sciences*, 34(1), 173–188.

Shin, H., & Benton, W. C. (2004). Quantity discount-based inventory coordination: Effectiveness and critical environmental factors. *Production and Operations Management*, 13(1), 63–76.

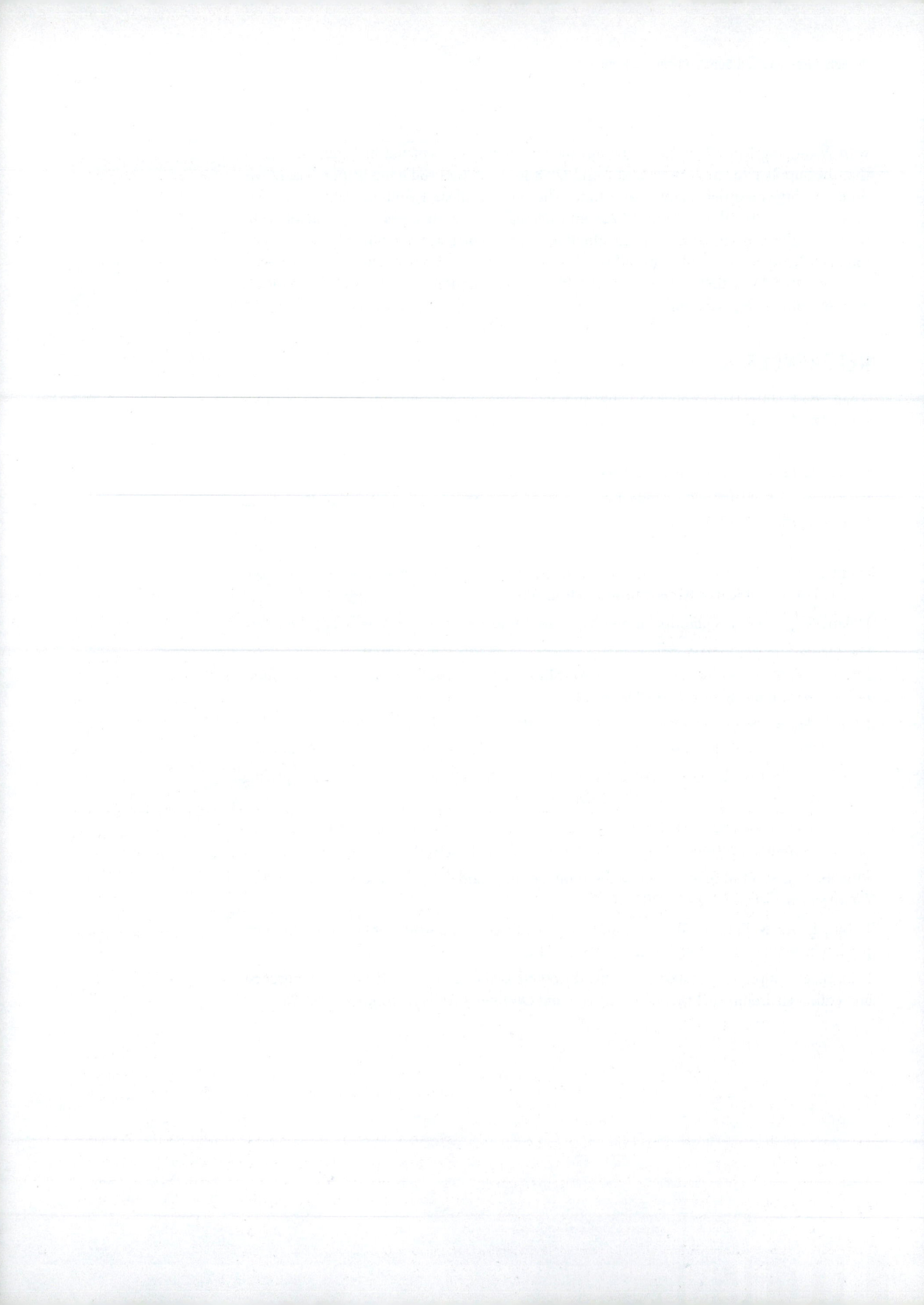

Appendix B: Glossary[1]

80-20 A term referring to the Pareto principle. The principle suggests that most effects come from relatively few causes; that is, 80 percent of the effects (or sales or costs) come from 20 percent of the possible causes (or items). See: *ABC classification.* A ratio less than 1.0 indicates the job is behind schedule, a ratio greater than 1.0 indicates the job is ahead of schedule, and a ratio of 1.0 indicates the job is on schedule.

A

ABC classification The classification of a group of items in decreasing order of annual dollar volume (price multiplied by projected volume) or other criteria. This array is then split into three classes called A, B, and C. The A group usually represents 10 percent to 20 percent by number of items and 50 percent to 70 percent by projected dollar volume. The next grouping, B, usually represents about 20 percent of the items and about 20 percent of the dollar volume. The ABC principle states that effort and money can be saved through applying looser controls to the low-dollar-volume–class items than will be applied to high-dollar-volume–class items. The ABC principle is applicable to inventories, purchasing, sales, and so on. Synonyms: ABC analysis, distribution by value, Pareto analysis. See: *80-20, Pareto's law.*

ABC inventory control An inventory-control approach based on the ABC classification.

absorption costing An approach to inventory valuation in which variable costs and a portion of fixed costs are assigned to each unit of production. The fixed costs are usually allocated to units of output on the basis of direct labor hours, machine hours, or material costs. Synonyms: allocation costing. See: *activity-based costing.*

acceptable quality level (AQL) When a continuing series of lots is considered, a quality level that, for the purposes of sampling inspection, is the limit of a satisfactory process average.

acceptance sampling (1) The process of sampling a portion of goods for inspection rather than examining the entire lot. The entire lot may be accepted or rejected based on the sample even though the specific units in the lot are better or worse than the sample. There are two types: attributes sampling and variables sampling. In attributes sampling, the presence or absence of a characteristic is noted in each of the units inspected. In variables sampling, the numerical magnitude of a characteristic is measured and recorded for each inspected unit; this type of sampling involves reference to a continuous scale of some kind. (2) A method of measuring random samples of lots or batches of products against predetermined standards.

accountability Being answerable for but not necessarily personally charged with doing the work. Accountability cannot be delegated, but it can be shared.

accounts payable The value of goods and services acquired for which payment has not yet been made.

accounts receivable The value of goods shipped or services rendered to a customer on which payment has not yet been received. Usually includes an allowance for bad debts.

accuracy The degree of freedom from error or the degree of conformity to a standard. Accuracy is different from precision. For example, four-significant-digit numbers are less precise than six-significant-digit numbers; however, a properly computed four-significant-digit number might be more accurate than an improperly computed six-significant-digit number.

active load Work scheduled that may not be on hand.

activity-based cost accounting (ABC) A cost accounting system that accumulates costs based on activities performed and then uses cost drivers to allocate these costs to products or other bases, such as customers, markets, or projects. It is an attempt to allocate overhead costs on a more realistic basis than direct labor or machine hours. Synonyms: activity-based costing, activity-based cost accounting. See: *absorption costing.*

activity-based costing Synonyms: activity-based cost accounting.

advanced planning and scheduling (APS) Techniques that deal with analysis and planning of logistics and manufacturing over the short-, intermediate-, and long-term time periods. APS describes any computer program that uses advanced mathematical algorithms or logic to perform optimization or simulation on finite-capacity scheduling, sourcing, capital planning, resource planning, forecasting, demand management, and other operations. These techniques simultaneously consider a range of constraints and business rules to provide real-time planning and scheduling, decision support, available-to-promise, and capable-to-promise capabilities. APS often generates and evaluates multiple scenarios. Management then selects one scenario to use as the "official plan." The five main components of APS systems are demand planning, production planning, production scheduling, distribution planning, and transportation planning.

aggregate forecast An estimate of sales, often time phased, for a grouping of products or product families produced by a facility or firm. Stated in terms of units, dollars, or both, the aggregate forecast is used for sales and production planning

[1]The glossary of terms and definitions is based on the accepted APICS Dictionary of definitions (APICS.org)

(or for sales and operations planning) purposes. See: *product group forecast.*

aggregate inventory The inventory for any grouping of items or products involving multiple stockkeeping units. See: *base inventory level.*

aggregate planning A process to develop tactical plans to support the organization's business plan. Aggregate planning usually includes the development, analysis, and maintenance of plans for total sales, total production, targeted inventory, and targeted customer backlog for families of products. The production plan is the result of the aggregate planning exist—production planning, and sales and operations planning. See: *sales and operations planning.*

agility The ability to successfully manufacture and market a broad range of low-cost, high-quality products and services with short lead times and varying volumes that provide enhanced value to customers through customization. Agility merges the four distinctive competencies of cost, quality, dependability, and flexibility.

alternate operation Replacement for a normal step in the manufacturing process. Antonym: primary operation.

alternate routing A routing, usually less preferred than the primary routing, but resulting in an identical item. Alternate routings may be maintained in the computer or offline via manual methods, but the computer software must be able to accept alternate routings for specific jobs.

alternate work center The work center at which an operation is not normally performed but can be performed. Antonym: primary work center.

andon (1) An electronic board that provides visibility of floor status and provides information to help coordinate the efforts to linked work centers. Signal lights are green (running), red (stop), and yellow (needs attention). (2) A visual signaling system.

anticipation inventories Additional inventory above basic pipeline stock to cover projected trends of increasing sales, planned sales promotion programs, seasonal fluctuations, plant shutdowns, and vacations.

APICS—The Association of Operations Management Founded in 1957 as the American Production and Inventory Control Society, APICS is a not-for-profit educational organization consisting of 70,000 members in the production/operations, materials, and integrated resource management areas.

assemble-to-order A production environment in which a good or service can be assembled after receipt of a customer's order. The key components (bulk, semifinished, intermediate, subassembly, fabricated, purchased, packing, and so on) used in the assembly or finishing process are planned and usually stocked in anticipation of a customer order. Receipt of an order initiates assembly of the customized product. This strategy is useful when a large number of end products (based on the selection of options and accessories) can be assembled from common components. Synonym: finish-to-order. See: *make-to-order, make-to-stock.*

assembly A group of subassemblies and/or parts that are put together and that constitute a major subdivision for the final product. An assembly may be an end item or a component of a higher-level assembly.

assembly lead time The time that normally elapses between the issuance of a work order to the assembly floor and work completion.

assembly line An assembly process in which equipment and work centers are laid out to follow the sequence in which raw materials and parts are assembled. See: *line, production line.*

assembly order A manufacturing order to an assembly department authorizing it to put components together into an assembly. See: *blend order.*

assembly parts list As used in the manufacturing process, a list of all parts (and subassemblies) that make up a particular assembly. See: *batch card, manufacturing order.*

asset value The adjusted purchase price of the asset plus any costs necessary to prepare the asset for use.

ATP Abbreviation for available-to-promise.

automatic rescheduling Rescheduling done by the computer to automatically change due dates on scheduled receipts when it detects that due dates and need dates are out of phase. Antonym: manual rescheduling.

automation The substitution of machine work for human physical and mental work, or the use of machines for work not otherwise able to be accomplished, entailing a less continuous interaction with humans than previous equipment used for similar tasks.

available inventory The on-hand inventory balance minus allocations, reservations, backorders, and (usually) quantities held for quality problems. Often called beginning available balance, net inventory.

available-to-promise (ATP) The uncommitted portion of a company's inventory and planned production maintained in the master schedule to support customer-order promising. The ATP quantity is the uncommitted inventory balance in the first period and is normally calculated for each period in which an MPS receipt is scheduled. In the first period, ATP includes on-hand inventory less customer orders that are due and overdue. Three methods of calculation are used: discrete ATP, cumulative ATP with lookahead, and cumulative ATP without lookahead. See: *discrete available-to-promise, cumulative available-to-promise.*

average cost per unit The estimated total cost, including allocated overhead, to produce a batch of goods divided by the total number of units produced.

average fixed cost The total fixed cost divided by units produced. This value declines as output increases.

average forecast error (1) The arithmetic mean of the forecast errors. (2) The exponentially smoothed forecast error. See: *bias, forecast error.*

average inventory One-half the average lot size plus the safety stock, when demand and lot sizes are expected to be relatively uniform over time. The average can be calculated as an average of several inventory observations taken over several historical time periods; for example, 12-month ending inventories may be averaged. When demand and lot sizes are not uniform, the stock level versus time can be graphed to determine the average.

average total cost The ratio of total costs (the sum of total fixed costs and total variable costs) over units produced.

average variable cost The ratio of total variable costs over units produced.

avoidable cost A cost associated with an activity that would not be incurred if the activity were not performed (e.g., telephone cost associated with vendor support).

B

backflush A method of inventory bookkeeping in which the book (computer) inventory of components is automatically reduced by the computer after completion of activity on the component's upper-level parent item based on what should have been used as specified on the bill of material and allocation records. This approach has the disadvantage of a built-in differential between the book record and what is physically in stock. Synonyms: explode-to-deduct, postdeduct inventory transaction processing.

backorder An unfilled customer order or commitment. A backorder is an immediate (or past-due) demand against an item whose inventory is insufficient to satisfy the demand. See: *stockout.*

backward scheduling A technique for calculating operation start dates and due dates. The schedule is computed starting with the due date for the order and working backward to determine the required start date and/or due dates for each operation. Synonym: backward scheduling. Antonym: forward scheduling.

balance (1) The act of evenly distributing the work elements between the two hands performing an operation. (2) The state of having approximately equal working times among the various operations in a process or the stations on an assembly line. See: *balance.*

balancing operations In repetitive just-in-time production, matching actual output cycle times of all operations to the demand or use for parts as required by final assembly and, eventually, as required by the market.

bar code A series of alternating bars and spaces printed or stamped on parts, containers, labels, or other media, representing encoded information that can be read by electronic readers. A bar code is used to facilitate timely and accurate input of data to a computer system.

base inventory level The inventory level made up of aggregate lot-size inventory plus the aggregate safety stock inventory. It does not take into account the anticipation inventory that will result from the production plan. The base inventory level should be known before the production plan is made. Synonym: basic stock. See: *aggregate inventory.*

base stock system A method of inventory control that includes as special cases most of the systems in practice. In this system, when an order is received for any item, it is used as a pricing ticket, and duplicate copies, called replenishment orders, are sent back to all stages of production to initiate replenishment of stocks. Positive or negative orders, called base stock orders, are also used from time to time to adjust the level of the base stock of each item. In actual practice, replenishment orders are usually accumulated when they are issued and are released at regular intervals.

basic stock Synonym: base inventory level.

batch bill of materials A recipe or formula in which the statement of components based on the standard batch quantity of the parent.

batch picking A method of picking orders in which order requirements are aggregated by product across orders to reduce movement to and from product locations. The aggregated quantities of each product are then transported to a common area in which the individual orders are constructed. See: *discrete order picking, order picking, zone picking.*

batch processing (1) A manufacturing technique in which parts are accumulated and processed together in a lot. (2) A computer technique in which transactions are accumulated and processed together or in a lot. Synonym: batch production.

benchmarking The continuous process of measuring the company's products, services, costs, and practices. Two types of benchmarking exist: competitive, a comparison against your industry best, and process, a comparison of a process to the best in-class. See: *competitive benchmarking, performance benchmarking, process benchmarking.*

bias A consistent deviation from the mean in one direction (high or low). A normal property of a good forecast is that it is not biased. See: *average forecast error.*

bid proposal The response to the written request from a potential customer asking for the submission of a quotation or proposal to provide goods or services. The bid proposal is in response to an RFP or RFQ.

bill of capacity Synonym: bill of resources.

bill of labor A structured listing of all labor requirements for the fabrication, assembly, and testing of a parent item. See: *bill of resources, capacity bill procedure, routing.*

bill of material (BOM) (1) A listing of all the subassemblies, intermediates, parts, and raw materials that go into a parent assembly. It is used in conjunction with the master production schedule to determine the items for which purchase requisitions and production orders must be released. A variety of display formats exist for bills of material, including the single-level bill of material, indented bill of material, modular (planning) bill of material, transient bill of material, matrix bill of material, and costed bill of material. (2) A list of all the materials needed to make one production run of a product, by a contract manufacturer, of piece parts/components for its customers. The bill of material may also be called the formula, recipe, or ingredients list in certain process industries.

bill of resources A listing of the required capacity and key resources needed to manufacture one unit of a selected item or family. Rough-cut capacity planning uses these bills to calculate the approximate capacity requirements of the master production schedule. Resource planning may use a form of this bill. Synonym: bill of capacity. See: *bill of labor, capacity planning using overall factors, product load profile, resource profile, rough-cut capacity planning, routing.*

bin (1) A storage device designed to hold small discrete parts. (2) A shelving unit with physical dividers separating the storage locations.

block scheduling An operation-scheduling technique in which each operation is allowed a "block" of time, such as a day or a week.

blocked operation An upstream work center that is not permitted to produce because of a full queue at a downstream work center or because no kanban authorizes production.

blocked operations A group of operations identified separately for instructions and documentation but reported as one.

blocking The condition requiring a work center that has parts to process to remain idle as long as the queue to which the parts would be sent is full or kanbans authorizing production are not present.

bottleneck A facility, function, department, or resource whose capacity is less than the demand placed upon it. For example, a bottleneck machine or work center exists where jobs are processed at a slower rate than they are demanded.

bottom-up replanning In MRP, the process of using pegging data to solve material availability or other problems. This process is accomplished by the planner (not the computer system), who evaluates the effects of possible solutions. Potential solutions include compressing lead time, cutting order quantity, substituting material, and changing the master schedule.

brainstorming A technique that teams use to generate ideas on a particular subject. Each person on the team is asked to think creatively and write down as many ideas as possible. The ideas are not discussed or reviewed until after the brainstorming session.

branch warehouse demand Synonym: warehouse demand.

break-even point The level of production or the volume of sales at which operations are neither profitable nor unprofitable. The break-even point is the intersection of the total revenue and total cost curves. See: *total cost curve.*

bucket A time period, usually a week.

bucketless system An MRP, DRP, or other time-phased system in which all time-phased data are processed, stored, and usually time displayed using dated records rather than defined time periods, or buckets.

budget A plan that includes an estimate of future costs and revenues related to expected activities. The budget serves as a pattern for and a control over future operations.

budgeted capacity The volume/mix of throughput on which financial budgets are set and overhead/burden absorption rates established.

buffer (1) A quantity of materials awaiting further processing. It can refer to raw materials, semifinished stores or hold points, or a work backlog that is purposely maintained behind a work center. Synonym: bank. (2) In the theory of constraints, buffers can be time or material and support throughput and/or due date performance. Buffers can be maintained at the constraint convergent points (with a constraint part), divergent points, and shipping points.

buffer management In the theory of constraints, a process in which all expediting in a shop is driven by what is scheduled to be in the buffers (constraint, shipping, and assembly buffers). By expediting this material into the buffers, the system helps avoid idleness at the constraint and missed customer due dates. In addition, the causes of items missing from the buffer are identified, and the frequency of occurrence is used to prioritize improvement activities.

bulk issue Parts issued from stores to work-in-process inventory, but not based on a job order. They are issued in quantities estimated to cover requirements of individual work centers and production lines. The issue may be used to cover a period of time or to fill a fixed-size container.

bullwhip effect An extreme change in the supply position upstream in a supply chain generated by a small change in demand downstream in the supply chain. Inventory can quickly move from being backordered to being excess. This is caused by the serial nature of communicating orders up the chain with the inherent transportation delays of moving product down the chain. The bullwhip effect can be eliminated by synchronizing the supply chain.

burden rate A cost, usually in dollars per hour, that is normally added to the cost of every standard production hour to cover overhead expenses.

business cycle a period of time marked by long-term fluctuations in the total level of economic activity. Measures of business cycle activity include the rate of unemployment and the level of gross domestic product.

business judgment rule Under common law, an absence of liability for corporate directors and officers if they have used rational business judgment and have no conflict of interest.

business plan (1) A statement of long-range strategy and revenue, cost, and profit objectives usually accompanied by budgets, a projected balance sheet, and a cash flow (source and application of funds) statement. A business plan is usually stated in terms of dollars and grouped by product family. The business plan is then translated into synchronized tactical functional plans through the production planning process (or the sales and operations planning process). Although frequently stated in different terms (dollars versus units), these tactical plans should agree with each other and with the business plan. See: *long-term planning, strategic plan.* (2) A document consisting of the business details (organization, strategy, and financing tactics) prepared by an entrepreneur to plan for a new business.

business process A set of logically related tasks or activities performed to achieve a defined business outcome.

business process reengineering (BPR) A procedure that involves the fundamental rethinking and radical redesign of business processes to achieve dramatic organizational improvements in such critical measures of performance as cost, quality, service, and speed. Any BPR activity is distinguished by its emphasis on (1) process rather than functions and products and (2) the customers for the process. Synonym: reengineering.

business service The software aspect of electronic commerce. It performs activities, such as encryption, that are required to support business transactions.

business unit A division or segment of an organization generally treated as a separate profit-and-loss center.

business-to-business commerce (B2B) Business being conducted over the Internet between businesses. The implication is that this connectivity will cause businesses to transform themselves via supply chain management to become virtual organizations, reducing costs, improving quality, reducing delivery lead time, and improving due-date performance.

business-to-consumer sales (B2C) Business being conducted between businesses and final consumers largely over the Internet. It includes traditional brick-and-mortar businesses that also offer products online and businesses that trade exclusively electronically.

C

CAD/CAM The integration of computer-aided design and computer-aided manufacturing to achieve automation from design through manufacturing.

calculated capacity Synonym: rated capacity.

calculated usage The determination of usage of components or ingredients in a manufacturing process by multiplying the receipt quantity of a parent by the quantity per each component or ingredient in the bill or recipe, accommodating standard yields.

can-order point An ordering system used when multiple items are ordered from one vendor. The can-order point is a point higher than the original order point. When any one of the items triggers an order by reaching the must-order point, all items below their can-order point are also ordered. The can-order point is set by considering the additional holding cost that would be incurred should the item be ordered easily.

capacity (1) The capability of a system to perform its expected function. (2) The capability of a worker, machine, work center, plant, or organization to produce output per time period. Capacity required represents the system capability needed to make a given product mix (assuming technology, product specification, etc.). As a planning function, both capacity available and capacity required can be measured in the short term (capacity requirements plan), intermediate term (rough-cut capacity plan), and long term (resource requirements plan). Capacity control is the execution through the I/O control report of the short-term plan. Capacity can be classified as budgeted, dedicated, demonstrated, productive, protective, rated, safety, standing, or theoretical. See: *capacity available, capacity required.* (3) Required mental ability to enter into a contract.

capacity control The process of measuring production output and comparing it with the capacity requirements plan, determining if the variance exceeds preestablished limits and taking corrective action to get back on plan if the limits are exceeded. See: *input/output control.*

capacity management The function of establishing, measuring, monitoring, and adjusting, limits or levels of capacity in order to execute all manufacturing schedules, that is, the production plan, master production schedule, material requirements plan, and dispatch list. Capacity management is executed at four levels: resource requirements planning, rough-cut capacity planning, capacity requirements planning, and input/output control.

capacity planning The process of determining the amount of capacity required to produce in the future. This process may be performed at an aggregate or product-line level (resource requirements planning), at the master-scheduling level (rough-cut capacity planning), and at the material requirements planning level (capacity requirements planning). See: *capacity requirement planning, resource planning, rough-cut planning.*

capacity planning using overall factors (CPOF) A rough-cut capacity planning technique. The master-schedule items and quantities are multiplied by the total time required to build each item to provide the total number of hours to produce the schedule. Historical work center percentages are then applied to the total number of hours to provide an estimate of the hours per work center to support the master schedule. This technique eliminates the need for engineered time standards. Synonym: overall factors. See: *bill of resources, capacity planning, resource profile, rough-cut capacity planning.*

capacity requirements The resources needed to produce the projected level of work required from a facility over a time horizon. Capacity requirements are usually expressed in terms of hours of work or, when units consume similar resources at the same rate, units of production.

Capacity-requirements planning (CRP) The function of establishing, measuring, and adjusting limits or levels of capacity. The term *capacity requirements planning* in this context refers to the process of determining in detail the amount of labor and machine resources required to accomplish the tasks of production. Open shop orders and planned orders in the MRP system are input to CRP, which, through the use of parts routings and time standards, translates these orders into hours of work by work center by time period. Even though rough-cut capacity planning may indicate that sufficient capacity exists to execute the MPS, CRP may show that capacity is insufficient during specific time periods. See: *capacity planning.*

capacity strategy One of the strategic choices that a firm must make as part of its manufacturing strategy. There are three commonly recognized capacity strategies: lead, lag, and tracking. A lead capacity strategy adds capacity in anticipation of increasing demand. A lag strategy does not add capacity until the firm is operating at or beyond full capacity. A tracking strategy adds capacity in small amounts to attempt to respond to changing demand in the marketplace.

capacity-related costs Costs generally related to increasing (or decreasing) capacity in the medium- to long-range time horizon. Personnel costs include hiring and training of direct laborers, supervisors, and support personnel in the areas related to the capacity increase. Equipment purchases to increase capacity are also considered. In contrast, costs related to decreasing capacity include layoffs, the fixed overhead spread over fewer units, the impact of low morale, and the inefficiencies of lower production levels.

capital asset A physical object that is held by an organization for its production potential and that costs more than some threshold value.

capital budgeting Actions relating to the planning and financing of capital outlays for such purposes as the purchase of new equipment, the introduction of new product lines, and the modernization of plant facilities.

capital expenditure Money invested in a long-term asset, one that is expected to last longer than one year. The investment is expected to generate a stream of future benefits.

carload lot A shipment that qualifies for a reduced freight rate because it is greater than a specified minimum weight. Since carload rates usually include minimum rates per unit of volume, the higher LCL (less than carload) rate may be less expensive for a heavy but relatively small shipment.

carrying cost The cost of holding inventory, usually defined as a percentage of the dollar value of inventory per unit of time (generally one year). Carrying cost depends mainly on the cost of capital invested as well as such costs of maintaining the inventory as taxes and insurance, obsolescence, spoilage, and space occupied. Such costs vary from 10 percent to 35 percent annually, depending on type of industry. Carrying cost is ultimately a policy variable reflecting the opportunity cost of alternative uses for funds invested in inventory. Synonym: holding costs.

cash conversion cycle (1) In retailing, the length of time between the sale of products and the cash payments for a company's resources. (2) In manufacturing, the length of time from the purchase of raw materials to the collection of amounts receivable from customers for the sale of products or services.

cellular layout An equipment configuration to support cellular manufacturing.

cellular manufacturing A manufacturing process that produces families of parts within a single line or cell of machines controlled by operators who work only within the line or cell.

centralized dispatching The organization of the dispatching function into one central location. This structure often involves the use of data-collection devices for communication between the centralized dispatching function, which usually reports to the production-control department, and the shop manufacturing departments.

Certified in Production and Inventory Management (CPIM) The APICS certification that is a recognition of a high level of professional knowledge.

Certified Purchasing Manager (CPM) The Institute for Supply Management (ISM) [formerly NAPM] certification.

co-product A product that is usually manufactured together or sequentially because of product or process similarities. See: *by-product.*

computer numerical control (CNC) A technique in which a machine tool controller uses a computer or microprocessor to store and execute numerical instructions.

computer-integrated manufacturing (CIM) The integration of the total manufacturing organization through the use of computer systems and managerial philosophies that improve the organization's effectiveness; the application of a computer to bridge various computerized systems and connect them into a coherent, integrated whole. For example, budgets, CAD/CAM, process controls, group technology systems, MRP II, financial reporting systems, and so forth are linked and interfaced.

configuration The arrangement of components as specified to produce an assembly.

confirming order A purchase order issued to a supplier, listing the goods or services and terms of an order placed orally or otherwise before the usual purchase document.

conformance An affirmative indication or judgment that a product or service has met the requirements of a relevant specification, contract, or regulation.

consumer's risk For a given sampling plan, the probability of acceptance of a lot, the quality of which has designated numerical value representing a level that is worse than some threshold value. See: *type II error.*

consuming the forecast The process of reducing the forecast by customer orders or other types of actual demands as they are received. The adjustments yield the value of the remaining forecast for each period. Synonym: forecast consumption.

consumption The amount of each bill-of-material component used in the production process to make the parent.

continuous process control The use of transducers (sensors) to monitor a process and make automatic changes in operations through the design of appropriate feedback-control loops. Although such devices have historically been mechanical or electromechanical, there is now widespread use of microcomputers and centralized control.

continuous process improvement (CPI) A never-ending effort to expose and eliminate root causes of problems; small-step improvement as opposed to big-step improvement. Synonym: continuous improvement. See: *kaizen.*

continuous production A production system in which the productive equipment is organized and sequenced according to the steps involved to produce the product. This term denotes that material flow is continuous during the production process. The routing of the jobs is fixed and setups are seldom changed. Synonyms: continuous flow (production), continuous process. See: *mass production, project manufacturing.*

contract administration Managing all aspects of a contract to guarantee that the contractor fulfills his obligations.

contract carrier A carrier that does not serve the general public but provides transportation for hire for one or a limited number of shippers under a specific contract.

contract labor Self-employed individuals or firms contracted by an organization to perform specific services on an intermittent or short-term basis.

contribution The difference between sales price and variable costs. Contribution is used to cover fixed costs and profits.

control chart A graphic comparison of process performance data with predetermined computed control limits. The process performance data usually consist of groups of measurements selected in regular sequence of production that preserve the order. The primary use of control charts is to detect assignable causes of variation in the process as opposed to random variations. The control chart is one of the seven tools of quality. Synonym: process control chart.

control system A system that has as its primary function the collection and analysis of feedback from a given set of functions for the purpose of controlling the functions. Control may be implemented by monitoring or systematically modifying parameters or policies used in those functions, or by preparing control reports that initiate useful action with respect to significant deviations and exceptions.

controllable cost A cost that is under the direct control of a given level of management.

conversion efficiency In e-commerce, a measure of how well an organization transforms visits to its website into customer orders. See: *attractability efficiency.*

core competencies Bundles of skills or knowledge sets that enable a firm to provide the greatest level of value to its customers in a way that is difficult for competitors to emulate and that provides for future growth. Core competencies are embodied in the skills of the workers and in the organization. They are developed through collective learning, communication, and commitment to work across levels and functions in the organization and with the customers and suppliers. For example, a core competency could be the capability of a firm to coordinate and harmonize diverse production skills and multiple technologies. To illustrate, advanced casting processes for making steel require the integration of machine design with sophisticated sensors to track temperature and speed, and the sensors require mathematical modeling of heat transfer. For rapid and effective development of such a process, materials scientists must work closely with machine designers, software engineers, process specialists, and operating personnel. Core competencies are not directly related to the product or market.

core process That unique capability that is central to a company's competitive strategy.

core team A cross-functional team of specialists formed to manage new product introduction. See: *cross-functional team.*

corporate culture The set of important assumptions that members of the company share. It is a system of shared values about what is important and beliefs about how the company works. These common assumptions influence the ways in which the company operates.

corrective maintenance The maintenance required to restore an item to a satisfactory condition.

correlation The relationship between two sets of data such that when one changes, the other is likely to make a corresponding change. If the changes are in the same direction, there is positive correlation. When changes tend to occur in opposite directions, there is negative correlation. When there is little correspondence or random changes, there is no correlation.

cost accounting The branch of accounting that is concerned with recording and reporting business operating costs. It includes the reporting of costs by departments, activities, and products.

cost analysis A review and an evaluation of actual or anticipated cost data.

cost center The smallest segment of an organization for which costs are collected and formally reported, typically a department; the criteria in defining cost centers are that the cost be significant and that the area of responsibility be clearly defined. A cost center is not necessarily identical to a work center; normally, a cost center encompasses more than one work center, but this may not always be the case.

cost control Applying procedures that monitor the progress of manufacturing operations against authorized budgets and taking action to achieve minimal costs.

cost driver analysis In activity-based cost accounting, the examination of the impact of cost drivers. The results of this analysis are useful in the continuous improvement of cost, quality, and delivery times.

cost element In activity-based cost accounting, the lowest subdivision of a resource, activity, or cost object.

cost engineer An engineer whose judgment and experience are used in the application of scientific principles and techniques to problems of cost estimation and cost control in business planning, profitability analysis, project management and production planning, scheduling, and control.

cost estimating In project management, creating an approximation of the resources and associated costs needed to complete a project.

cost management In activity-based cost accounting, control of activities to eliminate waste, improve cost drivers, and plan operations. This process should affect the organization's setting of strategy. Factors such as product pricing, introduction of new products, and distribution of existing products are examples of strategic decisions that are affected by cost management.

cost of capital The cost of maintaining a dollar of capital invested for a certain period, normally one year. This cost is normally expressed as a percentage and may be based on factors such as the average expected return on alternative investments and current bank interest rate for borrowing.

cost of goods sold An accounting classification useful for determining the amount of direct materials, direct labor, and allocated overhead associated with the products sold during a given period of time.

cost variance In cost accounting, the difference between what has been budgeted for an activity and what it actually costs.

cost-plus A pricing method in which the purchaser agrees to pay the supplier an amount determined by the cost incurred by the supplier to produce the goods or services plus a stated percentage or fixed sum.

cost-plus contract A pricing method in which the buyer agrees to pay the seller all the acceptable costs of the product or service up to a maximum cost plus a fixed fee. Synonym: cost-type contract.

cost-plus-fixed-fee contract A contract in which the seller is paid for costs specified as allowable in the contract plus a stipulated fixed fee.

cost-plus-incentive-fee contract A contract in which the seller is paid for costs specified as allowable in the contract plus a profit, provided certain provisions are met.

cost-volume-profit analysis The study of how profits change with various levels of output and selling price.

countertrade Any transaction in which partial or full payment is made with goods instead of money. This often applies in international trade.

CP A widely used process capability index. It is calculated by dividing the difference between the upper specification limit (USL) and the lower specification limit (LSL) by 6 times the standard deviations (s) or CP = upper specification limit (USL) − lower specification limit (LSL)6s.

CPIM Abbreviation for Certified in Production and Inventory Management.

crashing In project management, adding resources to critical-path or near-critical-path activities on a project to shorten project duration after analyzing the project to identify the most cost-effective course of action.

crew size The number of people required to perform an operation. The associated standard time should represent the total time for all crew members to perform the operation, not the net start-to-finish time for the crew.

critical characteristics The attributes of a product that must function properly to avoid the failure of the product. Synonym: functional requirements.

critical failure The malfunction of those parts that are essential for continual operation or the safety of the user.

critical mass Individuals who add value to the product or service. These individuals include personnel working directly on the product, personnel providing a service to the customer, and personnel who provide support for the product or service, such as after-sales service.

critical path In project management, the set of activities that defines the duration of a network. These activities have very little float or slack, usually zero. A delay in any critical-path activity will delay the entire project. See: *critical chain.*

critical process parameters A variable or a set of variables that dominates the other variables. Focusing on these variables will yield the greatest return in investment in quality control and improvement.

critical ratio A dispatching rule that calculates a priority index number by dividing the time to due date remaining by the expected elapsed time to finish the job. For example, critical ratio = time remaining = 30 = .75
work remaining 40

critical success factor One of a few organizational objectives whose achievement should be sufficient for organizational success.

Critical-path activity In project management, any activity on a network's critical path as determined by the critical-path method.

Critical-path lead time Synonym: cumulative lead time.

Critical-path method A network-planning technique for the analysis of a project's completion time used for planning and controlling the activities in a project. By showing each of these activities and their associated times, the critical path, which identifies those elements that actually constrain the total time for the project, can be determined. See: *critical chain method, network analysis.*

CRM Abbreviation for customer relationship management and custom relations management.

cross-docking The concept of packing products on the incoming shipments so they can be easily sorted at intermediate warehouses or for outgoing shipments based on final destination. The items are carried from the incoming vehicle docking point to the outgoing vehicle docking point without being stored in inventory at the warehouse. Cross-docking reduces inventory investment and storage space requirements. Synonym: direct loading.

cross-functional integration The establishment of processes among the business functions to improve communication and coordination in providing a good or service.

cross-training The providing of training or experience in several different areas, for example, training an employee on several machines rather than one. Cross-training provides backup workers in case the primary operator is unavailable.

cubic space In warehousing, a measurement of space available or required in transportation and warehousing.

cultural environment The sociocultural factors of the organization's external environment. It includes values, work ethics, education, religion, and consumer and ecological factors.

cumulative available-to-promise A calculation based on the available-to-promise (ATP) figure in the master schedule. Two methods of computing the cumulative available-to-promise are used, with and without lookahead calculation. The cumulative-with-lookahead ATP equals the ATP from the previous period plus the MPS of the period minus the sum of the differences between the backlogs and MPSs of all future periods until, but not to include, the period at which point production exceeds the backlogs. The cumulative-without-lookahead procedure equals the ATP in the previous period plus the MPS, minus the backlog in the period being considered. See: *available-to-promise.*

cumulative lead time The longest planned length of time to accomplish the activity in question. For any item planned through MRP, it is found by reviewing the lead time for each bill-of-material path below the item; whichever path adds up to the greatest number defines cumulative lead time. Synonyms: aggregate lead time, combined lead time, composite lead time, critical-path lead time, stacked lead time. See: *planning horizon, planning time fence.*

cumulative sum The accumulated total of all forecast errors, both positive and negative. This sum will approach zero if the forecast is unbiased. Synonym: sum of deviations.

current assets An accounting/financial term (balance sheet classification of accounts) representing the short-term resources owned by a company, including cash, accounts receivable, and inventories. See: *assets, balance sheet.*

current finish time In project management, the present estimate of an activity's finish time.

customer order servicing system An automated system for order entry, in which orders are keyed into a local terminal and a bill-of-material translator converts the catalog ordering numbers into required manufacturing part numbers and due dates for the MRP system. Advanced systems contain customer information, sales history, forecasting information, and product option compatibility checks to facilitate order processing, "cleaning up" orders before placing a demand on the manufacturing system. Synonyms: configuration system, sales order configuration.

customer relationship management (CRM) A marketing philosophy based on putting the customer first. The collection and analysis of information designed for sales and marketing decision support (as contrasted to enterprise resources-planning information) to understand and support existing and potential customer needs. It includes account management, catalog and order entry, payment processing, credits and adjustments, and other functions. Synonym: customer relations management.

customer service (1) The ability of a company to address the needs, inquiries, and requests from customers. (2) A measure of the delivery of a product to the customer at the time the customer specified.

customer service ratio (1) A measure of delivery performance of finished goods, usually expressed as a percentage. In a make-to-stock company, this percentage usually represents the number of items or dollars (on one or more customer orders) that were shipped on schedule for a specific time period, compared with the total that was supposed to be shipped in that time period. Synonyms: customer service level, fill rate, order fill ratio, percent of fill. Antonym: stockout percentage. (2) In a make-to-order company, it is usually some comparison of the number of jobs or dollars shipped in a given time period (e.g., a week) compared with the number of jobs or dollars that were supposed to be shipped in that time period.

customer–supplier partnership A long-term relationship between a buyer and a supplier characterized by teamwork and mutual confidence. The supplier is considered an extension of the buyer's organization. The partnership is based on several commitments. The buyer provides a long-term contract and uses fewer suppliers. The supplier implements quality-assurance processes so that incoming inspection can be minimized. The supplier also helps the buyer reduce costs and improve product and process designs. Synonym: customer partnership.

cybermarketing Any type of Internet-based promotion. Many marketing managers use the term to refer to any type of computer-based marketing.

cybernetic system The information flow or information system (electronic, mechanical, logical) that controls an industrial process.

cycle counting An inventory-accuracy audit technique in which inventory is counted on a cyclic schedule rather than once a year. A cycle inventory count is usually taken on a regular, defined basis (often more frequently for high-value or fast-moving item and less frequently for low-value or slow-moving items). Most effective cycle counting systems require the counting of a certain number of items every workday, with each item counted at a prescribed frequency. The key purpose of cycle counting is to identify items in error, thus triggering research, identification, and elimination of the cause of the errors.

cycle stock One of the two main conceptual components of any item inventory, the cycle stock is the most active component, that is, that which depletes gradually as customer orders are received and is replenished cyclically when supplier orders are received. The other conceptual component of the item inventory is the safety stock, which is a cushion of protection against uncertainty in the demand or in the replenishment lead time. Synonym: cycle inventory.

D

data Any representations, such as alphabetic or numeric characters, to which meaning can be assigned.

data collection The act of compiling data for recording, analysis, or distribution.

data communications The transmission of data over a distance.

data warehouse A repository of data that has been specially prepared to support decision-making applications. Synonyms: decision-support data, information data warehouse.

decision matrix A matrix used by teams to evaluate problems or possible solutions. After a matrix is drawn to evaluate possible solutions, for example, the team lists the solutions in the far left vertical column. Next, the team selects criteria to rate the possible solutions, writing them across the top row. Third, each possible solution is rated on a scale of 1 to 5 for each criterion and the rating recorded in the corresponding grid. Finally, the ratings of all the criteria for each possible solution are added to determine its total score. The total score is then used to help decide which solution deserves the most attention.

decision table A means of displaying logical conditions in an array that graphically illustrates actions associated with stated conditions.

decision tree A method of analysis that evaluates alternative decisions in a tree-like structure to estimate values and/or probabilities. Decision trees take into account the time value of future earnings by using a rollback concept. Calculations are started at the far right-hand side, then traced back through the branches to identify the appropriate decision.

decisions under certainty Simple decisions that assume complete information and no uncertainty connected with the analysis of decisions.

decisions under risk Decision problems in which the analyst elects to consider several possible futures, the probabilities of which can be estimated.

decisions under uncertainty Decisions for which the analyst elects to consider several possible futures, the probabilities of which cannot be estimated.

decoupling Creating independence between supply and use of material. Commonly denotes providing inventory between operations so that fluctuations in the production rate of the supplying operation do not constrain production or use rates of the next operation.

decoupling inventory An amount of inventory kept between entities in a manufacturing or distribution network to create independence between processes or entities. The objective of decoupling inventory is to disconnect the rate of use from the rate of supply of the item. See: *buffer.*

decoupling points The locations in the product structure or distribution network in which inventory is placed to create independence between processes or entities. Selection of decoupling points is a strategic decision that determines customer lead times and inventory investment. See: *control points.*

decryption Transformation of encrypted text into a readable format.

dedicated capacity A work center that is designated to produce a single item or a limited number of similar items. Equipment that is dedicated may be special equipment or may be grouped general-purpose equipment committed to a composite part.

dedicated equipment Equipment whose use is restricted to specific operations on a limited set of components.

defect A good's or service's nonfulfillment of an intended requirement or reasonable expectation for use, including safety considerations. There are four classes of defects: Class 1, Very Serious, leads directly to severe injury or catastrophic economic loss; Class 2, Serious, leads directly to significant injury or significant economic loss; Class 3, Major, is related to major problems with respect to intended normal or reasonably foreseeable use; and Class 4, Minor, is related to minor problems with respect to intended normal or reasonably foreseeable use. See: *blemish, imperfection, nonconformity.*

deficiency Failure to meet quality standards.

degrees of freedom A statistical term indicating the number of variables or data points used for testing a relationship. The greater the degrees of freedom, the greater the confidence that can be placed on the statistical significance of the results.

Delphi method A qualitative forecasting technique in which the opinions of experts are combined in a series of iterations. The results of each iteration are used to develop the next, so that convergence of the experts' opinions is obtained. See: *management estimation, panel consensus.*

demand A need for a particular product or component. The demand could come from any number of sources, such as customer order or forecast, an interplant requirement, or a request from a branch warehouse for a service part or for manufacturing another product. At the finished-goods level, demand data are usually different from sales data because demand does not necessarily result in sales (i.e., if there is no stock, there will be no sale). There are generally up to four components of demand: cyclical component, random component, seasonal component, and trend component.

demand curve A graphic description of the relationship between price and quantity demanded in a market, assuming that all other factors stay the same. Quantity demanded of a product is measured on the horizontal axis for an array of different prices measured on the vertical axis.

demand during lead time The quantity of a product expected to be withdrawn from stock or to be consumed during its replenishment lead time when usage is at the forecasted rate. See: *expected demand.*

demand forecasting Forecasting the demand for a particular good, component, or service.

demand lead time The amount of time potential customers are willing to wait for the delivery of a good or a service. Synonym: customer tolerance time.

demand management (1) The function of recognizing all demands for goods and services to support the marketplace. It involves prioritizing demand when supply is lacking. Proper demand management facilitates the planning and use of resources for profitable business results. (2) In marketing, the process of planning, executing, controlling, and monitoring the design, pricing, promotion, and distribution of products and services to bring about transactions that meet organizational and individual needs. Synonym: marketing management.

demand rate A statement of requirements in terms of quantity per unit of time (hour, day, week, month, etc.).

demand risk The risk that declining economic activity substantially reduces the demand for a firm's products or services.

demand uncertainty The uncertainty or variability in demand as measured by the standard deviation, mean absolute deviation (MAD), or variance of forecast errors.

dependent demand Demand that is directly related to or derived from the bill of material structure for other items or end products. Such demands are therefore calculated and need not and should not be forecast. A given inventory item may have both dependent and independent demand at any given time. For example, a part may simultaneously be the component of an assembly and sold as a service part. See: *independent demand.*

depreciation An allocation of the original value of an asset against current income to represent the declining value of the asset as a cost of that time period. Depreciation does not involve a cash payment. It acts as a tax shield and thereby reduces the tax payment. See: *capital recovery, depletion, double-declining-balance depreciation, straight-line depreciation, units-of-production depreciation.*

derived demand Demand for component products that arises from the demand for final design products. For example, the demand for steel is derived from the demand for automobiles.

design The conversion of a need or innovation into a product, process, or service that meets both the enterprise and customer expectations. The design process consists of translating a set of functional requirements into an operational product, process, or service.

design cycle The interval of time between the start of the design process of one model and the completion of the design process for the model.

design engineering The discipline consisting of process engineering and product engineering.

design for manufacturability Simplification of parts, products, and processes to improve quality and reduce manufacturing costs.

design for quality A product design approach that uses quality measures to capture the extent to which the design meets the needs of the target market (customer attributes), as well as its actual performance, aesthetics, and cost. See: *total quality engineering.*

designing in quality vs. inspecting in quality Synonym: prevention vs. detection.

deterministic models Models in which no uncertainty is included, such as inventory models without safety-stock considerations.

deviation The difference, usually the absolute difference, between a number and the mean of a set of numbers, or between a forecast value and the actual value.

diagnostic study A brief investigation or cursory methods of study of an operation, process, group, or individual to discover causes of operational difficulties or problems for which more detailed remedial studies may be feasible. An appropriate work-measurement technique may be used to evaluate alternatives or to locate major areas requiring improvement.

direct costs (1) In traditional cost accounting, variable costs that can be directly attributed to a particular job or operation. Direct material and direct labor are traditionally considered direct costs. (2) In activity-based cost accounting, a cost that can specifically be traced and is economically feasible to track to a particular cost object, such as units produced, a production line, a department, or a manufacturing plant. In contrast, if the cost must be allocated across various cost objects, it is an indirect cost. Based on the cost object under consideration, the classification of direct and indirect can change. Activity-based cost accounting assumes that more costs traditionally viewed as fixed costs are variable and can be traced to cost objects.

direct labor Labor that is specifically applied to the good being manufactured or used in the performance of the service. Synonym: touch labor.

direct labor cost The compensation of workers who are involved in converting material into a finished product.

direct marketing Communicating directly with consumers in an effort to elicit a response or a transaction.

direct material Material that becomes a part of the final product in measurable quantities.

direct materials cost The acquisition cost of all materials used directly in the finished product.

direct sales Sales from the manufacturer to the ultimate consumer without going through a distributor or retailer.

disassembly bill of material In remanufacturing, a bill of material used as a guide for the inspection in the teardown-and-inspection process. On the basis of inspection, this bill is modified to a bill of repair defining the actual repair materials and work required. Synonym: teardown bill of material. See: *repair bill of material.*

discontinuous demand A demand pattern that is characterized by large demands interrupted by periods with no demand, as opposed to a continuous or steady (e.g., daily) demand. Synonym: lumpy demand.

discount An allowance or deduction granted by the seller to the buyer, usually when the buyer meets certain stipulated conditions that reduce the price of the products purchased. A quantity discount is an allowance determined by the quantity or value of the purchase. A cash discount is an allowance extended to encourage payment of an invoice on or before a stated date. A trade discount is a deduction from an established price for goods or services made by the seller to those engaged in certain businesses. See: *price break.*

discount period The time allowed a customer to receive a cash discount for timely payment of an invoice.

discounted cash flow A method of investment analysis in which future cash flows are converted or discounted to their value at the present time. The net present value of an item is estimated to be the sum of all discounted future cash flows.

discrete manufacturing The production of distinct items such as automobiles, appliances, or computers.

dispatcher (1) A production control person whose primary function is dispatching. (2) A transportation worker who sends out and tracks cars, buses, trucks, railcars, and other vehicles.

dispatching The selecting and sequencing of available jobs to be run at individual workstations and the assignment of those jobs to workers.

distribution channel The distribution route, from raw materials through consumption, along which products travel. Synonym: marketing channel. See: *channels of distribution.*

distribution inventory Inventory, usually spare parts and finished goods, located in the distribution system (e.g., in warehouses and in transit between warehouses and the consumer).

distribution of forecast errors Tabulation of the forecast errors according to the frequency of occurrence of each error value. The errors in forecasting are, in many cases, normally distributed even when the observed data do not come from a normal distribution.

distribution requirements planning (DRP) (1) The function of determining the need to replenish inventory at branch warehouses. A time-phased order-point approach is used in which the planned orders at the branch warehouse level are "exploded" via MRP logic to become gross requirements on the supplying source. In the case of multilevel distribution networks, this explosion process can continue down through the various levels of regional warehouses (master warehouse, factory warehouse, etc.) and become input to the master production schedule. Demand on the supplying sources is recognized as dependent, replenishment inventory calculations, which may be based on other planning approaches such as period order quantities or "replace exactly what was used" rather than being limited to the time-phased order-point approach.

documentation The process of collecting and organizing documents or the information recorded in documents. The term usually refers to the development of material specifying inputs, operations, and outputs of a computer system.

downstream Used as a relative reference within a firm or supply chain to indicate moving in the direction of the end customer.

downstream operation The tasks subsequent to the task currently being planned or executed.

driver (1) In activity-based cost accounting, an operation that influences the quantity of work required and cost of an activity. Synonym: cost driver. (2) In the theory of constraints, an underlying cause that is responsible for several observed effects.

DRP Abbreviation for distribution resource planning.

dual-card kanban system Synonym: two-card kanban system.

due date The date when purchased material or production material is due to be available for use. Synonym: expected receipt date. See: *arrival date.*

due date rule A dispatching rule that directs the sequencing of jobs by the earliest due date.

dynamic lot sizing Any lot-sizing technique that creates an order quantity subject to continuous recomputation. See: *least total cost, least unit cost, part period balancing, period order quantity, Wagner-Whitin algorithm.*

E

earliest due date (EDD) A priority rule that sequences the jobs in a queue according to their (operation or job) due dates. See: *earliest operation due date.*

earliest operation due date (EODD) A dispatching rule that selects the job having the earliest due date for the impending operation. See: *earliest due date.*

earliest start date The earliest date an operation or order can start. It may be restricted by the current date, material availability, or management-specified "maximum advance."

early start date In the critical-path method of project management, the earliest time at which a given activity is estimated to begin. This date can change as the project is executed.

echelon A level of supply chain nodes. For example, a supply chain with two independent factory warehouses and nine wholesale warehouses delivering product to 350 retail stores is a supply chain with three echelons between the factory and the end customer. One echelon consists of the two independent factory warehouses, one echelon consists of the nine wholesale warehouses, and one echelon consists of the 350 retail stores. Each echelon adds operating expense, holds inventory, adds to the cycle time, and expects to make a profit. See: *disintermediation.*

economic indicator An index of total business activities at the regional, national, and global levels.

economic order quantity A type of fixed-order-quantity model that determines the amount of an item to be purchased or manufactured at one time. The intent is to maximize the combined costs of acquiring and carrying inventory. The basic formula is:

$$\text{Quantity} = \sqrt{\frac{2(d)(c)}{(i)(u)}}$$

where d = annual demand, c = average cost of order preparation, i = annual inventory carrying cost percentage, and u = unit cost. Synonyms: economic lot size, minimum cost order quantity. See: *total cost curve.*

effective date The date on which a component or an operation is to be added or removed from a bill of material or an assembly process. The effective dates are used in the explosion process to create demands for the correct items. Normally, bills of material and routing systems provide for an effectivity start date and stop date, signifying the start or stop of a particular relationship. Effectivity control also may be by serial number rather than date. Synonyms: effectivity, effectivity date.

efficiency A measurement (usually expressed as a percentage) of the actual output to the standard output expected. Efficiency measures how well something is performing relative to existing standards; in contrast, productivity measures output relative to a specific input, such as tons/labor hour. Efficiency is the ratio of (1) actual units produced to the standard rate of production expected in a time period or (2) standard hours produced to actual hours worked (taking longer means less efficiency) or (3) actual dollar volume of output to a standard dollar volume in a time period. Illustrations of these calculations follow. (1) There is a standard of 100 pieces per hour and 780 units are produced in one eight-hour shift; the efficiency is 780/800 converted to a percentage, or 97.5 percent. (2) The work is measured in hours and took 8.21 hours to produce 8 standard hours; the efficiency is 8/8.21 converted to a percentage or 97.5 percent. (3) The work is measured in dollars and produces $780 with a standard of $800; the efficiency is $780/$800 converted to a percentage, or 97.5 percent.

electronic data interchange (EDI) The paperless (electronic) exchange of trading documents, such as purchase orders, shipment authorizations, advanced shipment notices, and invoices, using standardized document formats.

electronic document The electronic representation of a document that can be printed.

empirical Pertaining to a statement or formula based upon experience or observation rather than on deduction or theory.

end item A product sold as a completed item or repair part; any item subject to a customer order or sales forecast.

Synonyms: end product, finished good, finished product. See: *good.*

ending inventory A statement of on-hand quantities or dollar value of an SKU at the end of a period, often determined by a physical inventory.

equivalent unit cost A method of costing that uses the total cost incurred for all like units for a period of time divided by the equivalent units completed during the same time period.

equivalent units A translation of inventories into equivalent finished goods units or of inventories exploded back to raw materials for period-end valuation of inventories. An equivalent unit can be the sum of several partially completed units. Two units 50 percent completed are equivalent to one unit 100 percent completed.

ERP Abbreviation for enterprise resources planning.

excess capacity A situation in which the output capabilities at a nonconstraint resource exceed the amount of productive and protective capacity required to achieve a given level of throughput at the constraint. See: *idle capacity, productive capacity, protective capacity.*

excess inventory Any inventory in the system that exceeds the minimum amount necessary to achieve the desired throughput rate at the constraint or that exceeds the minimum amount necessary to achieve the desired due date performance. Total inventory = productive inventory + protective inventory + excess inventory.

exchange rate The rate at which one currency converts to another.

exogenous variable A variable whose values are determined by considerations outside the model in question.

expected completion quantity The planned quantity of a manufacturing order after expected scrap.

expected demand The quantity expected to be consumed during a given time period when usage is at the forecast rate. See: *demand during lead time.*

expected value The average value that would be observed in taking an action an infinite number of times. The expected value of an action is calculated by multiplying the outcome of the action by the probability of achieving the outcome.

expedite To rush or chase production or purchase orders that are needed in less than the normal lead time; to take extraordinary action because of an increase in relative priority. Synonym: stockchase.

experience curve pricing The average cost pricing method, but using an estimate of future average costs, based on an experience (learning) curve.

experimental design A formal plan that details the specifics for conducting an experiment, such as which statistical techniques and responses, factors, levels, blocks, and treatments, are to be used.

expert system A type of artificial-intelligence computer system that mimics human experts by using rules and heuristics rather than deterministic algorithms.

explode to perform a bill-of-material explosion.

explosion Synonym: requirements explosion. Antonym: implosion.

exponential smoothing forecast A type of weighted-moving-average forecasting technique in which past observations are geometrically discounted according to their age. The heaviest weight is assigned to the most recent data. The smoothing is termed exponential because data points are weighted in accordance with an exponential function of their age. The technique makes use of a smoothing constant to apply to the difference between the most recent forecast and the critical sales data, thus avoiding the necessity of carrying historical sales data. The approach can be used for data that exhibit no trend or seasonal patterns. Higher-order exponential smoothing models can be used for data with either (or both) trend and seasonality.

exports Products produced in one country and sold in another.

exposures The number of time per year that the system risks a stockout. The number of exposures is arrived at by dividing the lot size into the annual usage.

extended enterprise The notion that supply chain partners form a larger entity. See: *supply chain community.*

external factory A situation in which suppliers are viewed as an extension of the firm's manufacturing capabilities and capacities. The same practices and concerns that are commonly applied to the management of the firm's manufacturing system should also be applied to the management of the external factory.

external failures cost The cost related to problems found after the product reaches the customer. This usually includes such costs as warranty and returns.

externality The costs or benefits of a firm's activities borne or received by others.

extranet A network connection to a partner's network using secure information-processing and Internet protocols to do business.

F

fabrication Manufacturing operations for making components, as opposed to assembly operations.

fabrication level The lowest production level. The only components at this level are parts (as opposed to assemblies or subassemblies). These parts are either procured from outside sources or fabricated within the manufacturing organization.

fabrication order A manufacturing order to a component-making department authorizing it to produce component parts. See: *batch card, manufacturing order.*

factory within a factory A technique to improve management focus and overall productivity by creating autonomous business units within a larger physical plant. Synonym: plant within a plant.

failure analysis The collection, examination, review, and classification of failures to determine trends and to identify poorly performing parts or components.

family A group of end items whose similarity of design and manufacture facilitates their being planned in aggregate, whose sales performance is monitored together, and occasionally, whose cost is aggregated at this level.

FAS (1) Abbreviation for final assembly schedule. (2) Abbreviation for free alongside ship.

feasibility study An analysis designed to establish the practicality and cost justification of a given project and, if it appears to be advisable to do so, to determine the direction of subsequent project efforts.

field service The functions of installing and maintaining a product for a customer after the sale or during the lease. Field service may also include training and implementation assistance. Synonym: after-sale service.

final assembly The highest-level assembled product, as it is shipped to customers.

final assembly department The name for the manufacturing department in which the product is assembled. See: *blending department, pack-out department.*

final assembly schedule (FAS) A schedule of end items to finish the product for specific customers' orders in a make-to-order or assemble-to-order environment. It is also referred to as the finishing schedule because it may involve operations other than just the final assembly; also, it may not involve assembly, but simply final mixing, cutting, packaging, and the like. The FAS is prepared after receipt of a customer order as constrained by the availability of material and capacity, and it schedules the operations required to complete the product from the level at which it is stocked (or master scheduled) to the end-item level.

finished-goods inventory Those items on which all manufacturing operations, including final test, have been completed. These products are available for shipment to the customer as either end items or repair parts. Synonym: finished products inventory. See: *goods.*

finishing lead time (1) The time that is necessary to finish manufacturing a good after receipt of a customer order. (2) the time allowed for completing the good based on the final assembly schedule.

finite loading Assigning no more work to a work center than it can be expected to execute in a given time period. The specific term usually refers to a computer technique that involves calculating shop priority revisions in order to level load operation by operation.

finite scheduling A scheduling methodology in which work is loaded into work centers such that no work-center capacity requirement exceeds the capacity available for that work center. See: *drum-buffer-rope, finite forward scheduling.*

firm fixed-price contract A contract in which the seller is paid a set price without regard to costs. Synonym: fixed-price contract.

firm planned order (FPO) A planned order that can be frozen in quantity and time. The computer is not allowed to change it automatically; this is the responsibility of the planner in charge of the item that is being planned. This technique can aid planners working with MRP systems to respond to material and capacity problems by firming up selected planned orders. In addition, firm planned orders are the normal method of starting the master production schedule. See: *planning time fence.*

first in, first out (FIFO) A method of inventory valuation for accounting purposes. The accounting assumption is that the oldest inventory (first in) is the first to be used (first out), but there is no necessary relationship with the actual physical movement of specific items. Synonym: first-come-first-served rule. See: *average cost system.*

first-come-first-served rule A dispatching rule under which the jobs are sequenced by their arrival times. Synonym: first-in, first-out.

first-order smoothing A single exponential smoothing; a weighted-moving-average approach that is applied to forecasting problems in which the data do not exhibit significant trend or seasonal patterns. Synonyms: single exponential smoothing, single smoothing.

five focusing steps In the theory of constraints, a process to continuously improve organizational profit by evaluating the production system and market mix to determine how to make the most profit using the system constraint. The steps consist of (1) identifying the constraint to the system, (2) deciding how to exploit the constraint to the system, (3) subordinating all nonconstraints to the constraint, (4) elevating the constraint to the system, and (5) returning to Step 1 if the constraint is broken in any previous step, while not allowing inertia to set in.

fixed budget A budget of expected costs based on a specific level of production or other activity.

fixed cost An expenditure that does not vary with the production volume; for example, rent, property tax, and salaries of certain personnel.

fixed order quantity A lot-sizing technique in MRP or inventory management that will always cause planned or actual orders to be generated for a predetermined fixed quantity, or multiples thereof, if net requirements for the period exceed the fixed order quantity.

fixed overhead Traditionally, all manufacturing costs, other than direct labor and direct materials, that continue even if products are not produced. Although fixed overhead is necessary to produce the product, it cannot be directly traced to the final product.

fixed-asset turnover Sales divided by net fixed assets. Fixed assets reflect asset acquisition price less depreciation.

fixed-cost contribution per unit An allocation process in which total fixed cost for a period is divided by total units produced in that given time period.

fixed-interval review system A hybrid inventory system in which the inventory analyst reviews the inventory position at fixed time periods. If the inventory level is found to be above a preset reorder point, no action is taken. If the inventory level is at or below the reorder point, the analyst orders a variable quantity equal to $M - x$, where M is a maximum stock level and x is the current quantity on hand and on order (if any). This hybrid system does not reorder every review interval. It therefore differs from the fixed-interval order system, which automatically places an order whenever inventory is reviewed.

fixed-location storage A method of storage in which a relatively permanent location is assigned for the storage of each item in a storeroom or warehouse. Although more space is needed to store parts than in a random-location storage system, fixed locations become familiar, and therefore a locator file may not be needed. See: *random-location storage.*

fixed-period quantity An MRP lot-sizing technique that sets the order quantity to the demand for a given number of periods. See: *discrete order quantity.*

fixed-period requirements A lot-sizing technique that sets the lot size equal to the net requirements for a given number of periods.

fixed-price-incentive-fee contract A contract in which the seller is paid a set price and can earn an additional profit if certain stipulations are met.

Fixed-reorder-quantity inventory model A form of independent-demand item-management model in which an order for a fixed quantity, Q, is placed whenever stock on hand plus on order reaches a predetermined reorder level, R. The fixed order quantity Q may be determined by the economic order quantity, by a fixed order quantity (such as a carton or a truckload), or by another model yielding a fixed result. The reorder point, R, may be deterministic of stochastic, and in either instance is large enough to cover the maximum expected demand during the replenishment lead time. Fixed-reorder-quantity models assume the existence of some form of physical tracking, such as a two-bin system, that is able to determine when the reorder point is reached. These reorder systems are sometimes called fixed-order-quantity systems, lot-size systems, or order point-order quantity systems. Synonyms: fixed-order-quantity system, lot-size system, order point-order quantity system, quantity-based order system. See: *fixed-reorder-cycle inventory model, hybrid inventory system, independent-demand item-management models, optional-replenishment model, order point, order-point system, statistical inventory control, time-phased order point.*

flexibility (1) The ability of the manufacturing system to respond quickly, in terms of range and time, to external or internal changes. Six different categories of flexibility can be considered: mix flexibility, design changeover flexibility, modification flexibility, volume flexibility, rerouting flexibility, and material flexibility (see each term for a more detailed discussion). In addition, flexibility involves concerns of product flexibility. Flexibility can be useful in coping with various types of uncertainty (regarding mix, volume, and so on). (2) The ability of a supply chain to mitigate, or neutralize, the risks of demand-forecast variability, supply-continuity variability, cycle-time-plus-lead-time uncertainty, and transit-time-plus-customs-clearance-time uncertainty during periods of increasing or diminishing volume.

flexible automation Automation that provides short setup times and the ability to switch quickly from one product to another.

flexible manufacturing system (FMS) A group of numerically controlled machine tools interconnected by a central control system. The various machining cells are interconnected via loading and unloading stations by an automated transport system. Operational flexibility is enhanced by the ability to execute all manufacturing tasks on numerous product designs in small quantities and with faster delivery.

flexible workforce A workforce whose members are cross-trained and whose work rules permit assignment of individual workers to different tasks.

flextime An arrangement in which employees are allowed to choose work hours as long as the standard number of work hours is worked.

float (1) The amount of work-in-process inventory between two manufacturing operations, especially in repetitive manufacturing. (2) In supply chains, the time necessary for items such as documents and checks to go from one supply chain partner to another. (3) In the critical-path method of project management, the amount of time that an activity's early start or early finish time can be delayed without delaying the completion time of the entire project. There are three types: total float, free float, and independent float. Synonyms: path float, slack.

floating inventory location system Synonym: random-location storage.

floating storage location Synonym: random-location storage.

floor stocks Stocks of inexpensive production parts held in the factory, from which production workers can draw without requisitions. Synonyms: bench stock, expensed stocks.

flow shop A form of manufacturing organization in which machines and operators handle a standard, usually uninterrupted, material flow. The operators generally perform the same operations for each production run. A flow shop is often referred to as a mass production shop or is said to have a continuous manufacturing layout. The plant layout (arrangement of machines, benches, assembly lines, etc.) is designed to facilitate a product "flow." Some process industries (chemicals, oil, paint, etc.) are extreme examples of flow shops. Each product, though variable in material specifications, uses the same flow pattern through the shop. Production is set at a given rate, and the products are generally manufactured in bulk. Synonyms: flow line, flow manufacturing, flow plant.

flowchart A chart that shows the operations, storages, delays, inspections, and so forth related to a process. Flowcharts are drawn to better understand processes. The flowchart is one of the seven tools of quality. See: *block diagram, flow process chart.*

focus forecasting A system that allows the user to simulate the effectiveness of numerous forecasting techniques, enabling selection of the most effective one.

focus group A set of people who are interviewed together for the purpose of collecting marketing data.

forecast An estimate of future demand. A forecast can be constructed using quantitative methods, qualitative methods, or a combination of methods, and it can be based on extrinsic (external) or intrinsic (internal) factors. Various forecasting techniques attempt to predict one or more of the four components of demand: cyclical, random, seasonal, and trend. See: *Box-Jenkins model, exponential smoothing forecast, extrinsic forecasting method, moving-average forecast, qualitative forecasting method, quantitative forecasting method.*

forecast accuracy A measurement of forecast usefulness, often defined as the average difference between the forecast value to the actual value. Synonym: sales forecast. See: *forecast error.*

forecast bias Tendency of a forecast to systematically miss the actual demand (consistently either high or low).

forecast error The difference between actual demand and forecast demand, stated as an absolute value or as a percentage. See: *average forecast error, forecast accuracy, mean absolute deviation, tracking signal.*

forecast horizon The period of time into the future for which a forecast is prepared.

forecast interval The time unit for which forecasts are prepared, such as week, month, or quarter. Synonym: forecast period.

forecasting The business function that attempts to predict sales and use of products so they can be purchased or manufactured in appropriate quantities in advance.

forward scheduling A scheduling technique in which the scheduler proceeds from a known start date and computes the completion date for an order, usually proceeding from the first operation to the last. Dates generated by this technique are generally the earliest start dates for operations. Synonym: forward pass. Antonym: back scheduling.

free float In the critical-path method of project management, the amount of time that a given activity can be delayed without delaying an immediately subsequent activity's early start time. See: *float, independent float, total float.*

free on board (FOB) The terms of sale that identify where title passes to the buyer.

Full-cost pricing Establishing price at some markup over the full cost (absorption costing). Full costing includes direct manufacturing as well as applied overhead.

functional manager A manager responsible for a specialized department such as accounting or engineering.

functional oriented The grouping of several employees who perform similar activities or work processes together in an organization. See: *team oriented.*

G

Gantt chart The earliest and best-known type of planning-and-control chart, especially designed to show graphically the relationship between planned performance and actual performance over time. Named after its originator, Henry L. Gantt, the chart is used (1) for machine loading, in which one horizontal line is used to represent capacity and another to represent load against that capacity; or (2) for monitoring job progress, in which one horizontal line represents the production schedule and another parallel line represents the actual progress of the job against the schedule in time. Synonym: job progress chart, milestone chart.

heijunka In the just-in-time philosophy, an approach to level production throughout the supply chain to match the planned rate of end product sales.

heuristics A form of problem solving in which the results or rules have been determined by experience or intuition instead of by optimization. Heuristics can be used in such areas as forecasting, lot sizing, or determining production, staff, or inventory levels.

house of quality (HOQ) A structured process that relates customer-defined attributes to the product's technical features needed to support and generate these attributes. This technique achieves this mapping by means of a six-step process: (1) identification of customer attributes; (2) identification of supporting technical features; (3) correlation of the customer attributes with the supporting technical features; (4) assignment of priorities to the customer requirements and technical features; (5) evaluation of competitive stances and competitive products; and (6) identification of those technical features to be used (deployed) in the final design of the product. HOQ is part of the quality function deployment (QFD) process and forces designers to consider customer needs and the degree to which the proposed designs satisfy these needs. See: *customer-defined attributes, quality function deployment.*

hybrid inventory system An inventory system combining features of the fixed-reorder-quantity inventory model and the fixed-reorder-cycle inventory model. Features of the fixed-reorder-cycle inventory model and the fixed-reorder-quantity inventory model can be combined in many different ways. Another hybrid inventory system is the optional-replenishment model. See: *fixed-reorder-cycle inventory, fixed-reorder-quantity inventory model, optional-replenishment model, order-point system.*

hybrid production method A production planning method that combines the aspects of both the chase and level production-planning methods. Synonym: hybrid strategy. See: *chase production method, level production method, production planning method.*

I

idle capacity The capacity generally not used in a system of linked resources. Idle capacity consists of protective capacity and excess capacity. See: *excess capacity, productive capacity, protective capacity.*

idle inventory The inventory generally not needed in a system of linked resources. Idle inventory generally consists of protective inventory and excess inventory. See: *excess inventory, productive inventory, protective inventory.*

implementation The act of installing a system into operation. It concludes the system project with the exception of appropriate follow-up or postinstallation review.

implode (1) Compression of detailed date in a summary-level record or report. (2) Tracing a usage and/or cost impact from the bottom to the top (end product) of a bill of material using where-used logic.

in-control process A process in which the statistical measure being evaluated is in a state of statistical control (i.e., the variations among the observed sampling results can be attributed to a constant system of chance causes). Antonym: out-of control process.

inactive inventory Stock designated as in excess of consumption within a defined period or stocks of items that have not been used for a defined period.

income statement A financial statement showing the net income for a business over a given period of time. See: *balance sheet, funds flow statement.*

incremental analysis A method of economic analysis in which the cost of a single additional unit is compared to its revenue. When the net contribution of an additional unit is zero, total contribution is maximized.

incremental available-to-promise Synonym: discrete available-to-promise.

incremental cost (1) Cost added in the process of finishing an item or assembling a group of items. If the cost of the components of a given assembly equals $5 and the additional cost of assembling the component is $1, the incremental assembly cost is $1, while the total cost of the finished assembly is $6. (2) Additional cost incurred as a result of a decision.

indented bill of material A form of multilevel bill of material. It exhibits the highest-level parents closest to the left margin, and all the components going into these parents are shown indented toward the right. All subsequent levels of components are indented farther to the right. If a component is used in more than one parent within a given product structure, it will appear more than once, under every subassembly in which it is used.

independent demand The demand for an item that is unrelated to the demand for other items. Demand for finished goods, parts required for destructive testing, and service parts requirements are examples of independent demand. See: *dependent demand.*

independent float In project management, the amount of float on an activity that does not affect float on preceding or succeeding activities. See: *float, free float, total float.*

independent-demand item-management models Models for the management of items whose demand is not strongly influenced by other items managed by the same company. These models can be characterized as follows: (1) stochastic or deterministic, depending on the variability of demand and other factors; (2) fixed quantity, fixed cycle, or hybrid (optional replenishment). See: *fixed-reorder-cycle inventory model, fixed-reorder-quantity inventory model, optional-replenishment model.*

indirect costs Costs that are not directly incurred by a particular job or operation. Certain utility costs, such as plant heating, are often indirect. An indirect cost is typically distributed to the product through the overhead rates.

indirect labor Work required to support production in general without being related to a specific product, such as floor sweeping.

indirect labor cost The compensation paid to workers whose activities are not related to a specific product.

industrial engineering The engineering discipline concerned with facilities layout, methods measurement and improvement, statistical quality control, job design and evaluation, and the use of management sciences to solve business problems.

industry analysis A major study of an industry, its major competitors, customer, and suppliers, and the focus and driving forces within that industry.

inefficiency risk The risk of losing customers because another firm has lower unit costs.

infinite loading Calculation of the capacity required at work centers in the time periods required regardless of the capacity available to perform this work. Synonym: infinite scheduling.

information Data arranged or presented so that they yield an understanding not available from any single data element.

information data warehouse Synonym: data warehouse.

information system Interrelated computer hardware and software along with people and processes designed for the collection, processing, and dissemination of information for planning, decision making, and control.

information technology The technology of computers, telecommunications, and other devices that integrate data, equipment, personnel, and problem-solving methods in planning and controlling business activities. Information technology provides the means for collecting, storing, encoding, processing, analyzing, transmitting, receiving, and printing text, audio, or video information.

innovation risk The risk of losing customers because another firm creates more innovative products.

input/output control A technique for capacity control in which planned and actual inputs and planned and actual outputs of a work center are monitored. Planned inputs and outputs for each work center are developed by capacity-requirements planning and approved by manufacturing management. Actual input is compared to planned input to identify when work-center output might vary from the plan because work is not available at the work center. Actual output is also compared to planned output to identify problems within the work center. Synonyms: input/output analysis, production monitoring. See: *capacity control.*

inspection Measuring, examining, testing, or gauging one or more characteristics of a good or service and comparing the results with specified requirements to determine whether conformity is achieved for each characteristic.

inspection ticket Frequently used as a synonym for an inspection order; more properly, a reporting of an inspection function performed.

Institute of Industrial Engineers (IIE) A nonprofit educational organization with members interested in the field of industrial engineering.

intangible costs Those costs that are difficult to quantify, such as the cost of poor quality or of high employee turnover.

integrated change control In project management, a system under which any changes are coordinated across the entire project.

integrated enterprise A business or organization made up of individuals who have acquired the knowledge and skills to work with others to make the organization a greater success than the sum of each individual's output. Integration includes increased communication and coordination between individuals and within and across teams, functions, processes, and organizations over time.

integrating mechanism A physical, organizational, or informational entity that allows people and functions to interact freely by transcending boundaries.

interactive A characteristic of those applications in which a user communicates with a computer program via a terminal, entering data and receiving responses from the computer.

interactive computer system A computer system that supports real-time interaction with a user. The response time to the user is similar to the actual timing of the business or physical process.

interactive scheduling Computer scheduling in which the process is either automatic or manually interrupted to allow the scheduler the opportunity to review and change the schedule.

interactive system A data-processing system in which the response to an inquiry is developed within a time period acceptable to the user and regarded as immediate.

interest (1) Financial share in a project or enterprise. (2) Periodic compensation for lending money. (3) In an economy study, synonymous with required return, expected profit, or charge for the use of capital. (4) The cost for the use of capital. Sometimes referred to as the time value of money.

interest rate The ratio of the interest payment to the principal for a given unit of time. It is usually expressed as a percentage of the principal.

intermediate part Material processed beyond raw material and used in higher-level items. See: *component.*

internal controls The policies and procedures, the documentation, and the plan for an organization that authorize transactions, safeguard assets, and maintain the accuracy of financial records.

internal environment The chosen domain or scope of activities within which an organization operates, for example, the tasks associated with goods or services to be delivered by the organization. See: *external environment.*

internal failure cost The cost of things that go wrong before the product reaches the customer. Internal failure costs usually include rework, scrap, downgrades, reinspection, retest, and process losses.

internal rate of return The rate of compound interest at which the company's outstanding investment is repaid by proceeds from the project.

Internet operations Operations performed over the Internet encompassing such things as email, telnet, newsgroups, file transfer protocol, and the World Wide Web.

interplant demand One plant's need for a part or product that is produced by another plant or division within the same organization. Although it is not a customer order, it is usually handled by the master production scheduling system in a similar manner. See: *interplant transfer.*

intransit inventory Material moving between two or more locations, usually separated geographically; for example, finished goods being shipped from a plant to a distribution center.

intransit lead time The time between the date of shipment (at the shipping point) and the date of receipt (at the receiver's dock). Orders normally specify the date by which goods should be at the dock. Consequently, this date should be offset by intransit lead time for establishing a ship date for the supplier.

inventory (1) Those stocks or items used to support production (raw materials and work-in-process items), supporting activities (maintenance, repair, and operating supplies), and customer service (finished goods and spare parts). Demand for inventory may be dependent or independent. Inventory functions are anticipation, hedge, cycle (lot size), fluctuation (safety, buffer, or reserve), transportation (pipeline), and service parts. (2) In the theory of constraints, inventory is defined as those items purchased for resale and includes finished foods, work in process, and raw materials. Inventory is always valued at purchase price and includes no value-added costs, as opposed to the traditional cost-accounting practice of adding direct labor and allocating overhead as work in process progresses through the production process.

inventory accounting The branch of accounting dealing with valuing inventory. Inventory may be recorded or valued using either a perpetual or a periodic system. A perpetual inventory record is updated frequently or in real time, while a periodic inventory record is counted or measured at fixed time intervals, such as every two weeks or monthly. Inventory valuation methods of LIFO, FIFO, or average costs are used with either recording system.

inventory control The activities and techniques of maintaining the desired levels of items, whether raw materials, work in process, or finished products. Synonym: material control.

inventory conversion period The time period needed to produce and sell a product, measured from procurement of raw materials to the sale of the product.

inventory costs Costs associated with ordering and holding inventory. See: *carrying costs, ordering cost.*

inventory cycle The length of time between two consecutive replenishment shipments.

inventory investment The dollars that are in all levels of inventory.

inventory issue (1) Items released from an inventory location for use or sale. (2) The inventory record transaction reducing the inventory balance by the amount released.

inventory management The branch of business management concerned with planning and controlling inventories.

inventory ordering system Inventory models for the replenishment of inventory. Independent-demand inventory ordering models include but are not limited to fixed-reorder-cycle, fixed-reorder-quantity, optional-replenishment, and hybrid models. Dependent-demand inventory ordering models include material-requirements planning, kanban, and drum-buffer-rope.

inventory planning The activities and techniques of determining the desired levels of items, whether raw materials, work in process, or finished products, including order quantities and safety stock levels. Synonym: material planning.

inventory policy A statement of a company's goals and approach to the management of inventories.

inventory returns Items returned to the manufacturer as defective, obsolete, overages, and so on. An inventory item record transaction records the return or receipt into physical stores of materials from which the item may be scrapped.

inventory shrinkage Losses of inventory resulting from scrap, deterioration, pilferage, and the like.

inventory turnover The number of times that an inventory cycles, or "turns over," during the year. A frequently used method to compute inventory turnover is to divide the average inventory level into the annual cost of sales. For example, an average inventory of $3 million divided into an annual cost of sales of $21 million means that inventory turned over seven times. Synonyms: inventory turns, inventory velocity, turnover.

inventory usage The value or the number of units of an inventory item consumed over a period of time.

inventory valuation The value of the inventory at either its cost or its market value. Because inventory value can change with time, some recognition is taken of the age distribution of inventory. Therefore, the cost value of inventory is usually computed on a first-in-first-out (FIFO) basis, last-in-first-out (LIFO) basis, or a standard cost basis to establish the cost of goods sold.

inventory velocity The speed with which inventory passes through an organization or supply chain at a given point in time as measured by inventory turnover. Synonym: inventory turnover.

inventory write-off A deduction of inventory dollars from the financial statement because the inventory is of less value. An inventory write-off may be necessary because the value of the physical inventory is less than its book value or because the items in inventory are no longer usable.

invitation for bid (IFB) Synonym: request for proposal.

issue (1) The physical movement of items from a stocking location. (2) Often, the transaction reporting of this activity.

issue cycle times The time required to generate a requisition for material, pull the material from an inventory location, and move it to its destination.

item Any unique manufactured or purchased part, material, intermediate, subassembly, or product.

item master file A file containing all item master records for a product, product line, plant, or company. See: *master file.*

item number A number that serves to uniquely identify an item. Synonyms: part number, product number, stock code, stock number.

item record The "master" record for an item. Typically, it contains identifying and descriptive data and control values (lead times, lot sizes, etc.) and may contain data on inventory status, requirements, planned orders, and costs. Item records are linked by bill of material records (or product structure records), thus defining the bill of material. Synonyms: item master record, part master record, part record.

J

jidoka The Japanese term for the practice of stopping the production line when a defect occurs.

JIT Acronym for just in time.

JIT supplier environment To effectively participate as a supplier under just-in-time (JIT), a company must supply components and subassemblies in exact quantities, delivery time, and quality. Shipments are made within narrow time windows that are readily enforced. Virtually every component must be delivered on time and be within specifications.

job (1) The combination of tasks, duties, and responsibilities assigned to an individual employee and usually considered his or her work assignment. (2) The contents of a work order.

job analysis A process of gathering (by observation, interview, or recording systems) significant task-oriented activities and requirements about work required of employees.

job costing A cost-accounting system in which costs are assigned to specific jobs. This system can be used with either actual or standard costs in the manufacturing of distinguishable units or lots of products. Synonym: job order costing.

job description A formal statement of duties, qualifications, and responsibilities associated with a particular job.

job design The function of describing a job with respect to its content and the methods to be used. Criteria, such as the degree of job specialization, job enrichment, and job enlargement, are useful in designing work content.

job enlargement An increase in the number of tasks that an employee performs. Job enlargement is associated with the design of jobs, particularly production jobs, and its purpose is to reduce employee dissatisfaction.

job enrichment An increase in the number of tasks that an employee performs and an increase in the control over those tasks. It is associated with the design of jobs and especially the production worker's job. Job enrichment is an extension of job enlargement.

job shop (1) An organization in which similar equipment is organized by function. Each job follows a distinct routing through the shop. (2) A type of manufacturing process used to produce items to each customer's specifications. Production operations are designed to handle a wide range of product designs and are performed at fixed plant locations using general-purpose equipment. Synonym: jobbing. See: *intermittent production, project manufacturing.*

job shop scheduling The production planning and control techniques used to sequence and prioritize production quantities across operations in a job shop.

job status A periodic report showing the plan for completing a job (usually the requirements and completion date) and the progress of the job against that plan.

joint replenishment Coordinating the lot sizing and order-release decision for related items and treating them as a family of items. The objective is to achieve lower costs because of ordering, setup, shipping, and quantity discount economies. This term applies equally to joint ordering (family contracts) and to composite part (group technology) fabrication scheduling. Synonym: joint replenishment system.

just-in-time (JIT) A philosophy of manufacturing based on planned elimination of all waste and on continuous improvement of productivity. It encompasses the successful execution of all manufacturing activities required to produce a final product, from design engineering to delivery, and includes all stages of conversion from raw material onward. The primary elements of just-in time are to have only the required inventory when needed; to improve quality to zero defects; to reduce lead times by reducing setup times, queue lengths, and lot sizes; to incrementally revise the operations themselves; and to accomplish these activities at minimum cost. In the broad sense, it applies to all forms of manufacturing—job shop, process, and repetitive—and to many service industries as well. Synonyms: short cycle manufacturing, stockless production, zero inventories.

K

kaizen The Japanese term for improvement; continuing improvement involving everyone—managers and workers. In manufacturing, kaizen relates to finding and eliminating waste in machinery, labor, or production methods. See: *continuous process improvement.*

kanban A method of just-in-time production that uses standard containers or lot sizes with a single card attached to each. It is a pull system in which work centers signal with a card that they wish to withdraw parts from feeding operations or suppliers. The Japanese word *kanban*, loosely translated, means card, billboard, or sign. The term is often used synonymously for the specific scheduling system developed and used by the Toyota Corporation in Japan. See: *move card, production card, synchronized production.*

keiretsu A form of cooperative relationship among companies in Japan in which the companies largely remain legally and economically independent, even though they work closely in various ways such as sole sourcing and financial backing. Supply chain keiretsus exist around linking companies from raw material suppliers to retailers.

knowledge creation The propensity for generating knowledge.

L

labor cost The dollar amount of labor performed during manufacturing. This amount is added to direct material cost and overhead cost to obtain total manufacturing cost.

labor efficiency (1) Synonym: worker efficiency. (2) The average of worker efficiency for all direct workers in a department or facility.

labor grade A classification of workers whose capability indicates their skill level or craft. See: *skill-based compensation, skills inventories.*

labor productivity A partial productivity measure, the rate of output of a worker or group of workers per unit of time compared to an established standard or rate of output. Labor productivity can be expressed as output per unit of time or output per labor hour. See: *machine productivity, productivity.*

labor ticket Synonym: labor claim.

late finish date In the critical-path method of project management, the last date upon which a given activity can be completed without delaying the completion date of the project.

lateness Delivery date minus due date. Lateness may be positive or, in the case of early jobs, negative. See: *earliness, tardiness.*

law of diminishing marginal returns A principle that as the quantity of a variable factor applied to a fixed factor is increased, the additional units of the variable factor will result in smaller and smaller increases in output. See: *marginal product.*

layout (1) Physical arrangement of resources or centers of economic activity (machines, groups of people, workstations, storage areas, aisles, etc.) within a facility. Layouts include product (linear or line), functional (job shop or process), cellular, and fixed position. (2) Synonym: kit.

lead time A span of time required to perform a process (or series of operations). (2) In a logistics context, the time between recognition of the need for an order and the receipt of goods. Individual components of lead time can include order-preparation time, queue time, processing time, move or transportation time, and receiving and inspection time. Synonym: total lead time. See: *manufacturing lead time, purchasing lead time.*

lead-time inventory Inventory that is carried to cover demand during the lead time.

lead-time offset A technique used in MRP in which a planned order receipt in one time period will require the release of that order in an earlier time period based on the lead time for the item. Synonyms: component lead-time offset, offsetting.

lean production A philosophy of production that emphasizes the minimization of the amount of all the resources (including time) used in the various activities of the enterprise. It involves identifying and eliminating non-value-adding activities in design, production, supply chain management, and dealing with the customers. Lean producers employ teams of multiskilled workers at all levels of the organization and use highly flexible, increasingly automated machines to produce volumes of products in potentially enormous variety. It contains a set of principles and practices to reduce cost through the simplification of all manufacturing and support processes. Synonyms: lean, lean manufacturing.

learning curve A curve reflecting the rate of improvement in time per piece as more units of an item are made. A planning technique, the learning curve is particularly useful in project-oriented industries in which new products are frequently phased in. The basis for the learning curve calculation is that workers will be able to produce the product more quickly after they get used to making it. Synonyms: experience curve, manufacturing progress curve.

learning organization An organization in which each of the individuals in the group is engaged in problem identification and solution generation. A learning organization is characterized by continuous experimentation and improvement in its capabilities in support of the organization's strategic direction.

least total cost A dynamic lot-sizing technique that calculates the order quantity by comparing the setup (or ordering) costs and the carrying cost for various lot sizes and selects the lot size at which these costs are most nearly equal. See: *discrete order quantity, dynamic lot sizing.*

least unit cost A dynamic lot-sizing technique that adds ordering cost and inventory carrying cost for each trial lot size and divides by the number of units in the lot size, picking the lot size with the lowest unit cost. See: *discrete order quantity, dynamic lot sizing.*

less than carload (LCL) Either a small shipment that does not fill the railcar or a shipment of not enough weight to qualify for a carload quantity rate discount.

less than truckload (LTL) Either a small shipment that does not fill the truck or a shipment of not enough weight to qualify for a truckload quantity (usually set at about 10,000 lbs.) rate discount, offered to a general commodity trucker.

level Every part or assembly in a product structure is assigned a level code signifying the relative level in which that part or assembly is used within the product structure. Often times the end items are assigned level 0 with the components and subassemblies going into it assigned to level 1 and so on. The MRP explosion process starts from level 0 and proceeds downward one level at a time.

level of service A measure (usually expressed as a percentage) of satisfying demand through inventory or by the current production schedule in time to satisfy the customers' requested delivery dates and quantities. In a make-to-stock environment, level of service is sometimes calculated as the percentage of orders picked complete from stock upon receipt of the customer order, the percentage of line items picked complete, or the percentage of total dollar demand picked complete. In make-to-order and design-to-order environments, level of service is the percentage of times the customer-requested or acknowledged date was met by shipping complete product quantities. Synonyms: measure of service, service level.

level schedule (1) In traditional management, a production schedule or master production schedule that generates material and labor requirements that are as evenly spread over time as possible. Finished-goods inventories buffer the production system against seasonal demand. See: *level production method.* (2) In JIT, a level schedule (usually constructed monthly) in which each day's customer demand is scheduled to be built on the day it will be shipped. A level schedule is the output of the load-leveling process. Synonyms: JIT master schedule, level production. See: *load leveling.*

liabilities An accounting/financial term (balance sheet classification of accounts) representing debts or obligations owed by a company to creditors. Liabilities may have a short-term time horizon, such as accounts payable, or a longer-term obligation, such as mortgage payable or bonds payable. See: *assets, balance sheet, owner's equity.*

life-cycle analysis A quantitative forecasting technique based on applying past patterns of demand data covering introduction, growth, maturity, saturation, and decline of similar products to a new product family.

life-cycle costing In evaluating alternatives, the consideration of all costs, including acquisition, operation, and disposition costs, that will be incurred over the entire time of ownership of a product.

line balancing (1) The balancing of the assignment of the tasks to workstations in a manner that minimizes the number of workstations and minimizes the total amount of idle time at all stations for a given output level. In balancing these tasks, the specified time requirement per unit of product for each task and its sequential relationship with the other tasks must be considered. (2) A technique for determining the product mix that can be run down an assembly line to provide a fairly consistent flow of work through that assembly line at the planned line rate.

line efficiency A measure of actual work content versus cycle time of the limiting operation in a production line. Line efficiency (percentage) is equal to the sum of all station task times divided by the longest task time multiplied by the number of stations. In an assembly-line layout, the line efficiency is 100 percent minus the balance delay percentage.

line haul costs Within physical distribution, such cost elements as fuel, drivers' wages, and wear and tear on the vehicle, that vary by distance traveled and not on weight carried.

line item One item on an order, regardless of quantity.

line loading The loading of a production line by multiplying the total pieces by the rate per piece for each item to come up with a finished schedule for the line.

line manager A manager involved in managing a department that is directly involved in making a product.

line manufacturing Repetitive manufacturing performed by specialized equipment in a fixed sequence.

line of balance planning A project-planning technique using a lead-time offset chart and a chart of required final assembly completions to graph a third bar chart showing the number of each component that should be completed to date. This bar chart forms a descending line, and aggregate component completions are then plotted against this line of balance. This is a crude form of material planning.

linear decision rules A modeling technique using simultaneous equations, for example, the establishment of aggregate workforce levels, based upon minimizing the total cost of hiring, firing, holding inventory, backorders, payroll, overtime, and undertime.

linear layout A layout of various machines in one straight line. This type of layout makes it difficult to reallocate operations among workers and machinery.

linear production Actual production to a level schedule, so that a plotting of actual output versus planned output forms a straight line, even when plotted for a short segment of time.

linearity (1) Production at a constant quantity. (2) Use of resources at a level rate, typically measured daily or more frequently.

load The amount of planned work scheduled for and actual work released to a facility, work center, or operation for a specific span of time. Usually expressed in terms of standard hours of work or, when items consume similar resources at the same rate, units of production. Synonym: workload.

load leveling Spreading orders out in time or rescheduling operations so that the amount of work to be done in sequential time periods tends to be distributed evenly and is achievable. Although both material and labor are ideally level loaded, specific businesses and industries may load to one or the other exclusively (e.g., service industries). Synonyms: capacity smoothing, level loading. See: *level schedule.*

load profile A display of future capacity requirements based on released and/or planned orders over a given span of time. Synonym: load projection. See: *capacity requirements plan.*

logistics (1) In an industrial context, the art and science of obtaining, producing, and distributing material and product in the proper place and in proper quantities. (2) In a military sense (where it has greater usage), its meaning can also include the movement of personnel.

logistics system The planning and coordination of the physical movement aspects of a firm's operations such that a flow of raw materials, parts, and finished goods is achieved in a manner that minimizes total costs for the levels of service desired.

lot A quantity produced together and sharing the same production costs and specifications. See: *batch.*

lot control A set of procedures (e.g., assigning unique batch numbers and tracking each batch) used to maintain lot integrity from raw materials, from the supplier through manufacturing to consumers.

lot cost In cost accounting, those costs associated with processing a common lot or quantity of parts having the same specifications.

lot operation cycle time The length of time required from the start of setup to the end of cleanup for a production lot at a given operation, including setup, production, and cleanup.

lot size The amount of a particular item that is ordered from the plant or a supplier or issued as a standard quantity to the production process. Synonym: order quantity.

lot sizing The process of, or techniques used in, determining lot size.

lot splitting Dividing a lot into two or more sublots and simultaneously processing each sublot on identical (or very similar) facilities as separate lots, usually to compress lead time or to expedite a small quantity. Synonym: operation splitting.

lot-for-lot A lot-sizing technique that generates planned orders in quantities equal to the net requirements in each period.

lot-size inventory Inventory that results whenever quantity price discounts, shipping costs, setup costs, or similar considerations make it more economical to purchase or produce in larger lots than are needed for immediate purposes.

low-level code A number that identifies the lowest level in any bill of material at which a particular component appears. Net requirements for a given component are not calculated until all the gross requirements have been calculated down to that level. Low-level codes are normally calculated and maintained automatically by the computer software. Synonym: explosion level.

M

machine center A production area consisting of one or more machines (and, if appropriate for capacity planning, the necessary support personnel) that can be considered as one unit for capacity requirements planning and detailed scheduling.

machine hours The amount of time, in hours, that a machine is actually running. Machine hours, rather than labor hours, may be used for planning capacity for scheduling, and for allocating costs.

machine loading The accumulation by workstation, machine, or machine group of the hours generated from the scheduling of operations for released orders by time period. Machine loading differs from capacity requirements planning in that it does not use the planned orders from MRP but operates solely from released orders. It may be of limited value because of its limited visibility of resources.

machine productivity A partial productivity measure. The rate of output of a machine per unit of time compared with an established standard or rate of output. Machine productivity can be expressed as output per unit of time or output per machine hour.

machine utilization A measure of how intensively a machine is being used. Machine utilization compares the actual machine time (setup and run time) to available time.

machine-limited capacity A production environment in which a specific machine limits throughput of the process.

machining center A machine capable of performing a variety of metal-, wood-, or plastic-removal operations on a part, usually operated by numerical control.

maintainability The characteristic of equipment design and installation that provides the ability for the equipment to be repaired easily and efficiently.

maintenance, repair, and operating supplies (MRO) Items used in support of general operations and maintenance such as maintenance supplies, spare parts, and consumables used in the manufacturing process and supporting operations.

maintenance, repair, and overhaul (MRO) An item for reprocessing in the remanufacturing industry.

make-or-buy cost analysis A comparison of all of the costs associated with making an item versus the cost of buying the item.

make-to-order A production environment in which a good or service can be made after receipt of a customer's order. The final product is usually a combination of standard items and items custom-designed to meet the special needs of the customer. Where options or accessories are stocked before customer orders arrive, the term *assemble-to-order* is frequently used. See: *assemble-to-order, make-to-stock.*

make-to-stock A production environment in which products can be and usually are finished before receipt of a customer order. Customer orders are typically filled from existing stocks, and production orders are used to replenish those stocks. See: *assemble-to-order, make-to-order.*

manufacturability A measure of the design of a product or process in terms of its ability to be produced easily, consistently, and with high quality.

manufacturing A series of interrelated activities and operations involving the design, material selection, planning, production, quality assurance, management, and marketing of discrete consumer and durable goods.

manufacturing cycle Synonym: manufacturing lead time.

manufacturing cycle efficiency The ratio of value-added time to manufacturing lead time or cycle time. Manufacturing cycle time can be improved by the reduction of manufacturing lead time by eliminating non-value-added activities such as inspecting, moving, and queuing.

manufacturing execution systems Programs and systems that participate in shop-floor control, including programmed logic controllers and process-control computers for direct and supervisory control of manufacturing equipment; process-information systems that gather historical performance information, then generate reports; graphical displays; and alarms that inform operations personnel what is going on in the plant currently and a very short history into the past. Quality-control information is also gathered, and a laboratory information management system may be part of this configuration to tie process conditions to the quality data that are generated. Thereby, cause-and-effect relationships can be determined. The quality data at times affect the control parameters that are used to meet product specifications either dynamically or off line.

manufacturing layout strategies An element of manufacturing strategy. It is the analysis of physical capacity, geography, functional needs, corporate philosophy, and product-market/process focus to systematically respond to required facility changes driven by organizational, strategic, and environmental considerations.

manufacturing lead time The total time required to manufacture an item, exclusive of lower-level purchasing lead time. For make-to-order products, it is the length of time between the release of an order to the production process and shipment to the final customer. For make-to-stock products, it is the length of time between the release of an order to the production process and receipt into finished goods inventory. Included here are order-preparation time, queue time, setup time, run time, move time, inspection time, and put-away time. Synonyms: manufacturing cycle, production cycle, production lead time. See: *lead time.*

manufacturing order A document, group of documents, or schedule conveying authority for the manufacture of specified parts or products in specified quantities. Synonyms: job order, manufacturing authorization, production order, production release, run order, shop order. See: *assembly parts list, batch card, blend order, fabrication order, mix ticket, work order.*

manufacturing resource A method for the effective planning of all resources of a manufacturing strategy—a collective pattern of decisions that acts upon the formulation and deployment of manufacturing resources. To be most effective, the manufacturing strategy should act in support of the overall strategic direction of the business and provide for competitive advantages (edges).

marginal analysis A decision rule that optimality occurs when incremental revenue equals incremental cost.

marginal cost The incremental costs incurred when the level of output of some operation or process is increased by one unit.

marginal cost of capital The cost of the next dollar, after taxes, that a firm expects to raise for investment.

marginal revenue The incremental sales dollars received when the level of output of some operation is increased by one unit.

market demand In marketing, the total demand that would exist within a defined customer group in a given geographical area during a particular time period given a known marketing program.

market plan The output of the market planning process. The market plan includes the current market position, opportunity and issue analysis, marketing objectives and strategies, action plans, programs, projects, budgets, and pro forma profit-and-loss statement and management controls. Synonyms: brand plan, product plan.

market segmentation A marketing strategy in which the total market is disaggregated into submarkets, or segments, sharing some measurable characteristics based on demographics, psychographics, lifestyle, geography, benefits, and so on.

marketing channel That set of organizations through which a good or service passes in going from a raw state to the final consumer. Synonym: distribution channel.

marketing strategy The basic plan marketing expects to use to achieve its business and marketing objectives in a particular market. This plan includes marketing expenditures, marketing mix, and marketing allocation.

mass customization The creation of a high-volume product with large variety so that a customer may specify his or her exact model out of a large volume of possible end items while manufacturing cost is low because of the large volume. An example is a personal computer order in which the customer may specify processor speed, removable storage device characteristics, and many other options when PCs are assembled on one line and at low cost.

mass production High-quantity production characterized by specialization of equipment and labor. See: *continuous production.*

master file A main reference file of information, such as the item master file and work center file. See: *detail file, item master file.*

master planning A group of business processes that includes the following activities: demand management (which includes forecasting and order servicing); production and resource planning; and master scheduling (which includes the master schedule and the rough-cut capacity plan.

master planning of resources A grouping of business processes that includes the following activities: demand management, which includes the forecasting of sales, the planning of distribution, and the servicing of customer orders; sales and operations planning, which includes sales planning, production planning, inventory planning, backlog planning, and resource planning; and master scheduling, which includes the preparation of the master production schedule and the rough-cut capacity plan.

master production schedule (MPS) The master production schedule is a line on the master schedule grid that reflects the anticipated build schedule for those items assigned to the master schedule. The master scheduler maintains this schedule and, in turn, it becomes a set of planning numbers that drives material requirements planning. It represents what the company plans to produce expressed in specific configurations, quantities, and dates. The master production schedule is not a sales item forecast that represents a statement of demand. The master production schedule must take into account the forecast, the production plan, and other important considerations such as backlog, availability of material, availability of capacity, and management policies and goals. Synonym: master schedule.

master schedule The master schedule is a format that includes time periods (dates), the forecast, customer orders, projected available balance, available-to-promise, and the master production schedule. The master schedule takes into account the forecast, the production plan, and other important considerations such as backlog, availability of material, availability of capacity, and management policies and goals. Synonym: master production schedule.

master schedule item A part number selected to be planned by the master scheduler. The item is deemed critical in its impact on lower-level components or resources such as skilled labor, key machines, or dollars. Therefore, the master scheduler, not the computer, maintains the plan for these items. A master schedule item may be an end item, a component, a pseudonumber, or a planning bill of material.

master scheduler Often the job title of the person charged with the responsibility of managing, establishing, reviewing, and maintaining a master schedule for select items. Ideally, the person should have substantial product, plant, process, and market knowledge, because the consequences of this individual's actions often have a great impact on customer service, material, and capacity planning.

master scheduling The process in which the master schedule is generated and reviewed and adjustments made to the master production schedule to ensure consistency with the production plan. The master production schedule (the line on the grid) is the primary input to the material requirements plan. The sum of the master production schedules for the items within the product family must equal the production plan for that family.

material requirements plan The result from the process of material requirements planning.

material requirements planning (MRP) A set of techniques that uses bill of material data, inventory data, and the master production schedule to calculate requirements for materials. It makes recommendations to release replenishment orders for material. Further, because it is time phased, it makes recommendations to reschedule open orders when due dates and need dates are not in phase. Time-phased MRP begins with the items listed on the MPS and determines (1) the quantity of all components and materials required to fabricate those items and (2) the date that the components and materials are required. Time-phased MRP is accomplished by exploding the bill of material, adjusting for inventory quantities on hand or on order, and offsetting the net requirements by the appropriate lead times.

materials management The grouping of management functions supporting the complete cycle of material flow, from the purchase and internal control of production materials to the planning and control of work in process to the warehousing, shipping, and distribution of the finished product.

matrix organizational structure An organizational structure in which two (or more) channels of command, budget responsibility, and performance measurement exist simultaneously. For example, both product and functional forms of organization could be implemented simultaneously, that is, the product and functional managers have equal authority and employees report to both managers.

maximum demonstrated capacity The highest amount of actual output produced in the past when all efforts have been made to "optimize" the resource, for instance, overtime, additional personnel, extra hours, extra shifts, reassignment of personnel, or use of any related equipment. Maximum demonstrated capacity is the most one could ever expect to produce in a short period of time but represents a rate that cannot be maintained over a long period of time. See: *demonstrated capacity.*

maximum inventory The planned maximum allowable inventory for an item based on its planned lot size and target safety stock.

maximum order quantity An order quantity modifier, applied after the lot size has been calculated, that limits the order quantity to a preestablished maximum.

mean absolute deviation (MAD) The average of the absolute values of the deviations of observed values from some expected value. MAD can be calculated based on observations and the arithmetic mean of those observations. An alternative is to calculate absolute deviations of actual sales data minus forecast data. These data can be average in the usual arithmetic way or with exponential smoothing. See: *forecast error, tracking signal.*

mean time between failures (MTBF) The average time interval between failures for repairable product for a defined unit of measures (e.g., operating hours, cycles, miles). See: *reliability.*

methods analysis That part of methods engineering normally involving an examination and analysis of an operation or a work cycle broken down into its constituent parts to improve the operation, eliminate unnecessary steps, and/or establish and record in detail a proposed method of performance.

min-max system A type of order point–replenishment system in which the "min" (minimum) is the order point and the "max" (maximum) is the "order up to" inventory level. The order quantity is variable and is the result of the max minus available and on-order inventory. An order is recommended when the sum of available and on-order inventory is at or below the min.

minimum order quantity An order quantity modifier, applied after the lot size has been calculated, that increases the order quantity to a preestablished minimum.

minor setup The incremental setup activities required when changing from one item to another within a group of items.

MIS Abbreviation for management information system.

mix flexibility The ability to handle a wide range of products or variants by using equipment having short setup times.

mix forecast Forecast of the proportion of products that will be sold within a given product family or the proportions of options offered within a product line. Product and option mix as well as aggregate product families must be forecasted. Even though the appropriate level of units is forecasted for a given product line, an inaccurate mix forecast can create material shortages and inventory problems.

mixed-flow scheduling A procedure used in some process industries for building process-train schedules that start at an initial stage and work toward the terminal process stages. This procedure is effective for scheduling in which several bottleneck stages may exist. Detailed scheduling is done at each bottleneck stage.

mixed-model master schedule The process of setting and maintaining the master production schedule to support mixed-model production.

mixed-model production Making several different parts or products in varying lot sizes so that a factory produces close to the same mix of products that will be sold that day. The mixed-model schedule governs the making and the delivery of component parts, including those provided by outside suppliers. The goal is to build every model every day, according to daily demand.

mixed-model scheduling The process of developing one or more schedules to enable mixed-model production. The goal is to achieve a day's production each day. See: *mixed-model production.*

model A representation of a process or system that attempts to relate the most important variables in the system in such a way that analysis of the model leads to insights into the system. Frequently, the model is used to anticipate the result of a particular strategy in a real system.

model number An item number for a finished good. This number may encompass other parts, such as a user's manual.

modular bill of material A type of planning bill that is arranged in product modules or options. It is often used in companies in which the product has many optional features, such as assemble-to-order companies like automobile manufacturers. See: *pseudo bill of material.*

modular system A system-design method that recognizes that different levels of experience exist in organizations and develops the system to provide for segments or modules to be installed at a rate compatible with the user's ability to implement the system.

module A self-contained unit of a computer program that communicates with other parts of the program solely through inputs and outputs.

monitoring The process of comparing actual to planned progress.

move The physical transportation of inventory from one location to another within a facility. Movements are usually made under the direction and control of the inventory system.

move card In a just-in-time context, a card or other signal indicating that a specific number of units of a particular item are to be taken from a source (usually an outbound stockpoint) and taken to a point of use (usually an inbound stockpoint). It authorizes the movement of one part number between a single pair of work centers. The card circulates between the outbound stockpoint of the supplying center and the inbound stockpoint of the using work center. Synonym: move signal. See: *kanban*.

move order The authorization to move a particular item from one location to another.

move ticket A document used in dispatching to authorize or record movement of a job from one work center to another. It may also be used to report other information, such as the actual quantity or the material storage location.

move time The time that a job spends in transit from one operation to another in the plant.

movement inventory A type of in-process inventory that arises because of the time required to move goods from one place to another.

moving-average forecast A forecasting technique that uses a simple moving average or a weighted moving average projected forward as a forecast.

MPC Abbreviation for manufacturing planning and control.

MPS Abbreviation for master production schedule.

MRO (1) Abbreviation for maintenance, repair, and operating supplies. (2) Abbreviation for maintenance, repair, and overhaul.

MRP Abbreviation for material requirements planning.

MRP II Abbreviation for manufacturing resource planning.

multilevel bill of material A display of all the components directly or indirectly used in a parent, together with the quantity required of each component. If a component is a subassembly, blend, intermediate, or similar item, all its components and all their components also will be exhibited, down to purchased parts and raw materials.

multilevel master schedule A master scheduling technique that allows any level in an end item's bill of material to be master scheduled. To accomplish this, MPS items must receive requirements from independent and dependent demand sources.

multiple sourcing Synonym: multisourcing.

multiple-item lot-sizing models Processes or systems used to determine the total replenishment order quantity for a group of related items.

multiprocessing The simultaneous use by a computer of two or more central processing units, with each executing its own instruction set and each controlled by a single operating system.

multisourcing Procurement of a good or service from more than one independent supplier. Synonym: multiple sourcing. Antonym: single sourcing.

N

negative float In project management, the amount of time that must be made up on an activity to get the project back on schedule.

negotiation The process by which a buyer and a vendor agree upon the conditions surrounding the purchase of an item.

nervousness The characteristic in an MRP system when minor changes in higher-level (e.g., level 0 or 1) records of the master production schedule cause significant timing or quantity changes in lower-level (e.g., level 5 or 6) schedules and orders.

net change MRP An approach in which the material requirements plan is continually retained in the computer. Whenever a change is needed in requirements, open-order inventory status, or bill of material, a partial explosion and netting is made for only those parts affected by the change. See: *requirements alteration*. Antonym: regeneration MRP.

net operating cash flow In finance management, the difference between cash inflow and cash outflow for a period. It is found by taking the change in net operating profit after taxes and adding the change in depreciation, then subtracting the increase in net working capital requirements.

net operating income The income before interest and taxes are subtracted. Synonyms: earnings before interest and taxes.

net present value The present (discounted) value of future earnings (operating expenses have been deducted from net operating revenues) for a given number of time periods.

net requirements In MRP, the net requirements for a part or an assembly are derived as a result of applying gross requirements and allocations against inventory on hand, scheduled receipts, and safety stock. Net requirements, lot-sized and offset for lead time, become planned orders.

net sales Sales dollars the company receives; gross sales minus returns and allowances.

netting The process of calculating net requirements.

network planning A generic term for techniques that are used to plan complex projects. Two of the best-known network planning techniques are the critical-path method (CPM) and the program evaluation and review technique (PERT).

node In project management, a point connected by arrows in a network.

non-value-added An activity that does not add value to a product, for example, moving the product from one work center to another inside a facility. One aspect of continuous improvement is the elimination or reduction of non-value-added activities.

nondurable goods Goods whose serviceability is generally limited to a period of less than three years (such as perishable goods and semidurable goods).

nonproduction material (NPM) Items (indirect materials and supplies) in the manufacturing process or in the maintenance or operation of a facility that do not generally become part of the final product.

nonrecurring material Tooling, gauges, and facilities necessary in the manufacturing of the final product and not consumed during manufacturing or shipping with the final product.

nonscheduled hours Hours when a machine is not generally available to be scheduled for operation, for example, nights, weekends, holidays, lunch breaks, major repair, and rebuilding.

nonsignificant part number A part number that is assigned to each part but does not convey any information about the part. Nonsignificant part numbers are identifiers, not descriptors. Antonym: significant part number.

normal distribution A particular statistical distribution in which most of the observations fall fairly close to one mean, and a deviation from the mean is as likely to be plus as it is to be minus. When graphed, the normal distribution takes the form of a bell-shaped curve.

normalize To adjust observed data to a standard base.

numerical control (NC) A means of operating a machine tool automatically by the use of coded numerical instructions.

O

objective function The goal or function that is to be optimized in a model. Most often it is a cost function that should be minimized subject to some restrictions, or a profit function that should be maximized subject to some restrictions.

obsolescence (1) The condition of being out of date. A loss of value occasioned by new developments that place the older property at a competitive disadvantage. A factor in depreciation. (2) A decrease in the value of an asset brought about by the development of new and more economical methods, processes, or machinery. (3) The loss of usefulness or worth of a product or facility as a result of the appearance of better or more economical products, methods, or facilities.

obsolete inventory Inventory items that have met the obsolescence criteria established by the organization. For example, inventory that has been superseded by a new model or otherwise made obsolescent. Obsolete inventory will never be used or sold at full value. Disposing of the inventory may reduce a company's profit.

OC curve Abbreviation for operating characteristic curve.

ODD Abbreviation for earliest operation date.

OEM Abbreviation for original equipment manufacturer.

offset quantity Synonym: overlap quantity.

offsetting Synonym: lead-time offset.

OJT Abbreviation for on-the-job training.

on-hand balance The quantity shown in the inventory records as being physically in stock.

on-the-job training (OJT) Learning the skills and necessary related knowledge useful for the job at the place of work or possibly while at work.

one-card kanban system A kanban system in which only a move card is employed. Typically, the work centers are adjacent; therefore, no production card is required. In many cases, squares located between work centers are used as the kanban system. An empty square signals the supplying work center to produce a standard container of the item. Synonym: single-card kanban system. See: *two-card kanban system.*

open order (1) A released manufacturing order or purchase order. Synonym: released order. See: *scheduled receipt.* (2) An unfilled customer order.

operating assets An accounting/financial term representing the resources owned by a company for productive purposes (to generate a profit), including cash, accounts receivable, inventories, equipment, and facilities.

operating characteristic curve (OC curve) A graph used to determine the probability of accepting lots as a function of the quality level of the lots or processes when using various sampling plans. There are three types: Type A curves, which give the probability of acceptance for an individual lot coming from finite production (will not continue in the future); Type B curves, which give the probability of acceptance for lots coming from a continuous process; and Type C curves, which, for a continuous-sampling plan, give the long-run percentage of product accepted during the sampling phase.

operating cycle The three primary activities of a company are purchasing, producing, and selling a product. The operating cycle is calculated by adding the inventory conversion period to the receivables conversion period.

operating efficiency A ratio (represented as a percentage) of the actual output of a piece of equipment, department, or plant as compared to the planned or standard output.

operating environment The global, domestic, environmental, and stakeholder influences that affect the key competitive factors, customer needs, culture, and philosophy of each individual company. This environment becomes the framework in which business strategy is developed and implemented. Synonym: business environment.

operating expense In the theory of constraints, the quantity of money spent by the firm to convert inventory into sales in a specific time period.

operating system A conglomeration of software that controls the hardware and application programs that perform the logical processing of the system. It is a system of

handling of goods, inspections, and setup costs, as applicable. See: *acquisition cost, inventory costs.*

overhead The costs incurred in the operation of a business that cannot be directly related to the individual goods or services produced. These costs, such as light, heat, supervision, and maintenance, are grouped in several pools (e.g., department overhead, factory overhead, general overhead) and distributed to units of goods or services by some standard allocation method such as direct labor hours, direct labor dollars, or direct material dollars. Synonym: burden. See: *expense.*

overlap quantity The number of items that need to be run and sent ahead to the following operation before the following "overlap" operation can begin. Synonym: offset quantity. See: *process batch, transfer batch.*

overlapped schedule A manufacturing schedule that "overlaps" successive operations. Overlapping occurs when the completed portion of an order at one work center is processed at one or more succeeding work centers before the pieces left behind are finished at the preceding work centers. Synonyms: lap phasing, operation overlapping, telescoping. See: *send ahead.* Antonym: gapped schedule.

overload A condition in which the total hours of work outstanding at a work center exceed that work center's capacity.

overrun (1) The quantity received from manufacturing or a supplier that is in excess of the quantity ordered. (2) the condition resulting when expenditures exceed the budget.

overstated master production schedule A schedule that includes either past-due quantities or quantities that are greater than the ability to produce, given current capacity and material availability. An overstated MPS should be made feasible before MRP is run.

overtime Work beyond normal established working hours that usually requires that a premium be paid to the workers.

P

***P* chart** A control chart for evaluating the stability of a process in terms of the percentage of the total number of units in a sample in which an event of a given classification occurs over time. *P* charts are used where it is difficult or costly to make numerical measurements or where it is desired to combine multiple types of defects into one measurement. Synonym: percent chart.

PAC Acronym for production activity control.

package to order A production environment in which a good or service can be packaged after receipt of a customer order. The item is common across many different customers; packaging determines the end product.

paperless purchasing A purchasing operation that does not employ purchase requisitions or hard-copy purchase orders. In actual practice, a small amount of paperwork usually remains, normally in the form of the supplier schedule.

parallel conversion A method of system implementation in which the operation of the new system overlaps with the operation of the system being replaced. The old system is shown to be working properly, thus minimizing the risk and negative consequences of a poor system implementation.

parallel schedule The use of two or more machines or job centers to perform identical operations on a lot of material. Duplicate tooling and setup are required.

parent item The item produced from one or more components. Synonym: parent.

Pareto analysis Synonym: ABC classification.

Pareto chart A graphical tool for ranking causes from most significant to least significant. It is based on Pareto's law, which was first defined with respect to quality by J. M. Juran in 1950. The Pareto chart is one of the seven tools of quality.

Pareto's law A concept developed by Vilfredo Pareto, an Italian economist, that states that a small percentage of a group accounts for the largest fraction of the impact, value, and so on. In an ABC classification, for example, 20 percent of the inventory items may constitute 80 percent of the inventory value. See: *ABC classification.*

part Generally, a material item that is used as a component and is not an assembly, subassembly, blend, intermediate, or other item.

part coding and classification A method used in group technology to identify the physical similarity of parts.

part family A collection of parts grouped for some managerial purpose.

part standardization A program for planned elimination of superficial, accidental, and deliberate differences between similar parts in the interest of reducing part and supplier proliferation.

part type A code for a component within a bill of material, for example, regular, phantom, reference.

partial order Any shipment received or shipped that is less than the amount ordered.

participative design/engineering A concept that refers to the participation of all the functional areas of the firm in the product-design activity. Suppliers and customer are often also included. The intent is to enhance the design with the inputs of all the key stakeholders. Such a process should ensure that the final design meets all the needs of the stakeholders and should ensure a product that can be quickly brought to the marketplace while maximizing quality and minimizing costs. Synonyms: co-design, concurrent design, concurrent engineering, neural network, parallel engineering, simultaneous design/engineering, simultaneous engineering, team design/engineering. See: *early manufacturing involvement.*

parts bank (1) In the narrow sense, an accumulation of inventory between operations that serves to keep a subsequent operation running although there are interruptions in the preceding operations. See: *buffer*. (2) In the larger sense, a stockroom or warehouse. The implication is that the contents of these areas should be controlled like the contents of a bank.

parts list A list of parts, materials, and components required to make an item.

parts requisition An authorization that identifies the item and quantity required to be withdrawn from an inventory. Synonym: requisition.

Past-due order A line item on an open customer order that has an original scheduled ship date that is earlier than the current date. Synonyms: delinquent order, late order. Synonym: order backlog.

patent A legal document giving exclusive rights to the production, use, sale, or other action regarding a product or process.

payback period The period of time required for a stream of cash flows resulting from a project to equal the project's initial investment.

PDCA Abbreviation for plan-do-check-action.

pegged requirement A requirement that shows the next-level parent item (or customer order) as the source of the demand.

pegging In MRP and MPS, the capability to identify for a given item the sources of its gross requirements and/or allocations. Pegging can be thought of as active where-used information. See: *requirements traceability.*

percent completed A comparison of work completed to the current projection of work.

performance criterion The characteristic to be measured (e.g., parts per million defective, business profit). See: *performance measure, performance measurement system, performance standard.*

performance efficiency A ratio, usually expressed as a percentage, of the standard processing time for a part divided by its actual processing time. Setups are excluded from this calculation to prevent distortion. A traditional definition includes setup time as part of operation time, but significant distortions can occur as a result of dependent settings.

performance measure In a performance-measurement system, the actual value measured for the criterion. Synonym: performance measurement. See: *performance criterion, performance-measurement system, performance standard.*

performance-measurement system A system for collecting, measuring, and comparing a measure to a standard for a specific criterion for an operation, item, good, service, business, and so forth. A performance-measurement system consists of a criterion, a standard, and a measure. Synonym: metrics.

performance rating Observation of worker performance to rate the productivity of the workers as a percentage in terms of the standard or normal worker performance.

period capacity The number of standard hours of work that can be performed at a facility or work center in a given time period.

period costs All costs related to a period of time rather than a unit of product, for example, marketing costs, property taxes.

period order quantity A lot-sizing technique under which the lot size is equal to the net requirements for a given number of periods, for example, weeks into the future. The number of periods to order is variable, each order size equalizing the holding costs and the ordering costs for the interval. See: *discrete order quantity, dynamic lot sizing.*

periodic inventory A physical inventory taken at some recurring interval, for example, monthly, quarterly, or annual physical inventory.

periodic review system Synonym: fixed-reorder-cycle inventory model.

perpetual inventory An inventory recordkeeping system in which each transaction in and out is recorded and a new balance is computed.

perpetual inventory record A computer record or manual document on which each inventory transaction is posted so that a current record of the inventory is maintained.

PERT Acronym for program evaluation and review technique.

pert period balancing (PPB) A dynamic lot-sizing technique that uses the same logic as the least-total-cost method but adds a routine called look ahead/look back. When the look ahead/look back feature is used, a lot quantity is calculated, and before it is firmed up, the next or the previous period's demands are evaluated to determine whether it would be economical to include them in the current lot. See: *discrete order quantity, dynamic lot sizing.*

piece rate The amount of money paid for a unit of production. It serves as the basis for determining the total pay for an employee working in a piecework system.

Piece-rate pay system A compensation system based upon volume of output of an individual worker.

piecework Work done on a piece rate.

pilot test (1) In computer systems, a test before final acceptance of a new business system using a subset of data with engineered cases and documented results. (2) Generally, production of a quantity to verify manufacturability, customer acceptance, or other management requirements before implementation of ongoing production. Synonyms: pilot, walkthrough.

pipeline inventory Synonym: pipeline stock.

pipeline stock Inventory in the transportation network and the distribution system, including the flow through intermediate stocking points. The flow time through the pipeline has a major effect on the amount of inventory required in the pipeline. Time factors involve order transmission, order processing, scheduling, shipping, transportation, receiving, stocking, review time, and so on. Synonym: pipeline inventory. See: *distribution system, transportation inventory.*

plan A predetermined course of action over a specified period of time that represents a projected response to an anticipated environment to accomplish a specific set of adaptive objectives.

plan-do-check-act cycle Synonym: plan-do-check-action.

plan-do-check-action (PDCA) A four-step process for quality improvement. In the first step (plan), a plan to effect improvement is developed. In the second step (do), the plan is carried out, preferably on a small scale. In the third step (check), the effects of the plan are observed. In the last step (action), the results are studied to determine what was learned and what can be predicted. The plan-do-check-act cycle is sometimes referred to as the Shewhart cycle (because Walter A. Shewhart discussed the concept in his book *Statistical Method from the Viewpoint of Quality Control*) and as the Deming circle (because W. Edwards Deming introduced the concept in Japan; the Japanese subsequently called it the Deming circle). Synonyms: plan-do-check-act cycle, Shewhart cycle of quality, Shewhart cycle. See: *Deming circle.*

planned load The standard hours of work required by the MRP–recommended (planned) production orders.

planned order A suggested order quantity, release date, and due date created by the planning system's logic when it encounters net requirements in processing MRP. In some cases, it can also be created by a master scheduling module. Planned orders are created by the computer, exist only within the computer, and may be changed or deleted by the computer during subsequent processing if conditions change. Planned orders at one level will be exploded into gross requirements for components at the next level. Planned orders, along with released orders, serve as input to capacity-requirements planning to show the total capacity requirements by work center in future time periods.

planned order receipt The quantity planned to be received at a future date as a result of a planned order release. Planned order receipts differ from scheduled receipts in that they have not been released.

planned order release A row on an MRP table that is derived from planned order receipts by taking that planned receipt quantity and offsetting to the left by the appropriate lead time. See: *order release.*

planned receipt (1) An anticipated receipt against an open purchase order or open production order. (2) Synonym: planned order receipt.

planning (MRP II) manufacturing company Ideally, it addresses operational planning in units, financial planning in dollars and has a simulation capability to answer what-if questions. It is made up of a variety of processes, each linked together: business planning, production planning (sales and operations planning), master production scheduling, material requirements planning, capacity requirements planning, and the execution support systems for capacity and material. Output from these systems is integrated with financial reports such as the business plan, purchase commitment report, shipping budget, and inventory projections in dollars. Manufacturing resource planning is a direct outgrowth and extension of closed-loop MRP.

planning-and-control process A process consisting of the following steps: plan, execute, measure, and control.

planning bill of material An artificial grouping of items or events in bill-of-material format used to facilitate master scheduling and material planning. It may include the historical average of demand expressed as a percentage of total demand for all options within a feature or for a specific end item within a product family and is used as the quantity per in the planning bill of material. Synonym: planning bill.

planning horizon The amount of time a plan extends into the future. For a master schedule, this is normally set to cover a minimum of cumulative lead time plus time for lot sizing low-level components and for capacity changes of primary work centers or of key suppliers. For longer-term plans, the planning horizon must be long enough to permit any needed additions to capacity. See: *cumulative lead time, planning time fence.*

planning time fence A point in time denoted in the planning horizon of the master scheduling process that marks a boundary inside of which changes to the schedule may adversely affect component schedules, capacity plans, customer deliveries, and cost. Outside the planning time fence, customer orders may be booked and changes to the master schedule can be made within the constraints of the production plan. Changes inside the planning time fence must be made manually by the master scheduler. Synonym: planning fence. See: *cumulative lead time, demand time fence, firm planned order, planned order, planning horizon, time fence.*

plant layout Configuration of the plant site with lines, buildings, major facilities, work areas, aisles, and other pertinent data, such as department boundaries.

***poka-yoke* (mistake-proof)** Mistake-proofing techniques, such as manufacturing or setup activity designed in a way to prevent an error from resulting in a product defect. For example, in an assembly operation, if each correct part is not used, a sensing device detects that a part was unused and shuts down the operation, thereby preventing the assembler from moving the incomplete part to the next station or beginning another operation. Sometimes spelled *poke-yoke.*

Synonyms: failsafe techniques, failsafe work methods, mistake-proofing.

population The entire set of items from which a sample is drawn.

postponement A product-design strategy that shifts product differentiation closer to the consumer by postponing identity changes, such as assembly or packaging, to the last possible supply chain location.

preexpediting The function of following up on open orders before the scheduled delivery date to ensure the timely delivery of materials in the specified quantity.

precedence relationship In the critical-path method of project management, a logical relationship that one node has to the succeeding node. The terms *precedence relationship*, *logical relationship*, and *dependency* are used somewhat interchangeably.

predecessor activity (1) In project management, in an activity-on-arrow network, the activity that enters a node. (2) In project management, in an activity-on-node network, the node at the tail of the arrow.

predetermined motion time An organized body of information, procedures, techniques and motion times employed in the study and evaluation of manual work elements. It is useful in categorizing and analyzing all motions into elements whose unit times are computed according to such factors as length, degree of muscle control, and precision. The element times provide the basis for calculating a time standard for the operations. Synonym: synthetic time standard.

predictive maintenance A type of preventive maintenance based on nondestructive testing and statistical analysis, used to predict when required maintenance should be scheduled. Synonym: predictable maintenance.

preferred stock A type of stock entitling the owner to dividends before common stockholders are entitled to them.

preferred supplier The supplier of choice.

prevention costs The costs caused by improvement activities that focus on the reduction of failure and appraisal costs. Typical costs include education, quality training, and supplier certification. Prevention costs are one of four categories of quality costs.

prevention vs. detection A term used to contrast two types of quality activities. Prevention refers to those activities designed to prevent nonconformances in goods and services. Detection refers to those activities designed to detect nonconformances already in goods and services. Synonym: designing in quality vs. inspecting in quality.

preventive maintenance The activities, including adjustments, replacements, and basic cleanliness, that forestall machine breakdowns. The purpose is to ensure that production quality is maintained and that delivery schedules are met. In addition, a machine that is well cared for will last longer and cause fewer problems.

price One of the four Ps (product, price, place, and promotion) that constitute the set of tools used to direct the business offering to the customer. Price is the amount charged for the product offering. The price set must take into account competition, substitute product, and internal business costs to return a desirable product margin. See: *four Ps*.

price analysis The examination of a seller's price proposal or bid by comparison with price benchmarks, without examination and evaluation of all of the separate elements of the cost and profit making up the price in the bid.

primary operation A manufacturing step normally performed as part of a manufacturing part's routing. Antonym: alternate operation.

primary work center The work center in which an operation on a manufactured part is normally scheduled to be performed. Antonym: alternate work center.

prime costs Direct costs of material and labor. Prime costs do not include general, sales, and administrative costs.

prime operations Critical or most significant operations whose production rates must be closely planned.

principle of postponement Synonym: order penetration point.

priority In a general sense, the relative importance of jobs, that is, the sequence in which jobs should be worked on. It is a separate concept from capacity.

priority control The process of communicating start and completion dates to manufacturing departments in order to execute a plan. The dispatch list is the tool normally used to provide these dates and priorities based on the current plan and status of all open orders.

priority planning The function of determining what material is needed and when. Master production scheduling and material requirements planning are the elements used for the planning and replanning process to maintain proper due dates on required materials.

private warehouse A company-owned warehouse.

probabilistic demand models Statistical procedures that represent the uncertainty of demand by a set of possible outcomes (i.e., a probability distribution) and that suggest inventory management strategies under probabilistic demands.

probability Mathematically, a number between 0 and 1 that estimates the fraction of experiments (if the same experiment were being repeated many times) in which a particular result would occur. This number can be either subjective or based upon the empirical results of experimentation. It can also be derived for a process to give the probable outcome of experimentation.

probability distribution A table of numbers or a mathematical expression that indicates the frequency with which each of all possible results of an experiment should occur.

probability tree A graphic display of all possible outcomes of an event based on the possible occurrences and their associated probabilities.

procedure manual A formal organization and indexing of a firm's procedures. Manuals are usually printed and distributed to the appropriate functional areas.

process (1) A planned series of actions or operations (e.g., mechanical, electrical, chemical, inspection, test) that advances a material or procedure from one stage of completion to another. (2) A planned and controlled treatment that subjects materials or procedures to the influence of one or more types of energy (e.g., human, mechanical, electrical, chemical, thermal) for the time required to bring about the desired reactions or results.

process average Expected value of the percentage defective of a given manufacturing process.

process batch The number of units made between sequential setups at a work center. See: *batch, exchange unit, overlap quantity.*

process benchmarking Benchmarking a process (such as the pick, pack, and ship process) against organizations known to be the best in class in this process. Process benchmarking is usually conducted on firms outside of the organization's industry. See: *benchmarking, best-in-class, competitive benchmarking.*

process capability Refers to the ability of the process to produce parts that conform to (engineering) specifications. Process capability relates to the inherent variability of a process that is in a state of statistical control. See: *Cp, Cpk, process capability analysis.*

process capability analysis A procedure to estimate the parameters defining a process. The mean and standard deviation of the process are estimated and compared to the specifications, if known. This comparison is the basis for calculating capability indexes. In addition, the form of the relative frequency distribution of the characteristic of interest may be estimated. Synonym: capability study. See: *process capability.*

process capability index The value of the tolerance specified for the characteristic divided by the process capability. There are several types of process capability indices, including the widely used *Cpk* and *Cp*.

process chart A chart that represents the sequence of work or the nature of events in process. It serves as a basis for examining and possibly improving the way work is carried out. See: *flow process chart.*

process control (1) The function of maintaining a process within a given range of capability by feedback, correction, and so forth. (2) The monitoring of instrumentation attached to equipment (valves, meters, mixers, liquid, temperature, time, etc.) from a control room to ensure that a high-quality product is being produced to specification.

process-control chart Synonym: control chart.

process costing A cost-accounting system in which the costs are collected by time period and averaged over all the units produced during the period. This system can be used with either actual or standard costs in the manufacture of a large number of identical units.

process design The design of the manufacturing method.

process engineering The discipline of designing and improving the manufacturing equipment and production process to support the manufacture of a product line. Synonym: manufacturing engineering.

process flexibility The speed and ease with which the manufacturing transformation tasks can respond to internal or external changes.

process-flow analysis A procedure to document and improve the flow of product through a production system.

process-flow chart Synonym: flow process chart.

process-flow production A production approach with minimal interruptions in the actual processing in any one production run or between production runs of similar products. Queue time is virtually eliminated by integrating the movement of the product into the actual operation of the resource performing the work.

process-flow scheduling A generalized method for planning equipment usage and material requirements that uses the process structure to guide scheduling calculations. It is used in flow environments common in process industries.

process focused A type of manufacturing organization in which both plant and staff management responsibilities are delineated by production process. A highly centralized staff coordinates plant activities and intracompany material movements. This type of organization is best suited to companies whose dominant orientation is to a technology or a material and whose manufacturing processes tend to be complex and capital intensive. See: *product focused.*

process improvement The activities designed to identify and eliminate causes of poor quality, process variation, and non-value-added activities.

process industries The group of manufacturers that produce products by mixing, separating, forming, and/or performing chemical reactions. Paint manufacturers, refineries, and breweries are examples of process industries.

process layout Synonym: functional layout.

process manufacturing Production that adds value by mixing, separating, forming, and/or performing chemical reactions. It may be done in either batch or continuous mode. See: *project manufacturing.*

process oriented A characteristic in which the focus is on the interrelated processes in a business environment. It includes the activities to transform inputs into outputs that have value.

process steps The operations or stages within the manufacturing cycle required to transform components into intermediates or finished goods.

process stocks Raw ingredients or intermediates available for further processing into marketable products.

process time The time during which the material is being changed, whether it is a machining operation or an assembly. Synonym: residence time.

procurement The business functions of procurement planning, purchasing, inventory control, traffic, receiving, incoming inspection, and salvage operations.

procurement lead time The time required to design a product, modify or design equipment, conduct market research, and obtain all necessary materials. Lead time begins when a decision has been made to accept an order to produce a new product and ends when production commences. Synonyms: procurement cycle, total procurement lead time. See: *time-to-market.*

producer One who creates a good or service.

producer's risk For a given sampling plan, the probability of not accepting a lot, the quality of which has a designated numerical value representing a level that is generally desired to accept. Usually the designated value will be the acceptable quality level (AQL). See: *type I error.*

producibility The characteristics of a design that enable the item to be produced and inspected in the quantity required at least cost and minimum time.

product (1) Any good or service produced for sale, barter, or internal use. (2) One of the four Ps (product, price, place, and promotion) that constitute the set of tools to direct the business offering to the customer. The product can be promoted as a distinctive item. See: *four Ps.*

product differentiation A strategy of making a product distinct from the competition on a nonprice basis such as availability, durability, quality, or reliability.

product diversification A marketing strategy that seeks to develop new products to supply current markets.

product engineering The discipline of designing a product or product line to take advantage of process technology and improve quality, reliability, and the like.

product family A group of products with similar characteristics, often used in production planning (or sales and operations planning).

product flexibility The ease with which current designs can be modified in response to changing market demands.

product focused A type of manufacturing organization in which both plant and staff responsibilities are delineated by product, product line, or market segment. Management authority is highly decentralized, which tends to make the company more responsive to market needs and more flexible when introducing new products. This type of organization is best suited to companies whose dominant orientation is to a market or consumer group and in which flexibility and innovation are more important than coordinated planning and tight control. See: *process focused.*

product layout Layout of resources arranged sequentially based on the product's routing.

product life cycle (1) The stages a new product goes through from beginning to end, that is, the stages that a product passes through from introduction through growth, maturity, and decline. (2) The time from initial research and development to the time at which sales and support of the product to customers are withdrawn. (3) The period of time during which a product can be produced and marketed profitably.

product line A group of products whose similarity in manufacturing procedures, marketing characteristics, or specifications enables them to be aggregated for planning, marketing, or, occasionally, costing. Synonym: product group.

product load profile A listing of the required capacity and key resources needed to manufacture one unit of a selected item or family. The resource requirements are further defined by a lead-time offset to predict the impact of the product on the load of the key resources by specific time period. The product load profile can be used for rough-cut capacity planning to calculate the approximate capacity requirements of the master production schedule. See: *bill of resources, resource profile, rough-cut capacity planning.*

product mix The proportion of individual products that make up the total production or sales volume. Changes in the product mix can mean drastic changes in the manufacturing requirements for certain types of labor and material.

product number Synonym: item number.

product or service liability The obligation of a company to make restitution for loss related to personal injury, property damage, or other harm caused by its good or services.

product positioning The marketing effort involved in placing a product in a market to serve a particular niche or function. Synonym: service positioning.

product profiling (1) A graphical device used to ascertain the level of fit between a manufacturing process and the order-winning criteria of its products. Product profiling can be used at the process or company level to compare the manufacturing capabilities with the market requirements to determine areas of mismatch and identify steps needed for realignment. (2) Removing material around a predetermined boundary by means of numerically controlled machining. The numerically controlled tool path is automatically generated on the system.

product quality Attribute that reflects the capability of a product to satisfy customers' needs.

product segments The shared information between a plan of resources and a production rule for a specific product. It is a logical grouping of personnel resources, equipment resources, and material specifications required to carry out the production step.

product specification A statement of acceptable, electrical, and/or chemical properties or an acceptable range of properties that distinguish one product or grade from another.

product structure The sequence of operations that components follow during their manufacture into a product. A typical product structure would show raw material converted into fabricated components, components put together to make subassemblies, subassemblies going into assemblies, and so forth.

product tree A graphical (or tree) representation of the bill of material.

product-mix flexibility The ability to change over quickly to other products produced in a facility, as required by demand shifts in mix.

production The conversion of inputs into finished products.

production activity control (PAC) The function of routing and dispatching the work to be accomplished through the production facility and of performing supplier control. PAC encompasses the principles, approaches, and techniques needed to schedule, control, measure, and evaluate the effectiveness of production operations. Synonym: shop floor control.

production and inventory management General term referring to the body of knowledge and activities concerned with planning and controlling rates of purchasing, production, distribution, and related capacity resources to achieve target levels of customer service, backlogs, operating costs, inventory investment, manufacturing efficiency, and, ultimately, profit and return on investment.

production capability (1) The highest sustainable output rate that could be achieved for a given product mix, raw materials, worker effort, plant, and equipment. (2) The collection of personnel, equipment, material, and process segment capabilities. (3) The total of the current committed, available, and unattainable capability of the production facility. The capability includes the capacity of the resource.

production card In a just-in-time context, a card or other signal for indicating that items should be made for use or to replace some items removed from pipeline stock. See: *kanban.*

production control The function of directing or regulating the movement of goods through the entire manufacturing cycle from the requisitioning of raw material to the delivery of the finished products.

production cycle Synonym: manufacturing lead time.

production cycle elements Elements of manufacturing strategy that define the span of an operation by addressing the following areas: (1) the established boundaries for the firm's activities, (2) the construction of relationships outside the firm's boundaries (i.e., suppliers, distributors, and customers), (3) circumstances under which changes in established boundaries or relationships are necessary, and (4) the effect of such boundary or relationship changes on the firm's competitive position. The production cycle elements must explicitly address the strategic implications of vertical integration in regard to (a) the direction of such expansion, (b) the extent of the process span desired, and (c) the balance among the resulting vertically linked activities.

production forecast A projected level of customer demand for a feature (option, accessory, etc.) of a make-to-order or an assemble-to-order product. Used in two-level master scheduling, it is calculated by netting customer backlog against an overall family or product-line master production schedule and then factoring this product's available-to-promise by the option percentage in a planning bill of material. See: *assemble-to-order, planning bill of material, two-level master production schedule.*

production line A series of equipment dedicated to the manufacture of a specific number of products or families.

production management (1) The planning, scheduling, execution, and control of the process of converting inputs into finished goods. (2) A field of study that focuses on the effective planning, scheduling, use, and control of a manufacturing organization thorough the study of concepts from design engineering, industrial engineering, management information systems, quality management, inventory management, accounting, and other functions as they affect the transformation process.

production plan The agreed-upon plan that comes from the production planning (sales and operations planning) process, specifically the overall level of manufacturing output planned to be produced, usually stated as a monthly rate for each product family (group of products, items, options, features, and so on). Various units of measurement can be used to express the plan: units, tonnage, standard hours, number of workers, and so on. The production plan is management's authorization for the master scheduler to convert it into a more detailed plan, that is, the master production schedule. See: *sales and operations planning, sales plan.*

production planning A process to develop tactical plans based on setting the overall level of manufacturing output (production plan) and other activities to best satisfy the current planned levels of sales (sales plan or forecasts) while meeting general business objectives of profitability, productivity, competitive customer lead times, and so on, as expressed in the overall business plan. The sales and production capabilities are compared, and a business strategy that includes a sales plan, a production plan, budgets, pro forma financial statements, and supporting plans for materials and workforce requirements, and so on is developed. One of its primary purposes is to establish production rates that will achieve management's objective of satisfying customer demand by maintaining, raising, or lowering inventories or backlogs, while usually attempting to keep the workforce relatively stable. Because this plan affects many company functions, it is normally prepared with information from marketing and coordinated with the functions of manufacturing, sales, engineering, finance, materials, and so on. See: *aggregate planning, production plan, sales and operations planning, sales plan.*

production planning and Control An element of manufacturing strategy that includes the design and control strategies development of manufacturing planning and control systems in relation to the following considerations: (1) market-related criteria: the required level of delivery speed and reliability in a given market segment; (2) process requirement criteria: consistency between process type (job shop, repetitive, continuous, etc.) and the production planning and control system; and (3) organization control levels: systems capable of providing long-term planning and short-term control capabilities for strategic and operational considerations by management. Production planning and control strategies help firms develop systems that enable them to exploit market opportunities while satisfying manufacturing process requirements.

production planning methods The approach taken in setting the overall manufacturing output to meet customer demand by setting production levels, inventory levels, and backlog. Companies can use a chase, level, or hybrid production planning method. See: *chase production method, hybrid production method, level production method.*

production process The activities involved in converting inputs into finished goods.

production rate The rate of production usually expressed in units, cases, or some other broad measure, expressed by a period of time, such as per hour, shift, day, or week. Synonym: production level.

production reporting and status control A vehicle to provide feedback to the production schedule and allow for corrective action and maintenance of valid on-hand and on-order balances. Production reporting and status control normally include manufacturing order authorization, release, acceptance, operation start, delay reporting, move reporting, scrap and rework reporting, order close-out, and payroll interface. Synonyms: manufacturing order reporting, shop order reporting.

production schedule A plan that authorizes the factory to manufacture a certain quantity of a specific item. It is usually initiated by the production planning department.

production scheduling The process of developing the production schedule.

production time Setup time plus total processing time, where total processing time is processing time per piece multiplied by the number of pieces.

productive capacity The maximum of the output capabilities of a resource (or series of resources) or the market demand for that output for a given time period. See: *excess capacity, idle capacity, protective capacity.*

productivity (1) An overall measure of the ability to produce a good or a service. It is the actual output of production compared to the actual input of resources. Productivity is a relative measure across time or against common entities (labor, capital, etc.). In the production literature, attempts have been made to define total productivity where the effects of labor and capital are combined and divided into the output. One example is a ratio that is calculated by adding the dollar value of labor, capital equipment, energy, material, and so forth and dividing it into the dollar value of output in a given time period. This is one measure of total factor productivity. See: *efficiency, labor productivity, machine productivity, utilization.* (2) In economics, the ratio of output in terms of dollars of sales to an input such as direct labor in terms of the total wages. This is called single-factor productivity or partial-factor productivity.

project An endeavor with a specific objective to be met within the prescribed time and dollar limitations and that has been assigned for definition or execution. See: *project manufacturing.*

project costing An accounting method of assigning valuations that is generally used in industries in which services are performed on a project basis. Each assignment is unique and costed without regard to other assignments. Examples are shipbuilding, construction projects, and public accounting firms. Project costing is opposed to process costing, in which products to be valued are homogeneous.

project duration The elapsed duration from project start date through project finish date.

project life cycle In project management, a set of project phases (objectives definition, requirements definition, external and internal design, construction, system test, and implementation and maintenance), whose definition is determined by the needs of those controlling the project.

project management The use of skills and knowledge in coordinating the organizing, planning, scheduling, directing, controlling, monitoring, and evaluating of prescribed activities to ensure that the stated objectives of a project, manufactured good, or service are achieved.

project manufacturing A type of manufacturing process used for large, often unique, items or structures that require a custom design capability (engineer-to-order). This type of process is highly flexible and can cope with a broad range of product designs and design changes. Product manufacturing usually uses a fixed-position type of layout. See: *batch* (fourth definition), *continuous production, job shop* (second definition), *process manufacturing, project, repetitive manufacturing.*

project production Production in which each unit or small group of units is managed by a project team created especially for that purpose.

project risk management In project management, a systematic process of controlling project risk. It includes maximizing the likelihood and effect of positive events and minimizing the likelihood and effect of negative events.

project schedule In project management, a list of activities and their planned completion dates that collectively achieve project milestones.

project scope In project management, the work required to create a product with given features and options.

projected available balance An inventory balance projected into the future. It is the running sum of on-hand inventory minus requirements plus scheduled receipts and planned orders. Synonym: projected available inventory.

projected available inventory Synonym: projected available balance.

projected finish date The current estimate of the date when an activity will be completed.

projected on hand Projected available balance, excluding planned orders.

projected start date The current estimate of the date when an activity will begin.

proprietary assembly An assembly designed by a manufacturer that may be serviced only with component parts supplied by the manufacturer and whose design is owned or licensed by its manufacturer.

protective capacity A given amount of extra capacity at nonconstraints above the system constraint's capacity, used to protect against statistical fluctuation (breakdowns, late receipts of materials, quality problems, etc.). Protective capacity provides nonconstraints with the ability to catch up to "protect" throughput and due date performance. See: *excess capacity, idle capacity, limiting operation, productive capacity, safety capacity.*

protective inventory The amount of inventory required relative to the protective capacity in the system to achieve a specific throughput rate at the constraint. See: *limiting operation.*

prototype A product model constructed for testing and evaluation to see how the product performs before releasing the product to manufacture.

provisioning The process of identifying and purchasing the support items and determining the quantity of each support item necessary to operate and maintain a system.

pseudo bill of material An artificial grouping of items that facilitates planning. See: *modular bill of material, phantom bill of material, planning bill of material, super bill of material.*

pull signal Any signal that indicates when to produce or transport items in a pull replenishment system. For example, in just-in-time production-control systems, a kanban card is used as the pull signal to replenish parts to the using operation. See: *pull system.*

pull system (1) In production, the production of items only as demanded for use or to replace those taken for use. See: *pull signal.* (2) In material control, the withdrawal of inventory as demanded by the using operations. Material is not issued until a signal comes from the user. (3) In distribution, a system for replenishing field warehouse inventories in which replenishment decisions are made at the field warehouse itself, not at the central warehouse or plant.

purchase order The purchaser's authorization used to formalize a purchase transaction with a supplier. A purchase order, when given to a supplier, should contain statements of the name, part number, quantity, description, and price of the goods or services ordered; agreed-to terms as to payment, discounts, date of performance, and transportation; and all other agreements pertinent to the purchase and its execution by the supplier.

purchase requisition An authorization to the purchasing department to purchase specified materials in specified quantities within a specified time. See: *parts requisition.*

purchased part An item sourced from a supplier.

purchasing The term used in industry and management to denote the function of and the responsibility for procuring materials, supplies, and services.

purchasing agent A person who is authorized by the company to purchase goods and services for the company.

purchasing capacity The act of buying capacity or machine time from a supplier. A company can then schedule and use the capacity of the machine or a part of the capacity of the machine as if it were in its own plant.

purchasing lead time The total lead time required to obtain a purchased item. Included here are order preparation and release time; supplier lead time; transportation time; and receiving, inspection, and put-away time. See: *lead time, supplier lead time, time-to-product.*

push (system) (1) In production, the production of items at times required by a given schedule planned in advance. (2) In material control, the issuing of material according to a given schedule or issuing material to a job order at its start time. (3) In distribution, a system for replenishing field warehouse inventories in which replenishment decision making is centralized, usually at the manufacturing site or central supply facility.

put-away Removing the material from the dock (or other location of receipt), transporting the material to a storage area, placing that material in a staging area and then moving it to a specific location, and recording the movement and identification of the location at which the material has been placed.

pyramid forecasting A forecasting technique that enables management to review and adjust forecasts made at an aggregate level and to keep lower-level forecasts in balance. The procedure begins with the rollup (aggregation) of item forecasts into forecasts by product group. The management team establishes a (new) forecast for the product group. The value is then forced down (disaggregation) to individual item forecasts so that they are consistent with the aggregate plan. The approach combines the stability of aggregate forecasts and the application of management judgment with the need to forecast many end items within the constraints of an aggregate forecast or sales plan. See: *management estimation, planning bill of material, product group forecast.*

Q

***Q* chart** A control chart for evaluating the stability of a process in terms of a quality score. The quality score is the weighted sum of the count of events of various classifications, where each classification is assigned a weight. Synonyms: quality chart, quality score chart.

QFD Abbreviation for quality function deployment.

QS-9000 Quality-management system requirements cooperatively developed and adopted by the "Big Three" automobile manufacturers, Chrysler, Ford, and General Motors, along with certain truck manufacturers. QS-9000 incorporates all of the main elements of the ISO 9001 standard and describes the minimum quality-system requirements to emphasize continuous improvement, defect prevention, consistency, and elimination of waste.

qualitative forecasting techniques An approach to forecasting that is based on intuitive or judgmental evaluation. It is used generally when data are scarce, not available, or no longer relevant. Common types of qualitative techniques include: personal insight, sales force estimates, panel consensus, market research, visionary forecasting, and the Delphi method. Examples include developing long-range projections and new product introduction.

quality Conformance to requirements or fitness for use. Quality can be defined through five principal approaches: (1) Transcendent quality is an ideal, a condition of excellence. (2) Product-based quality is based on a product attribute. (3) User-based quality is fitness for use. (4) Manufacturing-based quality is conformance to requirements. (5) Value-based quality is the degree of excellence at an acceptable price. Also, quality has two major components: (1) quality of conformance: quality is defined by the absence of defects; and (2) quality of design: quality is measured by the degree of customer satisfaction with a product's characteristics and features.

quality assurance/control Two terms that have many interpretations because of the multiple definitions for the words *assurance* and *control.* For example, *assurance* can mean the act of making certain; *control* can mean an evaluation to indicate needed corrective responses, the act of guiding, or the state of a process in which the variability is attributable to a constant system of chance causes. One definition of quality assurance is all the planned and systematic activities implemented within the quality system that can be demonstrated to provide confidence that a good or service will fulfill requirements for quality. One definition for quality control is the operational techniques and activities used to fulfill requirements for quality. Often, however, *quality assurance* and *quality control* are used interchangeably, referring to the actions performed to ensure the quality of a good, service, or process. See: *quality control.*

quality at the source A producer's responsibility to provide 100 percent acceptable-quality material to the consumer of the material. The objective is to reduce or eliminate shipping or receiving quality inspections and line stoppages as a result of supplier defects.

quality audit A systematic, independent examination and review to determine whether quality activities and related results comply with planned arrangements and whether these arrangements are implemented effectively and are suitable to achieve the objectives.

quality circle A small group of people who normally work as a unit and meet frequently to uncover and solve problems concerning the quality of items produced, process capability, or process control. See: *small group improvement activity.*

quality control The process of measuring quality conformance by comparing the actual with a standard for the characteristic and acting on the difference. See: *quality assurance/control.*

quality costs The overall costs associated with prevention activities and the improvement of quality throughout the firm before, during, and after production of a product. These costs fall into four recognized categories: internal failures, external failures, appraisal costs, and prevention costs. Internal failure costs relate to problems before the product reaches the customer. These usually include rework, scrap, downgrades, reinspection, retest, and process losses. External failure costs relate to problems found after the product reaches the customer. These usually include such costs as warranty and returns. Appraisal costs are associated with the formal evaluation and audit of quality in the firm. Typical costs include inspection, quality audits, testing, calibration, and checking time. Prevention costs are those caused by improvement activities that focus on reducing failure and appraisal costs. Typical costs include education, quality training, and supplier certification.

quality engineering The engineering discipline concerned with improving the quality of products and processes.

quality function deployment (QFD) A methodology designed to ensure that all the major requirements of the customer are identified and subsequently met or exceeded through the resulting product-design process and the design and operation of the supporting production management system. QFD can be viewed as a set of communication and translation tools. QFD tries to eliminate the gap between what the customer wants in a new product and what the product is capable of delivering. QFD often leads to a clear identification of the major requirements of the customers. These expectations are referred to as the voice of the customer (VOC). See: *house of quality.*

quality loss function A parabolic approximation of the quality loss that occurs when a quality characteristic deviates from its target value. The quality loss function is expressed in monetary units: The cost of deviating from the target increases quadratically as the quality characteristic moves farther from the target. The formula used to compute the quality loss function depends on the type of quality characteristic being used. The quality loss function was first introduced in this form by Genichi Taguchi.

quality tree An analytical tool that visualizes that quality is composed of four layers of achievement: (1) inspection, (2) process measurement and improvement, (3) process control, and (4) design for quality.

quantity discount A price-reduction allowance determined by the quantity or value of a purchase.

quantity-based order system Synonym: fixed-reorder-quantity inventory model.

queue A waiting line. In manufacturing, the jobs at a given work center waiting to be processed. As queues increase, so do average queue time and work-in-process inventory.

queue ratio The ratio of the hours of slack within the job to the queue originally scheduled.

queue time The amount of time a job waits at a work center before setup or work is performed on the job. Queue time is one element of total manufacturing lead time. Increases in queue time result in direct increases to manufacturing lead time and work-in-process inventories.

queuing theory The collection of models dealing with waiting line problems, for example, problems for which customers or units arrive at some service facility at which waiting lines or queues may build. Synonym: waiting line theory.

quick asset ratio An activity ratio of cash, marketable securities, and accounts receivable to current liabilities. This measurement of liquidity is more rigorous than the current ratio. Synonym: acid test ratio.

R

***R* chart** A control chart in which the subgroup range, *R*, is used to evaluate the stability of the variability within a process.

R&D Abbreviation for research and development.

random Having no predictable pattern. For example, sales data may vary randomly about some forecast value with no specific pattern and no attendant ability to obtain a more accurate sales estimate than the forecast value.

random cause Synonym: common cause.

random component A component of demand usually describing the impact of uncontrollable variation on demand.

random sample A selection of observations taken from all the observations of a phenomenon in such a way that each chosen observation has the same possibility of selection.

random variation A fluctuation in data that is caused by uncertain or random occurrences.

random-location storage A storage technique in which parts are placed in any space that is empty when they arrive at the storeroom. Although this random method requires the use of a locator file to identify part locations, it often requires less storage space than a fixed-location storage method. Synonyms: floating inventory location system, floating storage location. See: *fixed-location storage.*

range In statistics, the spread in a series of observations. For example, the anticipated demand for a particular product might vary from a low of 10 to a high of 500 per week. The range would therefore be 500 − 10, or 490.

rate of return on investment The efficiency ratio relating profit or cash flow incomes to investments. Several different measures of this ratio are in common use.

rate variance The difference between the actual output rate of product and the planned or standard output rate.

rate-based scheduling A method for scheduling and producing based on a periodic rate, for example, daily, weekly, or monthly. This method has traditionally been applied to high-volume and process industries. The concept has recently been applied within job shops using cellular layouts and mixed-model-level schedules in which the production rate is matched to the selling rate.

rated capacity The expected output capability of a resource or system. Capacity is traditionally calculated from such data as planned hours, efficiency, and utilization. The rated capacity is equal to hours available × efficiency × utilization. Synonyms: calculated capacity, effective capacity, nominal capacity, standing capacity.

rationing The allocation of product among consumers. When price is used to allocate product, it is allocated to those willing to pay the most.

raw material Purchased items or extracted materials that are converted via the manufacturing process into components and products.

raw materials inventory Inventory of material that has not undergone processing at a facility.

RCCP Abbreviation for rough-cut capacity planning.

real time The technique of coordinating data processing with external related physical events as they occur, thereby permitting prompt reporting of conditions. See: *online service.*

receivables conversion period The length of time required to collect sales receipts. Synonym: average collection period.

receiving point The location to which material is being shipped. Antonym: shipping point.

receiving report A document used by the receiving function of a company to inform others of the receipt of goods purchased.

reconciling inventory Comparing the physical inventory figures with the perpetual inventory record and making any necessary corrections.

record accuracy A measure of the conformity of recorded values in a bookkeeping system to the actual values, for example, the on-hand balance of an item maintained in a computer record relative to the actual on-hand balance of the items in the stockroom.

recycle (1) The reintroduction of partially processed product or carrier solvents from one operation or task into a previous operation. (2) A recirculation process.

redundancy (1) A backup capability, coming either from extra machines or from extra components within a machine, to reduce the effects of breakdowns. (2) The use of one or more extra or duplicating components in a system or equipment (often to increase reliability).

reengineering Synonym: business process reengineering.

reference capacity model A simulation model with accurate operational details and demand forecasts that can provide practical capacity utilization predictions. Various alternatives for system operation can be evaluated effectively.

regeneration MRP An MRP processing approach in which the master production schedule is totally reexploded down through all bills of material, to maintain valid priorities. New requirements and planned orders are completely recalculated or "regenerated" at that time. See: *requirements alteration. Antonym: net change MRP.*

regression analysis A statistical technique for determining the best mathematical expression describing the functional relationship between one response and one or more independent variables.

rejected inventory Inventory that does not meet quality requirements but has not yet been sent to rework, scrapped, or returned to a supplier.

release The authorization to produce or ship material that has already been ordered.

relevant costs Those costs incurred because of a decision. The costs would not have resulted unless the decision was made and implemented. They are relevant to the decision.

relevant range The range of activity planned for a firm.

reliability The probability that a product will perform its specified function under prescribed conditions without failure for a specified period of time. It is a design parameter that can be made part of a requirements statement. See: *mean time between failures, mean time for failures.*

reliability engineering The function responsible for the determination and application of appropriate reliability tasks and criteria during the design, development, manufacture, test, and support of a product that will result in achieving of the specified product reliability.

remanufactured parts Components or assemblies that are refurbished or rebuilt to perform the original function. Synonyms: refurbished goods, refurbished parts.

remanufacturing (1) An industrial process in which worn-out products are restored to like-new condition. In contrast, a repaired product normally retains its identity, and only those parts that have failed or are badly worn are replaced or serviced. (2) The manufacturing environment in which worn-out products are restored to like-new condition.

remanufacturing resource planning A manufacturing resource planning system designed for remanufacturing facilities.

reorder quantity (1) In a fixed-reorder-quantity system of inventory control, the fixed quantity that should be ordered each time the available stock (on-hand plus on-order) falls to or below the reorder point. (2) In a variable-reorder-quantity system, the amount ordered from time period to time period will vary. Synonym: replenishment order quantity.

repair bill of material In remanufacturing, the bill of material defining the actual work required to return a product to service. This bill is constructed based on inspection and determination of actual requirements. See: *disassembly bill of material.*

repairables Items that are technically feasible to repair economically.

repetitive industries The group of manufacturers that produce high-volume, low-variety products such as spark plugs, lawn mowers, and paper clips. See: *repetitive manufacturing.*

repetitive manufacturing The repeated production of the same discrete products or families of products. Repetitive methodology minimizes setups, inventory, and manufacturing lead times by using production lines, assembly lines, or cells. Work orders are no longer necessary; production scheduling and control are based on production rates. Products may be standard or assembled from modules. Repetitive is not a function of speed or volume. Synonyms: repetitive process, repetitive production.

replacement cost A method of setting the value of inventories based upon the cost of the next purchase.

replacement cost systems A method of inventory valuation that assigns an item cost based on the next item price incurred.

replacement order An order for the replacement of material that has been scrapped.

replacement parts Parts that can be used as substitutes that differ from completely interchangeable service parts in that they require some physical modification—for example, boring, cutting, or drilling—before they can replace the original part.

replanning frequency In an MRP system, the amount of time between successive runs of the MRP model. If the planner does not run MRP frequently enough, the material plan becomes inaccurate as material requirements and inventory status change with the passage of time.

replenishment Relocating material from a bulk storage area to an order-pick storage area and documenting this relocation.

replenishment interval Synonym: replenishment period.

replenishment lead time The total period of time that elapses from the moment it is determined that a product should be reordered until the product is back on the shelf available for use. Synonym: reorder cycle.

replenishment order quantity Synonym: reorder quantity.

replenishment period The time between successive replenishment orders. Synonym: replenishment interval. See: *review period.*

reprocessed material Goods that have gone through selective rework or cycle.

request for proposal (RFP) A document used to solicit vendor responses when the functional requirements and features are known but no specific product is in mind.

requirements definitions Specifying the inputs, files, processing, and outputs for a new system, but without expressing computer alternatives and technical details.

requirements explosion The process of calculating the demand for the components of a parent item by multiplying the parent item requirements by the component usage quantity specified in the bill of material. Synonym: explosion.

requirements traceability The capability to determine the source of demand requirements through record linkages. It is used in analyzing requirements to make adjustments to plans for material or capacity. See: *pegging.*

rerouting flexibility Accommodating unavailability of equipment by quickly and easily using alternate machines in the processing sequence.

rescheduling The process of changing order or operation due dates, usually as a result of their being out of phase with when they are needed.

research and development (R&D) A function that performs basic and applied research and develops potential new products.

reserve stock Synonym: safety stock.

reserved material Material on hand or on order that is assigned to specific future production or customer orders. Synonyms: allocated material, assigned material, obligated material.

resource Anything that adds value to a good or service in its creation, production, or delivery.

resource driver The objects that are linked to an activity that consume resources at a specified rate. For example, a resource driver is a purchase order (the object) that, when placed (the activity), consumes hours (the rate) of purchasing (the resource).

resource leveling The process of scheduling (and rescheduling) the start and finish dates of operations (or activities) to achieve a consistent rate of resource usage so that resource requirements do not exceed resource availability for a given time period. Synonym: leveling.

resource management (1) The planning and validation of all organizational resources. (2) The effective identification, planning, scheduling, execution, and control of all organization resources to produce a good or service that provides customer satisfaction and supports the organization's competitive edge and, ultimately, organizational goals. (3) An emerging field of study emphasizing the systems perspective, encompassing both the product and process life cycles, and focusing on the integration of organizational resources toward the effective realization of organizational goals. Resources include materials; maintenance, repair, and operating supplies; production and supporting equipment; facilities; direct and indirect employees; staff; administrative and professional employees; information; knowledge; and capital. Synonym: integrated resource management.

resource planning Capacity planning conducted at the business plan level. The process of establishing, measuring, and adjusting limits or levels of long-range capacity. Resource planning is normally based on the production plan, such as the business plan. It addresses those resources that take long periods of time to acquire. Resource-planning decisions always require top management approval. Synonyms: long-range resource planning, resource requirements planning. See: *capacity planning, long-term planning.*

resource profile The standard hours of load placed on a resource by time period. Production lead-time data are taken into account to provide time-phased projections of the capacity requirements for individual production facilities. See: *bill of resources, capacity planning using overall factors, product load profile, rough-cut capacity planning.*

resource-limited scheduling The scheduling of activities so that predetermined resource availability pools are not exceeded. Activities are started as soon as resources are available (with respect to logical constraints), as required by the activity. When not enough of a resource exists to do all tasks on a given day, a priority decision is made. Project finish may be delayed, if necessary, to alter schedules constrained by resource usage.

response time The elapse of time or average delay between the initiation of a transaction and the results of the transaction.

retention efficiency In marketing, a measurement of how well a company creates repeat customers.

return on assets Net income for the previous 12 months divided by total assets.

return on investment (ROI) A financial measure of the relative return from an investment, usually expressed as a percentage of earnings produced by an asset to the amount invested in the asset.

return on owner's equity (ROE) The net (after-tax) income divided by average owner's equity.

return to supplier Material that has been rejected by the buyer's inspection department and is awaiting shipment back to the supplier for repair or replacement.

revenue The income received by a company from sales or other sources, such as stock owned in other companies.

reverse engineering The process of disassembling, evaluating, and redesigning a competitor's product for the purpose of manufacturing a product with similar characteristics without violating any of the competitor's proprietary manufacturing technologies.

reverse flow scheduling A scheduling procedure used in some process industries for building process train schedules that starts with the last stage and proceeds backward (countercurrent to the process flow) through the process structure.

review period The time between successive evaluations of inventory status to determine whether to reorder. See: *replenishment period.*

rework Reprocessing to salvage a defective item or part.

rework lead time The lead time required to rework material in house or at a supplier's location.

rework order A manufacturing order to rework and salvage defective parts or products. Synonyms: repair order, spoiled work order.

right the first time A term used to convey the concept that it is beneficial and more cost-effective to take the necessary steps the first time to ensure that a good or service meets its requirements than to provide a good or service that will need rework or not meet customers' needs. In other words, an organization should engage in defect prevention rather than defect detection.

risk-adjusted discount rate A discount rate that is higher for more risky projects and lower for less risky projects.

risk analysis A review of the uncertainty associated with the research, development, and production of a product.

risk pooling The process of reducing the risk among customers by pooling stock in centralized warehouses. Statistically speaking, when one customer demands a large amount of a particular product, another customer demands only a little of the same product. The total inventory to maintain the customer service level is smaller, on average, with a centralized warehouse because the risk of a product stockout is pooled across all the customers.

risk response plan A document defining known risks including description, cause, likelihood, costs, and proposed responses. It also identifies current status on each risk.

rope In the theory of constraints' drum-buffer-rope system, the rope consists of the minimum set of instructions to ensure that (1) nonconstraint resources are used (and not overactivated or misallocated) and (2) material is released into the system and flows to the buffers in a way that supports the planned overall system throughput.

rough-cut capacity planning (RCCP) The process of converting the master production schedule into requirements for key resources, often including labor, machinery, warehouse space, suppliers' capabilities, and, in some cases, money. Comparison to available or demonstrated capacity is usually done for each key resource. This comparison assists the master scheduler in establishing a feasible master production schedule. Three approaches to performing RCCP are the bill-of-labor (resources, capacity) approach, the capacity-planning-using-overall-factors approach, and the resource-profile approach. See: *bill of resources, capacity planning, capacity planning using overall factors, product load profile, resource profile.*

routing (1) Information detailing the method of manufacture of a particular item. It includes the operations to be performed, their sequence, the various work centers involved, and the standards for setup and run. In some companies, the routing also includes information on tooling, operator skill levels, inspection operations and testing requirements, and so on. Synonyms: bill of operations, instruction sheet, manufacturing data sheet, operation chart, operation list, operation sheet, route sheet, routing sheet. See: *bill of labor, bill of resources.* (2) In information systems, the process of defining the path a message will take from one computer to another computer.

run A quantity of production being processed.

run chart A graphical technique that illustrates how a process is performing over time. By statistically analyzing a run chart, a process can be determined to be under or out of control. The most common types of data used to construct the charts are ranges, averages, percentages/count, and individual process attributes (e.g., temperature). See: *C chart, P chart, R chart, U chart, X-bar chart.*

run sheet A log-type document used in continuous processes to record raw materials used, quantity produced, in-process testing results, and the like. It may serve as an input document for inventory records.

run time The time required to process a piece or lot at a specific operation. Run time does not include setup time. Synonym: run standards.

running sum of forecast errors The arithmetic sum of the differences between actual and forecasted demand for the periods being evaluated.

runout list (1) A list of all items to be scheduled into production in sequence by the dates at which the present available stock is expected to be exhausted. (2) A statement of ingredients required to use up an available resource, for example, how much "a" resource is required to consume 300 pounds of *x*."

rush order An order that for some reason must be fulfilled in less than normal lead time.

S

***s*-curve** In project management, graphic display of cumulative project attributes such as costs, labor hours, or percentage of work. The name derives from the typical shape of the curve.

safety factor (1) The ratio of average strength to the worst stress expected. It is essential that the variation, in addition to the average value, be considered in design. (2) The numerical value used in the service function (based on the standard deviation or mean absolute deviation of the forecast) to provide a given level of customer service. For example, if the item MAD is 100 and a 0.95 customer service level (safety factor of 2.06) is desired, then a safety stock of 206 units should be carried. This safety stock must be adjusted if the forecast interval and item lead times differ. Synonym: service factor. See: *service function.*

safety lead time An element of time added to normal lead time to protect against fluctuations in lead time so that an order can be completed before its real need date. When used, the MRP system, in offsetting for lead time, will plan both order release and order completion for earlier dates than it would otherwise. Synonyms: protection time, safety time.

safety stock (1) In general, a quantity of stock planned to be in inventory to protect against fluctuations in demand of supply. (2) In the context of master production scheduling, the additional inventory and capacity are planned as protection against forecast errors and short-term changes in the back log. Overplanning can be used to create safety stock. Synonyms: buffer stock, reserve stock. See: *hedge, inventory buffer.*

sale-and-leaseback An agreement by which a firm first sells its assets to a financial institution and then leases these same assets from the financial institution.

sales and operations planning A process to develop tactical plans that provide management the ability to strategically direct its businesses to achieve competitive advantage on a continuous basis by integrating customer-focused marketing plans for new and existing products with the management of the supply chain. The process brings together all the plans for the business (sales, marketing, development, manufacturing, sourcing, and financial) into one integrated set of plans. It is performed at least once a month and is reviewed by management at an aggregate level (product family level). The process must reconcile all supply, demand, and new-product plans at both the detail and aggregate levels and tie to the business plan. It is the definitive statement of the company's plans for the near to intermediate term, covering a horizon sufficient to plan for resources and to support the annual business-planning process. Executed properly, the sales and operation planning process links the strategic plans for the business with its execution and reviews performance measurements for continuous improvement. See: *aggregate planning, production plan, production planning, sales plan, tactical planning.*

sales order number A unique control number assigned to each new customer order, usually during order entry. It is often used by order promising, master scheduling, cost accounting, invoicing, and so on. For some make-to-order products, it can also take the place of an end-item part number by becoming the control number that is scheduled through the finishing operations.

sales plan A time-phased statement of expected customer orders anticipated to be received (incoming sales, not outgoing shipments) for each major product family or item. It represents sales and marketing management's commitment to take all reasonable steps necessary to achieve this level of actual customer orders. The sales plan is a necessary input to the production-planning process (or sales and operations–planning process). It is expressed in units identical to those used for the production plan (as well as in sales dollars). See: *aggregate planning, production plan, production planning, sales and operations planning.*

sales planning The process of determining the overall sales plan to best support customer needs and operations capabilities while meeting general business objectives of profitability, productivity, competitive customer lead times, and so on, as expressed in the overall business plan. See: *production planning, sales and operations planning.*

salvage Property that, because of its worn, damaged, deteriorated, or incomplete condition or specialized nature, has no reasonable prospect of sale or use as serviceable property without major repairs or alterations but that has some value in excess of its scrap value.

salvage value (1) The cost recovered or that could be recovered from used property when removed, sold, or scrapped. A factor in appraisal of property value and in computing depreciation. (2) The market value of a machine or facility at any point in time. Normally, an estimate of an asset's net value at the end of its estimated life.

sample A portion of a universe of data chosen to estimate some characteristics about the whole universe. The universe of data could consist of sizes of customer orders, number of units of inventory, number of lines on a purchase order, and the like.

sample size The number of elements selected for analysis from the population.

sampling (1) A statistical process in which generalizations regarding an entire body of phenomena are drawn from a relatively small number of observations. (2) In marketing, the delivery of free trial goods to consumers.

sampling distribution The distribution of values of a statistic calculated from samples of a given size.

sawtooth diagram A quantity-versus-time graphic representation of the order point/order quantity inventory system showing inventory being received and then used up and reordered.

Scanlon plan A system of group incentives on a companywide or plantwide basis that sets up one measure that reflects the results of all efforts. The universal standard is the ratio of labor costs to sales value added by production. If there is an increase in production sales value with no change in labor costs, productivity has increased while unit cost has decreased.

scarcity A concept central to economics: that less of a good is freely available than consumers would like.

scatter chart A graphical technique to analyze the relationship between two variables. Two sets of data are plotted on a graph, with the y axis used for the variable to be predicted and the x axis used for the variable to make the prediction. The graph will show possible relationships (although two variables might appear to be related, they might not be; those who know most about the variables must make the evaluation). The scatter chart is one of the seven tools of quality. Synonyms: cross plot, scatter diagram.

schedule A timetable for planned occurrences, for example, shipping schedule, master production schedule, maintenance schedule, or supplier schedule. Some schedules include the starting and ending time for activities, such as a project schedule.

schedule chart Usually a large piece of graph paper used in the same manner as a control board. Where the control board often uses strings and markers to represent plans and progress, the schedule chart is typically filled in with pencil. See: *control board.*

schedule harmony In supply chains, the arrival of goods at a transfer point with a small buffer time in front of their departure via a different transportation mode.

scheduled downtime Planned shutdown of equipment or plant to perform maintenance or to adjust to softening demand.

scheduled finish date In project management, an activity's planned finish time and the late finish time. It may reflect resource limitations. Synonym: planned finish date.

scheduled load The standard hours of work required by scheduled receipts, that is, open production orders.

scheduled receipt An open order that has an assigned due date. See: *open order.*

scheduled start date In project management, an activity's planned start time, normally between the early start time and the late start time. It may reflect resource limitations. Synonym: planned start date.

scheduler A general term that can refer to a material planner, dispatcher, or a combined function.

scheduling The act of creating a schedule, such as a shipping schedule, master production schedule, maintenance schedule, or supplier schedule.

scheduling rules Basic rules that can be used consistently in a scheduling system. Scheduling rules usually specify the amount of calendar time to allow for a move, queue, load calculation, and so forth. Synonym: scheduling algorithm.

scientific inventory control Synonym: statistical inventory control.

scope In project management, the totality of products to be created by a project.

scope definition In project management, a change to a project's scope, usually requiring an adjustment to the project's budget and schedule.

scrap Material outside specifications and possessing characteristics that make rework impractical.

scrap factor A factor that expresses the quantity of a particular component that is expected to be scrapped upon receipt from a vendor, completion of production, or while that component is being built into a given assembly. It is usually expressed as a decimal value. For a given operation or process, the scrap factor plus the yield factor is equal to one. If the scrap factor is 30 percent (or 0.3), then the yield is 70 percent (or 0.7). In manufacturing planning and control systems, the scrap factor is usually related to a specific item in the item master but may be related to a specific component in the product structure. For example, if 50 units of a product are required by a customer and a scrap factor of 30 percent (a yield of 70 percent) is expected, then 72 units (computed as 50 units divided by 0.7) should be started in the manufacturing process. Synonym: scrap rate. See: *yield, yield factor.*

search models Operations research models that attempt to find optimal solutions with adaptive searching approaches.

seasonal component A component of demand, usually describing the impact of variations that occur because of the time of year (quarter, month, week) on demand. See: *decomposition, time series analysis.*

seasonal index A number used to adjust data to seasonal demand. Synonym: seasonal adjustment. See: *base series.*

seasonal inventory Inventory built up to smooth production in anticipation of a peak seasonal demand: seasonal stock.

seasonality A repetitive pattern of demand from year to year (or other repeating time interval) with some periods considerably higher than others.

second-order smoothing A method of exponential smoothing for trend situations that employs two previously computed averages, the singly and doubly smoothed values, to extrapolate into the future. Synonym: double smoothing.

semifinished goods Products that have been stored uncompleted awaiting final operations that adapt them to different uses or customer specifications.

semiprocess flow A manufacturing configuration in which most jobs go through the same sequence of operations even though production is in job lots.

semivariable costs Costs that change in increments. They remain fixed over a given range, and outside that range, the cost changes to a new level.

send ahead The movement of a portion of a lot of material to a subsequent operation before completion of the current operation for all units of the lot. The purpose of sending material ahead is to reduce the manufacturing lead time. See: *overlapped schedule.*

sensitivity analysis A technique for determining how much an expected outcome or result will change in response to a given change in an input variable. For example, given a projected level of resources, what would be the effect on net income if variable costs of production increased 20 percent?

sequencing Determining the order in which a manufacturing facility is to process a number of different jobs in order to achieve certain objectives.

sequential In numeric sequence, normally in ascending order.

serial number A unique number assigned for identification to a single piece that will never be repeated for similar pieces. Serial numbers are usually applied by the manufacturer but can be applied at other points, including by the distributor or wholesaler.

service Sometimes used to describe those activities that support the production or distribution functions in any organization, such as customer service and field service.

service function A mathematical relationship of the safety factor to service level, that is, the fraction of demand that is routinely met from stock.

service industry (1) In its narrowest sense, an organization that provides an intangible product, for example, medical or legal advice. (2) In its broadest sense, all organizations except farming, mining, and manufacturing. This definition of service industry includes retail trade; wholesale trade; transportation and utilities; finance, insurance, and real estate; construction; professional, personal, and social services; and local, state, and federal government.

service level Synonym: level of service.

service parts Those modules, components, and elements that are planned to be used without modifications to replace an original part. Synonyms: repair parts, spare parts.

service parts demand The need or requirement for a component to be sold by itself, as opposed to being used in production to make a higher-level product. Synonyms: repair parts demand, spare parts demand.

service time The time taken to serve a customer, for example, the time required to fill a sales order or the time required to fill a request at a tool crib.

service vs. investment chart A curve showing the amount of inventory that will be required to give various levels of customer service.

serviceability (1) Design characteristic that facilitates the easy and efficient performance of service activities. Service activities include those activities required to keep equipment in operating condition, such as lubrication, fueling, oiling, and cleaning. (2) A measurement of the degree to which servicing of an item will be accomplished within a given time under specified conditions. See: *maintainability.* (3) The competitive advantage gained when an organization focuses on aspects such as the speed and courtesy with which customer complaints and questions are answered, following up with customers after the sale to ensure satisfaction, and offering on-site service for product repairs.

setup (1) The work required to change a specific machine, resource, work center, or line from making the last good piece of item A to making the first good piece of item B. (2) The refitting of equipment to neutralize the effects of the last lot produced (e.g., teardown of the just-completed production and preparation of the equipment for production of the next scheduled item). Synonyms: changeover, turnaround, turnaround time.

setup costs Costs such as scrap costs, calibration costs, downtime costs, and lost sales associated with preparing the resource for the next product. Synonyms: changeover costs, turnaround costs.

setup time The time required for a specific machine, resource, work center, process, or line to convert from the production of the last good piece of item A to the first good piece of item B. Synonym: setup lead time.

seven tools of quality Tools that help organizations understand their processes in order to improve them. The tools are the cause-and-effect diagram, check sheet, control chart, flowchart, histogram, Pareto chart, and scatter chart.

Shingo's seven wastes Shigeo Shingo, a pioneer in the Japanese just-in-time philosophy, identified seven barriers to improving manufacturing. They are the waste of overproduction, waste of waiting, waste of transportation, waste of stocks, waste of motion, waste of making defect, and waste of the processing itself.

shipping lead time The number of working days normally required for moving goods between shipping and receiving points, plus acceptance time in days at the receiving point.

shipping manifest A document that lists the pieces in a shipment. A manifest usually covers an entire load regardless of whether the load is to be delivered to a single destination or to many destinations. Manifests usually list the items, piece count, total weight, and the destination name and address for each destination in the load.

shipping order debit memo The document used to authorize the shipment of rejected material back to the supplier and create a debit entry in accounts payable.

shipping point The location from which material is sent. Antonym: receiving point.

shop floor control A system for using data from the shop floor to maintain and communicate status information on shop orders (manufacturing orders) and on work centers. The major subfunctions of shop floor control are (1) assigning priority of each shop order; (2) maintaining work-in-process quantity information; (3) conveying shop order status information to the office; (4) providing actual output data for capacity-control purposes; (5) providing quantity by location by shop order for work-in-process inventory and accounting purposes; and (6) providing measurement of efficiency, utilization, and productivity of the workforce and machines. Shop-floor control can use order control or flow control to monitor material movement through the facility. Synonym: production activity control.

shop order close-out station A stocking point on the shop floor where completed production of components is transacted (received) into and subsequently transacted (issued) to assembly or other downstream operations. This technique is used to reduce material handling by avoiding the need to move items into and out of stockrooms while simultaneously enabling a high degree of inventory record accuracy.

shop planning The function of coordinating the availability of material handling, material, resources, setup, and tooling so that an operation or job can be done on a particular machine. Shop planning is often part of the dispatching function. The term *shop planning* is sometimes used interchangeably with *dispatching*, although dispatching does not necessarily include shop planning. For example, the selection of jobs might be handled by the centralized dispatching function, while the actual shop planning might be done by the foreman or a representative.

shortage cost The marginal profit that is lost when a customer orders an item that is not immediately available in stock.

shortest processing time rule (SPT) A dispatching rule that directs the sequencing of jobs in ascending order by processing time. If this rule is followed, most jobs at a work center per time period will be processed. As a result, the average lateness of jobs at the work center is minimized, but some jobs will be very late. Synonym: smallest processing time rule.

shrinkage Reductions of actual quantities of items in stock, in process, or in transit. The loss may be caused by scrap, theft, deterioration, evaporation, and so on.

shrinkage factor A percentage factor used to compensate for the expected loss during the manufacturing cycle of an item. This factor differs from the scrap factor in that it affects all components of the item, where the scrap factor relates to only one component's usage. Synonym: shrinkage rate.

sigma A Greek letter (Σ) commonly used to designate the standard deviation of a population.

significant part number A part number that is intended to convey certain information, such as the source of the part, the material in the part, or the shape of the part. Using numbers to represent this information usually makes these part numbers longer than corresponding nonsignificant part numbers. Antonym: nonsignificant part number.

significant variances Those differences between planned and actual performance that exceed established thresholds and that require further review, analysis, and action.

simple moving average A moving average in which the oldest data point is dropped and the newest data point is included in the calculation. All data points are assigned equal weights. See: *moving average, weighted moving average.*

simplex algorithm A procedure for solving a general linear programming problem.

simulation (1) The technique of using representative or artificial data to reproduce in a model various conditions that are likely to occur in the actual performance of a system. It is frequently used to test the behavior of a system under different operating policies. (2) Within MRP II, using the operational data to perform what-if evaluations of alternative plans to answer the question, Can we do it? If yes, the simulation can then be run in the financial mode to help answer the question, Do we really want to? See: *what-if analysis.*

single sourcing A method whereby a purchased part is supplied by only one supplier. Traditional manufacturers usually have at least two suppliers for each component part they purchase to ensure continuity of supply and (more so) to foster price competition between the suppliers. A JIT manufacturer will frequently have only one supplier for a purchased part so that close relationships can be established with a smaller number of suppliers. These close relationships (and mutual interdependence) foster high quality, reliability, short lead times, and cooperative action. Antonym: multi-sourcing. See: *sole source.*

single-card kanban system Synonym: one-card kanban system.

single-digit setup (SDS) The idea of performing setups in less than 10 minutes. See: *single-minute exchange of die.*

single-factor productivity The average amount of a given product (output) attributed to a unit of a given resource (input). Factors include labor and capital. Synonym: partial productivity factor.

single-level backflush A form of backflush that reduces inventory of only the parts used in the next level down in an assembly or subassembly.

single-level bill of material A display of components that are directly used in a parent item. It shows only the relationships one level down.

single-level where-used Single-level where-used for a component lists each parent in which that component is directly used and in what quantity. This information is usually made available through the technique known as implosion.

single-period inventory models Inventory models used to define economical or profit-maximizing lot-size quantities when an item is ordered or produced only once, for example, newspapers, calendars, tax guides, greeting cards, or periodicals, while facing uncertain demands. Synonym: static inventory models.

single-source supplier A company that is selected to have 100 percent of the business for a part although alternate suppliers are available. See: *sole-source supplier.*

six-sigma quality A term used generally to indicate that a process is well controlled: tolerance limits are ± 6 sigma from the centerline in a control chart. The term is usually associated with Motorola, which named one of its key operational initiatives Six-Sigma Quality.

skew The degree of nonsymmetry shown by a frequency of probability distribution.

skill-based compensation A method of employee compensation that bases the employee's wage rate on the number of skills the employee is qualified to perform. People who are qualified to do a wider variety of skills are paid more. See: *labor grade.*

skills inventories An organized file of information on each employee's skills, abilities, knowledge, and experience, usually maintained by a personnel office. See: *labor grade.*

SKU Abbreviation and acronym (pronounced skew) for stockkeeping unit.

slack Synonyms: float, slack time.

slack time In project management, the amount of time that an activity may be delayed from its early start without delaying the project finish date. Synonym: slack.

slack time rule A dispatching rule that directs the sequencing of jobs based on slack time. Slack time is equal to (days left until due date $\times$ hrs/day) minus standard hours of work left on this specific job: for example, $(5 \times 8) - 12 = 28$ hours of slack. The lower the amount of slack time, the higher the priority in sequencing of jobs.

slow-moving items Those inventory items with a low turnover, that is, items in inventory that have a relatively low rate of usage compared to the normal amount of inventory carried.

smoothing The process of averaging data by a mathematical process or by curve fitting, such as the least-squares method or exponential smoothing.

smoothing constant In exponential smoothing, the weighting factor that is applied to the most recent demand, observation, or error. In this case, the error is defined as the difference between actual demand and the forecast for the most recent period. The weighting factor is represented by the symbol α. Theoretically, the range of α is 0.0 to 1. Synonym: alpha factor.

sole source The situation in which the supply of a product is available from only one organization. Usually technical barriers such as patents preclude other suppliers from offering the product. See: *single source.*

sole-source supplier The only supplier capable of meeting (usually technical) requirements for an item. See: *single-source supplier.*

source document An original written or printed record of some type that is to be converted into machine-readable form.

source inspection Inspection at the source of supply or of production, for example, the supplier or the work center, as opposed to inspection following receipt from the supplier or following transfer of the items from one work center to another.

sourcing The process of identifying a company that provides a needed good or service.

SPC Abbreviation for statistical process control.

specific performance A contract remedy requiring defendants to do what they have contracted to do.

specification A clear, complete, and accurate statement of the technical requirements of a material, an item, or a service, and of the procedure to determine if the requirements are met.

split delivery A method by which a larger quantity is ordered on a purchase order to secure a lower price, but delivery is divided into smaller quantities and spread out over several dates to control inventory investment, save storage space, and the like.

split lot A manufacturing order quantity that has been divided into two or more smaller quantities, usually after the order has been released. The quantities of a split lot may be worked on in parallel, or a portion of the original quantity may be sent ahead to a subsequent operation to be worked on while work on the remainder of the quantity is being completed at the current operation. The purpose of splitting a lot is to reduce the lead time of the order.

spot demand Demand, having a short lead time, that is difficult to estimate. Usually supply for this demand is provided at a premium price.

SPT Abbreviation for shortest-processing-time rule.

SQC Abbreviation for statistical quality control.

SQL Abbreviation for structured query language.

stabilization stock An inventory that is carried on hand or above the base inventory level to provide protection against incurring overtime or downtime.

stacked lead time Synonym: cumulative lead time.

staging Pulling material for an order from inventory before the material is required. This action is often taken to identify shortages, but it can lead to increased problems in availability and inventory accuracy.

staging and consolidation Physically moving material from the packing area to a staging area, based on a prescribed set of instructions related to a particular outbound vehicle or delivery route, often for shipment consolidation purposes.

standard (1) An established norm against which measurements are compared. (2) An established norm of productivity defined in terms of units output per set time (minutes per unit). (3) The time allowed to perform a specific job, including quantity of work to be produced. See: *standard time.*

standard allowance The established or accepted amount by which the normal time for an operation is increased within an area, plant, or industry to compensate for the usual amount of personal, fatigue, and unavoidable delay times.

standard batch quantity (SBQ) The quantity of a parent that is used as the basis for specifying the material requirements for production. The quantity per is expressed as the quantity to make the SBQ, not to make only one of the parent. Often used by manufacturers that use some components in standard quantities or by process-related manufacturers. Synonym: run size.

standard containers Predetermined, specifically sized containers used for storing and moving components. These containers protect the components from damage and simplify the task of counting components.

standard cost-accounting system A cost-accounting system that uses cost units determined before production for estimating the cost of an order or product. For management control purposes, the standards are compared to actual costs, and variances are computed.

standard costs The target costs of an operation, process, or product, including direct material, direct labor, and overhead charges.

standard deviation A measurement of dispersion of data or of a variable. The standard deviation is computed by finding the differences between the average and actual observations, squaring each difference, adding the squared differences, dividing by $n - 1$ (for a sample), and taking the square root of the result. See: *estimate of error.*

standard error A measurement of the variability of statistics such as the sample mean.

standard industrial classification (SIC) Classification codes that are used to categorize companies into industry groups.

standard ratio A relationship based on a sample distribution by value for a particular company. When the standard ratio for a particular company is known, certain aggregate inventory predictions can be made, for example, the amount of inventory increase that would be required to provide a particular increase in customer service.

standard time The length of time that should be required to (1) set up a given machine or operation and (2) run one batch or one or more parts, assemblies, or end products through that operation. This time is used in determining machine requirements and labor requirements. Standard time assumes an average worker following prescribed methods and allows time for personal rest to overcome fatigue and unavoidable delays. It is also frequently used as a basis for incentive pay systems and as a basis of allocating overhead in cost accounting systems. Synonym: standard hours. See: *standard.*

standardization (1) The process of designing and altering products, parts, processes, and procedures to establish and use standard specifications for them and their components. (2) Reduction of the total numbers of parts and materials used and products, models, or grades produced. (3) The function of bringing a raw ingredient into standard (acceptable) range per the specification before introduction to the main process.

start date In project management, the time an activity begins; this may be defined as an actual start date or a planned start date.

start-to-finish In project management, a network requirement that activity A must start before subsequent activity B can finish. See: *logical relationship.*

startup That period starting with the date of initial operation during which the unit is brought up to acceptable production capacity and quality within estimated production costs. Startup is the activity that commences on the date of initial activity and has significant duration on most projects, but it is often confused (used interchangeably) with date of initial operation.

startup audit The technique of having an implementation team tour or visit the implementation site on a frequent basis and use the management-by-walking-around technique to identify problems and solutions.

startup costs The extra operating costs to bring the plant or product on-stream incurred between the completion of construction and the start of normal operations. In addition to the difference between actual operating costs during that period and normal costs, they include employee training, equipment tests, process adjustments, salaries and travel expenses of temporary labor staff and consultants, report writing, poststartup monitoring, and associated overhead. Additional capital required to correct plant problems may be included. Startup costs are sometimes capitalized.

statement of work (1) A description of products to be supplied under a contract. (2) In projection management, the first project-planning document that should be prepared. It describes the purpose, history, deliverables, and measurable success indicators for a project. It captures the support required from the customer and identifies contingency plans for events that could throw the project off course. Because the project must be sold to management, staff, and review groups, the statement of work should be a persuasive document.

statistical control The situation in which variations among the observed samples can be attributed to a constant system of chance causes.

statistical inventory control The use of statistical methods to model the demands and lead times experienced by an inventory item or group of items. Demand during lead time and between reviews can be modeled, and reorder points, safety stocks, and maximum inventory levels can be defined to strive for desired customer service levels, inventory investments, manufacturing and distribution efficiency, and targeted returns on investments. Synonym: scientific inventory control. See: *Fixed-reorder-quantity inventory model.*

Statistical-order-point system Synonym: order-point system.

statistical process control (SPC) The application of statistical techniques to monitor and adjust an operation. Often the term *statistical process control* is used interchangeably with *statistical quality control.*

statistical quality control (SQL) The application of statistical techniques to control quality. Often the term *statistical process control* is used interchangeably with *statistical quality control,* although statistical quality control includes acceptance sampling as well as statistical process control.

statistical safety stock calculations The mathematical determination of safety stock quantities considering forecast errors, lot sizes, desired customer service levels, and the ratio of lead time to the length of the forecast period. Safety stock is frequently the product of the appropriate safety factor and the standard deviation or mean absolute deviation of the distribution of demand forecast errors.

statute of limitations A statute restricting the length of time in which a lawsuit may be filed.

step-function scheduling Scheduling logic that recognizes run length to be a multiple of the number of batches to be run rather than simply a linear relationship of run time to total production quantity.

stochastic models Models in which uncertainty is explicitly considered in the analysis.

stock (1) Items in inventory. (2) Stored products or service parts ready for sale, as distinguished from stores, which are usually components or raw materials.

stock dividend A dividend paid to shareholders in stock rather than cash.

stock order An order to replenish stock, as opposed to a production order to make a particular product for a specific customer.

stock status A periodic report showing the inventory on hand and usually showing the inventory on order and some sales or usage history for the products that are covered in the stock status report.

stockkeeping unit (SKU) (1) An inventory item. For example, a shirt in six colors and five sizes would represent 30 different SKUs. (2) In a distribution system, an item at a particular geographic location. For example, one product stocked at the plant and at six different distribution centers would represent seven SKUs.

stockless purchasing Buying material, parts, supplies, and so on for direct use by the departments involved, as opposed to receiving them into stores and subsequently issuing them to the department. The intent is to reduce inventory investment, increase cash flow, reduce material handling and storage, and provide better service. See: *dock-to-stock inventory.*

stockout A lack of materials, components, or finished goods that are needed. See: *backorder.*

stockout costs The costs associated with a stockout. Those costs may include lost sales, backorder costs, expediting, and additional manufacturing and purchasing costs.

stockout percentage A measure of the effectiveness with which a company responds to actual demand or requirements. The stockout percentage can be a measurement of total orders containing a stockout to total orders, or of line items incurring stockouts to total line items ordered during a period. One formula is: stockout percentage = (1 − customer service ratio) × 100 percent. Antonym: customer service ratio.

stockpoint A designated location in an active area of operation into which material is placed and from which it is taken. Not necessarily a stockroom isolated from activity, it is a way of tracking and controlling active material.

storage The retention of parts or products for future use or shipment.

storage costs A subset of inventory carrying costs, including the cost of warehouse utilities, material handling personnel, equipment maintenance, building maintenance, and security personnel.

stores (1) Stored materials used in making a product. (2) The room in which stored components, parts, assemblies, tools, fixtures, and so forth are kept.

straight-line depreciation A method of depreciation whereby the amount to be recovered (written off as an expense) is spread uniformly over the estimated life of the asset in terms of time periods. See: *depreciation.*

strategic business unit (SBU) An approach to strategic planning that develops a plan based on products. A company's products are typically grouped into strategic business units (SBUs) with each SBU evaluation in terms of strengths and weaknesses vis-à-vis similar business units made and marketed by competitors. The units are evaluated in terms of their competitive strengths, their relative advantages, life cycles, and cash flow patterns.

strategic drivers Factors that influence business unit and manufacturing strategies.

strategic mission Defines the business, including the goods or services offered, the scope of coverage (customers and markets), and any geographic scope for the business. The mission is used to define the extent of external and internal analysis (strengths, weaknesses, opportunities, and threats, often called SWOT analysis) necessary to determine specific action plans, often called strategies.

strategic plan The plan for how to marshal and determine actions to support the mission, goals, and objectives of an organization. Generally includes an organization's explicit mission, goals, and objectives and the specific actions needed to achieve those goals and objectives. Synonym: strategy. See: *business plan, operational plan, strategic planning, tactical plan.*

strategic sourcing The development and management of supplier relationships to acquire goods and services in a way that aids in achieving the immediate needs of a business. It is entirely aligned with the sourcing portion of managing the procurement process. See: *tactical buying.*

subassembly An assembly that is used at the next level of the bill of material to build another assembly.

suboptimization A solution to a problem that is best from a narrow point of view but not from a higher or overall company point of view. For example, a department manager who would not have employees work overtime to minimize the department's operating expense may cause lost sales and a reduction in overall company profitability.

subplant An organizational structure within a factory, consisting of a compact entrepreneurial unit, either process oriented or product oriented and structured to achieve maximum productivity.

summarized bill of material A form of multilevel bill of material that lists all the parts and their quantities required in a given product structure. Unlike the indented bill of material, it does not list the levels of manufacture and lists a component only once for the total quantity used.

sunk cost (1) The unrecovered balance of an investment. It is a cost, already paid, that is not relevant to the decision concerning the future that is being made. Capital already invested that for some reason cannot be retrieved. (2) A past cost that has no relevance with respect to future receipts and disbursements of a facility undergoing an economic study. This concept implies that since a past outlay is the same regardless of the alternative selected, it should not influence the choice between alternatives.

super bill of material A type of planning bill, located at the top level in the structure, that ties together various modular bills (and possibly a common parts bill) to define an entire product or product family. The quantity per relationship of the super bill to its modules represents the forecasted percentage of demand of each module. The master-scheduled quantities of the super bill explode to create requirements for the modules that also are master scheduled. See: *pseudo bill of material.*

superflush A technique to relieve all components down to the lowest level using the complete bill of material, based on the count of finished units produced or transferred to finished goods inventory.

supplier (1) Provider of goods or services. See: *vendor.* (2) Seller with whom the buyer does business, as opposed to vendor, which is a generic term referring to all sellers in the marketplace.

supplier alternative A seller other than the primary one. The supplier alternative may or may not supply the items purchased but is usually approved to supply those items.

supplier clustering Deliberately sole sourcing remote suppliers within a small geographical area to facilitate joint shipments of what would otherwise be less-than-truckload quantities.

supplier lead time The amount of time that normally elapses between the time an order is received by a supplier and the time the order is shipped. Synonym: vendor lead time. See: *purchasing lead time.*

supplier number A numerical code used to distinguish one supplier from another.

supplier quality assurance The confidence that a supplier's goods or services will fulfill its customers' needs. This confidence is achieved by creating a relationship between the customer and supplier that ensures that the product will be fit for use with minimal corrective action and inspection. According to J. M. Juran, nine primary activities are needed: (1) define product and program quality requirements, (2) evaluate alternative suppliers, (3) select suppliers, (4) conduct joint quality planning, (5) cooperate with the supplier during the execution of the contract, (6) obtain proof of conformance to requirements, (7) certify qualified suppliers, (8) conduct quality-improvement programs as required, and (9) create and use supplier quality ratings.

supplies Materials used in manufacturing that are not normally charged to finished production, such as cutting and lubricating oils, machine repair parts, glue, or tape. Synonyms: general stores, indirect materials.

supply (1) The quantity of goods available for use. (2) The actual of planned replenishment of a product of component. The replenishment quantities are created in response to a demand for the product or component or in anticipation of such a demand.

supply chain design The determination of how to structure a supply chain. Design decisions include the selection of partners, the location and capacity of warehouse and production facilities, the products, the modes of transportation, and supporting information systems.

supply chain execution Execution-oriented software applications for effective procurement and supply of goods and services across a supply chain. It includes manufacturing, warehouse, and transportation execution systems and systems providing visibility across the supply chain.

supply chain management The design, planning, execution, control, and monitoring of supply chain activities with the objective of creating net value, building a competitive infrastructure, leveraging worldwide logistics, synchronizing supply with demand, and measuring performance globally.

supply chain planning The determination of a set of policies and procedures that govern the operation of a supply chain. Planning includes the determination of marketing channels, promotions, respective quantities and timing, inventory and replenishment policies, and production policies. Planning establishes the parameters within which the supply chain will operate.

support costs In activity-based cost accounting, activity costs not directly related with producing a product, such as the cost of the information system.

surge capacity The ability to meet sudden, unexpected increases in demand by expanding production with existing personnel and equipment.

surplus A situation in which an oversupply exists at a given price and a decline in price would eliminate the surplus.

sustaining activity In activity-based cost accounting, an activity that is not directly beneficial to any specific cost object but does benefit the organization as a whole.

SWOT analysis An analysis of the strengths, weaknesses, opportunities, and threats of and to an organization. SWOT analysis is useful in developing strategy.

synchronized production A manufacturing management philosophy that includes a consistent set of principles, procedures, and techniques in which every action is evaluated in terms of the global goal of the system. Both kanban, which is a part of the JIT philosophy, and drum-buffer-rope, which is a part of the theory-of-constraints philosophy, represent synchronized production control approaches. Synonym: synchronous manufacturing. See: *drum-buffer-rope, kanban, synchronous scheduling.*

synchronous scheduling Scheduling processes (kanban in just-in-time and drum-buffer-rope in theory-of-constraints environments) that focus on synchronizing all operations to the constraint of the system. See: *synchronized production.*

T

tactical buying The purchasing process focused on transactions and nonstrategic material buying. It is closely aligned with the "ordering" portion of executing the purchasing transaction process. The characteristics for tactical buying include stable, limited fluctuations, defined standard specifications, noncritical to production, no delivery issues, and high reliability concerning quality standard material with very little concern for rejects. See: *strategic sourcing.*

tactical planning The process of developing a set of tactical plans (e.g., production plan, sales plan, marketing plan, and so on). Two approaches to tactical planning exist for linking tactical plans to strategic plans—production planning and sales and operations planning. See: *operational planning, strategic planning, tactical plan.*

Taguchi methodology A concept of offline quality control methods conducted at the product- and process-design stages in the product development cycle. This concept, expressed by Genichi Taguchi, encompasses three phases of product design: system design, parameter design, and tolerance design. The goal is to reduce quality loss by reducing the variability of the product's characteristics during the parameter phase of product development. Synonym: Taguchi methods.

takt time Sets the pace of production to match the rate of customer demand and becomes the heartbeat of any lean production system. It is computed as the available production time divided by the rate of customer demand. For example, assume demand is 10,000 units per month, or 500 units per day, and planned available capacity is 420 minutes per day. The takt time – 420 minutes per day/500 units per day = 0.84 minutes per unit. This takt time means that a unit should be planned to exit the production system on average every 0.84 minutes. Synonym: tact time.

tangibles Things that can be quantitatively measured or valued, such as the costs of physical assets.

tank inventory Goods stored in tanks. Theses goods may be raw materials, intermediates, or finished goods. The description of inventory as tank inventory indicates the necessity of calculating the quantity on hand from the levels within the tanks.

tardiness For jobs that are late, the delivery date minus the due date. See: *earliness, lateness.*

tare weight The weight of a substance, obtained by deducting the weight of the empty container from the gross weight of the full container.

target costing The process of designing a product to meet a specific cost objective. Target costing involves setting the planned selling price, then subtracting the desired profit as well as marketing and distribution costs, thus leaving the required manufacturing or target cost.

target inventory level In a min-max inventory system, the equivalent of the maximum. The target inventory is equal to the order point plus a variable order quantity. It is often called an order-up-to inventory level and is used in a periodic review system. Synonym: order-up-to level.

target market (1) A fairly homogenous group of customers to whom a company wishes to appeal. (2) A definable group of buyers to which a marketer has decided to market.

target marketing The process of focusing marketing activities specifically on those people who are most likely to buy a company's products and services. Data gathered on people who use the Internet are enabling companies to identify and focus on more likely candidates.

task (1) In project management, the lowest level to which work can be subdivided on a project. (2) In activity-based cost accounting, a task, a subdivision of an activity, is the least amount of work. Tasks are used to describe activities.

team A cross-functional group of employees assembled for a period of time to accomplish either a specific task or ongoing production of goods and services. See: *team oriented.*

team design/engineering Synonym: participative design/engineering.

teardown bill of material Synonym: disassembly bill of material.

teardown time The time needed to remove a setup from a machine or facility. Teardown is an element of manufacturing lead time, but it is often allowed for in setup or run time rather than separately. See: *teardown.*

technologies The terms, concepts, philosophies, hardware, software, and other attributes used in a field, industrial sector, or business function.

technology transfer The transmission of technology (e.g., knowledge, skills, software, hardware, etc.) from one country, organization, business, or entity to another country, organization, business, or entity.

theory of constraints (TOC) A management philosophy developed by Dr. Eliyahu M. Goldratt that can be viewed as three separate but interrelated areas—logistics, performance measurement, and logical thinking. Logistics include drum-buffer-rope scheduling, buffer management, and VAT analysis. Performance measurement includes throughput, inventory and operating expense, and the five focusing steps. Thinking process tools are important in identifying the root problem (current reality tree), identifying and expanding win-win solutions (evaporating cloud and future reality tree), and developing implementation plans (prerequisite tree and transition tree). Synonym: constraint theory. See: *constraint management.*

third-party logistics A buyer and supplier team with a third party that provides product delivery services. This third party may provide added supply chain expertise.

third-party logistics company A company that manages all or part of another company's product delivery operations.

third-party warehousing The outsourcing of the warehousing function by the seller of the goods.

Thomas Register A privately produced reference set that includes a listing of part suppliers by product type and geographic area.

throughput (1) The total volume of production through a facility (machine, work center, department, plant, or network of plants). (2) In the theory of constraints, the rate at which the system (firm) generates money through sales. Throughput is a separate concept from output. See: *machine-limited capacity.*

time bucket A number of days of data summarized into a columnar display. A weekly time bucket would contain all of the relevant data for an entire week. Weekly time buckets are considered to be the largest possible (at least in the near and medium term) to permit effective MRP.

time buffer The amount of time that materials are released to the production process ahead of the scheduled due date. Time buffers protect against uncertainty.

time card A document recording attendance time, often used for indicating the number of hours for which wages are to be paid. Synonym: clock card.

time fence A policy or guideline established to note where various restrictions or changes in operating procedures take place. For example, changes to the master production schedule can be accomplished easily beyond the cumulative lead time, while changes inside the cumulative lead time become increasingly more difficult to a point at which changes should be resisted. Time fences can be used to define these points. See: *demand time fence, hedge, planning time fence.*

time-period safety stock A safety stock that is based on usage over a designated time frame. The period can be set as days, weeks, or months. Safety stock varies directly with the demand. This differs from statistical-based safety stocks in that the amount is not based on deviation from demand.

time series A set of data that is distributed over time, such as demand, supply, and inventories, by time period. Various patterns of demand must be considered in time series analysis: seasonal, trend, cyclical, and random.

time series analysis Analysis of any variable classified by time in which the values of the variable are functions of the time periods. Time series analysis is used in forecasting. A time series consists of seasonal, cyclical, trend, and random components. See: *cyclical component, random component, seasonal component, trend component.*

time standard The predetermined times allowed for the performance of a specific job. The standard will often consist of two parts, that for machine setup and that for actual running. The standard can be developed through observation of the actual work (time study), summation of standard micromotion times (predetermined or synthetic time standards), or approximation (historical job times).

time ticket An operator-entered labor claim. Synonym: job ticket.

time value of money (1) The cumulative effect of elapsed time on the money value of an event, based on the earning power of equivalent invested funds. See: *future worth, present value.* (2) The interest rate that capital is expected to earn.

time-based competition (TBC) A corporate strategy that emphasizes time as the vehicle for achieving and maintaining a sustainable competitive edge. Its characteristics are (1) it deals only with those lead times that are important to the customers; (2) the lead-time reductions must involve decreases in both the mean and the variance; and (3) the lead-time reductions must be achieved through system/process analysis (the processes must be changed to reduce lead times). TBC is a broad-based strategy. Reductions in lead times are achieved by changing the processes and the decision structures used to design, produce, and deliver products to the customers. TBC involves design, manufacturing, and logistical processes.

time-based order system Synonym: fixed-reorder-cycle inventory model.

time to market The total time required to design, build, and deliver a product (timed from concept to delivery). See: *procurement lead time.*

time to product The total time required to receive, fill, and deliver an order for an existing product to a customer, timed from the moment that the customer places the order until the customer receives the product. See: *purchasing lead time.*

TOC Abbreviation for theory of constraints.

TOC performance measures In the theory of constraints, throughput, inventory, and operating expense are considered performance measures that link operational decisions to organizational profit.

tolerance Allowable departure from a nominal value established by design engineers that is deemed acceptable for the functioning of the good or service over its life cycle.

tolerance limits (1) The upper and lower extreme values permitted by the tolerance. (2) In work measurement, the limits between which a specified operation time value or other work unit will be expected to vary. See: *lower specification limit, upper specification limit.*

tool Any instrument, such as a saw blade, that is the working part of a machine.

tool calibration frequency The recommended length of time between tool calibrations. It is normally expressed in days.

tool number The identification number assigned to reference and control a specific tool.

top management commitment (quality) In the total-quality-management philosophy, participation of the highest-level official in the organization's quality-improvement efforts. Participation includes establishing and serving on a quality committee, establishing quality policies and goals, deploying those goals to lower levels of the organization, providing the resources and training that the lower levels need to achieve the goals, participating in quality-improvement teams, reviewing organizationwide progress, recognizing those who have performed well, and revising the current reward system to reflect the importance of achieving the quality goals.

total cost concept In logistics, the idea that all logistical decisions that provide equal service levels should favor the option that minimizes the total of all logistical costs and not be used on cost reductions in one area alone, such as lower transportation charges.

total cost curve (1) In cost-volume-profit (breakeven) analysis, the total cost curve is composed of total fixed and variable costs per unit multiplied by the number of units provided. Breakeven quantity occurs when the total cost curve and total sales revenue curve intersect. See: *break-even chart, break-even point.* (2) In inventory theory, the total cost curve for an inventory item is the sum of the costs of acquiring and carrying the item. See: *economic order quantity.*

total costs All the costs of operating a firm; total variable costs plus total fixed costs.

total float In project management, the length of time an activity can be late without delaying succeeding activities. See: *float, free float, independent float.*

total lead time Synonym: lead time.

total productive maintenance (TPM) Preventive maintenance plus continuing efforts to adapt, modify, and refine equipment to increase flexibility, reduce material handling, and promote continuous flows. It is operator-oriented maintenance with the involvement of all qualified employees in all maintenance activities.

total quality control (TQC) The process of creating and producing the total composite good and service characteristics by marketing, engineering, manufacturing, purchasing, and the like, through which the good and service will meet the expectations of consumers.

total quality engineering (TQE) The discipline of designing quality into the product and manufacturing processes by understanding the needs of the customer and performance capabilities of the equipment. See: *design for quality.*

total quality management (TQM) A term coined to describe Japanese-style management approaches to quality improvement. Since then, total quality management (TQM) has taken on many meanings. Simply put, TQM is a management approach to long-term success through customer satisfaction. TQM is based on the participation of all members of an organization in improving processes, goods, services, and the culture in which they work. The methods for implementing this approach are found in teachings of such quality leaders as Philip B. Crosby, W. Edwards Deming, Armand V. Feigenbaum, Kaoru Ishikawa, J. M. Juran, and Genichi Taguchi.

total value analysis A method of economic analysis in which a model expresses the dependent variable of interest as a function of independent variables, some of which are controllable.

tracking signal The ratio of the cumulative algebraic sum of the deviations between the forecasts and the actual values to the mean absolute deviation. Used to signal when the validity of the forecasting model might be in doubt. See: *forecast error, mean absolute deviation.*

transactions Individual events reported to the computer system, for example, issues, receipts, transfers, adjustments.

transfer batch The quantity of an item moved between sequential work centers during production. See: *batch, overlap quantity.*

transfer price Price that one segment (subunit, department, division, etc.) of an organization charges for a good or service supplied to another segment of the same organization.

transfer pricing The pricing of goods or service transferred from one segment of a business to another. See: *interplant transfer.*

transformation process The process of converting inputs into finished goods or services. In a service firm, the input may be a customer. Synonym: transformation system. See: *manufacturing process, production process.*

transit inventory Inventory in transit between manufacturing and stocking locations. See: *transportation inventory.*

transit time A standard allowance that is assumed on any given order for the movement of items from one operation to the next. Synonym: travel time.

transport stocks A carrier material to move solids in solution or slurry or to dilute ingredients to safe levels for reactions.

transportation inventory Inventory that is in transit between locations. See: *pipeline stock, transit inventory.*

traveling purchase requisition A purchase requisition designed for repetitive use. After a purchase order has been prepared for the goods requisitioned, the form is returned to the originator, who holds it until a repurchase of the goods is required. The name is derived from the repetitive travel between the originating and purchasing departments. Synonym: traveling requisition.

traveling requisition Synonym: traveling purchase requisition.

trend General upward or downward movement of a variable over time, for example, demand or process attribute.

trend analysis An analysis to determine whether trend (general upward or downward change) exists in data. See: *trend forecasting models.*

trend component A component of demand, usually describing the impact of increasing or decreasing growth on demand.

trend control chart A control chart in which the deviation of the subgroup average, *X*-bar, from an expected trend in the process level is used to evaluate the stability of a process.

trend forecasting models Methods for forecasting sales data when a definite upward or downward pattern exists. Models include double exponential smoothing, regression, and triple smoothing.

trigger level Synonym: order point.

triple smoothing A method of exponential smoothing that accounts for accelerating or decelerating trends, such as would be experienced in a fad cycle. Synonym: third-order smoothing.

truckload lot A truck shipment that qualifies for a lower freight rate because it meets a minimum weight and/or volume.

turnover (1) Synonym: inventory turnover. (2) In the United Kingdom and certain other countries, annual sales volume.

turnover ratio An indicator of whether a company is using its assets efficiently. It is measured by dividing sales by average assets during a particular period.

two-bin inventory system A type of fixed-order system in which inventory is carried in two bins. A replenishment quantity is ordered when the first bin (working) is empty. During the replenishment lead time, material is used from the second bin. When the material is received, the second bin (which contains a quantity to cover demand during lead time plus some safety stock) is refilled and the excess is put into the working bin. At this time, stock is drawn from the first bin until it is again exhausted. This term is also used loosely to describe any fixed-order system even when physical "bins" do not exist. Synonym: bin reserve system. See: *visual review system.*

two-card kanban system A kanban system in which a move card and production card are employed. The move card authorizes the movement of a specific number of parts from a source to a point of use. The move card is attached to the standard container of parts during movement to the point of use of the parts. The production card authorizes the production of a given number of parts for use or replenishment. Synonym: dual-card kanban system. See: *one-card kanban system.*

two-level master schedule A master scheduling approach in which a planning bill of material is used to master schedule an end product or family, along with selected key features (options and accessories). See: *hedge, multilevel master schedule, production forecast.*

U

***U* chart** A control chart for evaluating the stability of a process in terms of the average count of events of a given classification per unit occurring in a sample. Synonym: count-per-unit chart.

U-lines Production lines shaped like the letter U. The shape allows works to easily perform several nonsequential tasks without much walk time. The number of workstations in a U-line is usually determined by line balancing. U-lines promote communication.

UCL Abbreviation for upper control limit.

unattainable capability The portion of the production capability that cannot be attained. This is typically caused by factors such as equipment unavailability, suboptimal scheduling, or resource limitations.

uncertainty Unknown future events that cannot be predicted quantitatively within useful limits, such as an accident that destroys facilities, a major strike, or an innovation that makes existing products obsolete.

undertime A condition occurring when more personnel are on the payroll than are required to produce the planned output.

uniform-delivered pricing A type of geographic pricing policy in which all customers pay the same delivered price regardless of their location. A company allocates the total transportation cost among all customers.

unit cost Total labor, material, and overhead cost for one unit of production, for example, one part, one gallon, one pound.

units-of-production depreciation A method of depreciation whereby the amount to be recovered (written off as a period expense) is calculated based on estimated life of the equipment in units to be produced over the life and the number of units produced in a given time period. See: *depreciation.*

universe The population, or large set of data, from which samples are drawn. Usually assumed to be infinitely large or at least very large relative to the sample.

upstream Used as a relative reference within a firm or supply chain to indicate moving in the direction of the raw material supplier.

URL Abbreviation for uniform resource locator.

usage The number of units or dollars of an inventory item consumed over time.

usage variance Deviation of the actual consumption of materials as compared to the standard.

user-friendly Characteristic of computer software or hardware that makes it easy for the user or operator to use the programs or equipment with a minimum of specialized knowledge or recourse to operating manuals.

utilization (1) A measure (usually expressed as a percentage) of how intensively a resource is being used to produce a good or service. Utilization compares actual time used to available time. Traditionally, utilization is the ratio of direct time charged (run time plus setup time) to the clock time available. Utilization is a percentage between 0 percent and 100 percent that is equal to 100 percent minus the percentage of time lost due to unavailability of machines, tools, workers, and so forth. See: *efficiency, lost time factor, productivity.* (2) In the theory of constraints, utilization is the ratio of the time the resource is needed to support the constraint to the time available for the resource, expressed as a percentage. See: *activation.*

V

value added (1) In accounting, the addition of direct labor, direct material, and allocated overhead assigned at an operation. It is the cost rollup as a part goes through a manufacturing process to finished inventory. (2) In current manufacturing terms, the actual increase of utility from the viewpoint of the customer as a part is transformed from raw material to finished inventory. It is the contribution made by an operation or a plant to the final usefulness and value of a product, as seen by the customer. The objective is to eliminate all non-value-added activities in producing and providing a good or service.

value analysis The systematic use of techniques that identify a required function, establish a value for that function, and finally provide that function at the lowest overall cost. This approach focuses on the functions of an item rather than the methods of producing the present product design.

value chain The functions within a company that add value to the goods or services that the organization sells to customers and for which it receives payment.

value chain analysis An examination of all links a company uses to produce and deliver its product and services, starting from the origination point and continuing through delivery to the final customer.

value engineering and/or analysis A disciplined approach to the elimination of waste from products or processes through an investigative process that focuses on the functions to be performed and whether such functions add value to the good or service.

value stream The processes of creating, producing, and delivering a good or service to the market. For a good, the value stream encompasses the raw material supplier, the manufacture and assembly of the good, and the distribution network. For a service, the value stream consists of suppliers, support personnel and technology, the service "producer," and the distribution channel. The value stream may be controlled by a single business or a network of several businesses.

variable A quantity that can assume any of a given set of values. Antonym: constant.

variable cost An operating cost that varies directly with a change of one unit in the production volume, for example, direct materials consumed or sales commissions.

variable costing An inventory valuation method in which only variable production costs are applied to the product; fixed factory overhead is not assigned to the product. Traditionally, variable production costs are direct labor, direct material, and variable overhead costs. Variable costing can be helpful for internal management analysis but is not widely accepted for external financial reporting. For inventory-order-quantity purposes, however, the unit costs must include both the variable and allocated fixed costs to be compatible with the other terms in the order quantity formula. For make-or-buy decisions, variable costing should be used rather than full-absorption costing. Synonym: direct costing.

variable overhead All manufacturing costs, other than direct labor and direct materials, that vary directly with production volume. Variable overhead is necessary to produce the product but cannot be directly assigned to a specific product.

variable yield The condition that occurs when the output of a process is not consistently repeatable either in quantity, quality, or combinations of these.

variables data Measurement information. Control charts based on variables data include average (X-bar) charts, range (R) charts, and sample standard deviations charts.

variance (1) The difference between the expected (budgeted or planned) value and the actual. (2) In statistics, a measurement of dispersion of data. See: *estimate of error.*

variation A change in data, a characteristic, or a function that is caused by one of four factors: special causes, common causes, or structural variation.

VAT analysis In the theory of constraints, a procedure for determining the general flow of parts and products from raw materials to finished products (logical product structure). A V logical structure starts with one or a few raw materials, and the product expands into a number of different products as it flows through divergent points in its routing. The shape of an A logical structure is dominated by converging points. Many raw materials are fabricated and assembled into a few finished products. A T logical structure consists of numerous similar finished products assembled from common assemblies, subassemblies, and parts. Once the general parts flow is determined, the system control points (gating operations, convergent points, divergent point, constraints, and shipping points) can be identified and managed.

velocity (1) The rate of change of an item with respect to time. See: *inventory turnover, lead time.* (2) In supply chain management, a term used to indicate the relative speed of all transactions, collectively, within a supply chain community. A maximum velocity is most desirable because it indicates higher asset turnover for stockholders and faster order-to-delivery response for customers.

vendor Any seller of an item in the marketplace. See: *supplier.*

vendor managed inventory (VMI) A means of optimizing supply chain performance in which the supplier has access to the customer's inventory data and is responsible for maintaining the inventory level required by the customer. This activity is accomplished by a process in which resupply is done by the vendor through regularly scheduled reviews of the on-site inventory. The on-site inventory is counted, damaged or outdated goods are removed, and the inventory is restocked to predefined levels. The vendor obtains a receipt for the restocked inventory and accordingly invoices the customer. See; continuous replenishment.

vendor measurement The act of measuring the vendor's performance to a contract. Measurements usually cover delivery reliability, lead time, quality, and price.

vendor-owned inventory (VOI) Synonym: consigned stock.

vertical dependency The relationship between a parent item and a component in its bill of material that defines the need for the component based on producing the parent, without regard to the availability of other components at the same level in the bill of material. See: *horizontal dependency.*

vertical display A method of displaying or printing output from an MRP system in which requirements, scheduled receipts, projected balance, and so forth are displayed vertically. Vertical displays are often used in conjunction with bucketless systems. Antonym: horizontal display.

vertical integration The degree to which a firm has decided to directly produce multiple value-adding stages from raw material to the sale of the product to the ultimate consumer. The more steps in the sequence, the greater the vertical integration. A manufacturer that decides to begin producing parts, components, and materials that it normally purchases is said to be backward integrated. Likewise, a manufacturer that decides to take over distribution and perhaps sale to the ultimate consumer is said to be forward integrated. See: *backward integration, forward integration.*

vertical merger An alliance of two firms in which one firm is a supplier to the other.

virtual corporation The logical extension of outpartnering. With the virtual corporation, the capabilities and systems of the firm are merged with those of the suppliers, resulting in a new type of corporation in which the boundaries between the suppliers' systems and those of the firm seem to disappear. The virtual corporation is dynamic in that the relationships and structures formed change according to the changing needs of the customer.

virtual factory A changed transformation process most frequently found under the virtual corporation. It is a transformation process that involves merging the capabilities and capacities of the firm with those of its suppliers. Typically, the components provided by the suppliers are those that are not related to a core competency of the firm, while the components managed by the firm are related to core competencies. One ability found in the virtual factory is that it can be restructured quickly in response to changing customer demands and needs.

vision The shared perception of the organization's future: what the organization will achieve and a supporting philosophy. This shared vision must be supported by strategic objectives, strategies, and action plans to move it in the desired direction. See: *vision statement.*

visual inspection Inspection performed without test instruments.

volume flexibility The ability of the transformation process to quickly accommodate large variations in production levels.

W

Wagner-Whitin algorithm A mathematically complex, dynamic lot-sizing technique that evaluates all possible ways of ordering to cover net requirements in each period of the planning horizon to arrive at the theoretically optimum ordering strategy for the entire net requirements schedule. See: *discrete order quantity, dynamic lot sizing.*

wait time The time a job remains at a work center after an operation is completed until it is moved to the next operation. It is often expressed as a part of move time. Synonym: idle time.

waiting line theory Synonym: queuing theory.

waiver Authorization to accept an item that, during production or upon inspection, is found to depart from specified requirements, but nevertheless is considered suitable for use as is or after rework.

walkthrough Synonym: pilot test.

wall-to-wall inventory An inventory-management technique in which material enters a plant and is processed though the plant into finished goods without ever having entered a formal stock area. Synonym: four-wall inventory.

wandering bottleneck Describes the problem of a bottleneck seeming to move around from one resource to another. Wandering bottlenecks are "pseudoconstraints." Wandering bottlenecks can be caused by policies such as large lot sizes or transfer batch that is equal to process batch.

warranty A commitment, either expressed or implied, that a certain fact regarding the subject matter of a contract is presently true or will be true. The word should be distinguished from *guarantee*, which means a contract or promise by an entity to answer for the performance of a product or person. Synonyms: general warranty, special warranty. See: *guarantee.*

waste (1) In just-in-time, any activity that does not add value to the good or service in the eyes of the consumer. (2) A by-product of a process or task with unique characteristics requiring special management control. Waste production can usually be planned and somewhat controlled. Scrap is typically not planned and may result from the same production run as waste. See: *hazardous waste.*

waybill A document containing a list of goods with shipping instructions related to a shipment.

weighted moving average An averaging technique in which the data to be averaged are not uniformly weighted but are given values according to their importance. See: *moving average, simple moving average.*

withdrawal (1) Removal of material from stores. (2) A transaction issuing material to a specific location, run, or schedule.

work breakdown structure In project management, a hierarchical description of a project in which each lower level is more detailed.

work center A specific production area, consisting of one or more people and/or machines with identical capabilities, that can be considered as one unit for purposes of capacity-requirement planning and detailed scheduling. Synonym: load center.

work center where-used A listing (constructed from a routing file) of every manufactured item that is routed (primary or secondary) to a given work center.

work in process (WIP) A good or goods in various stages of completion throughout the plant, including all material from raw material that has been released for initial processing up to completely processed material awaiting final inspection and acceptance as finished goods inventory. Many accounting systems also include the value of semifinished stock and components in this category. Synonym: in-process inventory.

work order (1) An order to the machine shop for tool manufacture or equipment maintenance; not to be confused with a manufacturing order. Synonym: work ticket. (2) An authorization to start work on an activity (e.g., maintenance) or product. See: *manufacturing order.*

work rules (1) Compensation rules concerning such issues as overtime, vacation, and shift premiums. (2) Employee and employer job rights and obligation rules, such as performance standards, promotion procedures, job descriptions, and layoff rules. Work rules are usually a part of a union contract and may include a code of conduct for workers and language to ensure decent conditions and health standards.

work sampling The use of a number of random samples to determine the frequency with which certain activities are performed.

workers' compensation The replacement of an employee's loss of earnings capacity caused by an occupational injury or disease. Formerly known as workmen's compensation.

working capital Synonym: net working capital.

workstation The assigned location in which a worker performs the job; it could be a machine or a workbench.

world-class quality A term used to indicate a standard of excellence: the best of the best.

X

***X*-bar chart** Synonym: average chart.

Y

yield The amount of good or acceptable material available after the completion of a process. Usually computed as the final amount divided by the initial amount converted to a decimal or percentage. In manufacturing planning and control systems, yield is usually related to specific routing steps or to the parent item to determine how many units should be scheduled to produce a specific number of finished goods. For example, if 50 units of a product are required by a customer and a yield of 70 percent is expected, then 72 units (computed as 50 units divided by 0.7) should be started in the manufacturing process. See: *scrap factor, yield factor.*

yield factor A measurement of the yield of a process. For a specific process or operation, yield factor + scrap factor = 1. Synonym: material yield. See: *scrap factor, yield.*

Z

zero defects A performance standard developed by Philip B. Crosby to address a dual attitude in the workplace: People are willing to accept imperfection in some areas, while in other areas, they expect the number of defects to be zero. This dual attitude has developed as a result of the condition that as people commit themselves to watching details and avoiding errors, they can move closer to the goal of zero defects. The performance standard that must be set is "zero defects," not "close enough."

zero-based budgeting A budget procedure used primarily by governmental agencies in which managers are required to justify each budgetary expenditure anew, as if the budget were being initiated for the first time rather than being based on an adjustment of prior-year data.

Index